Why Do You Need This New Edition?

If you're wondering why you should buy this new edition of *Cognitive Psychology*, here are 7 good reasons!

1. The third edition includes topics that weren't covered in the second edition, such as low-prevalence visual search, magic and attention, distracted driving, stress and working memory, mind wandering, and techniques for improving attention.

2. There has been a veritable explosion of research on visual attention since the second edition was published. The study of attentional control (i.e., executive attention) has also been burgeoning in recent years. To reflect these trends, coverage of both topics has been expanded.

3. Discussions of visual attention, multi-sensory integration, and essentialist theories of categorization have been expanded and updated.

4. Coverage of language now spans two chapters; Chapter 9 discusses general language principles and speech, and Chapter 10 focuses primarily on reading comprehension.

5. Topics on memory that have been enhanced include recovered memories of abuse, memory for trauma, childhood memories, and memories for the events of 9/11.

6. The themes reflecting unifying and cutting-edge research areas have been reconfigured for this edition. These research themes include Evolution, Emotion, Embodied Cognition, Culture, and Metacognition.

7. New *Reality Check* sections discuss and critique commonly held beliefs and assumptions related to how we think, as purveyed in the (cognitive) pop-psychology literature.

Contents

Chapter 2

Perception and Consciousness: Basics of Information Intake   45

Chapter 3

Mechanisms of Attention: Monitoring and Noticing Information   83

Chapter 4

Immediate Memory: The Control and Manipulation of Information   129

Chapter 5

Objects and Concepts: Identifying and Classifying Information   171

Chapter 8

Malleability in Memory: Processes of Forgetting, Editing, and Distortion   305

Chapter 9

Language I: Basic Issues and Speech Processing   348

Chapter 10

Language II: Reading and Comprehending Text   400

Chapter 11

Judgments and Decisions: Using Information to Make Choices   446

Chapter 12

Problems and Goals: Using Information to Arrive at Solutions   492

Preface

To the Student

The book you're about to read is about something with which you're intimately familiar yet haven't really stopped to think about. It's about something you engage in every single day, but you rarely give it notice unless something goes wrong. You couldn't live day to day without it, but you seldom stop to truly appreciate it. Is it TV? No. Coffee? No. Sleep? Nope. It's **thinking**. Ironically, although the mind is in constant use, most people take it for granted, only noticing it when it misfires. Consider the following examples of annoying little disturbances in thought:

- Why did I just put the cereal in the refrigerator and the milk in the cabinet?
- Why did I just get a D on an exam when I thought I knew everything "cold"?
- Why do I always find that answers to exam questions are right on "the tip of the tongue," but I can't quite spit them out?
- Why do I find it so difficult to listen to a professor lecture and take notes (not to mention stay awake) at the same time?

Your average Joe/Jane understands relatively little about how it works or how to improve it. But take heart! Thousands of scientists who call themselves cognitive psychologists have performed countless investigations on the thinking processes that we engage in every day, shedding tremendous light on the mechanics of thought. After reading this book, you will not be the average Joe/Jane.

What Is Cognitive Psychology?

Cognitive psychology is the subdiscipline of psychology that employs the scientific method to answer fundamental questions about how the mind works. By using controlled research (mostly experiments), cognitive psychologists attempt to explain the thinking processes that we use every day. A cognitive psychologist would have a more analytic view of the problems just described and would view them more technically, through the lens of a scientist. The following questions are how a cognitive psychologist might rework each of the questions posed:

- What are the cognitive factors that underlie action slips? How does this relate to automatic processing?
- Why do people sometimes fail to monitor their own level of comprehension? What are the components of successful *metacognition*?
- What factors play a role in *retrieval failures*, and how can retrieval failures be successfully overcome?
- How do people successfully *divide their attention* between multiple sources of stimulation, given the limited nature of attention?

Why Study Cognition?

The study of cognition has tremendous ramifications for an overall understanding of how you "tick" on a day-to-day basis; it is in some ways the most applied (and applicable) of psychology's subdisciplines. As noted, cognitive psychologists are attempting to understand the processes that you use every day: perception, attention, memory, language, and reasoning. It's important for gaining a basic understanding of how people think and behave, which is the focus of psychology. And it's important for improving our lot in everyday life—who hasn't been frustrated by the (sometimes more than) occasional "brain lapse" and other difficulties in attention, memory, and the like?

Let's broaden the issue a bit. A full understanding of cognition is critical to an understanding of other subdisciplines in the field of psychology. This makes sense—psychology is typically defined as the scientific study of thinking and behavior, and questions of thinking are at the core of every other subdiscipline of psychology. Consider the following questions from other arenas of psychology:

- *Clinical Psychology*: Do depressed people remember events from their lives differently than nondepressed people?
- *Neuropsychology*: What's happening in different areas of the brain's cortex as people engage in cognitive processes like memory and problem solving?
- *Developmental Psychology*: How do cognitive processes like memory and problem solving change with age?
- *Personality*: Does a person's personality play a role in the types of decisions they make?
- *Social Psychology*: What factors influence our ability to remember an individual?

These questions have quite a range, but there are two common threads. First, they are fundamental psychological questions, and second, they all involve cognition. Unlocking and understanding the mechanisms that are involved in cognition is fundamental to psychological explanation.

Cognitive psychology can be a bit of a challenge to master for a number of reasons. First, the subject matter of cognitive psychology (mental processes) can be difficult to grasp—you can't really see or touch them, and most often they take place quickly and outside of conscious awareness. As a result, the discussion of mental processes often takes place on a rather abstract level, and discussions of findings from research on cognition are full of jargon that can be difficult to decipher. Second, cognitive psychology's roots are firmly in experimental methodology. So to understand cognitive psychology, you need to understand experimental methodology. Third, cognitive psychology is a sprawling field; no one has provided the one unifying theory of cognition or even of a simpler subprocess, like memory. Findings and theories tend to conflict with one another due to the relative youth of the field (experimental cognitive psychology has only been around for about 60 years). As a result, students don't gain a good sense of "the big picture." Fortunately, this text offers a number of features designed to help you organize, integrate, and apply the material you'll be reading about cognition research.

First, the overall structure of the book parallels the progression of thinking. Take a simple cognitive process—looking at an animal at a zoo and realizing it's a duck-billed platypus. This involves (a) perceiving the animal, (b) paying attention to the animal, (c) retrieving the matching label for the animal from our store of concepts in memory, and (d) saying "duck-billed platypus." Then, we may remember the summer when we had a duck-billed platypus for a pet and, when it got too big, having to decide what to do with it. In line with this intuitive progression through the cognitive system, our text (after an initial foray into the history of cognitive psychology), proceeds from perception (initial perception of the animal), to attention and immediate memory (paying attention to the animal), to pattern recognition and concept representation (retrieving the label "duck-billed platypus" from memory). From there it's on to higher-level mental processes, including autobiographical memory, language, decision making, and problem solving (relating the story of the summer when we had a duck-billed platypus for a pet, and when it got too big, having to decide what to do with it, and then actually carrying out the solution).

A second feature that will help you integrate the material is our inclusion of a number of recurring empirical threads in each chapter. These "threads" are topics that cut across all areas of cognition and will be highlighted throughout the book:

- **Emotion:** How does affect, or feeling, impact basic cognitive processes like memory and attention?
- **Embodied Cognition**: The mind is just one element of an interactive system that includes the body and the situation. Thinking is inextricably tied to body and action.
- **Metacognition:** How do we understand our own processes of thought, and what role does this understanding play in improving cognition?
- **Evolution:** How might cognitive processes serve as adaptations that aid us in everyday functioning?
- **Culture:** It's probably not a big surprise to you that not everyone thinks exactly the same way; what are the differences and similarities in thinking across cultures?

A third feature that will assist you in integrating and applying the material is chapter-opening points that highlight thought-provoking questions or applications that will get you thinking about the material to be covered in the chapter.

In addition to features that assist you in organizing, integrating, and applying cognitive psychology research, our text provides several tools that we hope will help you in understanding and remembering the material. These features include:

- **Stop and Review!:** To help you assess whether you've learned the important material from what you've just read, each major section of a chapter will conclude with a short quiz. Following the quiz, a brief summary of the main points from the section (including the points covered in the preceding quiz) will be presented. As you'll read in Chapter 7, testing yourself on material you've already learned is one of the best ways to retain information for the long term.

- **Stop and Think!:** One of the best ways to understand and remember material is to become actively engaged with it. To help you accomplish this, each chapter will feature a number of exercises titled "Stop and Think!" These exercises will involve a number of hands-on and "mind-on" activities that will help you to give closer consideration to the material being discussed. The exercises will include demonstrations of cognitive processes and principles through "mini-experiments," questions about how you might design a study to investigate some cognitive process, opinion questions about controversial issues in the field, and questions that require you to examine your own cognitive processing and evaluate it in the context of the topic being discussed. Each chapter also features a Stop and Think! exercise designed specifically to encourage you to consider material from an earlier chapter, connecting to the topics currently being discussed.

- **Reality Checks:** Wacky claims about brain and mind abound. You only use 10 percent of your brain; hypnosis unlocks buried (fully intact) memories; subliminal messages are controlling your behavior. Fortunately, cognitive psychology researchers have data that bear on these sorts of claims and that debunk many "mind myths." We discuss some of this work in a feature termed "Reality Check."

As noted earlier, the newness, complexity, and breadth of cognitive psychology make it a challenging topic. However, these characteristics also make cognitive psychology an exciting and dynamic topic of study. Its newness means that there are many more exciting areas to explore and an endless array of questions waiting to be answered. Its complexity makes learning about it a great exercise in critical thinking. In reading this text, we hope that you gain a firm understanding of how seemingly vague questions about mental processes can be translated into experiments that provide concrete empirical answers. The breadth of cognitive psychology makes it one of the most interesting and applicable of psychology's subdisciplines. Topics included in the text range from visual perception to eyewitness memory to language comprehension to problem solving, with many fascinating stops in between. Our sincere hope is that you enjoy learning about cognitive psychology as much as we enjoy talking and teaching about it. Turn to page 1, and start thinking about thinking!

To the Instructor

As in our previous two editions, our goal in this text is to engage students in cognitive psychology with a lively, entertaining, and (most importantly) accessible presentation of the fascinating research in cognitive psychology. Cognitive psychology can be technical, dry, and more than a little intimidating, and students aren't always as grabbed by the field as we feel they should be. So our goal always has been to combine the engaging with the rigorous. We attempted to continue this approach in the present edition.

Organizational Structure.   In organizing the chapters of the text, we attempted to follow the flow of a piece of information that enters the cognitive system. The information is perceived, attended to and placed in immediate memory, identified, and committed to memory. Later, the information serves as the basis for the higher-level processes of language, decision making, and problem-solving. Admittedly serial, but we think it provides for a nice intuitive description of cognition that will enhance understanding.

Although our text does feature a fairly standard approach to explaining the flow of cognition, there are a couple of notable exceptions. One is that work on attention spans two chapters. Basic work on both visual and auditory attention is discussed in Chapter 3. We continue the discussion of attention in Chapter 4, in the context of short-term/working/immediate memory. It always struck us (and our students) that when we're discussing the control processes of attention and the control processes used in short-term/working/immediate memory, we were talking about many of the same things. The two seem to be (in many ways) flip sides of the same coin. This view is certainly not new—indeed, much of the research on immediate memory has characterized it in terms of attentional control (i.e., executive attention). We thought it highly appropriate to discuss attention and immediate memory together. Another distinctive feature of our layout is that object recognition occurs *after* discussion of attention and immediate memory. We placed it here because conscious recognition of a stimulus only occurs as the stimulus is processed by immediate memory. In other words, pattern recognition can be viewed as the first task of attention/immediate memory. In this edition, we've re-ordered the material on memory a bit, placing the discussion of memory editing and distortion after discussion of basic memory processes and autobiographical memory. In addition, we omitted the chapter on knowledge representation, integrating much of that material throughout the text in appropriate locations.

We've also tried to provide some organizational structure by referring to several different research themes in each chapter, including evolution, embodiment, emotion, metacognition, and culture. These themes capture some of the most interesting and dynamic questions that currently define the field. We hope that their inclusion will enhance students' sense of some of the overarching issues that currently define the field.

We've strengthened organizational flow by making the interrelatedness of cognitive processes very apparent. The separate discussion of perception, attention, memory, and so on, is completely a descriptive convention; when it comes to everyday thinking, these processes are inseparable. We've tried to give students a sense of this by pointing out, whenever possible, the relationship between the cognitive processes currently being discussed, those already covered, and those to come.

Everyday Relevance.   Cognition is constant; thinking is what we do. Despite the obvious relevance of thinking to our everyday lives, we sensed that students didn't appreciate this relevance as fully as they should. To enhance this appreciation in class, we make liberal use of everyday examples and give students thought-journaling assignments and experiments to do outside of class. The students really enjoy these and often are surprised at how interesting this stuff can be (needless to say, we're never surprised). We've adopted this tactic in our book, sprinkling the discussion with numerous examples and sprinkling each chapter with exercises—titled Stop and Think!—to entice students to do just that. These exercises could serve as homework assignments, as discussion generators for the classroom, or both.

Cool Experiments.   We also were never completely satisfied with the research presented in cognition texts. There are classic findings that merit extensive discussion, to be sure. But there are also some really intriguing empirical investigations, perhaps a little more off the beaten track, that merit mention and analysis. These investigations might be distinctive in their setting or in their empirical question (out-of-body experiences in touch caused by visual stimuli), but they still address fundamental questions of cognition. We've tried to include a good number of studies like this because they're likely to pique student interest and still convey the critical points.

Thanks for taking a look at our book. We hope your students enjoyed reading it as much as we enjoyed putting it together. We'd love to get your feedback and suggestions. If you spot errors or misrepresentations, know of an interesting study that may merit discussion, or otherwise want to comment on the text, please feel free to e-mail us (robinson@augsburg.edu and/or glriegler@stthomas.edu).

Changes for the Third Edition

The third edition of the text features extensive changes, primarily in content, but some in pedagogy, that we believe strengthen the text. These changes are based on the comments of users of the first and second editions, other reviewers, and our own experience with the text.

Content.   One major change to the content in this edition is the considerable expansion of coverage for three areas in particular. First, there has been a veritable explosion of research on visual cognition, especially visual attention. The study of attentional control (i.e., executive attention) has also been burgeoning in recent years. To reflect these trends, we expanded coverage of both topics considerably. Previously, perception, attention, and immediate memory were covered over only two chapters. In this edition, we devote separate chapters to basic perceptual issues, visual attention, and immediate memory. Another major content change is a second chapter on language. Moving from the first edition, we had condensed language into only one chapter; however, this seemed to be sacrificing too much, and in this edition, we have moved back to two— one on general language principles and speech and another that focuses primarily on reading comprehension.

One change intended to streamline coverage is that there is no longer a separate chapter on research methods in cognition. The material introducing cognitive neuroscience and neuroscience techniques is now in Chapter 1, and the basic information on research design will be available to interested instructors as an online supplement.

The major content change is an extensive updating of the material in all chapters, with addition of dozens of references to and discussions of sources from the last several years. The following is a comparative overview of the chapter structure from the previous edition and this new edition, along with a sampling of topics added for this edition.

2nd Edition	3rd Edition	E = Expanded Coverage N = New topic
Chapter 1 Introduction and History	Chapter 1 Cognitive Psychology: A Brief History and Introduction	E-Neuroscience techniques
Chapter 3 Basic Perceptual Processes	Chapter 2 Perception and Consciousness: Basics of Information intake	E-Subliminal processing E-Global precedence E-Synesthesia and cross-modal interaction N-Affordances E-Embodied perception E-Authorship processing
Chapter 4 Attending to and Manipulating Information	Chapter 3 Mechanisms of Attention: Monitoring and Noticing Information	N- Subitizing N- Low-prevalence search E- Visual Search N- Distracted Driving E-Space-based attention E-Object-based attention N-Search asymmetries N-Guided search N-Attentional blink E-Change blindness N-Magic
Chapter 5 Object Recognition and Concepts	Chapter 4 Immediate Memory: The Control and Manipulation of Information	N-Unitary views of immediate memory E-Role of inhibition in executive control E-Critique of WM N-Irrelevant speech effect N-Mind-wandering N-Effects of stress on immediate memory N-Improving executive function
Chapter 6 Encoding and Retrieval in LTM	Chapter 5 Objects and Concepts: Identifying and Classifying Information	E-Expertise view vs special mechanism view of facial recognition N-Gender and facial recognition N-Culture and facial recognition N-Self-enhancement bias E-Essentialist approach to categorization
Chapter 7 Memory Distortions	Chapter 6 Basic Processes in Long-Term Memory: Encoding and Retrieving Information	N-Fitness relevant processing E-Spacing effect N-Effects of ownership on memory N-Actors' memories N-Neural correlates of availability and accessibility E-Prospective memory N-Neural correlates for memory and emotion
Chapter 8 Reconstructing the Personal Past	Chapter 7 Autobiographical Memory: Recalling Important Events from Life	N-Feelings of nearness of remoteness of memories N-Culture and childhood amnesia E-Offset of childhood amnesia

2nd Edition	3rd Edition	E = Expanded Coverage
		N = New topic
		E-Reminiscence bump
		N-Culture and specificity of AM
		N-Embodiment and AM
		E-Self-memory system view
		N-Basic systems view
		E-Involuntary memories
		E-Memory for 9/11
		E-Memory for trauma
Chapter 9 Knowledge Representation	Chapter 8 Malleability in Memory: Processes of Forgetting, Editing, and Distortion	N-Baseline ability to recognize a face
		E-Stress and trauma in eyewitness memory
		E-Other race effect
		N-Change blindness and unconscious transference
		E-Lineup structure
		E-Effects of pictures on false memory
		N-Doctored evidence effect
		N-Positive application of false memory
		N-Fuzzy trace theory
		N-Memorability-based strategy for reality monitoring
		E-Recovered memory debate
Chapter 10 Language	Chapter 9 Language I: Basic Issues and Speech Processing	N-Phoneme production
		N-Critique of cohort model
		N-Emotional prosody in word recognition
		N-Embodiment and Language
		E-Top-down and bottom-up processes in word recognition
		N-Bilingual lexicon
		N-Learning word labels
		N-Critique of transformational grammar
		N-Universal grammar debate
		E-Child-directed speech
		N-Gender and conversation
		E-Self-monitoring stage of language production
		E-Motor theory of speech perception
		E-Auditory theory of speech perception
Chapter 11 Problem Solving	Chapter 10 Language II: Reading and Comprehending Text	E-Eye fixations during reading
		N-Phonological processing in visual word recognition
		N-Dyslexia
		N-Anglocentric language research
		N -Reading text messages
		N-Discourse comprehension
		N-Discourse memory and representation
		N-Speed reading

(continued)

2nd Edition	3rd Edition	E = Expanded Coverage
		N = New topic
Chapter 12 Decision Making	Chapter 11 Judgments and Decisions: Using Information to Make Choices	E-Dual-Process approach
		N-Myside bias
		N-Spacing effect and induction
		E-Hot-hand phenomenon
		N-Credit card minimum payment and anchoring and adjustment
		E-Hindsight bias
		E-Overconfidence
		N-Temporal value asymmetry in decision making
		N-Stress/emotion in decision making
		N-Physical touch and decision making
		E-Heuristics as adaptive tools
		N-Improving decision making
	Chapter 12 Problems and Goals: Using Information to Arrive at Solutions.	E-Individual differences in problem representation
		E-Stereotype threat
		E-Anological problem solving
		E-Dual process views of problem solving
		N-Expertise and age related deficits
		E-Costs of Expertise
		E-Insight
		E-Incubation
		E-Creativity

Pedagogy.   We've reconfigured the current research threads that we feature in the text. For this edition, we focus on five broad research themes, each of which makes an appearance across most chapters: Embodied Cognition, Emotion, Culture, Metacognition, and Evolution. These trends have become areas of increasing interest in cognitive research and seemed to warrant frequent mention and more extensive coverage.

We've added some new Stop and Think critical thinking exercises. In each chapter, we now feature a Stop and Think Back in which we deliberately focus students' attention on a previous chapter topic and how it relates to the topic being discussed. One motivation for this was the growing evidence of the value of retrieval of information in promoting later retention. A second pedagogical device is the addition of Reality Checks, discussions of topics about which students are likely to be misinformed or, at the least, underinformed. Some examples are speed reading, distracted driving, and confidence in memory.

Supplements

Pearson Education is pleased to offer the following supplements to qualified adopters.

For Instructors

Instructor's Manual and Test Bank (**0205050093**). Offered electronically, the Instructor's Manual is a wonderful tool for classroom preparation and management. Each chapter in the manual section includes an at-a-glance grid, brief and detailed outlines, elaborations on the text's Stop and Think exercises, discussion starters, and Internet resources. The test bank contains a set of questions for each chapter, including 50 multiple-choice questions with correct answers, page references, and difficulty ratings (1 = easy, 2 = medium, 3 = difficult), and 10 to 15 essay questions.

PowerPoint Presentation **(0205050085).** The PowerPoint Presentation is an exciting interactive tool for use in the classroom. Each chapter pairs key concepts with images from the textbook to reinforce student learning.

For Students

CourseSmart eTextbook **(ISBN: 0205050077).** This new Pearson Choice offers students an online subscription to *Cognitive Psychology,* 3/e at a 60% savings. With the CourseSmart eTextbook, students can search the text, make notes online, print our reading assignments that incorporate lecture notes, and bookmark important passages. Ask your Pearson sales representative for details or visit www.coursesmart.com.

For Instructors and Students

MyPsychLab. MyPsychLab offers students useful and engaging self-assessment tools, and offers instructors flexibility in assessing and tracking student progress. To instructors, MyPsychLab is a powerful tool for assessing student performance and adapting course content to students' changing needs—without investing additional time or resources. Students benefit from an easy-to-use site on which they can test themselves on key content, track their progress, and utilize individually tailored study plan. MyPsychLab includes an eBook plus simulated experiments for students to participate in, audio, video, simulations, animations, and controlled assessments to completely engage students and reinforce learning. MyPsychLab is designed with instructor flexibility in mind—you decide the extent of integration into your course—from independent self-assessment for students tracked in a gradebook to total instructor-driven course management. Instructors are provided with the results of student diagnostic tests in a gradebook and can view performance of individual students or an aggregate report of their class. Instructors can access the remediation activities students receive within their customized study plans, and can also link to extra lecture notes, video clips, and activities that reflect the content areas their class is struggling with. Instructors can bring these resources to class, or easily post them online for students to access. Ask your Pearson sales representative for details or visit www.pearsonhighered.com. To ensure that your students receive a MyPsychLab access code with their book, please use ISBN 9780205176748.

Acknowledgments

There are a host of people to thank for their help with the preparation of this edition. Thanks to our editor, Susan Hartman, for her calm and steady guidance (not to mention getting us a bit more time when we needed it!). Thanks to associate editor Kara Kikel for being on top of the details and providing us with quick and helpful answers to our many questions. Thanks to student assistants of Greg's, Angie Duffy and Dani Blackowiak, for all of their invaluable assistance in keeping track of references, permissions, and figures/ photos. They saved us many a headache! Thanks to Bridget's students Lani Deluna, Roman Hascall, Anita Singh, and Tiffany Tyus for insightful examples of cognitive processing used/adapted in this text.

We'd like to thank all of our colleagues who have e-mailed us with helpful comments on previous editions and would particularly like to thank the reviewers of the third edition for their helpful insights: Tatiana Ballion, University of Central Florida; Kim Christopherson, Morningside College; Patricia Costello, Gustavus Adolphus College; Kara Federmeier, University of Illinois; Todd Haskell, Western Washington University; Jeffrey Karpicke, Purdue University; Joshua Landau, York College of Pennsylvania; Dani McKinney, SUNY-Fredonia; Suzanna Penningroth, University of Wyoming.

Thanks to Greg's colleagues at St. Thomas Roxanne Prichard and Uta Wolfe for helpful comments on the discussion of neuroscientific techniques in Chapter 2. We are indebted to our colleagues who provided original materials from their research for this and previous editions, including Jodi Davenport, Julian Keenan, Vera Kempe, Dennis Proffitt, Sue Savage-Rumbaugh, Dan Simons, Kimberly Wade, Daniel Wegner, and Jeremy Wolfe. We deeply appreciate their gracious and generous cooperation.

CHAPTER OUTLINE

1

Cognitive Psychology: A Brief History and Introduction

What is thinking, exactly? How can there be a scientific discipline focusing on a process that is so complex, varied, and unobservable?

What are the roots of cognitive psychology? The study of mind sounds like it might involve philosophy—how does cognitive psychology differ? What were the important historical developments in study of mind?

Can thinking be broken down into subprocesses? What are the different types of thinking in which you engage throughout the course of a day, and what sorts of questions might be asked about these processes?

The mind seems to be a sort of "thinking machine"; technological devices like computers, cell phones, and Blackberries seem to have "minds of their own." Might those "minds" work in a way similar to ours?

What Is Cognition?

Psychology is generally defined as the scientific study of mental processes and behavior. **Cognitive psychology** could be defined by eliminating the last two words of that definition—the scientific study of mental processes. Behavior is examined by cognitive psychologists, but primarily as an avenue into the underlying mental processes, in the same way that physicists infer the force of gravity from the behavior of objects in the world. And the study of *mental processes* covers a lot of ground. These processes include attending, remembering, producing and understanding language, solving problems, and making decisions. It is hard to imagine that we take such vital processes for granted. Thinking is something that is constantly happening, yet we rarely stop to...well...think about it. However, for the past six decades, cognitive psychologists have done exactly that, using the methods of science to answer questions about the mind. With the experimental method as their primary tool, these researchers approach the mind as a type of machine, attempting to elucidate its inner workings. Given that thinking is at the heart of everything we do on a day-to-day basis, it's difficult to imagine a more important field of study.

The Omnipresence of Cognitive Processes

One of our goals in this text is to help you appreciate and understand the importance of the cognitive processes in which you are constantly engaged. As an exercise in thinking about thinking, consider the mental processes that you go through on the first day of class.

Perception.   Imagine the visual and auditory information processing that occurs on the first day of class. Based on a quick glance of the room, you immediately separate the tables from the chairs and make out the back row, your area of choice. Scanning the room, you spot a couple of old friends from last semester. You take your seat and listen to the professor outline the thrilling experience you're about to have in their course. This scenario involves perception—the set of front-end processes through which you organize and interpret incoming information.

Attention.   Should you drift off in one of your classes, you may hear your professor bellow, "Pay attention!" Attention is the set of processes through which you focus on incoming information. Your ability to attend is flexible—you can divert your attention to that juicy gossip being discussed behind you. But it's also limited—if you shift your attention, you're not likely to remember much of what the professor has said.

Immediate Memory.   It's not enough to simply "zero in" on what the professor is saying at any given moment in time. In order to fully process and understand the facts and figures being discussed in class, you've got to perform a sort of mental juggling act. As the material is being presented, you've got to repeat it to yourself and/or jot it down in your notes. The online processor that makes this possible is immediate memory, also referred to as short-term memory or working memory.

Identifying and Classifying Objects.   Two of the most important, yet most taken for granted sets of cognitive processes in which we engage are those involved in identifying and classifying. Without thinking, you distinguish the professor from the students, you pull out your notebook rather than your planner to take notes, and you (without looking) reach into your backpack to turn off that infernal cell phone. How do these acts of identification occur so seamlessly?

Long-Term Memory. Let's go back to your juggling act. It's not over when the class winds to a close. When the class is finished, you must catch the balls you're juggling and put them in your pocket until the next juggling act. In cognitive psychology lingo, you have to store the information for later use. Taking notes helps serve this purpose—that is, if you engage in the note-taking process seriously and think about concepts as you are writing them down. Through conscientious note taking, you start to commit information to long-term memory. In our discussion of memory, we'll examine some of the processes involved in remembering, both when you're studying information and when you're trying to retrieve it.

Autobiographical Memory. Chances are good that the first day of classes will be one of the better-remembered days of your entire school year. You can probably think of some reasons for this: you meet new professors, hear about new classes, get reacquainted with old friends, and make new ones. Research on how we remember our personal past has exploded, and the study of autobiographical memory has become one of the most dynamic and interesting topics within the field of cognitive psychology.

Memory Distortion. Memory's not perfect; far from it. It serves us well most of the time, but there are systematic ways in which it fails us. We're sure you've had the exasperating experience—especially on tests—of completely blanking on or misremembering information that you thought you knew. We'll discuss some of the processes involved in forgetting and memory distortion.

Language. Your seamless processing of all the information from your first day is a testament to your skill in yet another important set of cognitive processes—those involved in the use of language. As the professor speaks, your implicit knowledge of and practice with sentence structure allows you to follow along just fine. What would happen if the professor came into class and said, "Class, and textbook turn your get page out OK to 28"? How about, "Pretty textbooks fly to the bookstore"? No doubt you'd be calling campus security. Your implicit knowledge of syntax (word arrangement rules) and semantics (rules for expressing meaning) allows you to comprehend instantly what makes sense and what doesn't. Your knowledge of language also allows you to ask questions that professors just love to hear, like, "Do we have to know this?" or "Will this be on the test?"

Decision Making. You're going to have to make many decisions throughout the semester. "How much time should I devote to studying for each of my classes?" "If I miss class once in a while, am I going to pay for it in my final grade?" (Do you really need an answer to that one?) The process through which you arrive at decisions involves a complex interplay among other cognitive processes such as attention, memory, and knowledge retrieval.

Problem Solving. After you've been to all of your classes, you've got another juggling act to perform. Somehow, you're going to have to fit studying for 15 to 20 tests, writing for 15 to 20 papers, and attending class for about 150 one-hour periods all into the space of 14 or so weeks. And you've got to do it well. This is a fairly hefty example of problem solving. Problem solving involves operating within constraints (such as time) and reaching a goal from a starting state that is nowhere near that goal.

Stop&*Think* | THINKING ABOUT THOUGHT PROCESSES

Look at the list of cognitive processes that begins on page 2. You engage in all of these in some manner every day. Come up with an example of each of these from your daily life.

An Interdisciplinary Perspective

Not only is cognitive psychology central to everything we do in our day-to-day lives, it is also central to psychology's quest to understand how people think and act. As noted in the definition of psychology, cognition comprises half of the subject matter! Because cognition is so fundamental to understanding how humans "tick," it is crucial to psychology's other subdisciplines. Social psychologists investigate the mental processes involved in thinking about others. Clinical psychologists investigate the role that mental processes play in psychopathology. Developmental psychologists are interested in the ways that cognitive processes change throughout the life span. Neuropsychologists are interested in the association between mental processing and brain activity. Industrial/organizational psychologists are interested in how cognitive processes such as remembering and decision making play out in the workplace. Understanding the fundamental mechanisms of human cognition provides critical insights into the other subdisciplines that define psychology.

The study of cognition also lends insights beyond psychology. Cognitive psychology is a key player within the interdisciplinary field of study termed "cognitive science." **Cognitive science,** simply defined, is an interdisciplinary effort to understand the mind. It includes a number of (seemingly disparate) disciplines, five of them plus cognitive psychology lying at its "core" (Gardner, 1985). Philosophy, the first discipline to systematically examine the mind, helps to formulate and examine the fundamental questions that define the field. Neuroscience attempts to specify the relationship between mind and brain. Artificial intelligence addresses issues of mind by modeling human thought processes with computer hardware and software. The field of linguistics investigates the structure of language and the specifics of language use and what they tell us about the mind. Anthropology explores the mind through quite a different lens—the lens of culture. How do our physical and cultural surroundings impact our thinking? Given that each of these disciplinary approaches is reflected to some degree in the work of cognitive psychologists, you'll be getting a taste of most of these disciplines in this text.

Stop&*Review*

1. Identify the major topics covered by cognitive psychologists.
2. True or false? Cognitive science is a specific field within cognitive psychology.
• Cognitive psychology can be defined as the scientific study of mental processes.

• Cognitive psychologists study a wide range of abilities—perception, sensory memory, attention, working memory, pattern recognition, concept representation, long-term memory, knowledge representation, language, problem solving, and decision making.

- Cognitive psychology lies at the core of an interdisciplinary approach termed cognitive science. Cognitive science attempts to bring together research from the fields of philosophy, neuroscience, artificial intelligence, linguistics, and anthropology in an effort to understand the mind.

Psychology B. C. (*Before Cognitive Psychology*)

As pioneering cognitive psychologist Hermann Ebbinghaus observed, psychology has a long past but a short history. Thinking has long been a topic of interest—no doubt since we, as humans, started thinking. It shouldn't be a surprise that philosophy is generally considered to be the primary disciplinary "parent" of psychology, particularly cognitive psychology. Ancient philosophers such as Aristotle were interested in the mechanics of mind. He (and others) sought to establish **laws of association** to explain why the activation of some concepts seems to automatically lead to the activation of others. Consider a word association task: What is the first word that pops to mind when we say "black"? How about "chair"? We'd be willing to bet that you thought of the concepts "white" and "table." Aristotle assumed, as do modern-day cognitive psychologists, that mental processes are lawful and predictable.

    Although philosophers have long been interested in the mind, the subject was not thoroughly examined with the scientific method of controlled observation until the 1800s. At that point a second disciplinary "parent" of psychology, physiology, had begun to establish itself as a legitimate area of scientific inquiry. Physiologists looked at the body as a sort of machine and employed scientific methods to determine its inner workings. How do nerve impulses travel? How does information from the outside world enter into our sensory systems? How is this information interpreted? These latter two questions bring physiology right to the doorstep of psychology because they are questions of human experience and thinking. Once physiologists started applying their methods to these types of questions, a complete science of mind was inevitable.

Stop&*Think* | COMPARING COGNITIVE PSYCHOLOGY TO ITS FORERUNNERS

Philosophy and physiology are generally recognized as the parent disciplines of psychology.

- Do you consider cognitive psychology to be more like philosophy or more like physiology?

- Why do you think so?
- What are some of their similarities and differences?

Psychophysics

The scientific study of mind can be traced back to a number of origins, none more important than the work of early psychophysicists. **Psychophysics** refers to the study of the relationship between the physical properties of a stimulus and the properties taken on when the stimulus is filtered through subjective experience. For instance, suppose we see two lights in succession. The first light is double the luminance of the second light. Does the first light *seem* twice as *bright*? Note that while luminance is a physical measure of light intensity, *seem* is a subjective term and *brightness* is a psychological dimension, not a physical one.

Mapping out the relationship between the physical and the psychological was a primary concern of early psychophysicists such as Gustav Fechner (1801–1878). One of Fechner's major contributions was his quantification of the relationship between incoming stimuli and corresponding perceptions. Fechner demonstrated that there is not a one-to-one relationship between changes in the physical intensity of a stimulus and changes in its *psychological* (or perceived) intensity. Think about it. If someone snaps their fingers at a rock concert, no one would notice. If somebody snaps their fingers in a quiet room, you notice it easily. Clearly, there is some process of translation occurring between the presentation of the physical stimulus and the actual experience of that stimulus.

Hermann von Helmholtz (1821–1894) influenced the newly developing science of mind primarily through his work on visual perception, which Helmholtz argued involved a process of **unconscious inference.** An inference is a conclusion that we arrive at through some type of evidence. According to Helmholtz, our visual systems are constantly making inferences about the external world based on the information gathered as well as on the "evidence" of previous experience. Consider what happens when you pick up your alarm clock in the morning and hold it close enough to read it (leaving aside the revulsion you feel that it's 7:30 and you have to get up for an 8:00 class). The image picked up by the retina in the back of your eye gets larger as you move the clock close to your face. Do you recoil in horror at the sight of a giant clock? Perhaps, if you had a particularly rough evening immediately before, but we're betting you don't. Based on life experiences, you make an unconscious inference that alarm clocks (and other objects) do not spontaneously increase in size. Therefore, you know that the clock is closer, not larger. Three important principles are highlighted by Helmholtz's concept of unconscious inferences. First, the perceiver plays an interpretive role in what is perceived; perception is not just a passive process of registering incoming physical energy. Second, perceptual and cognitive processes are influenced by previous experience. Third, perceptual and cognitive processes often occur outside of conscious awareness (as implied in the term *unconscious inference*).

Stop&*Think* | COGNITIVE PROCESSES—CONSCIOUS OR UNCONSCIOUS?

In proposing the concept of unconscious inference, Helmholtz helped make it clear that many cognitive processes occur outside conscious awareness. Look again at the list of cognitive processes that begins on page 2. Rate each process on the following continuum and explain your rating.

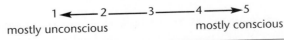

1 ←— 2 ——3——— 4 —→ 5
mostly unconscious   mostly conscious

It's not difficult to see why the work of early psychophysicists provided an important step toward a science of cognition. Psychophysicists were among the first to apply the scientific method to bridge the physical and the mental. Both psychophysicists and cognitive psychologists are interested in how stimulation and information in the outside world are linked with internal processes, representations, and conscious experience.

While psychophysicists tend to focus on the early stages of how we process information, cognitive psychologists focus on *all* stages of information processing. Let's turn our attention back to that blasted alarm clock that shatters your nighttime reverie. Psychophysicists might be interested in how bright the LED read-out on the clock needs to be for you to read it, or on how loud the alarm has to be for you to hear it, or on whether you think the light is as bright as the alarm is loud—in other words, your psychological interpretation of physical experiences. A cognitive psychologist, on the other hand, would be interested in these processes and more: How do you focus your attention on the clock? How do you recognize and understand the sound coming from it? What are the processes that may lead you to decide to sleep in?

Structuralism: The Contents of Mental Experience

Although psychophysics may have helped lay the foundation, modern experimental psychology is generally traced back to 1879, when Wilhelm Wundt (1832–1920) established the first psychological laboratory at the University of Leipzig in Germany. Wundt believed that a science of psychology should be concerned with how people consciously experience the world. Given that psychology was a fledgling scientific enterprise, some thought it wise to model psychology after a well-established science—chemistry. Simple chemical elements combine to form more complex compounds. The structuralists, as they would later be dubbed, wondered whether this approach could be applied to conscious experience. Perhaps the complexities of how we experience everyday events could be broken down into distinct and basic elements of consciousness. According to the structuralists, these elements could likely be classified into three broad categories: sensations (the basic sensory dimensions that we encode from a stimulus), feelings (emotions aroused by a stimulus), and images (mental impressions that seem sensory in nature).

Consider an example: Wundt and his colleagues might characterize looking at a sunrise as a complex experience made up of simpler ones. These would include simple sensations (e.g., warmth on the skin), simple images (e.g., hearing bird calls), and simple feelings (e.g., contentment). Wundt attempted to identify these simple components of complex experiences through the use of **introspection,** a procedure that requires participants to provide a rigorous, unbiased report of every element of the conscious experience that accompanies the presentation of some stimulus (e.g., the presentation of a tone). It was hoped that applying this method of thorough, objective analysis to a wide range of everyday experiences would yield the elemental sensations, images, and feelings that combine to produce everyday consciousness. One of Wundt's students, Edward Titchener (1867–1927), popularized this approach in the United States, terming it **structuralism.** While this early approach to the study of psychology may seem simplistic at best, you must remember the context in which it emerged. Psychology was new and trying to establish itself as a scientific discipline, so it made sense to emulate the approach used by another science.

Functionalism: The Functions of Mental Experience

At about the same time that structuralists were attempting to distill consciousness into its basic elements, a decidedly different approach was evolving. William James (1842–1910) and others were highly critical of the structuralist approach (see Kimble, 1985), contending that their atomistic approach to consciousness was wrong-headed. James invoked the well-known phrase *stream of consciousness* to capture the continuous, ever-changing nature of our experience. Analyzing it at any discrete point in time (as the structuralists did with introspection) violates its very nature. A related point is that the mere act of scrutinizing and analyzing one's conscious experience changes the experience. You're no longer studying consciousness.

Rather than using introspection to provide moment-to-moment snapshots of what was currently in mind, James thought psychology should devote itself to figuring out the *functions* of the mind—what it does in everyday life (hence the name given to this approach—**functionalism**). While a structuralist would attempt to determine the basic images, feelings, and sensations that comprise the conscious experience of being angry, a functionalist would study the emotion of anger by trying to determine the purpose or function of being angry. Given its emphasis on mental processing rather than mental structure, functionalism ultimately had a more profound influence on cognitive psychology than did structuralism. Indeed, the table of contents of James's famous text *Principles of Psychology* reads like a "what's what" of the study of cognition, including chapters on attention, remembering, emotions, and thinking.

Behaviorism: The Rejection of Mental Experience

While the structuralists and functionalists were debating the proper focus of a scientific study of consciousness, a storm was brewing. The study of the mind and conscious experience was entering what might be termed a sort of "dark age." Psychologist John B. Watson (1878–1958), intensely dissatisfied with psychology's lack of progress, suggested a shift that he believed would make the fledgling enterprise of psychology truly scientific. Watson's radical notion was the banishment of consciousness from scientific study. Why would he propose such a radical move? The hallmarks of scientific study are observation, measurement, and repeatability. The study of consciousness lends itself to none of these. It cannot be reliably observed or measured, and the results of an introspective analysis cannot be reliably reproduced. But behavior can be observed, measured, and repeated; hence, it should serve as the focus of scientific psychology. Watson's approach, termed **behaviorism,** discarded both the subject matter and the approach of the structuralists and functionalists, instead emphasizing the study of observable responses and their relation to observable stimuli. Given its emphasis on observable stimuli and responses, it makes sense that behaviorism is sometimes referred to as **S-R psychology.** According to behaviorists, psychology should dedicate itself to discovering these S-R connections. Between stimulus and response is a "black box" that houses consciousness. Investigation of the contents of the black box is a futile enterprise, according to the behaviorists, because the contents do not lend themselves to scientific investigation.

The behaviorists were not denying that we experience consciousness; for example, they wouldn't have a problem with acknowledging that people have the conscious experience of hunger. They simply rejected the idea that this conscious experience could be meaningfully studied, owing to its inherently subjective nature. They also gave consciousness no causal role in producing behavior; we don't eat because we *feel hungry*. Eating is an observable response that occurs in the presence of some verifiable stimulus, such as low insulin levels or a plate of fresh-out-of-the-oven cookies. The complete rejection of consciousness from scientific study was a radical move, but it struck a resounding chord. In the United States, the behaviorist approach dominated experimental psychology for the first half of the 20th century.

Laying the Foundation for Cognitive Psychology

The rejection of consciousness as a topic for scientific study was not without good intent. The behaviorists wanted to establish psychology as a rigorous experimental science alongside other disciplines more readily acknowledged as "scientific," such as biology and chemistry. Their sincere belief was that the study of mind was never going to get us there. But scientists throughout the short history of psychology have demonstrated time and time again that rigorous observation and measurement of mental processes is possible. In fact, even before the behaviorists "threw down the gauntlet" to scientists interested in human behavior, Hermann Ebbinghaus was quietly conducting a strikingly methodical and precise series of experiments on remembering.

Ebbinghaus: Pioneering Experiments on Memory.　In the late 1800s, Ebbinghaus embarked on an investigation of his own memory—an investigation that demonstrated convincingly that complex mental processes could be submitted to experimental test. Ebbinghaus was a truly dedicated researcher; he served as his only participant, tirelessly testing and retesting his own memory under rigorously controlled conditions of presentation and testing. He did this by memorizing list after list of nonsense syllables—letter strings that do not form words (e.g., DBJ). For a given list, he would record the number of study trials it took to learn the list to perfection. Then, after varying periods of time, he would attempt to relearn the list to perfection again. As you might imagine, it took him fewer trials to relearn a list than it initially did to learn it. Ebbinghaus coined the term **savings** to refer to this reduction in the number of trials it took to relearn a list. His previous experience in perfectly learning the material *saved* him some trials the second time he tried to learn it. Think about it: If you've already learned to do something well and then take some time off, you're not going to have to start from scratch when you attempt to redo or relearn the task.

　　Using the method of savings, Ebbinghaus revealed a number of fundamental principles of memory. He found that recall was more difficult as list length increased, a harbinger of later research that would investigate the limited nature of immediate memory. He found that his ability to retain the nonsense syllables increased with the frequency of repetitions (if you study more, you'll remember more). And he captured a pattern of forgetting that has been termed the **forgetting curve,** memory performance declines over the time interval since study. Early in the time interval, forgetting occurs rapidly, then slows down considerably. This pattern has been replicated in countless investigations of memory, but as you'll read later, the precise function that relates what we remember and forget to the passage of time depends on a myriad of variables.

Ebbinghaus' research was significant for a number of reasons. First, it demonstrated that precise and well-controlled experimental methods could be applied to study complex mental processes, setting the stage for the experimental approach to cognition that was to follow. Second, it provided a well-conceived research paradigm for the study of memory that inspired a legion of later researchers. Finally, as noted, it established a number of core principles of memory that are still being replicated and extended in laboratory research today.

Bartlett's Memory Research.   Sir Frederick Bartlett objected to the use of tightly controlled laboratory procedures for revealing memory function. He believed that if psychological research was to be generalizable, it should be as naturalistic as possible. Following this principle, his procedure involved the presentation of materials that were meaningful rather than nonsensical. Therefore, he assessed participants' memory for stories and folk tales and discovered a fair amount of reconstruction (Bartlett, 1932). Some details were left out of the story; other details were inserted. Based on his results, Bartlett characterized memory as a reconstructive process rather than a reproductive one. This reconstruction was guided by what Bartlett termed *schemata,* generalized knowledge structures about events and situations that are constructed based on past experience.

Note that in contrast to the behaviorist explanations of the day, Bartlett was postulating that mental structures (schemata) exerted a causal influence over behavior. Bartlett's work was distinctive and important in a couple of ways. First, it provided an alternative to the mechanistic S-R view of remembering, Second, it showed incredible prescience, foreshadowing some major concerns that have taken center stage in present-day cognitive psychology—the reconstructive nature of memory. A social anthropologist at heart, Bartlett was interested in remembering as a dynamic, social process that helps us make sense of our daily lives. His classic book was titled *Remembering: A Study in Experimental and <u>Social</u> Psychology* (emphasis added). Cognitive psychology's current emphasis on the study of cognition within natural contexts owes much to Bartlett's early investigations.

It's interesting to note the strong contrast between the methods used by Ebbinghaus and those used by Bartlett to study remembering. Ebbinghaus's method involved the precisely controlled presentation and remembering of lists of nonsense syllables, while Bartlett's method (though somewhat controlled) left more to chance, as participants were exposed to stories and asked to remember them. The tension between precise control and realism will be seen in studies discussed throughout the text.

Stop&*Think* | TWO APPROACHES TO THE STUDY OF COGNITION

Look at the list of cognitive processes that begins on page 2 (again!). For each process, give a brief description of how you would study it

- in the laboratory
- in the real world

Gestalt Psychology. Developed in Germany, the Gestalt perspective in psychology was very active in the first half of the last century. It emphasized the role that organizational processes play in perception and problem solving. Roughly translated, the German word *gestalt* means something like *configuration*. Psychologists who adopted the **Gestalt approach** were interested in the organizational principles that guide mental processing. So a Gestalt psychologist would be interested in investigating the way you organize visual stimuli in your environment—do you see the items in Figure 1.1 as rows or columns of X's? The Gestaltists believed that the answer to this question revealed something fundamental about visual perception.

Figure 1.1
Three rows or five columns?

The spirit of the Gestalt approach is captured well by their oft-cited credo "The whole is different than the sum of its parts." One cannot capture the essence of conscious experience by analyzing it into its elements, as the structuralists attempted to do. Experience is more than just a summary of elementary sensations, images, and feelings. When combined in a particular way, these elements of experience form a particular gestalt, or whole. And one cannot understand human experience and behavior by eliminating all talk of conscious experience, as the behaviorists attempted to do. Current cognitive psychology embodies the spirit of the Gestalt view by placing the mind center stage and viewing it as an active processor of information. In addition, the Gestalt approach still has a strong influence on how we view particular cognitive processes, most notably, perception and problem solving, as we'll see in Chapters 2 and 12.

Stop&Review

1. True or false? Philosophy provided the content of cognitive psychology, while physiology provided the method used by cognitive psychology.

2. True or false? Functionalism ultimately had a greater influence on psychology than did structuralism.

3. The behaviorist approach in psychology
   a. was theoretically aligned with Gestalt psychology
   b. followed the assumptions and methods established by structuralists and functionalists
   c. emphasized the study of observable phenomena
   d. focused on the role of mind in behavior

4. What are the basic ideas of Ebbinghaus, Bartlett, and the Gestalt approach to psychology?

- The scientific study of thinking has its roots in philosophy, which provided the basic questions that empirical research in cognition attempts to answer. The science of physiology provided a basic method for the investigation of perceptual processes. Modern attempts to understand the mind can be traced to the psychophysicists, who studied the relationship between physical stimulation and psychological experience.

- Psychology was established in 1879, when the structuralists began to formally investigate the elements of conscious experience. Their primary method was introspection, an intensive analysis of the contents (images, feelings, and sensations) of one's own consciousness. The functionalists were concerned with specifying the functions of consciousness rather than its structure, and ultimately had a much larger impact on the field.

- Behaviorists favored the elimination of consciousness as a topic of study, given its subjective nature. Behaviorists believed a science of psychology should focus on observables like behavior. Behaviorism is sometimes referred to as S-R psychology because of its emphasis on the analysis of observable stimuli and responses and their relation to one another.

- Ebbinghaus demonstrated that rigorous experimental work on cognition was possible. His research on memory for nonsense syllables established a number of key principles of memory that are still recognized today. Bartlett investigated memory for more realistic materials and, based on his results, argued that memory involves processes of reconstruction. Gestalt psychologists were interested in the organizational tendencies of the mind and had a significant influence on views of perception and problem solving.

The Emergence of Cognitive Psychology

Although behaviorism had struck a chord, to many it rang hollow in failing to capture the richness and diversity of human behavior and creativity. The challenges to behaviorism came from outside and from within and were both empirical and theoretical. From within the behaviorist camp, some studies of animal behavior were producing results that were problematic for S-R accounts, results revealing that rats could rightfully be described as "thinking" under some circumstances. The momentum from these research challenges began to build in the 1930s, posing a threat to the behaviorist stronghold on scientific psychology. In addition, psychologists were growing increasingly frustrated with the narrowness of explanations offered within the behaviorist paradigm, arguing that such explanations captured virtually nothing of what human beings do on a day-to-day basis, such as our use of language. Another major influence on the emergence of cognitive psychology was the development of new technologies like calculators, computers, and communication systems. These developments revolutionized how humans viewed machines and their capabilities. This, in turn, revolutionized the way humans viewed *themselves* and *their* own capabilities.

S-R Explanations: *Seriously wRong?*

Failure to Account for the Data.   As we've seen, behaviorists viewed reference to mental states or mental representations as useless, preferring to focus only on behavior, and using only the concepts of stimuli, responses, and the associations between them. Consider the following example: Suppose we have a rat that we place in a T-maze; the rat has to learn to run down the straightaway and choose the side with food in it. Over a series of trials, what do you suppose happens? As you might suspect, the rat starts to make the correct turn to obtain the food. Rats may not be the brightest of animals, but they can learn that simple association. A behaviorist would explain the rat's learning of the maze with three simple concepts: stimuli, responses, and reinforcement.

Associations are formed between stimuli and responses, with reinforcement as the "glue" that holds the associations together. When placed in a particular *stimulus* situation (the feel and smell of a maze), the rat engages in a particular *response* (running forward in the maze). If it receives reinforcement at the end of the maze, this bonds the stimulus and the response together—an S-R association. The next time the rat is confronted with the feel and smell of the maze (the S), the response of running (the R) will be triggered. Each time the rat is placed in the maze, this association plays itself out again and becomes stronger with each reinforcement. The rat runs faster. Over time, it zips down the alley and without hesitation makes the correct turn, without asking for directions.

The behaviorist account of the learning process is simple and elegant and does not rely on reference to unobservable mental processes, like the rat *expecting* or *knowing* that the food is on the right. The rat doesn't "know" anything; it is simply executing a chain of S-R associations that have been built up over a series of trials. But the trouble is that there are too many scenarios in which this simple account doesn't apply. Let's briefly review a few of these findings.

Learning Without Responding. According to the behaviorists, responding is absolutely essential for learning. It's the R in the S-R association link. Demonstrating that learning occurs in the absence of R would be difficult, if not impossible, to explain. A study by McNamara, Long, and Wike (1956) investigated whether learning would occur in this type of situation. Rats were tested in a T-maze, described previously. Some of the rats ran the maze themselves, eventually learning that they had to turn right to get to the food. Other rats were pushed by the experimenters down the alleyway in small carts. At the end of the runway, the experimenters turned the cart to the right and let the rat out to eat the food.

Which group of rats will *know* where the food is? "Isn't it obvious?" you must be thinking. They both will. They both saw the maze and saw that food was on the right. So now they *expect* the food to be on the right. But this is exactly the type of mentalistic explanation that behaviorists rejected. Behaviorists would say only the group of rats that ran on their own would learn the correct response. Why? Because R is required for learning. The results, however, failed to support the behaviorist prediction. When allowed to run on their own, the rats that had previously gotten a ride to the food showed a preference for the right side, just like the rats that had run there on their own from the beginning. Clearly, the hitchhiking rats learned—and without responding.

Learning Without Reinforcement. Recall that, according to the behaviorist view, reinforcement is necessary for learning to occur; as described earlier, it's the "glue" that holds the S and the R together. Without reinforcement, the stimulus and response will not be bonded, and there will be no learning. Tolman and Honzik (1930) tested this in a classic study. Over the course of two weeks, they placed three different groups of rats in a complex maze like the one in Figure 1.2 and had them explore it. One group of rats was reinforced every time they reached the goal box, starting on day 1. A second group was never reinforced. A third group was not reinforced during the first 10 days but began receiving a reinforcement in the goal box on the 11th day.

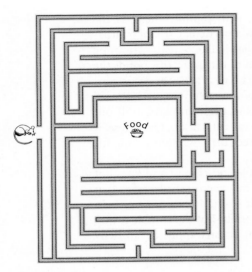

Figure 1.2

A complex garden-style maze used in some early studies of simple learning.

Consider the prediction of the S-R view. The rats in group 1 should show a steady decrease in error rate. The reinforcement in the goal box strengthens the response (R) of running when placed in the stimulus (S) of the maze. Group 2 rats should show no decrease in error rate; they were never reinforced, so S and R were never bonded. Group 3 should look exactly like group 2 until day 11, when the rats receive food in the goal box. Then, starting on day 12, group 3 rats should show the same gradual decrease in error rate shown in group 1, as the goal box reinforcement gradually strengthens the S-R connection.

The findings were surprising, at least to those operating from an S-R perspective. The rats in groups 1 and 2 behaved exactly as predicted, showing a gradual decrease in error rate and no decrease in error rate, respectively. But the results from group 3 proved problematic for the behaviorists. As you can see in Figure 1.3, starting on day 12, these rats were as error free as rats in group 1. Clearly, they had been learning the maze all along, even without reinforcement. Tolman termed this phenomenon **latent learning.** This finding is difficult to handle from a behaviorist standpoint: How could learning occur if the stimulus and response were never associated? Once again, a cognitive explanation seemed reasonable. The rats wandered around the maze for 11 days and picked up what Tolman (1948) termed a general "lay of the land." They were well aware of the maze layout, and once there was a reason to demonstrate what they had learned, they did.

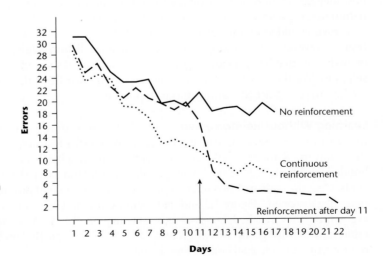

Figure 1.3

Latent learning; results from Tolman and Honzik's (1930) study.

From Tolman, E. C., & Honzik, C. H. (1930). Introduction and removal of reward, and maze performance in rats. *University of California Publications in Psychology, 4,* 257–275.

Cognitive Maps.   In 1948, Tolman conducted a classic study that would put another fly in the behaviorists' ointment. In this experiment, rats were faced with a maze like the one pictured in Figure 1.4. There are three possible routes to the destination—three possible *responses:* path 1, path 2, and path 3. Which one would you pick if you were hungry? The shortest one, of course, and this is what S-R theory would predict. In behaviorist terms, path 1 has the strongest S-R association because the reinforcement is obtained the most quickly, and the less time that elapses between responding and reinforcement, the stronger the association. Following this logic, path 2 has the next-strongest S-R association because food can be obtained quicker via this path relative to path 3. Path 3 has the weakest S-R association because taking this path would take the longest to get to the food.

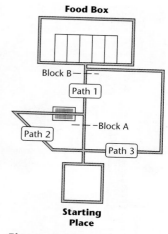

Figure 1.4

Maze used to study latent learning. On different trials, blocks were placed at various places in the maze.

From Tolman, E. C. (1948). Cognitive maps in rats and men. *Psychological Review, 55,* 189–208.

The cognitive view of rat behavior in this situation is quite different. Recall Tolman's proposal that rats acquired a "lay of the land" as they explored the maze. Another way of putting this is that the rats formed a **mental map** of the maze layout and consulted it to determine which path would get them to the food most quickly. Note that this explanation is exactly the type of view that the behaviorists railed against because it appeals to the notion of mental representations (i.e., mental maps) and their influence on behavior. Behaviorists believed that behavior could be explained without any appeal to such factors.

In his study, Tolman allowed rats to freely explore the maze over a series of trials. True to S-R predictions, the rats preferred path 1, choosing it the most. Then the investigators teased the rats by placing a block at point A (see Figure 1.4). When rats ran into this block, they were forced to retreat to the choice point and go a different way. The S-R approach would predict that at this point, the rats should behave according to the next-strongest S-R association and take path 2. The cognitive approach would also make this prediction, because when placed in this situation, the rats would consult their mental map and realize that path 2 was shorter than path 3.

The key condition was when a block was placed at point B (see Figure 1.4). What is a rat to do? The behaviorist and cognitive predictions diverge in this case. According to the behaviorist view, the rats will take path 1, because path 1 has the strongest S-R association. When blocked, they will go back to the choice point and take path 2, which has the next-strongest S-R association. Finally, when blocked again, they should return to the choice point and choose path 3. The cognitive view gives the rats a little more credit. According to this view, the rats have a general mental map for the entire maze arrangement, so when the rats see the block at point B, they'll realize that path 2 is also blocked. Therefore, they won't even bother with it. They'll run back to the choice point and take path 3. This is exactly what Tolman found. On the first trial with the block at point B, the rats chose path 3 over 90% of the time.

Because behaviorists claim that both reinforcement and responding are necessary for learning, they were bedeviled by the discovery of learning without a response or reinforcement, as well as by the seeming reality of mental maps. Theorists such as Clark Hull (1943) attempted to repair the damage done to behaviorist theory by postulating

Simple as a rat turning left?

additional mechanisms and processes, but these changes (postulating unseen mechanisms) brought S-R theory perilously close to cognitive theory. Change was afoot; the failure of S-R theory was helping to set the stage for the new science of mind.

Lashley Lashes Out.   As the middle of the 20th century approached, the theoretical tide was shifting away from behaviorist explanations of action. In 1948, a group of scientists convened at the Hixon Symposium in what was to be a seminal event for the emergence of the scientific study of mind. As described by Gardner (1985), this conference featured a number of papers that championed a new approach to studying mind and brain and cast severe doubt on behaviorism's rigidity.

One of the most devastating blows was dealt by Karl Lashley, who argued that any science of behavior must be able to explain forms both simple (rats running in a T-maze) and complex (the aerial stunts of a snowboarder). Complex behaviors, Lashley argued, could not possibly play out via a series of S-R connections, as the behaviorists claimed. Consider snowboarder Shaun White as he performs the double McTwist 1260. According to the behaviorists, the performance of this insane trick can be explained through S-R connections. Shaun's aerial twisting movements are the *responses* that are connected to the *stimuli* (the snowboard) by some type of *reinforcement* (be it audience applause, an adrenaline rush, or a gold medal (or 3) at the Winter X Games). The problem is, the sequence of movements required to perform the stunt play out with such speed that there is no conceivable way that a chain of S-R connections could be the explanation. Complex behaviors like this need to be planned out and organized in advance, according to Lashley. Any complete science of behavior should have to address the question of internal mental plans for action. It was becoming more and more apparent that the banishment of mental representations from scientific explanations of behavior was threatening to lead psychology to a dead end.

Chomsky's Challenge.   Challenges to standard behaviorist explanations came not only from inside the domain of animal learning research, but also from disciplines outside of psychology, such as linguistics. Remember that behaviorism offered a general explanation of all behavior, animal and human. Indeed, renowned behaviorist B. F. Skinner termed language *verbal behavior* and applied an S-R analysis to the acquisition of language, arguing that even complex abilities like language could be captured in purely S-R terms. Skinner viewed language as the acquisition of a set of responses, explainable through the principles of reinforcement. Linguist Noam Chomsky (1959) wrote a scathing review of Skinner's analysis in what Leahey (1992) calls "perhaps the single most influential psychological paper published since Watson's behaviorist manifesto of 1913." In his review, Chomsky completely rejected the S-R view of language, characterizing it as more vague and unscientific than the very cognitive explanations that Skinner himself criticized (Lachman, Lachman, & Butterfield, 1979).

Behaviorists explained language, as they did all human behavior, in terms of stimulus, response, and reinforcement. When little two-year-old Jimmy drinks his favorite drink, looks up at Mommy, and happily says, "Chocolate!", his mother says enthusiastically, "That's *right*, Jimmy!" Skinner applied a simple S-R account to such scenarios. The stimulus is the beverage Jimmy is drinking, the response is "Chocolate!", and the reinforcement is Mommy's smile and exclamation that solidifies the bond between the stimulus and the response. In Skinnerian terms, the *response* "Chocolate" comes under control of the *stimulus,* a glass of chocolate milk. This mechanism is typically labeled "stimulus control."

Chomsky challenged this conceptualization, pointing out gaping holes in Skinner's account. He argued that the concept of stimulus control has no meaning in language. Consider an example. If we hand you a glass filled with a brown-colored bubbling liquid (the stimulus), you could respond by saying, "Coke?" or "cold" or "tasty." No matter what you said, a behaviorist would say that your response was elicited by some stimulus property; but there would be no way of predicting *which* stimulus property. Skinner would just say that whatever response you gave was elicited by a stimulus property. Chomsky pointed out that this explanation is no explanation at all. The term *stimulus* might mean something when a rat runs in a maze, but it loses virtually all meaning when applied to the subtleties and complexities of language.

Consider the following sentence: *After the storm, the sun came out, and the leprechaun started searching for the gold.* We just created this sentence. We've never heard it before. We've never been reinforced for saying it or writing it. It seems kind of silly to say that the *response* of typing it came about because of the *stimulus* of the laptop computer. The behaviorists really have no satisfactory explanation for how this sentence was created. They also have no explanation for the wonder of sentence comprehension—the process by which you understood the sentence and probably inferred that the leprechaun would first need to find a rainbow or his search would be unsuccessful. The term *reinforcement* doesn't hold up very well either. It's not really apparent what the reinforcement is for speaking. What's reinforcing about people talking to themselves or a little girl talking to her dolls at a tea party? Skinner's explanation was *automatic self-reinforcement;* but once again, if such a slippery concept is allowed as an explanation of language, then we really have no explanation at all. Chomsky argued that Skinner's account of language learning was nothing more than a fuzzy, metaphorical description of language learning that happened to sound vaguely scientific.

Automatically self-reinforcing? Sounds like thinking.

Chomsky's critique of Skinner was so devastating that it was met by silence from the behaviorists for over a decade (Lachman, Lachman, & Butterfield, 1979); they simply didn't have an answer for it. The basic premise of Chomsky's account was that the productivity and novelty observed in language use can be explained only by appealing to mental representations—"rules in the head" that allow a person to produce and comprehend language. As you'll see throughout the text, the concept of mental representation is central to the study of cognition, and Chomsky deserves much of the credit for legitimizing it.

The movement toward a new science of mind now had undeniable momentum. Conceptually, behaviorism was failing as a satisfactory explanation of behavior. The issues discussed in the preceding sections were all converging on a single, very important point that lies at the heart of cognitive psychology—any satisfactory account of behavior must make reference to mental processes and mental representations. The time was right for a new approach to the study of mind to emerge.

Technological Influences

Around the same time that behaviorism was faltering, emerging technologies, such as communication systems and computers, provided useful models for describing the process of thinking and investigating its components.

Communications Engineering.   Communication devices such as televisions, radios, and cell phones are all examples of information transmission systems. In 1948, Bell Telephone mathematician Claude Shannon developed a general theory of how such systems work. According to Shannon, any communications system has several key components, including an information source, a transmitter, a channel through which a message is transmitted, and a receiver. An effective communications system will transmit information with as much fidelity as possible, minimizing distortion and the effects of outside interference, or "noise." These issues are obviously of interest to engineers working with communications systems. But this description of a communications system is also a fairly good model of how humans process information. Consider yourself as you listen to your professor's riveting lecture on the history of cognitive psychology. The professor is the information source, and the lecture is the transmitter. You listen to the message via your auditory channel, and after reception, the message is interpreted. The noise in the system could be the students behind you whispering or someone's cell phone ringing. Shannon's concept of a communications system provided a fruitful metaphor for considering how human thought processes might work and suggested ways they might be analyzed and investigated.

Computer Science.   A second technological advance that had a dramatic impact on the newly developing science of mind was the development of the computer. It became apparent that machines could be programmed to perform some of the intelligent functions thought to be the exclusive province of humans. Simply put, computers could, in a sense, "think." It wasn't long before the analogy was actively pursued. Could the way computers "think" be similar to the way humans think? After all, like communications systems, the computer provides a good descriptive model of how the mind might work. Computers handle information in three basic stages: input, some type of processing, and output. Humans can be thought of in exactly the same way. We take in information through our sensory systems, process it in some way, and respond to it in some way. A promising direction for a science of mind might be to specify the mechanisms whereby humans process data and how the data are stored, retrieved, and used. As you'll see, cognitive psychology research has these basic aims.

The computer has been a rich metaphor for conceptualizing mental processing.

Stop&*Think* | CONSIDERING COGNITION'S HISTORICAL INFLUENCES

Look over the developments that led to the decline of behaviorism and the ascendance of cognitive psychology, and think about their relative importance. Provide a ranking of the following developments, from most important to least important, and explain your ranking.

Lashley's argument	learning-without-reinforcement study
Chomsky's argument	learning-without-responding study
cognitive map study	advances in communications engineering

Stop&*Review* |

1. True or false? Research has shown that learning can occur without responding.
2. Explain Chomsky's objection to the behaviorist account of language learning.
3. True or false? Lashley argued that many behaviors are carried out too slowly for an S-R explanation to be correct.

4. Describe the ways in which technology was instrumental in the development of cognitive psychology.

- According to behaviorism, learning requires both a response and reinforcement. Contrary to this view, research indicated that rats were capable of learning in the absence of reinforcement and in the absence of a response, suggesting that behavior is guided by mental representations like maps and expectations.

- Chomsky sharply criticized Skinner's simplistic S-R view of learning language, citing the tremendous novelty and generativity of language.

- Lashley pointed out the inadequacy of the behaviorist approach in explaining rapid behavioral sequences, like those involved in playing the piano.

- The development of new technologies such as computers and communication systems provided new models of how the mind might work and helped inspire the new science of cognition.

Psychology A. D. (After the *Decline* of Behaviorism)

By the mid-1950s, cognitive psychology was well on its way to establishing itself as a legitimate paradigm within psychology. The failure of the S-R approach, coupled with the promise and excitement generated by new theoretical approaches and new technologies, fueled what some have termed the *cognitive revolution.* One of cognitive psychology's pioneers, George Miller (cited in Gardner, 1985), fixed the birth date of cognitive psychology as September 11, 1956. On this date, psychologists interested in the study of mind gathered at the Massachusetts Institute of Technology for the Symposium on Information Theory. As outlined by Gardner (1985), this conference featured a number of seminal papers that employed the new approach to mind. Chomsky presented his newly developed theory of language; computer scientists Allen Newell and Herbert Simon presented a paper detailing their "Logic Theory Machine"—a complete theorem proof carried out by a computing machine; and George Miller presented his now-classic view of short-term memory as a limited information-processing mechanism that could hold approximately 7 ± 2 items. Clearly, times had changed.

Behaviorism Reconsidered

But before we kick the last bit of dirt onto the behaviorists' grave, we should emphasize the immeasurable positive influence they had on the study of mind. As you'll see, the methodologies employed by modern-day cognitive psychologists are truly impressive in their objectivity and precision, almost to a fault. Whereas introspection was an "easy mark" in terms of criticism, the same cannot be said of today's investigations of mind, which are rigorously controlled and feature careful measurement and observation. Behaviorists threw down the gauntlet of challenge to investigators of mind, and the challenge was answered.

And, as it turns out, behaviorism never really went away after all. In an essay entitled "What Happened to Behaviorism," Roediger (2004) gives his answer: not much.

Behaviorism is still alive and well, and is well represented in much of the research and theorizing in current cognitive psychology. For example, all psychologists (including cognitive psychologists) must ultimately measure behavior to reach any type of conclusion. And, as Roediger points out, "The scientist's hope is to discover fundamentally interesting principles from simple, elegant experimental analyses," and when cognitive psychologists engage in this process of discovery, they use behavioral measures to arrive at the "fundamentally interesting principles." So the behaviorist approach continues to hold some sway, although different from its heyday.

Information Processing: A Computer Metaphor for Cognition

As cognitive psychology evolved, the **information-processing model** emerged as the pre-eminent paradigm in cognitive psychology. This paradigm uses the computer as a model for human cognition and has dominated theory and research in cognitive psychology for its first five decades.

Lachman, Lachman, and Butterfield (1979) identified some of the major assumptions of the information-processing approach. The first assumption is that humans are *symbol manipulators* who encode, store, retrieve, and manipulate symbolic data. Flowing from this is the idea of *representation;* the data of the human information-processing system consist of representations that correspond to information from the environment (e.g., objects and events) and processes (e.g., remembering and problem solving). Another assumption is that human thought is best characterized as a *system* of interrelated capacities and processes that all affect each other. The components cannot be fully understood in isolation from one another. This view also assumes that humans are active and creative information scanners and seekers; we don't just passively react to the environment. This idea contrasts powerfully with the behaviorist approach, which considers humans to be passive responders waiting for the environment to elicit responses. According to the information-processing approach, thinking is a step-by-step process in which the products of a given stage serve as the input for the next stage, and so on. Each of these processes takes time and can be examined separately, to some extent. For example, we can attempt to isolate processes such as encoding, processing, and retrieval and estimate their duration. This assumption paved the way for using reaction time to measure mental processing.

Connectionism: A Brain Metaphor for Cognition

One might say that the information-processing approach would characterize the brain as the "hardware" of the human computer system and the numerous cognitive processes as the "software"; engaging in different mental operations is analogous to running different software packages. This analogy has proven to be a fairly appropriate characterization, as thousands of studies have helped to specify the "software" that is cognitive processing. However, some feel that the human-computer analogy has been taken to (perhaps beyond) the limits of its usefulness. Do humans really process information in a way similar to computers? It turns out there are some major differences between the two. The most important difference is that computers typically have some type of central processing unit that does things one at a time; that is, computers tend to operate in a serial (step-by-step) fashion. This is not how the human brain works. Investigations of the brain's basic function have failed to reveal any central processor and have made it apparent that much of the brain's functioning occurs in a parallel, not a serial manner.

Instead of a very rapid and serially operating computer, the mind seems better characterized as a set of slower computers that operate in parallel, all working on relatively specific tasks (Martindale, 1991). Computers can do things that humans find difficult (e.g., error-free calculation), and humans can do things that computers find difficult (e.g., recognizing variations in a familiar pattern). Unlike a computer, we can quickly recognize **A**, *A*, A, **A**, A, A, *A* as all representing the same thing; consequently, it's clear that information is processed differently in each system. The inadequacies of the information-processing metaphor have led most psychologists to abandon it as a model for the way cognitive processes work. As you'll see throughout the text, however, this metaphor is employed as a descriptive device. Although significant differences exist in how humans and computers process information, certain similarities do remain.

In a continuing search for a good model, many cognitive psychologists have turned to structural aspects of the brain for answers to the riddle of cognition. A different model of cognitive processes has evolved and threatens to replace information processing as the dominant paradigm for exploring and explaining cognition. This approach, termed **connectionism,** uses the brain (rather than the computer) as a basis for modeling cognitive processes (e.g., McClelland & Rumelhart, 1981; Rumelhart & McClelland, 1986). This model attempts to account for cognition solely in terms of the underlying "hardware" (in the computer terms used earlier) without the need to postulate extra "software" that "runs" on the hardware. In addition, psychologists (and scientists) prefer simpler theories to more complex ones, all things being equal. (The simplicity of a theory is termed *parsimony*.) Explaining cognition solely in terms of existing brain structure and function has a theoretically appealing simplicity—and it also makes a great deal of intuitive sense. It's not difficult to understand why these models generate a great deal of interest and enthusiasm.

According to connectionist models, the cognitive system (which corresponds to the brain) is made up of billions of interconnected nodes (corresponding to the billions of interconnected neurons in the brain) that come together to form complex networks. Nodes within a network can be activated, and the pattern of activation among these nodes corresponds to conscious experience. Let's examine some of the basic assumptions underlying this approach. First, the approach proposes that the networks underlying cognitive processing operate largely in parallel; information processors throughout the brain work simultaneously on some specific component of a cognitive task. Second, the processing involved in a given task (e.g., retrieving a memory) does not occur in only one specific location. Rather, the networks involved in cognitive processing are distributed throughout the brain. This idea of parallel processing contrasts strongly with the idea of cognition as a serial (step-by-step) process, as proposed in the information-processing approach.

If cognition is characterized as the parallel activity of a complex series of networks distributed throughout the brain, you might be asking yourself, "How are these networks formed?" The basic building block of these networks is a connection between two individual nodes. Once again, the dynamics of interconnection between nodes is modeled

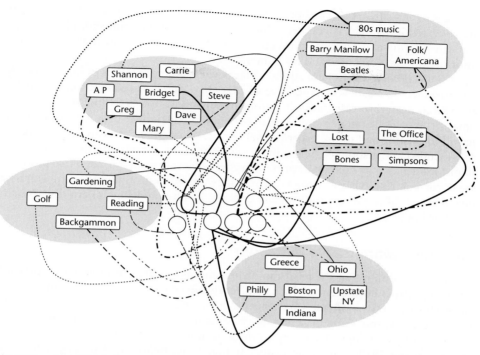

Adapted from Rumelhart, D. E., & McClelland, J. L. (1986). *Parallel distributed processing: Explorations in the microstructure of cognition.* Cambridge, MA: MIT Press. Reprinted by permission of the author.

on the way neurons interact. The effect of one neuron on another may be excitatory, inhibitory, or nonexistent. So, within a neural network, nodes may have an excitatory connection (activation of one node makes activation of another node more likely), an inhibitory connection (activation of one node makes activation of another node less likely), or no connection (activation of one node has no effect on another node). These connections are built up, solidified, and modified as we experience the world day to day, just as our memories, general knowledge, and skills are built up, solidified, and modified. Connectionist models postulate some type of learning rule to model this process. One intuitively sensible rule often employed is that connections between nodes are strengthened if they are activated at the same time.

Consider this simple example: Imagine that you meet Greg (one of your authors) at a party. It probably won't be more than about 15 minutes before he makes some reference to either *The Simpsons* ("Homer Simpson is the greatest comic creation in TV history") or the Beatles ("The Beatles are bigger than cognitive psychology"). From this encounter, you will have the beginnings of a connectionist network that corresponds to your memory of Greg—essentially, it *is* your memory of him. The nodes distributed throughout your neural network correspond to the bits of information you have about Greg and are connected one to another. There are excitatory connections between Greg's name, *The Simpsons,* the Beatles, and whatever other information you might pick up. Every time you meet Greg and he bores you with yet another piece of trivia about the Beatles, that particular connection gets stronger. When you are asked about him, all of the nodes in your network that are Greg are activated in parallel as you bring him to mind. From this simpleminded example, you can imagine how your brain might encode the thousands of memories and bits of information that you know and encounter.

Connectionist models have advanced far beyond simple accounts of how knowledge is represented. In recent years, cognitive scientists have developed connectionist models of everything from face recognition to problem solving to how we form attitudes about other people. These models are used to generate predictions, which are assessed with regard to existing and future experimental results. When predictions are correct, models are extended and elaborated; when incorrect, they undergo revision. Although connectionist modeling may hold an important key to truly understanding cognitive processes, most current research in cognitive psychology focuses on straightforward empirical investigations of cognitive processes and does not involve modeling, so our discussion of it will be limited.

The Brain: More than a Metaphor

There is little doubt that the most rapidly expanding research frontier within psychology is **cognitive neuroscience,** which involves relating cognitive processes to their neural substrates—in other words, what the brain is doing when the mind is thinking. Gazzaniga, Ivry, and Mangun (2002) describe cognitive neuroscience as a coalescence of biology and psychology. According to these authors, cognitive neuroscience began to emerge in the 1970s out of necessity. At that time, neuroscientists began to move beyond the simple destruction of brain tissue and the consequent behavioral changes of that destruction to the use of increasingly sophisticated methods to address more complex questions, such as how visual cells process and combine information to produce percepts. As neuroscientists advanced beyond simple approaches, so did cognitive psychologists. Recall that by the 1960s, cognitive psychologists were developing theories and models of cognition and action that were based on mental representations (whose basis, ultimately, is the brain). Given that the interests of many neuroscientists were getting more cognitive and that the interest of many cognitive psychologists was turning toward brain representation, a union of the two approaches was inevitable.

An Overview of the Nervous System.   Throughout the text, we'll be discussing cognitive neuroscience research. Before we do, it would be helpful to review some basics about the nervous system. We'll start at the most basic level with a discussion of the basic nerve cell, the neuron. We'll then proceed to the brain, highlighting its structure and discussing some of the important questions posed by cognitive neuroscientists as well as their tools of investigation.

The Neuron.   The nervous system is the body's system for processing information, and the **neuron,** or nerve cell, is its basic unit. It is estimated that there are about 100 billion neurons throughout the nervous system. Many of these are located in the brain's cerebral cortex, the seat of complex thought. A simple neuron is pictured in Figure 1.5. This is a general representation; there are many different types of neurons, with different sizes, shapes, and

functions. Given that there are billions of them, you might imagine that they're interconnected in incredibly complex networks. Indeed, this aspect of brain structure forms the basis for the connectionist approach to cognition, just discussed.

Neurons are electrochemical information processors. Within a neuron, communication is basically an electrical process whereby a signal travels from the dendrites to the cell body down the length of the axon. This process is called an **action potential,** and it occurs in an all-or-none fashion if the stimulation of the neuron reaches some critical value, or threshold. At this point, the communication process becomes chemical; the action potential causes the release of neurotransmitters into the tiny gap between neurons, the synapse. The neurotransmitters released into the synapse interact with dendrites of many receiving neurons, leading to their excitation or inhibition. This system of excitatory and inhibitory connections between these basic units of the nervous system underlies all thinking and behavior. Indeed, many believe it *is* thinking

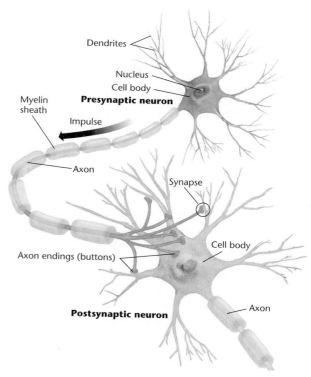

Figure 1.5

A neuron and its major structures.

(e.g., LeDoux, 2002), although this assertion generates some philosophical argument.

Hebb (1949) suggested a basic principle of neuronal functioning. According to Hebb, "When an axon of cell A is near enough to excite a cell B, and repeatedly takes part in firing it, some growth process or metabolic change takes place in one or both cells such that A's efficiency as one of the cells firing B is increased" (p. 62). In other words, the association between neurons can become stronger with experience; neural networks can learn. Hebb's suggestion has been supported by research and has served as a partial basis for the connectionist approach to mental processes, which attempts to explain thinking in terms of the strengthening and weakening (i.e., the changes) in association among simple units. These simple units and their interconnections correspond to the brain's neurons and neural networks. Researchers have attempted to simulate thinking tasks like problem solving or object recognition with computer models that have architecture similar to that of the brain, in hopes that these models might provide some insight into how the activity of the brain subserves cognitive processes.

Research in cognitive neuroscience has not progressed to the point of explaining cognition in terms of how individual neurons and neural networks actually work in their seemingly infinite complexity and variety. But researchers have come a long way in modeling how cognition *might* work, given the properties of neurons (e.g., Pinker, 1994b). So while we can't map out the exact grouping and activity of neurons that underlie the cognitive processes that occur as we're deciding what to watch on TV tonight, we are fairly certain where in the brain the relevant activity takes place and how some of the component processes may play themselves out in a system modeled on the neural networks of the brain. So some of the pieces of the puzzle about how the brain works are in place, and cognitive neuroscientists continue to look for the remaining ones.

The Brain.   The brain serves as the primary focus of cognitive neuroscience because the brain is the center of information processing. Cognitive neuroscientists investigate a number of questions about brain structure and its relation to cognitive processing. A great deal of research has investigated exactly what brain areas are active during different mental processes. Based on this general information, researchers can pinpoint more specifically the brain substrates of cognition.

A Terminology Tour.   Neuroscience can be a challenging topic, in part because of the sheer volume of new terminology one encounters; anterior commissure, parahippocampal gyrus, anterior thalamic nucleus—it's enough to give one dorsal-ventricular cerebral distress (i.e., a headache). Knowing some of the standard terminology going in will help you understand some of the neuroscience research you'll read about throughout the text. As a convention, anatomists (and neuroscientists) use certain terms to refer to different areas of the brain. The term **anterior** (or **rostral**) refers to the front portion of the brain or brain region, while **posterior** (or **caudal**) refers to the back portion. **Dorsal** (or **superior**) refers to the top surface of the brain or brain region (like the famous dorsal fin of a shark), while **ventral** refers to the bottom. Other general terms you might hear in conjunction with specific brain structures are **lateral** (to refer to brain structures closer to the periphery) and **medial** (to refer to areas closer to the brain's midpoint).

Neuroscientists commonly divide the brain into three major areas (see Figure 1.6). The **hindbrain** is located at the base of the brain, just above the spinal cord, and its primary function is to monitor, maintain, and control basic life functions such as breathing and heartbeat. Just above the hindbrain, a relatively small area termed the **midbrain** contains areas that are involved in some sensory reflexes and help to regulate brain arousal. The remainder of the brain, the forebrain, is the area of primary interest for cognitive neuroscientists. The **forebrain** comprises most of the brain and consists mainly of the **cerebral cortex,** the familiar wrinkled outer shell of the brain, which is actually a sheet of billions of neurons. The cerebral cortex is the primary neural substrate for what might be termed *higher cognitive functions*—remembering, planning, deciding, communicating—essentially, all the stuff that you'll be reading about in this text. Beneath the cortex lies an array of important subcortical structures

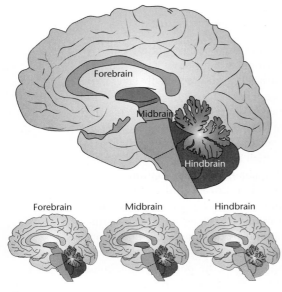

Figure 1.6
Three major areas of the brain

that are involved in basic processes such as the regulation of memory and emotion.

The Cerebral Cortex. The cerebral cortex consists of two hemispheres that are made up of layered sheets of neurons that form tremendously complex interconnections and networks. Each hemisphere can be subdivided into four major areas, or *lobes* (see Figure 1.7). The frontal lobe is the anterior portion (i.e., the "front part") of your cortex, located immediately behind your forehead and running back to about the middle of the top of your head. The posterior area (i.e., the "back part") of the frontal lobe, the motor cortex, plays an important role in carrying out voluntary movements. Areas in the anterior portion of the frontal lobe (commonly called the *prefrontal cortex*) are important in higher aspects of motor control, such as planning and executing complex behaviors. The frontal lobe also includes Broca's area, an important region that's related to the physical production of speech. Behind the frontal lobe lies the parietal lobe, centered more or less under the crown of your skull. In terms of cognitive processes, the parietal lobe houses areas important in regulating (among other things) the processes of attention and working memory. Beneath the parietal lobe in the posterior portion of the cortex is the occipital lobe, which contains the primary visual cortex, the area of the brain primarily responsible for vision and the ability to recognize visual patterns. (So you really do have "eyes" in the back of your head!) Finally, the temporal lobe is appropriately located behind the ears because it contains the auditory cortex, the brain's primary sensory area for audition. It also includes Wernicke's area, which is involved in speech comprehension. Many areas of the cortex are not specifically devoted to motor or sensory function and have been dubbed "association areas." Association areas of the cortex are believed to integrate the processing of other brain areas, serving as the basis for higher mental processes that require integration, such as language processing, problem solving, and decision making.

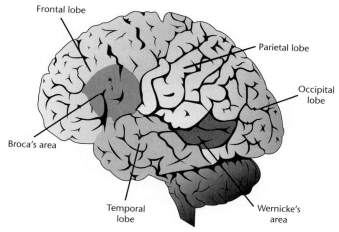

Figure 1.7
The major areas of the cerebral cortex

Hemispheric Asymmetries. The cerebral cortex is made up of two hemispheres, the right and the left. The hemispheres appear more or less symmetrical in their appearance, but as we'll see, each features some interesting processing differences. In general, the operation of the hemispheres is lateralized—that is, the left hemisphere receives information from and controls the right side of the body, while the right hemisphere receives information from and controls the left side of the body. The two hemispheres communicate primarily by means of the corpus callosum, a nerve bundle located in the center of the brain above the limbic system.

The fact that the brain is divided into two separate hemispheres is a happy coincidence for brain researchers, because the asymmetries in the processing of the hemispheres have revealed some interesting features of brain processing. The main distinction between the brain's hemispheres relates to verbal ability. In most people, the left hemisphere is specialized for verbal processing, while the right hemisphere is relatively nonverbal. One major source of evidence for this asymmetry has been research on **split-brain patients,** people who have had their corpus callosum severed to alleviate the severity of epileptic seizures. While successful in alleviating seizures, cutting the main source of communication between the right and left hemispheres does lead to some oddities in processing that have illuminated some of the differences in hemispheric functions. These oddities are revealed only in a special laboratory setup. Were you to meet a split-brain person on the street, you likely wouldn't notice anything.

Split-brain research takes advantage of the wiring of the visual system, which is structured so that if you were to stare straight ahead, information right of center would go predominantly to the left hemisphere, while information left of center would go predominantly to the right hemisphere. When a split-brain patient is presented with a stimulus (e.g., a word) left of center fixation, it goes to the right hemisphere, but cannot get to the left due to the severed corpus callosum. If the patient is asked to read aloud the word, they will have a great deal of difficulty because the right hemisphere is relatively poor in its verbal ability. But interestingly, if asked to take their left hand and reach behind a screen to pick up the item that the word names, they are able to do so because the right hemisphere directs the left hand. The right hemisphere "knows" the word it saw, but is limited by its inability to demonstrate the knowledge verbally. However, if a word is presented right of center fixation, it goes to the left hemisphere, and the patient will have no trouble reading it aloud because the left hemisphere is specialized for verbal processing.

Differences in left and right brain function also can be seen in people with intact brains. This research has revealed that the left hemisphere is specialized for language processing, while the right hemisphere is specialized for spatial tasks like assembling the pieces of a puzzle or orienting oneself within the environment. And there are some other asymmetries in processing, some of which you'll learn about in subsequent chapters. But one should be careful not to overgeneralize—the two hemispheres of the brain form an elegantly integrated system that features close interactions between right and left.

Subcortical Structures.   Beneath the cerebral cortex lies a complex system of structures that play an important role in a variety of cognitive processes. Most of the structures are grouped together and termed the *limbic system*. The **limbic system** is integral to learning and remembering new information as well as the processing of emotion. Important structures in the limbic system include the *hippocampus*, which is vital for encoding new information into memory and the *amygdala* which plays a key role in regulating emotions and in forming emotional memories. Other subcortical structures include the *thalamus*, which primarily serves as a relay point that routes incoming sensory information to the appropriate area of the brain (directing visual information to the visual cortex and so on) and also seems to play a role in attention. Below the thalamus lies the *hypothalamus* ("hypo" means "under" in Latin), which controls the endocrine system (the body's system of hormones) and plays an important role in emotion as well as the maintenance of important and basic survival processes, such as temperature regulation and food intake. Together, the thalamus and hypothalamus are termed the *diencephalon*. The basal ganglia play a critical role in controlling movement and are important for motor-based memories, such as the procedures involved in riding a bike.

Although brain areas and brain structures are to a considerable extent specialized for certain types of functions, it is important not to lose sight of the brain as an integrated system. No function (particularly cognitive functions like remembering) takes place in a single brain structure or area. While some subcomponents of cognitive processes may be localized in one area, complex cognition involves an intricate interplay between brain areas and brain structures that are distributed throughout the brain.

The Tools of Cognitive Neuroscience.   Cognitive neuroscientists rely on a number of investigative techniques to discover the neural underpinnings of cognition. Before the development of sophisticated technologies, much of the information we know about the brain, and what happens where, was discovered through investigations of people who had suffered brain damage. In the last 25 years, there has been an explosion in the development of brain investigation techniques. Some of these techniques involve the assessment of the electrophysiological activity occurring in the brain during cognitive processes, while others involve "taking a picture" of the brain activity that accompanies mental processing.

There are a number of criteria for assessing the utility of brain investigation techniques. One is how well the technique informs the precise nature of brain activity down to the level of *how* a given brain structure might be involved in cognitive processing; that is, what structures or mechanisms underlie a given cognitive process. A related criterion, applied to any of the techniques that "take a picture" of the brain, is the *spatial resolution* of that map. Imagine being told that Greg is from the United States. This isn't as informative as telling you he's from the Delhi neighborhood of Cincinnati, Ohio, within the United States. *Temporal resolution* refers to how well the technique pinpoints *when* the neural activity occurs. If I told you that Greg called Bridget around 3:00. That does not have as fine a temporal resolution as if I told you Greg called Bridget at 3:02 and 58 seconds.

Brain Trauma and Lesions.   Much of the early knowledge about what brain areas are involved in various cognitive functions came from studies of patients who had suffered some sort of trauma to the brain through injury or disease. A prominent example relevant to cognitive psychology is the work of Paul Broca, a neuroscience pioneer in the mid-1850s. Broca had a famous patient who was dubbed "Tan" because this syllable was all he could say. In spite of this inability to speak normally, Tan's ability to understand was relatively unimpaired. Broca discovered that this patient had damage to the left frontal lobe in an area now called Broca's area. Later, in the 1870s, Carl Wernicke had a patient who could speak, but what he said was gibberish. Furthermore, he was unable to understand written or spoken language. Wernicke discovered that this patient had damage to the left temporal lobe in an area now called Wernicke's area. Based on these and other patients with language impairment, researchers were able to clearly delineate the role of left-hemisphere areas in language processing.

The most severe limitation of using cases such as these to study cognitive processes is that they allow absolutely no control. A researcher can't map out the human brain by systematically damaging different areas and observing the associated deficits. (How would you like to volunteer for that study?) Studies of brain trauma cases also suffer limitations in generalizability. There may be critical differences in the functioning of a normal and a damaged brain. And finally (and this is true of most brain investigation techniques), the evidence yielded is purely descriptive. It provides a relatively simple sketch of the relationship between brain areas and cognitive function.

Single and Double Dissociations.   So what modes of assessment do cognitive neuroscientists use in studying individuals with brain damage? Often they will compare performance on two tasks that differ in the use of one proposed cognitive process. Let's consider an example from Coltheart (2001). It is important to note that the following example is fictional and does not necessarily depict any actual brain structure; the names of the possible brain structures have been changed to protect their identity.... Suppose we find a person who has brain damage in area X and exhibits deficits in comprehending written language (i.e., reading) but has no deficits in comprehending spoken language. This would be an example of a *single dissociation*—performance deficits in one task but no performance deficits in another task. Based on these data, it's tempting to conclude that area X is responsible for written comprehension but not for spoken comprehension. Perhaps spoken comprehension depends on some other area, Y. Do you see a problem with this conclusion? Maybe area X is responsible for *both* written and spoken comprehension, but the damage is not severe enough to reveal the deficits in spoken comprehension.

So what can researchers do? They could examine patients with different areas of brain damage—X *and* Y. Suppose we found a patient with damage to area X who shows deficits in reading but not in understanding spoken language *and* a patient with damage to area Y who has deficits in understanding spoken language but not in reading. This pattern is termed a **double dissociation.** This double dissociation data serves as stronger evidence than the single dissociation data that area X is responsible for written comprehension and area Y is responsible for spoken language comprehension. Although double dissociations are quite informative, they do not provide conclusive evidence that any two processes are based on *completely* different brain processes and structures. However, the double dissociation in this fictional example certainly suggests that written comprehension and spoken comprehension are partially independent and controlled by areas X and Y, respectively.

The value of double dissociations extends well beyond cognitive neuroscience. Double dissociations also have been used to argue that the performance on two different experimental conditions or tasks relies on different mental processes, or different cognitive systems. Throughout this text, you'll encounter numerous examples of dissociations that indicate the operation of distinct brain systems, or distinct sets of cognitive processes.

Relatively few neuroscientific studies involve patient populations and lesion/brain trauma investigations we've just discussed. According to Chatterjee (2005) this is disappointing because of the explanatory potential offered by patient studies. In contrast, the techniques we will be discussing next are limited to telling us "where it is" or "when it occurs" whereas neuropsychological investigation of patients and lesions offers greater potential for telling us "how it works."

Encephalographic Techniques.   Remember the way neurons work—they are electrochemical information processors. Because the activity of neurons is electrical in part, some research techniques involve recording the electrical activity of the brain and relating it to cognitive functioning. The **electroencephalograph (EEG)** uses electrodes placed on the scalp to pick up the electrical current being conducted through the skull by the activity of neurons underneath, essentially providing a global recording of the action potentials occurring in the brain. Although researchers have used this method to localize the brain processes underlying cognition, the results have been somewhat disappointing. The electroencephalograph simply records a combination of the activity of millions of neurons at the brain's surface, making it difficult to pinpoint specific areas underlying cognitive processes. Also, because the neural impulses are traveling over the brain and through the skull and scalp, some distortion in the recorded signal is inevitable, further confounding attempts to localize where the important brain processing is occurring. Some have likened the use of the EEG to trying to diagnose a computer malfunction by holding up a voltmeter in front of it. As we'll see later in the chapter, neuroscientists have developed much better techniques for mapping out brain function.

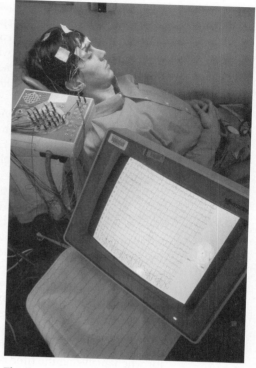

The EEG allows a researcher to record summed action potentials from different brain sites.

Event-Related Potentials.   Although electroencephalography leaves something to be desired in terms of brain-mapping precision, it does have one advantage over some other techniques. It has fairly good temporal resolution, or precision, in specifying the time course of events. Researchers can observe EEG tracings over time and look for *changes* in the brain's electrical activity at certain critical points, like when something surprising occurs. These changes are termed **event-related potentials (ERP)** because they represent the action *potentials* that occur in *relation* to some *event*. These potentials allow researchers to plot out *when* (in addition to a rough idea of *where*) important brain activity is occurring.

Event-related potentials have become increasingly popular in recent years because of their unique ability to pinpoint highlights of cognitive processing in real time—something the brain-imaging techniques that we'll be talking about later cannot do. Let's take a closer look at the makeup of an event-related potential (see Figure 1.8) and review some of the terminology. The x-axis represents time in milliseconds, and the y-axis represents the magnitude/direction of the brain's electrical response, typically measured in millivolts. The plot defined by these axes represents the brain's response to a stimulus over time. As you can see, shortly after stimulus presentation, the ERP response begins. The response curve

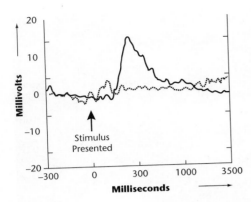

Figure 1.8
An event-related potential (ERP).

has several features to note. First is the *amplitude* of response, indicated by the distance of the response from a control condition that serves as a baseline. Second is whether the change in amplitude occurs in a positive or a negative direction (i.e., deflection above or below the baseline condition). Third is the point in time at which the peak level of response occurs relative to stimulus presentation. Also keep in mind that ERPs are being collected from a myriad of points along the surface of the scalp, so a given ERP may represent activity from a particular location on the scalp (and, correspondingly, the brain).

As noted earlier, ERP responses always involve a comparison between at least two conditions. Let's make this concrete with an example. A researcher might compare the brain's response to "Jocelyn put the cookies into the *oven*" and the response to "Jocelyn put the cookies into the *shoe*" in order to find out the brain's response to a semantic (i.e., meaning) anomaly. It turns out that the pattern generated in response to the aforementioned kooky cookie sentence would be a pronounced *negative* deflection in the wave, *400* ms after stimulus presentation, relative to the normal (i.e., baseline) cookie sentence. This pronounced deflection is termed an **N400 response** (Kutas & Hillyard, 1980); this response (often shortened to N4) tends to be larger over the parietal and temporal regions of the right hemisphere (Atchley & Kwasny, 2003).

The N400 response is just one of a number of typical responses that researchers look for when analyzing the time course and location of various cognitive processes. Another informative pattern is the **P300 response** (Sutton, Tueting, Zubin, & John, 1967), a pronounced *positive* deflection in the brain's response *300* ms after stimulus presentation, relative to a baseline condition. Actually, this response (often shortened to P3) is probably the most analyzed component of the ERP response (Key, Dove, & Maguire, 2005). It occurs in response to an unexpected stimulus—sometimes termed an "oddball." For example, if someone had been observing a series of bird pictures, an oddball picture of a panda bear inserted in the middle would result in a P300 response. Although sources of the P300 are unclear, the medial (i.e., toward the middle) temporal regions of the brain seems to be the probable location.

The P300 and N400 components are only two of many that researchers attempt to extract from the EEG in order to plot out the time course and locations of cognitive processing. All components are affected by a host of independent variables like stimulus probability, presentation time, modality of presentation (visual vs. auditory), and more. Indeed, observing the variation in ERP components as a function of these independent variables is critical in mapping out brain function. You'll be encountering more of these component-variable interactions in subsequent chapters, within the context of specific cognitive processes and paradigms, such as face recognition, autobiographical remembering, and problem solving.

Magnetoencephalography.   The changes in electrical potential in the brain produce more than electrical signals. They also produce magnetic fields. This fact forms the basis for another encephalographic technique termed **magnetoencephalography,** or MEG. When large groups of neurons fire at the same time, the fields they generate are strong enough to be picked up by a detector outside the skull, termed a SQUID (superconducting quantum interference device) magnetometer. These detectors can determine which brain areas were active in response to different types of stimuli, and like the EEG, provide a more precise analysis of the time course of neural processing than do the brain imaging techniques. In fact, the MEG is capable of producing an even finer-grained analysis of the time course of a neural event than the EEG. Second, the MEG's spatial resolution is much better than that of the EEG, allowing for a finer precision of localization.

Transcranial Magnetic Stimulation.   Electromagnetic principles form the basis for a quite different technique of brain investigation: **transcranial magnetic stimulation,** or TMS. As you can tell from its title, this method is fundamentally different than MEG, and from all of the other techniques we're discussing for that matter, because it involves stimulation of the brain, rather than recording or imaging of brain activity. Transcranial magnetic stimulation is based on a principle introduced by physicist Michael Faraday (not the one from TV's *Lost*; the other physicist Faraday). Faraday demonstrated that running an electrical current through one coil leads to a magnetic field that can induce an electronic current in a second nearby coil. For TMS, the brain is like the second coil; neural activity is stimulated by the magnetic field produced by an electrical current. Transcranial magnetic stimulation can be used to interfere with brain activity (basically by producing temporary and transient brain lesions!). Impeding or disrupting brain processing (a la the brain trauma work described previously) even temporarily allows researchers to gain insights about what areas are involved in brain processing, and what the time course of the processing might be. The spatial and temporal resolution of TMS is fairly good, compared to other neuroscientific techniques; one can get a decent bead on the time course and the location of neural processing.

Imaging Techniques: PET, fMRI Scans.   The most commonly used techniques in the field of cognitive neuroscience (to the chagrin of some; see Chatterjee, 2005) are functional imaging techniques. These imaging techniques have proven much more successful than EEGs in precisely localizing the brain areas associated with various cognitive processes. Unlike EEGs, imaging techniques do not involve the direct measurement of neural activity. Rather, changes in blood flow are used as indices of where brain activity is occurring during various cognitive processes, essentially providing a map of brain activity.

Imaging techniques involve a comparison between an active and a (relatively) inactive brain. In a test scan, researchers present some type of task that is thought to reflect a given cognitive process. For example, to investigate how we access words from our mental dictionary, researchers might have participants generate synonyms for words as they are presented. Brain activity would be monitored as participants engage in this task, and the results would yield an *image* of what the brain is doing. But this image isn't enough to indicate the brain centers important for performing the task. These brain centers might be active anyway, because the brain is never simply "turned off." Therefore, researchers must also get an image of the brain activity that occurs when the brain is at rest or is involved in some simpler task. This image is termed a *baseline,* or *control scan.* By comparing the *difference* in the two images, researchers can extract the areas of the brain that seem to be consistently associated with the task in question.

A **positron-emission tomography scan** (**PET scan**) uses radioactive substances ingested (in harmless amounts!) by a willing participant to trace brain activity. The technique is based on one feature of brain metabolism: active areas of the brain are associated with increased blood flow, and a radioactive substance can gauge where this blood flow is occurring. Detectors pick up this blood flow and convert it into a visual image—essentially a map of the brain in which "hot" colors, like red and yellow, indicate increased activity and "cool" colors, like blue and green, indicate less active brain areas.

Functional magnetic resonance imaging (**fMRI**) is similar to a PET scan in that it reflects brain activity through changes in blood flow. But fMRI picks up this activity with magnetic detectors that are sensitive to hemoglobin levels in the blood. Basically, a magnetic scanner picks up differences in hemoglobin that is oxygenated (carrying oxygen) or nonoxygenated (no longer carrying oxygen). The larger the difference, the more neuronal activity is occurring in that area (Gazzaniga, Ivry, & Mangun, 2002). This activity is displayed in much the same way as in PET scanning—as a multicolored map of more and less active brain areas.

fMRI offers a number of advantages over PET scanning. First, it's noninvasive. In other words, no foreign agent has to be introduced into the body, like the radioactive substance used in PET scan studies. Functional magnetic resonance imaging is also cheaper than PET scans. Equipment that's already present in many hospitals and clinics can be modified to conduct fMRI, whereas PET scanning equipment is relatively exotic.

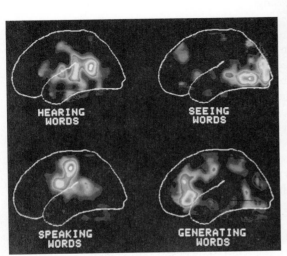
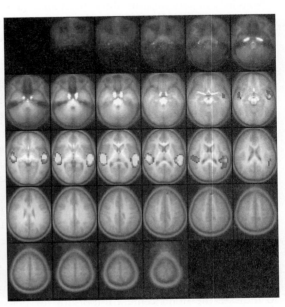

Both PET scans (left) and fMRI images (right) allow researchers to note active and less active areas of the brain.

A third advantage of fMRI is a little more subtle, and relates to how the brain scans are collected over time. Because a PET scan uses a radioactive substance to trace brain activity, some time must elapse between test and control scans to allow the substance to dissipate; the next scan needs to start with a "clean slate." Therefore, over a given period of time, only a limited number of scans can be taken, and these scans are combined into an average image. In fMRI research, there is no decaying radioactive tracer to worry about, so test and control scans can be interspersed with much greater frequency. In other words, researchers can collect many more control scans and many more test scans in a given period of time. Why is this important? Common sense probably tells you that the more participants in an experiment, the higher the likelihood is that the results of the experiment will be valid and representative. The same principle applies here; the more scans that are obtained, the more likely it is that a researcher is getting a valid and representative idea of brain activity.

Imaging techniques such as PET and fMRI have led to crucial insights about where the neural substrates for cognitive activity may lie. These techniques do have a number of limitations, however. One major limitation is their relative inability to provide a time-based analysis of cognition. Most basic cognitive processes occur on the order of fractions of a second, and the temporal (time) resolution of imaging techniques is not nearly this precise, so what we get is only a global picture of brain functioning.

Cognitive Neuroscience Techniques: A Comparison.   In an informative review of various brain investigation techniques, Chatterjee (2005) notes the prevalence of neuroimaging techniques, particularly fMRI. Chatterjee culled the 2005 proceedings of the Cognitive Neuroscience Society to count the number of investigations that used each of several different neuroscientific techniques. Imaging techniques dominated in that count, representing the highest proportion of studies reviewed (about 35%). Electrophysiological techniques were next in terms of commonality, representing about 25% of the studies. As mentioned earlier, a disappointingly small proportion of studies (about 15%) were patient studies focusing on brain damage and lesion. Behavioral techniques, which are cognitive psychology studies with neuroscientific implications comprised 15% of the studies. TMS constituted only 2% and the last category (the grab bag "other") consisted of studies related to such things as behavioral genetics and pharmacology (about 5%). A recent PsycINFO citation search (2006–2010) for abstracts that included fMRI/PET, EEG/ERP/MEG, or TMA yielded similar results; however, electrophysiological techniques and TMS are becoming increasingly prevalent (the new count did not include the other categories from Chatterjee's review).

Table 1.1 provides a quick and rough summary of how each of the neuroscientific techniques fare on the dimensions discussed previously. The indicators in the table are designed primarily to give you an idea of how each technique compares to the others on the various dimensions. It is important to note a couple of important qualifications about the table. First, the list of techniques that we describe is by no means exhaustive; there are a number of other techniques that researchers employ, particularly when working with simpler organisms, to develop models of brain functioning in humans. Second, these techniques are rarely used in isolation. In using combinations of techniques, researchers can get a more complete "picture" of the neural substrates of a given cognitive process.

Table 1.1 **Comparison of brain investigation techniques. See text for explanation.**

	EEG/ERP	MEG	PET	fMRI	TMS	Naturally Occurring Lesion/Trauma
How/What? Specification of Mechanism/ Structure	🧠	🧠	🧠	🧠🧠	🧠🧠	🧠🧠
Where? Spatial Resolution	🧠	🧠	🧠🧠🧠	🧠🧠🧠	🧠🧠🧠	🧠
When? Temporal Resolution	🧠🧠🧠	🧠🧠🧠	🧠🧠	🧠🧠🧠	🧠🧠🧠	🧠
COST	$$	$$$$	$$$$	$$$	$$	NA

Brain-based Explanations: Caveat Emptor. There can be no denying that breathtaking strides have been made in delineating the neural substrates of cognition. At the same time, there can be no denying that we know very little about how any specific daily cognition—getting a book out to study and reading the first page, for example—is realized at the level of specific neural networks. On a microlevel, we know a good deal about the general mechanics of how neurons fire action potentials; on a macrolevel, brain-imaging techniques have provided a good deal of information about the brain areas that are active during certain cognitive processes. However, a gaping chasm continues to exist between these two levels of analysis, and work continues to build a critical bridge between them.

Neuroimaging: The New Phrenology? Despite the need to bridge the gap between these macrolevels and microlevels of analysis, it is clear that much of the current research still focuses on the macrolevel as indicated by the prominence of neuroimaging techniques in brain research. Therefore, you may think that they are the magic key to unlocking the secrets of the brain. Before you draw that conclusion, it is important to remember that that these techniques only provide *descriptive* information about the location of the brain activity that accompanies a given set of cognitive processes. Some think this concern is grave enough to question the entire enterprise of mapping the brain with neuroimaging, referring to it as "the new phrenology" (e.g., Uttal, 2003). You may recall phrenology from your introductory psychology course; it's the (now totally discredited) attempt to link brain functions to bumps on the skull, popular in the 19th century. Although functional imaging has certainly not been discredited (indeed, it has been enthusiastically embraced), the criticism would seem to be well

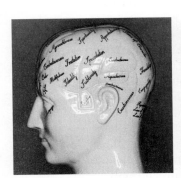
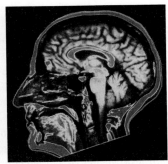

The new phrenology?

taken. The concern is that simply pointing to brain areas and saying, for example, "These three areas are quite active when people make a decision" doesn't really say much about the underlying processes.

Poldrack (2006) points out another serious problem that relates to a logical flaw in the conclusions drawn from studies that use these techniques. The problem is easiest to understand in the context of an example. Let's say that the hippocampus has been shown to be active during memory processing. In other words, memory processing leads to activation of the hippocampus. When another study finds that the hippocampus is active during task X, it is assumed that task X must involve memory processes. But this is a classic logical flaw, which you'll read about in Chapter 11, termed *affirming the consequent*. Consider the following example; if you flunk the final, you fail the course. Now say that you failed the course—does this mean that you flunked the final? Not necessarily; there could be myriad other reasons why you flunked the course. Basically, if A then B does not imply if B then A. So just because hippocampus is active does not mean that memory processes are being used. The hippocampus is involved in many different processes, not just memory. Imaging researchers and consumers of brain imaging research have to be careful to avoid this pernicious flaw in reasoning.

In spite of these reservations, researchers continue to plot brain function with functional imaging techniques. Although the comparison to phrenology seems on the mark in some ways, it is a bit extreme. After all, we have excellent reasons to attribute (or at least to relate) cognitive processes to the operation of the brain's neural networks. The same cannot be said of attempts to relate cognitive processes to skull bumps. But the comparison to phrenology serves as an important caveat and guide to researchers: general information about *where* cognitive processes seem to be taking place is only one piece of the puzzle that, when complete, will describe exactly *how* they take place. No one would deny that a combination of all of the methods available to cognitive neuroscientists will be necessary to discover the holy grail of mind-brain interaction.

Wacky Brain Claims.　Although neuroscience hurdles ahead, we are at least several orders of magnitude away from anything approaching a complete understanding of how the brain subserves cognition. Indeed, that full understanding may never come. But alas, there are always hucksters eager to make a buck by watering down what is known about brain and mind, and serving it up as oversimplified tripe. Let's briefly examine two examples. First is the claim that we use only 10% of our brains. Given that the brain is the center for cognitive processing, it's no surprise that you hear claims about "unleashing your brain power" or "tapping into the unused portion of your brain." There is no evidence whatsoever for this ridiculous assertion (except maybe the fact that people make the assertion), yet it persists like the weeds in our backyard. Radford (1999) contends that the origin of the claim may lie in the prevalence of association areas in the cerebral cortex. Some have misinterpreted their lack of specialization as a lack of important function that, if used, could enhance our "brain power." It's almost as if the association areas are perceived as just lying there, doing nothing. Nothing could be further from the truth! There are no unused areas in the brain. Areas that are not specialized for particular functions are critical for combining and integrating information from other brain areas.

A second wacky brain claim is based in empirical fact. As you read earlier, scads of research evidence support the notion that the left and right hemispheres of the brain are

Reality Check

specialized for different sorts of functions. No one would deny this. But in the decades that have ensued since this discovery and subsequent investigations, pop psychology schlockmeisters have taken the distinction to unfounded extremes. Rather than subtle differences between the hemispheres in their responses to certain types of stimuli, you hear about the logical, linear, mathematical, and verbal left hemisphere and the creative, freethinking, spatial, and nonverbal right hemisphere. An associated claim is that the abilities of the right hemisphere go largely untapped relative to those of the left (which also may relate to the 10% myth), and that the right hemisphere needs selective exercise.

This over-dichotomization of hemispheric specialization represents a series of gross over-simplifications. First, the difference between the hemispheres on these various tasks is a matter of degree. Neither hemisphere lies there completely inactive during *any* cognitive task. Second, tasks and abilities are much more intricate and complex than implied by these wacky claims. *Nothing* we do can be pigeonholed as purely a left-hemisphere or a right-hemisphere task. Take reading a novel, for example.... Verbal task, right? Well, in some ways, yes. We're reading, following a linear plot, analyzing the logic of the characters' actions, and so on. But at the same time, we're no doubt engaged in some serious "right-hemisphere activity" as well, as we form mental images of the events in the novel, create our own alternate plotlines, and attempt to follow the stream-of-consciousness writing of an author like William Faulkner. The point is, nothing is simple. Everything we do requires a complex interplay of processing between the hemispheres and can't be neatly classified as "right-brained" or "left-brained."

Cognitive Neuroscience: The Future?   There are some differences of opinion about where the yellow-brick road of neuroscience will lead. One seemingly radical view is that someday neuroscience will supplant psychology completely! Marshall (2009) provides an informative review of the relationship between psychology and neuroscience, as well as a provocative preview of what might be to come. Marshall proposes that, in spite of their common interests and goals, there has always been somewhat of a gap between the cognitive and neuroscientific approaches. According to Marshall, the information-processing approach that evolved as the dominant approach to the study of cognition in the 1950's was influenced primarily by artificial intelligence and has always been more interested in computational, rather than neurological, explanations of thinking. Cognitive psychologists have focused on the mental representations (e.g., memories, rules, symbols) that underlie cognition, and the processes whereby they are formed, organized, stored, and retrieved. They've never been particularly concerned with the neurological underpinnings of those representations and processes. As we pointed out earlier that's considered a serious shortcoming of the information-processing approach, and is one reason why it's become somewhat outmoded, not necessarily as a descriptive device, but as a complete theory.

The typical approach of cognitive neuroscience represents a sort of unification of the two markedly different disciplines of neuroscience and information processing. The strategy of cognitive neuroscience is to use the findings of cognitive researchers as sort of a guide or description of the cognitive processes that need to be explained or modeled. The neuroscience half of cognitive neuroscience then attempts to specify where, when, and how those processes play themselves out in the brain. According to Bechtel

(2002), this collaboration manifests itself in two different specific ways. First, neuro-science data can be used to test theories of information processing; for example, if brain imaging reveals that two different cognitive processes each activate different areas of the brain, this would suggest that the processes are in some way fundamentally different. A second use of neuroscience data is to focus on one particular cognitive task, and dissect it into different components with the help of neuroscientific data. The primary aim of this approach is to find out how cognitive processes are implemented or realized at the neurological level. Some have wondered whether taking this approach to its logical end will result in the reduction of all cognitive processes to a neurological explanation, thereby rendering the study of cognition superfluous.

Marshall (2009) is not so pessimistic, however. In summarizing the history and approaches of neuroscience and cognitive psychology, and their sometimes tenuous asso-ciation, Marshall contends that both have been constrained by the view of the mind as a sort of "disembodied" computer. This disembodied view led to a longstanding neglect of neuroscience by cognitive researchers, a neglect that has largely been addressed by the cog-nitive neuroscience approach. But the information-processing view has had its constrain-ing effect on neuroscience as well, viewing the brain as simply an isolated information processor, rather than as a critical component of a dynamic system. Marshall argues that the future of cognitive neuroscience lies within the realm of embodied approaches. Embodied approaches to mind attempt to understand thinking processes in the context of the dynamic interactions between brain, mind, and the particular context or situation in which they occur (sometimes the approach is termed "situated cognition"). Neuroscience will not replace psychology; as Marshall puts it, "neuroscience is not a reductive force, but rather a way to relate internal and external aspects of representations through the sensori-motor interface of an organism that is deeply embedded in the world."

Current Trends in the Study of Cognition

An important distinction in cognitive psychology is between basic and applied research. Basic research in cognitive psychology involves investigating the mechanisms of thought in terms of their simplest components: neurons, neural networks, and (speaking concep-tually) knowledge representations. Understanding what's happening to a person as they try to drive and text at the same time would require an analysis at this level. However, this analysis will not enable any sort of remediation, improvement, or safety directive. Research that focuses on these sorts of "real-world" problems and remedies is termed applied research. The primary concern in applied research is not reducing thought and behavior down to their simplest mechanisms; it's to figure out the answer to some every-day issue or problem, and perhaps provide a solution.

This foray into basic and applied research provides a brief glimpse of an important issue in any research-based field—the tension between internal and external validity. Basic research tends to emphasize internal validity over external validity. Internal validity refers to the extent to which it can be concluded that the manipulated (i.e., independent) vari-ables by the researchers were the sole causes of change in the measured (i.e., dependent) variable(s). Simply put, it's a reflection of the degree of precision in the experimental design. Applied research on the other hand, tends to emphasize external validity over internal validity. External validity refers to the naturalness of the research setting, or the degree to which it represents everyday life. External validity is sometimes termed ecological validity. External and internal validity typically have an inverse relationship; you trade off one to get more of the other. The addition of more realism to an experimental procedure often comes at the expense of experimental control.

Consider the research discussed earlier in the chapter conducted by pioneering memory researchers Ebbinghaus and Bartlett. Bartlett's procedures and materials were more in the tradition of applied research, and were not as tightly controlled as Ebbinghaus's, opening up the possibility that Bartlett's results may have been the product of uncontrolled variables. However, if you impose too much control, you may create a situation that doesn't really mirror real life, thereby limiting your findings. Some might claim that Ebbinghaus's basic research, while rigorously controlled, is of limited value because nonsense syllables do not resemble the types of material that we encode and remember on a daily basis.

But it also serves to highlight an important development in cognitive psychology research over the past quarter-century. Research has begun to move beyond the confines of the laboratory into "messier" contexts like the classroom, the car, and group interaction. This growing trend will be reflected in many of the studies reviewed in this text. Although we do discuss a fair amount of basic research, we stress its application, and focus on cognition as it occurs in everyday contexts (i.e., the **ecological approach to cognition**).

The Problem of Meaning.   The trend toward more applied research on cognitive processes is in large part a response to what cognitive developmental psychologist Jerome Bruner (1990, 1996) has termed the *problem of meaning.* Just as John Watson believed that psychology had lost its way by examining unobservable mental constructs, Bruner believes that cognitive psychology has lost its way, albeit for different reasons. The computer-based information-processing approach, with its antiseptic view of the thinking machine, has tended to remove cognitive processes from any type of meaningful setting. In so doing, cognitive psychology has largely ignored the processes whereby we use our everyday experiences to make some type of broader sense of the world. In other words we have not gone far enough in our examination of mental constructs, and have been overly confined by the behaviorist methodology from which we evolved. This sounds a bit like the functionalist school of thought and it may sound a bit touchy-feely, but the point is well-taken. As an example, think about memory. Memories are our personal histories; they're critical to our identity, and to our place in the world. Practically, they serve as a critical basis for many important cognitive processes, such as reminiscing, telling stories, or making important life decisions. How much does the retention of a list of nonsense syllables really tell us about these meaningful uses of memory? Not much, according to Bruner's view. What is needed is a broad and rich evaluation of memory (and other cognitive processes) in *meaningful* situations, complete with the concomitant, albeit "messy," influences of personality and emotion that cognitive psychology has traditionally taken great pains to avoid.

Dualism and Its Aftermath.   Another prominent influence on current cognitive psychology—for better and for worse—comes from the work of a renowned philosopher whom many credit as the father of modern-day psychology: the French philosopher Rene Descartes. One of Descartes' many claims to fame was his dualistic view of human beings. **Dualism** refers to the belief that mind and body are separable entities. This distinction is implicit in the definition of cognitive psychology that we gave earlier—the scientific study of mental processes. In other words, cognitive psychology is the study of "mind," separate from behavior.

A number of "frustrations" have resulted from the Cartesian roots of cognitive psychology. One is dualism itself—most cognitive psychologists would probably consider themselves *materialists* rather than dualists. **Materialism** is the view that mind and body are one and the same—they are both "material." In fact, the mind doesn't really exist at all, except as a label for the processes of the brain. And once neuroscience has delineated the functions of the human brain, there will be nothing else to explain with regard to mind, soul, or consciousness because these are all just manifestations of brain activity. A recent issue of the flagship journal for the Association for Psychological Science, *Perspectives on Psychological Science,* was devoted in part to the tension between the levels of explanation offered by neuroscientists and cognitive psychologists. As noted by Marshall (2009) in that issue, some expect that once neurobiological mechanisms in the brain are specified, we'll know everything we need to know, and the level of explanation offered by cognitive psychologists will become essentially obsolete. Happily for us cognitive psychologists, that day isn't here yet. Neuroscientists are far from delineating the functions of the human brain; so we still have jobs.

Embodied Cognition: Keeping Body in Mind.

As a result of Cartesian dualism cognitive psychologists have tended to "disconnect" their investigation of mind *from* the action of the body. As we stated earlier in our introduction to cognitive neuroscience, this approach to studying cognition might be considered "disembodied." It's almost as if the researchers conducting these studies conceive of the mind as a machine that's been plopped into our skull—and the task is to take the machine out and learn how it works. A recent trend in cognition research and theory is attempting to counter this with an approach appropriately termed **embodied cognition.** Embodied cognition applies to a constellation of ideas about how we think and interact with the world. It makes the important point that thinking is dynamic and situated—it occurs in conjunction with action and within a broad context that guides and shapes it. As you'll see, cognition and action are inextricably linked, each affecting and shaping the other. Throughout the chapters we'll be discussing some studies that highlight this dynamic interplay.

Research Theme
Embodied
Cognition

Emotion: The Mind in Touch With its Feelings.

Another "frustration" that dualism has created is an embedded assumption of an "idealized" thinking mechanism that is "untainted" by extraneous influences. As a result, investigators have tended to study cognition in (unrealistically) idealized settings. Essentially, researchers have strived to remove any "impure" influence from the picture in order to figure out how the "thinking machine" works. One of the "impurities" that has typically been removed from cognitive research (until recently, at least), is emotion. It has been a common habit of Western philosophical traditions to separate reason and emotion. To Descartes, reason was a function of mind, separate from the sullying effects of body-bound, animalistic

Research Theme
Emotion

"emotion." This tendency carried over to modern-day cognitive psychology. Much of the early research within the information-processing paradigm went out of its way to avoid ostensibly confounding factors like previous experience and personal reactions to stimuli, fearing that these would obscure the investigation of "pure" cognitive processing. This has proven to be a regrettable omission; far from being an impurity or confounding factor, emotion turns out to be key player in cognitive processing, as you'll see throughout the text.

Research Theme
Culture

Culture: We Don't All Think Alike.   Another set of "extraneous" factors that cognitive psychologists have often taken great pains to control, or avoid altogether, are individual difference variables such as gender and cultural background. There's been a decided bias toward trying to figure out how the mind works in a basic sense, outside of the influences of one's particular perspective on the world. But it seems more than a bit presumptuous to assume that everyone around the world remembers, speaks, solves problems, and makes decisions in the same way. The processes of mind cannot be separated from one's particular perspective on the world, so perhaps it should be considered in the mix. Therefore, current research is dealing more and more with the relationship between culture and cognition. Throughout the text, we'll be taking a look at some of the ways cognition varies among individuals. Does everyone in the world have the same basic cognitive machinery, or are there different habits of mind in different parts of the world? How might culture have shaped the manner in which individuals think?

Research Theme
Metacognition

Metacognition: The "I" in Cognition.   In emphasizing only behavior, the behaviorists (implicitly at least) were fully endorsing the dualistic view. They were interested only in body (i.e., behavior), and considered questions of mind or subjectivity to be a waste of time and effort. Introspection and other self-report techniques were rejected as unreliable. But as the study of mind returned to prominence, investigators once again became interested in the nature of cognitive processes, including the thoughts of the thinker.

Much of this work has been done under the general label of metacognition, which refers to the processes whereby we reflect on our own thinking. Essentially, it's "cognition about cognition" or "thinking about thinking." Not only will we discuss the research related to this important area of cognition, but many of the Stop and Think! activities will ask you to pause and cogitate on your own cognitions.

We'd like to mention one more feature that is intended to help you cogitate about your own (and others') cognition. Throughout the text, we'll be featuring what we'll term "reality checks." Earlier in this chapter you saw one of these "reality checks" when we discussed wacky brain claims. In these brief sections we will critically evaluate everyday claims or beliefs about mental processes. It turns out that when it comes to issues of mind, far too many people think they're experts, and empirical evidence often flies in the face of so-called "common sense."

Research Theme
Evolution

The Evolutionary Perspective: Upright Thinking.   Behaviorists emphasized the investigation of simple behaviors in simple organisms. In so doing, they made the implicit assumption that the principles underlying actions and behaviors in rats are similar to those in humans. This assumption is based on the notion that the differences between rats and humans are, in large part, quantitative, rather than qualitative. That is, the processes underlying human thought and behavior are in some sense more evolved than those of the rat, rather than fundamentally different in kind. Rats most likely have a fine life but they are no match for humans in a battle of wits. An **evolutionary perspective** on cognitive psychology (and psychology in general) views cognitive processes as adaptations that have evolved because of their survival value. In a variety of contexts throughout the text, we will discuss cognitive processes as adaptations that may have developed over the course of human evolution.

Stop&*Review*

1. True or false? The information-processing model has been the dominant paradigm for explaining cognition since the 1950s.
2. The connectionist approach uses _____ as a model for how cognitive processing takes place.
   a. communication systems
   b. a library
   c. an interstate highway system
   d. the brain
3. What is the basic unit of processing in the nervous system?
4. Describe the basic idea behind the EEG.
5. True or false? Imaging techniques are the most-used brain investigation technique.
6. True or false? Since the 1970's there has been a trend toward conducting more ecologically valid research.

- The information-processing approach compares mental processing to the serial operation of a computer. Humans, like computers, encode and store information for later retrieval and use. This model has proved to be an extremely useful framework for investigating cognitive processes and has been the dominant approach to describing and investigating cognition since the 1950s.

- The connectionist approach uses the neural networks of the brain, rather than the computer, as a model for how thinking takes place. According to this approach, the interactive and parallel activity of neural networks distributed throughout the brain forms the basis for mental representations and processes.

- The basic unit of processing in the brain is the neuron. The neuron transmits information electrically within a neuron, via an action potential and chemically between neurons. The brain can be subdivided into the hindbrain, midbrain, and forebrain. The majority of higher-level processing that underlies cognition occurs in the forebrain, particularly in the cerebral cortex.

- The EEG involves recording brain potentials (through the scalp) from different sites in the cortex. Event-related potentials can reveal the time course of brain activity in response to stimuli. Electromagnetic properties of neural interaction form the basis for two other techniques, magnetoencephalography (a recording technique) and trans-cranial magnetic stimulation (a brain stimulation technique).

- Neuroimaging techniques (PET scanning and fMRI) allow researchers to pinpoint brain regions active in conjunction with cognitive processes. The cognitive neuroscience field is dominated by the use of neuroimaging techniques but it is important to remember that these techniques are limited to simple descriptions of the localization of brain activity. Researchers need to avoid logical reasoning flaws in inferring brain function solely from imaging investigations of cognitive tasks.

- Since the late 1970s, the trend in cognitive research has been to feature investigations of cognition in ecologically valid contexts. In this spirit, more researchers are investigating cultural and individual differences in basic cognitive processes.

2

Perception and Consciousness: Basics of Information Intake

Look up from what you're doing right now, and reflect on what's happening as you view the scene. As soon as you set your sights on it—instantly—it's neatly organized, everything is sorted and separated. How does this "perceptual packaging" occur?

How might people differ in their perceptual reports? No doubt you've experienced sights or sounds that others around you haven't. Have you ever heard a "bump in the night" that someone else swears didn't happen? What could give rise to such different perceptions?

You hear the claims and the warnings—subliminal messages are all around us, in magazine ads, in music, and who knows where else? Can we really be influenced by things that we can't even perceive?

Basic Issues in Perception

Perception is truly a masterful achievement. Consider vision. A two-dimensional array of light appears on the retina, which houses the visual receptors. Instead of a random array of color dots, we instantaneously experience a rich, coherent, veridical, three-dimensional perception of an object, person, or event (i.e., a **percept**). Perhaps the most astonishing fact is that this all occurs instantaneously, mostly outside of conscious awareness. You're aware only of the product, not the process. Perception is indeed an incredible achievement, not to mention a brilliantly engineered one. Attempts at computer vision and speech recognition—basically, getting computers to "see" and "hear"—have met with extremely limited success. No machine can yet match the speed and flexibility of human perceptual systems.

Sensation and Perception

Given that cognition is often characterized in terms of information processing, it makes sense to say that cognition begins as soon as "information" enters the cognitive system. A series of processes is responsible for the transformation from "two-dimensional array of light," "air vibration," and "pressure" to the percepts of "cat," "car horn," and "kiss." Because the resulting percept forms the basis of all subsequent cognition and action, a complete understanding of cognitive processes requires an understanding of the basic processes that lead to these percepts.

Psychologists usually distinguish between *sensation* and *perception*. Although the distinction is somewhat artificial, there are a number of bases for making it. The most relevant basis for our purposes is a distinction between the physiological and the psychological. The term **sensation** is sometimes loosely associated with the physiological processes that underlie information intake. In the previously mentioned examples, this would include the processes whereby eye, ear, and skin receptors take the initial stimuli (the light, vibration, and pressure, respectively), and register them in the chemical language of the nervous system. From there, it's on to the neurons and then to the brain, where the processes typically labeled "perception" transform this electrochemical message into a rich percept (cat, car horn, and kiss). This latter set of processes, termed **perception,** refers to the psychological processes involved in the immediate organization and interpretation of sensations.

We sense and perceive through a myriad of channels that include the ubiquitous five major senses of vision, audition, touch, taste, and smell. Information taken in through any of these channels can and does initiate information processing. However, there can be little doubt that thinking is dominated by things we see and hear. As a result, most of the research done by cognitive psychologists focuses on information from these two sense modalities.

Fans of the other senses shouldn't lose heart! In this chapter we will have some brief discussion of how the senses commingle and interact. Also, information processing initiated by the other senses will make brief appearances in subsequent chapters as we consider identification via touch (Chapter 5) and smell as a cue for autobiographical memories (Chapter 7).

Bottom-Up and Top-Down Processing

The processes of perception are the product of what are commonly termed *bottom-up* and *top-down processing*. **Bottom-up processing** basically refers to a flow of information that proceeds from the stimulus to the neural activity driven by this stimulus to its eventual identification. Bottom-up processing is sometimes termed **data-driven processing,** because it refers to the processes whereby the stimulus itself (i.e., the *data*) leads to a sensible percept. **Top-down processing** refers to the processes whereby we bring to bear what we expect, what we know, and what we experience from the surrounding context in determining what it is we're sensing and subsequently perceiving. Because it refers to the application of concepts to perception, top-down processing is sometimes dubbed **conceptually driven processing.**

Are Our Perceptions Constructions?   The distinction between bottom-up and top-down processing is related to another fundamental question that arises in perceptual research and theory—to what degree are our percepts *constructed* by interpretive processes or *directly experienced* (with little or no interpretation) from the external environment? This issue has been debated most thoroughly with regard to visual perception, although the basic arguments apply to any modality. The **constructive view** emphasizes the role of active construction and interpretation in arriving at a three-dimensional percept of the world. This view has its psychological roots in the work of Helmholtz, whom you read about in Chapter 1. Recall that Helmholtz advanced the notion of *unconscious inference* in perception. His basic idea was that we *infer* or construct a percept based on the sensory information we're receiving and our previous knowledge and experience. This view emphasizes the role of top-down factors in perception. Perception, in this view, is a process of problem solving. Take golf, which often (always, for Greg) involves the difficult perceptual task of locating where one's drive off the tee ended up. Finding a golf ball requires the detection of a round, light-colored speck in a field of green. There is no doubt that Greg's ability to locate the ball depends on expectations—he watched it as it flew away from him, he knows that he doesn't typically hit it far (a pathetic 150 yards at best), and he knows he usually hits it straight. This cluster of knowledge, which cognitive psychologists term a **schema,** "tunes" his perception of the ball as he searches for it.

According to an alternative view proposed by theorist J. J. Gibson (1966, 1987), perception is not a matter of construction or interpretation. What we perceive about our visual environment is picked up directly, hence the name: the **direct view.** This view is closely aligned with the concept of bottom-up processing because it emphasizes the actual data being analyzed by visual mechanisms. Let's go back to our golf example. According to the direct view of perception, when Greg searches for his golf ball and scans the surrounding grass (which is usually very deep), two important pieces of data guide his search. One is *optical flow*—as you move through a given environment (say, a particular fairway on a golf course), the image on your retina changes; as you move toward some object or destination, that image expands, and the rate of expansion offers information about how fast you're moving and how close you are to objects. *Texture gradients* also serve as unambiguous sources of information. As you move closer to an object in the environment (say, the golf ball and surrounding grass), the perceived detail of the object changes; this change provides information about depth that needs no interpretation. The constructive and direct views aren't necessarily oppositional. It's almost certainly the case that both "modes" of perception are at work as we take in visual information.

Stop&*Review*

1. Sensation is to perception as:
   a. physiological is to psychological
   b. vision is to the other senses
   c. responding is to information intake
   d. organization is to interpretation
2. Describe the basic difference between bottom-up processing and top-down processing.
3. True or false? According to the direct view of perception, top-down processing is more important to perception than is bottom-up processing.

- Sensation generally refers to the physiological processes that underlie information intake, while perception generally refers to the psychological processes involved in the immediate organization and interpretation of those sensations.

- Some perceptual processes are primarily bottom-up, or data-driven, featuring a flow of information that proceeds from the stimulus to subsequent neural activity to stimulus identification. These processes are complemented by top-down, conceptually driven processes through which we bring our expectation, our knowledge, and the surrounding context to bear in identification.

- The constructive view of visual perception emphasizes the role of top-down, active interpretation in perception. The direct view of visual perception emphasizes the bottom-up processing of information inherent in the stimulus itself, and minimizes the role of interpretation.

The Basic Tasks of Visual Perception

Palmer (2003) separates the processes of visual perception into two major subsets that correspond neatly to the progression of information processing that will structure the next few chapters. The first subset of processes involves the organization of an incoming stimulus array into discrete perceptual parts and elements; the second set of processes involves the identification and further processing of these elements and their categorization as people, golf balls, computers, books, etc. This chapter will deal primarily with the first set of processes—those whereby we impose some initial order on incoming information. These processes have been characterized as preattentive (i.e., before attention is directed at a stimulus) and postattentive (i.e., those that occur as soon as attention has been directed to a stimulus). This chapter will focus primarily on preattentive processing. In the next chapter we'll move into discussion of postattentive processes and how attentional focus impacts processing. In Chapters 4 and 5 we'll discuss the second set of processes proposed by Palmer (2003), those that are responsible for identification and further processing of perceptual inputs. Chapter 4 will focus on the control and manipulation of information, and Chapter 5 will focus on the identification and classification of incoming information.

Perceptual Organizational Processes

Palmer (2003) proposes that when confronted with a stimulus array, the first major task of the visual system—one of the preattentive tasks just mentioned—is to impose structure on it. In other words, we must figure out which parts of the image go together and which do not.

Grouping and Region Segmentation. A vital aspect of visual organization is **grouping,** our ability to sort things in our environment so that the percept is a neat, orderly package rather than a jumbled mess of randomly arranged stimulus patterns. It is important to note that principle of grouping applies not only to visual objects but to auditory ones as well (Bergman, 1990). However, our discussion will be limited mainly to visual perception as that is the primary context in which these principles are applied.

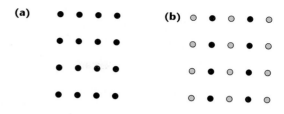

Figure 2.1

The Gestalt grouping principles that guide perceptual organization.

As noted by Tversky (2006), the mind groups objects on just about any basis it can find. But the early work of Wertheimer (1923/1938) and other Gestalt psychologists (briefly introduced in Chapter 1) were the first to formalize the basic principles by which we do this. These psychologists were interested in the processes underlying perceptual and mental organization. Perhaps most notable were their proposed **principles of visual organization.** These principles account for most of the "order" that we see in our visual environment. The Gestalt psychologists believed that these principles were the cornerstone of perception.

Several of the Gestalt grouping principles are depicted in Figure 2.1. **Proximity** refers to the tendency for objects that are near one another (i.e., proximal) to be grouped together. The elements of Figure 2.1a look like rows rather than columns because the row elements are closer to one another than are the column elements. The principle of **similarity** refers to the tendency for similar objects to be grouped together. The elements of Figure 2.1b seem to be columns rather than rows because the columns have like elements. The principle of **good continuation** refers to our tendency to perceive lines as flowing naturally, in a single direction. For example, the letter X seems to be two lines that cross rather than two connected 45° angles. According to the principle of **closure,** we tend to complete the incomplete, perceptually connecting contours that are almost, but not quite, connected. Finally, **common fate** refers to our tendency to group elements together if they are moving in the same direction or at the same speed. Palmer and his colleagues added a few other organizational cues to these "classics." **Common region**

Element connectedness in the real world.

indicates that elements belonging to a common designated area, or region, will be grouped together. **Synchrony** refers to our tendency to group elements that occur at the same time. **Element connectedness** specifies that elements tend to be grouped together if they are connected to other elements. It's important to note that these principles of organization are all interrelated and that one may dominate another, given the particular nature of the visual stimulus. For example, in Figure 2.1c, the principle of common region dominates the principle of similarity.

Stop&*Think* | GROUPING

Right now, stop reading, look up, and make a list of all of the Gestalt grouping cues that are assisting you in organizing your visual environment. If you're near a window, walk to it and see if any other grouping cues seem apparent.

As noted by Palmer (2003), it's tempting to think of these organizational tendencies as vague generalizations that don't really apply to our perception of objects in the real world. Nothing could be further from the truth. Can you find the camouflaged object in Figure 2.2? The difficulty you're having results from the breakdown of grouping cues. So if these cues were not available in your everyday visual experience, you'd be missing objects you reach for, failing to recognize friends' faces, and walking into walls in much the same way that you were unable to identify the camouflaged object as a Dalmatian sniffing something on the ground.

Palmer and Beck (2007) provide empirical evidence for the power of these principles. Participants were presented with a *repetition discrimination task* in which they received a series of displays like the ones in Figure 2.3. For each display, the participants indicated, as quickly as possible, whether the repeated elements were circles or squares. Reaction time for this judgment was the dependent variable. The critical independent variable was the status of these repeated elements. On some trials (labeled "within-group" trials) the repeated elements were part of the same perceptual group indicated by a particular cue (e.g., similarity, common region, or element connectedness). On other trials (labeled "between-group" trials), the repeated elements were from different perceptual groups. Grouping tendencies would be indicated by faster responding when the repeated elements were in the same perceptual group than when the repeated elements were in different perceptual groups.

Let's look at the sample trials shown in Figure 2.3. If participants group elements by the designated grouping principle (similarity, common region, element connectedness), they would tend to indicate "square" when presented with the within-group trials more quickly than

Figure 2.2

when presented with the between-group trials. The results showed clear evidence of the power of each cue in grouping. In each case, within-group RTs were much faster than between-group RTs. Clearly, the perceptual grouping cues of similarity, common region, and element connectedness had exerted an effect on participants' tendency to group particular elements together.

Figure-Ground. Another fundamental principle of organization, termed **figure-ground,** refers to our tendency to segregate visual scenes into a background and a figure that appears to be superimposed against that background. Several cues allow us to parse figure from ground. Regions identified as figure tend to be smaller and have more symmetrical features than regions designated as background. In addition, a region is seen as figure to the degree that it is meaningful (a person is more meaningful than a wall) and is surrounded by other elements of the visual array (Palmer, 2003). Vecera, Vogel, and Woodman (2002) add another feature to the mix. Elements in the lower region of the visual field are more likely to be seen as figure than elements in the upper region of the visual field. According to Vecera et al., this tendency develops with visual experience; in most natural scenes, regions below the horizon line are close and comprise the figure.

A recent computational analysis by Fowlkes, Martin and Malik (2007) reveals the ecological validity of the figure-ground principle. You'll recall from Chapter 1 that ecological validity refers to the real-world generalizability of an empirical finding or theoretical account. Fowlkes et al. collected a large number of natural images and had participants assign the labels of "figure" and "ground" to the elements in the images. In line with Vecera et al, they found that one of the characteristics most commonly associated with perceiving an element as "figure" was its appearance in a lower region of the scene. In addition, convexity and size are cues to an element's designation as figure rather than ground. As you can see in Figure 2.4, the tiger is relatively low in the scene, big, and features convexity (rather than concavity) in its appearance. Fowlkes et al. give their conclusions an evolutionary spin, noting that an evolutionary process would favor organisms that exploit these cues to distinguish between figure and ground. Certainly in the case of our

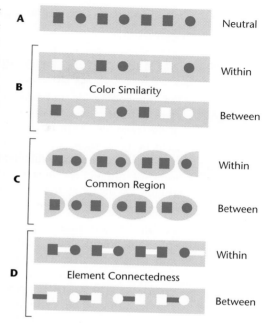

Figure 2.3

Sample displays from Beck and Palmer's study of perceptual grouping.

Figure 2.4

Characteristics of "figure": Which tiger is the figure?

friend in the picture, exploiting these cues might minimize the chances of becoming an oversized kitty treat.

Stop&*Think* | FIGURING OUT FIGURE-GROUND

Put this book aside and take note of the scene in front of you. Jot down all elements of the scene. Take your list and classify each element as (a) figure or (b) ground. See if you notice any general differences in the sorts of things comprising figure and ground. Do the things that seem like "figure"

reflect the characteristics discussed in the text and summarized below?

- Smaller
- More symmetrical
- More meaningful
- Lower region of visual scene

Global Precedence.   When we hear a symphony or look at a painting, it seems that (phenomenologically, at least) we tend to blend the elements into an integrated whole rather than to perceive isolated separate elements. The Gestalt credo that "the whole is different from the sum of its parts" does a nice job of capturing this phenomenological experience. The Gestaltists viewed perception (and thinking in general) as a process of apprehending whole configurations or relationships—and this apprehension is more than just the sum of a group of independent sensations and thoughts. Basically, the Gestalt view is that apprehending wholes or configurations is what is sometimes termed a primitive. It's the natural tendency of our perceptual system and, as such, is done fairly easily and automatically. In other words, we see the "forest" before we see the "trees."

A classic study by Navon (1977) provides some hard evidence for the validity of this adage. Navon was interested in how people process visual displays. More specifically, would this processing be dominated by the specific and individual features within the pattern (i.e., local features), or would it be dominated by the overall pattern (i.e., global features)? Navon addressed this question rather cleverly, by composing stimuli that could be perceived in one of two ways, depending on whether participants were influenced by global or local features. He pitted these two modes of processing against one another by using letter stimuli that were made up of other letters or neutral symbols to see which would dominate. (See sample stimuli at the top of Figure 2.5.) When viewed globally, each stimulus is an H; however, the local features are

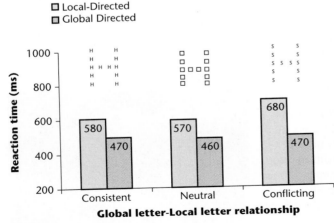

Figure 2.5

Sample stimuli and results from Navon (1977) study.

From Navon, D. (1977). Forest before trees: The precedence of global features in visual perception. *Cognitive Psychology, 9,* 353–383. Reprinted by permission.

made up of a different letter or symbols (S, H or □). When you glance at these figures, what do you notice first?

Navon (1977, Experiment 3) investigated this question with a fairly straightforward procedure. Participants viewed letters like the ones in Figure 2.5 under different instructional conditions. In the *global-directed* condition, the task was to indicate whether the global figure was H or S; in the *local-directed* condition, the task was to indicate whether the component letters were H's or S's. The big letters presented to participants were of three types: (1) the global and local features were consistent (a big H made of little H's); (2) the global and local features conflicted (a big H made of little S's); (3) the global and local features were neutral with respect to one another (a big H made of little rectangles).

The results are shown in Figure 2.5. The first thing you see in the graph is that the reaction time (RT) for the big letters (global-directed) was much less than that for the small ones (local-directed). This demonstrates that perceptually, it's easier to "grab" what's represented by the big letter. This could be due simply to the size of the stimulus— it's easier to identify something that's big than something that's small. This explanation would suffice, were it not for the striking interaction that's apparent in the graph. The effect of a conflicting letter had markedly different effects on global-directed and local-directed conditions. In the global-directed condition (identify the large letter), it didn't matter whether the local (small component) letters were consistent, conflicting, or neutral. The global (large) letter was easily apprehended. This was not the case for the local-directed condition (identify the small letters); whether the global letter was consistent or conflicting made a huge difference. If the large letter conflicted, participants' RT was slowed by about 100 milliseconds (relative to the neutral and consistent conditions), a sizable inhibition effect. This implies that even when instructed to look for the local letters, participants couldn't help but encode the global one. This finding, termed the **global precedence** effect has been viewed as quite general in that it has been demonstrated in a variety of contexts (see Kimchi, 1992, for a review).

However, is this effect universal? There is evidence that a number of perceptual tendencies vary as a function of cultural context (e.g., Nisbett, Peng, Choi, & Norenzayan, 2001). That is, based on the traditions, customs, values, and experiences of cultures around the world, different habits of perception and cognition develop. Might a culture with different experiences show the opposite of a global precedence effect—a local precedence effect?

Research Theme
Culture

Davidoff, Fonteneau, and Fagot (2008) studied the tendency toward global and local processing in a remote culture known as the Himba, who hail from the northern portion of Namibia, a country on the southwestern coast of Africa.

Davidoff and colleagues began with two observations about this culture: the first was that when asked to sort colors, the Himba tended to form many different categories, placing relatively few hues and shades within each. A second observation relates to a phenomenon

The Himba.

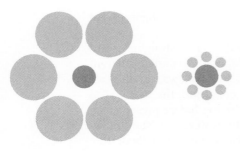

Figure 2.6

The Ebbinghaus Ilusion: Believe it or not, the center circles are the same size!

Target

Shares global features   Shares local features

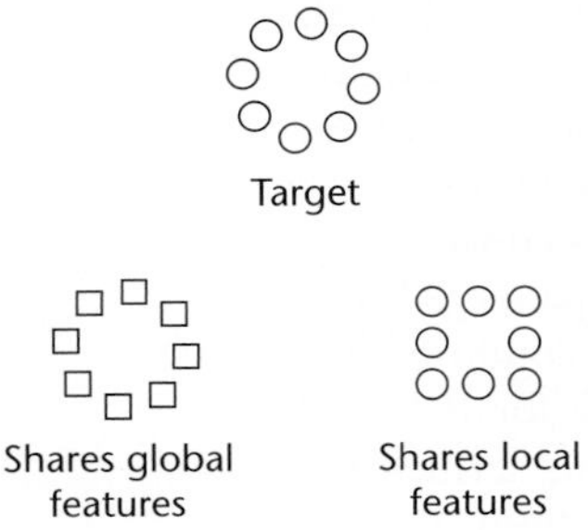

Figure 2.7

Sample stimuli Davidoff et al. study of cross-cultural differences in global/local processing.

known as the *Ebbinghaus illusion,* depicted in Figure 2.6. You are quite likely thinking that the inner circle in the left-hand panel is smaller than the inner circle in the right-hand panel. If so, you are experiencing the Ebbinghaus illusion. As you might be able to guess, the source of the illusion is the context of the surrounding circles. The central circle on the left seems dwarfed by them, while on the right, the central circle does the dwarfing. Interestingly, DeFockert, Davidoff, Fagot, Parron, and Goldstein (2007) observed that the Himba were strikingly less susceptible (in fact, not really susceptible at all) to this illusion, ostensibly because of their ability to focus on the target circle independent of its context. This finding suggests that the global processing effect found by Navon and others might not occur in the Himba.

To test this hypothesis, Davidoff et al. had the Himba and U.K. participants perform a simple matching task. They were presented with a target stimulus (big circle or big square) along with two comparison stimuli below it (Figure 2.7). Their task was to choose which of the two comparison stimuli "was most like" the target stimulus. One comparison stimulus shared the global feature (stimulus on the left in Figure 2.7) but not the local features of the target (e.g., circle comprised of small squares). The other comparison stimulus shared the local features (stimulus on the right in Figure 2.7) but not the global feature of the target (e.g., circles were used to create the global shape of a square). The global precedence effect would dictate that the stimulus on the left would be chosen, as it "globally" represents a circle. The fact that the elements of it are squares should be overruled by the global similarity. U.K. participants showed the typical global precedence effect, choosing the comparison stimulus that shared the global feature with the target 86% of the time. However, the Himba showed a dramatic reversal of the global precedence effect, choosing the comparison stimulus that shared *local* features with the target 77% of the time.

Stop&*Review*

1. Which of these is not one of the Gestalt principles of visual organization?
   a. similarity
   b. proximity
   c. common fate
   d. figure-ground
2. Describe the figure-ground principle.

3. True or false? The global precedence effect is universal (i.e., unaffected by cultural factors).

- A first basic task of visual perception is to organize the incoming information into sensible groups and regions. This is accomplished in part with the help of

Gestalt principles of visual organization, which include similarity, proximity, common fate, synchrony, common
region, and closure.

- Another fundamental organization
principle is figure-ground, which refers
to our tendency to segregate visual
scenes into a background and a figure
superimposed upon it.

- The global precedence effect refers to
the finding that global elements of a
visual scene tend to dominate local
elements; all other things being equal,
people tend to see "forest" before they
see "trees." This effect is not universal
as some cultures (the Himba) show
an opposite effect—a local precedence
effect.

Multisensory Interaction and Integration

Devoting separate discussions to perception, attention, memory, and the like is largely a
matter of descriptive convenience. Parsing the processes into separate chapters might
lead one to lose sight of the interrelation among cognitive processes. The same is true
(albeit on a smaller scale) for perceptual processes. For example, what we see affects what
we hear; what we hear impacts our sense of touch.

Synesthesia

An intriguing example of interactions between sensory systems is involved in the phenomenon known as synesthesia. **Synesthesia** refers to experiences in which input from
one sensory system produces an experience not only in that modality but in another as
well. For example, synesthetes, as they're termed, might experience a particular musical chord as green. These cases, termed *strong synesthesia* by Martino and Marks
(2001), are very rare (occurring in fewer than 1 out of every 2,000 individuals); interestingly, female synesthetes outnumber males about 6 to 1 (Baron-Cohen, Burt,
Smith-Laittan, & Harrison, 1996). This disproportionate distribution combined with
the fact that synesthesia runs in families (Baron-Cohen et al., 1996) indicates that the
phenomenon may have a genetic basis.

Synesthesia is generally thought to be unidirectional in nature (e.g., Mills, Boteler, &
Oliver, 1999). For example, a synesthete may see the number 9, and have an experience of
orange. However, the converse experience does not occur; the experience of orange does
not lead to the experience of 9. However, some recent evidence indicates that there is
some bidirectionality in the association between colors and digits in synesthetes
(e.g., Knoch, Gianotti, Mohr, & Brugger, 2005). In addition, there tends to be consistency
in the associations made. For example the number 9 will always produce the color orange
but never another color.

The type of association just described (a link between numbers or letters and colors)
turns out to be the most-studied form of synesthesia. The experience has been labeled
grapheme-color synesthesia (Ramachandran & Hubbard, 2001). Bargary, Barnett,
Mitchell, and Newell (2009) attempted to isolate the stage of processing that gives rise to
this type of "strong" synesthetic experience. Does synesthesia result from characteristics
of early, low-level information processing, or from later stages of information processing

that involve identification and attention? It is a bit oversimplified, but the question can be boiled down to the distinction we described at the beginning of the chapter: Is synesthesia more the result of sensation or perception?

Bargary et al. (2009) addressed this question by employing another interesting phenomenon of sensory integration termed the **McGurk effect** (e.g. McGurk & MacDonald, 1976). This effect occurs upon simultaneous presentation of a speech sound (e.g., /b/) and a (silent) visual display of a speaker pronouncing a different speech sound (e.g., /g/). The McGurk effect refers to the resulting perception, which turns out to be a sort of "average" of the two speech sounds (e.g., /d/). You'll learn in Chapter 9 that by varying the way a consonant is formed, the /b/ sound can be transformed into the /d/ sound which then can be transformed into the /g/ sound. If you think about this as a continuum of sound, the /d/ sound is "between" the /b/ and /g/ sounds. The visual-auditory integration observed in the McGurk effect is generally agreed to be the result of later, higher-level processing (e.g. perception).

Bargary et al. put a clever spin on the McGurk effect to determine the locus of grapheme-color synesthesia. They presented McGurk-style stimuli to synesthetes as inducers. Their logic was that if synesthesia is an early, sensory phenomenon, the color induced by the McGurk stimulus should correspond to the auditory sensation of the stimulus (/b/) and not the blended perception (/d/). Alternatively if synesthesia is the result of later, perceptual processing, the color induced should correspond to the blended perception (/d/) and not the auditory sensation (/b/). For example, let's imagine that there is a synesthete who experiences the color purple when hearing a /b/ sound and the color pink when hearing the /d/ sound. If the synesthetic experience is due to early sensory processing they will see the color purple. The /b/ sound is registered by the sensory system which produces the synesthetic experience. However, if the synesthetic experience is due to later perceptual processing they will see the color pink. The synesthetic experience does not occur until the sound is perceived as a /d/; this blended perception occurs later in processing. The results supported the latter prediction. The induced colors experienced by synesthetes corresponded to the blended perception rather than the auditory sensation of that stimulus, suggesting that synesthesia is the product of later perceptual processing rather than early sensory processing.

Although synesthesia may seem like a unique and rare experience, some (e.g., Kadosh & Henik, 2008) believe it may provide important insight into basic cognitive processes, including numerical cognition, automatic processing, and sensory integration. In addition, many view synesthesia as a window into how we use metaphor and language (e.g., Cacciari, 2008). Everyone is familiar with linguistic phrases that mix senses; consider the ideas of "warm" colors, "sharp" tastes, and "bright" sounds. Most people resonate with these metaphors, which involve cross-modal experiences. Martino and Marks (2001) term these garden-variety synesthetic experiences *weak synesthesia*. Weak synesthesia is also evident in controlled laboratory settings. For example, in a study by Martino and Marks (2001), tones were presented and participants were to rapidly classify them as high or low. Tones were accompanied either by a black or a white square. Results indicate a cross-modal interaction (weak synesthesia); high-pitched tones were more quickly classified when presented along with white squares than when presented with black squares. The opposite pattern held for low-pitched tones. This pattern is termed a *congruence effect*.

Like Bargary et al. (2009), Martino and Marks propose that synesthetic effects arise from higher-level mechanisms. More specifically, they propose that the associations between sensory modalities that give rise to synesthetic effects are the product of knowledge (i.e., top-down processing). Synesthetic effects derive from the way we think about and linguistically code our sensory experiences. According to Martino and Marks, as we experience and describe our perceptions, we build an abstract network of concepts that applies to these experiences. With experience, some of these concepts become strongly associated (e.g., white and high pitched, black and low pitched) such that one automatically activates the other. So the experience of light blue activates a related concept (at least within this network) of coolness.

Comparing the Senses

As mentioned at the outset of the chapter, vision tends to dominate research on sensation and perception, no doubt because it is the dominant sensory modality for information intake. The visual sense's domination over the other modalities has been demonstrated empirically in a variety of research paradigms.

Vision and Audition. A great deal of information processing involves the joint intake of visual and auditory stimuli, so it's not surprising that there are some powerful interactions between the two. In each, vision tends to dominate audition. Two examples involve the process of sound localization. In a movie theater, the sound appears to be coming from the appropriate sources on the screen—the actors, the ringing phones, and so on. But in reality, the sound is coming from speakers positioned around the theater. Ventriloquism relies on the same effect; the voice seems to be coming from the dummy, not from the ventriloquist. The so-called **ventriloquist effect** (Alais & Burr, 2004; Bertelson, 1999) occurs when a visual cue that is presented simultaneously with an auditory stimulus biases the localization of that auditory stimulus toward the location of the visual cue.

Another interesting cross-modal illusion was discovered by Schutz and Lipscomb (2007). They presented videos of a world-class musician playing single notes on a marimba using either a "long" gesture (used to play long notes) or a "short" gesture (used to play short notes). The notes played were all of equal duration. When asked to estimate the duration of the notes (without the video), participants correctly judged them to be equal. However, when the notes were accompanied by the corresponding video that included long or short gestures, estimations were biased; notes

America's Got Talent! And multisensory interaction!

Our favorite marimba player and his biggest fans.

produced with long gestures were judged to be longer in duration than notes produced with short gestures. As in the previous case, visual information exerts a biasing effect on auditory processing. But in this case, the biasing is especially surprising. Typically, in temporal (i.e., time-based) tasks, auditory information dominates visual information because of the auditory system's superior temporal acuity. The illusion represents a reversal of this relationship. Schutz and Kubovy (2009) propose the explanation is cross-modal causality. That is, integration among sensory stimuli is especially likely to occur in situations where the relationship seems to be causal (e.g., when a marimba player "causes" a note by striking the marimba). An interesting side note on the original Schutz and Lipscomb (2007) study (as related in Schutz & Kubovy, 2009) is that the research was motivated by a difference between two schools of marimba playing that differ on whether changing the playing gesture can actually modulate the marimba note. As the investigators note (p. 1809) "what was wrong in theory was right in practice." The notes weren't longer, but they *seemed* longer.

Vision and Chemical Senses. It takes only a moment's reflection to realize that there's probably an association between the look of a plate of food and how good it smells/tastes (aside from the obvious fact that spoiled food doesn't look good). Morrot, Brochet, and Dubourdieu (2001) showed evidence of just such an interaction within the context of smelling wine. They presented a white wine that had been artificially colored to look like red wine, and gave the concoction to a panel of 54 wine experts. They then performed an analysis of the words the experts used to describe the smell of the wine. They found what might be termed a "smell illusion." The wine experts described the white wine with words typically associated with red wine (e.g., *cherry, clove, cocoa*). Basically, visual information led the experts to discount the olfactory information they were receiving. These results were replicated and extended by Parr, White, and Heatherbell (2004). And for the sommerliers out there, consult Parr (2008), which might be the first extended application of cognitive psychology to wine tasting expertise.

Vision and Touch. Vision and touch allow us to gather richly elaborate information about objects in the world. But what happens when these two senses are placed in conflict? Evidence indicates that vision exerts undue influence, just as it does in the cases of conflict between vision and audition.

Pavani, Spence, and Driver (2000) devised a unique test of the possible dominance of vision over touch. They placed participants in the setup pictured at the top of Figure 2.8. In this experiment, participants wore rubber gloves, and their hands were placed out of sight. Each participant held a small sponge cube with their forefinger (top of cube) and thumb (bottom of cube). The top and bottom of each cube were equipped with tiny vibrators. Directly above the handheld sponge cubes were two

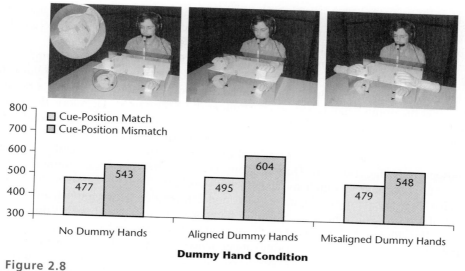

Figure 2.8

From Pavani, F., Spence, C., & Driver, J. (2000). Visual capture of touch: Out-of-body experiences with rubber gloves. *Psychological Science, 11,* 353–359. Copyright 2000 by Blackwell, Inc. Reproduced by permission.

visible sponge cubes. These sponge cubes were equipped with an LED at the top and bottom that would light up simultaneously when the respective handheld cube below vibrated. The relationship between which LED was activated (top or bottom) and which position received the vibration (top or bottom) was random on any given trial; sometimes they matched, and sometimes they mismatched. But activation of the lights and vibration always occurred at the same time. The participants were to identify the source of the vibration (bottom or top), and reaction time to make this judgment was recorded. The question of interest was the possible facilitatory or inhibitory effect of the light. Would the location of the light on the visible cube (top or bottom) affect the reaction time to identify the source of the vibration (top or bottom)?

Here's where the fun starts: On half of the trials, dummy hands in rubber gloves were placed on the visible cubes (the ones with the LEDs). Participants' hands (situated below, and out of sight) were in identical rubber gloves, and the fake hands were positioned so that they looked like they could have been the participants' hands. Imagine what participants would experience in this condition. They'd be looking at "hands" that are holding cubes; the LEDs on these cubes would light up at the same time they'd feel a vibration directly underneath. So what happens when the visual cue and tactile stimulation match or mismatch?

The results are presented at the bottom of Figure 2.8. Reaction time to identify the source of the vibration is plotted as a function of whether the viewed light matched or mismatched the location of the vibration and whether or not there were dummy hands holding the cubes. As you can see, the reaction time to identify the source of the vibration was slower when the light mismatched the vibration location than when it matched. More importantly, the presence of the dummy hands significantly accentuated this interfering effect! In the dummy hand condition, participants were even slower (reaction time was greater) at identifying the source of the vibration when the light mismatched the vibration location than when it matched. Seeing the light at a given position on the dummy hand gave rise to an illusory sensation of feeling that vibration in the corresponding position below.

Perhaps, you might think, participants were confused because they saw another set of hands. In a second experiment, Pavani et al. replicated the same procedure but with misaligned dummy hands that were clearly fake. The results, shown in Figure 2.8 make it clear that the dummy hands had no effect under these conditions. Therefore, the results of the first experiment show that participants experienced (at least to some extent) the dummy hands as their own. This has been termed the *rubber hand illusion*.

This illusion has inspired a great deal of research over the past several years (e.g., Constantini & Haggard, 2007; Durgin, Evans, Dunphy, Klostermann, & Simmons, 2007. Ehrsson, Holmes, & Passingham, 2005; Schütz-Bosbach, Tausche, & Weiss, 2009) and yielded some fascinating examples of cross-modal interaction between touch and vision. One of the most intriguing is a study of upper-limb amputees by Ehrsson, Rosén, Stockselius, Ragnö, Köhler, and Lundborg (2008). These researchers used a procedure similar to that of Pavani et al. A visible rubber hand holding a sponge cube with LEDs on the top (forefinger) of the cube was displayed. The LED lit up at the same time as a vibration to the amputee's stump. This led to an illusion of sensing touch on the rubber hand rather than on the stump. As in the case of phantom limb pain, the amputees experienced a sensation in a nonexistent hand. This also led to a reported feeling of ownership of the hand. In addition, the sense of ownership was indicated by physiological measures. For example, when the rubber hand was about to be stabbed with a needle, skin conductance tests indicated anxiety in the participants, but only for those who earlier had experienced the LED light up simultaneously with vibrations on their stump. Ehrsson et al. propose that their results have important applications for neuroprosthetics, one of the major goals of which is to develop artificial limbs that feel like the real thing. Their results indicate that the brain can essentially be "tricked" into accepting the prosthetic as a real body part.

Audition and Touch.   Another interesting study of a cross-modal interaction involving touch was conducted by Hötting and Röder (2004). These researchers were interested in the degree to which life experience shapes multisensory integration and function. They compared blind and sighted individuals in a task that involved both the tactile and the auditory modalities. Participants were presented with a series of one to four tactile stimuli to the right index finger; simultaneously, they heard a series of one to four tones. Their task was simply to judge the number of times their index finger had been touched. If multisensory integration occurs, then the number of tactile stimulations subjectively experienced would be influenced by the number of tones heard. You may be thinking, "Why did they compare sighted and blind individuals?" Blind individuals are bound to have profoundly different perceptual experiences and combinations of perceptual experiences than sighted individuals. Therefore, one might expect a difference in the processes involved in multisensory integration.

As in the Pavani, Spence, and Driver (2000) study, the sense of touch was fooled. There was an effect of the number of tones. As the number of tones increased, so did the reported number of tactile stimulations. In addition, there was an interaction between the number of tones presented and the type of participant. The disruptive effect of the tones on tactile perception was more pronounced in sighted individuals than congenitally blind individuals. This supports the notion that the processes involved in multisensory integration differ in congenitally blind and sighted individuals. However, a possible confound is present in this experiment. All of the blind participants were experienced Braille readers. Due to this tactile expertise, they may have had more confidence in their tactile judgments, and therefore were less susceptible to the auditory interference. So while it's apparent that multisensory integration is different in blind and sighted individuals, it remains an open question whether the difference is due to enhanced tactile expertise in blind individuals or a fundamental difference in the way the senses interact.

Perception and Action

So far, we've been talking about perception in pretty passive contexts, sitting around having your fingers stimulated, smelling wine, hearing marimbas playing...provocative research to say the least. But truth be told, much of your perception occurs not while you're sitting around, but *while you are moving*. The study of action and its role in cognition is finally getting the attention it deserved all along. In fact, Rosenbaum (2005) dubbed the study of action and motor control the "Cinderella" of psychology, due to what he terms "the neglect of motor control in the science of mental life and behavior." Rosenbaum describes a number of reasons for the neglect, the most notable being what he terms the "neuroscientists have it covered" hypothesis. Rosenbaum makes his point by comparing the number of times various topics are cited in two well-known reference works: The Science Citation Index (which focuses primarily on neuroscience and brain journals) and the Social Science Citation Index (which includes psychology and cognitive psychology journals). These indexes include encyclopedic lists of all research articles published in these academic arenas. In reviewing these citation indexes and doing his own count of where different cognition topics get mentioned and how often, Rosenbaum found that motor control and action receive a great deal of attention from brain scientists, and relatively little from social scientists. The situation is regrettable, as Rosenbaum points out, because motor control lies at the heart of the science of mental life and behavior—it connects the two! Other topics, such as problem solving and decision making, receive far more attention from cognitive psychologists than they do from neuroscience.

Much of this "new wave" of attention on motor control and action occurs in the context of visual perception research. This makes sense given that perception often occurs in the context of action. Not only that, sometimes the objects you're perceiving are moving as well. Let's take a look at some research on perception as it occurs in the dynamic context of our interaction with the world.

Affordances. Earlier in the chapter we discussed Gibson's view of direct perception. According to this approach, perception is not a matter of using previous knowledge to construct a representation of the environment. Rather, perception is dynamic, immediate, and requires no previous knowledge to "construct" some sort of representation. One important concept emphasized by the Gibsonian view is the notion of **affordances,** which are the action possibilities offered by a particular object. How

C'mon…sit down…you can afford it.

many times have you found yourself mindlessly sitting on a rock, ledge, a stone wall, counter, stairs, or some other type of structure? According to the direct view of perception, these surfaces *afford* sitting. It's almost as if your (direct) perceptual tendencies and the structure itself force you to sit. Chairs afford sitting; thankfully, stoves do not.

As you might imagine, our perception of affordances is critical for our successful interaction with and navigation through the world. And, as Ishak, Adolph, and Lin (2008) note, the problem is far from trivial. Affordances can change with changing environmental circumstances, physical propensities, and one's physical makeup. Consider your authors' recent trip to Linville Caverns in North Carolina. There's little doubt that affordances played some role in their successful navigation through various nooks and crannies, without getting any stalactites in the face. As luck would have it, Ishak et al.'s study dealt with just this aspect of affordances. Consider how common this problem is as you shimmy your way to seat 10 in a crowded ballpark or reach down inside the couch for your cell phone (which is where Bridget seems to keep hers).

Stop&*Think* | CAN YOU AFFORD IT?

Gibson's notion of affordances suggests that we directly and naturally perceive properties and functions ("action possibilities"; Gibson, 1979) of objects. Look around and take note of which objects in your environment "invite" or "afford" certain action possibilities, like reaching into, grasping, sitting, or leaning. Similarly, notice which objects do not to have these action possibilities? What distinguishes the two sets? What do the members within each set seem to have in common?

Research Theme
Embodied
Cognition

Ishak, Adolph, and Linn investigated people's perception of affordances by inviting them to reach their hands through small apertures (i.e., openings), as depicted in Figure 2.9a. As enticement to reach into the aperture, candy was placed in the center at the end of a long flat stick; participants had to reach through the aperture to retrieve the candy and they were allowed to keep all the candy they collected. On each trial, three outcomes were possible. The participant (1) attempted to reach the candy but got stuck because the aperture size was too small for their hand, (2) successfully reached the candy, or (3) did not attempt to reach the candy. For the sake of simplicity,

(a)

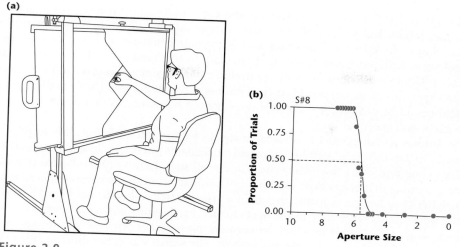

Figure 2.9

Aperture apparatus used in Ishak et al. (2008) study, and representative data from a participant, showing reach attempts as a function of aperture size.

we only will discuss two of the dependent variables used in the study—the motor decision function (the % of trials on which they attempted to reach for the candy, regardless of success) and the affordance threshold (the aperture size at which the participant attempted to reach the candy and was successful 50% of the time).

If a participant had highly sensitive aperture perception (i.e., they knew when the aperture was big enough for them to successfully reach the candy), their motor decision function would be highest at the affordance threshold but would drop precipitously below the affordance threshold. In other words, participants would make the most attempts to reach the candy when they perceived that they would succeed, and in fact, would *only* reach for it when they were sure they'd succeed. As you can see in Figure 2.9b, this is exactly what happened. The graph presents data for a typical participant, and plots the proportion of attempted reaches through the aperture as a function of aperture size. For aperture sizes greater than the affordance threshold, participants always attempted to get their hand through the aperture but for aperture sizes smaller than the threshold, participants almost never attempted to get their hand through it. They seemed to know which apertures they could fit their hand through without even trying to do it. In two subsequent experiments, Ishak et al. found that the nondominant hand was just as accurate as the dominant one, and participants would "recalibrate" their aperture perception when wearing a prosthesis that increased the size of their hand.

Ishak et al. also note that although participant perception and behavior was pretty accurate overall, people tended to err on the side of reaching into too-small apertures. The investigators offer a number of interesting reasons for this. First, the cost-benefit ratio was favorable; treats were available, and failure had no consequence; no one lost a hand. In addition, people seemed to find it compelling to reach into the aperture— they just seemed to want to do it! But overall, the authors conclude that affordance perception is highly accurate. With large apertures, participants reached through without hesitation, and with small ones, they simply said no and didn't even attempt it. Reaching is an extremely common and important behavior, and one that requires finely tuned perception of things that are close to the hands (in other words, within reach). Things within our immediate physical environment are in some sense the most important things in our world at that moment, so having good information about them would be critical for successful responses or behaviors. Is that a jelly bean or a roach in that aperture?

Research Theme
Embodied
Cognition

Studies revealing enhanced visual analysis of information that is close in physical proximity typically (and sensibly) have had participants physically close to the visual display in question. But a fascinating study by Davoli and Abrams (2009) showed that simply imagining that one is close to a visual display can result in the same enhanced visual analysis! They had participants engage in a visual search task, a test of visual attention that we'll discuss more fully in the next chapter. Participants looked at a series of trials on a computer monitor in which letters were presented. Their task was to determine whether a particular target letter was present. The search was either difficult (many letters in the display) or easy (few letters in the display). The key manipulation was what participants were told to imagine while they did the task. In one condition, they were told to imagine that they were holding the sides of the monitor; in the other, they were told to imagine that they had their hands behind their back. In reality, they had their hands on the computer keyboard while performing the task.

The reaction time results revealed no effect of imagination condition. There was, however, an effect of the number of letters in the display. It took longer to search through eight letters than it did to search through four. The intriguing finding was an interaction between the two variables of imagination and display size. When participants imagined they were grasping the computer monitor, the increase in RT was greater than when they imagined themselves with their hands behind their back! According to the investigators, this implies that the participants in the "imagine hands on monitor" condition were giving the visual display a more careful analysis (i.e., spent more time looking at it) than participants in the "imagine hands behind the back" condition. This makes adaptive sense; wouldn't it be beneficial to have a finely-tuned view of the elements in your visual world that are within your reach? These elements have greater potential to figure into future action than do more distant elements so they require a detailed visual analysis. Let's consider the practical implications of this finding. In any situation in which we have to solve a perceptual problem, we might enhance our perception of the situation by simply imagining an appropriate posture or action. In the Ishak, et al. (2008 study, participants may have imagined putting their hand through the aperture and this may have aided their decision about whether to stick their hand into the aperture or not.

Embodied Perception.   As we've seen, perception involves an intricate interplay among sensory processing, action, environment, and even imagination. This takes us pretty far afield of the traditional "disembodied" view of the brain as a computer that sits on top of the body and takes in information and issues commands. Mind, brain, and body combine to form a dynamic system. Work by Proffitt and his colleagues (e.g., Proffitt, Steanucci, Banton, & Epstein, 2003; Witt & Proffitt, 2005) enriches the picture even more. Proffitt's perspective is termed **embodied perception.** According to this view, perception doesn't involve "thinking" as much as it involves the body "reacting." And this "reaction" is influenced by a variety of nonvisual factors such as bodily state, emotional state, and a person's goals. In fact, Proffitt (2006) makes the provocative statement that "A principal function of perception is to defend people from having to think" (p. 119).

Research Theme
Embodied
Cognition

Some fascinating research on perception of distance and slant supports these claims. Proffitt and his colleagues have shown that perception of these two factors is quite mutable in some unexpected ways. For example, Proffitt, Bhalla, Gossweiler, and Midgett (1995) looked at the effects of fatigue on judgments of slant. They recruited participants who were regular runners and asked them to have their most demanding run of the week coincide with the experiment. Upon arriving at the experiment site, the runners stood at the foot of a hill and were asked to make three estimates of its slant. For the verbal estimate, they simply looked at the hill and estimated how steep it was, in degrees. For the visual estimation, they took a handheld pie chart and adjusted a "piece of the pie" to reflect their estimate of the hill's slant (see Figure 2.10). For the haptic estimation, they stood at the foot of the hill and placed a hand on a movable palmboard (see Figure 2.11). They then adjusted the palmboard (without looking at their hand) to reflect their judgment of the hill's slant. The actual slant of the hill was 5°. After making these estimates, the participants took their demanding run and arrived at a second 5° slant hill where the same estimates were made.

Figure 2.12 presents the results for the estimations of the two different 5° hills. The independent variables are the time the slant of the hill was estimated (before or after a run; you might also label this independent variable "fatigue") and type of estimation (verbal, visual, or haptic). The dependent variable is slant estimation. The results are striking. The visual and verbal estimates of slant weren't great to begin with, and the effects of fatigue were powerful. Estimates of slant for the (postfatigue) second hill were nearly 10° greater than the estimates for the (prefatigue) first hill, in spite of the fact that the slant of the hills was the same! And it's not just that we're poor estimators of slant to begin with; the haptic judgments were pretty good, and unaffected by fatigue. These findings indicate that visual perception—in this case, the perception of geographic slant—is modulated by what Proffitt (2006) terms "energetic considerations," in order to promote "efficient energy expenditure." In other

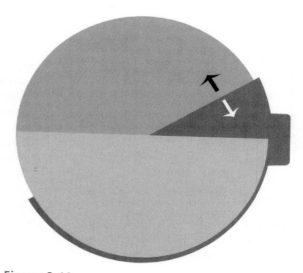

Figure 2.10

Device used for visual estimation in the Proffitt, Bhalla, Gossweiler, and Midgett (1995) study of embodied perception. Subjects estimated the slant of a hill by adjusting a small segment of the pie chart device to match the degree of slant.

From Proffitt, D.R. (2006). Embodied perception and the economy of action. *Perspectives on Psychological Science, 1*(2), 110–122. Published by Blackwell, Inc. Reprinted with permission of the author.

Figure 2.11

Device used for haptic estimation in the Proffitt, Bhalla, Gossweiler, and Midgett (1995) study of embodied perception. Subjects estimated the slant of a hill by placing a hand on the movable palmboard and adjusting it (without looking at their hand) to reflect their judgment of the hill's slant.

From Proffitt, D.R. (2006). Embodied perception and the economy of action. *Perspectives on Psychological Science, 1*(2), 110–122. Published by Blackwell, Inc. Reprinted with permission of the author.

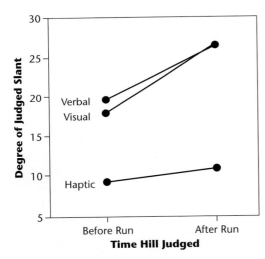

Figure 2.12

Results from the Proffitt, Bhalla, Gossweiler, and Midgett (1995) study on the effects of fatigue on slant estimation.

From Proffitt, D.R. (2006). Embodied perception and the economy of action. *Perspectives on Psychological Science, 1*(2), 110–122. Published by Blackwell, Inc. Reprinted with permission of the author.

Research Theme
Evolution

words, if you feel dead-tired (an energetic consideration), you probably need to rest. The illusory perception of a 5° hill as a 15° hill is more likely to prompt you to rest, which in this case, would aid the goal of "efficient energy expenditure."

The finding and conclusions just described would imply that any consideration—energetic or otherwise—that implies the necessity of increased effort will impact perception. So that hill would look overly steep not only to someone who's tired, but also to someone who is in pain. To test this extension of the basic idea, Witt, Linkenauger, Bakdash, Augustyn, Cook, and Proffitt (2009) recruited participants who suffered from minor, but chronic, pain of the back and/or lower extremities. Patients were approached after an appointment and were taken to a hallway for a distance estimation task. They viewed traffic cones placed at different points along the hallway and were asked to estimate their distance from each cone. They were given an 18" ruler to use as a reference. Their estimates were compared with those of control participants, who had no chronic pain. The results were consistent with Proffitt's view: chronic pain sufferers' estimate of the distance to each cone was greater than the estimates given by the controls.

It's important to note that Proffitt's view of perception is expressly evolutionary. The basic idea behind the evolutionary approach is that we evolve in ways that maximize our chances of survival. A key principle in survival is that energy consumption has to exceed energy expenditure. So how does this tie in with perception? Well, as Proffitt points out, perception aids in the process whereby we "economize our actions." If the energy we need to expend to accomplish something exceeds the amount of energy we have, then the action isn't worth doing. Our perceptual processes have evolved to aid in making these decisions.

Stop&*Think* | EMBODIED PERCEPTION

Proffitt's (2006) embodied perception notion emphasizes how perceptual processes help assess how much energy we're going to need to expend to accomplish something, aiding us in deciding whether or not to engage in the action. Proffitt et al demonstrated that fatigue can make hills look steeper than they are. Might fatigue make backpacks seem heavier than they are?

For this demonstration, annoy your friends by having them make perceptual estimates under different conditions of fatigue. Get a backpack, fill it with several books, and weigh it. Then ask your friends for weight estimates from just glancing at it (keep the backpack open so they can see what is inside). Do this in the following conditions (test different people in each one):

a. early in the morning
b. midday
c. late in the evening

These different conditions are meant as a manipulation of fatigue. You should also have "subjects" rate their fatigue on a 1 to 10 scale after they make their estimate. In which conditions should the estimates of weight be the heaviest? Did your results match the prediction?

The examples just discussed demonstrate how aversive (or at least, taxing) physical states can impact our perceptions and quite possibly limit our behavior. Other work within this paradigm has revealed a positive complement to these findings. The effects need not always be limiting. In fact, bad golfers, might find the next finding liberating. Witt, Linkenauger, Bakdash, and Proffitt (2008) investigated the relationship between golfing skill and perceived hole size. They had participants attempt a putt into a practice putting hole. Afterwards, they estimated the size of the hole while sitting next to it. The putt required of the participants was either difficult (a bit over seven feet) or easy (just under a foot and a half). Note that the estimate should be no different if the only factor in making the estimate is the participants' visual ability and the size of the hole. But surprisingly, estimates of the hole size made after easy putts were larger than estimates made after more difficult ones. Similarly, in another study, the authors found a negative relationship between a golfers' round score and their estimate of hole size. The higher the score (high scores are bad in golf), the lower the estimate of hole size. Similar patterns have been revealed in studies of softball players' perception of ball size (Witt & Proffitt, 2005). Hence, we have yet another example of how one's ability to perform an action impacts action-related perception.

The astute student (this means you) might wonder which way the "causal arrow" points in this relationship. Does being a good golfer lead the player to perceive the holes as bigger or is it the perception of the hole being bigger that leads to being a good

Research Theme
Embodied
Cognition

golfer? Studies thus far haven't addressed this question. Regardless, the previous discussion makes it apparent that our perception of the world around us isn't some static process of our sensory receptors obtaining information and subsequently calculating their respective inputs. Rather, it's a dynamic process that involves an exquisite orchestration and integration of input from all of the sensory systems, a process that occurs within the rich context of our previous experiences as well as our motives and goals.

Stop&Review

1. Define synesthesia, and distinguish between strong and weak synesthesia.
2. True or false? Vision tends to dominate all senses with the exception of audition.
3. What is an affordance?
4. Which of these is NOT true of the embodied perception view?
   a. It fits well with Gibson's view of direct perception.
   b. It characterizes perception as dynamic and not constructed.
   c. It characterizes perception as an evolved survival mechanism.
   d. It proposes that previous knowledge guides perception.

- Strong synesthesia refers to experiences in which input from one sensory system produces an experience not only in that modality but in another as well. Synesthesia is the product of later perceptual processing rather than early sensory processing. A weaker form of synesthesia involves cross-modal associations between concepts that are based in different modalities, like dark and low-pitched tones.
- Vision tends to dominate the other senses. Dominance of audition is shown by the *McGurk effect,* which occurs when a visual stimulus distorts the identification of an auditory (speech) stimulus, and the *ventriloquist effect,* which occurs when a visual cue that is presented simultaneously with an auditory stimulus biases the localization of that auditory stimulus toward the location of the visual cue. Audition dominates the sense of touch.

- A good deal of recent research deals with the interplay between perception and action, the study of which has been somewhat neglected. One example of this interplay is the notion of an affordances, or the action possibilities offered by an object.
- Embodied perception (similar to Gibson's notion of direct perception) describes the view that perception is dynamic, immediate, and requires no previous knowledge to "construct" some sort of representation. This evolutionary view proposes that perception aids in the process whereby we "economize our actions."

Consciousness

Have you ever had the experience of driving somewhere via a familiar route and, upon arriving at your destination, have no memory whatsoever of the drive? It's a common, yet striking, phenomenon. It's frankly amazing that in spite of being engaged in the highly complex set of activities that comprise driving, you aren't particularly aware of what you're doing. Have you ever been operating in this mode, and then a squirrel darts out in front of your car? All of a sudden, you're in full-thinking mode! The squirrel (as squirrels so often do) prompted a profound change in your **consciousness** (our awareness of internal and external events). Your "autopilot" process of driving became a conscious one.

Consciousness-altering squirrel.

Within the study of cognition, no general topic has stimulated more interest than the notion of consciousness, and how consciousness relates to cognitive processing. Our consciousness of the world around us is at the very root of how we experience daily life, and many believe it is at the very root of who we are. It's an elusive concept, and has proven exceedingly difficult to define or pin down. The proliferation of terms thrown around to describe things outside of conscious awareness attests to this—we hear about things being nonconscious, subconscious, preconscious, and unconscious—and there is relatively little agreement about exactly what *non-*, *sub-*, *pre-*, and *un-* refer to, much less exactly what *conscious* means. The quest to account for the phenomenon of consciousness is currently one of the hottest topics within the interdisciplinary field of cognitive science (discussed in Chapter 1). In 2005, this quest—finding the biological basis for consciousness—was designated by the prestigious journal *Science* as one of the top 25 unanswered questions facing modern-day scientists.

Varieties of Consciousness

Block (1995) offers a helpful framework that distinguishes between four different senses of consciousness (which Block contends is a "mongrel concept" that refers to a number of different phenomena). *Monitoring* consciousness refers to one's ability to reflect on our own thinking processes; this concept was briefly mentioned in Chapter 1 as *metacognition*. *Self-*consciousness refers to one's general knowledge about oneself. For example, Bridget knows she's from Indiana, knows she loves to teach, and knows she loves to read mystery novels. **Access consciousness** is used when you're manipulating representations, and manipulation of representations has the potential to influence your mental processing or behavior. For example, the processes that underlie your ability to drive a car would be considered access consciousness. Whenever we process information, we're demonstrating access consciousness. But this doesn't mean that we're aware of the fact that we're processing information. The subjective awareness of what our mind is currently doing is termed **phenomenal consciousness.**

Let's return to our driving example. When you're cruising along, not a care in the world, plenty is going on at the level of access consciousness. All of your mental processes are whirring and clicking, with predictable results: you stop at the red, go at the green, and make all the necessary turns. The fact that you barely notice it and don't remember it later indicates that you had little phenomenal consciousness of the act of driving—it's almost as if you had no subjective experience of driving at all. But the picture changes drastically when the squirrel makes its appearance. When that happens, you are jolted into phenomenal consciousness as you stop and pay attention to what you were thinking, doing, and feeling. The vast majority of the research you'll read about in the rest of the text deals with the processes of access consciousness. Cognitive psychology research is all about the nature of the representations that allow us to reason and communicate, and how those representations are accessed and manipulated. And, as implied by our driving example, many of these processes operate outside of our phenomenal consciousness.

The fact that cognitive processes lie largely outside of our phenomenal consciousness creates a bit of a pickle for researchers. It renders subjective experience highly suspect; I can't just ask you how you read, remember, or perceive things, because these processes in large part are not open to introspection. Indeed, this is a major reason the structuralist approach to cognition discussed in Chapter 1 was doomed to fail.

Let's examine this point within the context of perception. As you might imagine, access consciousness and phenomenal consciousness are associated with quite different dependent variables. If I want to assess your phenomenal consciousness, I simply ask you what you're perceiving and take careful notes on your responses. But, as noted earlier verbal report isn't a complete or unbiased reflection of cognitive processing. It involves more than the ability of our sensory system to detect the stimulus. Perception also involves a willingness to report an event. Think about bumps you may have heard in the night. Did you really perceive them, or were they a product of your imagination? The important point here is that perception involves two processes: a discrimination process based on the sensitivity of the particular sensory system (e.g. vision, audition, etc.) and a *decision* process whereby we determine if a stimulus was actually perceived. This important insight forms part of the basis for **signal detection theory,** an approach to psychophysics that characterizes perceptual experiences as the joint product of **sensitivity** and **response bias.** For example, if a sound is made and two people witness it, one may succeed at hearing it and the other fail to hear it. This could result because one observer is more sensitive than the other, or because one observer is more willing to report that they perceived the stimulus than the other. Due to response bias and other possible biases on the part of the participant, not many studies rely on phenomenal consciousness to assess cognitive processing. A final strike against the reliance on phenomenal consciousness as a tool for assessing cognitive processing is that most of the cognitive processes of interest take place rapidly. Therefore, subtle measures like reaction time and accuracy are needed to reveal their intricacies.

Dissociations in Consciousness

As you've probably gathered from the discussion up to this point, one of the most interesting topics in perception involves conditions in which access consciousness and phenomenal consciousness diverge. Another way of stating this is that different types of consciousness dissociate from one another. They behave in different ways and are influenced by different variables.

Authorship Processing.   Stop reading right now, and raise your hand. Go ahead, do it! Now, how would you describe the sequence of events that led you to raise your hand? Sounds like a stupid question, right? You're probably thinking, "I read a command to raise my hand, processed those instructions, and decided to raise my hand." So your belief is that you had *authorship* of that action. Consciousness led to will, and will caused you to raise your hand. This is your subjective experience of what happened (i.e., your phenomenal consciousness), but this is what Wegner and his colleagues (Wegner, 2003; Wegner & Sparrow, 2004) term the **illusion of conscious will**—the "mind's best trick."

It's quite a challenging notion, that our conscious experience of will is illusory; it's a notion that fits uncomfortably well with the idea that free will itself is an illusion. Now that's a metaphysical quagmire into which we dare not tread. We'll settle for explaining Wegner's major assumptions. Subjectively (phenomenal consciousness), the apparent causal path is from our conscious will to an action. However, both the feeling of conscious will and the action itself are caused by separate, unconscious processes. It is just like the phrase you probably heard (or will hear) in your research method courses: correlation does not equal causation. Although our feeling of will is highly correlated with our actions, that association does not necessarily indicate a causal relationship.

This illusion is a product of **authorship processing,** the set of processes that leads us to attribute events to the entities that are thought to have caused them. Why would we even question this feeling? Aren't we pretty good at figuring out whether we (or someone else) authored an action? Not according to Wegner, who points out many instances of mistakes in authorship processing. One such example is the infamous Ouija board; a game in which users place their fingers on a device termed a *planchet,* and (supposedly) spirits guide their movements to spell out messages from beyond the grave. This certainly seems to be a situation in which our attribution of authorship is mistaken. We believe we do not have authorship of the planchet's movement but in reality we are "the author."

What are the preconditions for a subjective experience of conscious will that might be mistaken? Wegner and Sparrow (2004) mention several, including direct bodily feedback, feedback from visual perception, and action-relevant thoughts. For example, at the start of this section, we asked you to raise your hand. You no doubt had the subjective experience that you consciously willed your arm up. This experience (illusory, in Wegner's view) was encouraged by the facts that (a) you felt your arm raise, (b) you saw your arm raise, and (c) this was in close coincidence with the thought that "the authors want me to raise my arm."

A more detailed account of the theory, along with critiques from other researchers and theorists, can be found in Wegner (2004). But a closer look at one of the studies supporting this view is warranted. Wegner, Sparrow, and Winerman (2004) were interested in the conditions that might lead one to have an illusory experience of control over the movements of others. To investigate this question, they used a unique setup in which they recruited pairs of participants and put them in the situation pictured in Figure 2.13. As you can see, the setup was rather odd. The person in back was the one moving their own arms, but the situation was arranged so that it appeared to the person in front (passive observer) that it was their own arms that were moving. The person in front is the participant of interest. Wegner et al. wanted to find out whether that person might experience an illusion of conscious will over the movements of another—in this case, the person behind them. The person in back was given commands (e.g., raise arm, wave hand, etc.) while the person in front stood passively (arms down and covered by a smock), and watched the odd scenario in a mirror that they

Figure 2.13

A passive observer participant from the study by Wegner, Sparrow, and Winerman (2004).

From Wegner, D. M., Sparrow, B., Winerman, L. (2004). Vicarious agency: experiencing control over the movements of others. *Journal of Personality and Social Psychology, 86(6),* 838–848. Reprinted with permission from the American Psychological Association and the author.

Research Theme
Metacognition

were facing. Now, here's the critical manipulation: In one condition, the passive observer was hearing the instructions through headphones as they were given; in another condition, the passive observer heard nothing.

Recall Wegner et al.'s idea that the experience of conscious will is having a relevant thought in close conjunction with an action. Therefore, if the passive observer was listening to the commands being given to the person in back, this would increase the feeling that they were somehow controlling or willing the action that occurred. Obviously this feeling would be in striking error, as the passive observer did nothing. Wegner et al. assessed the observer's experience with a simple rating scale in which participants rated the degree to which they felt they were consciously willing the arm movement that they were viewing in the mirror. Consistent with the authors' suspicions, passive observers who heard the instructions gave higher ratings of conscious will and control than did those who had not heard the instructions. So basically, people had a strong experience of phenomenal consciousness. But they had absolutely no access consciousness of the action, because they weren't doing anything!

Metcalfe and Greene (2007) were interested in people's metacognition about their own sense of agency (i.e., amount of perceived control). As we discussed in Chapter 1, metacognition refers to one's knowledge of, sensitivity to, or insight about one's own thinking processes. Let's consider the examples given by Metcalfe and Greene. When using a Ouija Board, metacognition of agency is poor; people think they're not in control. The converse is the feeling you have in a responsive car. You feel in complete control. In both situations you *are* in control but your metacognitive awareness of this control is accurate in the driving example and inaccurate in the Ouija board example. So in general, how accurate is our metacognition about our sense of agency, and what factors influence it? In order to address this question, Metcalfe and Greene (2007) had participants play a simple video game in which X's and O's were moving downward on a computer screen. The task involved using the mouse to move the cursor so that it touched the X's but avoided touching the 0's. They received a point for each X they touched. At various points, the game stopped and participants were asked to rate the degree to which they had been in control of the cursor during that period (these were termed judgments of agency).

The researchers manipulated three independent variables: (1) the speed at which the X's and O's moved down the screen; (2) the fidelity of the mouse-cursor relationship (termed turbulence). In the no turbulence condition, the move of the cursor corresponded perfectly with the participants' movement of the mouse. In the turbulence condition, random "noise" was introduced, so that there was a loose correspondence between the mouse movement and the cursor movement; (3) how close the participant had to get to an X to receive credit for touching it (termed "magic" by the authors). In the no magic condition, the cursor needed to touch the X to receive credit. In the magic

Feeling in control.

Feeling out of control.

condition, the cursor only needed to get within 10 pixels of the X to receive credit. This super-lenient criterion made it seem like points were being accumulated almost "by magic." The study had two dependent variables: hit rates (proportion of X's that were touched) and judgments of agency (How in control was I?).

The results are presented in Figure 2.14. Hit rates should show patterns similar to judgment of agency (JoA) ratings if performance is the basis for the agency ratings. This makes intuitive sense; when we are doing well we tend to believe we are the causal agent of our performance and when we perform poorly we tend to believe that some external factor is the causal agent. If hit rates and JoA ratings are not similar, it indicates that something other than performance is basis for the JoA ratings (i.e., participants believe something other than their ability is the cause of their performance).

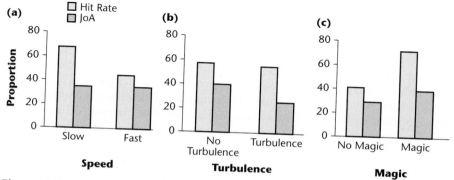

Figure 2.14
Results from Metcalfe & Green's (2007) study of metacognition and agency.

The results in Figure 2.14a show that performance (hit rates) was better in the slow condition than the fast condition but the JoA ratings were the same in the two conditions. The JoA ratings indicate that participants did not attribute their performance to their own ability. Rather, they seemed to have had good metacognitive awareness that the speed at which the targets were falling was the cause for their improved performance. If they had attributed the performance increase to their own ability, the JoA rating would have been greater in the fast condition than the slow condition, just like it was for the hit rates.

The results in Figure 2.14b show that there was little difference (albeit significant) in performance between the no turbulent and turbulent conditions (hit rates were almost identical). However, the JoA ratings were much greater in the no turbulent than turbulent condition. This reflects the metacognitive awareness that participants had less control over their performance in the turbulent condition. This realization was accurate as there was less correspondence between the mouse movement and cursor movement in the turbulent condition. If they were not metacognitively aware of this, their JoA ratings would have mirrored their hit rates. As previously stated performance is typically the basis for the judgment of how much control we have over our actions. Given that performance did not differ that much between the two conditions, neither would their JoA ratings. But this did not happen, indicating the accuracy of the participant's metacognition.

The results in Figure 2.14c reveal that hit rates and JoA ratings were greater in the magic condition than the no magic condition but the difference was greater for hit rates than JoA ratings. This indicates that the participants were metacognitively aware that they basically were being given points in the magic condition. Consequently, they modulated their sense of having produced the outcome (i.e., the JoA ratings did not increase as much as the hit rates). If they did not know this, the difference between JoA ratings and hit rates would have been the same in the magic and no magic conditions. But again, this did not happen, indicating the accuracy of the participant's metacognition.

Overall the results of this study indicate that people do have good metacognitve awareness of the extent to which they are the causal agents of their performance. Therefore, the illusion of authorship created in the Wegner and Sparrow (2004) study might be the exception rather than the rule. Its occurrence may be limited to special circumstances rather than evidence of error-prone processing.

What vs. Where: Blindsight.   The illusion of conscious will reflects the presence of phenomenal consciousness in the absence of access consciousness. We have the subjective experience (presence of phenomenal consciousness) of controlling a movement but we are not producing it (absence of access consciousness). Now let's consider a case in which a person has no subjective experience of something but their behavior is affected by it. In other words, there is access consciousness in the absence of phenomenal consciousness. This is what happens in the surprising phenomenon termed **blindsight,** detailed in a case study by Weiskrantz (1986). His patient, D. B., was blind to the entire left side of his visual field as the result of surgery to remove enlarged blood vessels in his right visual cortex. The wiring of the visual system is such that information presented to the left visual field ends up being processed in the right visual cortex (and vice versa for information presented to the right visual field). Consistent with this, D. B. reported no awareness of objects or events on his left. However, there were some intriguing suggestions that he had some knowledge of them. For example, he could accurately reach for a person's outstretched hand in order to shake it. He attributed this type of success to lucky guessing, swearing up and down that he didn't see it.

In order to systematically investigate D. B.'s deficits and abilities, Weiskrantz (1986) placed him in a controlled visual settings in which a variety of visual stimuli were presented to his left and right visual fields. Whenever stimuli were presented to the left visual field, D. B. reported seeing nothing (self-reported blindness). Weiskrantz then employed a *forced-choice procedure* to find out what if anything D. B. knew about the stimulus he claimed not to see. In a forced-choice procedure, participants are given two alternative answers and are *forced* to choose one—"I don't know" is not an acceptable answer. D. B. was asked to make a forced choice about some aspect of the stimulus presented to his left visual field (e.g. where it occurred). His performance under these conditions was quite surprising—his accuracy was well above chance. In spite of his lack of visual awareness (i.e., no phenomenal consciousness), he was able to process some information about the stimuli (i.e., there was access consciousness). Weiskrantz termed the phenomenon blindsight to underscore the seeming contradiction between the ability to perceive some aspect of a presented stimulus while being unaware that it had been presented.

Subsequent research on blindsight (along with other research on the visual system) has indicated that blindsight is not simply a case of degraded vision (Squire, 2009) and that there are two distinct neurological systems underlying vision that are dissociated in the case of blindsight. One of these systems, based primarily in the visual cortex, is responsible for identifying, recognizing, and becoming aware of visual stimuli. This is often termed the *what system.* The other system, which functions at an earlier point in visual processing (i.e., a subcortical system), is concerned with detection and localization (i.e., the *where system*). So basically, the patient D. B. had an intact "where" system but a deficient "what" system. Analogous "what versus where" systems seem to exist in audition (e.g., Rauschecker & Tian, 2000) and touch (e.g., Reed, Klatzky, & Halgren, 2005).

Subliminal Perception

An issue that has been the subject of hot debate both in the public arena and in cognition laboratories is the relative influence of stimuli of which we are unaware. In the case of blindsight, such stimuli do have an influence. In the lay literature, the effects of **subliminal perception** can allegedly be seen in many different guises. Many proponents (e.g., Key, 1973) claim that ice cubes in vodka ads, heavy metal rock songs, and frames of movies contain insidious subliminal messages that exert an influence on our behavior. One of the most famous examples of supposed subliminal influence (the example most students relate when they claim that subliminal influence is real) was reported in 1957 by advertising expert James Vicary, who (self-) reportedly embedded the messages "eat popcorn" and "drink Coke" in a movie, resulting in a rush of movie watchers to the concession stands to buy refreshments. Almost everyone has heard some version of this story. However, almost no one knows that Vicary later admitted that it was a hoax—a story he cooked up to generate some publicity for a struggling advertising firm (see Weir, 1984). But based on stories like this and other anecdotal evidence, people tend to believe in the reality of subliminal influence. So let's discuss the extent to which semantic (i.e., meaning-based) processing can occur outside of consciousness.

Reality Check

Preconscious Identification.   Is there any evidence of semantic processing for stimuli registered completely outside of consciousness? The intriguing answer is yes. One paradigm that has recently been employed to investigate the possibilities of unconscious processing is semantic priming. Semantic **priming** refers to the tendency for the processing of one stimulus to enhance the speed at which another related stimulus is processed. For example, seeing "cat" would increase the speed at which you are able to identify the related word "dog" but would have no effect on the speed with which you are able to identify the unrelated word "doll." Costello, Jiang, Baartman, McGlennen, and He (2009) used the binocular rivalry paradigm to investigate the possibility of whether consciously presented words could prime unconsciously presented words.

In their investigation, Costello et al. used the procedure depicted in Figure 2.15. They presented a prime word to both eyes (salt). These words were visible and consciously perceived by the participants. Immediately after the presentation of the prime, a related target word (pepper) or unrelated target word (basket) was presented to one eye, and a color patch was presented to the opposite eye. The color patch was constructed so that participants consciously perceived the color patch but not the word. In essence the target word was invisible due to the presentation of the color patch to the other eye. This effect is termed binocular suppression. To test for the possibility of unconscious processing, Costello et al. gradually increased the brightness of the target word until it became visible (i.e., was consciously perceived). When this happened the stimulus was considered to have "emerged from suppression."

When participants saw a related prime word (salt), the invisible target word (pepper) emerged from suppression (i.e., became visible) more quickly than if the target was unrelated (basket). This indicates that even when the target word was completely

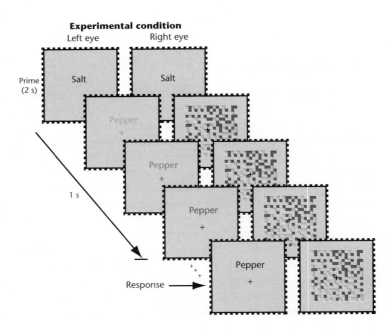

Figure 2.15
Stimulus sequence from Costello et al.'s (2009) study of subliminal semantic processing.

invisible, it was undergoing semantic processing and therefore could be primed by the visibly presented prime word.

Effects of Subliminal Primes.

So it appears that at least some processing of incoming information occurs outside of our conscious awareness. And the processing isn't just superficial. Information about the identity and meaningfulness is apparently processed well before conscious awareness is brought to bear. Now the question is, does subliminal processing influence later responding? It is commonly believed that it does. This is basically the reverse of the Costello et al. paradigm. In the studies to be described now, the prime is presented subliminally, and researchers observe the effect of that subliminally presented prime on some later response. Controversy still rages regarding the effects of subliminally presented primes; their influence depends critically on how exactly "subliminal" and "later responding" are defined.

Questions of Definition and Method.

As you'll see, controlled experimental research has revealed extremely subtle (though consistent) effects of subliminally presented primes, but not the large-scale effects claimed by Vicary and others. So why the gulf between popular opinion and the empirical facts? The question "Can there be subliminal influences on behavior" can be answered in a myriad of ways, depending on what you mean by *subliminal,* and *influence behavior.* Put in terms that might be familiar to you from your research methods course, the debate over the existence of subliminal influences on behavior is an intricate lesson in the importance of operational definitions and experimental methodology.

What is meant by subliminal? When your local newscaster or your Aunt Edna says something about subliminal perception, the term *subliminal* could simply mean "not attended." This is unfortunate, because the difference between "not attended" and "not perceived" proves to be critical when assessing whether a stimulus is likely to affect processing. As you'll see in Chapter 3, it's clear that unattended stimuli can exert an influence on behavior. In Chapter 6, you'll see that information we don't remember also can influence our behavior. But subliminal literally means "below threshold"—that is, it cannot be perceived. So the sound of people murmuring behind you in class is not subliminal; it's simply not attended to (hopefully!). The real question of subliminal influence is whether stimuli that aren't even judged as being present at all can influence behavior. As you'll see, there are even subtler definitional shadings to the notion of subliminal.

Marcel (1983) conducted a series of studies to investigate the possibility of subliminal priming. The procedure involved a task in which participants were presented with a color patch on a screen and the task was to name the color as quickly as possible. The presentation of the color patch was preceded by a prime word that either was neutral (table—orange patch) or matched the color patch (orange—orange patch). Reaction time should be faster when the color patch is preceded by a matching prime word, relative to when it is preceded by a neutral prime word.

To test for subliminal influence the prime word was (on some trials) presented subliminally—that is, participants could not see it. To ensure that the prime could not be seen, Marcel ran a pretest for each participant in which color words were presented extremely quickly. He basically wanted to find the point at which the participants achieved approximately chance performance in saying that they had detected a word. In the subliminal prime condition, these individualized exposure times were used to present the prime words. He also tested participants in a **supraliminal** (above the threshold of conscious awareness) prime condition, in which the prime words were clearly visible.

Would a prime presented at a level at which participants had reported not seeing anything produce an effect on responding? Marcel's results showed that it did. If the prime word matched the color of the patch, it facilitated (speeded) responding, relative to a condition in which the prime word was neutral. The prime words influenced the speed of color naming even if the primes were presented at a level in which participants reported not being aware of them (i.e., subliminally). It's important to note that the priming effect was much greater in the supraliminal condition than the subliminal condition.

Marcel (1983) defined subliminal in terms of what participants *said* they perceived. You might say that Marcel defined the threshold *subjectively*—solely in terms of the participants' phenomenal consciousness. Others (e.g., Cheesman & Merikle, 1984) emphasized the importance of what is termed an objective threshold—that is, the level at which *performance on some task* (not participants' self-report) indicates that the prime was not perceived. They point out that in the Marcel procedure, in which awareness was defined subjectively, participants may have perceived the prime but were conservative in reporting it. So even though they said they were unaware, they may have been aware. This relates to the two concepts of psychophysics discussed earlier. When participants reported that they hadn't perceived the subliminal prime, it may have been a matter of *sensitivity* (they truly did not detect it; no access or phenomenal consciousness), or a matter of *response bias* (they were conservative in their reporting). A third possibility is that they truly were not aware of the stimulus (i.e., they had no phenomenal consciousness), but some processing occurred outside of their conscious awareness (i.e., they were engaged in access consciousness). In this case, their report of "I don't see it" was only partially true.

Cheesman and Merikle (1984) were concerned about this third possibility and attempted to replicate Marcel's study while adding a twist of their own. They used the same task—a primed color identification task—but they used a stringent criterion to determine that a prime was presented *subliminally*. Recall that Marcel defined subliminal as the level at which participants indicated a word was presented half the time. Cheesman and Merikle defined it differently—in a pretest, they presented prime words for different durations. After each presentation, participants were asked (as they were in the Marcel study) if they had seen anything. In cases where they failed to detect a word, they were then presented with four color names and forced to choose which they had seen. Note that if their guessing performance matched their self-report, they shouldn't have been able to guess the correct color more than 25% of the time. But even under conditions in which participants reported seeing nothing, they guessed the color they had seen at a level much higher than chance (>25%). This demonstrates that some information about the stimulus must had been processed (which is evidence of access consciousness); otherwise, guessing would have been at chance levels.

Cheesman and Merikle tested the effects of prime words presented under the conditions identified in the pretest. In the objective threshold condition, primes were presented under conditions that had led to chance levels of performance in the forced-choice pretest (25%). The authors believed that this was the condition that truly involved subliminal presentation because at this level of exposure participants couldn't guess what color had occurred with any level of proficiency. Thus, this condition used what was termed an **objective threshold.** In a second condition, they presented primes under conditions that had led to 50% accurate guessing in the "did you see something or not" pretest (percentage used by Marcel). This latter condition used what Cheesman and Merikle termed a **subjective threshold**—participants *reported* that they couldn't see the prime words, yet their guessing performance indicated otherwise. An analysis of the amount of priming as a function of prime condition—supraliminal, subjectively subliminal, and objectively subliminal—confirmed Cheesman and Merikle's suspicion. Primes presented below an objective threshold failed to influence performance (i.e., reaction time did not differ from a neutral prime condition). But primes that were presented below a subjective threshold did produce a statistically significant (albeit small) degree of priming, replicating Marcel's results; priming occurred even though participants reported not being aware of the prime. Cheesman and Merikle concluded that the reality of subliminal perception depends on how one defines the threshold of awareness below which the stimuli presented are deemed *subliminal.* Defined subjectively, subliminal perception exists; objectively, subliminal perception does not exist.

What is Meant by "Influence Behavior"? It's important to note that even when subliminal influences are found, they tend to be small effects, on the order of 1/20th of a second (see a recent review by Van den Bussche, Van den Noortgate, and Reynvoet, 2009) for a complete discussion of subliminal priming effects). This brings us to the second question: What is meant by "influence behavior"? This question is important if we're to think critically about the insidious claims that illicit subliminal forces are omnipresent and attempting to manipulate our thoughts and actions. We've just seen that many of the studies of subliminal influence have operationalized "influence behavior" as "primed responding in a speeded reaction time task." You may be skeptical that these findings generalize to any real effects in everyday settings.

However, social psychologists have found effects of subliminal messages and claim that some of the empirical tests have not been fair. Karremans, Stroebe, and Claus (2006) criticize much of the research on subliminal influence. They point out that the subliminal messages used in some of the studies are much too long to have any effect and point out that subliminal priming increases the accessibility or activation of a concept, which is unlikely to result in long-range effects on behavior. Consistent with this view, there is some evidence that priming a concept relevant to a current goal or motive can lead to subliminal priming effects. For example, Karremans et al. found that subliminally presented drink brand names influenced preference and choice of that particular brand, but only for participants who were thirsty. Bermeitinger, Goelz, Johr, Neumann, Ecker and Doerr (2009) provided a conceptual replication of this finding, showing that participants' consumption of a particular brand of dextrose (sugar) pills was influenced by subliminally presented logos, the effect only occurring for participants who were tired. And some researchers have found long-range effects of subliminally presented information. Lowery, Hardin, Eisenberger, and Sinclair (2007) primed student participants with a word related to intelligence, and found that primed participants did better on the midterm exam, days after the experimental session that featured the priming task!

In spite of the occasional positive finding, many researchers remain skeptical, mostly due to what they see as the methodological shortcomings of studies that do find subliminal effects. Another reason for skepticism is the healthy imaginations of the credulous consumer, who are sometimes too easily convinced of subliminal influence after being told that it's there. In other words, the effect depends on the top-down processing of the "subliminal perceiver." One common application of what might be termed *subliminal perception technology* involves presenting subliminal messages on tapes. Such tapes claim to offer assistance with everything from weight loss to alleviating depression to curing acne (see Druckman & Bjork, 1991, for a more complete list). Is there any evidence that such tapes work? Usually, their advertisers cite the evidence of testimonials from satisfied customers. But even if these testimonials are real, they aren't very compelling evidence. Satisfied customers represent a biased sample; people who listen to self-help tapes are certainly motivated to make the change targeted by the tape. Any observed behavioral change may simply be the result of these motivational factors.

To separate the possible effects of subliminal self-help messages from motivational effects, one needs to conduct a double-blind study of the effects. Greenwald, Spangenberg, Pratkanis, and Eskenazi (1991) conducted a double-blind study on the effectiveness of subliminal message tapes. They used commercially manufactured tapes that had subliminal messages embedded within classical music, popular music, or nature sounds. In a clever procedure, they gave participants one of two tapes with an embedded subliminal message; the message was designed to improve either self-esteem or memory. However, the label on each tape was randomly assigned. So, sometimes a tape labeled "memory improvement" was actually a self-esteem tape and a tape labeled "self-esteem improvement" was actually a memory improvement tape. Participants were given pretests that included measures of memory and self-esteem and were then instructed to listen to the tapes every day for one month. They then returned for a series of posttests, including retests of memory and self-esteem. Participants also were asked to rate whether they believed their self-esteem and memory had improved.

The results were clear: the posttest measures of self-esteem and memory showed none of the expected improvement over the pretest measures in any of the conditions. The only consistent effect that emerged was a participant-expectancy effect. When asked about their perceived improvement, participants indicated that they had improved in whatever quality (memory or self-esteem) was on the tape label (even if the tape had been labeled incorrectly). For example, participants who saw a "self-esteem improvement" label on their tape thought that they had made improvements in their self-esteem, regardless of what was actually on the tape.

Another example of top-down processing was demonstrated by Vokey and Read (1988). In one of their studies, they investigated the phenomenon of backmasking—the alleged presence and influence of messages on record albums (which were all the rage before CDs) that are supposedly discernible if the records are played backward. According to some, these backmasked messages embedded in rock albums are capable of eliciting negative effects in listeners. In an especially tragic case, the heavy metal band Judas Priest was sued by the parents of two teenagers who jointly attempted suicide. Sadly, one of the boys succeeded and the other died from drug complications a few years later (Moore, 1996). The plaintiffs alleged that subliminal messages in the music played a role in prompting this tragedy. After hearing expert testimony on both sides, the judge ruled in favor of the defendants. (See Moore, 1996, for an excellent discussion of this case, as well as an informative discussion of the lay and legal beliefs about the effectiveness of subliminal messaging.)

Vokey and Read demonstrated that you can hear just about anything in a garbled message, as long as you have an expectation that you're going to hear something. They made backward recordings of Lewis Carroll's *Jabberwocky* ("Twas Brillig and the Slithy Toves…") and the 23rd Psalm ("The Lord is my shepherd…"). The experimenters did some (in their words) "creative listening" to these backward tapes and detected a few sequences that could be heard as something meaningful. Among these were "Saw a girl with a weasel in her mouth" and "I saw Satan." Now, mind you, these messages weren't really there; the garbled noise that was there could be construed into these messages by the creative listener. The experimenters found six such passages for each of the two recordings. They then gave participants a simple task: they were to listen to the backward recordings to see if they could hear the messages designated by the experimenter. Each participant was given the six "creatively heard" messages for one of the passages (experimental passage); for the other passage, they listened without any prior prompting about what they might hear (control passage). As Vokey and Read suspected, participants were very good at hearing the backmasked messages, but only the ones they were told to expect. The six messages in the control passage, extracted by the experimenters but not mentioned to the participants, were never heard. So in essence, the participants "heard" the backmasked messages because they expected to hear them; when they didn't expect them, they didn't hear them. Clearly, top-down processing is at work here: the data are garbled, but expectations and knowledge impose order on this garbled data.

In spite of findings like these, and strong skeptical views of some who claim there is voluminous evidence against the effectiveness of subliminal persuasion (e.g., Brannon & Brock, 1994; Pratkanis & Aronson, 2001), controversy still rages. Dijksterhuis, Aarts, and Smith (2005) summarize their review of the literature with three good reasons to continue investigating the possibility of subliminal effects. First, there are potential benefits that might be had, as seen in studies indicating positive effects of priming constructs related to desirable characteristics and behaviors. Second, it's likely that no one would want to be manipulated by subliminal messages, so understanding them thoroughly and informing the public about how they work would be one effective tool for preventing their misuse and abuse. Third, these authors view the abandonment of subliminal perception research as an overreaction to the fallacious and preposterous claims of proponents like Vicary. While the conclusions were undoubtedly based on shoddy research, that is no reason to suspend empirical investigation of the phenomenon. Doing so would be tantamount to throwing the baby out with the bath water.

Stop&Review

1. Phenomenal consciousness is to access consciousness as:
   a. aware is to unaware
   b. sensation is to perception
   c. manipulation is to subjective experience
   d. mind is to brain
2. True or false? Blindsight is an example of access consciousness in the absence of phenomenal consciousness.
3. How does the presence of a subliminal priming effect relate to how the threshold of awareness is defined?
4. True or false? Top down processing plays a role in whether or not effects of subliminal perception are found.

- Phenomenal consciousness refers to subjective awareness of what our mind is currently doing; access consciousness refers to the manipulation of representations in the service of thinking. Dissociations between these types of consciousness (i.e., one is present in the absence of the other) are commonplace.

- A dissociation related to authorship processing is called the illusion of conscious will, believing that you consciously willed an action when in reality, you did not. Blindsight occurs when an individual reports not seeing a stimulus (absence of phenomenal consciousness) that had been presented. In spite of this, they often guess correctly about the location of the stimulus (presence of access consciousness).

- There is evidence of semantic priming when the prime is presented supraliminally and the target is presented subliminally. Semantic priming when the prime is presented subliminally depends on the definition of subliminal. If subjectively defined then semantic priming is found, when defined objectively, it is not.

- The long-term effects of subliminal stimuli are limited and seemed to depend on top-down processes such as motivation and expectations. However, social psychologists have found some positive effects of subliminal persuasion.

CHAPTER OUTLINE

3

Mechanisms of Attention: Monitoring and Noticing Information

Why is it sometimes so easy and sometimes so difficult to notice something, or to pay attention? Under what circumstances do we have to "pay attention" and when does attention just seem to "happen"?

How is it that you can be completely engrossed in something like a conversation or a movie, yet somehow you happen to hear your name? How much processing occurs when we aren't paying attention to something?

Have you ever put the milk in the cabinet and the cereal in the refrigerator? Walked into a room, and then forgot what you went there for? Responded to someone who says, "How's it going?" with a brilliant response of, "Not much!" Are you losing your mind?

Is it really that risky to talk on a cell phone and drive at the same time? It seems easy enough, and it seems that a lot of people do it with no problem. Do hands-free devices help?

Attention: What Is It?

As was evident from the previous chapter, we're constantly being bombarded by information moving in and out of our conscious awareness. As I write this, I can hear the air conditioner humming; water from the sprinkler is hitting the windows because it isn't set quite right; a baseball game is on TV; and my laptop computer is threatening to fall and become a floortop computer. Obviously, there is a nearly constant need to monitor the events that are occurring in our external environment, not to mention the "events" in our internal environment (i.e., thoughts). Cognitive psychologists call this monitoring process **attention.** You'll learn in this chapter that attention is strategic and actively manipulated as we take in the unceasing ebb and flow of objects and events occurring in our environment. Given the sheer dynamic nature of ongoing experience, a process that allows us to monitor and notice important information would seem critical to survival and success.

Turning our…attention…to the title of this section, there seems to be some serious disagreement on the answer to the question "What is attention?" Pioneering psychologist William James had a ready answer: "Everyone knows what attention is." James was confident about people's lay knowledge about attention because (provided we're awake) we are constantly engaged in this monitoring process. Our waking existence involves a continuous focusing and refocusing of what might be termed *mental effort.*

Given that everyone knows what it is, this should be an especially short chapter, right? Well, consider another more recent view on attention, modern-day attention researcher Harold Pashler's view that "No one knows what attention is." Pashler (1998) and others lament that the concept of attention is thrown around so frequently and used to describe so many different phenomena, that it really isn't a very useful concept (e.g., Pashler & Carrier, 1996). So the question of what exactly attention "is" remains difficult to pin down. But researchers have done their best to try and delineate the basic processes whereby we take in information, choose the important stuff, and filter out the unimportant.

Perhaps not surprisingly, attention researchers have focused on the two senses that are probably most prominent in your attentional stream right now. There's no doubt vision is a key player, given that you're reading this. Audition is likely to be shifting around as well, as your focus drifts to the latest episode of *Family Guy* on TV, your roommate's whining, or the next song on your iPod. These two senses—vision and audition—have been the focus of researchers' attention over the past 50 years, and will be ours as well.

Attention: Basic Characteristics

The most noteworthy aspect of attentional processing is its limited capacity. This also might be the most subjectively salient aspect of attention. Think of all of the times you've felt overwhelmed this semester, with the immediate demands of your visual and auditory environment, not to mention the events, worries, and future tasks to which your mind wanders as you lose focus.

Think of attentional processing in terms of the juggler's ability to keep a certain number of balls in the air. No matter how good the juggler is, there is going to be a limit. Only so many things can be kept in the air. Likewise, you are (severely) limited in the number of things you can mentally "keep in the air." There is a critical difference between the juggler and the attender. Juggling is probably more responsive to practice than is attention; you can't get better at dividing your attention by spending more time talking on your cell phone while driving. So in spite of how often you practice "mental juggling," you probably aren't getting much better at it. However, at the end of this chapter we will discuss some interesting and somewhat surprising ways to improve your attentional control. In addition, we will return to this issue in Chapter 4 when we discuss the limited capacity of working memory.

Limits in capacity express themselves somewhat differently within the contexts of visual and auditory attention and correspondingly, researchers describe them with different metaphors. As we'll see, the limits of visual attention are often expressed as a spotlight that only focuses on a portion of what we see. Auditory attention limits are often discussed in terms of a gateway that only can let a limited amount of information through at a given time, or a limited pool of central resources that we draw from during listening and comprehension.

Limits in attentional capacity would seem to present a serious problem, given the number of potential suitors for our attention. If there weren't some way to deal with attentional overload, we would either sit frozen in a chair, overwhelmed with the stimulation around us, or would move recklessly through our environment, likely to be knocked over by something we failed to see. The limit in attentional capacity seems to necessitate, in an adaptive sense, the next two characteristics.

One of these adaptive characteristics is *flexibility;* we can easily shift our attention based on the demands of the current environment and moment. Attentionally, we are light on our feet. In fact, it's likely that you've shifted attention several times during this reading (however fascinating the text might be) by something that caught your eye or ear. So it's apparent that attention is quite pliable and dynamic. A central question in attention research—and one that will serve as a focus for our discussion—involves identifying the characteristics of stimuli that draw and maintain our attention.

The other adaptive characteristic of attention is that it allows for *voluntary control* of how we deal with incoming information (i.e., strategic deployment). While it is true that our attention is drawn or captured by certain types of stimuli, it is also the case that we can direct our attention based on interests, goals, or other aspects of the situation. Visually, this implies that we can willfully search for stimuli of a certain type. If you know that your good friend always wears Hawaiian shirts, you can basically tune your attention to look for people wearing that type of shirt (which might not be too difficult as few people make such a wardrobe choice). Auditorily, strategic deployment means that you can choose to listen to your professor's lecture rather than the gossiping in the row behind you.

Pre-Attentive vs. Post-Attentive Processing

Much research on the nature of attention distinguishes between what are termed pre-attentive and post-attentive (or simply attentive) processes. Pre-attentive processing is generally characterized as occurring quickly, before the focus of attention is brought to a stimulus. It's almost as if you arrive at a conclusion before you start thinking. Most of the processes discussed in the previous chapter—global processing, perceptual grouping,

Pupitizing

synesthetic experiences—are thought to occur pre-attentively. Post-attentive processing occurs once attention has been focused on a stimulus.

To contrast pre-attentive and post-attentive processes within the context of a single ability, let's consider enumeration, or the ability to accurately count instances of an object. How many puppies are in the picture in the upper right of the page? How many kittens are in the picture on the lower right? Chances are you used two different processes to arrive at your answers, one thought to be pre-attentive, and the other post-attentive. The difference was probably salient phenomenologically—can you come up with it?

In the case of the puppies, you probably engaged in a process termed subitizing. **Subitizing** refers to the quick and effortless (i.e., pre-attentive) enumeration of a small number of objects (Kaufman, Lord, Reese, & Volkmann, 1949). As soon as you looked at the puppies, you just knew there were three; "counting" doesn't seem to be involved at all. This evaluation was fast, effortless, and likely didn't demand any attention (Trick & Pylyshyn, 1994). The kittens are another matter. Here, you probably did exert mental effort (i.e., attention), counting each kitten to arrive at your answer. Subitizing is much faster than counting and is virtually unaffected by changes in number, up to about three or four (Mandler & Shebo, 1982).

Subitizing is instructive for another reason in that it demonstrates an important methodological convention in studies of visual attention. Researchers often gauge attentional involvement by noting how reaction time varies as a function of the amount of information in a visual display. There is little or no difference in the ability or speed to enumerate one to three items. However, there is a steady increase in the effort and time expended to enumerate more than four or so items (e.g., six items takes longer than five items, which takes longer than four items.) This signifies that enumerating up to three items is thought to indicate attention-free (i.e., pre-attentive) processing. The steady rise in RT when enumerating a greater number of items signifies attentional (i.e., post-attentive) processing.

Countin' Kittens

Stop&*Think* | SUBITIZING

For this demonstration, you're going to observe your friends enumerating objects pre-attentively and post-attentively. You'll need 7 or 8 small items of the same type—pennies, paper clips, pencils, etc. While your friend isn't looking, gently "toss" the objects in front them so they end up in a random arrangement. Have them look and estimate the number of items. Do this for many trials, changing the number of items each time, jumping back between subitizing range (1 to 3 or 4) and counting range (about 4 or over). Through your own observations of their enumeration, and their own introspections about it, see where the transition between subitizing and counting occurs.

An interesting variation might be to group differing numbers of items in some familiar or obvious way. For example, you could employ Gestalt grouping cue of proximity to group items. Out of sight, you might place six items in two groups of three, and observe whether your "participants'" enumeration seems to be more like subitizing or counting. Another alternative is to lay out items (without your participant looking) in a familiar configuration (e.g., like the five-spot on a die). Does the resulting enumeration seem more pre- or post-attentive?

Given that "no one knows what attention is," it's no surprise that not all researchers are fond of the distinction between pre-attentive and post-attentive processing. Nevertheless, the labels are convenient descriptors that retain a great deal of intuitive and phenomenological validity, and more importantly, empirical validity. The problem lies in attempting to make hard and fast distinctions between the two. Pre- and post-attentive processing are probably best conceived of as ends of a continuum. Also, it's likely that processing in any given context involves some mix of both.

Stop&*Review*

1. Name the three major characteristics of attention.
2. What is subitizing? Is it considered to be primarily pre-attentive or post-attentive?
3. Large increases in reaction time as a function of display size would indicate that:
   a. pre-attentive processes are involved
   b. post-attentive processes are involved
   c. subitizing is being done
   d. attention is independent of reaction time

• Attention refers to the processes we use to monitor incoming events. Most research has focused on attention in the visual and auditory domains. Attention is limited in capacity (only so much can be processed), flexible (attention shifts to different stimuli depending on importance), and voluntary (we can control our attentional focus).

- Pre-attentive processes are those that occur before the focus of attention is brought to a stimulus. Post-attentive processes occur after a stimulus has been brought into the focus of attention. Subitizing refers to the fast enumeration of a small number of objects, and is thought to be pre-attentive.

- An important tool in the assessment of attention is an assessment the time it takes to process a visual display as a function of the number of items in the display. Pre-attentive processes are indicated by minimal increases in processing time as a function of display size, while post-attentive processes are indicated by moderate or large increases.

Visual Attention

As discussed in the last chapter and previously in this chapter, we are constantly bombarded by visual stimuli that differ in size, shape, color, movement, salience, relevance, friendliness...well, you get the idea. The bombardment is simultaneous and constant, but eminently manageable. How can this be? How can such varied and constantly changing input be managed so efficiently and responded to so appropriately (most of the time, that is)? Let's examine some of the processes of visual attention.

Types of Visual Attention

In spite of the pessimistic assessment by Pashler (1998) that "No one knows what attention is," researchers have made a number of basic distinctions between different attentional modes. In visual attention, one critical distinction goes all the way back to pioneering psychologist William James. In his seminal text *Principles of Psychology,* James (1890) noted both *active* and *passive* modes of attention. In an active mode of attention, the observer has a goal in mind, and guides the attentional process in the service of that goal. Modern researchers are likely to label this type of attention **goal-driven attention.** Note that this mode of attention is an example of top-down processing because the observer is guiding attention based on their own knowledge, goals, and expectations.

In a *passive* mode of attention, observers simply take in the environment as attention is occasionally "grabbed" by some aspect of the visual scene. That is, the stimulus itself (rather than the observer) guides attention; hence it has been termed **stimulus-driven attention.** As you might have guessed, this mode of attention is an example of bottom-up processing because it is driven by the characteristics of the stimulus. Moment-to-moment visual processing no doubt involves a combination of both (Yantis, 1998), but let's take a close look at each of them in isolation.

Goal-Driven Attention.

As just noted, the goal-driven mode is defined by the willful direction of one's attentional focus—that is, what one chooses to look at and focus on. When you look at someone with whom you're conversing, you look them in the eye. When you watch your favorite show on TV, you direct your attention to the center of the

TV screen. When you listen to class lecture, you focus your attention on the notes appearing on the screen in the front of the room.

Space-Based Attention.   In all of the cases just described, you're focusing attention on a particular spatial location (**space-based attention**) in front of you, almost as if you're turning on a spotlight. A spotlight illuminates the center of one's view most intensely, with more diffuse light falling on the periphery. Outside this ring of peripheral light (i.e., outside the spotlight), things are barely, if at all, discernible. In some ways, attention seems to work in much the same way, with areas within central attentional focus receiving more thorough processing than areas on the periphery of that focus, which receive more diffuse attentional processing (e.g., Posner, 1980).

Consider a study by Laberge (1983) that empirically demonstrated the validity of the spotlight analogy. The basic task in this study was target detection in a visual display. Participants were shown a series of trials that consisted of five positions in which letters or numbers might be presented. There were two types of trials. Regular trials (presented 75% of the time) consisted of letters that spelled out a common word; probe trials (presented 25% of the time) consisted of a 7, T, or Z in one of the positions (chosen at random) and + signs in the other positions. Different trial types were randomly interspersed. Participants were told to focus on the middle position. When presented with a regular trial, they were instructed to press a key if the center position was the letter A-G and do nothing if the letter was N-U (H-M were never presented in the center position). When presented with a probe trial they were to press a key if they saw a 7 and do nothing if they saw a T or Z.

The probe trials yield the data of primary interest. The dependent variable was the reaction time to press the key when a 7 was presented. Figure 3.1 presents the RT results from the probe trials, as a function of where the probe stimulus appeared. The pattern is precisely what you would expect based on the idea of an attentional spotlight. Reaction time was fastest when the probes were presented in the center position, fell off a bit one position out (2nd and 4th position), and were slowest when probes were presented at either end (1st or 5th position). In terms of the spotlight analogy, the attentional spotlight was shining on the middle position. That position was "well illuminated" and RT was fast when the stimulus appeared there. But the "intensity" of the "light" became more diffuse the farther the position was from the center, with a concomitant slowing of RT.

A number of other studies (e.g., Eriksen & Eriksen, 1974; Posner, 1980) support the general notion of a strategic "spotlight" whereby we "zero in" on a particular region in space. Note that the idea of a spotlight fits nicely with the characterization of attention as flexible and strategic. We can choose where we focus the spotlight and we can move the spotlight to focus on other aspects of the environment when needed.

The spotlight metaphor and supporting data reveal that visual attention is, to some degree, spatial. However the spotlight metaphor is deficient in a number ways as outlined by Cave and Bichot (1999). For example, if attention is a spotlight, when the spotlight moves (i.e., as attention shifts), the space along the way

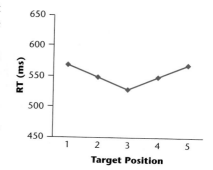

Figure 3.1
Results from Laberge (1983) study, demonstrating a "spotlight" effect in visual attention.

should be temporarily illuminated by the spotlight. Also, the time it takes to shift attention should vary according to how far the spotlight has to travel. Neither of these predictions is clearly borne out by the data. Variations of the metaphor have been proposed, such as a jumping spotlight (e.g., Eriksen & Murphy, 1987) or a blinking spotlight (Van Rullen, Carlson, & Cavanagh, 2007). The general notion of a spotlight is alive and well. However the precise nature of space-based attention remains a matter of empirical debate.

Object-Based Attention.   The most significant way in which the spotlight metaphor falls short is the observation that visual attention is not always based on location. We certainly can choose to pay attention to locations in space but we also can choose to pay attention to particular *objects* in our visual field. Attention can be guided by *what* something is, not just *where* it is; that is, attention can be object-based (Duncan, 1984) as well as space-based.

The possibility of **object-based attention** is demonstrated in a study by Egly, Driver, and Rafal (1994). Their clever procedure allowed for the assessment of both space-based and object-based attention. The procedure is depicted in Figure 3.2. Participants were told to fixate on the middle of the screen (indicated by a +). A trial consisted of 4 events. In event 1, participants saw two grey rectangular boxes. The boxes could be presented vertically to the right and left of fixation (see Figure 3.2a for an example of this trial) or horizontally above and below fixation. In event 2, one of the ends of one of the rectangles brightened to white (Figure 3.2b). This was a cue that indicated where the participants should focus their attention. In event 3, the rectangles returned to their original grey color (Figure 3.2c). Event 4 was the critical event. One end of one of the rectangles darkened to black (the target); participants were to press a button as soon as they detected this target.

The location of the target was the independent variable. In a valid trial (which occurred 75% of the time), the target appeared in the same location as the cue in event 2 (1st panel of Figure 3.2d). In an invalid trial (which occurred 25% of the time), the target did not appear in the same location as the cue (right three panels of Figure 3.2d). The dependent variable was RT to detect the target.

The location of the target on invalid trials allowed for the assessment of object-based and space–based attention. The target could be in one of three locations—the opposite end of the same rectangle that was cued in phase 2 or either end of the other

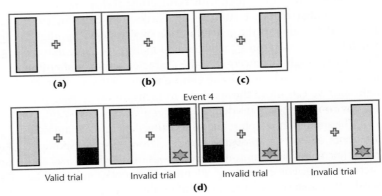

Figure 3.2
A sample trial from Egly et al.'s study of object-based attention. On a given trial participants would get one of the events in panel (d).

rectangle. The critical invalid events are depicted in the middle two panels of Figure 3.2d. In both events, the target is equidistant from the focus of the participant's attention (i.e., the cued location in event 2 and indicated by a star). If attention is space-based, RT for detecting targets in either of these positions should be comparable. The spotlight is focused on the cued location and the amount of "light" reaching either target location should be the same as they are equidistant from the center of the spotlight. However, if attention is object-based, RT to respond to the trial depicted in the 2nd panel of Figure 3.2d (where the target is in the same rectangle as the cue) should be faster than the trial depicted in the 3rd panel of Figure 3.2d (where the target is in a different rectangle than the cue). The idea behind object-based attention is that attention is directed to objects, rather than locations. When asked to respond to a feature of an attended object (2nd panel of Figure 3.2d), RT should be faster than when asked to respond to a feature of an unattended object (3rd panel of Figure 3.2d). The object-based prediction was supported by the data. Research since has highlighted the importance of both space-based and object-based modes of attention (Matsukura & Vecera, 2007). Intuitively, it makes sense that the flexibility of attention would allow you to orient to space or to objects of interest or relevance.

Stop&*Think Back* | SPOTLIGHTS, OBJECTS, AND GESTALT CUES

The notions of paying attention to regions in space (space-based attention) or to objects (object-based attention) is related to the Gestalt principles of grouping (discussed in Chapter 2). Reflect on why (in Gestalt terms) attention would be guided by space. What Gestalt cues would be involved in space-based attention? Similarly, reflect on why (in Gestalt terms) attention would be guided by objects. What Gestalt cues would come into play in this mode?

Stimulus-Driven Attention.   Often, attention is not driven by the goals of the observer, but by the characteristics of the stimuli to which we're attending. Consequently, a great deal of research has been done on the particular characteristics of visual displays and scenes that are likely to draw our attention. This notion, called **attentional capture,** has become central to studies of visual attention. Much of the research on stimulus-driven attention and attentional capture has been done using a visual search task. If you think about it, you'll realize that most everyday problems of visual attention involve searching for something: Your misplaced keys, your friend's face at a party, Honey-Nut Cheerios in the cereal aisle, the app you want to go to on your iPhone... it should come as no surprise that researchers investigating visual attention have relied heavily on a laboratory version of the searches just described.

Visual Search.   In a **visual search task,** people are presented with some type of computerized visual display and are asked to determine whether a particular target is present or absent. The independent variable of interest is the number of distractors (that is, nontargets) in the visual display. This would correspond to the number of cereal boxes in the

Silly rabbit! Visual search is for kids.

grocery aisle when you're looking for the Honey-Nut Cheerios. Intuitively, you would suppose that the more stuff that has to be searched through, the more difficult the visual search will be. Turns out you're right, but only under certain circumstances. It depends on the nature of the target, the distractors, and their relationship to one another. This simple visual search procedure allows researchers to explore a variety of questions central to attention. What factors make it easy or difficult to find a visual target? What features of a visual scene are especially salient? What captures attention?

To get the basic idea behind a visual search task, let's look at a classic study by Treisman and Gelade (1980). One of their basic assumptions is that when searching for a visual stimulus, it would be easier to search for a single feature than it would be to search for a conjunction of features. Think about your trip down the cereal aisle at the grocery store. If I told you to be on the lookout for Quaker Oats, it would be pretty easy to spot because that's the only cereal in a cylindrical box. If I told you to look for Trix, you would need to really attend closely, because seeing red could mean Lucky Charms, Froot Loops, or Trix. Therefore, you need to look for the conjunction between red and a silly rabbit.

Participants in the Treisman and Gelade (1980) study performed visual search tasks. In Experiment 1 participants looked at displays and had to indicate whether a particular stimulus was present or absent by pressing a key; as is so often the case, reaction time was the measure of interest. The distractor items were brown T's and green X's. In the feature search condition, the target was a blue T. In this condition, participants only had to notice whether a blue T was in the display or not, an easy determination, because they only had to look for "blue." In the conjunction search condition, participants had to search for a green T. In this condition, noticing a single feature (green or the letter T) in the display wasn't enough as some of the distractor stimuli were green and some were T's. They had to watch for the *conjunction* of those two features in the same stimulus. Another key variable was the number of distractors in the display.

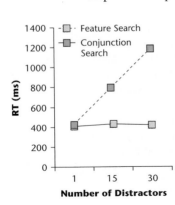

Figure 3.3
Visual search RTs on target present trials from Triesman and Gelade (1980).

The basic result is presented in Figure 3.3, which displays search times for target-present trials. The most apparent effect is that, on average, searching for conjunctions took much longer than searching for single features. Most critical perhaps—indeed *the* critical finding in most studies of visual search—is an interaction between the type of search and the number of distractors in the display. As you can see, when participants had to search for a single feature (e.g., color), the number of things they had to look through (i.e., the number of distractors) didn't matter. However, when searching for the conjunction of features (e.g., color and shape), the number of distractors mattered tremendously. Search time nearly tripled from displays with just a few distractors to those with a few dozen.

Based on this and other findings, Treisman and her colleagues (Treisman & Gelade, 1980; Treisman, Sykes, & Gelade, 1977) proposed the **feature integration theory.** According to this account, visual search is a two-stage process. In the first stage, basic perceptual features (e.g., size, shape, color, etc.) are registered quickly and efficiently. This is why RT to perform a feature search is unaffected by the number of distractors. The target simply seems to "pop out" of the visual display. This **pop-out effect** has been used as a sign of a highly efficient visual search. If an item cannot be classified as a target or distractor based on the first stage, the second stage is performed. At this stage, attention must be focused on each item. This individualized search increases RT. A conjunction search necessitates the use of this second stage of processing. Each item must become the focus of attention in order to determine whether it is or is not a target. This is relatively inefficient as distractors and targets must both be searched. Consequently, the number of distractors has a significant and severe effect on RT.

Earlier in this chapter we discussed how RT can be used to determine if a process is pre-attentive or post-attentive—attentional involvement can be gauged by noting how reaction time varies as a function of the visual display. We discussed this in context of subitizing (remember the cute puppies and kittens?). Fast RT was indicative of pre-attentive processing (enumerating 3 or fewer items) and slow RT was indicative of post-attentive processing (enumerating 6–8 items). Applying the same logic to the feature integration model leads to the conclusion that Stage 1 of the model involves pre-attentive processing and Stage 2 involves post-attentive processing.

Guiding Attributes and Search Asymmetries.   A great deal of research has been done to determine which features of visual stimuli lead to highly efficient searches (i.e., pre-attentive processing). In a review covering two decades of research, Wolfe and Horowitz (2004) propose some likely candidates for stimulus features that are salient enough to support pre-attentive detection. Dimensions with strong supporting evidence include color, size, motion, and orientation.

Treisman and her colleagues (Treisman & Gormican, 1988; Treisman & Souther 1985) also observed that the relationship between the target and distractors led to variations in the efficiency of a visual search. In one of their studies, participants either (a) searched for a stimulus that included a feature that was not present in the distractors (Figure 3.4a: find the circle that contains the line; target has a line but distractors do not) or (b) search for a stimulus that does not have a feature that is present in the distractors (Figure 3.4b, find the circle that does not have the line; target does not have a line but distracters do). These two conditions produced the same pattern of findings discussed previously—pre-attentive (i.e., efficient) searches for targets that included a feature and post-attentive (i.e., inefficient) searches for targets missing a feature.

The finding just discussed is an example of a peculiar phenomenon known as a **search asymmetry.** Generically, searching for targets of type A amongst distractors of type B

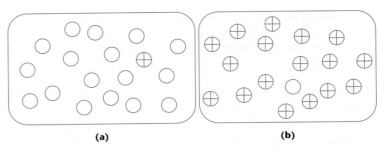

Figure 3.4

What pops out? The unique stimulus that includes an extra feature, or the unique stimulus that's missing a feature?

(a)   (b)

could be more or less efficient than searching for targets of type B amongst distractors of type A. In this case, it's easier to find targets that have a feature amidst distractors that do not. Another example of a search asymmetry is motion. It is much easier to detect something moving in the midst of stationary objects than the converse. Color also can lead to a search asymmetry; for example Triesman and Gormican (1988) found that searching for an orange circle amidst red circles is easier to detect than a red circle amongst orange ones. Really? Why? The color orange, relative to red, is defined by the presence of yellowness while red, relative to orange, is defined by the absence of yellowness. So this odd asymmetry is the product of the difference in searching for the presence or absence of a feature, just like the circle with line stimulus.

Feature Integration vs. Guided Search. Although there is little doubt that Treisman's feature integration theory has had tremendous influence in the field, many researchers have questioned some of its basic assumptions. The most serious issue relates to the distinction between the two stages of visual attention proposed by the theory and the key result that seems to support this distinction. As you've read, conjunction searches are thought to be especially difficult due to the necessity of a focused attention (i.e., post-attentive) stage following a pre-attentive stage. However, a number of researchers (e.g., Nakayama & Silverman, 1986; Wolfe, 1998; Wolfe, Cave, & Franzel, 1989) have found evidence for an efficient conjunction search; in fact, conjunction searches can sometimes be as efficient as feature searches. This should never be the case, according to feature integration theory's assumption that the binding of multiple features involves a slow individualized search process.

Another problem with the two-stage proposal of feature integration theory (and one that relates to its inability to predict an efficient conjunction search) is that the two stages are portrayed as distinct and noninteractive. If the first stage fails to detect a target, the slow second stage must be performed. It's almost as if the search process has to start all over again, which as noted by Wolfe and Horowitz (2004), wouldn't make much sense. After all, some information has been registered in first stage, and it would make sense that this information is ultimately used in target detection. Consider an example outlined by Wolfe, Cave, and Franzel (1986), a search for a red X among green Xs and red 0s. The target red X is a conjunction of the features "red" and "X," so will not be detected by the pre-attentive stage. However, the pre-attentive process *does* differentiate the green items from the red items. Given that none of the green items could possibly be the red X, it would make sense that this information garnered from the pre-attentive stage might feed forward, and inform subsequent stages of processing to enhance efficiency. This is the basic idea behind **guided search,** a proposal by Wolfe and colleagues that retains the distinction between pre-attentive and post-attentive processes, but emphasizes the role of pre-attentive processes in guiding later stages of visual attention.

Limits in Visual Attention

Everyone knows that attention is limited. Limits in attentional capacity are the price we pay for an efficient, flexible, and responsive brain. But these limitations can lead to some pretty dramatic results with serious ramifications. In this section, we'll consider some of the ways in which visual attention goes wrong—or doesn't go at all.

Low Target Prevalence.   Real world applications of visual search are numerous, but there are at least a couple of applied situations that seem to have a bit more gravity than most. One is medical diagnostics—radiologists and doctors are constantly faced with the task of scanning medical images for abnormalities. Another is airport security screening—agents are constantly faced with the task of scanning luggage for knives, guns, potential explosives and the like.

Thankfully for all of us, tumors and bombs don't appear all that often. But surprisingly (not to mention alarmingly), "low-target prevalence" represents a real problem in visual search. Wolfe, Horowitz, and Kenner (2005) presented an artificial baggage screening task in which participants viewed complex displays meant to resemble those faced by a baggage screener (see Figure 3.5) On each trial, participants were shown these semi-transparent images containing different numbers of objects, and noisy backgrounds. They were asked to identify a specific target by hitting one key if the target was present and another key if the target was absent. The critical independent variable was

Real world visual search for potentially dangerous anomalies.

Figure 3.5

Sample stimulus from Wolfe, Horowitz, & Kenner's (2005) studies of low-prevalence search.

target prevalence—how often a target appeared over the course of trials. In the high- and medium-prevalence conditions, participants saw 200 trials, with targets appearing in 50% and 10% of the trials, respectively. In the low prevalence condition, participants saw 2000 trials, with only 20 target-present trials; a prevalence rate of only 1%.

What Wolfe et al. found was disconcerting to say the least. The percentage of target-present trials in which the target was missed increased dramatically from the highest to lowest prevalence condition, with nearly 1/3 of all targets being missed in the lowest prevalence condition! The RT data reported by Wolfe et al. provide an interesting possibility for why low-prevalence conditions led to such error-prone responding. In a typical visual search task, declaring the absence of a target (with a keypress) typically takes longer than detecting its presence. But Wolfe et al. found precisely the opposite in their lowest-prevalence condition; target-absent responses were *faster* than target-present responses! The researchers contend that in low-prevalence conditions, "no" responses (i.e., indicating absence of the target) are almost always correct, so they get faster and faster, with the observer relying on less and less evidence to support their fast response. To put it in terms of a Chapter 2 concept, their response bias changes; they don't demand as much evidence to make their no response, so the response is faster. This doesn't occur in the high (50%) prevalence condition, where incorrect "no" responses are as likely as "yes" responses.

Fleck and Mitroff (2007) suspected that the low-prevalence effect found by Wolfe et al. might be due to overly fast responding, and wondered whether participants might realize that they missed a target immediately after the trial was over, when it was too late to change their response. If this is the case, then performance should improve if participants are given the opportunity to correct their response. However, if the problem is perceptual and they just flat-out missed the target, then giving an opportunity for correction should have little or no effect. They tested their idea with a procedure and design similar to Wolfe et al. but tested participants with search displays like the one pictured in Figure 3.6. In addition,

Figure 3.6

Sample display used in Fleck and Mitroff (2007) study of low-prevalence search.

they had a critical manipulation to test their hypothesis. Some participants were allowed to hit the ESC key after their response if they felt their response had been incorrect. Thus, if they actually noticed a target and just responded "no" too quickly, the rate of misses should go down. This is precisely what happened, as you can see in Figure 3.7. The no-correction condition replicated the findings of Wofe et al. However, if participants were allowed to correct their mistakes, error rates were low and constant across prevalence conditions.

We're not finished yet; in the latest volley in this empirical debate, Van Wert, Horowitz, and Wolfe (2009) ran the correction condition of Fleck and Mitroff (2007) with the Wolfe et al. (2005) displays, and found little effect of the correction option, replicating the basic result found by Wolfe, et al. So, what's going on? The authors suggest that the low-prevalence effect depends critically on the nature of the display. The displays used by Wolfe et al. and those by Fleck and Mitroff were considerably different. In the Wolfe et al. display detecting a target was difficult. Consequently, when participants incorrectly responded "no," they probably didn't recognize their error. In the simple displays used by Fleck and Mitroff, detecting a target would be relatively easy. So when participants incorrectly responded "no," they were able to detect their error.

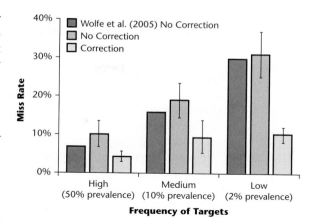

Figure 3.7

Does a second chance ("correction" condition) improve low-prevalence search?

So where do we go from here? Who's right? Well, the most likely answer is that both sets of results are "right." Van Wert et al. make the important point that when one considers variations in methodology (e.g., different visual displays and levels of task difficulty, etc.), it is not surprising that the effect of low target prevalence varies as well. Given this, it is incumbent upon applied researchers to fully understand real-world visual search scenarios in order to discover the effects of variables like low-target prevalence across a wide range of task variations. Generalizability of any empirical result requires that the finding be tested with different participants and materials, using different measures and experimental contexts.

As if the potential problem with low-prevalence targets wasn't enough cause for concern as you approach airport security, consider the results of a study by Menneer, Cave, and Donnelly (2009), who looked at visual search proficiency as a function of the number of targets. To return to our radiologist or baggage screener, it's certainly the case that they're engaging in multiple-target searches; that is, there are a number of different items for which they need to be on the lookout. Menneer et al. found that the requirement to search for multiple targets led to poorer performance than a search for a single target. This deficit was lessened if the multiple targets shared features (e.g. color, shape). Menneer et al. make the practical suggestion that screening performance might be improved by having multiple screeners, each specialized at the detection of one object rather than one screener who needs to detect multiple objects.

Stop&*Think* | VISUAL SEARCH FOR TARGETS AT TARGET

Shopping involves visual search. You are constantly faced with displays that differ in size, location, shape, color, and arrangement. Consider the following questions before your next trip to the store. When you go, reflect on the processing that occurs. What would "stimulus driven" and "goal-driven" search be at the grocery store? When might you be in one mode vs. the other? How would "search processes" differ in these modes?

Wolfe et al. found that misses are common for low-prevalence targets.

When you're shopping, there are "high-prevalence items" (i.e., you buy them a lot) and "low-prevalence items" (i.e., you occasionally buy them) as well as items that have characteristics that make them easy to locate and items that have characteristics that make them difficult to locate. What types of items fit into these two categories? What commonalities do you see among them, in terms of their characteristics, how you find them, and "search efficiency"?

In spite of the seeming ramifications of this research, you shouldn't cancel your airline reservations. These studies were done within the confines of the cognitive psychology laboratory, with artificial displays, keypress responses, and relatively unmotivated students as participants, rather than in airports with real bags and real baggage screeners who know that much depends on their judgments. But there's no doubt that there's a pressing need for applied research on these potential problems, and the ways in which they might be ameliorated.

The Attentional Blink.   As it turns out, the old saying "blink and you'll miss it" has some empirical support but might be more appropriately stated "blink and you won't attend to it." We're not talking about the literal "blink of the eye" but the so-called **attentional blink,** which refers to a period of time after the detection of a visual stimulus during which another stimulus cannot be detected (Shapiro, Arnell, & Raymond, 1997). Given the rapidly changing stream that likely is your visual world, some things simply don't get "seen." This limit in visual attention is often demonstrated within a paradigm termed **RSVP, or rapid serial visual presentation.** (This does lead to some confusion in the rare event that a cognitive psychologist throws a party, and asks you to RSVP). The paradigm is pretty much what it says—a series of visual stimuli is presented rapidly in some type of sequence, and some type of response is required after the series is presented.

Upon presentation of a visual stimulus, there is a short period of time in which nothing else can be processed (i.e., the attentional blink). If the second stimulus is presented during the attentional blink, it will never be processed. If presented after the attentional blink, it will be processed. Therefore, as the length of time increases between the presentations of the two stimuli, the likelihood of detecting the second stimulus increases. After a sufficiently long delay, it's near-perfect.

Research Theme
Emotion

Let's look at the attentional blink in the context of processing emotional stimuli. It would make evolutionary sense for our cognitive systems to be especially sensitive to potentially threatening or otherwise aversive stimuli. In other words, it would be beneficial if such stimuli received prioritized processing. After all, you should avoid or minimize contact with these stimuli. Maratos, Mogg, and Bradley (2008) used the attentional blink paradigm to determine whether angry faces receive prioritized attentional processing. Because angry faces are important, they hypothesized that they would emerge from the attentional blink faster than a less threatening face. Metaphorically, the attentional "eye" reopens more quickly when it needs to detect important information.

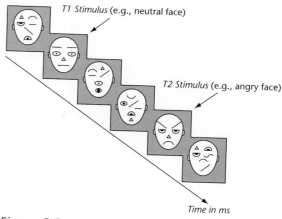

T1 Stimulus (e.g., neutral face)

T2 Stimulus (e.g., angry face)

Time in ms

Figure 3.8

Sample stimuli sequence from Maratos et al. study of attentional blink.

Several schematic faces were used in the study but for the sake of simplicity we will limit our discussion to the angry and neutral faces (see Figure 3.8). Participants were presented with a rapid sequence of faces made up of two target faces (designated T1 and T2) and masks interspersed between them. The number of distractor "masks" between T1 and T2 varied on every trial. At the end of each trial participants were to indicate if one or two faces had been presented. If they indicated that two had been presented, they were asked to identify the expression on the second face. The dependent variable was accuracy in identifying this expression. If angry faces receive prioritized processing, they should be identified after fewer intervening masks (i.e., they should emerge from the attentional blink faster) than a neutral face.

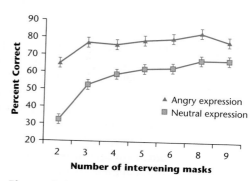

Figure 3.9

Results from Maratos et al. study, showing a briefer attentional blink for angry faces.

The results are displayed in Figure 3.9, which shows the classification percentage for the second face as a function of the number of intervening masks. Angry faces were classified more accurately than neutral faces. In addition, there was clear evidence of the attentional blink. Overall, classification of the second face became increasingly easy as the number of intervening masks from the first face increased. More importantly, the emergence from the attentional blink was faster for angry faces relative to neutral faces. For example, after 2 intervening masks identification of an angry face was over 60% but just over 30% for a neutral face. So it seems that some of the limitations in visual attention are attenuated when the stimuli to be processed are emotional in nature.

Research Theme
Evolution

Change Blindness.   Just as the blinking eye momentarily obscures vision, the attentional blink momentarily obscures attention. Surprisingly, at times, the disruption isn't all that momentary—it's more like blindness than a blink, which explains the name of the phenomenon we're about to discuss: **change blindness** or **inattentional blindness** (e.g., Mack & Rock, 1998; Rensink, 1997; Rensink, 2002). This phenomenon refers to the failure to notice

Figure 3.10

Still photo from film shown to subjects in the Simon and Chabris (1999) study. (Photos provided by Daniel Simons.)

Simons, D. J., & Chabris, C. F. (1999). Gorillas in our midst: Sustained inattentional blindness for dynamic events. *Perception, 28*, 1059–1074.

obvious changes or events in our visual environment. Basically, you can be staring right at something and not see it. This phenomenon has been demonstrated in many studies using a variety of research paradigms (O'Regan, Rensink, & Clark, 1999; Davies & Hine, 2007; Simons & Levin, 1998). Failure to detect significant stimulus changes has also been demonstrated in nonvisual senses, including hearing (Gregg & Samuel, 2008) and touch (Auvray, Gallace, Hartcher-O'Brien, Tan, & Spence, 2008).

In what's become a modern classic, Simons and Chabris (1999) showed observers an experimenter-created video of two teams passing a basketball around. The players moved, threw bounce passes, waved their arms, and generally kept moving around while passing to one another. One team was dressed in black T-shirts, the other in white. The task was to watch the "game" and keep track of some activity—for example, the number of bounce passes thrown by the black-shirted team. The twist was that right in the middle of the game, an extremely bizarre event occurred: A person in a gorilla suit strolled into the scene in plain view, beat its chest a few times, and strolled off (see Figure 3.10). Would participants notice the unusual event, and what variables might affect the probability of noticing it?

Simons and Chabris (1999) had participants attend to one of the two teams. They manipulated task difficulty and the perceptual similarity to the critical event. In the easy condition, participants counted the total number of passes made by the attended team. In the difficult condition, participants kept separate counts of bounce and aerial passes made by the attended team. In the similar condition, the attended team wore a t-shirt that was perceptually similar to the unusual event (black t-shirt/black gorilla suit). In the different condition, the attended team wore a t-shirt that was perceptually different from the unusual event (white t-shirt/black gorilla suit).

After watching the video, participants reported their pass count, and were asked if they had noticed anything unusual during the game. You're probably thinking that every participant noticed the gorilla. But astoundingly, a significant proportion completely missed it! (See Table 3.1). A demanding visual task essentially compromised their ability to notice other things that occurred *in the same visual space*. As you can see, the probability of noticing was dependent on two variables. First, participants were less likely to notice

Table 3.1 **Results from the Simon and Chabris (1999) study. Numbers refer to the percentage of subjects who noticed the gorilla, as a function of attentional task difficulty and visual similarity to the gorilla.**

	Easy Attentional Task	Difficult Attentional Task
Similar	83	58
Different	42	50

the unusual event in the difficult condition than the easy condition. The more demanding the task, the less likely they were to notice the event. Interestingly, this effect was qualified by visual similarity. The gorilla suit was black, and was easier to notice when counting passes of the black-shirted team, relative to those of the white-shirted team. Participants attending to the black T-shirts were "tuned" to black, so were more likely to catch the gorilla's appearance. Conversely, catching the gorilla in the different condition was so challenging that making the attentional task more difficult didn't really even matter.

Striking failures to notice obvious changes in a visual scene also has been investigated using a change detection paradigm in which participants are presented with two versions of a scene that rapidly alternate with one another (termed a **flicker paradigm;** see Rensink, 2002). One feature changes between the two versions, essentially disappearing and reappearing. Although the difference is obvious when the scenes are viewed side by side, viewing them in rapid alternation makes it surprisingly difficult to detect the change.

The phenomenon of change blindness highlights two important concepts in visual attention. One is **coherence**—the notion that visual attention is necessary to hold the elements of a visual scene together (Rensink, 2002). Visual attention is like "perceptual glue," and when it is absent, features become transient and difficult to perceive—in a word, "unglued." In the Simons and Chabris (1999) gorilla-noticing study, participants were so focused on counting the basketball passes (in other words, on keeping that scene glued together) that they had precious little attention left to notice the gorilla; to stretch the metaphor to its limit, the gorilla didn't "stick."

The second concept is **attentional set,** which refers to one's strategy or mind-set when watching a visual scene (Most, Scholl, Clifford, & Simons, 2005). Again, consider the participants in the Simon and Chabris study. They watched a scene in which individuals continually passed basketballs to one other, and were instructed to count the number of passes for a given team (e.g. wearing black t-shirts). This gave them the attentional set "OK, I have to watch this game and pay particular attention to the passes made by people wearing the black T-shirts." This basically "tuned their attention to a certain frequency," if you will. Note that they were more likely to notice the surprising event when the features of that event matched (black gorilla suit, black T-shirts) rather than mismatched (black gorilla suit, white t-shirt) that "frequency." This idea of attentional set also explains why the deficits found in searching for multiple targets in the Meneer et al. (2009) study lessened when the multiple targets shared features (e.g. color, shape). Their attentional set could tune into objects of a particular shape or color, thus improving their detection ability compared to when the multiple targets did not share features.

Cultural Differences.

Based on a well-established difference between Eastern (e.g., Japan, China) and Western (e.g., United States, Europe) cultures, Nisbett and Masuda (2003) hypothesized a difference in change blindness between these two cultures. Eastern cultures tend to de-emphasize the importance of central objects in a visual scene. Instead they emphasize the importance of the background upon which the object is superimposed. Western cultures have converse inclinations. The investigators believed that these deeply rooted differences might be associated with a **perceptual set,** or a tendency to attend to visual scenes in a particular way. Specifically, they hypothesized that Eastern participants would be better at detecting changes that occurred in the background, rather than in central objects.

Research Theme
Culture

They made the converse prediction for Western participants; they would be better at detecting changes that occurred in central objects rather than in the background. And this is exactly what they found. A recent study by Boduroglu, Shah, and Nisbett (2009) replicated the cultural difference found in the previous study. U.S. participants were much faster than Asian participants at detecting the appearance of a centrally presented square. These cross-cultural differences in change blindness may indicate differences in ability, preference, or some combination of the two.

After reading the last few pages, you're probably afraid to walk out the front door for fear of missing a step or getting hit by a bus. But take heart—your visual attention is outstanding. You'll notice that many studies revealing error quite deliberately set out to strain visual attention (and other cognitive processes) to the breaking point. The reason for this is that discovering the boundary conditions beyond which cognitive processes fail is quite informative in regard to how they operate in everyday situations. The errors that seem so common in studies of visual attention are really exceptions to the rule, and represent the relatively low cost for cognitive processes that for the most part, operate efficiently and accurately.

Magic and the Misdirection of Visual Attention.   However, there is one real-world situation in which your normally efficient attentional processing can be manipulated to let you down; however, in this case, it's not dangerous—it's fun! The bewildering and bedeviling skills of the magician owe a great deal to the tendencies of visual attention, a fact that has no doubt been recognized by prestidigitators. Some recent work (e.g., Kuhn, Tatler, Findlay, & Cole, 2008; Kuhn, Amlani, & Rensink, 2008) has begun to investigate how the magician exploits the processes of visual awareness and attention. A recent paper in the prominent journal *Nature Reviews Neuroscience* by Macknik, King, Randi, Robbins, Teller, Thompson, and Martinez-Conde (2008) represents the collaboration of magicians and cognitive scientists. It provides a fascinating overview of the magician's bag of cognitive tricks. A side note—the Teller in the list of authors is the silent half of the famous magician team of Penn and Teller.

To invoke a metaphor for attention discussed earlier, magicians seem especially deft at manipulating the attentional spotlight. Recall our discussion of goal-driven and stimulus-driven attention; goal-driven attention is top-down and guided by the observer. Stimulus-driven attention is bottom-up and guided by external events (i.e., the stimulus). Macknik et. al. describe how some of the standard techniques employed by magicians involve the misdirection of attention from the bottom-up by doing things that grab attention such as having a dove appear suddenly. This is a pretty cool trick but it is probably covering something else that the magician doesn't want you to notice. Another example provided by Macknik et al. is the old magician's axiom that "a big move

Grabbing your attention, from the bottom up.

covers a small move." If a magician wants to distract you from noticing a subtle maneuver or action, they're also likely to engage in a more salient one, and this is the one you're likely to notice. The magician also manipulates attention from the top-down by asking the audience to engage in some sort of attention-demanding activity. For example, "look at the card you picked and memorize it" is a manipulation of top-down (goal-driven) perceptual processes, and might serve to distract you from other activities critical to the trick.

Well, that's enough fun, let's get back to the lab.....

Stop&*Review*

1. Describe the two different modes in which goal-driven attention can operate. How is goal-driven attention "top-down"?
2. How does object-based attention differ from space-based attention?
3. What two stages of visual attention does feature integration theory propose?
4. True or false? Visual detection is particularly good when the targets to be searched for are rare.
5. What is the attentional blink?

- Visual attention can be goal-driven or stimulus-driven. Goal-driven attention is top-down, and driven by knowledge and expectations. Goal-driven attention can be spaced-based or object-based. Space-based attention refers to our tendency to focus on a region in space. One such theory likens visual attention to a spotlight.
- Space-based attention refers to our tendency to isolate and attend to specific locations in the visual scene. Some evidence suggests that our attention can be directed to objects rather than to locations in space (object-based attention). It seems likely that we use both space-based and object-based attentional mechanisms, based on the specific demands of the situation.
- Stimulus-driven attention is bottom-up, and occurs when some stimulus "grabs" attention. This type of attention is investigated with a visual search task. Feature integration theory proposes that visual attention is a two-stage process, with an automatic (pre-attentive) stage followed by an effortful (post-attentive) stage. Some attributes of stimuli (e.g., color, size) can be detected based solely on the first stage. Guided search emphasizes the role of pre-attentive processes in guiding later stages of visual attention.
- One limitation of visual attention is seen during a visual search task for low-prevalence targets, which refers to situations in which the object being searched for is extremely rare. In these cases, failure to detect targets is quite common and it is particularly difficult if multiple low-prevalence targets need to be detected.
- Other limitations in visual attention include the attentional blink, a period of time after the detection of a visual stimulus during which another stimulus cannot be detected. Change blindness (or, inattentional blindness) refers to a failure to notice obvious changes or events in our visual environment. These failures can also be revealed by the flicker paradigm, and highlight the importance of visual attention in providing a coherent view of the visual world.

Auditory Attention

Many of the phenomena of perception and attention just discussed within the visual domain have an auditory analog. In fact, much if not most of the pioneering work on the limited nature of attention and the fate of unattended stimuli were conducted using the auditory sense. Much of the pioneering work, done in the middle of the 20th century, was inspired by the applied problems of the day. British psychologists Donald Broadbent (1958) and Colin Cherry (1953) were interested in the difficulties pilots encountered in World War II. These pilots faced complex control panels with a bewildering combination of visual and auditory displays. Monitoring these displays and responding appropriately presented an incredible challenge—a situation of sensory overload! Therefore, early theories of attention attempted to explain how our cognitive systems operate under these conditions.

Recall the "spotlight" analog in visual attention—we shine our spotlight on certain locations that we need to "illuminate." The analogous mechanism for auditory attention is a "gateway"—a sort of passive filtering mechanism that allows only some of the information through into conscious awareness. The questions that emerge in auditory attention parallel those from visual attention: What are we aware of when we are focusing our auditory attention on one aspect of an auditory scene? Are we "deaf" to some aspects of the auditory scene, just like we're blind to some aspects of a visual scene? Do certain auditory stimuli get privileged access through the gateway of auditory attention, just as certain visual stimuli manage to grab the spotlight?

Selective Attention

The gateway analogy has been used to describe auditory **selective attention tasks** in which some information must be processed and responded to and some must be ignored. Before we venture into the theories that view attention as a gateway, let's take a look at the methodological implementation of a selective attention task in the context of a classic study by Cherry (1953). Participants engaged in **dichotic listening**—specially rigged headphones presented a different message to each ear. But simply having a person listen to two messages doesn't allow the researcher a window into their attentional processes. To control attention, Cherry had participants perform **speech shadowing** (repeating a message, word for word) for the information coming into one ear. Speech shadowing forced participants to selectively attend to one message (the *attended message*) while ignoring the other (the *unattended message*).

One of the most intriguing questions that emerges from this situation is whether participants notice or process the ignored elements of the auditory scene (i.e., the unattended message). It turns out that participants were fairly successful in their attempts to shadow the attended message, but they seemed to know very little about the content of the unattended message. They *were* aware that a message was being played and tended to notice some of its physical characteristics such as changes in pitch (e.g., whether the speaker was male or female). But as for what actually was said, they were aware of practically nothing. This basic pattern—minimal processing of information presented in an unattended channel—was a common finding in early studies of selective attention (e.g., Moray, 1959).

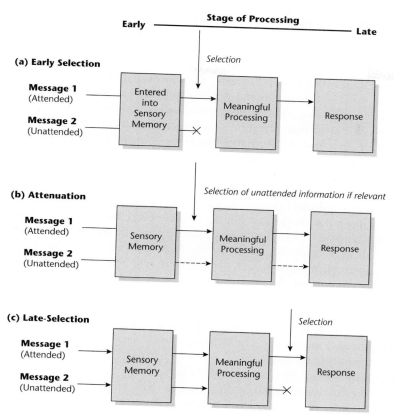

Figure 3.11

Attentional processing according to (a) early selection theory, (b) attenuation theory, and (c) late-selection theory.

Early Selection Theories. The basic findings of studies like those conducted by Cherry led to the development of a theory typically referred to as **early selection theory,** which is depicted in the top panel of Figure 3.11. First, the initial processing of auditory information encodes each source of information in terms of its physical characteristics. At this point, the information sources are *filtered* on the basis of this information, with only one source selected for further processing. This approach is termed *early selection* because the *selection* process whereby we designate information for further processing occurs *early,* as the information is first registered by the senses. The process of early selection was evident in Cherry's study—the only things that participants seemed to notice about the unattended message were its physical characteristics—exactly what would be expected if all messages were processed only to an early stage of analysis. After the selection of the attended message, the other messages were essentially discarded. However, further investigation of auditory selective attention made it clear that more is going on than meets the ear. Just as your visual attention can be grabbed by a squirrel darting out in front of your car, your auditory attention can be grabbed by a similarly salient stimulus.

Consider the **cocktail-party phenomenon.** You've no doubt been at a party where there were many conversations occurring all at once, yet you had little or no trouble focusing on only one (the kids no longer call these "cocktail parties," but you get the idea; at least it sounds better than "the kegger phenomenon"). This is an everyday example of selective attention. According to early selection theories, the unattended conversations are like static—you're really not processing them. Yet (and this is where the problem lies) if someone in another conversation says your name, you are very likely to notice. Based on a strict interpretation of early selection theory, this shouldn't happen; the analysis of unattended information stops *early,* at the point of noticing only sensory characteristics. Therefore, you shouldn't be able to recognize your name (or anything else), because doing so requires analysis at the level of meaning (i.e., analysis at a *later* stage of processing).

Now, this demonstration doesn't necessarily give psychologists cause to toss out the theory—after all, it is just a demonstration. But the results of a classic (not to mention ingenious) study by Treisman (1960) lends empirical support to this phenomenon. Treisman employed dichotic listening in her study, but with an interesting twist: Participants heard a different message in each ear and were required to shadow one of them. Occasionally, *the meaning of the shadowed message switched ears,* as depicted in Figure 3.12. The question is whether this switch in meaning grabs the listener's attention so that they will say, "Psychology is a really interesting major for students..." (the meaningful response) or "Psychology is a really interesting walk on the beach..." (the correct response). As you might have anticipated, the meaningful message grabbed participants' attention, leading to shadowing mistakes.

The intriguing results from Treisman's (1960) classic study demonstrate clearly that we process a good deal more of the auditory scene than we might be aware of, and that, when appropriate, an auditory stimulus can grab our attention. But what if a stimulus doesn't grab our conscious attention—do we still register it on some level?

Right Ear
Psychology is a really interesting / walk on the beach.

Left Ear
On our vacation we went for a / major for students.

"an interesting— uh—major for students"

Figure 3.12
The procedure employed in the Treisman (1960) selective attention study.

Adapted from Treismam, A. (1960). Contextual cues in selective listening. *Quarterly Journal of Experimental Psychology, 12,* 242–248.

Corteen and Wood (1972) conducted a two-phase study to find out. In the first phase, participants listened to a series of words. Each list contained three city names (e.g., Minneapolis, Lafayette, Cincinnati) that were each followed by a slight electric shock. The shock produced an autonomic nervous system response called a *galvanic skin response (GSR)*—slight sweating in the fingertips. In the second phase, participants performed a dichotic listening and shadowing task. The unattended message was a word list that contained 12 critical words—6 words presented in phase 1 (3 shock-associated city words plus 3 nouns not associated with shock) and 6 words not presented in phase 1 (3 new city words and 3 new nouns). When the dichotic listening/shadowing task was complete, some of the participants reported hearing words in the unattended ear but were unaware that some of these words were city names. To put it in terms of a distinction presented in Chapter 2, participants had no phenomenal consciousness of identifying these words. But did they show evidence of access consciousness?

Indeed they did; during the dichotic listening task, the 3 shock-associated city words from phase 1 produced a higher galvanic skin response relative to that produced by the 3 nonshock-associated nouns from phase 1 (37.7% vs. 12.3%). As noted earlier, these words were not consciously identified (or at least they weren't remembered shortly after their presentation). But they must have been meaningfully identified because they produced a GSR. In addition, the 3 new city words produced a more intense GSR than the 3 new nouns (22.8% vs. 8.7%). The fact that the heightened GSR generalized to new items from the same semantic category (i.e., city names) is further evidence that the city names presented in the unattended channel in phase 1 were indeed recognized at some level.

Attenuation Theory.
To account for the apparent fact that unattended events in the auditory scene are being processed and even may overtly grab our attention, Treisman (1960) proposed the **attenuation theory.** This theory is essentially a slight modification of early selection theories and it is depicted in the middle panel of Figure 3.11 (p. 105). According to this model, unattended information is not completely blocked from further analysis. Rather, it is *attenuated* or "turned down," if you will. So the early filtering of messages is partial, not complete. Unattended information does make it through the filter, but weakly. So how does this weak trickle of information grab our attention?

Treisman proposed that some words in our "mental dictionary" are permanently more available than others because of personal importance (e.g., one's name). Similarly, other words are temporarily more available due to present circumstances (e.g., the context of the sentence in Treisman's ear-switching study or the words that indicated the arrival of a shock in the Corteen and Wood study). Therefore, even the small trickle of information that makes it through the attenuating filter might be enough to grab our attention. To put it in terms of a basic issue discussed in Chapter 2, some stimuli require less information from bottom-up processing to trigger recognition because of the facilitatory effect of top-down processing (e.g., personal importance or current circumstances).

Late-Selection Theories.
Of course, Treisman's attenuation theory is only one way to account for how unattended information grabs our attention; another is a **late-selection theory** (e.g., Deutsch & Deutsch, 1963). This theory is depicted in the bottom panel of Figure 3.11 (p. 105). According to late-selection theories, *all* incoming information is identified or recognized. *After* the information is identified, only the selected piece of information emerges into phenomenal consciousness.

The late-selection approach easily accounts for how unattended elements of an auditory scene grab our attention. For example, the cocktail-party phenomenon is no surprise—because unattended stimuli are identified, one's name certainly would be, leading to an attention switch. The experimental demonstrations of Treisman (1960) and Corteen and Wood (1972) also are explained quite easily. All incoming information in the unattended message is identified. This identification leads to an attention switch (as in the Treisman study) or to a physiological reaction (as in the Corteen and Wood study).

You might find it difficult to differentiate between attenuation and late-selection because both theories seem to make similar predictions and allow for the identification of unattended information. Driver (2001) provides a useful way to distinguish the two approaches. Attenuation theory proposes that identification of unattended information is the *exception rather than the rule*. Whether or not information is identified depends on the context or the exact nature of the information. Conversely, late-selection theories argue that the identification of meaning is the *rule rather than the exception*. The identification of meaning is obligatory; all information (attended and unattended) is identified. So which is correct? Driver (2001) indicates that neurological studies of attention are consistent with an attenuation-type account. While the attenuation theory proposed by Treisman may be a bit simplistic, it is clear that attention is influenced by the type of top-down processing (e.g., context, current task demands, goals of the attender, etc.) proposed by the attenuation theory. A review of attention research from both the visual and auditory domains turns the clock back to the beginnings of cognitive psychology, claiming that on balance, there's no reason to doubt Broadbent's (1958) proposal of a strict early filter for incoming stimuli (Lachter, Forster, & Ruthruff, 2004). Couched in recent terminology, early filtering is based on bottom-up processing of the stimuli. But now we know this is mediated by top-down processing.

Our discussion of auditory attention seems to imply that how we focus our attention is passive. Nothing could be further from the truth. Rather, the *way in which* we pay attention can be strategically varied according to the situational demands. This may remind you of the notion of attentional set within the context of visual attention. Recall that in vision, you basically can decide what you're going to look at and attend to visually; what you notice and don't notice depends on this set. Similarly, in auditory attention you can make the same decision, choosing what you are going to listen to and attend to auditorily. Both situations demonstrate two of the characteristics of attention discussed at the beginning of the chapter: flexibility and voluntary control.

Multimode Theory.   A series of investigations by Johnston and Heinz (1978) provides evidence for the strategic nature of auditory attention. According to the **multimode theory,** attention is flexible in that people can shift from early modes of attention (processing only the physical characteristics of incoming stimuli) to late modes (processing the meaning of incoming stimuli). Given that we have voluntary control over how we deal with incoming information, we are capable of determining the basis upon which we select information for further processing (an early or late processing mode). However, attending in each of these modes has an associated set of costs. As selection proceeds to a later point in the information-processing system, attending takes more mental effort. To test their multimode theory of attention, Johnston and Heinz developed a clever attention task. Participants were given two tasks—speech shadowing lists of words and light

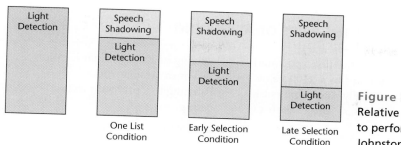

Light Detection	Speech Shadowing	Speech Shadowing	Speech Shadowing
	Light Detection	Light Detection	
			Light Detection
	One List Condition	Early Selection Condition	Late Selection Condition

Figure 3.13

Relative amounts of attention needed to perform each of the tasks in the Johnston and Heinz (1978) study.

detection. During the speech shadowing task, participants had to watch for a light signal and press a key as quickly as possible when they saw it.

They varied the mode of attention (early vs. late) by manipulating the nature of the shadowing task. In the one list condition, the speech shadowing task was easy; participants simply had to repeat (i.e., shadow) one list. In the other two conditions, the shadowing task required *selecting* between two lists (i.e., dichotic listening). In one of these conditions, the difference between the two lists was physical; one was read by a female voice, the other by a male voice. Participants had to shadow one. Repeating one of these lists required only a simple discrimination of the lists' physical characteristics; in other words, only early selection was required. In a more challenging condition, the two lists had similar physical characteristics (i.e., they were read by speakers of the same gender), so an easy selection based on physical characteristics wasn't possible. For these two lists, only the meaning differed. Therefore, the shadowing task required late selection.

The difference in attentional capacity required by the various shadowing tasks was assessed by examining performance on the light detection task (see Figure 3.13) in each condition. According to the multimode theory, early and late selection modes are both possible, but late selection costs more in terms of capacity. The condition requiring late selection (two lists spoken by the same gender) was expensive in terms of attentional capacity. Therefore, there would be little capacity left to detect the light. The condition requiring early selection (two lists spoken by different genders) was cheap in terms of attentional capacity, leaving more capacity to perform the light detection task.

The dependent variable was RT cost, which is calculated by subtracting simple reaction time (light detection task only) from reaction time to detect the light in each of the other three conditions. The dichotic listening task exacted a RT cost in each condition. More importantly, the "price" was different, depending on the degree of selection required. The one-list condition exacted only a slight cost on RT. But the requirement to listen to two lists and select one for shadowing was much more challenging and more costly in terms of attention. Consistent with Johnston and Heinz's analysis, the cost was greater in the late-selection condition, in which participants had to discriminate between two lists on the basis of meaning. These findings support Johnston and Heinz's view that both early and late selection are possible, but late selection requires a greater amount of mental effort or capacity.

Stop&*Think* | THE PRICE OF ATTENDING

Imagine that all of the attention you could focus on some task that has a $100 value. That is, the most mentally challenging task costs $100. Based on this, "price" each of the following tasks.

> watching TV
> listening to music
> taking notes
> cell phone conversation
> walking

> driving in an unfamiliar location
> driving a familiar route
> listening to a professor lecture
> eating

Based on your "pricing system,"

- Which pairs of tasks would/would not send you "over budget"?

- What makes tasks easy or difficult to combine?

Divided Attention

The results of the Johnston and Heinz (1978) study clearly demonstrate the strategic nature of attention. This characteristic of auditory attention is even more obvious when one considers the processes of divided attention. Whereas selective attention tasks involve choosing one input to process at the expense of others, **divided attention tasks** involve the processing of multiple inputs. The ability to divide attention and the factors that affect this ability have been investigated within a variety of dual-task paradigms in which participants are faced with juggling two tasks at once.

The PRP Paradigm.   One simple yet classic method for investigating dual-task interference is termed the *psychological refractory period (PRP) paradigm* (Telford, 1931; see Pashler, 1994, for a review); it's sort of a "double reaction time" task in which two different signals are presented in rapid succession, and each of the signals requires a separate fast response. Either task on its own would be trivially simple, but when they're paired, responding becomes quite challenging. The major independent variable of interest in this paradigm is **stimulus onset asynchrony (SOA),** the time that lapses between the presentations of the two stimuli. The major dependent variable of interest is reaction time to the second stimulus (RT2). The typical finding can be seen in Figure 3.14, which plots RT2 as a function of stimulus onset asynchrony. As you can see, reaction time to respond to the second stimulus

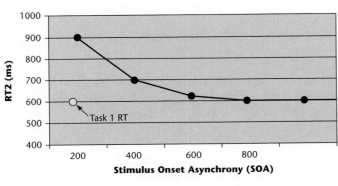

Figure 3.14
The psychological refractory period. Reaction time to second stimulus (RT2) is elevated the more closely in time it occurs after a first stimulus.

relative to performing that task alone (single-task RT) is greatly elevated when the second stimulus is presented immediately after the first stimulus. As this interval between presentations (the SOA) increases, RT2 becomes faster, finally mirroring single-task reaction times at long SOAs. This improvement in RT as a function of time is taken as evidence of a **psychological refractory period,** a period of time during which the response to a second stimulus will be significantly slowed because of the processing still occurring on the earlier stimulus. This is analogous to the attentional blink found in visual attention in which the presentation of a visual stimulus blocks the ability to attend to another stimulus presented immediately after it.

Dual-Task Paradigm.   Another way to assess divided attention is to present concurrent tasks to participants, who must engage in both behaviors at the same time. The lay term for this practice is "multitasking." A host of studies on the ability to multitask demonstrate that it is possible, but not without a serious cost to performance on each component task. Also, it's not really possible to do more than two tasks at once without a total attentional breakdown (which would simply mean abandoning one or more of the tasks).

One combination of tasks with which you're intimately and painfully aware is writing while listening. Think of the hours you spend in class listening to your professors' lectures and jotting down everything important that comes out of their mouths (all the while attempting to make judgments about what's important). Throw in some PowerPoint slides, and you have a great example of the need for divided attention. There has been some research on the ability to divide attention in situations that involve concurrent writing and listening. For example, Olive and Kellogg (2002) were interested in the relative demands of different sorts of writing processes, such as transcribing and composing text. They also were interested in possible developmental differences in the writing process and how those differences might alter the effect of divided attention.

They had children (third-graders) and adults (college students) write a brief persuasive essay. The children were asked to write about inviting friends to a birthday party; adults were asked to write on the pros and cons of increasing tuition to cover college expenses. After completing the essay, all participants were asked simply to transcribe what they had written. Throughout the entire experiment, all participants had to listen for auditory probes, and press a key whenever one was detected. RT to detect the probe was measured. The dependent variable was "attentional cost" which was calculated by subtracting simple reaction time (auditory probe task only) from reaction time to detect the auditory probe in each of the dual task conditions.

The results are shown in Figure 3.15. As you can see, the RT cost was greater when adults were writing than when they were simply transcribing. The converse was true for children. Another way of stating the results is that adults devoted more attentional resources to writing than they did to transcribing, while children

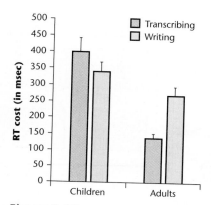

Figure 3.15

Results from Olive and Kellogg's (2002) study of divided attention.

had the opposite allocation pattern. Olive and Kellogg conclude that children do not have the level of verbal skill required for planning, reading, and editing text, so they fail to engage in these processes during writing, leaving plenty of resources to perform the auditory probe detection task.

The dual-task methodology allows researchers to explore the boundary conditions of our attentional abilities by combining different types of tasks and mapping out patterns of interference. The dual-task methodology also allows researchers to investigate (as in Olive & Kellogg, 2002) the ways in which individuals direct their attention, a concept sometimes termed executive control, which we'll be assessing in-depth in the next chapter.

Accounts of Dual-Task Interference.   It may be obvious that trying to do two things at once is more difficult than doing just one. But what are the underlying mechanisms that may lead to these deficits? In this section, we lay out a couple of theories often proffered to account for findings of dual-task interference.

One model appeals to the metaphor of a bottleneck (e.g., Pashler, 1992; see Lien, Ruthruff, & Johnston, 2006, for a recent overview). You've no doubt been in bottlenecked traffic, where only one lane of cars is moving. Everyone has to stop, get into the queue, and wait their turn. Recall the classic finding from the PRP paradigm—that reaction time to a second stimulus increases as SOA decreases. It makes sense—if a first stimulus is already being processed, any other stimulus that occurs in that time is going to have to wait its turn, due to the bottleneck in processing; only one thing can be dealt with at a time. This will delay responding to the second stimulus—and the delay will be longer the more closely in time it occurs to the first stimulus.

A diagram of this type of model is presented in Figure 3.16. The two sets of bars represent two different tasks (T1 and T2). For ease of understanding, let's assume that three cognitive processes must be engaged in order to perform the tasks (represented by the three different squares). Time is moving from left to right—note that this is a serial (i.e., step-by-step) depiction of stimulus processing. In this particular depiction, there is a bottleneck in the middle process. In the diagram, the first stimulus has been presented, progressed through the first process, and is currently undergoing the second process, when the next stimulus is presented. The second stimulus proceeds through the first stage, but because of the bottleneck in the second process, it needs to wait until those processes finish with the first stimulus. So basically, processing of the second stimulus gets temporarily postponed, lengthening overall RT. And of course, the postponement will be longer, the closer in time T2 is to T1 (i.e., at shorter SOAs).

Although this type of model applies most readily to the simple PRP paradigm, it isn't hard to imagine how such bottlenecks and "waiting in line" would play themselves out in a more complex scenario like driving and talking on a cell phone.

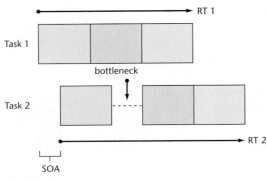

Figure 3.16

Dual-task interference in the psychological refractory period paradigm.

Both of these complex tasks have simpler subtasks in common; for example, you need to process numbers to think about and dial a cell phone number and also to check your speed and how many miles it is to the next destination. You need to interpret words to have the cell phone conversation and also to read and interpret highway signs. It's not hard to imagine how the specific processes that ultimately comprise driving and conversing would be cued up behind one another, waiting, which would lead to slow and error-prone performance.

Another way of capturing what is going on in situations that require the division of attention between two tasks is by appealing to the notion of limited mental resources, or capacity that must be shared when doing two tasks at once (e.g., Kahneman, 1973; Navon & Gopher, 1979). Two tasks can be performed simultaneously by sharing the common "pool" of resources, as long as they don't empty the pool; when this happens, performance on either task, both tasks, or neither task could suffer. The major difference between this view and the bottleneck view is that the capacity view proposes no information-processing bottleneck that "holds up" processing in terms of time. According to the capacity view, processing of multiple tasks can be simultaneous; tasks don't have to wait in line for the others to be processed.

One issue that has been bandied about within the context of capacity theories is whether the capacity is unitary or not. In other words, do we have one general type of resource from which we draw to perform tasks, or do we have multiple specific resources? And if there are multiple types of resources, what differentiates them? Consider your ability to balance two tasks at once—you have no doubt noticed that this ability depends on the nature of the two tasks. For example, you probably find it relatively easy to talk and drive at the same time. However, you would find it much more difficult to drive and read at the same time (although we have seen people reading their papers while driving!). Performing two visual monitoring tasks seems more difficult than performing one visual task along with one auditory task. No doubt a great deal of the ease or difficulty relates to the physical operations required by each of the tasks, but some researchers (e.g., Navon & Gopher, 1979; Wickens, 1984) have proposed that it also relates to a likely difference in the type of mental capacity required.

What differentiates these types, or pools, of capacity? Wickens (1984) suggests that pools are differentiated according to a number of factors, such as whether the input modality is visual or auditory, and whether the response required is vocal or manual. According to this view, tasks interfere to the degree that they tap into the same pool of resources. For example, an auditory and visual task will interfere less with each other than will two visual tasks. This may get you thinking about driving and cell phone usage—driving relies primarily on the visual modality, while talking on a cell phone relies primarily on the auditory modality. Therefore, you might figure that, given the previous analysis, the two should not interfere with one another. But even if two tasks are in different modalities, there is a central limit to the total amount of capacity that can be devoted to them together, with predictable results when that amount is exceeded. And it is important to note that less interference does not mean NO interference. We will discuss the issue of driving and cell phone use in more depth at the end of this chapter.

In spite of the general success of the notion of capacity as a descriptor of task sharing, the concept has some pretty harsh critics (e.g., Logan, 1997). Whether we have one general type of resource from which we draw to perform tasks or multiple specific resources begs a more fundamental question—what exactly *is* a mental resource? The term is just a vague concept that's used as an explanation of attention, but it doesn't really explain anything; it simply redescribes it. In addition, the definition of resources is circular. That is, the notion of limited resources is used to explain why sharing two tasks is difficult; but the fact that two tasks are difficult to share is used as the reason for limited resources! Using a concept to explain some phenomenon, and then using that phenomenon as evidence of the original concept is shoddy theorizing. There needs to be some concrete measure or definition of a *resource* that is independent of increases in the difficulty of a task; however, a satisfactory one has not yet emerged. Given the difficulty in pinning down the concept, some (e.g., Logan, 1997) have urged restraint in using the term.

So which model provides a better account of divided-attention data? It's hard to say. When one gets down to the nitty-gritty of the models, they are actually more difficult to tell apart than it would seem. In a very broad sense, the approaches are similar in that they each propose some sort of basic limit on the amount of mental activity in which we can engage. Some even propose that the bottleneck notion is subsumed by the capacity approach (e.g., Navon & Miller, 2002); the serial bottleneck mechanism could be considered a mental resource, and indeed may be a part of a more complex system. As is so often the case when theories conflict, it is quite likely the case that the division of attention features both the "queueing" of the bottleneck approach and the "sharing" of the capacity approach.

Research Theme
Culture

Culture. In an investigation of cross-cultural differences in patterns of divided attention, Correa-Chávez, Rogoff, and Arauz (2005) were interested in how different *modes* of attention might be employed by children from European American and indigenous North and Central American cultural backgrounds. More specifically, they were interested in comparing what they termed *simultaneous* and *focused* styles of managing attention. A *focused* attentional style is characterized by concentration on one activity at a time. A *simultaneous* attention style is seen when, as stated by Correa-Chávez et al., "...people attend keenly and actively in a broad manner that focuses skillfully on several events at once" (p. 664).

The researchers hypothesized that differences in ethnic and cultural backgrounds, in addition to differences in formal education, lead to divergent patterns of paying attention. Specifically, children from indigenous North and Central American families and communities are expected to learn by participating in family and social activities, keenly and closely observing everything that is going on—a kind of a "hands-on" approach to absorbing the customs, traditions, and history of the community (e.g., Rogoff, Paradise, Mejía Arauz, Correa-Chávez, & Angelillo, 2003). Through these sorts of interactions, children might be expected to develop a more simultaneous "try and absorb as many things as you can" attentional style. The authors are careful to point out that this *simultaneous attention* does not necessarily imply a lack of focus.

In contrast, children from European American families are less likely to participate in the activities of the adult community, and are more likely to have highly structured and formal educational experiences focused exclusively on them (the individual child). The type of attention that emerges from these experiences is a "try and learn these individual facts" attentional style. Children with this type of style are more likely to pay attention to one thing at a time, and alternate that attention when required to perform multiple tasks. From this point on, we will label this style *alternating attention*.

The procedure used by Correa-Chávez et al. involved groups of children (7–8 years of age) learning the paper-folding art of origami. The children were instructed by a first-grade teacher who was blind to the researchers' hypotheses. The interaction between the teacher and the children (tested in groups of three) took a total of about 15 minutes and involved a few minutes of getting acquainted and playing with some already-made figures. The rest of the period involved the teacher showing the children how to make the figures. The teacher was instructed to interact with the students informally, as an "auntie" rather than as a teacher; children were free to attend or not attend, to fold figures on their own, or to help their classmates. These interactions were videotaped and later coded in terms of the type of attention the children engaged in as they struggled with the most difficult phase of the instructions, learning how to fold an origami frog.

Two critical types of attention were operationally defined and subsequently coded from the videotaped interactions. *Simultaneous attentional style* was defined as instances in which children managed to attend to at least two events effectively, without stopping one in favor of another. *Alternating attentional style* was marked by instances in which children were attending to multiple events in a serial fashion such that they were interrupting one event in order to switch to another. The dependent variable was the percentage of 10-second periods in which the children engaged in these two types of attention. The predicted dissociation was observed. Children from indigenous North and Central American family backgrounds spent more of their time engaged in simultaneous attention relative to alternating attention, while children from European American backgrounds showed the opposite pattern.

Stop&Review

1. How are dichotic listening and speech shadowing combined to study auditory attention?

2. True or false? Early-selection theory fixes the problems with attenuation theory.

3. According to multi-mode theory:
   a. we perform both late-selection and early selection at the same time
   b. early selection costs more than late selection
   c. late selection costs more than early selection
   d. we perform early selection after we've already performed late selection

4. What happens in the psychological refractory period paradigm?

5. Distinguish between bottleneck and capacity theories of divided attention.

- Auditory attention is studied with dichotic listening (having people listen to two distinct messages) and speech shadowing (requiring that they repeat one of the messages). These techniques show that attention is limited; people seem able to attend to only one stimulus at a time. In spite of these limits, unattended information does sometimes receive meaningful analysis. A gateway often is used as an analogy for auditory attention.

- Early selection theories propose that the processes whereby we designate information for further processing occur as the information is first registered by the senses. This view fails to account for cases in which the meaning of unattended information grabs our attention. A variation, attenuation theory, accounts for these cases by proposing that early filtering of messages is partial, so especially salient stimuli can be noticed.

- Late-selection theories propose that *all* incoming information is identified or recognized. According to multimode theory, attenders can choose to attend in either early or late selection "modes," but this choice has consequences in terms of the capacity that is needed; late selection requires more attentional capacity.

- Divided attention can be investigated with the psychological refractory period paradigm, in which two RT tasks are presented in rapid succession, resulting in delayed responding to the second stimulus. Divided attention can also be assessed with dual-task paradigm, which requires participants to execute two tasks simultaneously.

- Bottleneck theories of divided attention propose that when one stimulus is already being processed, any other stimulus that occurs in that time is going to have to wait in line to be processed. In contrast, capacity theories of divided attention propose that we have mental resources that are shared among tasks. When the attention demanded exceeds capacity, task performance will suffer.

Automatic Processing

You have probably noticed that many of the daily activities in which you engage seem to involve little or no attention. Tasks such as these are said to involve *automatic processing*. This **automaticity** typically develops as the result of extensive practice. After years of repeatedly engaging in a set of processes, they occur with relatively little effort.

The Stroop Effect

Perhaps the most celebrated demonstration of automatic processing is the Stroop effect. First demonstrated by J. Ridley Stroop (1935), the **Stroop effect** refers to the finding that the ability to name the ink color in which a word is printed is inhibited if that word happens to name a conflicting color. For example, if the word red is printed in blue ink, it's quite difficult to name the ink color (blue) without suffering some interference. How does this demonstrate automatic processing? One common explanation for the effect is that reading is an automatic process; it's obligatory—you can't not do it. Therefore, the ability to name the ink color of the word suffers tremendous interference because you are automatically reading a color word that conflicts with the ink color. It is important to note that this effect is not limited to the traditional task of naming color words. Words that are closely associated with a given color can also have an inhibitory effect on naming a conflicting color (e.g., if the word grass is written in red, it's very difficult to name the color red without first thinking of grass which is green (Klein, 1964).

Stop&*Think* | STROOPING

Try these variations on the Stroop task. Have a friend name the number of characters in each grouping as quickly as possible. Test each list separately, and time how long it takes your friend to finish each of the lists.

List 1	List 2
FFF	222
GGGGGGG	8888888
PPPPP	66666
VVVVVV	555555
JJ	33
DDDDD	44444
NN	11
LLLLLL	777777
SSSSSSSS	99999999

- How did their reaction time vary across list?

- What two processes seem to be in competition?

The Stroop Effect Reconsidered.   Work on the Stroop effect by Besner and his colleagues (Besner, Stolz, & Boutilier, 1997; Risko, Stolz and Besner, 2005) casts some doubt on the automaticity interpretation of the Stroop effect. Besner, Stolz, and Boutilier (1997) tested this interpretation with a disarmingly simple task. Participants were presented with words in the center of a computer screen. Either one letter of the word (randomly chosen) was colored, or the whole word was colored. Participants' task was to name the color they saw—of the entire word or the single letter. Note that according to the automaticity interpretation of the Stroop effect, there should be equal interference in both conditions, because in both conditions, participants should be automatically drawn to read the word. However, Besner et al. found the Stroop effect to be greatly reduced in the letter condition.

Besner and his colleagues have an account of the Stroop effect that is markedly different from the over 500 articles (Besner, Stolz, & Boutilier, 1997) that chalk it up to the automatic reading of words. These researchers claim that the Stroop effect is an instance of mental set. Mental set refers to our tendency to revert to well-practiced and routine mental processes when faced with a cognitive task. We'll be talking more about mental set in Chapter 12. But in the present example of the Stroop effect, participants fall into a familiar mental set when faced with a word—they read it. Give them an alternative mind set (i.e., search the letter strings for the colored letter), they are able to disregard the typical mind set and not read the word, contrary to what the automaticity view would predict. Indeed, such a manipulation does serve to reduce Stroop interference substantially (Besner, Stolz, & Boutilier, 1997).

Characteristics of Automatic Processing

In a review of research and theory, Moors and De Houwer (2006; also see Posner & Snyder, 1975; Saling & Phillips, 2007) summarize the characteristics generally thought to differentiate between automatic and nonautomatic (i.e., controlled) processes. One of the most salient distinctions between automatic and controlled processes is the degree to which actions are subjected to conscious *control*. Control involves the ability or propensity to monitor, alter, change, or stop doing something. This control is lessened to the degree that a task is automatic. A related difference is the degree to which there is a conscious *intention* present. When activities are automatic, you aren't really consciously intending to engage in them; they're more autonomous, seeming to occur on their own, without any central control. A third characteristic of automatic processes is their *attentional efficiency*. Activities involving automatic processes take place with a minimum of attentional capacity, which leaves more capacity for the performance of other tasks.

Accounts of Automaticity

One example of automatic processing is the development of simple math skills (e.g., Ashcraft, 1992). We'll use this example to compare two major accounts of what's happening as a task becomes automatic. Greg was quite into mental arithmetic while in college—no, not as a hobby but as a mail clerk. One of a mail clerk's many exciting tasks is the tabulation of mail charges for bundles of mail. When Greg was a mail clerk, a piece of mail cost 17¢ (yes, he's that old). His first few months on the job, he would painstakingly multiply 17 by any and all numbers laboriously in his head, or sometimes on paper. But after two years of clerking, he was extremely fast at multiplying any number by 17 (a feat that now serves no useful purpose, other than to win the occasional bet at a party).

There are a number of accounts of what's happening as a given task, (e.g. Greg's multiplication of any number by 17) becomes automatic, and how automatic processes differ from controlled processes. Saling and Phillips (2007) distinguish between quantitative and qualitative accounts of the difference. Quantitative accounts assert that automatic processes are for the most part similar to the controlled version—they're just faster. Qualitative accounts contend that once a behavior has become automatic, there is an essential change in the way the behavior is carried out—that is, the processes are *qualitatively* different.

One quantitative account of the transition from controlled processing to automatic processing might be termed a sort of *increased speed approach* (e.g., Schneider & Shiffrin, 1977). According to this view, as the performance of a task undergoes the transition from controlled to automatic, the component processes required to perform the task get increasingly faster with practice. So Greg's ability to rapidly multiply numbers after extended practice occurred because each of the component processes of multiplication (i.e., multiply the 1's, carry over 10's, multiply 10's) got faster. In addition, this view proposes a gradual transition from serial (step-by-step) processing to parallel (all-at-once) processing. In the case of mental arithmetic, this might mean that the three stages of multiplication mentioned parenthetically above might eventually progress to the point where they could be done in a somewhat overlapping (i.e., parallel) fashion.

Logan (1988) has a qualitative view of what is happening as a task becomes automatic. According to his approach, termed the *instance-based view,* there is a fundamental change in the way tasks are performed as people get more and more practice. Performance of a task in the early stages tends to be conscious and deliberate, involving effortful memory search and information manipulation. Each encounter with the task leads to the formation of a new memory trace, so after a great deal of practice, there are countless *instances* of having performed the task stored in memory. After sufficient practice, performance of the task switches from a conscious and deliberate mode to the quick and simple retrieval of an instance from memory. So after a great deal of practice, instead of having to rely on repeating a mental computation, a person performs the task by quickly retrieving relevant information from memory.

Turning again to Greg's party trick......According to Logan's view, after years of practice, the way Greg accomplished this task changed fundamentally. Instead of carrying out the actual multiplication each time he was holding 23 envelopes ($3.91!!), he was instantly and directly retrieving an instance from the hundreds of memories of having multiplied 17 by 23. This transition from computation to memory retrieval is what is happening as a task becomes automatic.

A study by Tronsky (2005) demonstrates this transition quite nicely and, coincidentally, in an empirical setting that mirrors Greg's real-world experience. Tronksy was interested in investigating how automaticity develops in complex multiplication. To find out, he assessed participant skill and strategy in computing single-digit/multiple-digit multiplication problems (e.g., 9 x 17). Participants solved 60 different multiplication problems more than 120 times each! In addition to the multiplication task, Tronsky also required the participants to provide regular assessments of the strategies they were using to calculate the products.

Needless to say, accuracy of calculation wasn't of much interest in the study. For their purposes, the most interesting findings were those from the strategy assessment. Reported strategies from early multiplication trials were formulaic or algorithmic. Participants followed the sometimes arduous rules of multiplication. However, over time, their strategies had changed completely. By the end of the experiment, they were relying almost exclusively on memory to retrieve the products of the multiplication problems. Rather than getting faster and faster at carrying out the same computations, it seems that (consistent with Logan's 1988 view), participants were changing how they performed the task, moving from the relatively slow and laborious application of an algorithm to the quick and efficient retrieval of an answer from memory. Not surprisingly, Rawson and Touron (2009) found that the transition from computational to memory-based processing tends to occur more slowly for older adults than younger adults. As you'll see in other chapters, cognitive processing tends to slow as we age.

Costs of Automaticity

Although the nature of automaticity is still debated, there is little doubt about the practical implications of automatic processing. Automaticity seems to be largely a good thing; after all, we perform tasks more quickly and efficiently and are better able to share attention between tasks. But there is a downside to automaticity. Automatic processes can be quite difficult to abort or modify, due in part to the fact that they involve relatively little in the way of conscious monitoring. Therefore, it's often the case that people make absentminded mistakes when they are engaged in automatic processing. These mistakes can range from the amusing to the downright dangerous. Norman (1981) coined a term for these all-too-common bouts of absentmindedness—action slips.

Action Slips.   We've all done it—put the cereal in the refrigerator; gone to a room to fetch something only to return with the wrong object; called someone on the phone and forgotten who it was we were calling. Norman (1988) would label each of these an **action slip,** which tend to occur in the absence of attention (hence the term *absentmindedness*). Recall that one characteristic of automatic processes is that they are performed with relatively little conscious control or monitoring. Given this, it's not surprising that many action slips occur in the context of automatic processing; quite literally, when we do things automatically, *we aren't thinking.*

Norman (1988; see also Cooper & Shallice, 2006) proposes that highly learned action sequences (like driving a car) are controlled by organized memory structures termed *schemas*—an organized body of knowledge (or set of movements) that guides motor activities. Each schema is assumed to cover only a limited range of knowledge. Therefore, a given action sequence must be made up of a number of hierarchically organized schemas. The highest-level schema is called the *parent schema* that consists of a series of *child schemas* that are initiated by the parent schema at the appropriate time. A sample parent schema might be driving to school in the morning, which is made up of many child schemas, such as walking to the car, starting the car, and parking. Norman contends that once an action becomes highly skilled, only higher-level (parent) schemas need to be activated in order to set a behavior chain in motion; once set in motion, it basically "runs" fairly mindlessly.

Action slips can occur at any time during this schema activation. Some action slips occur when schemas are triggered inappropriately. A *data-driven error* occurs when external events cause the (inappropriate) activation of a schema and forces some type of unwanted behavior. Have you ever been typing an e-mail, when a word from the music you are listening to appears on your screen? If so, you've experienced a data-driven error. Another type of slip, termed a *capture error,* occurs when an intended action is similar to one that is very familiar and well practiced. The schemas controlling the well-practiced action sequence may become activated and take over. For example, if you're in a mall store and a salesperson approaches you and asks, "So how many inches of snow are on the ground? Has it stopped snowing yet?" You respond "No, I'm just looking." Typically, when a salesperson asks you a question, the prototypical (i.e., familiar) response is "No, I'm just looking" and not "about 6 inches and it's still coming down." In this example, the more familiar "no, I'm just looking" response is uttered rather than the intended one. This type of slip is similar to another slip called the *associative activation error,* but it occurs for a slightly different reason. This slip occurs when your intention to do or say something activates a strongly related but inappropriate schema. For example, you might respond to a friend's question, "What's up?" with "Great!" This happens because what might be termed a *greeting schema* activates a number of *reply schemas* that are closely associated, and the wrong one wins. The response is not more familiar than the intended one; it simply is related to it.

Given that the associative-activation error, the capture error, and the data-driven error all occur because an inappropriate schema is activated, you may find it difficult to differentiate between them. To distinguish them, think about the familiarity level and the nature of the intruding action sequence. If the intruding action sequence is more familiar than the intended action sequence, then a capture error has occurred. If the intruding action sequence is not more familiar but simply related to the intended action sequence, then an associative activation error has occurred. If the intruding action sequence is initiated by some aspect of the environment, regardless of whether it was more familiar or less familiar, then a data-driven error has occurred.

Activation of inappropriate schemas isn't the only route to an action slip. Some slips involve a failure to completely activate or maintain the activation of a schema. One of the most frustrating types of slips is the *loss-of-activation error,* which basically involves going to do something and forgetting what it was you wanted to do. This occurs when an activated schema loses activation because of interference (a mechanisms for forgetting we'll discuss in Chapter 4). Some slips can occur because an intention to do something is formed, but not correctly or completely. In other words, an incomplete description of what to do is formed, leading to what Norman terms a *description error.* This occurs when you carry out the action you wanted but on the wrong object. For example, in a rush to put things away in the kitchen, you may find yourself putting cereal in the refrigerator and milk in the cupboard. The actions are appropriate, but they're performed on the wrong objects.

According to Norman (1981), all of these action slips occur because their prevention and/or detection require feedback from the information-processing system about ongoing processing. Because such conscious monitoring is at a relatively low level when actions are automatic, slips are likely to occur. But automaticity is not the only situation characterized by lowered conscious monitoring. Are you more likely to make mistakes when you're tired? Undoubtedly you responded yes to that question. When you are tired, you do not have the mental energy needed to carefully monitor your actions, and as a result, are more likely to commit action slips and other cognitive errors.

Another example is stress. Van Der Linden, Keisjers, Eling, and Van Schaijk (2005) investigated the occurrence of cognitive errors in the context of work burnout. Participants clinically diagnosed as suffering from burnout and nonburnout control participants performed a target detection task. They were instructed to press a key whenever a target appeared in the middle of the computer screen, except when the target was the number 3. When the number 3 appeared, they were instructed to do nothing. The percentage of errors (pressing the key when the number 3 appeared) was recorded. Participants diagnosed with burnout made more errors than the nonburnout control participants.

Research Theme
Metacognition

In order to determine if these errors might extend beyond the lab, they had participants complete the cognitive failure questionnaire. This instrument assesses one's metacognitive knowledge of the frequency with which cognitive errors are committed. Scores for burnout participants indicated high levels of metacognitive awareness that they were committing cognitive errors in their daily life. This provides converging evidence of the effect of stress on cognitive processing.

Stop&*Think* | ABSENTMINDEDNESS

Start a diary of absentminded mistakes you make over the next couple of weeks. Classify each according to Norman's scheme. Detail what happened, what should have happened, and what was going on externally (i.e., around you) and internally (your thoughts, how you felt).

- When do slips seem to occur?
- Relate their occurrence to automatic processing.

Stop&*Review*

1. The Stroop effect involves difficulty in:
   a. making a task automatic
   b. naming colors
   c. reading words
   d. using a mental set
2. Which of these is not one of the characteristics of an automatic process?
   a. they are intentional
   b. they operate outside of conscious awareness
   c. they are attention demanding
   d. they may be associated with a shift from algorithm to memory retrieval
3. What is an action slip, and how do they relate to automatic processing? What is the effect of being tired or stressed on action slips?

- Automaticity characterizes tasks that have received extensive practice and, as a result, seem to operate with little or no attention. A common example of automaticity is the Stroop effect, which refers to the finding that the ability to name the ink color in which a word is printed is inhibited if that word happens to name a conflicting color. Some claim that it is not an example of automaticity but an example of a mental set.

- Automatic processes operate without intention, outside of conscious awareness, and with a minimum demand on attention. One view of their development is that there is a dramatic increase in the speed of processing. An alternative account is that, with practice, processing shifts from algorithm to memory retrieval.

- Action slips refer to absentminded actions that occur during the course of automatic processing due to a lack of conscious monitoring. These slips also are more likely to occur when tired or stressed.

Driving: A Case Study in Attention

Gadgets are all around us—GPS devices, Blackberries, Razors, iPhones, iPods—and the activities performed with these gadgets are unceasing: listening, navigating, browsing, talking, friending, tweeting, and texting. Combine all of this with attentional spotlights, bottlenecks and blinks, and put it behind the wheel of a car and quite literally, you've got an accident waiting to happen. Distracted driving has become an epidemic. It's become so bad that Oprah has mobilized her legion of fans to fight it (http://www.oprah.com/oprahshow/End-Distracted-Driving) and the U.S. government has a Web site devoted exclusively to it (www.distraction.gov). Check out these statistics from the Web site (operated by the U.S. Department of Transportation).

Research Theme
Reality

- In 2008, there were a total of 34,017 fatal crashes in which 37,261 individuals were killed; 5,870 of them were killed in crashes involving driver distraction (16% of total fatalities).

- The proportion of drivers reportedly distracted at the time of the fatal crashes has increased from 8% in 2004 to 11% in 2008.

- The under-20 age group had the highest proportion of distracted drivers involved in fatal crashes (16%). The age group with the next greatest proportion of distracted drivers was the 20- to 29-year-old age group (12%).

- An estimated 21% of 1,630,000 injury crashes were reported to have involved distracted driving.

Clearly we have a problem, and it falls squarely within the bailiwick of cognitive psychologists. The research and theory discussed in this chapter is directly relevant to this pressing real-world problem. Now it's not just general conceptual and theoretical work, it's literally a matter of life and death. Consequently, the field has placed the problem of distracted driving squarely within its attentional spotlight. A PsycINFO search of the empirical literature, using the terms driving and attention and distracted driving reveals a dramatic increase in the number of relevant investigations. Between 1998 and 2004, just under 400 such investigations had been done. In the six years since, nearly 700 more investigations have been done, an increase of over 150%! This steady and large growth of the research literature mirrors the intensity of the problem.

Stop&*Think* | BACK-SEAT DRIVING

This exercise could get pretty involved, and will require a partner. Your partner has to agree to drive you around town; alternatively, you could do this while a passenger in someone's car. When you can get a good view of other drivers, (e.g., in slow traffic, while passing, or while stopped at lights), note the distractions in which they are engaged. Keep a record, and note the frequency of each, and when they occur. Also note any problems with their driving (if any). After the observations, draw some general conclusions regarding the commonality of distracted driving, the most common types of distractions, when they occur, and the problems they may create.

And please, no dirty looks or obscene gestures to the distracted drivers...but you could hold up a sign in your window that says "Got Attention?"

As cell phone usage increased in the '90s, and the dangers of driving while talking on them became increasingly evident, most figured "Well of course...your hands are on the phone, instead of on the wheel!" Basically, it was perceived as a problem of physical movement and control. Turns out, that's only part of the problem, and it's smaller than you probably think. Groeger (1999) provides a useful framework for considering the possible effects of adding an additional task (e.g., eating, conversing, and texting) to driving performance. The *operational level* refers to the movements and actions required to keep a car on the road. A deficit here might be shown as you drift to the side of the road while reaching for a french fry or your cell phone. The *tactical level* involves maneuvering a vehicle within traffic. This level entails more cognitive control. A problem at this level might be miscalculating one's clearance from oncoming traffic when making a left-hand turn (or a right-hand turn, for you Brits), or putting on the brakes too late to stop safely at a light. Finally, the *strategic level* of performance relates to goal-related aspects of driving such as route planning or navigational thinking.

Most research has dealt with the problems created by drivers chatting on the ubiquitous, omnipresent, omni-on cell phones. This is a perfect example of the dual-task situation we discussed in the context of auditory attention. And, as sad as at it may seem, when drivers talk on their cell phones their conversation becomes their primary task while driving becomes the probe RT task. So let's talk about the impact of talking on the cell phone on the secondary task of driving.

Figure 3.17
A participant in the simulator employed by Drews and colleagues.

Driving and Auditory Attention

David Strayer, Frank Drews and their colleagues at the University of Utah (Cooper & Strayer, 2001; Strayer & Drews, 2006; Strayer & Drews, 2007; Strayer, Drews, & Crouch, 2006; Strayer & Johnston, 2001) have led the charge to investigate the dangerous dynamic that takes place when a driver engages in their distraction of choice. Most of their work involves a realistic driving simulator (see Figure 3.17) due to the intractable problem of conducting experimental studies with drivers in a real-life driving context.

Drews, Pasupathi, and Strayer (2008) investigated the impact of conversations on simulated driving at each of the performance levels identified by Groeger (1999): operational, tactical, and strategic. They also addressed another rationalizing FAQ of the cell-phone obsessed driver: "Is it really any worse than talking to someone in the car?" After all, as these researchers note, a conversation is a conversation. But upon closer scrutiny, maybe not—imagine yourself as the conversation partner of someone driving a car. Certainly your conversational behavior varies depending on whether you're in the car or not. A traveling passenger can see the driver, the traffic, and other elements of the context, and adjust their behavior accordingly. The cell phone partner is completely unaware of the driving conditions and their conversation will continue in blissful ignorance of the rapidly changing environment.

In the practice phase of the experiment by Drews et al., participants were given practice in the simulator. Then, they were randomly given the role of driver or passenger/cell phone partner for the test phase. One of the two was randomly designated to get the conversation rolling by telling a "close call" story about a time when they were in some danger (a topic meant to lead to an engaging conversation). The two participants were told to engage in a conversation prompted by the story as the driver made their way down the simulated highway to a rest stop about eight miles away, forewarned by an exit sign. Both the driver and passenger were aware of the destination and the instructions. In the cell phone condition, the driver used a hands-free device to conduct the conversation. All drivers also took part in a single task version (no conversation) of the driving route to provide a baseline for comparison. The simulator replicated a typical highway driving situation, in that it simulated an irregular flow of traffic with other drivers changing lanes and speeds. Therefore, it wasn't possible for the simulated driver to just stay in one lane for the duration of the route.

Drews et al. used a variety of dependent variables to assess performance. For the operational level, they assessed how well the driver stayed in the center of their lane and avoided drifting. Drivers on cell phones were more often "off-center" in their driving lanes, relative to the single task condition and drivers with passengers. For the tactical level, they measured speed and following distance. Drivers on cell phones had a greater following distance than drivers in other conditions. Speed of the vehicle did not differ among conditions; previous results had indicated that cell-phone using drivers typically travel at a slower speed. For the strategic level, they noted whether or not the driver successfully carried out the mission of pulling off at the rest stop. The results were rather disturbing. Everyone in the passenger condition was successful, but in the cell phone condition, nearly 50% of drivers missed their exit!

These results indicate clear deficits (at the operational and strategic level) of driving performance when talking on the cell phone, but not when conversing with a passenger. The conversation data collected by Drews et al. provide some indication of why in-car conversations aren't as likely to lead to driving deficits. Overall (and not surprisingly) cell-phone partners made significantly fewer references to traffic than passengers, and when references to traffic were made, there was more turn-taking in the conversation with the passenger than the cell-phone partner. That is, passengers and drivers were much more likely to have traffic as the focus of their conversation than drivers and cell-phone partners. This no doubt aided the driver, helping to ensure their successful exit at the rest stop.

Driving and Visual Attention

Change Blindness.   The phenomena of change blindness underscore the importance of visual attention in providing a coherent view of the world around us. Simply looking is not enough. A growing body of research (e.g., Galpin, Underwood & Crundall, 2009; Lee, Lee, & Boyle, 2007; Strayer, Drews, & Johnston, 2003) reveals that the disconcerting phenomenon of change blindness is likely to occur in the context of driving. This fact become even more disturbing in the context of the findings from a study by Clifasefi, Takarangi, and Bergman (2006), who investigated the influence of alcohol on change blindness. They employed the gorilla video of Simons and Chabris (1999) and compared gorilla detection in sober and mildly intoxicated participants (.04 blood alcohol content, well below the legal limit). The proportion of participants who noticed the gorilla differed dramatically between conditions. Nearly half of the sober observers (46%) detected the gorilla, compared to a miserable 18% of those who were mildly intoxicated. Although this was not a driving study, when combined with the investigations of driving discussed to this point, the results are truly sobering. The combined effects of drinking and driving will drastically compromise attention, leading to potentially catastrophic results. Take heed.

Other Visual Distractions.   Unfortunately, talking on the cell phone isn't the only form of distraction in a car. Drivers also are constantly fiddling with radios and MP3 players, and in bouts of astounding attentional stupidity, receiving and sending text messages (both of your authors are mystified by this practice!). Cognitive researchers have begun to investigate the effects of these distractions, and the results aren't surprising. Drews, Yazdani, Godfrey, Cooper, and Strayer (2010) investigated the effects of texting while driving, with a focus on braking behavior. You may be familiar with the video gone viral of the bus driver who texted his way into a dramatic rear-end collision, all caught on surveillance video. Given what Drews et al. found, the collision was not the least bit surprising. These investigators used the same driving simulator mentioned above, but assigned drivers a different task. They were to follow a "pace car" that was part of the simulation. The pace car stayed in the same lane and its brake lights would come on intermittently. The brake lights remained on until the participant put on the brakes of the simulator. Participants were tested in dual-task (texting and driving) and single-task (driving only) conditions.

The effects of texting while driving were evident across a variety of variables. For example, *braking onset* took 25% longer when drivers were texting relative to when they were just driving. The dependent variable of *following distance* revealed an interesting result; the minimum following distance was considerably shorter for texters, and their following distance was considerably more variable. This indicates that the texters were moving up and dropping back, probably with the ebb and flow of their attention. In addition, inadvertent lane changes and swerving back and forth in a lane were more likely to occur in dual-task situations. Rear-end collisions occurred only seven times across all conditions, but six of the seven occurred in the dual-task condition. So the effects of texting are even more severe than talking on the cell phone. As the investigators note, this isn't surprising, given that texting requires task-switching, not just task sharing.

One final task that people often share with driving is the operation of an MP3 player, like the proverbial iPod. This is one distraction Greg engages in (to Bridget's chagrin). He argues that it's always simple, brief, and he's well practiced at it. Chisholm, Caird, and Lockhart (2008) investigated the effects of MP3 operation on driving, and also looked at the effects of practice. In their study, participants drove in a simulator and had to engage in a braking response to each of three different events, including a pedestrian, a braking car, and a car pulling out in front of them. Each event occurred in conjunction with iPod tasks that were easy (turn it off, skip two songs) or difficult (get to a specific song) and three trials of each were given to assess the effects of practice. The results revealed that difficult iPod tasks (e.g., selecting particular songs and artists) had a sizeable effect on RTs to the critical events, and the effect did not diminish with practice. Easy iPod tasks (e.g., stopping it, advancing songs) also influenced responding, but not as acutely, and the effects were eliminated with practice. So although the effects of interacting with your MP3 player might not be as dramatic as those of texting, it's probably best if you just put the thing on "Shuffle songs" and drive.

Improving Visual Search.   Earlier in the chapter, we discussed the theoretical and empirical nuances that define the study of visual attention. You may have felt the whole enterprise seemed a little esoteric or arcane. But rest assured—the answers to those questions matter tremendously, and the distance between the basic issues and their application can be as short as the distance between you and that car you were tailgating this morning....oh wait, that was me. Speaking of brakes, did you ever think of detecting brake lights as a visual search task? It is—consider the rich information in your visual field as you drive, and the amount of information you are required to process. Detection of brake lights in the "visual display" ahead of you is a critical task. McIntyre (2008) wondered whether current brake displays—featuring a red light that lights up within a red taillight—might be improved by using a different color. You might recall that color is one of the guiding attributes that is processed pre-attentively; it's possible that a striking change in color when someone brakes would be processed more efficiently and quickly than detecting the change in luminance that occurs with the current brake light systems. In addition, the fact that drivers are accustomed to seeing red taillights might make their response to the red brake lights a bit sluggish. Essentially, the cue "red" is a bit overloaded in the driving task.

McIntyre had participants view colored slides of driving scenes in which the cars had "normal" brakes lights or yellow brake lights. Participants' task was to indicate (with a "present" or "absent" keypress) whether or not brake lights were illuminated for any cars in the scene. The results were dramatic. Average RT for displays that featured yellow brake lights was 2000 ms (2 sec) and for displays with the typical red brakelights the average RT was 3000 ms (3 sec). One second might not seem like a big deal, but it could be the difference between life and death.

Stop&*Review*

1. Name the three performance levels that might be assessed in the distracted driver.
2. True or false? Talking on the cell phone is no worse than talking to someone who is riding in the car.
3. True or false? Less demanding visual tasks like MP3 operation do not interfere with driving.

- Divided attention and distraction have become pressing issues in the context of driving. Interference from nondriving tasks can occur at multiple levels of, including operational (physically manipulating the steering wheel), tactical (maneuvering within traffic), and strategic (route planning).

- Deficits in auditory attention have found that talking on the cell phone while driving causes more driving errors than talking to a person who is present in the car. These deficits occur at the operational and strategic levels.

- Deficits in visual attention are evident in driving, which becomes a major concern when considering that alcohol accentuates change blindness. Visual distractions such as texting and using an MP3 player have been shown to adversely affect various aspects of driving.

4

Immediate Memory: The Control and Manipulation of Information

How good are you at ignoring all of the little distractions that are going on in the background while you study or listen to your professor's lecture? Why do some people seem to be so good at it, and others, not so much?

Why *does* listening in class and taking good notes present so much of a challenge? The words are all familiar, the individual sentences are comprehensible; you obviously understand English pretty well. Yet the combined demands of comprehending and writing down the main points of a lecture can be exceedingly difficult. What's the problem?

You may notice sometimes that when you're keeping information in mind, you're "replaying it" in some way, either by "listening" to it, or by "seeing it" in terms of a visual image. How do these sorts of processes operate? Are listening and seeing things in consciousness the only modes of processing open to us?

You're golfing, playing tennis, or (fill in your favorite skill here) and have a pesky habit of making the same mistake over and over. And when you really try to tell yourself not to make the mistake, and pay extra close attention. . . . you're even *more* likely to make the mistake! What's going on?

Multitasking is everywhere; it seems that no one is ever doing just one thing. People are always mixing and matching 2 or 3 concurrent tasks. Does this serve as practice that makes people better at multitasking? Or are the constant strains on attention detrimental? If so, are there any remedies for society's seeming attention deficits?

The Importance of Executive Attention

Recall our discussion of the strategic nature of attention in the previous chapter. The multimode theory proposed that we can choose to attend selectively in either an early or late-selection mode. Later you saw that capacity theories of attention emphasize the strategic nature of divided attention. To some extent, we can parcel out our attention to ongoing events as we see fit. This is illustrated well by our orchestration of events as we're driving, also discussed in Chapter 3. As we make our way through traffic, we must constantly engage in the visual monitoring of signs, other moving vehicles, honking horns, blinking lights, and so on. These demands must often be shared with the demands of attentive listening to the radio, conversation partners, honking horns, or approaching sirens. Clearly the control of attention in these situations is of critical importance. The processes whereby we strategically direct our attention in response to situational demands is termed **executive attention.** The nature of executive attention has become an object of intense focus in recent years (e.g., Banich, 2009; Ophir, Nass, & Wagner, 2009; Engle, 2002; Unsworth & Engle, 2007), as researchers attempt to specify the nature of what might be termed "cognitive control."

Engle (2002; see also Engle & Kane, 2004) discusses the importance of *inhibition* in the control of attention. It's easy to acknowledge the value of attending to important information and keeping it active in consciousness. What may not be as obvious is the role of inhibition in attention (Dempster, 1992). We have to be able to screen out what isn't immediately important because of the interference it may produce. Let's take a look at the role of inhibition within the context of a couple tried-and-true research paradigms discussed in Chapter 3: the cocktail party phenomenon and the Stroop task.

Conway, Cowan, and Bunting (2001) were interested in the relationship between attentional control and the cocktail-party phenomenon. As you'll recall, this refers to our tendency to overhear our name (or other personally salient information) even if it occurs in unattended sources of stimulation. At first blush, this might seem like a good thing but it also might be considered a failure of attention, given that information that was supposed to be unattended intrudes on consciousness. In other words, the cocktail party phenomenon is a failure of inhibition. We're willing to bet that you've had some similar failures of inhibition as you're reading the text right now; potential suitors for your attention are abundant. In their study, Conway and colleagues gave participants a screening measure to assess their capacity for attentional control. The measure is called operation span, and assesses a person's ability to keep track of multiple streams of information. The task is depicted in Figure 4.1. Individuals are presented with math problems and are asked to read them aloud and solve them. Each problem is presented with a word. After completing varying numbers of problems (three in this example), participants recall the words that accompanied each problem. The operation span task is essentially a divided-attention situation; participants must process and answer the simple math problems and at the same time, keep track of the words in order to recall them.

After using this task to classify participants as high-span and low-span, Conway et al. (2001) placed them in a dichotic listening situation in which separate word lists were presented to each ear. The relevant list was presented in a female voice, and the list to be ignored was presented in a male voice (as you'll recall from Chapter 3 this is a relatively easy selective attention task). Each participant's name was inserted in the to-be-ignored list. The results are depicted in Figure 4.2.

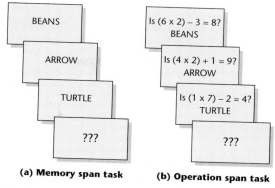

(a) Memory span task   **(b) Operation span task**

Figure 4.1

Comparison of (a) memory span task and (b) operation span task.

The results (plotted a bit differently in that the y-axis corresponds to the number of participants making errors) revealed that low-span participants were more than three times as likely to hear their name than high-span participants. Further analyses of shadowing errors revealed the effects of noticing the irrelevant information (i.e., their name). Immediately after hearing their name some high-span participants made shadowing errors; however, low-span participants were more than four times as likely to make errors. By three words after hearing their name, more low-span participants than high-spans were still making errors. In fact, there were more low-span participants making errors at that point than there were high-span participants making errors immediately after hearing their name.

High-span participants, who demonstrated superior divided attention in the operation span task, also demonstrated superior selective attention in the shadowing task. They were able to inhibit their name from significantly impairing performance on the primary task (speech shadowing).

Another paradigm requiring the ability to inhibit irrelevant information is the Stroop task. As you may remember, Stroop interference occurs when an individual must name the color of a printed word when the color conflicts with the word label (e.g., the word green printed in blue). The irrelevant information is the word, as the task is to name the color, not read the word.

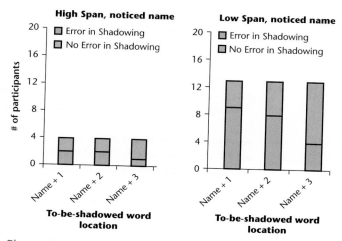

Figure 4.2

Operation span and susceptibility to distraction.

Results from Conway, Cowan, & Bunting (2001).

Kane and Engle (2003) compared high- and low-span participants on a Stroop task. In the 100% condition, the proportion of incongruent trials (e.g., word-color mismatch—the word green printed in blue) was 100%; every trial was set up to produce Stroop interference. In the 25% condition, only 25% of the trials were incongruent; the remaining 75% of the trials were congruent trials (word-color match—the word blue printed in blue). So in this condition, the majority of trials did not produce Stroop interference. The dependent variable was the number of errors made on the incongruent trials (i.e., saying the word label rather than the color in which the word was printed).

As noted by Kane and Engle, the goal of the participants in the Stroop task is to ignore the word (i.e., inhibit reading) and focus on the color. Let's see how this applies within the present procedure. In the 100% condition, participants would have a relatively easy time ignoring the word, given that they knew there would be a color-word mismatch on every single trial. But in the 25% condition, the word and the color *matched* most of the time (75%), so reading the word was especially tempting, given that it helped identify the color. Inhibiting the word-reading response on incongruent trials in this condition should be extremely difficult. In addition, this difficulty should be more pronounced for low-span participants because high-span participants are better able to inhibit irrelevant information. In other words, high-span participants should be less susceptible to Stroop interference than low-span participants.

This is exactly what Kane and Engle found. In the 100% condition, both groups were reasonably successful at ignoring the word and naming the color. However, in the 25% condition, error rates on the incongruent trials for high-span and low-span participants diverged. Error rates for low-span participants were nearly double those of high-span participants, indicating that it was difficult for them to inhibit reading the word when doing so was especially tempting.

Executive attention and its component processes (one of which is inhibition) are thought by many researchers to be a fundamentally important function of consciousness. You might be thinking, "OK, the last two studies make it clear that executive attention is important in the area of attention; but isn't that like saying problem solving is important in problem solving?" Point taken, but the importance of executive attention reaches far beyond this one area of cognitive psychology. Research has revealed that a person's ability to control their attention (as indicated by tasks like operation span) is a strikingly good predictor of a broad range of complex abilities like spoken and written language comprehension, writing, note taking, vocabulary learning, and even bridge playing! Why might executive attention play such a key role in complex task performance? According to Engle and colleagues, the processing needed to perform complex tasks involves keeping track of multiple streams of information, keeping some of it active and easily retrievable even in the face of interference from other material that may be more relevant at the time. For example, if you have professors like us, who simultaneously lecture and use PowerPoint, executive attention is critical as you attempt to get down what's on the PowerPoint while also tracking what the professor is saying.

McVay and Kane (2009) have an apt metaphor for executive attention; they refer to it as "conducting the train of thought." Continuing with the metaphor, you might conceive of attentional failures (e.g., Stroop interference, cocktail party phenomenon) as instances of the train running off the rails. We'll return to this topic later in the chapter. But for now, let's examine the main purpose of executive attention; it is the linchpin in the set of processes collectively referred to as **immediate memory,** which allows for the maintenance and manipulation of information currently in consciousness. The stream of incoming information is constant, therefore the maintenance and manipulation of this information is a continual, never-ending, process that we engage in during every waking moment of our life. All aboard!

Stop&*Review*

1. Define executive attention.
2. How does the ability to control attention relate to the cocktail party phenomenon and to the Stroop effect?
3. True or false? Executive attention is central to immediate memory.

- The processes whereby we strategically direct our attention in response to situational demands is termed executive attention, which can also be termed "cognitive control." One important process of cognitive control is inhibition of irrelevant information.

- Operation span is a task that can be used to assess one's ability to control attention. People with high span are better at inhibiting irrelevant information, as indicated by a lowered susceptibility to the cocktail-party phenomenon, and to Stroop interference.

- Executive attention and its component processes are thought to be a fundamentally important function of consciousness and serve as the centerpiece for immediate memory, the set of processes that allows for the manipulation of information currently in consciousness.

Immediate Memory: Basic Characteristics

As previously stated, immediate memory can be defined as the active processing and manipulation of information in consciousness, which can be contrasted with the more permanent version of memory that includes all of our acquired knowledge and skills. The distinction between a temporarily activated, conscious form of memory and a non-active, nonconscious store of knowledge that can be brought into an active state when necessary is not a new one. William James (1890) himself proposed such a distinction, labeling the former "primary memory" and the latter "secondary memory. Let's take a look at some of immediate memory's general characteristics.

Limits in Duration

When keeping track of your instructor's riveting lectures, you've no doubt experienced one of the defining characteristics of immediate memory—the fact that it has a limited duration. The information seems to be gone quickly after it is presented. Given that information is active only temporarily, the information must be rehearsed in order to maintain it in immediate memory. In Chapter 6, you'll read more about the basic rehearsal of information and its effect on long-term retention.

The limited duration of immediate memory most often has been demonstrated with the **Brown-Peterson task** (Brown, 1958; Peterson & Peterson, 1959). In this task, people receive a brief presentation of a consonant trigram (e.g., JDL) immediately followed by the presentation of a three-digit number. Participants must count backward by threes from that number. The purpose of the counting task is to prevent rehearsal of the material. The amount of time they're required to count defines the **retention interval.** The amount of time that lapses between encoding and retrieval is a common independent variable in memory experiments. Peterson and Peterson found that forgetting was quite extreme and quite quick; within about 20 seconds, the probability of recalling the trigram was only 0.10 (or 10%).

Limits in Capacity

Duration isn't the only limit on immediate memory processing. As you're well aware from frenzied attempts to write down what your professor is saying, there are severe limits in what immediate memory can handle at one time. A loose analogy can be drawn between immediate memory and storage on an old-fashioned audiotape, which can hold only a finite amount of information. Analogously, the amount of information we can hold in immediate memory is also limited (we'll return later to this analogy).

Limitations in immediate memory capacity were noted by George Miller, one of the leading figures in the cognitive revolution of the 1950s. In a classic paper, Miller (1956) notes the prominence of what he coined the **magical number 7 ± 2.** He was referring to a strikingly consistent limitation in the number of items we can hold in immediate memory. Miller noted that this number is applicable across a wide array of different stimulus types, from letters to numbers to words to musical notes. So "magical" was this number that it was the basis for our seven-digit phone numbers. Most people can easily remember seven digits and seven digits seemed more than adequate to allow for the various unique phone number combinations needed, at least at that point in time. Given the proliferation of cell phones, expansion to 10 digits has been necessary. Given that 10 digits exceeds immediate memory capacity, phone numbers are no longer so easy to remember—thank goodness for cell-phone address books!

The limited capacity of immediate memory most often is assessed through **memory span,** the longest string of information (e.g., numbers, letters) that a person can immediately recall. A legion of research findings using this task confirm what Miller originally proposed: we have a fundamental limit in our ability to keep track of incoming information (e.g., Baddeley, 1993; Shiffrin & Nosofsky, 1994). Nairne (1996) likens the limited capacity of immediate memory to the capacity of a juggler. Just as a juggler can keep only so many balls in the air at a time, our immediate memory can keep only so much information "in the air" at a time. Miller puts the limit at 7 ± 2 items. Now the question is, what exactly constitutes an item?

Chunking.   It turns out that our immediate memory is considerably more powerful than the magic number would imply. Although there is no doubt that there is a limit to memory span, we can functionally increase the limits by recoding information, combining it into larger and larger "chunks." Through this process, called **chunking** or **recoding,** you translate incoming information into a more manageable form. The capacity limits of immediate memory never get beyond the magic number, but with efficient use of recoding strategies, we can functionally increase the capacity. In the juggling analogy of immediate memory, we can think of this as being able to juggle seven large balls or seven small balls, but seven is all that can be juggled. And according to Cowan (2001), it's not even really seven. He contends that Miller's "magic number" mainly was meant to be a rough estimate, almost a rhetorical device to describe the capacity limit of immediate memory (which, by the way, does fit with the folksy manner in which Miller lays out his argument). Cowan's thorough review of the immediate memory literature post-Miller suggests that the limit is actually about four chunks of information, with a chunk defined as ". . . a collection of concepts that have strong associations to one another and much weaker connections to other information currently in use" (p. 89). Cowan terms this limit the focus of attention. More recently, some (e.g., McElree, 2001; Verhaeghen & Basak, 2005) have even made the claim that only one or two items can be held in immediate memory! We'll return to this debate a bit later in the context of the various theoretical views of immediate memory. But for now, suffice it to say that immediate memory is limited.

Regardless of how one conceives of the limits in immediate memory, chunking functionally increases its capacity but the process of chunking also has limitations. First, the rate of presentation can be a limiting factor. For instance, when someone tells you a phone number too quickly, with no pauses, you have a difficult time chunking the number. Chunking also is affected profoundly by *knowledge base.* When you're taking notes based on a professor's lecture, you are recoding the information. This ability is enhanced the more you know about the topic; previous knowledge aids your reorganization of the information. (That's why it helps to read the material from the textbook before you come to class!)

Coding

How is information typically coded in immediate memory? When you're listening to something, whether it's a phone number or an important fact from class discussion, how do you keep track of it in consciousness? Your answer is almost certainly that you repeat it to yourself. A great deal of research indicates that *auditory coding* is the dominant mode of processing in immediate memory. That is, we "hear" information as it is being rehearsed via a sort of "inner voice." In addition, it's easy to show that we have an inner eye as well. Close your eyes, and imagine the front of your house and count the number of windows. Chances are you found that pretty easy to do. The ears and eyes of immediate memory dovetail nicely in most everyday circumstances.

This dovetailing was demonstrated in a study by Brooks (1968), who was interested in the use of verbal and visual/spatial processing during recall from immediate memory. His experiments manipulated the mode by which information would be coded. One of the tasks relied primarily on visual/spatial processing. He had participants hold a block letter F in mind and scan it to determine whether each corner was at the extreme top or bottom.

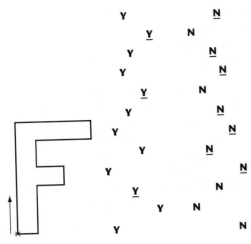

Figure 4.3
Stimulus (left) and response sheet (right) for visual/spatial mode in Brooks (1968).

Look at the F in left panel of Figure 4.3. If one starts scanning at the point of the asterisk, the correct sequence would be "yes, yes, no, no, no, no, no, no, yes, yes." (Your author had a dreadful time coming up with that, by the way.) The other condition relied primarily on the verbal processing. In this condition, participants had to hold a sentence in mind and indicate whether each word was a noun or not. One sentence was "A bird in the hand is not in the bush" so the correct series of responses would be "no, yes, no, no, yes, no, no, no, no, yes."

Brooks (1968) also manipulated the mode by which the participants responded "yes" and "no." One mode was verbal; participants simply said "yes" and "no" as appropriate. The other mode was visual/spatial; participants answered by pointing to a sheet of paper that had a Y and N corresponding to each word or corner to which the participant had to respond (see right panel of Figure 4.3). At each decision point, they were to point to the appropriate "Y" or "N." The coding mode was completely crossed with the responding mode, leading to 4 conditions: verbal coding with visual/spatial responding, visual/spatial coding with verbal responding, verbal coding with verbal responding, or visual/spatial coding with visual/spatial responding. The dependent variable was the time it took to finish the sequence of responses. Brooks was interested in the conditions under which participants could and could not perform the tasks together.

Performing each task in isolation was ridiculously easy, but in combination, some interesting results emerge. Take a look at Table 4.1. As you can see, there is a dramatic interaction between task and response mode. When participants were required to scan a visual image of the block letter F (visual/spatial coding task), they had a much easier time saying yes and no (verbal response mode) rather than pointing to Y's or N's (visual/spatial response mode). Now you might speculate that this is because pointing to Y's and N's on a piece of paper is an unfamiliar and therefore difficult task. But look at the visual/spatial mode of responding in the context of the verbal coding task (sentence); the visual/spatial response mode turns out to be much *easier* than the verbal response mode. Brooks had revealed two critical characteristics of immediate memory. First, it can operate via both verbal and visual/spatial codes. Second, it's considerably easier to

Table 4.1 Response time (seconds) for participants in the Brooks study as a function of response mode and stimulus type

		Task Mode	
		Verbal (Sentence)	Spatial (Block Letter F)
Response Mode	Verbal (speaking)	28.2	11.3
	Spatial (pointing)	9.8	13.8

combine two tasks that use different modes than it is to combine two tasks that share the same mode. We'll discuss these modes of processing in more detail later in the chapter.

Stop&*Review*

1. What limit in immediate memory is revealed by the Brown-Peterson task?
2. What is "the magic number" and to what does it refer?
3. True or false? Visual-spatial coding is the dominant mode of processing in immediate memory.

- The Brown-Peterson task requires people to hold information in mind for some time. During the retention interval, distraction is introduced, and information is lost relatively quickly, revealing the limited duration of immediate memory.

- Limits in the capacity of immediate memory are evidenced through memory span, the longest string of information that a person can immediately recall. These limits are often described with Miller's "magic number 7+ 2," but are actually probably more constrained to 3 or 4 chunks of information. These chunks occupy the focus of attention. Chunking can stretch the functional limits of immediate memory. This ability relates to characteristics of presentation (e.g., speed), and knowledge base.

- Auditory coding is the dominant mode of processing in immediate memory; we "hear" information as it is being processed in immediate memory. Coding can also be visual-spatial. These two forms of coding tend not to interfere with one another.

Theoretical Frameworks for Immediate Memory

Since the opening shots of the cognitive revolution, immediate memory has been a central topic of investigation. A PsycINFO search of research abstracts since 1960 for the terms short-term memory and working memory (the terms most often used to describe immediate memory) reveals over 17,000 investigations! These models have tried to account for the characteristics just discussed and along the way discovered refinements and extensions for each of them. Most of that work has been motivated by two theoretical frameworks: Atkinson-Shiffrin's modal model of memory and Baddeley's working memory model. However, the most recent work eschews the need for the notion of a designated set of processes called immediate memory, instead claiming that immediate memory is just an active part of long term memory that is currently the focus of attention. We'll begin by discussing the two standard models of immediate memory.

The Modal Model

Waugh and Norman (1965) and Atkinson and Shiffrin (1968) formalized and popularized the distinction between a transient, momentarily activated memory store and a permanent form of storage. The Atkinson-Shiffrin view has been so influential that it is often termed the **modal model.** The model is clearly in the tradition of information-processing, postulating a series of chronologically arranged stages (sensory memory, short-term memory and long-term memory) through which incoming information passes. Although current researchers do not espouse this stage-like progression or the idea of three distinct memory stores, at a descriptive level, the model provides an extremely useful way to characterize different types of memory processing.

Three Memory Systems.   Atkinson and Shiffrin (1968) propose three different types of memory storage: sensory memory, short-term memory, and long-term memory. As originally conceptualized, **sensory memory** serves as an initial storage system and refers to an extremely brief representation of a just-presented stimulus. Although some type of sensory memory is thought to exist for all major senses, it's easiest to imagine in the context of vision; Atkinson and Shiffrin label this quickly fleeting form of visual storage "iconic memory." The notion of an icon is evident when viewing a scene during a lightning flash. Although the flash lasts only about 50 ms, the scene illuminated by the flash seems to be visible for much longer. In the laboratory, this phenomenon was demonstrated by very briefly presenting a stimulus array to participants and having them report as many letters as possible. The results of these studies indicated that when presented with a stimulus array, the entire array remained available for about 1/4 of a second (a la the lightning flash). Basically, for that brief period, participants could "read off" any part of the array, as if they were looking at an "icon" that displayed the items. However, the icon was found to fade almost instantly.

The notion of a rapidly decaying iconic memory store has become a bit outmoded in the eyes of many researchers (e.g., Massaro & Loftus, 1996; Nairne, 2002b). Rather than viewing iconic memory as a passive buffer or "box" that holds information for a brief time, iconic memory is usually conceived of as a phenomenon of **visual persistence** that results from the way the visual system processes stimuli over the course of time. Put another way, the *decaying icon* is simply a by-product of the way our neural system processes visual information. For example, when a visual stimulus is presented, the presentation begins a neural response that lasts for a few hundred milliseconds. If the stimulus is removed immediately after presentation (as it is in many studies of iconic memory), the neural response will continue to its natural end; this continuation is experienced as the fading icon.

The centerpiece of the modal model has proven to be the other two memory stores and the postulated distinction between them. **Long-term memory (LTM)** can be conceptualized as a vast repository that houses all of the experiences, knowledge, and skills that we have accumulated throughout our lifetime. (Keep in mind that this simple spatial metaphor is only a convenient description of LTM and fails to capture anything about LTM storage on a physiological level.) We'll address issues of LTM in more depth in Chapters 6 through 8.

So what lies between the transient sensory buffer and the long-term storage of everything we know? Atkinson and Shiffrin proposed a processing store termed **short-term memory (STM),** which is their version of the processes we've been discussing thus far in the chapter. However, their concept of immediate memory was narrowly proscribed as a limited-capacity holding buffer for information currently being processed.

This *temporary* form of memory can be conceptualized as a sort of mental workbench in which we rehearse or recycle information. Information can flow back and forth between STM and LTM meaning that rehearsal in STM is thought to result in LTM storage. And when information in LTM is appropriate for dealing with present circumstances, it is brought back into STM.

Evidence for a STM-LTM Distinction.   Back in the old days of the information-processing approach, there seemed to be solid, if not overwhelming evidence for distinguishing between STM and LTM. Consider the **serial position effect,** which is really the combination of two different effects: especially good memory for the first few items (i.e., **primacy effect**) and the last few items (i.e., **recency effect**) of a just-presented list (Glanzer & Cunitz, 1996). The standard explanation for this effect relies on a distinction between an immediate memory store (i.e., STM) and a remote memory store (i.e., LTM). Items that occur at the end of a list are assumed to be active in STM as the recall cue is given. Consequently, these items are directly "dumped" from STM leading to high levels of recall. Items that occurred early in a list are the beneficiaries of increased rehearsal. The first few items will receive more rehearsal than other items on the list, leading to storage in LTM. Consequently, the items will be well recalled.

This account is bolstered by the results of a study by Glanzer and Cunitz (1996) in which they delayed the presentation of the cue to recall by 0 seconds, 10 seconds, or 30 seconds. Delaying the recall cue robbed the participant of the benefits of recency. At the 10 second delay, the recall advantage enjoyed by recent items was weakened, and by 30 seconds, it was completely gone. The primacy effect was untouched. This supports the distinction just described. The last items on the list are stored in short-term memory. As time passes, they fade—leading to low levels of recall at long delays (i.e., a recency effect is not observed). However, this delay has no effect on retention of the first items, which have already received their rehearsal, and are now represented in long-term memory.

Glanzer and Cunitz also varied the spacing between presented items. This manipulation should enhance the primacy effect but not the recency effect. Why is this the case? Additional spacing between items provides more time for rehearsal and storage in LTM. It shouldn't have much impact later on items, given that the last few items are in STM at the time of recall. Consistent with this prediction, item spacing enhanced the primacy effect but did not change the recency effect.

Another early source of evidence for separate STM and LTM stores came from the study of amnesics, most notably H.M. and K.F. Consider the case of H.M. (e.g., Corkin, 1968), quite possibly the most famous amnesic of them all. He passed away in 2009 after graciously allowing researchers to probe his memory for over 50 years and left his brain for them to dissect after his death! H.M. exhibited normal STM functioning; he could hold information in consciousness, and keep track of things like phone numbers or the last thing said in a conversation. But his long-term memory for events since the onset of his amnesia was extremely poor. He had great difficulty forming new memories (we'll discuss amnesia and LTM further in Chapter 6). The case of H.M. contrasts sharply with that of K.F., another renowned amnesic (e.g., Shallice & Warrington, 1974; Warrington & Shallice, 1972). His situation is one that is fascinatingly rare; his long-term retention of information was normal, yet his memory span, an indicator of STM capacity, was gravely impaired. The results from studies of H.M and K.F., considered together, represent a double dissociation. A double dissociation occurs when one pattern of (in this case) brain damage is associated with deficits in task A and preserved function in task B, and another pattern of damage is associated with deficits in task B and preserved function in task A. This is a potent indicator that A and B are apples and oranges, that is, the product of separate systems (in this case STM and LTM).

But as is often the case in scientific research, the picture isn't quite so simple. As you'll see in Chapter 6, H.M.'s inability to retain new information was not complete. And K.F.'s poor short-term retention was interestingly selective. Although he could not keep track of auditorily presented verbal information (e.g., word or digit lists), he could retain nonlanguage sounds like birds chirping or phones ringing. This selective deficit led to more complex multicomponent views of immediate memory which we'll be discussing next.

The Working Memory Model

Based on years of research demonstrating the richness and variety of processing in immediate memory, investigators have proposed increasingly elaborate models of its function. The most widely influential one is Baddeley's **working memory model** (WM) (Baddeley, 1986, 2000, 2007; Hitch & Baddeley, 1976). The model captured researchers' fancy to such a degree that working memory is how many psychologists refer to the collective set of processes we've been discussing. Baddeley's model has served as an extremely useful descriptive guide for organizing and explaining much of what researchers have found about the duration, capacity limitations, and coding mechanisms in immediate memory. And although recent research has challenged the status of the model, it has pretty much defined the study of immediate memory processing, and we'll use it as a descriptive framework to organize much of the research we discuss in this chapter.

The working memory model is certainly a more complete account of immediate memory processing than proposed in the modal model, which characterized immediate memory as a relatively static holding place for information. According to the working memory model, immediate memory is actually a number of closely interacting subsystems that combine to subserve a host of higher-level mental processes, including language comprehension, problem solving, and reasoning. Two of the subsystems incorporate notions of verbal (phonological loop) and visual-spatial (visuo-spatial sketchpad) coding demonstrated by the Brooks (1968) study mentioned earlier. Another subsystem serves as a "go-between" that allows for the integration among the phonological loop and the visuo-spatial sketchpad and long-term memory (episodic buffer). The keystone of the working memory model is what Baddely terms the central executive, which serves as the "boss," supervising the operation of the other subsystems and carrying out important duties of its own. Let's take a closer look at the processes that comprise immediate memory, according to Baddeley's model.

The Phonological Loop.   In order to work with information in our current awareness, we need to be able to hold and manipulate it in some type of active form.

According to the working memory model, this is partially accomplished by a set of processes called the **phonological loop.** The name gives you some idea of its function and operation. Phonological implies that we are using the aforementioned inner voice to "hear" the information internally. The notion of a *loop* implies the repetitive recycling function of immediate memory proposed in the original modal model. In the block letter F/sentence study by Brooks (1968), this component of working memory was used to read the sentence and indicate if each word was a noun or not. And as demonstrated in that study, this component has its limits. Using it to (a) think about the words in a sentence and (b) verbally indicate if each word is a noun or not proved to be pretty difficult. Similar overloads can occur for the visual-spatial component of working memory as well. But for now, let's take a closer look at verbal processing in working memory.

The phonological loop is the most investigated aspect of Baddeley's model. In fact, Buchsbaum and D'Esposito (2008) refer to it as "the most studied 'box' in the history of cognitive psychology" (p. 762). The model proposes two subcomponents of the phonological loop. The *phonological store* holds information temporarily and as such represents the time-limited nature of immediate memory. Therefore, information in the phonological store will be lost if not rehearsed. The second component, the *subvocal rehearsal mechanism* is responsible for this rehearsal. According to the model, coding with the phonological loop is obligatory (i.e., it must happen). As a result, even visually presented information is quickly converted into a form that that can be processed by the phonological loop (i.e., a verbal form).

The Effect of Phonological Interference.

One piece of experimental evidence supporting the phonological loop is the **irrelevant speech effect** (e.g., Salame & Baddeley, 1982). The effect is simple but powerful. Any spoken stimulus presented during the processing of information has the potential to disrupt memory for that information, even if the spoken stimulus is irrelevant and participants are told to ignore it. Because coding by the phonological loop is obligatory, all information, relevant and irrelevant, will be processed. However, irrelevant information will be an unwelcome visitor in the phonological store, making it more difficult to process the relevant information. Irrelevant speech also disrupts the processing of visually presented information. This is because visual information is quickly converted into a verbal form and is ultimately processed by the phonological loop. Given that this effect is found for verbal as well as visual information, the effect might be more appropriately called the irrelevant information effect.

Regardless of the effect's label, it has serious implications for how you study. Think about the television or iPod you have on while you're studying. You might be under the impression that it helps you concentrate, or at the very least, doesn't hurt. After all, you would argue that the information (e.g., the words spoken by the actors or sung by singers) is irrelevant to the content you're studying. Well now you know that this irrelevance is, well, ... irrelevant. A study by Alley and Greene (2008) provides empirical support for our recommendation to turn off the TV or iPod before reading any further. The authors compared digit spans for college students in a variety of distraction conditions. Participants attempted to keep track of a series of digits while being simultaneously presented with vocal music, nonvocal music (the karaoke

Reality Check

version of the vocal condition), speech, and silence. The results indicated that the silence condition was associated with better digit spans than the speech and vocal music conditions. However, digit span was the same in the silence and nonvocal music conditions. So listening to classical music is OK? Unfortunately, the answer is no. In Chapter 6, we'll discuss a reason why even listening to nonvocal music can be detrimental to your studying. Until then....when you're studying, you're probably better off heeding the old adage, "silence is golden."

Stop&*Think Back* | IRRELEVANT STUDYING?

Most students study with background noise—TV, music, roommates, the ambient white noise of the library or coffee shop—and they think they're doing just fine in spite of it. To what theory of attention are they implicitly subscribing? Can their experience be reconciled with the irrelevant speech effect? Which theory of attention in Chapter 3 would be most consistent with this effect? What differences do you think there may be between the research that demonstrates negative effects of irrelevant noise, and your own experiences?

Research Theme
Metacognition

Your metacognitive processing (your "thinking about thinking") might tell you that you're the exception to the rule...that you study just fine with music playing in the background or through your headphones. If so, you're probably mistaken. Alley and Greene also found that people were relatively poor judges of which background stimuli were more or less distracting; their estimates did not reflect the reality evident in their performance. So don't trust the self-assessment of your abilities; it's not a good indicator. Trust the empirical evidence and turn off your music!

The Effect of Word Length.   Since Miller's (1956) original formulation of the magic number, research has demonstrated that this number may not be as "magical" as was first thought. Immediate memory span seems to be limited not necessarily by the number of items being encoded but by the time it takes to encode them. Consider again the old-fashioned audio tape analogy: the amount of information that will fit on a tape is not only determined by the capacity of the tape, but also by how fast you talk. (The faster you talk, the more information you can get on the tape.) Similarly, retaining 7 ± 2 long items (e.g., *hippopotamus*) in immediate memory proves to be much more difficult than retaining 7 ± 2 short items (e.g., *cat*). This **word-length effect** is a consistent finding in studies of immediate memory (e.g., Baddeley, Thompson, & Buchanan, 1975; Schweickert, McDaniel, & Riegler, 1993). Remember the phonological store is time limited and information will be lost if it is not rehearsed. Given that long words take longer to pronounce than shorter ones, the subvocal rehearsal mechanism cannot rehearse the information quickly enough to maintain it in the phonological store. So the information fades away. Short words, on the other hand, can be rehearsed at a rate that allows them to be maintained in the phonological store. This differential rate of rehearsal is responsible for the word length effect.

The Effect of Phonological Similarity.   The **phonological similarity effect** refers to the finding that lists of similar-sounding items are more difficult to keep track of in immediate memory than lists of different-sounding items. This basic effect has been replicated many times (e.g., Baddeley, 1966; Conrad, 1964; Schiano & Watkins, 1981). It even occurs when material is presented visually, further supporting the obligatory nature of phonological coding. Similar-sounding words share phonemic (speech sound) features; therefore, similar sounding words sound similar because similar motor movements are required to articulate them. The term, phonological similarity effect, implies that the critical factor is sound; however, the real issue is articulation. Therefore, it might be more appropriate to call this effect the similar articulatory features effect. Regardless of how we label it, the existence of this effect indicates that the phonological loop relies on the way in which we articulate information. When the items share similar articulatory features, they are likely to get confused when held in the phonological store.

Stop&*Think* | SPANNING IMMEDIATE MEMORY LIMITS

Present the following lists of items to some of your friends, and ask them (after each list) to recall as many items from the list as possible. A variation would be to change presentation rate (e.g., 1 item per second, 2 items per second, etc.). Ask your participants to tell you the strategies they used to keep the items in mind.

  cake, lake, bake, sake, take, make, rake
  ham, dog, gem, skill, heart, bag, ring, jaw

mystery, vanilla, bicycle, pyramid, condiment, television, automobile

- How did the type of item you presented influence the participants' memory span? Why do you think the type of item had an influence?

- How did changing the rate of presentation impact performance? Did the effect of rate interact with the type of list?

The Effect of Articulatory Suppression.   Given that articulation is the critical factor in the operation of the phonological loop, what would happen if we prevent a person from articulating the information they are attempting to rehearse? When you were a child (or maybe even as an adult!) did you ever say "la la la…" when you didn't want to hear what someone was saying? Well, it turns out this rather childish form of self-distraction is a favorite task of working memory researchers, who term it **articulatory suppression.** The task is designed to prevent a person from using articulation mechanisms to rehearse information by tying up their the subvocal rehearsal mechanism with a silly task (saying, "la, la, la,…). Therefore, the information decays and is lost from the phonological store. As you might expect, this makes the retention of information much more difficult, decreasing memory span (Murray, 1968).

Recall that visually presented stimuli (e.g., printed words or nameable pictures) seem to be quickly translated into a verbal form (Posner & Keele, 1967) and therefore are subject to the negative effects of phonological similarity. However, something interesting happens when you introduce articulatory suppression during the encoding of visually presented items: there is no negative effect of phonological similarity (e.g., Coltheart, 1993; Murray, 1968). It makes sense if you think about it. Seeing a picture of a tiger will lead you to silently rehearse "tiger" using the subvocal rehearsal mechanism which activates a verbal representation of a tiger in the phonological store. But this can't happen if the subvocal rehearsal mechanism is tied up doing the silly "la, a, la" task. Consequently, these words must be maintained using another store (possibly, the visuo-spatial sketchpad we'll talk about a little later). Given that the items are not in the phonological store, the similar articulatory features are not a problem and the typical phonological similarity effect is not found.

Articulatory suppression leads to a similar result for the word-length effect (e.g., Baddeley, Lewis, & Vallar, 1984). An articulatory suppression task prevents rehearsal. Without rehearsal, items are rapidly lost from the phonological store. The word-length effect results from long words taking longer to pronounce and subsequently rehearse than short words. If the words aren't being rehearsed, then long words and short words will decay from the phonological store at the same rate, hence eliminating the word length effect.

The Phonological Loop in the Deaf: An Oxymoron?   The label "phonological loop" implies that working memory is based on sound. But based on the previous discussion you know this is misleading. When the model was first introduced, this may have been a reasonable conclusion because the participants used speech to communicate and so this was the basis for storage in the phonological loop. It didn't take people long to realize that this conclusion was erroneous as it would seem to suggest that speech is necessary for working memory processing. But a moment's consideration tells us that can't be true. Deaf individuals are obviously capable of processing information in immediate memory. Therefore, the mechanism by which the phonological loop operates is more general than the processing of sound (i.e., speech). As indicated earlier, the mechanism is articulation, the coordination of the various motor movements used to produce the basic units of an individual's communication system.

Hearing individuals use speech to communicate, so items in the phonological store include speech-related motor movements (i.e., articulatory) features. When items in the phonological store share these features, we find a phonological similarity effect. So what should we find for deaf individuals? The basic unit of their communication system (American Sign Language—ASL) is hand movements and gestures. Given that the determining factor in obtaining the phonological similarity effect is the sharing of articulatory features, we should expect to obtain an analogous finding for users of ASL in their articulatory mode—namely, signing. In other words, deaf signers of ASL should show a sign-based similarity effect. Similar-looking signs should be more difficult to keep track of than different-looking signs, because similar-looking signs share similar motor movements. This has been found by several investigators (e.g., Beluggi, Klima, & Siple, 1974; Hanson, 1982; Wilson & Emmorey, 1997); signs that share the same hand movements are more difficult for deaf signers to retain in immediate memory than are signs that vary in hand movements.

Second, one would expect to find a word-length effect; long signs should be just as difficult for deaf signers to keep straight as long words are for hearing speakers. To test this idea, Wilson and Emmorey (1998) presented deaf users of ASL with signs that varied in terms of movement features. Long signs featured movements that were large and circular, covered distance, or featured a change in direction; short signs involved short

All uses of language—including American Sign Language—involve the articulatory loop.

movements, with no change of direction. Importantly, the long and short signs were matched for other features, such as the hand shapes used. The signs were filmed and presented to participants via videotape. At the end of each sign sequence, a probe sign was presented that signaled participants to recall the list. The researchers did find a word-length effect for sign language. Signs involving distance, changes in direction, or large circular motions were difficult to remember (i.e., memory span was less for long signs than short signs). But would articulatory suppression make this effect go away, as it does for hearing individuals? And what would articulatory suppression *look* like in ASL?

Wilson and Emmorey (1998) looked at the effects of suppression in a second condition of their study. To do this, half of the participants engaged in an articulatory suppression task. These participants were required to touch their middle fingers to their respective thumbs (the ASL sign for "8") while at the same time having their hands circle one another, with contact at the end of each circle (this is the sign for "world"). Just as saying "La, la, la" prevents a hearing person from using the "inner voice" to vocally rehearse, making hand motions should prevent a deaf person from using what might be termed the "inner hands" to manually rehearse. Wilson and Emmorey found that articulatory suppression not only disrupted immediate memory performance overall, it also eliminated the effects of sign length. And interestingly, an earlier study by Wilson and Emmorey (1997) produced the corresponding finding: articulatory suppression eliminated the sign-based similarity effect. So whether you're dealing with the spoken word or ASL hand movements, it's pretty clear that the articulatory features of words are represented in the phonological store. But these articulatory features are based on one's customary language and developmental experience (Wilson & Emmorey, 1998), which is not necessarily auditory as implied by the term "phonological."

However, some work does suggest a difference between signed working memory and spoken working memory, specifically in their capacity. A number of studies, reviewed by Emmorey (2002) reveal a smaller capacity (measured by memory span) for native signers of ASL relative to native speakers of English. One explanation attributes the difference in capacity to the fact that it takes more time to sign the average word than it does to say it; consequently, memory span is smaller in signers than speakers. Remember, the phonological store is time-limited. As mentioned earlier, the longer it takes to *pronounce* a word, the fewer of them can be maintained because the subvocal rehearsal mechanism cannot rehearse them fast enough to prevent them from decaying from the phonological store.

Wilson and Emmorey (2006) put this explanation to the empirical test to determine if the signed-spoken difference in memory span is "real" or just an artifact of length. They controlled the length of the items by using a sequence of letters that in ASL would take about the same amount of time to articulate as in spoken English. With these stimuli, memory span for signers and speakers was equivalent. This suggests that the time-limited nature of the phonological store is universal. It is important to note that the ramifications of this capacity difference for everyday communication are minimal, because sign language conveys information in a simultaneous fashion. But in the serial recall situation characteristic of memory span tasks, the extra time to sign greatly affects span.

The Phonological Store Reconsidered.   As previously mentioned, Baddeley's model postulates that the phonological store is simply the passive holding buffer for words being processed by the phonological loop. Therefore, factors not related to articulation (i.e., meaning) should not affect how information is stored. In order to test this idea, Acheson, Postle, and MacDonald (2010) investigated the possible interactive effects of phonological similarity and the semantic (i.e., meaning-based) aspects of encoded words. Acheson et al. decided to test this by manipulating a semantic property of incoming words—their concreteness, which refers to how easily they are to imagine (*giraffe* is higher in concreteness than *honesty*). A well-established finding in the memory literature is that concrete words are recalled better than abstract words. The researchers presented participants with short lists of words in four conditions: phonologically similar and concrete (e.g., flag and bag), phonologically similar and abstract (e.g., brag and nag), phonologically dissimilar and concrete (e.g., kite and frog), and phonologically dissimilar and abstract (sour and fund). The dependent variable was memory span.

Two completely unsurprising main effects were found. Memory span was greater for phonologically dissimilar words than phonologically similar words, replicating scores of earlier studies revealing the phonological similarity effect. In addition, memory span was greater for concrete words than abstract words (another well-established finding in the memory literature). The interesting finding was an interaction between the two variables. Interestingly, the effect of concreteness interacted with the effects of phonological similarity. The phonological similarity effect was larger for concrete words than abstract ones. Put another way, phonological similarity disrupted the storage (as measured by memory span) of concrete words to a greater extent than abstract words. This indicates that not only are articulatory features represented in the phonological store, the phonological store is more than phonological. More recent research on the nature of the phonological store has led some researchers (e.g., Buchsbaum & D'Esposito, 2008; Jones, Macken, & Nicholls, 2004; Jones, Hughes, & Mackin, 2007) to abandon the concept completely. The nature of this argument is beyond the scope of this text but suffice it to say that many believe that phonological store (a) is not phonological and (b) is not a store at all because it doesn't really have phonological (articulatory or speech-based) characteristics.

The Visuo-Spatial Sketchpad.   The nature of the code (phonological, articulatory, or neither) does not negate the observation that information is coded in some type of "verbal" code. The findings of the Brooks (1968) block letter F/sentence study revealed that information also can be processed visually/spatially. Based on these findings, Baddeley's model proposes a second subsystem, termed the **visuo-spatial sketchpad,** which is responsible for the storage and manipulation of visual and spatial information. This subsystem seems to operate (in large part) independently of the other subsystem (the phonological loop). In other words, the two systems do not interfere with one another. Recall this was the conclusion from the Brooks (1968) study; a double dissociation was found for visual and verbal tasks. The verbal response mode (saying yes/no) interfered with the verbal task (sentence) but not

the visual/spatial task (block letter F) while the visual/spatial response mode (pointing) interfered with the visual/spatial task but not the verbal task. As you may remember from Chapter 1, a double dissociation is considered to be evidence that the two tasks rely on different underlying mechanisms. Therefore, Baddeley proposed two separate systems (i.e., the phonological loop and the visuo-spatial sketchpad), each responsible for processing one type of information.

Some evidence indicates a further division of duties within the visuo-spatial sketchpad. Della Sala, Gray, Baddeley, Allamano, and Wilson (1999) propose separable components corresponding to *spatial* processing and *visual* processing. To see the difference, take a look at the tasks used by Della Sala et al. to assess each subcomponent. Figure 4.4a presents the visual processing task (VPT); Figure 4.4b presents the spatial processing task (SPT). For the VPT, participants are presented with a visual matrix—a checkerboard pattern with randomly alternating black and white squares. After a three-second presentation, participants must replicate the pattern by filling in squares in a blank matrix. The SPT is called the *Corsi blocks test.* The participants watch the experimenter tap out a pattern on wood blocks. Once the pattern has been tapped out, the participant has to replicate it. Like the VPT, this SPT is visual, but it ups the ante by adding the requirement of

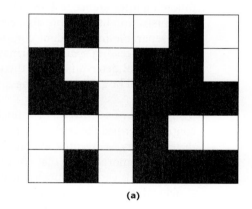

(a)

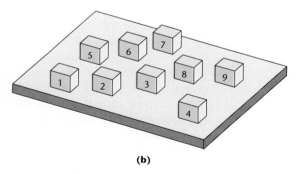

(b)

Figure 4.4

Tasks used by Della Sala et al. (1999) to assess processing of the visuo-spatial sketchpad. The figure in (a) depicts the visual processing task; the figure in (b) depicts the spatial processing task.

remembering a positional sequence. Whereas the VPT requires only memory for the appearance of a matrix, the SPT requires that participants mentally reason about distance, direction, and order. Della Sala et al. tested the notion of separate visual and spatial processes by using an interference paradigm. On noninterference trials, participants were presented with a visual or a spatial pattern and were tested on the pattern after an unfilled 10-second interval. On interference trials, the 10-second interval was filled with an interference task. On half of these interference trials, the participants had to view irrelevant pictures before reconstructing the visual matrix. This task was primarily thought to involve visual processing, and was expected to interfere primarily with the VPT. On the other half of the interference trials, participants had to reach under a screen and haptically (i.e., by touch) follow a sequence of pegs. This task was primarily thought to involve spatial processing, and was expected to interfere primarily with the SPT.

The data revealed a double dissociation. Performance on the VPT was disrupted much more by the picture-viewing interference task than it was by the peg-following task. The converse was true of the SPT, which was disrupted much more by the peg-following interference task than by the picture-viewing task. Once again, the empirical demonstration of a double dissociation led to the conclusion that the model needed to have separable independent components, one for processing visual information and one for processing spatial information. The empirical demonstration of dissociations was a critical determinant for the model's structure. As you'll see later in the chapter, this also will be a critical finding demonstrating its limitations.

The Central Executive. The linchpin component of Baddeley's WM model is a central controller, termed the **central executive.** At the opening of the chapter, we discussed immediate memory as executive attention. Baddeley's central executive is the component of the working memory model that corresponds to this particular function. When a particular task demands extensive involvement of either the phonological loop or the visuo-spatial sketchpad, the central executive deploys the necessary resources. The central executive is also thought to be responsible for the higher-level thought processes involved in reasoning and language comprehension. Because the capacity of the attentional system is limited, the central executive has only so much to give; if a task is too demanding, the central executive's resources will be drained, and complex thinking will suffer. Once again, let's consider the Brooks (1968) study. In one condition, the participants were required to scan an imaginary block letter F and decide if each corner was an extreme one or not by saying yes or no. The central executive would be responsible for comprehending the instructions (knowing what F and "extreme corner" mean), initiating the task, deciding when the task was done, and a responding appropriately. It also would be responsible for monitoring the two subsystems needed to complete the task: the phonological loop, which is used to respond "yes" and "no" and the visual-spatial sketchpad that is holding the block letter F in mind.

In sum, the central executive of the working memory model is in charge of all tasks thought to involve executive control. If this description sounds a bit vague, many researchers would agree! In fact, Baddeley himself (Baddeley, 1986) once referred to the concept as something of a "conceptual ragbag"; every function that isn't articulatory, visual, or spatial, gets thrown into it. It serves as little more than a place-holder term for "everything else." Another potential problem with the central executive is that it represents what some critics term a homunculus or "little person in the head" that plagues many theories of cognition. Postulating a central process (i.e., a little man in the head) that essentially runs the show is really no explanation at all.

The homunculus

Recently, Baddeley (1996; 2002) proposed the *fractionation* of the central executive into functions that include (Bunge & Souza, 2009) selective attention, manipulation of information currently in working memory, task switching, and response inhibition. Hester and Garavan (2005) investigated the possible role of the central executive in two of these attention-controlling functions: task switching (Experiment 1) and response inhibition (Experiment 2). In Experiment 1 participants performed a primary task in which they held a series of letters in mind (i.e., the *memory set*), and decided whether a presented letter was a member of the memory set. Occasionally, they were presented a letter in color; in these cases, they were required to *switch tasks*. Instead of making the memory set decision, they were required to determine whether the colored letter was a consonant or a vowel. Imagine yourself in this study; a letter in the memory set appears, and you're set to respond "yes," that it's in the memory set but then you realize it's in color, so you have to switch tasks and make a consonant-vowel decision. Working memory load was manipulated by increasing memory set size (i.e., how many items had to be held in mind).

The results were consistent with the notion that task switching involves executive function. Increasing memory load made it more difficult to switch tasks. The switching cost—the extra time it took to change gears from a memory set decision to a consonant-vowel decision—increased as memory load increased. The results demonstrate that the contents of working memory influence the ability of the central executive to control attention; the more information that is being held, the harder it is to switch attention to another task.

Experiment 2 investigated the role of the central executive in another attention-controlling function: inhibition. The experiment employed a paradigm commonly used to measure inhibition, termed a go-no go task. As in Experiment 1, participants held a memory set in mind, and were asked to respond only when they saw a distractor item (termed *go* trials). In other words, if a target from the memory set appeared, they were to *inhibit a response* and do nothing (termed *no-go* trials). The task was made especially difficult by having 55 of the 60 trials be *go* trials in which a distractor was presented. That created an especially strong tendency to respond and made it extremely difficult to withhold a response on *no-go* (memory set) trials. So response inhibition presented a particular challenge. The results indicated that the ability to inhibit responding decreased as the memory load increased; in other words, the more occupied the central executive was, the less able it was to inhibit a response.

The Working Memory Model Reconsidered.   Baddeley's approach is not without its problems. One of them is the vague specification of the central executive just discussed. Neath (2000) summarizes a number of other problems with this model. One criticism is that the label "working memory" is somewhat misleading. As you just read, what working memory is (supposedly) all about is the executive control of attention; this is the centerpiece of the theory. So, working memory isn't really about memory; it's about attention. The term "working attention" might therefore be more apt (Kintsch, 1998).

A related problem is the mechanism proposed to account for the forgetting that occurs in working memory. Baddeley's model is a "rehearsal and decay" model that emphasizes the importance of activation in maintaining information in the face of decay. But, as you'll see in our later discussion of forgetting, decay is not an explanation for memory loss. It's simply a restatement of the phenomenon: information is lost. As Neath (2000) points out, Baddeley's model fails to specify exactly what is lost and doesn't specify the mechanisms whereby it's lost.

Another problem with the model is that it focuses on sensory (i.e., visual and auditory) processing of incoming information, but is mute on the concept of meaning. As you saw in the discussion of research on the phonological store, immediate memory is sensitive to the meaning of encoded information. Obviously, then, contact with long-term memory occurs in working memory. The **episodic buffer** was added to provide for a mechanism of contact between working memory and long-term memory, but the mechanism is vaguely specified. This concept was not in the original model, and given its recent foray into theory, the jury is still out on how well the episodic buffer accounts for the interaction among the memory systems.

In reviewing the literature on working memory, one thing is crystal-clear. Baddeley's multicomponent view has ruled the day, and has just about single-handedly framed many of the 17,000 research investigations of immediate memory mentioned at the beginning of the chapter. As alluded to earlier, Baddeley's working memory model appears to be suffering a fate similar to the information-processing approach, discussed in Chapter 1. You'll recall that even though the information-processing approach proved extremely useful as a descriptive heuristic for cognitive processes in general, subsequent research made it clear that it falls short as a complete theoretical account of cognitive processes and their origins in brain activity. In much the same way, Baddeley's model seems to have lost the theoretical foothold that it has held for some 30 years, as more recent approaches and neuroscientific evidence have combined to challenge the assumptions of the model.

Separable and (largely) independently operating components (e.g., the phonological loop and visuospatial sketchpad) is one of the basic assumptions of the working memory model. As stated earlier, dissociations were used to support the need for these separate components. Ironically, the existence of dissociations, an important piece of evidence for the model when it was first proposed, now are threatening to become its undoing. Postle (2006) reviews a series of dissociations that have been revealed in the last decade of neuroscientific research on working memory. For example, neuroimaging studies indicate that working memory for faces and houses can be dissociated (Ranganath, Cohen, Dam, & D'Esposito, 2004) as can working memory for faces and outdoor scenes (Ranganath, DeGutis, & D'Esposito, 2004). Within the auditory domain, working memory for pitch, loudness and location can all be dissociated from one another (e.g., Clement, Demany, & Semal, 1999). These dissociations are problematic because the existence of a dissociation suggests another specialized subsystem is needed to explain it. Well, based on the partial list just summarized, Baddeley's model would have to add a half-dozen more subsystems. And the news gets worse; research indicates that working memory for tactile (Harris, Miniussi, Harris, & Diamond, 2002) and olfactory (Dade, Zatorre, Evans, & Jones-Gottman, 2001) information are both robust phenomena, and neither are included in Baddeley's model.

A Unitary View of Memory

The aforementioned problems has led some to question more than just the working memory model. Some have begun to question the need for a separate immediate memory store at all. These theorist are reassessing the dissociation data from the 60's and 70's that was used to argue for the distinction between long-term memory (LTM) and immediate memory (Jonides, Lewis, Nee, Lustig, Berman, & Sledge-Moore, 2008). This distinction is the basis for what are termed **memory systems views.** Both the modal model and the working memory model are examples, because they espouse the need for separate memory systems to explain memory function.

The recent dissociation evidence that undermines the multiple systems approach has led some to abandon the approach entirely, and instead propose a **unitary view of memory** which suggests that immediate memory is not a separate set of mechanisms or processes; it's basically just the currently activated portion of long-term memory. This view was actually proposed by Atkinson & Shiffrin (1971) and Anderson (1983) but never really gained traction due to the dominance of Baddeley's multistore model. But over the last 20 years (e.g., Cowan, 1988, 1995, 2001; McElree, 2001; Postle, 2006) unitary views of immediate memory have become increasingly popular.

Let's examine one of the dissociations that was used to support the distinction between immediate memory and LTM and the recent evidence that casts doubt on the finding and consequently the memory systems view. You'll recall that the amnesic H.M. (as well as many other amnesics) show normal immediate memory functioning but impaired LTM functioning. If you meet an amnesic they will be able to interact with you (normal immediate memory), but once you leave, they won't remember you (impaired LTM). The amount of time that passes appeared to be the critical variable. Amnesics are able to process information in current consciousness, but as time passes the information fades and due to impaired LTM functioning the information is lost. H.M., as well as other amnesics, suffered damage to the medial-temporal lobe (MTL) so it was assumed that the MTL was not involved in immediate memory. If it was, an amnesic also would have immediate memory impairment, but they don't. Different brain mechanisms seem to be involved, suggesting two different memory processes at work: LTM and immediate memory. But what if the MTL was found to be involved in immediate memory? This would mean that the same brain mechanism is involved in the two different memory processes. Therefore, there is no longer a need to make the distinction; LTM and immediate memory processes are the same.

This is the idea behind the unitary view of memory. Recent research indicates that the MTL *is* involved in immediate memory (e.g., Nicholls, Kao, & Verfaeille, et al. 2006). More specifically, the MTL seems to be responsible for encoding novel relations among objects and events. Therefore, the important function of the MTL has nothing to do with the time course of information presentation and retrieval as suggested by the memory systems view. This means that "preserved immediate memory" in amnesics isn't necessarily "preserved immediate memory" and "impaired LTM" isn't necessarily "impaired LTM;" it simply reflects an inability to encode novel connections and the preserved ability to reactivate old ones (Jonides et al., 2008).

Given that new things are happening every day, and for that matter, each moment (nothing is ever repeated in exactly the same way except in the movie *Ground Hog Day*), an amnesic will be unable to remember what happened. It has nothing to do with the inability to hold the information for longer than a few minutes. Amnesics can perform immediate memory tasks (used to support the need for a separate immediate memory store that is preserved in amnesics) but recent research reveals they cannot perform immediate memory tasks when it involves novel materials or encoding novel relations (e.g., Olson, Moore, Stark, & Chatterjee, 2006; Olson, Page, Mooore, Chatterjee, & Verfaellie, 2006). In order for the memory systems view to be valid, the immediate memory system must either function or not function; it can't depend on the task. But it does depend on the task, which supports the unitary view.

Unitary views of memory have one basic tenet: They assume that only one set of representations comprise our knowledge store. These representations are those ascribed to LTM and these representations differ in their level of activation. Those that are activated are the focus of attention. Postle (2006; Postle & Pasternak, 2009) proposes that immediate memory is simply an emergent property of mind and brain. According to this view, immediate memory arises as the result of the manner in which we sense, perceive, and attend to incoming information. According to Postle's view, brain systems have evolved to accomplish a number of different functions necessary for the effective processing of incoming information. Combine these with the flexible manner in which we deploy attention and what you have is immediate memory. It is not some special set of dedicated mechanisms for manipulating information within phonological loops or visual-spatial sketchpads. Immediate memory is simply the coming together of sensation, perception, attention, and action-related mechanisms.

Embedded-Process View

Another conceptualization of immediate memory is proposed by Cowan (1988; 1995; 2001). This view might be considered a hybrid of the memory systems and unitary views. His **embedded-process view** is depicted in Figure 4.5. As you can see, it bears a resemblance to the unitary view in that immediate memory is subsumed under LTM. Like the views just summarized, Cowan characterizes immediate memory as the momentary and temporary activation of information in long-term memory. Embedded within this temporarily activated information is the information that we're consciously aware of: the focus of attention. Like the memory systems view, Cowan proposes executive processes that are responsible for the movement of information in and out of the attentional focus. As you recall, Cowan revisioned the Miller magical number 7 ± 2 as 3 ± 1 chunks of information, which he proposed as the number of things that can share attentional focus.

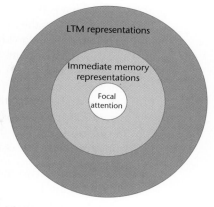

Figure 4.5

Is immediate memory embedded within LTM?

Something We All Can Agree On: Capacity Limits and Forgetting

Believe it or not, there is still a fair amount of disagreement over the seemingly simple question of exactly how much information can be held in immediate memory. No one questions the notion that it is subject to capacity limits, but the precise nature of the limit is a matter of fairly intense debate. We've dropped from the magical number seven to a magical number four. Some even propose that the magic number is only one or two!

Capacity Limits Revisited.   Garavan (1998) presented participants with a sequence of triangles and squares and required them to keep a running count of each type of stimulus. The sequence was self-paced; participants controlled how long they looked at each stimulus. This allowed Garavan (1998) to determine how much time was necessary to process each stimulus. He found that when the type of item switched (e.g., from a triangle to a circle), the participants took 500 ms longer to move on to the next item than when the item stayed the same (e.g., a triangle followed by another triangle). Now, if the capacity of immediate memory were seven, or even four items, you would expect that two running counts could easily be held at the same time. But the Garavan results indicate that only one number (the current running count) could be held at a time! Oberauer (2002) proposes that perhaps multiple items (i.e., Cowan's four) are highly accessible in immediate memory, but only a limited number (i.e., Garavan's one) can be in the focus of attention. So in the Garavan study both counts are highly accessible but only one count is the focus of attention. When the trial changes from triangle to circle, the 500 ms increase in RT represents the time needed "to move" the circle count into the focus of attention.

So what is the take-home message? Which is the "correct" view of immediate memory? As is always the case with the cumulative knowledge base that addresses any scientific question, we still don't have "the answer" but with each new study we are getting closer to a possible answer (equivocation intended). But practically, whether immediate memory is conceptualized as a set of interacting systems, the manifestation of focal attention, or as emergent property of long-term memory is of relatively little practical consequence. The issue central to immediate memory's real-world significance (which is consistent with all theoretical approaches) is that there is a limit on the amount of information we can hold in consciousness and this information is easily lost. So now, before we forget, let's turn our attention to this issue.

Forgetting.   Two mechanisms have received a great deal of attention as the primary culprits in this loss of information: decay and interference. Decay-based accounts of forgetting focus on the role of time passage in loss of information while interference-based accounts tend to invoke notions of similarity between, displacement by, or overwriting of one source vs. another. Let's examine each of these in a bit more detail.

Decay.   The loss of information from immediate memory due to the passage of time is referred to as **decay.** The initial evidence for this rather simple view consists of findings from early studies that employed the Brown-Peterson technique. Forgetting in this task seemed to occur even with minimal interference. It was assumed that counting backward did not interfere with the maintenance of information in immediate memory because the corresponding stimuli (letters and numbers) are so dissimilar. Therefore, any forgetting that occurred could be attributed to decay.

The decay view of forgetting may be seen as a little insufficient. Time passes, and we forget. A classic criticism of this notion was offered by McGeoch (1932). The fact that iron rusts over time does not mean that the rust was caused by time's passage. It's caused by something that happens over the time interval—namely, oxidation. As Jonides, Lewis, Nee, Lustig Berman, and Sledge-Moore (2008) point out, decay theorists need to describe the oxidation process that works on immediate memory.

Jonides et al. review a few possible mechanisms that would manifest themselves as time-based decay. It's possible that as new information is added to immediate memory, older, previously encoded information is not brought into the focus of attention as frequently. A way of viewing this in terms of neural activity is to consider a memory representation as a synchronized pattern of neural firing (that is, a neural network is activated in a particular dynamic pattern). Jonides et al. propose that with passing time, neurons in a given network grow increasingly out of sync unless they are "reset" by retrieval of the memory. As they get more and more out of sync, they get increasingly difficult to discriminate from other neural patterns (Lustig, Matell, & Meck, 2005). In other words, memories become noise.

Interference.   According to the notion of **interference**, information is lost from immediate memory because information currently being processed is negatively influenced by the presentation of other information. In a broad sense, interference can occur in one of two basic patterns. When previously encoded information interferes with the ability to remember new information, it's termed **proactive interference.** The complementary case, when newly encoded information interferes with the ability to remember previously encoded information, it's termed **retroactive interference.** These two can be distinguished by considering the temporal relationship between the to-be-remembered information and the interfering information. Figure 4.6 should help you determine which type of interference is operating in a given situation.

So what causes forgetting in immediate memory—a simple process of erosion, or the confusion that arises when we encode additional information? There still exists a fair amount of disagreement on this score, although most researchers probably look to interference as the most likely culprit. There are a number of findings that cast serious doubt on the simple decay theory. For example, Keppel and Underwood (1962) used the Brown-Peterson task to assess forgetting, and found that there was virtually no forgetting on the first trial of the Brown-Peterson task and the length of the delay interval didn't matter. Even at long delays, there was almost no forgetting on the initial trial. In other words, there seemed to be little or no effect of delay until there was significant potential for interference. Hence, interference is implicated as the more important cause of forgetting. What type of interference did Keppel and Underwood find—proactive or retroactive? Use the information in Figure 4.6 to figure it out.

Although interference may be the explanation of choice for immediate memory forgetting, the exact manner in which it inhibits immediate memory is a matter of some debate (Nairne, 1996). The negative effects of interference on immediate memory could result from a problem in storing or retrieving the information.

Here's a scheme that should help you discriminate between retroactive and proactive interference. Imagine that you've spent your weekend studying for two tests—psychology and sociology. You studied psychology on Saturday and sociology on Sunday.

Which information was learned first? Write it down:

psychology

Which information was learned second? Write it down to the right of the item that was learned first; it was learned after the first item:

psychology   **sociology**

Which of the two pieces of information is trying to be remembered? Let's say you're taking your psychology exam. Underline that item and draw an arrow from the nonunderlined item (i.e., the item that is not being remembered) to the underlined item (i.e., the item that is being remembered).

If the arrow is pointing in the backward direction (pointing backward in time from what was learned second to what was learned first), the type of interference is *retroactive* (*retro* means "backward"). Sociology information is retroactively interfering with your ability to remember information for your psychology exam.
Now let's imagine you are in your sociology exam.

If the arrow is pointing in the forward direction, the type of interference is *proactive* (*pro* means "forward"). Psychology information is proactively interfering with your ability to remember information for your sociology exam.

Figure 4.6

Scheme/mnemonic for distinguishing retroactive and proactive interference.

From Robinson-Riegler, M. B., & Robinson-Riegler, G., and Kohn, A. J. (1999). *Instructor's resource guide* for J. Kalat, *Introduction to psychology* (5th ed.). Belmont, CA: Wadsworth. Copyright 1999. Reprinted by permission of Wadsworth, a division of Thomson Learning.

Interference may have damaging effects on immediate memory because it makes the storage of information difficult. The *displacement view* suggests that when a new item enters immediate memory, it "bumps out" (or *displaces*) a previously stored item. The *overwriting view* assumes that when a new item enters immediate memory, it overwrites a previously stored item. A study by Proctor and Fagnani (1978) indicates that the overwriting view may be a better description of the effects of interference in immediate memory than the displacement view. They found more interference in a Brown-Peterson task if newer information was presented in the same modality as previously stored information (i.e., both visual or both auditory) than if the two were presented in different modalities (i.e., one visual and one auditory). If the interference effect was due to items being "bumped out" of immediate memory, the new information would bump the old stuff out, regardless of presentation modality. The fact that the similarity of the information led to more interference indicates that similarity caused confusion among the items whereas the lack of similarity reduced confusion. Reduced confusion leads to more effective storage, hence more effective retrieval.

On the other hand, it is possible that interference does not affect how information is encoded but affects how it's retrieved. Any time you're required to remember something, a process of retrieval is involved. And as you'll see in Chapter 6, long-term memory retrieval is not perfect; it is a reconstructive, rather than a reproductive, process. The same is true in immediate memory; the rememberer must reconstruct the information that has just been presented in order to report it. Some accounts of interference place the locus of the effect at the point of retrieval (Nairne, 1990; Schweickert et al. 1993). According to the notion of *blurring* and *deblurring,* items in immediate memory can blur into one another and become difficult to tell apart (or *deblur*) at retrieval. Let's examine these views by taking a look at a classic experiment by Wickens, Dalezman, and Eggemeier (1976). In this study, Wickens et al. employed the Brown-Peterson task, but used categorized lists (fruits, vegetables, flowers, meats, or professions) instead of letters; so, for example, on a given trial, you would read 3 flowers (daisy, rose, daffodil) and then be required to count backward for 18 seconds. After the distractor period, you'd be asked to recall the flowers. Wickens et al. presented 3 of these *Brown-Peterson trials* in a row, each time using three more items from the same category. Can you imagine what might happen over the course of these three trials? Try it and see in Figure 4.7.

You probably found that as you were required to remember the second and third groups from a category, you became more and more confused about what had actually occurred on these lists, largely because the previously encoded items were interfering

Trial 1	Recall	Trial 2	Recall	Trial 3	Recall
daisy		tulip		orchid	
rose		sunflower		carnation	
daffodil		hyacinth		marigold	

Figure 4.7
A rendition of the Wickens et al. (1976) procedure for demonstrating release from proactive interference.

Adapted from Wickens, D. D., Dalezman, R. E., & Eggemeier, F. T. (1976). Multiple encoding of word attributes in memory. *Memory and Cognition, 4,* 307–310.

with your ability to remember the new items; this is proactive interference. (The same type of interference found by Keppel and Underwood a few paragraphs ago—did you manage to figure it out?) And as you can see in Figure 4.8, participants in this study were profoundly affected by this interference; recall fell by 60% from the first to third trials. But the most intriguing finding from this study emerged from performance on a fourth trial. Recall that participants had received three successive lists from the same category. On the fourth trial, Wickens et al. presented participants with three items (again!) but this time from a *different* category—fruits (plum, peach, banana). A control group received fruits on all four trials. The last data point in the figure shows the surprising results—recall bounced back up. This bounce-back effect is termed **release from proactive interference.** Interestingly, the degree of release from interference is greater, the greater the difference between the original lists and the final list.

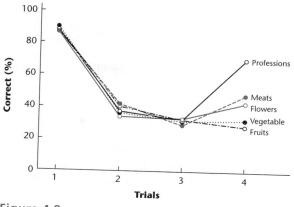

Figure 4.8

Trial-by-trial recall in the Wickens et al. (1976) study.

From Wickens, D. D., Dalezman, R. E., & Eggemeier, F. T. (1976). Multiple encoding of word attributes in memory. *Memory and Cognition, 4*, 307–310. Reprinted by permission of the Psychonomic Society, Inc.

Imagine what might be happening in this experiment according to the different notions of interference. Let's look at the memory performance for the first three trials. If interference is a storage problem, new items entering immediate memory get confused with the old items. As a result, these newer items are poorly encoded. Confusion can also make it difficult to retrieve or reconstruct the information. So many items are associated with the retrieval cue *flowers* that it no longer serves as an effective hint when the rememberer thinks of it (Nairne, 2001). On the fourth trial (when the category switches), the confusion is greatly reduced. New words interfere less with old words because they come from a new category. Why, an astute reader may be asking—the words were presented in the same modality so why should they be less interfering?

As it turns out, the Wickens et al. study is a classic not only for its demonstration of proactive interference and release from proactive interference, but also for revealing another dimension of immediate memory—it is sensitive to *meaning*. When the category shifted, the words were less likely to be confused with old ones because the *meaning* had changed. Furthermore, the cue that the rememberer thinks of (fruits) is fresh and new, and only has been associated with three items, so it does a better job of cuing the items from that trial. So confusion at storage and/or retrieval results in proactive interference and a reduction in that confusion results in release from proactive interference.

The finding that immediate memory is sensitive to semantic information (i.e., meaning) may have reminded you of the study by Acheson et al. (2010) discussed in the context of the phonological loop. As you'll recall, these investigators showed that word concreteness, (a semantic dimension) interacted with phonological similarity to affect performance in a memory span task. This demonstrated that immediate memory is sensitive to the meaning of encoded information and, given that the meaning of words is stored in LTM, any model of immediate memory would need to account for the influence of LTM on immediate memory. Consequently, the episodic buffer was added to the working memory model. Others have solved this problem by espousing a unitary view of immediate memory; immediate memory is simply the activated portion of LTM so it makes sense that meaning of information would influence processing. So while Wickens et. al. may have been the first to demonstrate this characteristic of immediate memory, the importance of this finding is still evident over 30 years later and theorists are still figuring out how to account for it.

Both decay and interference remain viable as accounts of forgetting from immediate memory, but as noted by Jonides et al., further research needs to be done to specify the nature of the breakdown processes dictating memory decay, and/or the precise rules that govern the overwriting or displacement of information presumed to be responsible for interference.

Stop&Review

1. Recency effects are often attributed to _____; primacy effects are often attributed to:_____.
   a. LTM; LTM
   b. STM; STM
   c. STM; LTM
   d. LTM; STM
2. What are the three major components of Baddeley's working memory model?
3. Name one piece of empirical evidence that supports the existence of the phonological loop.
4. True or false? Articulatory suppression can eliminate the phonological similarity effect.
5. Name two of the specific processes thought to involve the central executive.
6. Unitary views of working memory:
   a. include Baddeley's view
   b. have recently fallen out of favor
   c. suggest that there is no real distinction between immediate memory and LTM
   d. suggest that there is immediate memory STM, but no LTM
7. Distinguish between proactive and retroactive interference.

- The information-processing approach (i.e., the modal model) has been the dominant explanatory framework for working memory. It proposes three memory systems, and most importantly, a distinction between short-term and long-term memory. Sensory memory is now viewed as neural persistence rather than a store for immediately presented items. Evidence for the distinction between STM and LTM includes serial position effects (recency effect, ostensibly due to STM, and primacy effect, ostensibly due to LTM). In addition, case study data from amnesics indicates separable STM and LTM memory systems or processes.

- Baddeley's working memory model proposes immediate memory as a number of closely interacting subsystems that combine to subserve a host of higher-level mental processes, including language comprehension, problem solving, and reasoning. The three major components of the model are the phological loop, the visual-spatial sketchpad, and the central executive.

- The phonological loop is responsible for the articulatory coding of incoming information. Subcomponents include the phonological store and the subvocal rehearsal mechanism. Evidence for the phonological loop includes the irrelevant speech effect, the finding that any spoken stimulus can disrupt working memory, even if it's irrelevant. The word length effect shows that longer words are more difficult to hold in working memory, relative to short words. Working memory can also be disrupted by phonological similarity; similar-sounding items are more difficult to hold in memory than are dissimilar items.

- Articulatory suppression (engaging in a task that requires articulation) disrupts processing in working memory, and can eliminate the phonological similarity effect and word length effect. Research on deaf individuals reveals "motor versions" of the working memory effects, demonstrating that articulation need not only be auditory or phonological. The visual-spatial sketchpad is responsible for the storage and manipulation of visual and spatial information. Some evidence indicates that the sketchpad is separable into two distinct components, one visual and one spatial.

- The central executive is the set of working memory processes that comprise executive attention. It is also responsible for directing the other components of working memory. Fractionation refers to isolating separate functions of the executive, and these include task switching, response inhibition, and attentional control. The working memory model has been criticized for its vagueness, particularly with regard to the functions of the central executive.

- Numerous dissociations among working memory tasks suggests that a multicomponent view of working memory is not very feasible. Unitary views of working memory provide an alternative, postulating memory is simply the conscious portion of long-term memory. One such view is Cowan's embedded process view.

- Two general accounts of forgetting are interference and decay. Decay refers to the loss of information from immediate memory due to the passage of time. This explanation is cited by many as incomplete, with the mechanism causing decay often left unspecified. Interference refers to the loss of information due to the influence of other information. Proactive interference occurs when something learned initially interferes with memory for information learned later. Retroactive memory occurs when something learned recently interferes with information learned earlier. Interference might take place through displacement or overwriting.

Who's the Boss? Problems in Executive Control

As you've gathered from reading the chapter, the focus of attention in immediate memory research has moved toward addressing the question of how things move in and out of attentional focus. Or, as we discussed at the outset of the chapter, on the nature of the executive processes that allow this to happen. In this section, we take a look at some of this work.

Mind Wandering

How many times has your attention drifted while reading this chapter? Be honest; we're betting at least a dozen. Keeping things in the focus of attention isn't easy. Come to mention it, keeping things *out* of your focus of attention can be just as difficult (as we mentioned at the beginning of the chapter inhibition is an important aspect of executive attention). What factors are associated with this "attentional drift? Said another way, what cognitive processes underlie daydreaming? It's interesting to note that until recently, such a question would be considered on the fringes of psychology, as it deals directly with the subjective experience of consciousness, and relies heavily on introspective evidence. Smallwood and Schooler (2006) note that "mind wandering has largely been relegated to the backwaters of mainstream psychology." (p. 956). This is not because it's an uncommon experience; in their review of the **mind-wandering** phenomenon, Smallwood and Schooler note that as much as 15–50% of a person's thinking time is spent wandering. While this may be an overestimate because of boring laboratory tasks, there is no denying the pervasiveness of mind-wandering. And, as the processes of consciousness and attention have come back into vogue, so too, have seemingly subjective mental states and processes like mind wandering. So chain your mind down and read on!

Smallwood and Schooler review work on what they term the "restless mind," noting our propensity to let our consciousness wander and how this fits quite neatly with the notion of executive control. Their framework proposes that mind wandering is particularly likely when the task at hand (the primary task, as it were) does not require much in the way of executive control. In these circumstances, our consciousness is quite likely to stray towards some internal stimulus, like memories. Even mind-wandering requires some expenditure of mental effort, so it isn't as likely to occur when we're engaged in an especially demanding task. A second fact about mind wandering is that it's associated with a reduced awareness of the external environment, because attention is being directed inward. According to Smallwood and Schooler, the processing of the primary task (the external world) is superficial as our mind wanders to an internal event. Finally, and perhaps counter-intuitively, our mind wanders without our intention to do it. It's almost as if a personal goal becomes activated and proceeds to hijack the goal of the task at hand.

If your mind hasn't been wandering, you might notice a parallel between Smallwood and Schooler's framework for mind-wandering and our discussion of action slips at the end of the last chapter. Indeed, there are some definite parallels. Both involve going off-task, and both are likely to occur when we're on "auto-pilot." Both can be described in terms of one schema or set of processes "hijacking" another. One difference between the two may be that action slips do not serve a purpose; they simply are an error. Conversely, mind wandering may be serving a cognitive "higher purpose." For example, Smallwood and Schooler propose that perhaps the hijacking of cognition that occurs in mind wandering aids problem solving. It may even lie behind the insightful "AHA!" moments (i.e., insight), which we'll be discussing in the final chapter. In this way, mind wandering might be an important component of creativity.

Smallwood and Schooler's assumptions about when mind-wandering is likely to occur have some interesting implications for techniques that might aid in its prevention. When we're doing something that's boring or not all that demanding, cognitive processes are likely to drift off. But this mind-wandering might be thwarted by engaging in some other task that helps to hold one's focus. A recent study suggests one such task: doodling! Andrade (2009) proposes that the little squiggles and stars that you've drawn in your notes may have aided your ability to stay focused on the task at hand (the scintillating lecture on attention). In her study, she had people monitor a fairly monotonous telephone conversation about people going to a party. Their task was to take note of all individuals who planned to attend. The conversation included a great deal of irrelevant information including the mention of eight place names. One group was asked to doodle by shading in simple shapes on a sheet of paper (they were told it might help relieve the boredom of the task). The no doodling control group only did the monitoring task. After the telephone conservation, participants were asked about intentionally encoded information (the names) as well as information obtained incidentally (place names).

Surprisingly, doodlers not only recalled the names (intentionally monitored) better than nondoodlers; they also recalled the places (incidentally monitored) better than nondoodlers. Andrade (2009) proposes a few explanations for this counterintuitive finding. One explanation relates to the mind-wandering we've been discussing. Basically, doodling serves as a tangible destination to which your mind can wander, and a relatively harmless one. It doesn't take much mental effort to doodle, so resources are not being taken from the task at hand, and it's preventing you from mind-wandering to something more demanding and thus detrimental to primary task performance.

Stop&*Think* | HEY! GET BACK HERE! (MIND WANDERING)

It might seem a little odd and will no doubt be somewhat of a challenge, but do your best to keep a mind wandering journal. Whenever you catch your mind wandering away from the task on which you're working, stop what you're doing (if feasible! Don't do this in the middle of your professor's lecture!!) and reflect on/answer the following:

- What were you doing when your mind wandered? Do you see any pattern?
- What were the surroundings when your mind wandered?
- To what type of other thought did your mind wander? Do you see any pattern?

- Did the requirement to keep a journal of mind wandering have any effect on mind wandering?

If you are in the middle of something important, and can stop on the spot to make these observations, you might just note the episode by jotting a couple of words (perhaps a brief two-word cue that describes the content to which your mind wandered). Then, when you have some time, find those notes, and reflect back on when your mind wandered.

Ironic Processes of Control

It seems like you should be able to control the tendency of your mind to drift off just by telling yourself "Concentrate!" or "Stay on task!" Sadly, attempts to do just that lead to what Wegner (1994) terms "ironic" effects. In other words, the processes involved in guarding against some type of mistaken action actually *encourage* the mistaken action to occur! Wegner, Ansfield, and Pilloff (1998) summarize it well: "Our bodies mock us as we double dribble, slice into the rough, miss our first serve, and otherwise work our way out of the record books and into blooper videos" (p. 196).

Wegner and his colleagues (Wegner, 1994, 2003; Wegner, Ansfield, & Pilloff, 1998) propose a two-factor theory of cognitive control to account for situations in which we make the very mistakes we're trying to avoid. According to this account, two different control processes come together in the service of action. The first process is termed an *intentional operating process,* and it is responsible for activating thoughts relevant to the goal at hand (e.g., hitting a golf ball off a tee). The second process is termed the *ironic monitoring process,* and it is responsible for keeping track of thoughts that might foil the goal at hand (e.g., the desire to lift your head to see where the drive went). It searches for these goal-thwarting thoughts so that they can be identified and eradicated. According to Wegner's (1994) analysis, the intentional operating process is conscious and effortful, while the ironic monitoring process is not conscious, does not demand effort, and is usually less influential. In other words, it works "behind the scenes."

The two systems usually combine happily to produce the desired outcome. The intentional operating process fills the mind with goal-achieving thoughts and feelings while the ironic monitoring process concurrently tracks goal-thwarting thoughts or emotions. If the ironic monitoring process finds evidence of these, the intentional operating process initiates an act of control to keep the thoughts and emotions at bay. Here's where the irony starts to rear its ugly head: Because the ironic monitoring process is tracking unwanted thoughts and feelings, these thoughts and feelings are in an activated state. This is fine when the intentional operating process has sufficient capacity (say, when you're engaging in a task that's highly practiced, and you have nothing else on your mind). But if mental capacity is drained in some way (you're engaged in a task that takes a good deal of effort, or you're distracted or nervous), the intentional operating process is compromised in its ability to keep these now highly activated thoughts and feelings at bay, so they spill over into consciousness and impact behavior.

Wegner, Ansfield, and Pilloff (1998) tested this account in the context of what can be an exquisitely difficult motor skill to execute—putting a golf ball. If you've ever partaken in the grand game of golf, you know that you spend almost as much time considering how things could go wrong as you do considering how things could go right. This is certainly true of putting. And, according to the **ironic process of control theory,** this is OK—monitoring for unwanted thoughts is an important part of mental and physical control. But problems will arise in cases of increased mental load. Wegner et al. had all participants make a baseline putt (they putted to a spot that was highlighted on the floor). Then, for their next (experimental) putt, they were given an extra instruction—they were told to be particularly careful not to overshoot the spot. For this second putt, half of the participants were told to keep in mind a six-digit number that they would have to report after the putt (i.e., extra mental load). The other half was given no extra task.

According to the ironic process theory, the group given the extra mental load should have been especially likely to overshoot. Can you figure out why? The intentional operating process would be activating all the thoughts that lead to a good putt, while the ironic monitoring process would be trying to find all of the thoughts related to overshooting. When found, the intentional operating process would deal with it, making the proper adjustment. But in the mental load group, participants were distracted by the requirement to keep a six-digit number in mind. Hence, the intentional operating process would be compromised in its ability to adjust—and wouldn't be able to do so, leading to the very thing the participant was trying to avoid, overshooting the spot.

Right in line with the predictions, overshooting proved to be a problem for participants who were given a mental load; they overshot the putt by an average of over 20 cm! Participants not given a mental load actually undershot the target by an average of 11 cm, which makes sense. Because there was no extra mental load, the intentional operating process could make the proper adjustments to avoid overshooting. This may be the reason why some coaches encourage their players to "turn off your mind and let your body do the work." They most likely don't know the theoretical basis for this recommendation but they do seem to intuit that "thinking too much" can be problematic for performance. So the lesson here may be that to avoid these ironic effects, you have to try not to think about the mistakes you tend to make. Unfortunately, that sets up a sort of double-irony situation (not to mention a syntactic disaster).

The ironic effects of control seem evident in situations far more serious than your occasional trip out to the Pirate's Cove Mini-Golf. Clinical psychologists have found the paradigm to be applicable to disorders that feature the inability to control anxiety-producing thoughts, such as insomnia (Harvey, 2005), post-traumatic stress disorder (e.g., Shipherd & Beck, 2005), depression (Wenzlaff & Luxton, 2003), and obsessive-compulsive disorder (Smári, 2001). Trying not to think about the things that make a person anxious or sad can lead to ironic effects. So attempts to relieve one's own anxiety have the potential to worsen it.

The Effects of Stress

Obviously, the ability to control one's attention has some important implications. And you've no doubt noticed how hard it is to do when you're overrun, tired, spread too thin, "too busy to breathe"....fill in your own metaphor for stress here. Your concentration is off; you can't focus. Recall our discussion of action slips in Chapter 3; you learned that job-related stress and burnout was associated with more frequent action slips. Stated in terms of the concepts we've been discussing in this chapter, stress has a negative impact on executive function. The stress can be physiological, mental, and/or emotional. Indeed, the distinction among these sources of stress is to some degree arbitrary anyway.

In a rather unique applied study, Leach and Griffith (2008) propose that compromised immediate-memory function due to the intense situational stress induced by skydiving might be a cause of "no-pull fatalities." A significant percentage of sport-parachuting accidents are linked to cases in which a jumper failed to deploy the reserve parachute by pulling the appropriate handle. Leach and Griffin (2008) speculate that this might be due to immediate memory failure. To evaluate their hypothesis, the investigators gave expert (>40 jumps) and novice (<10 jumps) parachutists an operation span task. As you'll recall, this task requires participants to perform simple but effortful mathematical computations while holding short lists of words in mind. Parachutists were tested at three different times: in the jump phase (within 10 minutes prior to a jump), in the landing phase (immediately after landing), and in a baseline condition (no jump scheduled).

The results showed clear evidence of an immediate memory deficit for both expert and novice parachutists prior to a jump, as operation span scores were lower than baseline. Obviously, the authors had no way to assess their hypothesis about the role of immediate memory in no-pull fatalities, but their research demonstrates that the anxiety endemic to preparing to jump out of an airplane lowers immediate memory capacity. We can only imagine the stress induced when the main parachute fails to open. This incredibly high level of stress could reduce immediate memory functioning so badly that the parachutist is unable to figure out what to do next and fails to deploy the reserve parachute. Interestingly, in the moments after a jump, the immediate memory performance of the experts recovered to their baseline level. Not so for novice jumpers, who continued to exhibit a disruption in executive function.

Immediate memory is also impacted by stress of a different sort—the chronic physiological and mental stress imposed by long-term exposure to impoverished socioeconomic conditions. A great deal of social scientific research has revealed an income-achievement gap, such that family income is a reliable predictor of various measures of cognitive performance and academic achievement (e.g., test scores, educational advancement). The gap appears early in development and only grows wider with time. In summarizing this evidence, Evans and Schamburg (2009) speculate that this gap can be traced to the chronic stress associated with poverty, which in turn manifests itself through (among other things) immediate memory performance. Although previous studies (e.g. Noble, McCandiliss, & Farah, 2007) had demonstrated a link between socio-economic status and cognitive abilities, they had not demonstrated the causal chain running from poverty to chronic stress to immediate memory deficits.

In an elaborate multivariate correlational analysis, Evans and Schamburg show that the correlation between poverty and poor immediate memory depends most critically on the chronic stress associated with poverty. These chronic effects of stress were measured by calculating allostatic load (a measure of chronic wear and tear on the body), as reflected in a number of physiological measurements, including blood pressure, body mass index, and cortisol (stress hormone) levels. When allostatic load was removed (mathematically) from the multivariate analysis, there was no longer a relationship between poverty and immediate memory. So, the chronic stress effects produced by a life of poverty and their physiological impact are the source of immediate memory deficits and consequently the achievement gap.

Improving Executive Function

What's someone with the attention span of a 5-year old to do? Can our executive functioning benefit from on-the-job training, as it were? Let's conclude our discussion of immediate memory by exploring some possible interventions that might improve our attentional control. One immediate thought you might have is that simple practice might improve attentional dexterity. After all, we live in an age of multi-tasking. People combine all manner of activities: eating, reading, watching TV, talking on the phone....and the list goes on. You might guess that multitasking practice would serve to improve someone's ability to do it. After all, practice makes perfect, right? Guess again.

Ophir, Nass, and Wagner (2009) were interested in how the current saturation of technology might be impacting attentional control. Ophir et al. separated their participants (via a questionnaire) into heavy and light multitaskers. The questionnaire asked about the number of hours spent per week using particular media, such as print media, internet, cell phones, text messaging, e-mail, and others. They also reported the degree to which they used these media in tandem (i.e., the degree to which they engaged in multi-tasking). The

Reality Check

researchers related the questionnaire scores to performance on a series of tasks measuring immediate memory and attentional control. One task measured breadth of attention and the ability to notice change. They presented displays of red targets amidst varying numbers of blue distractors. The task was to determine, upon the presentation of a second display, whether or not the red distractors had changed orientation. As in the studies of visual search discussed in Chapter 3, the authors were interested in how the number of distractors would impact search. As you can see in Figure 4.9, the answer depended on

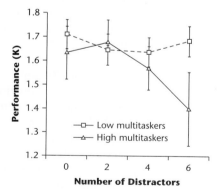

This person's attentional boss is likely to get fired.

your multitasking habits. The addition of distractors impaired visual task performance, but only for the high multitaskers. These participants demonstrated difficulty in ignoring extraneous information.

Visual search wasn't the only task to reveal deficits in high multitaskers. Ophir et al. also compared high-and low-multitaskers in 2-back and 3-back tasks. These tasks assess one's ability to monitor and update immediate memory representations by presenting a series of stimuli (digits or letters) one at a time to participants. Upon seeing the stimulus, the participant was to indicate if it was identical or not to the stimulus present "n" slots earlier ("n" referring to the number of slots they had to "think back"). This is quite a demanding task; participants continually have to update which digits or letters have occurred in the last 2 or 3 presentation slots (depending on condition), in addition to monitoring whether it matches the one they're currently looking at. Performance in this task is shown in Figure 4.10, which presents the decline in performance from the 2-back to 3-back task, in terms of both hit rate (number of "matches" correctly identified) and false

Figure 4.9

Visual attention and memory in multitaskers.

Results from Ophir et al. (2009)

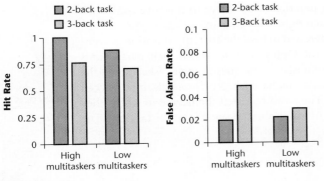

Figure 4.10

Executive control as indicated by the 2- and 3-back tasks, as a function of media multi-tasking.

Results from Ophir et al. (2009)

alarms (number of incorrectly identified "matches"). As you can see, the decline in hit rate from the 2-back to 3-back tasks was similar for high and low multitaskers. The false alarm rates is where things got interesting. Moving from the 2-back to 3-back task proved to be much more challenging for high multitaskers than for low multitaskers; High multitaskers were much more likely to commit false alarms in the 3-back condition. The multitaskers falsely responded that the current target matched the one that had appeared 3 slots back when it actually didn't. The supposed "match" *had* occurred previously but not in the 3-back position. These false alarms were more likely for frequently occurring stimuli (i.e., participants were more likely to falsely identify a target that had appeared frequently in precious slots). In other words, high multitaskers had trouble inhibiting prior sequences that were familiar.

Ophir et al. (2009) conclude that high and low multitaskers have fundamentally different information-processing tendencies and capabilities. High multitaskers have broader-based attention with a concomitant difficulty in screening out irrelevant stimuli. Basically, high multitaskers seemed to be more distractible than low multitaskers. Low multitaskers seem to be better at executive control of attention, and focusing on a single task in the face of distraction. In the case of attentional control: practice makes imperfect!

Our advice for improving? Log out of Facebook, turn off your cell phone, and go for a walk in a quiet park. This advice is based on the notion that executive attention can be improved by our experiences, just not experiences involving practice with multitasking. In a recent review, Tang and Posner (2009) distinguish between two approaches designed to improve one's control over attentional processing: Attention training and attention state training.

Attention Training.   Attention training techniques involve attempts to explicitly train immediate memory mechanisms via repetitive trials of executive attention tasks that are meant to "exercise" the brain's ability to focus and manipulate attention. You might be thinking "wait, I thought you said you can't improve attentional control with practice." True, but this "practice" does not involve the repeated performance of a multitasking activity but repeated performance of the skills needed to control attention.

A number of studies have revealed the value of explicit and repeated engagement in tasks that specifically train executive function. Diamond, Barnett, Thomas, and Munro (2007) describe an educational intervention termed Tools of the Mind that attempts to train three key features of executive function, including inhibitory control (resisting habits or distractions), immediate memory (holding and manipulating information), and cognitive flexibility (adjusting to change). This curriculum, designed for preschoolers, combines the academic curriculum with tasks designed to improve executive control. These tasks included dramatic role playing, private speech to deal with the changing rules of a game and the regulation of behavior, and turn taking by alternately reading to and listening to a "reading buddy." These and other tasks required children to exercise each element of executive function: inhibitory control, immediate memory, and cognitive flexibility. The comparison (control) curriculum covered the same academic content, but did not include training in executive function. After a substantial period (1–2 yrs) of exposure to their respective curricula, the children were given a number of tests of executive function (different from what they had seen before, so there was no chance of a straight practice effect for the Tools children).

In the *Dots task,* a red heart or a flower appeared on the right or left of a screen. In the congruent condition, children were given one simple rule to remember, "press the key on the same side as the heart/flower." The incongruent condition was a bit tougher; children were given instructions to "press the key on the opposite side as the flower/red heart." It is easier to press the key on the same side as the stimulus, so the requirement to do the opposite requires the inhibition of this natural tendency. In the *flanker task,* children were presented with one shape embedded within another, and they were to respond with the shape that was on the inside. The two shapes were always a circle and a triangle. For example, when presented with a circle embedded in a triangle, children would be required to screen out the "triangle" and respond "circle." There's a stronger tendency to perceive an outside shape rather than an embedded shape, so the requirement to do the opposite requires the inhibition of a natural tendency.

Across both of these tasks, all three core executive functions described above were in play. Both required inhibition (natural tendency to respond on the same side as the presented stimulus and the outside shape), flexibility (required response changed from trial to trial), and immediate memory (the need to remember the specific stimulus-response pairings). The dependent variable was accuracy, which is the most sensitive measure for children in these types of tasks. The results demonstrate the effectiveness of the Tools of Mind curriculum in improving executive function. For every measure, children educated with the Tools of Minds curriculum outperformed those in the control curriculum. Based on this study it is clear that executive functions are subject to training, with important ramifications for education (Thorell, Lindqvist, Nutley, Bohlin, Klingberg, 2009). The importance of executive attention cannot be overestimated. Diamond et al. report that poor executive function in students is associated with teacher burnout, student dropout, ADHD, drug use, and crime. This relationship is especially disconcerting in light of the relationship between poverty and immediate memory discussed earlier. Clearly, any intervention capable of training attention and executive control would be well worth the effort and expenditure.

Attention State Training. Attention state training techniques have their roots in Eastern contemplative traditions and involve methods designed to produce altered states of mind and body through some type of experiential intervention. Recall our earlier advice to log off of Facebook and take a walk in a quiet park. This advice is based on evidence for the effectiveness of attention state training, in particular, a study by Berman, Jonides, and Kaplan (2008). Berman et al. contrast top-down control of attention (basically, the executive processes we've been discussing throughout the chapter) with bottom-up control (the grabbing of attention by some salient stimulus). Top-down (voluntary) attentional control is effortful, and benefits from down time by engaging in activities like encountering nature. Why wouldn't urban encounters do the same? According to Berman et al.'s view of attentional control, the level of stimulation present in an urban setting results in intense bottom-up attentional capture that forces movement to top-down attentional processing in an attempt to deal with the barrage of incoming stimuli. However, nature is not as "busy" as an urban setting; encounters with nature lead only to a gentle bottom-up attentional capture that does not initiate top-down attentional processing, so this type of processing gets a break.

To understand this distinction, let's imagine you are in Glacier National Park and wake up to see a beautiful sunrise off the balcony of your lodge room (see left panel of Figure 4.11). When viewing this sunrise (gentle bottom-up attentional capture) there is no need to exert any top-down attentional control. You can simply enjoy it, giving your top-down attentional processing a breather. But now imagine you are in the city with streetlights, people, and you're walking down the boulevard (see right panel of Figure 4.11). This excursion requires constant vigilance of your surroundings in order to avoid being mowed down by pedestrians, taxis, or police officers on horses (intense visual capture). In this situation you must exert top-down attentional processes in order to react and avoid getting knocked over; your top-down attentional processing is sweating-it out, and this processing is effortful and draining.

To test their idea, Berman, Jonides, and Kaplan (2008) gave participants a backwards digit-span task before and after exposure to a nature or urban setting. Backwards digit span is basically the memory span task we described earlier in the chapter, with added difficulty. Rather than repeat back a series of digits in the order they were presented, backwards digit span ups the ante in terms of executive control element. The order of the items must be reversed as the sequence is recalled. According to Berman et al.'s analysis, exposure to nature should rest voluntary attention, leading to improvements in immediate memory task relative to a condition in which they're exposed to an urban environment. Consistent

Attentional back rub . . .

Figure 4.11

Attentional workout . . .

with this hypothesis, Berman et al. (2008) found that backwards memory span improved after participants went on a 1-hour walk in a campus arboretum. Walking for an hour in downtown Ann Arbor led to no such benefit. In a second experiment, the investigators replicated the finding using pictures of nature settings and pictures of urban settings. You might find it hard to believe that a simple picture could have such a dramatic effect. But look again at the pictures in Figure 4.11. Do you feel calmer looking at the mountains than the city street? Probably, and that difference impacts your cognitive processing. As Berman et al. conclude the eye- (and attention) catching beauty of nature is just gentle enough to have restorative effects on focused attention.

Perhaps the most well-known example of attention state training is meditation, which explicitly focuses on producing a relaxed state and the attempt to calm the mind and body. A number of studies have shown that training in meditative techniques can lead to improvements in stress levels and cognitive control (e.g., Shapiro, Carlson, Astin, & Freedman, 2006). Recall the attentional blink phenomenon discussed in the previous chapter. If you'll recall, when stimuli are presented in rapid succession, the attentional processing of a stimulus essentially blocks the processing of the following stimulus. Slagter, Lutz, Greischar, Francis, Nieuwenhuis, Davis, and Davidson (2007) showed that three months of intensive meditation training was associated with a decrease in the magnitude of the attentional blink (i.e., improved processing of second stimulus), as well as a reduction in the brain resources to process the first target. The authors suggest that this combination of results suggests that meditation leads to efficient brain networks.

Based in ancient Chinese medicine, **integrative mind-body training (IBMT)** attempts to achieve a mind-body balance by using meditation in combination with a broad concept called mindfulness. **Mindfulness** refers to an acute awareness of the present moment, including one's present thoughts, emotions, and actions. IBMT attempts to heighten both bodily and mental awareness through a state of mindful relaxation. Tang et al. (Tang, et al., 2007) investigated IBMT in a sample of Chinese students. Participants received IBMT training or simple relaxation training 20 minutes a day for five days. On later tests of attention, the IBMT group showed more improvement in their executive function than the simple relaxation group. In addition, there were emotional effects, including lessened anxiety, anger, depression, and fatigue, as well as lowered cortisol (stress hormone) release in reaction to a stressful event!

Although the initial training in these meditation-type techniques is difficult and challenging, the later use of these techniques is relatively effortless. And the initial effort is worth it as a growing body of evidence points to their effectiveness. However, these techniques might seem a

The path to attentional enlightenment?

little mysterious or exotic given their basis in Asian meditative traditions, but there are some who feel their effectiveness has a "Western" explanation. According to attention restoration theory (Kaplan, 1995) sustained mental effort produces fatigue and leads to a reduction in systemic glucose. Attention state training techniques (e.g., meditation) serve to replenish glucose supply which improves performance. Regardless of the explanation, the fact that immediate memory in the form of attentional control seems to be trainable is good news indeed for our chaotic, multitasking society.

Stop &*Think* | TAKE A DEEP ATTENTIONAL BREATH—MINDFULNESS

Mindfulness and meditation offer islands of calm in our stressed-out society. These practices offer benefit for one's ability to control attention. This exercise is to see if you can derive some of this benefit. Visit one of the following sites, and make your way to some mindfulness and/or meditation exercises. Devote at least 10 minutes a day exercising mindfulness, and journal your experience, in terms of your own subjective experience "in the moment" of the mindfulness/meditation exercise, and perhaps more importantly, in terms of any benefit to your everyday attentional functioning.

Mindfulness in Action: http://www.mindfulness.org.au/InAction.htm

Mindful Awareness Research Center: http://marc.ucla.edu/

Mindful Living Programs: http://www.mindfullivingprograms.com/

Stop &*Review*

1. How does mind wandering relate to executive control?
2. Why are ironic control processes "ironic"?
3. True or false? Meditation is an example of attention state training.

- Mind wandering is one example of a problem in executive control. One account of mind wandering is that consciousness is "decoupled," and there are simultaneous streams of information-processing going on. Some research suggests that doodling might be an effective means of preventing mind-wandering.

- Sometimes, processes involved in guarding against some type of mistaken action actually *encourage* the mistaken action to occur; these are termed ironic processes.

Ironic processes are particularly likely to occur under conditions of divided attention. Attentional control can be adversely affected by emotional and physiological stress. Executive control is adversely impacted by multitasking. Heavy multitaskers seem to be more distractible than light multitaskers.

- A number of procedures have been proposed to improve attention and executive control. Attention state training techniques are based in Eastern contemplative traditions, and include meditation. Attention training techniques involve repetitions of specific cognitive tasks related to the control of executive attention.

CHAPTER OUTLINE

5

Objects and Concepts: Identifying and Classifying Information

It seems pretty amazing that you can instantly recognize a chair as a chair, no matter if it's upright, lying on its side, or in a picture that you're looking at upside down. Furthermore, you recognize all different kinds of chairs—rocking, folding, and high chairs. What processes might underlie this ability?

As many types of chairs as there may be in the world, there seem to be several orders of magnitude more faces. How in the world do we ever manage to distinguish between them? Are we specially equipped to deal with the recognition of faces?

Have you ever watched ESPN and wondered why you were watching poker, dance competitions, or hunting? Are these things really sports? Football, baseball, and basketball sure seem to fit the sports category. What are the possible bases for categorization?

Identification and Classification: An Overview

In this chapter, we continue our "tour" through the early components of the information-processing system. Up to this point, we've talked about how we look or listen, pay attention, and hold information in immediate memory for further processing. The first step in further processing involves *identifying* and *classifying* what it is you've latched onto through attentional processing. The process of identification is typically labeled **object recognition**—the processes whereby we match an incoming stimulus with stored representations for the purpose of identification. The fact that we can look at a pattern of stimulation and say "bird," "football," "tree," or "chair" begs the question of how we know what birds, footballs, trees, and chairs are. That is, how do we represent these **concepts,** and how did we arrive at these representations? What is a tree, exactly? You've probably never thought too much about questions like this (unless you major in philosophy), but this chapter will introduce you to some of the answers that cognitive psychologists have proposed to these questions.

The fact that we are able to identify and classify everything around us raises a fundamental issue: What is the classification database, and how is it formed, organized, and accessed? In the latter half of the chapter, we'll explore some of the answers that have emerged to these basic questions. But first let's start off with the basics.... Think about how quickly and effortlessly you recognize: bird, football, tree, and chair. Notice that we didn't write "animal," "sports equipment," "plant," or "piece of furniture." Those seem to be too general. Nor did we say "black-capped chickadee," "Rawlings Collegiate Size Composite Leather Football," "white dogwood," or "beanbag chair." These seem to be ridiculously specific (not to mention much more wordy and space consuming!). What we've just done is outline three fundamental **levels of categorization,** or gradations of specificity that can be used in describing everyday categories.

In a classic discussion, Rosch (1976) summarizes these levels of categorization. The superordinate level of categorization—animal—is the most general; the subordinate level of categorization—black-capped chickadee—is the most specific. The midpoint between these two levels is termed the **basic level of categorization:** bird. Rosch also discusses a number of features that characterize items at the basic level. At this level of categorization, items (a) share similar shapes, (b) require the same movements and postures to interact with them, and (c) lead to the formation of a single mental image. Rosch notes that this level of categorization is by far the most salient, and dominates our cognitive processing. Intuitively, this makes sense—superordinate terms like *animal* would seem to provide too little information to be of much use. Subordinate terms like *black-capped chickadee* often provide more information than is necessary. The basic level is "just right" in that it provides enough detail to specify the type of object (i.e., bird) yet doesn't bore you with the details.

As you'll see, the differing levels of specificity of everyday categories and concepts have important ramifications for the task of object recognition. In more concrete terms, it seems that distinguishing between two quite different objects like chairs and birds (which differentiate at the basic level) might involve a different set of recognition processes than distinguishing between two quite similar objects like a black-capped chickadee and a tufted titmouse (which differentiate at the subordinate level). Another way of saying this is that the basic level turns out to be the **entry point for recognition.** The entry point refers to the default level of categorization that we use for familiar objects.

Recognizing from the Bottom Up and the Top Down

In Chapter 2, we discussed the basic processes of visual perception through which an incoming stimulus is translated into a percept. In order to deal with these incoming stimuli, we need to identify them (*recognize* these objects). It turns out that a distinction we introduced in Chapter 2 is critical to an account of object recognition—namely, the notions of *bottom-up* and *top-down processing*. Bottom-up processing employs the information in the stimulus itself (what you might call "data") to aid in its identification. That is, we build and identify stimuli "from the bottom up." For example, you recognize a chair because of the data of cylindrical lines, four pointing to the ground and a couple pointed in the air, and two flat surfaces, one parallel to the ground and one perpendicular to it. It's not difficult to see that bottom-up processing is necessary for recognizing objects. It's obvious that we can't identify something without any data at all; there would be nothing to identify. While bottom-up processing may be necessary to account for object recognition, it isn't sufficient. A fundamental fact about object recognition is that both bottom-up and top-down processing play an important role.

The importance of top-down processing may not be as obvious, but it does play a vital role in our ability to recognize what we see. Quite often, incoming data are incomplete or obscured in some manner and are thus unidentifiable. In these cases, we must rely on expectations, knowledge, and/or surrounding context to supplement the data (i.e., top-down processing). Even if the aforementioned chair were partially obscured, chances are you'd be able to identify it, particularly if it were in a familiar context (e.g., a living room or furniture store). Our knowledge of chairs enhances identification. In other words, we identify what things are "from the top down."

The number of objects we are able to recognize is nothing short of phenomenal. Look around you and identify all of the things you can. Chances are you were able to name at least 10 or so things in the space of 10 or so seconds. A computer recognition system can't touch this level of performance. Decades of work in artificial intelligence have not cracked the problem of getting computers to recognize and classify objects in the rapid, flexible, and accurate manner that humans can. In the first section of the chapter, we'll examine some of the mechanisms researchers propose to account for object recognition.

Object Recognition

Consider the processes of recognition, as outlined by Tarr (2000). A messy array of light information strikes the retina, where early visual processes extract some basic information and impose some basic order on the chaos via the perceptual organizational processes we discussed in Chapter 2. These processes include the discernment of boundaries, edges, contours, and surfaces

Can you identify me?

as well as more global organizational processes that lead us to discern the shapes and objects that will ultimately lead to recognition. The next step in recognition is a matching process whereby the now-analyzed visual pattern is compared with representations in memory. Evidence accumulates for the most likely candidates, and ultimately, we come to the conclusion that the object in the picture is indeed....a...bunny rabbit!

In theory, the process of recognition seems pretty straightforward, but keep in mind what it's up against. The view of an object that falls on the retina (the "stuff" of recognition) is woefully inconsistent. A given object is rarely, if ever, viewed in exactly the same way. Objects can rotate, shift, change position; viewers can move and radically change their perspective on an object; the lighting on the object can change; parts of the object can be blocked out. There are also incredible variations in the object itself. Are you viewing it live, in a movie, in a photo, or in a pencil sketch? You can also recognize the bunny rabbit at the different levels of categorization—you could recognize it as an animal, a mammal, a rabbit, a jackrabbit, the Easter bunny, or Bugs Bunny. In spite of these challenges, you're nearly flawless in execution. Before discussing theoretical accounts of the process, let's talk about "nuts and bolts"—empirical research on how recognition occurs.

Effects of Orientation and Perspective.   It's obvious, for practical purposes at least, that the particular perspective from which we view objects doesn't really affect our ability to identify them. We know what they are in a split second. But are the processes of recognition really impervious to orientation and perspective when viewed with a fine-grained analysis? This question—whether recognition is *viewpoint invariant*—is a critical one for evaluating the theories of recognition that we'll talk about a little later. It also turns out that the answer to the question is, well,...yes and no.

A classic study of perspective effects on recognition was done by Palmer, Rosch, and Chase (1981). These investigators collected ratings from participants regarding how well each of several photos represented a particular object. Then they gave a separate

Canonical (left photo) and non-canonical (right photo) of Bridget's Prius.

group of participants an identification task in which they were to name as quickly as possible the objects pictured. Recognition turned out to be fastest for objects in a canonical perspective—that is, the perspective rated as the best representation of the object. For the lower-rated perspectives, recognition was slower. You might think that perhaps this RT pattern occurs because the canonical perspective is the most familiar one. Good intuition, but it turns out that similar effects are found for unfamiliar objects (e.g., Edelman & Bülthoff, 1992).

Because one's perspective of an object seems to affect object recognition, object rotation itself must, too, right? Well, no…answers in cognitive psychology are rarely so simple. Some pioneering work done by Biederman and his colleagues (Biederman & Cooper, 1991; Biederman & Gerhardstein, 1993) suggests that orientation might not matter all that much in object recognition. They used a technique commonly employed in all sorts of studies of cognition, a technique termed *priming*. As you read in Chapter 2, priming refers to a benefit gained from earlier exposure to a stimulus. After having thought about or identified an object once, you're "primed" to think of it or identify it more easily afterward. Biederman and Gerhardstein (1993) presented participants with a series of objects like the flashlight pictured in Figure 5.1a, and participants were simply to name each one as quickly as possible (phase 1). In the second phase of the experiment, participants were once again presented with a series of objects to name. Half of these objects were the same as those seen in phase 1, but presented at varying degrees of rotation. The other half of the objects were different examples of the same objects (e.g., a different type of flashlight), also presented at varying degrees of rotation. Their measure of performance was priming—would the first presentation speed up the identification time in the second phase? And would priming depend at all on rotation?

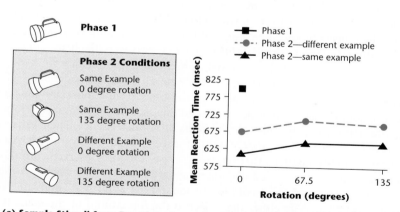

(a) Sample Stimuli from Experiment   **(b) Effect of Rotation on Object Recognition**

Figure 5.1

Sample stimuli from the Biederman and Gerhardstein (1993) study, and graph of the major results.

Figure 5.1b shows phase 1 reaction time as a single point because degree of rotation was not varied in this phase. Phase 1 provided a baseline identification reaction time, which was needed for comparison with phase 2 reaction times. The graph also depicts phase 2 reaction times for the same objects and for different examples, plotted as a function of degree of rotation. As you can see, for both types of objects, reaction time was faster in phase 2 than in phase 1. Seeing a flashlight in phase 1 primed identification of all flashlights (whether the same object or a different example)—this is termed *semantic priming*. However, same object reaction times were faster than different example reaction times. Seeing the same object produced more priming than seeing a different example. But most important for the present discussion were the effects of rotation, which were negligible. This indicates that rotation doesn't really matter to object recognition.

Effects of Context.   Our discussion of recognition thus far is missing something; we've been talking about lab studies that investigate the speed of recognition for isolated objects. But in everyday life you rarely see things in complete isolation. Instead, you view them within some sort of meaningful context. You see a bunny rabbit sitting in the grass underneath a tree; you see a pencil in the hand of someone sitting in a classroom taking notes. One classic demonstration of the beneficial effects of context on recognition was conducted by Palmer (1975). In his study, simple sketches of various everyday scenes were presented, and then sketches of single objects were presented briefly for identification. Palmer varied the relationship between the objects and the scenes: In some cases, the preceding scene (e.g., a kitchen) was consistent with the object to be identified (e.g., a loaf of bread), while in other cases it was inconsistent (e.g., a drum). In others, it was inconsistent *and* misleading (e.g., a mailbox, which has features in common with a loaf of bread). Identification of objects was best when the objects followed a scene that was consistent and worst when the objects were misleading. In fact, in this condition, participants were likely to name the object with a scene-appropriate label (i.e., a loaf of bread and not a mailbox).

Another study by Davenport and Potter (2004) shows the interactive effect that objects and scenes have on identification of the other. While most previous investigations of scenes and object recognition had used line sketches, these investigators decided to use more naturalistic stimuli—photographs of familiar scenes. Their general procedure involved a brief (80 ms) presentation of a scene, followed by a mask. A *mask* is a briefly presented visual pattern that serves to "erase" the just-observed stimulus so that identification can't be based on a fleeting visual afterimage. They wanted to isolate the identification process to the presentation of the photograph itself. Following the mask, participants had to identify either the object in the foreground or the scene itself. The figure was either consistent with the background scene (e.g., quarterback on a football field, cardinal in church) or inconsistent (e.g., quarterback in a church, cardinal on football field). See Figure 5.2 for sample photos from the inconsistent condition. The dependent variable was the accuracy of the identification.

The results are presented in Table 5.1. As you can see participants had an easier time identifying foreground objects than background scenes. This makes sense, as we're no doubt more used to identifying objects than their backgrounds, a finding that fits well

Figure 5.2

Sample of photos from the inconsistent conditon in Davenport and Potter (2004).

From Davenport, J. L. & Potter, M. C. (2004). Scene Consistency in Object and Background Percerption. *Psychological Science, 15,* 559–564. Reprinter with permission from the author and from Elsevier.

with our discussion of basic figure-ground processing in Chapter 2. More importantly, there was a strong effect of consistency between the object and background scene. Both objects and scenes were recognized more easily in cases in which the corresponding background scene and object were consistent than when they were inconsistent.

As Oliva and Torralba (2007) note, the beneficial effect of context on recognition likely represents two different levels of processing. First, the presence of contextual information leads to the preactivation of memory representations for things related to the context. This activation allows for perceptual "educated guesses" to be made about the classes of objects that are likely present in the scene. This influence could be considered top-down in nature, as knowledge of the presented context aids in recognizing its components. A second way in which context aids in recognition is through bottom-up processing, as the presentation of context enhances the integration of component features themselves, enhancing the ability to recognize the object. Although a good deal of evidence does suggest that context can facilitate object recognition, not all researchers are in agreement (e.g., Hollingworth & Henderson, 1998).

Theories of Visual Object Recognition

Now that we've looked at some of the factors that influence recognition, let's consider some of the processes that might be involved. The last 20 years or so have witnessed a lively theoretical debate regarding the nature of recognition processes. As noted earlier, any theory of recognition needs to explain how various changes in an incoming stimulus can have little or no effect on our recognition processes. Two basic approaches have been proposed; let's introduce them briefly within the context of our proverbial bunny rabbit. **Parts-based approaches** propose that the incoming pattern of stimulation produced by the rabbit is parsed into its component parts (little sphere; bigger sphere; long, thin triangles); we

Table 5.1 Results from Davenport and Potter (2004) Study

	Object-Background Relationship	
	Consistent	Inconsistent
Objects	.82	.68
Backgrounds	.70	.54

then compare this set of components to information in memory, and recognize that this set of basic components in this particular combination equals a rabbit. **Image-based approaches** propose a more holistic process whereby we take the whole image of the rabbit, in the orientation that we're viewing it, and compare it to corresponding representations in memory until we find a match. Let's look at these approaches in a little more detail.

Parts-Based (PB) Approach.   According to a *parts-based approach* to visual recognition (e.g., Biederman, 1987; Marr & Nishihara, 1982), we compare the features of the object we've just encoded to a description of the object's structure stored in memory. This description includes a list of the parts (features) of the object, as well as the relationship among them. Given the emphasis on features, it may not surprise you that some parts-based approaches are often given the label **feature analysis.** An important feature of PB approaches is that the representation stored in memory is *not* visually or spatially analogous to the object being recognized. Rather, we compare the features of the incoming visual stimulus to an abstract description of those features in memory.

Recognition based on parts offers an obvious advantage; the particular orientation or view of the object is not important. No matter the perspective, objects are broken down into component parts and compared to a set of features. So orientation or transformation of objects doesn't matter, as long as the component parts are still identifiable. Therefore, these approaches are also termed *viewpoint-independent* because identification of the object does not depend on the particular view that we have of the object; identification depends only on the component features of the object itself.

One influential parts-based theory has been proposed by Biederman and colleagues (e.g., Biederman, 1987; Biederman & Cooper, 1991; Biederman & Gerhardstein, 1993). Its name—**recognition-by-components (RBC)**—makes the general approach clear. Object recognition is a matter of separating, analyzing, and recombining the features of whatever we're looking at. The features into which we parse objects are basic three-dimensional shapes that Biederman terms **geons** (derived from the phrase "geometrical ions"). A sample of these shapes is presented in Figure 5.3, along with a variety of ways in which they might combine to form everyday objects. According to Biederman's theory, there are a total of 36 geons that serve as *visual primitives*—simple shapes that can combine to form most complex shapes. Importantly, these geons are viewed the same way regardless of orientation; a cylinder almost always looks like a cylinder, no matter what visual perspective you happen to have on it.

The RBC theory proposes a series of hierarchically arranged stages whereby information about component features is used to identify the object. First, information about edges is extracted from the retinal image. This edge-extraction process looks for differences in features (e.g., texture, luminance, and color) which results in a simple line drawing of the object. Following this edge extraction, we encode the *nonaccidental features* of the retinal image. Nonaccidental features are those that are almost sure to be actual features of the stimulus rather than some accident of the perspective the observer has on the object. Put simply, we detect features of the stimulus and assume they don't vary with the particular viewpoint. This should sound familiar. Recall from Chapter 2 that Gestalt psychologists were particularly interested in how cognitive processes impose organization on incoming

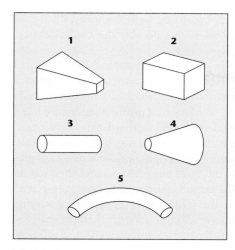 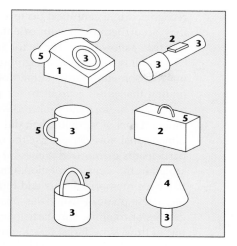

Figure 5.3

Some of the 36 geons proposed by Biederman (1987) and how they combine to form simple objects.

From Biederman, I. (1985). Human image understanding: Recent research and a theory. *Computer Vision, Graphics, and Image Processing, 32*, 29–73. Copyright 1985. Reprinted by permission of Elsevier Science.

information. A basic theme underlying their principles of organization is *simplicity;* we tend to parse objects in the simplest way possible. The segmentation of objects, as proposed by RBC theory, is guided by this basic assumption (Biederman, 1987).

Concurrently with this search for regularities, the visual system is also parsing the object at areas where there appear to be boundaries between the parts of the object. Next, with the information gained to this point, the components of the figure (the geons) are determined, and this set of components is matched with object representations in memory. When a match is found, the object is identified. You may be wondering whether 36 geons is a sufficient number, given the incredible variety of objects we view on a daily basis. Biederman argues that it is; he estimates that humans are familiar with up to 30,000 visually discriminable objects (see Biederman, 1987, for more information on how this estimate was derived). This estimate is no match for the number of objects that could be formed by the 36 geons. Given only two geons—and considering differences in their size, where they join together, and their position relative to one another—over 50,000 shapes are possible. Add a third geon to the mix, and the estimate goes to over 150 million! Clearly, 36 geons provide enough representational power to account for the power of object recognition.

The RBC approach does a fairly good job of accounting for the general processes of object recognition as described earlier. As you saw, Biederman and Gerhardstein (1993) found that object rotation had minimal to no effect on object recognition. This fits with the RBC assumption that recognition of an object should be unaffected as long as the component parts (i.e., the geons) are identifiable. But what about the effects of perspective found by Palmer, Rosch, and Chase (1981)? Recall their finding that objects are best

Figure 5.4
Sample stimuli from
the Tarr and Pinker
(1989) study.

From Tarr, M. J., & Pinker, S.
(1989). Mental rotation and
orientation-dependence in
shape recognition. *Cognitive
Psychology, 21,* 233–282.
Copyright 1989, Elsevier
Science (USA). Reprinted by
permission.

recognized in a canonical perspective. According to RBC theory, this result may occur because certain orientations—most notably the canonical perspective—allow more readily for geon recovery.

So, all is well for the recognition-by-components approach? Well, it turns out that sometimes orientation does have an impact on visual recognition, a finding that poses a problem for parts-based approaches. Consider a study conducted by Tarr and Pinker (1989), which used a priming procedure but a different sort of stimulus than did Biederman and Gerhardstein (1993): two-dimensional novel shapes like the ones in Figure 5.4. During a training phase, participants memorized names for three such shapes, which were always presented in the same orientation. Once the three target shapes and their names had been memorized, Tarr and Pinker assessed participants' recognition during a test phase. During this phase, the targets were presented at varying degrees of rotation, and participants were asked to identify them by pressing one of three keys. Target reaction times showed a significant effect of rotation; participants responded quickly if the shapes were presented in the same orientation as in training, but responded successively slower as the degree of rotation from that original position increased, indicating that visual recognition might be tuned to specific views, or a particular perspective, on an object.

Image-Based (IB) Approach. In contrast to a PB approach, an **image-based (IB) approach** to object recognition contends that objects are recognized holistically through a process of comparison with a stored analog. When a match is found, the object is recognized. In contrast to PB approaches, IB approaches are considered *viewpoint-dependent,* because identification of an object depends critically on the particular perspective of the viewer. To identify the object, an image matching this particular view must be found, or the incoming stimulus image must be manipulated in some way (e.g., rotated) until a match is found.

The first systematic attempt to account for recognition in the early history of cognitive psychology was an IB approach (although at the time, PB and IB were not classifications for theories of recognition). Neisser (1967) suggested that recognizing simple line patterns (e.g., letters) was a process of *template matching.* According to this **template-matching theory,** our store of general knowledge includes a set of **templates,** or copies, of every pattern that we might encounter. You may have seen (or used) plastic stencils that allow you to trace perfect forms (provided you have a steady hand). You might picture templates this way—as perfect forms or replicas of a pattern. The basic notion behind template-matching theory is that when we encounter some pattern that needs to be identified, the mind quickly rifles through its set of templates, and when a match is found, the pattern is given the label stored with the template (i.e., the pattern is recognized).

Template matching is an IB approach in that pattern recognition involves a comparison with a stored analog. Many simple computer-based recognition systems are based on this sort of process. For example, the somewhat odd-looking numbers at the bottom of your checks are rigidly structured such that they fit the templates that computers use for recognition. These recognition systems are "stupid" in that even the slightest change in the pattern will lead to a recognition failure. This strict version of the template-matching theory is too limited to account for the tremendous flexibility of human object recognition.

We have no problem recognizing objects that are distorted, upside down, backward, tilted, partially blocked, bent, twisted…you get the idea. Another problem is the lack of economy implied by the template approach. We'd need countless templates to recognize all the objects we encounter every day. Also, we'd need different templates for different versions of objects (tilted, upside down, partially blocked). This means we'd need to have an essentially infinite number of templates, something that just doesn't seem feasible.

The strict version of the template-matching theory is really a sort of straw-man argument that's easy to dismiss. But this general approach is not without its merit. The basic mechanism—matching our view of an object with a representation of that image stored in memory—is quite sensible. The problems arise from the rigidity implied in the original approach. Based on our overwhelming "hit" rate in correctly identifying objects in the world, it seems apparent that misorientation and distortion don't seem to hurt visual recognition as much as the template-matching theory would imply. The Biederman and Gerhardstein study that was discussed earlier lent empirical support to this intuition, revealing minimal effects of orientation on object recognition.

To deal with these sorts of issues, IB theorists (e.g., Tarr & Pinker, 1989) propose that through experience with objects in many different orientations and viewed from many different perspectives, we develop multiple representations, or *views,* of the objects. These *multiple views* serve as the templates for later recognition. The reason orientation tends not to affect our visual recognition under most circumstances is that everything we must recognize has received extensive exposure from different perspectives. For example, think of all the different perspectives from which you've viewed your car. Based on extensive exposure to these different perspectives, you've developed multiple views of your car that you use in recognizing it.

The importance of multiple views in allowing for object recognition received some early support from studies of basic visual processing in monkeys (who have visual systems comparable to our own). Logothetis, Pauls, and Poggio (1995) taught monkeys to recognize novel three-dimensional objects from a variety of different perspectives, and like humans, the monkeys eventually became equally proficient at recognizing these objects, given any of the rotations. Especially compelling was the neural activity associated with recognition during a later testing phase; different sets of cells responded most strongly to certain objects, indicating that certain networks were devoted to certain objects. More importantly, a given set of cells responded most strongly when that object appeared in the same orientation as it had during training. The responses of these cells decreased systematically with increases in the rotation from that perspective. Consistent with the basic assumption of the multiple-views approach, these monkeys seemed to have what might be termed *physiological templates* that were devoted to recognizing a specific object in a specific orientation (Tarr, 2000).

Palmeri and Tarr (2008) describe a critical difference between PB and IB views of object recognition. This difference centers on the role of experience. According to PB theories like Biederman's, object representations are constructed by assembling visual primitives (i.e., geons) via a fixed processing mechanism. Experience plays no role in determining the primitives or the architecture of the system; those are fixed. Experience comes in as we learn the *configurations* of primitives that distinguish objects from one another. That is, we learn through experience that a telephone represents a different configuration of primitives than does a car. Compare this with image-based theories, which propose that we build up a representation of phones and cars through specific experiences with phones and cars. So basically, object recognition is the same as visual memory; when we recognize something, we're remembering it. This distinction has an interesting parallel in the theories of concept representation that we'll discuss later in the chapter.

Object Recognition: Parts or Images?   So we've seen conflicting evidence regarding whether object recognition is impacted by orientation or perspective of the viewer. As you've read, both the image-based and the parts-based approaches to recognition have garnered support. Tarr and Bülthoff (1995) provide one example of how the two sets of mechanisms might combine. These authors suggest that object recognition can be conceived as a continuum. At one end are heavily viewpoint-independent mechanisms like those proposed by the PB approaches. These mechanisms will be recruited when more gross categorical judgments are required, such as when we need to distinguish among two different basic-level category members, like a hammer and a blue jay. In this sort of judgment, orientation is not likely to matter much. At the other end of the continuum are heavily viewpoint-dependent mechanisms like those proposed by the IB approaches that are used for making subtle discriminations among subordinate-level category members like a blue jay and a cardinal. Here, orientation is likely to play a role, particularly if we're not experts in the particular domain (e.g., birds). Another way to consider how to combine these two approaches is provided by Palmeri and Tarr (2008). They suggest that parts-based models like Biederman's recognition-by-components theory highlight the importance of the parts of an object and their spatial relations, while image-based theories highlight the importance of specific visual memories of objects. Regardless of the particular manner in which view-dependent (i.e., image-based) and view-independent (i.e., parts-based) combine to produce object recognition, a hybrid view is favored by many researchers (e.g., Ullman, Vidal-Naquet, & Sali, 2002; Thoma, Hummel, & Davidoff, 2004; Barenholtz & Tarr, 2007).

The processes used to distinguish between two subordinate-level category members (two types of birds) may be different from those used to distinguish between two basic-level category members (a bird and a hammer).

Nonvisual Recognition

Although there would be little disagreement that vision is the most important and prominent mode for the recognition of objects, recognition also occurs in the other senses. The most important task of auditory recognition occurs within the context of language use and will be discussed further in Chapter 9. Along with vision and audition, we do gain a good deal of information that aids in our identification from both the tactile and chemical senses.

Tactile Recognition.   Given our tendency to think of vision as the primary mode for environmental exploration and information intake, we fail to notice how much information is available through touch (i.e., **haptics**) (Gibson, 1966). Klatzky, Lederman, and Reed (1987) suggest the following thought experiment: think of what you would likely see if you were looking at a cat. Chances are, this visual image includes a head, pointy ears, whiskers, four legs, and a tail, along with the respective sizes and layout of these features. If you were asked to think of how a cat feels to the touch, you'd likely come up with quite different attributes: furriness, warmth, and softness. There's a great deal of information about objects you can't get from looking at it.

So how do you gain this information? Klatzky, Lederman, and Metzger (1985) coined the term **exploratory procedures (EPs)** to describe the precise motor patterns performed by the hands in the exploration and identification of an object. They asked participants to identify 100 common objects using nothing but their hands. It may seem surprising that participants were able to identify each object in a matter of one to two seconds, with virtually no wrong identifications. Clearly, we can gather an incredible amount of information with what Klatzky and Lederman (1995) call a *haptic glance*.

Based on their observations of participants' haptic exploration, Klatzky, Lederman, and Metzger (1985) identified six exploratory procedures (depicted in Figure 5.5): static

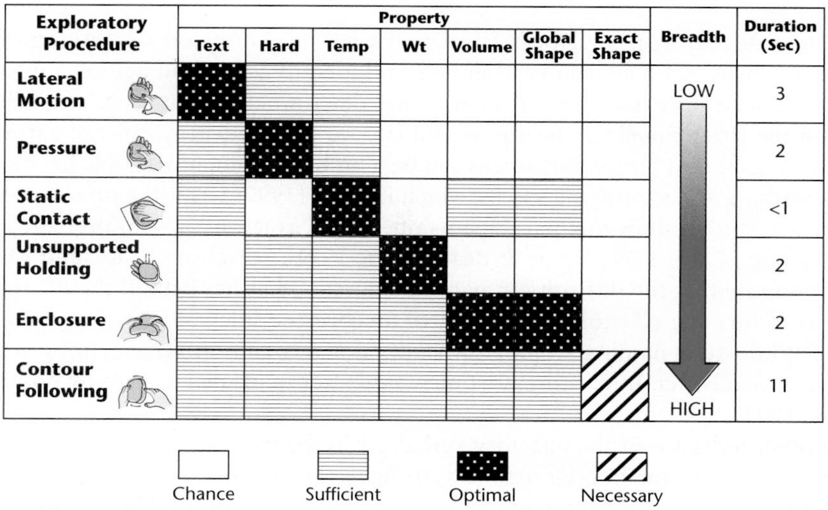

Exploratory Procedure	Property							Breadth	Duration (Sec)
	Text	Hard	Temp	Wt	Volume	Global Shape	Exact Shape		
Lateral Motion	Optimal	Sufficient						LOW	3
Pressure		Optimal							2
Static Contact			Optimal			Sufficient	Sufficient		<1
Unsupported Holding		Sufficient		Optimal					2
Enclosure					Optimal	Sufficient			2
Contour Following						Sufficient	Necessary	HIGH	11

Legend: Chance — Sufficient — Optimal — Necessary

Figure 5.5

Exploratory procedures and their properties (from Klatzky and Lederman 2008).

contact, unsupported lifting, lateral motion, pressure, contour following, and enclosure. Figure 5.5 also presents some of the information gained about these EPs over two decades of research. This information includes the nature and amount (i.e. breadth) of the information extracted, as well as the time each takes to perform. Klatzky and Lederman (2008) note a few important principles that can be gleaned from this table. For example, judging from the number of EPs that provide certain types of information, it is apparent that the material properties of objects (e.g., texture, temperature) are easier to ascertain than their geometric properties (e.g., shape, size). Also, some EPs have more breadth (i.e., provide a wider range of information) than others. However, this breadth comes with a cost. The most informative exploratory procedure—contour following—also takes the longest amount of time to perform. In general, compared with visual object recognition, tactile recognition tends to be relatively slow and painstaking.

Stop&*Think* | EXPLORING EPs

Gather three easily-held objects and keep them hidden. Recruit some friends and test their haptic identification. You'll have to direct your "subjects" to close their eyes. Take note of hand movements as they attempt to identify each object and classify each hand movement in terms of the Klatzky and Lederman scheme.

- Do they use hand movements not identified by Klatzky, Lederman, and Metzger? If so, explain what they are.
- Do the hand movements seem to take place in a particular order?

Olfactory Recognition.   Not much research has been done on recognition of basic tastes and smells. After all, you typically see and identify your food before you eat it or smell it. Because taste is strongly related to and determined by our sense of smell, we'll focus on the latter. Smell can be a powerful cue we use to identify objects, particularly foodstuff like peanut butter. But smells can be a bit bedeviling, too. People have a tough time describing and identifying smells, which Lawless (1997) terms the **olfactory-verbal gap.** In fact, studies show that participants often label as few as 50% of presented odors correctly (e.g., Cain, 1977; Desor & Beauchamp, 1974). Stevenson, Case, and Mahmut (2007) propose that the difficulty in naming odors is what lies behind the oft-reported difficulty in forming olfactory images (try to imagine the smell of a rose, vs. the sight of a rose). While odor naming is quite difficult, odor recognition (given choices of odor labels) is much better. Interestingly, women are better than men at naming odors (e.g., Lehrner, 1993).

Another indicator of the olfactory-verbal gap is the frustrating inability to come up with the verbal label for an odor despite a strong feeling that one knows what the odor is, termed tip of the nose phenomenon by Lawless and Engen (1977). This is a specific and sensory example of a phenomenon termed **tip-of-the-tongue (TOT) state.** The TOT state occurs when we are quite certain that we know a piece of information, but feel blocked from retrieving it. The type of information that is most likely to sit on the tip of your tongue, refusing to come out, turns out to be people's names. We'll discuss that later, in the context of face and name recognition.

Research into the TOT experience has proved to be an important inroad to metacognition, or people's sensitivity to and knowledge about their own cognitive processes. One trademark characteristic of the TOT state is a palpable *feeling of knowing*. Even when blocked from retrieving the information, we have a strong subjective feeling that we know it. One question of interest is the accuracy of these feelings-of-knowing. When researchers collect feeling-of-knowing judgments from someone experiencing a TOT, they can test metacognitive accuracy by having that person attempt to pick out the answer, given some choices. If the feeling of knowing is accurate, people should be able to pick out the answer at a level above chance. For the most part, research shows that feelings of knowing are usually accurate.

Research Theme
Metacognition

Jonsson and Olsson (2003) conducted an investigation of olfactory metacognition on the tip-of-the-nose phenomenon. They presented a wide variety of "odorants" (e.g., oregano, vanilla, peppermint), and asked participants to name the odor. If they were unable to name it, they were asked to make a feeling-of-knowing judgment, guessing the probability that they would be able to determine whether a label presented after the odor was correct. After this judgment, they were presented a label and had to determine whether it was the correct label for the odor. Consistent with the general difficulties found previously in odor-naming, participants attempted to guess the odor only 28% of the time, and 16% of the time were correct. Typically, odors that could not be named were associated with a feeling of knowing. These feelings of knowing were indeed correlated with recognition performance, indicating that participants had some sensitivity to their state of knowledge with regard to the odors. So although people are often poor at naming odors, they do seem to have some sensitivity to their ability to recognize the odor.

Stop&*Review*

1. Distinguish between the role of bottom-up and top-down processing in object recognition.

2. Objects are identified most easily if they are viewed from a _____ perspective.

3. Parts-based views state that object recognition is _____; Image-based views state that object recognition is _____ .
   a. viewpoint-independent; viewpoint-independent
   b. viewpoint-dependent; viewpoint-dependent
   c. viewpoint-independent; viewpoint-dependent
   d. viewpoint-dependent; viewpoint-independent

4. Describe how the two major views of object recognition map onto levels of categorization.

5. True or false? Exploratory procedures are the processes that we use to identify smells

• Object recognition refers to the processes whereby we match an incoming stimulus with stored representations for the purpose of identification. There are three levels of categorization: superordinate level (animal), basic level (bird), subordinate level (cardinal). Bottom-up processing employs the information in the stimulus itself to aid in identification. Top-down processes rely on expectations, knowledge, and/or surrounding context to help identify an object.

- Object recognition is influenced by a number of variables including one's perspective on an object. Objects seem to be identified most easily when viewed from a canonical perspective, the perspective that serves as the best representation of the object. Context also aids in object recognition; objects are recognized more easily in an appropriate context than in an inappropriate context.

- According to parts-based approaches, object recognition is based on an analysis of object parts. These approaches are termed *viewpoint-independent;* identification does not depend on perspective. Image-based (IB) approaches contend

that objects are recognized holistically through a process of comparison to a stored analog. These approaches are termed *viewpoint-dependent* because they contend that identification does depend on perspective.

- Some contend that object recognition is likely to involve both parts-based (viewpoint-independent) and image-based (viewpoint-dependent) mechanisms, depending on the nature of the identification task. Recognition at the basic level may involve primarily parts-based mechanisms, while the finer discriminations required at the subordinate level involve primarily image-based mechanisms.

- The olfactory-verbal gap refers to the difficulty people have in identifying smells. Exploratory procedures are the hand movements we use for tactile identification. These procedures include contour following, enclosure, lateral motion, static contact, unsupported lifting, and pressure.

Face Recognition

If there's one class of stimuli for which recognition is the most important, significant, and frequent, it's the recognition of faces. Without the ability to recognize familiar faces, we would be awash in a sea of strangers. Indeed, this is the disconcerting dilemma faced by those suffering from **prosopagnosia,** an inability to recognize familiar faces. Farah (1992) recounts the story of a prosopagnosic who was sitting in a country club wondering why another gentleman was staring so intently at him. He asked one of the servers to investigate and found that the man staring at him was his own reflection in a mirror!

Face Inversion

Let's take a closer look at face recognition and a revealing finding—that turning a face upside down has a disproportionately disrupting effect on the recognition of faces relative to its effects on the recognition of objects (Yin, 1969). Look at the man in the photo on page 187. Do you recognize him? He is none other than the "Governator," Arnold Schwarzenegger. If you hesitated in recognizing him, it is because he is upside down.

The Thatcher Illusion.   The effects of face inversion have been studied quite extensively within what has come to be known as the Thatcher illusion (Thompson, 1980). Take a look at the left-hand panel of Figure 5.6. What you see is an upside down picture of Britney Spears. The right-hand panel shows the same picture…or does it? Flip the book over, and be horrified. When placed in the proper orientation you can see that the picture is actually a seriously distorted version of the "normal" picture. (In the original study, pictures of former British Prime Minister Margaret Thatcher were used. Pity poor Margaret Thatcher, whose frightening upside-down visage has become a staple of psychology books.) Anyway, the point of the demonstration is that turning a face upside down—that is, inverting it—is severely disruptive to face recognition.

I'll be back….Who am I?

What makes the recognition of faces so different from that of other objects, and how does this lead to the inversion effect? Diamond and Carey (1986) propose that to recognize objects, we need *first-order relational information*—that is, information about the parts of an object and how those parts relate to one another. For face recognition, this would involve an analysis of the person's facial features and the relationship among those features. However, first-order relational information is not enough to recognize faces; simply noticing that two eyes are above the nose, which is above the mouth, may be enough for recognizing that something is a face but doesn't allow for recognition of who the face is.

To recognize faces, we need what Diamond and Carey term *second-order relational information*. Second-order relational information involves comparing the first-order analysis to facial features of a "typical," or "average," face. This typical face is built up through experience and serves as an implicit standard against which we compare the

Figure 5.6
An example of the Thatcher illusion.

faces we see. Inverting a face disrupts the encoding of second-order relational information. Given that this information is most important for recognizing faces, inversion disproportionately harms face recognition.

Holistic Processing

As you've read, face recognition seems to depend on second-order relational information, or the relationship among the features. Inverting a face disrupts these relationships profoundly, and thus disrupts face recognition. This underscores the fact that faces are encoded as whole configurations (like templates) that are best processed holistically. The upright face is a unique pattern, and when that pattern is disrupted (e.g., is turned upside down), so is recognition. This is true in spite of the fact that none of the individual parts has changed. This isn't the case with objects—rearranging the parts of objects doesn't disrupt their recognition too much.

This difference between face and object recognition was evident in a study by Tanaka and Farah (1993). These authors reasoned that to the degree that a given pattern (e.g., a face or some other object) is stored as a set of features, those features ought to be useful cues in retrieving the remaining information about the object. However, if a pattern is stored as a whole configuration (as seems to be the case with faces), then presenting part of that whole will not be particularly helpful in recognition.

To test their hypotheses, Tanaka and Farah presented participants with sketches of faces and sketches of houses, both decomposable in terms of distinct features. Each face and house was given a label, such as "Larry's house" or "Larry's face." On a later recognition test, participants were asked about the faces and houses in either an isolated-part condition or a whole-object condition. In the isolated-part condition, they were given a choice of two object parts and had to pick which one of them had been part of an object presented earlier (e.g., "Which of these is Larry's nose?" or "Which of these is Larry's door?"). In the whole-object condition, they were given a choice of two whole objects and had to pick out the one they had seen earlier (e.g., "Which of these is Larry's face?" or "Which of these is Larry's house?").

The results are presented in Table 5.2. As you can see, the type of question asked didn't matter for recognition of houses; participants were just as good at recognizing parts of houses as they were at recognizing whole houses. But for faces, the type of question did matter. Participants were not as good at recognizing face parts as they were at recognizing whole faces.

Table 5.2 **Results from Tanaka and Farah (1993); Proportion Correct as a Function of Presentation Condition and Type of Stimulus**

| | | Type of Stimulus | |
		Houses	Faces
Presentation Condition	**Isolated-Part**	.80	.66
	Whole-Object	.78	.77

Is Face Recognition "Special"?

The finding that face recognition is based on the recognition of whole configurations rather than individual parts indicates that face recognition is more akin to the mechanisms proposed by image-based approaches to object recognition than to parts-based approaches. Recall that image-based approaches assume holistic processing of objects whereas parts-based approaches assume an analysis and assembly of component features. This would explain why rotation harms face recognition disproportionately. As you saw earlier, parts-based recognition is unaffected by rotation, while image-based recognition is affected by it. While the theoretical position that face recognition is akin to image-based approaches to recognition is well-accepted, one issue remains hotly debated. Are the mechanisms used to recognize faces "special?" In other words, are there a set of processes specialized for the sole purpose of recognizing faces? A specialized mechanism for this type of processing certainly would seem to make evolutionary sense. It would be hard to come up with a more important thing to recognize and respond to than a human face.

The main evidence to support the **special mechanism view** is the existence of dissociations found between object and face recognition. Recall the concept of dissociations from Chapter 1—dissociations are taken as evidence that two different abilities are based on different processes. Farah (1992, 1996) reports several double dissociations in her examination of neurological patients with deficits in face recognition. For example, she reports that some patients show intact object recognition without face recognition, while others show the converse pattern. Another dissociation used to support the special mechanism view is the face-inversion effect; inversion hurts the recognition of faces but not objects, Dissociations like these indicate that face and object recognition are based on different mechanisms. Put another way, faces would appear to be a "special" class of objects, recognized with different (face-specific) mechanisms.

Research Theme
Evolution

The most prominent alternative to the special mechanism view is the **expertise view** (e.g., Gauthier & Curby, 2005; Tanaka, 2001; Tarr & Cheng, 2003). Expertise refers to the superior knowledge and skill that develops after extensive practice in some domain, and there's no doubt that all human beings (except perhaps infants) could be considered experts in the domain of face recognition. Tarr and Cheng (2003) propose that the recognition of faces differs from that of other objects because of the typical *entry point* required for recognition. As you read earlier in the context of levels of categorization, the entry point refers to the default level of categorization that we assign to familiar objects. In our earlier discussion, we noted that the basic level serves as the most common entry point for recognition. But given the seemingly infinite variety of faces that we encounter in our lives, recognition at the basic level would not be enough. No one looks at their best friend and thinks, "Hey, there's a human"; they don't even recognize a face at the subordinate level: "Hey, there's a young Caucasian American." Instead, they recognize individuals: "Hey, there's Allyson." So the entry point required for recognition of human faces is at the *individual* level, a more specific level than we've addressed thus far.

Recall our discussion of recognition theories and the resolution of those theories proposed by Tarr and Bulthoff (1995). They propose that parts-based mechanisms are important for making gross discriminations (i.e., at the basic level), while more holistic image-based mechanisms are used for making fine discriminations (i.e., at the subordinate level). Tarr and Cheng (2003) apply this distinction to the recognition of objects and faces. Given that the individual level is more specific than the subordinate level, objects at this level (i.e., faces) would require an even finer level of discrimination to differentiate between them than objects at the subordinate level. Therefore, faces can be recognized only holistically, in terms of the particular configuration of their features. According to Tarr and Cheng (2003) expertise leads one to shift the default level of categorization and recognition from the basic level to the individual level. Faces aren't special; expertise is.

A recent issue of the journal *Cognition* featuring an exchange between leading proponents of the special mechanism view and the expertise view (Gauthier & Bukach, 2007; McKone & Robbins, 2007; Robbins & McKone, 2007) indicates that a definitive answer regarding the "special" status of face recognition has yet to be determined. But while we don't know the answer to the theoretical question, there is absolutely no denying that from a practical standpoint, face recognition is prioritized and unique given the ubiquity of the human face and our interactions with them. Whether face recognition is special because of dedicated special mechanisms or because of our extensive expertise in identifying them, there is no doubt that face recognition is special.

Stop&*Think Back* | FACE IT! PRIORITIES IN FACE RECOGNITION

Evidence indicates that not only are we good at perceiving and recognizing faces; they also receive attentional priority. Recall the finding from Chapter 3 that angry faces are subject to a shorter attentional blink than neutral faces. This makes adaptive sense; there would be a survival advantage to noticing threatening faces. What other specific reasons can you think of for the advantage humans would have in speed and efficiency of recognizing faces? What characteristics or types (i.e., expressions) of human faces might be particularly recognizable?

Individual Differences

Regardless of whether a special mechanism exists for the recognition of human faces, there is growing evidence that the mechanisms we use for recognition are tuned differently for different individuals, most likely as a function of visual and social experience. So let's see how one's gender and cultural background influence facial recognition.

Gender.   It is well known that women have an advantage over men at recognizing facial emotions (see McClure, 2000 for a review). McBain, Norton, and Chen (2009) wanted to determine if this difference was related to superior face recognition ability, in general. In one experiment, participants were shown line-drawings of an object embedded within a larger array or lines. The objects were an upright face (Figure 5.7a), an inverted face (Figure 5.7b) or an upright tree (Figure 5.7c). The line drawings were shown for various durations ranging from 13 to 104 milliseconds. The participant's task was to indicate if the face or tree appeared on the left or right side. The dependent variable was accuracy.

Detector Task

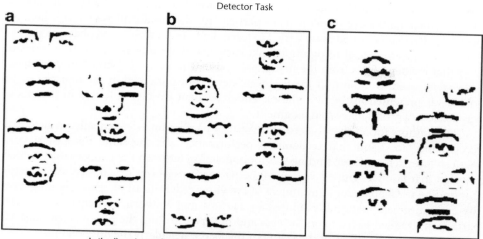

Is the line-drawn face/tree on the left or the right side of the drawing?

Figure 5.7

Sample stimuli used in the McBain, Norton, and Chen (2009) study on face recognition.

Not surprisingly, performance was better the longer the stimulus was displayed. However, regardless of stimulus duration, women were more accurate than men in the upright and inverted face conditions. However, accuracy was the same for male and female participants in the tree condition. The participants were equated on age, IQ, years of education, and visual acuity. Therefore, this finding cannot be attributed to any other differences between the groups. So it seems that woman do possess a general advantage in facial identification. Assuming the female performance advantage is due to gender role socialization, it remains unclear which specific factor leads to this enhanced performance or when in development this advantage emerges.

The authors indicate that given the critical role that face recognition plays in social interaction (Haxby, Hoffman, & Gobbini, 2002), these results might help to explain some clinical findings related to schizophrenia and autism. Both of these populations show poor performance on basic face processing tasks (Lee, Kwon, Shin & Lee, 2007) and under-developed social skills. Moreover, 76% of people with autism are male (Nicholas, Charles, Carpenter, King, Jenner, & Spratt, 2008) and female schizophrenics tend to have less social impairment than male schizophrenics (Usall, Araya, Ochoa, Busquets, Gost, Márquez, 2001). These findings combined with the results of the McBain et al. study suggests that enhanced face recognition in woman may moderate the clinical symptoms of these disorders.

Culture.   Differences in face recognition tendencies are not limited to gender. Blais, Jack, Scheepers, Fiset, and Caldara (2008) examined variation in face recognition between Eastern and Western cultures. Their investigation included two independent variables: culture of the participant (Eastern or Western) and ethnicity of the faces to be learned (Western Caucasian or East Asian). In the first phase of the experiment, participants were

Research Theme
Culture

given a set of Western Caucasian or East Asian faces to learn. One dependent variable involved tracking the eye movements of participants during this phase to see where on the face participants fixated as they tried to learn the faces. In the second phase, all participants were given a facial recognition task. Participants were presented with a series of faces that included faces from the first phase and new faces not presented in that phase. They were asked to indicate if the face was "new" (not presented in the first phase) or "old" (was presented in the first phase). The dependent variable collected in this phase was the accuracy of the new/old judgment.

The authors found that Eastern and Western participants were equally proficient at recognizing faces, and that recognition performance was the same for Eastern and Western faces. The striking finding was an interaction between the two variables, which revealed that face recognition was much better for faces of one's own race. We'll revisit this finding in Chapter 8, in the context of eyewitness identification. Also revealing were the eye movement patterns exhibited by Eastern and Western participants. Western participants tended to fixate on the eyes and the areas around the eyes whereas Eastern participants tended to look at the center of the face, particularly the nose region.

What factors lie at the root of these processing differences? Blais, Jack, Scheepers, Fiset, and Caldara (2008) have a few ideas. First they propose that due to social norms Eastern participants might be in the habit of avoiding direct gaze; excessive eye contact is considered to be rude in East Asian cultures (e.g., Argyle & Cook, 1976); this may have tuned Eastern participants to look in regions other than the eyes. The cultural difference might also reflect differences in visual processing found in each culture, which was discussed in Chapter 2. Research indicates that individuals from Western cultures prefer an analytic mode that emphasizes the processing of salient focal elements of a visual scene. Individuals from Eastern cultures tend toward a holistic mode that emphasizes the processing of contextual elements. Blais et al. speculate that the Western participants' tendency to focus on the eyes is consistent with the notion that people from Western cultures tend to focus on salient focal features. The Eastern participants' tendency to focus on the central region of the face is consistent with the notion that people from Eastern cultures tend to focus on contextual elements; the central region of the face is the optimal area in which to fixate if one wants an integrated and holistic view of the face.

Self-Recognition

Let's return to the plight of the man in the anecdote related by Farah (1992) who failed to recognize his own face. His visual recognition deficit is striking, reminding us of the degree to which we take this ability for granted. Our knowledge of our own face seems inseparable from our general knowledge of self—who we are, our likes and dislikes, our personal history. Whether face recognition involves a special mechanism or is simply a matter of perceptual expertise, there does seem to be evidence to suggest that recognition of one's own face may be particularly special. One indicator of this is that although nonhuman primates have shown face-recognition ability, they fail on tests of self-recognition even after extended training (Keenan, Wheeler, Gallup, & Pascual-Leone, 2000). Might our own face recognition rely on different brain areas than general face recognition?

Keenan and colleagues (Keenan, Freund, Hamilton, Ganis, & Pascual-Leone, 2000; Keenan, McCutcheon, Freund, Gallup, Sanders, & Pascual-Leone, 1999) have found some intriguing evidence that self-recognition may involve the right prefrontal area of the cortex. This evidence is especially intriguing in light of what others have found—that this same area is especially active during other tasks involving the self, such as recalling the events from one's own life story (Fink, Markowitsch, & Reinkemeier, 1996). (We'll talk more about recall of one's life story—autobiographical memory—in Chapter 7.)

This right-hemisphere advantage in self-recognition was demonstrated in a study by Keenan et al (1999). In this study participants saw a series of rapidly presented faces—a sort of "face movie." The series of faces began with the person's own face and ended with the face of a famous person (e.g., Bill Clinton or Marilyn Monroe). In between was a sequence of morphed pictures that were combinations of the two (see Figure 5.8). The researchers also used the opposite sequence in which the famous face would gradually morph into the participant's face. Participants were told to watch the series and press a key when they felt that each picture had become more "not themselves" than "themselves" (or vice versa, in the reverse condition), using either their right or left hand to respond. As you may recall, given the contrateral organization of the brain's hemispheres, a left-hand response is controlled by the right hemisphere while the converse is true for a right-hand response. If the right hemisphere is specialized for self-recognition, then one might expect that a left-handed response should exhibit a self-recognition bias. This is precisely what happened; When using the left hand (the right hemisphere) the "not themselves" transition was judged as occurring significantly earlier than when participants responded with their right hand. This indicates right-hemisphere advantage in self-recognition.

A recent study—aptly named "Mirror Mirror on the Wall"—used a face-morphing procedure similar to the one just described in order to investigate a different sort of bias in self-recognition. Rather than a bias in hemispheric processing, Epley and Whitchurch (2008) were interested in a self-enhancement bias. They hypothesized that people are likely to see themselves as more attractive or desirable than they actually are. Such a finding would be consistent with a growing body of evidence showing that people perceive things about themselves as objectively positive (Koole & DeHart, 2007). The procedure was relatively simple. In an initial session, participants had their pictures taken, and were

Figure 5.8

Facial morph like that used by Keenan et al. (1999). Over a series of pictures, a subject's face morphs into a famous face.

From Keenan, J. P., McCutcheon, B., Freund, S., Gallup, G. G., Sanders, G., & Pascual-Leone, A. (1999). Left-hand advantage in a self-face recognition task. *Neuropsychologia, 37,* 1421–1425. Copyright 1999. Reprinted by permission of Elsevier Science.

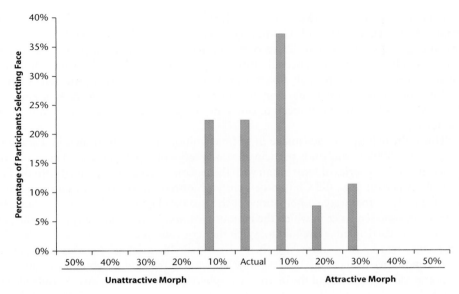

Figure 5.9
Results from Epley and Whitchurch (2008); choices of the attractive morph indicate a self-enhancement bias.

told to return for another experimental session a few weeks later. In the interim, the experimenters created 10 more versions of their face by computer-morphing to varying degrees with an unattractive or attractive face. On their second visit, participants were presented with all 11 versions of their face and were asked to select the original picture. The amusing results are presented in Figure 5.9. As you can see, less than 25% of participants correctly recognized the original photo of their face, and the recognition errors were not random. People were much more likely to err on the side of the attractive morph rather than the unattractive morph. Interestingly, follow-up studies revealed the same bias for participants' evaluation of friends.

Based on extensive research on self-face recognition and other domains of self-relevant processing, Feinberg, Keenan and colleagues (Feinberg & Keenan, 2005; Keenan & Gorman 2007; Keenan, Gallup, & Falk, 2003) have proposed that one's self-awareness, indeed, their very sense of identity is localized largely in the right hemisphere, more specifically, the right prefrontal cortex. Further research (e.g, Platek, Wathne, Tierney, & Thomson, 2008) reveals that the unique and specialized processing associated with self extends to the processing of important others, such as family and friends (as with our cell phones, we seem to have a "friends and family" network!).

Retrieving Names of Faces: Person Recognition

It is perhaps a cruel irony that our phenomenal abilities to perceive and recognize human faces is accompanied by an accursed difficulty—an inability to remember names.

Retrieving names might be seen as the final stage of face recognition, and it's the stage that quite often fails. Tip-of-the tongue experiences, described earlier in the chapter, are quite common for names, and are often accompanied by generally strong and accurate feelings of knowing (e.g., Hosey, Peynircioğlu, & Rabinowitz, 2009).

Hanley and Cowell (1988) conducted a study that highlighted the special difficulty in retrieving people's names. Participants were presented with familiar faces and asked to recognize them as familiar, provide biographical information about them, and, finally, name them. The pattern of errors was quite revealing; in many instances, people could recognize that a face was familiar but couldn't provide any biographical information about the person or name the person. Other times, participants could recognize the face as familiar and provide some biographical information but could not name the person. And, revealingly, the converse was almost never true; it was almost never the case that the name was retrieved in the absence of any other information about the person.

These results indicate a gradient of difficulty in the processes of person recognition, with the most difficult task being name retrieval. Young, Ellis, and Flude (1988) provided converging evidence for the notion of a difficulty gradient using a reaction time (RT) task. The RT for recognizing a face as familiar is reliably faster than the RT for retrieving biographical information about the person; and this RT is faster than the RT for retrieving the name. Based on this evidence, some propose that the retrieval of names and the retrieval of biographical information comprise different processes and stages within a person-recognition system.

Serial and Parallel Accounts.

Two basic approaches have been offered to explain why the retrieval of a person's name is more difficult than the retrieval of other information about that person. The Bruce and Young (1986) model proposes a serial process for accessing information about a person. First, a face must activate a face recognition unit (FRU)—a stored representation of that face in memory. If activated, the person is recognized as familiar. Next, the FRU must activate the person identity node (PIN), which stores biographical information about the person. If activated, this biographical information becomes available. Next, the PIN must activate the terminal node, which stores the name of the person. This model accounts for the finding that names are retrieved slower than other information about a person; name retrieval is the last node activated in the system. It can also explain why a name is sometimes not remembered while other information about the person is; information about the person must be retrieved before the name can be retrieved. Therefore, a name will never be activated in the absence of information retrieval about the person.

In contrast to the serial nature of the Bruce and Young (1986) model, the *interactive activation and competition (IAC) model* (Burton & Bruce, 1992) proposes that parallel processes allow us to access names. The IAC model assumes that there are separate FRUs (stored representations of faces), PINs (which in this model are multimodal general representations of people), and semantic information units (SIUs). An SIU contains both biographical information and names; there is no separate representation for names. In addition, the activation and retrieval process is parallel, not serial. So the face of David Letterman will simultaneously activate his PIN, his FRU, and his SIU. His SIU will include "talk show host," "from Indiana," and the name "David Letterman." "Talk show host" will also be linked to the Jay Leno PIN, and "from Indiana" will also be linked to the Michael Jackson PIN. But the name "David Letterman" will be linked only to the David Letterman PIN (see Figure 5.10).

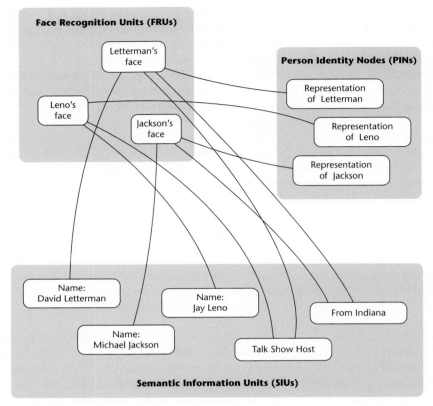

Figure 5.10

A portion of the knowledge network representing names and faces, according to the interactive activation and competition (IAC) model.

Adapted from Burton, A. M., & Bruce, V. (1992). Naming faces and naming names: Exploring an interactive activation model of person recognition memory. *Memory, 1,* 457–480.

Superior access to biographical information like "talk show host" and "from Indiana" relative to the name "David Letterman" can be explained by a faster buildup of activation for his biographical information relative to his name. For example, when we encounter the funniest man in late-night TV, activation spreads from the David Letterman PIN to "talk show host" and "from Indiana" back to the David Letterman PIN, but also to the Jay Leno PIN and the Michael Jackson PIN, respectively. The David Letterman PIN and the Jay Leno PIN will reactivate "talk show host," and the David Letterman PIN and the Michael Jackson PIN will reactivate "from Indiana." But the name "David Letterman" receives activation only from the David Letterman PIN. So over time, nodes that refer to more general pieces of biographical information (e.g., "from Indiana" and "talk show host") will receive more activation than the person's name, which is completely unique and corresponds only to that person. Due to this faster buildup of activation, biographical information will be in a state of higher activation than will a specific name and hence will be more retrievable.

The parallel approach to name retrieval receives some solid support from a study by Brédart, Brennen, Delchambre, McNeill, and Burton (2005). They reasoned that it might be possible to reverse the commonly found effect that names are more difficult to retrieve than biographical information. You'll recall that this effect is one basis for supposing that name retrieval is a serial process. Brédart and colleagues subscribe to the parallel view, which assumes that the difficulty of name retrieval stems from the fact that names have chronically lower levels of activation, as described previously. They reasoned, however, that not all names have such low levels of activation. One's own names, as well as the names of family members and close friends, are frequently activated, so one might suspect that they would be at a chronically high level of activation, just waiting to be recognized. In fact, one might expect the activation of the name to exceed the activation of other biographical information.

To test this hypothesis, Brédart et al. (2005) asked colleagues in the same psychology department who had known each other for several years to participate in a face recognition experiment. The task was simple; participants were presented with one of three different cue words—*name*, *educational level*, or *nationality*. Immediately following the cue, they were presented with a picture of themselves or one of their coworkers. The dependent variable was reaction time to correctly identify if the cue belonged to the face. The researchers' hypothesis was supported. Contrary to previous findings, and to the assumptions of the serial model of name retrieval, retrieval of names was significantly *faster* than the retrieval of biographical information. This finding fits quite nicely with the notion that extremely familiar names rest at a relatively high level of activation, and thus are apt to be retrieved quickly and easily. Calderwood and Burton (2006) replicated and extended the finding, showing that children as young as 8 years of age demonstrate the same patterns as adults: difficulty in retrieving names, relative to other sorts of information, and a reversal of these difference in the case of highly familiar individuals.

Stop&*Review*

1. The Thatcher illusion shows that:
   a. turning a face upside down impacts recognition of the faces of celebrities, but not faces of noncelebrities.
   b. turning a face upside down impairs the ability to recognize it.
   c. people recognize the parts of a face, but can't recognize the whole face.
   d. faces can't be recognized as faces if they're presented upside down.
2. Briefly describe the claims of the "specialized module" and "perceptual expertise" accounts of how we recognize faces.

3. True or false? The right hemisphere seems especially proficient at recognizing one's own face.
4. Describe the gradient of difficulty in person recognition tasks.

- The Thatcher illusion demonstrates that inverting a face has a disproportionate effect on recognition, relative to its effect on objects. This suggests that faces are encoded and subsequently recognized holistically, while objects are encoded more in terms of separate elements. Inversion has much more of an effect on faces than it does on other objects due to the strong configural properties of faces.

- Some view faces as "special" stimuli, with a dedicated brain module or set of mechanisms devoted specifically to their recognition. Others characterize the proficiency of face recognition as an instance of perceptual expertise.

- Research on individual differences in face recognition indicate that females have superior facial identification abilities, relative to males. Also, individuals within a given culture tend to recognize same-culture faces more readily than different-culture faces. Evidence of the ability to recognize one's own face demonstrates a hemispheric asymmetry. The right hemisphere seems to be selectively involved in self-face recognition.

- Studies on memory for names indicate that names are particularly difficult to retrieve. There is a gradient of difficulty in person-recognition tasks. Recognizing a face as familiar is least difficult, while name retrieval is most difficult. Researchers have proposed models of name retrieval that emphasize either serial or parallel processing of person information.

Networks and Concepts: The Classification Database

Throughout this chapter, we've been discussing the recognition of various things (objects, faces, etc.) but this begs a number of questions about the knowledge needed for identification. How is this knowledge acquired, stored, accessed, and retrieved? Perhaps a more vexing question is what makes a thing what it is? Look at the photo on this page. All are instantly recognizable as animals, and as mammals. But, nearly as quickly, we notice that they are fundamentally different, quickly coming up with the labels "dogs," "cat," "mouse" and "rabbit." Why doesn't the black and white coloring place these items into the same category? What differentiates the three animals we recognized as dogs? And what distinguishes those 3 animals from the other similar looking animals and leads us to give them the same label—dog? In this section of the chapter, we'll discuss some fundamental work on how knowledge is represented. First, we'll describe a popular metaphor for how knowledge is represented in memory. After that, we'll turn to the basic question of how a given concept (e.g., dog) is defined and organized.

Which one of these is not like the others?

Semantic Networks

One common way to describe the representation of categories and concepts is in terms of semantic networks. According to this approach, knowledge is stored in the form of associative networks in which concepts are represented by nearby nodes that correspond to related concepts or features of a given concept. A **category verification task** can be used to determine how we access categorical knowledge. In this task, participants are asked to verify or deny simple statements like "A penguin is a bird" or "A robin is a bird" as quickly as possible. A **feature verification task** is used to assess how the *features* of categories are stored and accessed. Participants are asked to verify or deny sentences like "A cat has pointy ears" or "A cat has skin."

As you might suspect, accuracy is not really of concern in these studies; in general, these questions are relatively easy, and people almost never make mistakes unless they're trying to answer too quickly. *Speed* is the more informative dependent variable in studies of category and feature verification. The fact that participants consistently verify "A robin is a bird" more quickly than "A penguin is a bird" tells us something about how knowledge is organized—in some way, *robin* is more tightly connected with the general concept "bird" than *penguin* is. In addition, the fact that we tend to verify "A cat has pointy ears" faster than a "A cat has skin" tells us something about the *proximity* of these features to the concept "cat." So let's take a look at some general theoretical notions that have been suggested to account for the way we retrieve words and their associates.

Consider the example presented in Figure 5.11 As you can see, like concepts are "close to" one another, as are a given concept's features. It's important to note that within these models, the phrases "close to" and "nearby" are in the colloquial sense; that is, the concept "canary" is figuratively close to the concept "bird." Another important clarification—this type of model is *not* the same (indeed, it's quite different from) the *neural* network approaches to knowledge and cognition that we've discussed elsewhere. The networks we're about to discuss are not based on brain structure, as are neural networks (although you might consider the two approaches kindred theoretical spirits). In neural network models, the representations (nodes) correspond to neurons, and the connections between the nodes correspond to the complex interconnections between neurons that form neural networks. In the neural network approach, these nodes and links are not specifically dedicated to particular words and characteristics—that is, there is no neuron that corresponds to "canary" and no neural connection that connects this concept to a neuron for "bird."

In contrast, the nodes in semantic network models *do* correspond to specific concepts (i.e., "canary"), and the links between these nodes do correspond to relationships among concepts (i.e., "canary" would be connected to "pet"). These sorts of metaphorical networks provide a convenient way to describe and represent the relationships among concepts. Knowledge retrieval is described within the framework offered by these models as a process of traversing the nodes by gliding along the associative links. As we just noted, however, the neural network and semantic network approaches are similar in at least one basic way. Both architectures rely on the concept of excitatory connections between representations as a way of explaining knowledge activation and retrieval. As you'll see, semantic network models posit spreading activation, a process whereby the activation of one node spreads to other, related nodes. Neural network models posit a similar mechanism whereby activation of one node or network can lead to the activation (or inhibition) of other nodes or networks. So the two approaches are not without their similarity.

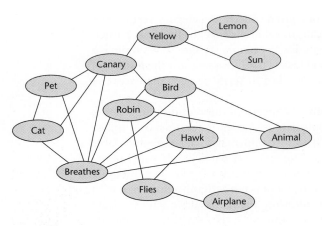

Figure 5.11
A semantic network.

Semantic network approaches to knowledge representation are exemplified by the **spreading activation model** proposed by Collins and Loftus (1975). This approach makes a number of assumptions about the representation of knowledge in addition to the central assumption that concept nodes are linked in an associative network. The links that connect concepts represent a wide variety of relationships. As you can see in the network pictured in Figure 5.11, the relationships include category membership (canary to bird), property to concept (yellow to canary) relationships, and more subtle relationships like those between canary and cat.

Collins and Loftus (1975) propose a number of processing assumptions. When a given concept is presented, the corresponding node is activated, and the activation spreads out to other concepts in the network. The strength of activation decreases as a function of time, distance, and the number of concepts activated: the more concepts that are activated, the less activation any one concept receives. Finally, the activation that reaches any concept node is summed up, and if the activation passes some threshold value, that concept will be activated.

The spreading activation model provides a straightforward account of an oft-replicated finding in studies of knowledge representation: semantic priming. This aspect of cognitive processing was introduced in Chapter 2. Semantic priming refers to the tendency for the processing of one stimulus to enhance or speed up the processing of a related stimulus. Priming will result when a concept like "lemon" is activated beyond a threshold level. So consider what happens in the network when a prime (e.g., "yellow") is presented. Presentation of the word *yellow* activates that concept, and the activation spreads out from there; concepts receiving activation would no doubt include "sun," "canary," and, "lemon." The activation gives these concepts a "head start" toward the threshold that needs to be reached for identification. So when the word *lemon* is actually presented, the responder is almost ready (primed and ready, as it were) to verify it as a word. The architecture espoused by network models—that of an associative network—has become part and parcel of several influential accounts of knowledge representation and cognitive processes in general.

Concepts and Categories

Much of the work on knowledge representation is less concerned with the precise nature of the knowledge structure or "network" that might represent everything we know, than with the precise nature of the representation of specific concepts. It's back to the question we posed at the beginning of the chapter. What gives a category its underlying structure?

What makes Monopoly, dodge ball, and hop-scotch all games, despite wide varieties in their characteristics?

Functions of Concepts. Just reading through the different sorts of concepts that we use in everyday thought and language ought to give you some feel for just how important concepts are. Indeed, as succinctly summarized by Solomon, Medin, and Lynch (1999), "Concepts are the building blocks of thought." Their functions go well beyond just providing us with labels that are convenient for grouping things. Medin and Rips (2005) review the various and sundry functions of concepts. They serve as a sort of mental shorthand that allows for quick and efficient *understanding*. They also allow us to go beyond the present moment and make *predictions*. Suppose someone tells you that their favorite TV show is a reality show; they probably don't need to add that the show features real people rather than actors, that it involves some sort of competition with prize money for the winner, that it's often, but not always, devoid of quality, and high on the

I won a reality show! And Simon loved me!

embarrassment factor, and that you can watch it on a little box that projects color images. "Reality show" immediately evokes all of these ideas. Put another way, our knowledge of concepts allows us to infer knowledge not explicitly stated. In addition, if you don't like reality shows, based on the label "reality show" you can predict that you won't like the show. Concepts also can support new *learning*. Reality shows weren't even a category 20 years ago. Now they're as pervasive and annoying as the common cold, and everyone knows what one is.

Finally, concepts are important for communication. As you'll see in Chapters 9 and 10, people are wizards in their ability to combine concepts via language in order to get their idea across. For example Greg makes a distinction between "restaurant coffee" and "real coffee," and he's willing to bet that many if not most readers of this text know what he means. Restaurant coffee is weak—hot water flavored with a hint of coffee bean. Real coffee is the kind you get at a coffee shop—it packs more flavor and gives you more of a jolt. Clearly, concepts are subtle and complex entities.

Categories as a Concept. It turns out that the notion of *categories* is rich enough and pervasive enough in our everyday thinking that categories themselves serve as an organizing concept. In other words, there are types of categories, just as there are types of dogs. There are a number of different schemes one might use to distinguish between category types (see Medin, Lynch, & Solomon, 2000 for an extensive consideration of this issue). Goldstone and Kersten (2003) suggest that different types of categories can be ordered in terms of how similar members of the category seem to be to one another. **Natural kinds** (also termed **natural categories**) are those that occur naturally in the world; they essentially define themselves. Members within these types of categories seem to share important characteristics or features. For example, all flowers are grouped into a single category by virtue of the naturally occurring attributes that they share. These naturally occurring concepts are labeled only after their discovery (Medin & Heit, 1999). **Artifacts** (also termed **artifact categories**) include objects or conventions designed or invented by humans to serve particular functions (e.g., tools, sports, furniture). Members of artifact categories don't seem to share the same sorts of basic features shared by members of a natural category. For example, soccer and cross-country (two members of the artifact category *sport*) don't quite hang together as well as rose and daisy (two members of the natural kind category *flower*).

Two other sorts of categories seem even more loosely associated than natural kinds and artifacts; however, there's no question that there is a concept underlying them. For example, **ad hoc categories** (Barsalou, 1983) are those formed in the service of some goal. The members of the category cohere only by virtue of their relation to the context at hand. For example, we doubt that *things to take on vacation* has the same presence in your knowledge representation as does the natural kind category *fruit.* Nonetheless, asking for *things to take on vacation* would lead to consistent responses across individuals within a particular cultural context, suggesting that we can form categories "on the fly," given a particular goal. These categories are labeled "ad hoc" because they're formed only for a purpose. In Goldstone and Kersten's (2003) similarity scheme, members of ad hoc categories would seem to be pretty low in terms of their similarity. It seems that, other than all belonging to the ad hoc category *things people take on vacation,* there's virtually nothing in common among suitcases, swimsuits, cameras, and books. Even less coherent is the *metaphorical concept.* An example of this type of concept is an emotional prison, which could describe an unrewarding job, a relationship that can't be ended for some reason, or a person who can't share some dark secret. The specific situations underlying these three category members may be radically different, yet there is a common underlying theme that unites them.

Similarity-Based Categorization

Similarity-based approaches to concept representation assert that categorization is a matter of judging the similarity between the target object and some standard in long-term memory. That standard might be a clearly specified set of features or characteristics, an abstracted "best example" version of the category, or all of the other members of the category. We now examine each of these possibilities.

The Classical View.   The earliest and perhaps most straightforward account of how we use concepts is termed the **classical view.** According to the classical view, items are

classified into particular categories if they have certain features or characteristics (e.g., Bruner, Goodnow, & Austin, 1956). These features are both necessary and sufficient for defining the concept. For example, the concept "triangle" is a closed, three-sided figure whose angles sum to 180°. Shapes that have these characteristics are triangles; shapes that don't are not. The classical view is considered similarity based, because categorization is based on whether the set of features that characterize a given entity is similar to the features that define the concept.

Problems with the Classical View. Although the classical view provides a ready description of how we might classify concepts that have clearly defined properties, closer inspection reveals some serious flaws. The most significant criticism gets at the very core of the approach: it's very difficult to specify many concepts in terms of features that are both necessary and sufficient. For example, take our earlier example of the concept "game," which can include Monopoly, dodge ball, and hopscotch. What on earth are the common features that define them as games and make them members of that category? Which features are necessary and sufficient for something to be called a game?

Another serious problem with the classical view is that it can't explain a fundamental characteristic of categorization—the fact that our representations of categories have a **graded structure.** When we think of a category like "furniture," it's not the case that all examples of furniture are created equal. When asked to name a member of the category "furniture," the vast majority of respondents will say "table," "chair," or "couch." The classical view of concepts has no way to deal with this finding, termed the typicality effect. According to the classical view, if something has all of the features that define "furniture," then it's a piece of furniture; if it doesn't, then it's not. The view has no mechanism that explains why certain category members (e.g., tables) are more "furniturey" than others. An interesting side note: even members of ad hoc categories, like "things to take on vacation," vary in their typicality (typical: "swimsuit"; less typical: "deck of cards"). The graded nature of category representation is evident from many research studies, most notably the work of Eleanor Rosch and colleagues (e.g., Rosch, 1973; Rosch & Mervis, 1975). When participants are asked to rate which members of categories are typical, there is overwhelming agreement about which members are more and less typical.

The final problem with the classical view is the implication that categories are separated by absolute, clear-cut boundaries. If something has the necessary and sufficient features of a category, then it's a member; if not, it's not. If the categories of "game" and "sport" were well defined, it would be a trivial task to classify "bowling." But in reality, categories have what have been called **fuzzy boundaries;** one person's game is another person's sport. When we invite opinion from our students regarding whether bowling is a sport, we invariably get a split. Bowling is "kind of" a sport; like other sports, it requires well-coordinated motor movements, and it's shown on the sports channel. But still, it seems (at most) like "sort of" a sport. But the classical view doesn't allow for this "sort of" view of categories. Something is a sport or it isn't. This absolute view fails to capture many of the categories we think about every day.

The Prototype Approach. The **prototype approach** to categorization provides a more flexible view. Rather than specifying necessary and sufficient features that each category member must have, the prototype approach contends that there are features of the category that members are likely to have. Instances of the category are evaluated and classified based on their resemblance to other members. Instances that have a high **family resemblance** (i.e., those that share many features with other category members) are classified as typical members of the category and serve as the standard to which other category members are compared (this standard is called the **prototype**). Those with a low family resemblance are seen as less typical members. For example, typical bird features might be the following: flies, chirps, has feathers, has a beak. The instance "robin," because it is characterized by all four of these features, is perceived as more typical than "penguin," which is characterized by only two. (Penguins are one of the aberrations of the bird category.) This is why the prototype approach is classified as similarity based. Category membership is determined by an item's similarity to the prototype.

The prototype approach solves the problems encountered by the classical view. First, it avoids the view's rigidity. One doesn't need to come up with the set of features that absolutely defines a category. The prototype approach contends that there are features that tend to be present. The second problem—the fact that some category members are perceived as more typical, or "better," members than others—certainly poses no difficulty. In fact, it's the very basis for the prototype approach. Finally, the fuzzy boundary issue isn't really a problem for the prototype approach. The fuzzy boundary between the categories of "game" and "sport" fits well with this view. "Bowling" is difficult to classify because it lies near the boundaries for each category (about equidistant from each category's prototype), and the category boundaries aren't really clear.

How does a category member become a prototype? Prototypes are thought to be abstracted through repeated experience with category members. Through repeated encounters with birds, we arrive at a representation of a "bird" that includes the features we've seen the most often; smallish, flies, builds nests, has feathers, and so on. A particularly compelling demonstration of prototype formation is provided by Posner, Goldsmith, and Welton (1967). These investigators used an unusual sort of category—dot patterns—to investigate prototype formation. Figure 5.12 presents some sample patterns. Unbeknownst to the participants, all of the dot patterns presented were statistically generated distortions of a prototype; the presented examples differed from the prototype by varying amounts. However, the prototype itself was never presented. During a test phase, participants were presented with both old (previously presented) and new dot patterns and were to determine whether or not they had seen each pattern in the earlier phase.

Sport, or not a sport?

The most compelling result came from test trials on which the prototype pattern was presented. Participants tended to confidently confirm that they had seen the prototype pattern, even though they never had. They were considerably less likely to make this same mistake with other new patterns. Later in the session, after only the one test presentation, the prototype was recognized just as well as patterns that had been presented throughout the experiment, almost as if the prototype itself had been repeatedly presented. In a sense, it had, according to the prototype approach. Throughout the initial presentation trials, participants were abstracting a prototype that represented the average of all the patterns they were observing.

As previously mentioned, the term *prototype* refers not only to the theoretical approach to concept representation but also to the most representative member (or members) of a given category. These anchoring, or standard, category members are afforded advantages in processing. They're more quickly and easily accessed from memory, they're learned more quickly, and they're more likely than other category members to be "primed" by the category name. Put in terms of the network models discussed earlier, the distance between category prototypes and category labels is relatively short.

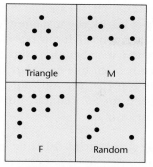

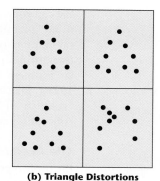

(a) Prototypical Pattern   **(b) Triangle Distortions**

Figure 5.12

Stimuli used in the Posner et al. (1967) study of prototypes.

From Posner, M. I., Goldsmith, R., & Welton, K. E. (1967). Perceived distance and the classification of distorted patterns. *Journal of Experimental Psychology, 73,* 28–38. Copyright 1967 by the American Psychological Society. Reprinted by permission.

Problems with the Prototype Approach.   There is no question about the descriptive value of the term prototype. As just discussed, the idea that certain category members serve as the basis to which other members are compared is not in doubt. But prototype as a theoretical explanation for how we represent concepts has fared less well than prototype as a descriptive term. One problem is that people's representations of categories and their characteristics seem to be much more complex than would be implied by the prototype approach. Categorical knowledge extends beyond the simple average representation suggested by the prototype approach. Evidence indicates that people are sensitive to the ways in which certain properties of category members do and do not go together. For example, people are sensitive to the fact that small birds tend to sing but large birds tend to squawk (Mervis & Rosch, 1981); furthermore, people use this type of information in classifying objects. It's not clear how an average representation could allow for this rather sophisticated representation of object properties and their intercorrelations.

The prototype approach also fails to capture another key feature of category representation—the fact that it's sensitive to context (Roth & Shoben, 1983). Research shows that what we view as a typical category member depends on how we think about the category. For example, if I ask you to name a musical instrument, you're quite likely to say "piano;" but if I ask you to name a "campfire musical instrument," you're likely to say "guitar" or "harmonica." If our representation of a category is centered on one (or two or three) typical member(s), it's not clear why context should matter at all. A similar problem arises when one considers the conjunction of two concepts (Hampton, 1993). Take the concept "pet fish," for example; most people would say "guppy" or "goldfish" if asked for an example, but neither is prototypical of either individual concept ("pet" or "fish").

The Exemplar Approach.   Partially in response to the problems encountered with the prototype approach, some researchers have proposed the **exemplar approach,** which suggests that we represent categories in terms of examples, or category exemplars. According to this view, there is no single representation of a category that is abstracted over time. There are a number of different versions of the exemplar approach (e. g., Brooks, 1978; Hintzman, 1986; Nosofsky, 1984). The extreme version of the exemplar view proposes no abstraction or generalization process. Rather, our representation of a concept (i.e., "guitar") consists of every single encounter we've had with it. When we think about the concept, we retrieve one of these encounters (e.g., Brooks, 1987). Note that like the prototype approach, the exemplar approach is similarity based: objects and events are assessed in terms of their similarity to a standard. But in this case, the standard is a specific example of the category rather than a generalized representation. Also, the standard that is used (i.e., the particular example) will depend on circumstances. When asked if an eagle is a bird, the exemplar retrieved will be some relatively large bird of prey (Ross & Spalding, 1994).

Like the prototype approach, the exemplar approach can deal readily with the difficulties of the classical view. The effect of typicality poses no problem for the exemplar approach. The reason we're most likely to think of "robin" when we encounter the concept "bird" is that the majority of our stored examples of birds are robins (or similar to robins). When we retrieve an instance, we're more likely to retrieve one that's been encoded frequently.

The exemplar approach can also deal quite readily with some of the problems encountered by the prototype approach. The biasing effect of context ("harmonica" as an example of "a campfire musical instrument") is no problem for the exemplar approach, which claims that a particular context can activate certain exemplars, essentially *priming* their retrieval. When we're in the middle of the Christmas season, for example, Christmas songs abound. So if asked in December to give an example of the category "song," "Jingle Bells" may well be the answer; in this case, temporal context serves to make this particular exemplar especially retrievable. The exemplar approach also has no problem with the finding that people are sensitive to correlations in the properties of category members (Malt & Smith, 1984). (Remember the previous example that little birds sing and big birds squawk?) Given that we store every single encounter with category members, all the information about the category's members is available. So although you may not be particularly aware that small birds tend to sing and big birds tend to squawk, you are able to arrive at this conclusion if asked. (Of course, who would ask but a cognitive researcher?)

Problems with the Exemplar Approach. But alas, it seems that every theory has its problems, and the exemplar approach is no exception. For one thing, it seems that in some circumstances people are truly using an abstracted representation—one that's constructed from repeated encounters. Think back to the dot-pattern classification study conducted by Posner and colleagues (1967). In that study, people were very likely to say they had seen the prototype they had never seen, so there was no corresponding exemplar. Obviously, the exemplar approach has no explanation for these results. How would one recognize an exemplar that was never encoded? Another problem with extreme versions of the exemplar approach is one of economy (Komatsu, 1992). It strains credulity to think that every single encounter with every single object is stored in memory. (This recalls the problem of economy faced by the template view of pattern recognition.) Even if only some exemplars are stored, what determines the ones that are?

As is often the case in theoretical debates, it appears that both the prototype approach and the exemplar approach have some merit and that both may serve as accurate descriptions of concept representations. Malt (1989) demonstrated that under different circumstances, people may classify based on either exemplars or prototypes. It seems that the boundary between these two categories of theories is definitely fuzzy!

Essentialist Approach: Concepts as Theories

Similarity-based approaches to categorization take what might be termed a bottom-up approach to categorization. These approaches emphasize the processing of the particular features possessed by members of the concept; a robin is a bird because it has the features of a bird, or is similar in features to some prototypical bird or to an exemplar. Alternatively, one might conceive of categorization in more of a top-down manner. It could be that categorization is not based on encoding the particular properties of entities in the external world and comparing these properties to those of stored exemplars or prototypes. Instead, categorization of external entities may be based on a person's general idea (or "theory") regarding the essence of the concept—what *is* the concept, at its very core? And this essence isn't always obvious, or even related closely to physical appearance or obvious characteristics. Because of this notion—that categories have some underlying nature or essence—these accounts are sometimes labeled as **essentialist approaches** (Medin & Ortony, 1989).

One critical implication of the notion of an essence is that categories are not represented or thought of solely in terms of their characteristics or features. And by extension, when we compare categories, we aren't just doing some type of simple comparison and arriving at some judgment of similarity, as the classical, prototype, and exemplar approaches would propose. Categorization goes well beyond superficial comparison of perceptual similarity.

A study by Rips (1989) provides a compelling demonstration of the inadequacy of the similarity-based approaches, and of the validity of the essentialist approaches. He used an intriguing procedure in which he presented participants with stories that involved made-up organisms—but although they were made up, participants were

Table 5.3 **Transformation Stories Used in the Study by Rips (1989)**

Accident Condition:

There was an animal called a sorp which, when it was fully grown, was like other sorps, having a diet which consisted of seeds and berries found on the ground or on plants. The sorp had two wings, two legs, and lived in a nest high in the branches of a tree. Its nest was composed of twigs and other fibrous plant material. This sorp was covered with bluish-gray feathers.

The sorp's nest happened to be not too far from a place where hazardous chemicals were buried. The chemicals contaminated the vegetation that the sorp ate, and as time went by it gradually began to change. The sorp shed its feathers and sprouted a new set of wings composed of a transparent membrane. The sorp abandoned its nest, developed a brittle iridescent outer shell, and grew two more pairs of legs. At the tip of each of the sorp's six legs an adhesive pad was formed so that it was able to hold onto smooth surfaces; for example, the sorp learned to take shelter during rainstorms by clinging upside down to the undersides of tree leaves. The sorp eventually sustained itself entirely on the nectar of flowers.

Eventually this sorp mated with a normal female sorp one spring. The female laid the fertilized eggs in her nest and incubated them for three weeks. After that time normal young sorps broke out of their shells.

During an early stage of the doon's life it is known as a sorp. A sorp's diet mainly consists of seeds and berries found on the ground or on plants. A sorp has two wings, two legs, and lives in a nest high in the branches of a tree. Its nest is composed of twigs and other fibrous plant material. A sorp is covered with bluish-gray feathers.

Essence Condition:

After a few months, the doon sheds its feathers, revealing that its wings are composed of a transparent membrane. The doon abandons its nest, develops a brittle, iridescent outer shell, and grows two more pairs of legs. At the tip of each of the doon's six legs an adhesive pad is formed so that it can hold onto smooth surfaces; for example, doons take shelter during rainstorms by clinging upside down to the undersides of tree leaves. A doon sustains itself entirely on the nectar of flowers.

Doons mate in the late summer. The female doon deposits the eggs among thick vegetation where they will remain in safety until they hatch.

From Rips, L. J. (1989). Similarity, typicality, and categorization. In S. Vosniadu & A. Ortony (Eds.), *Similarity and analogical reasoning* (pp. 21–59). Cambridge, UK: Cambridge University Press. Reprinted by permission of Cambridge University Press.

likely to label them as a member of a familiar category, like a bird or insect (importantly, however, these labels were never presented to participants). They compared two conditions (see Table 5.3 for example stories from each condition). In the *accident* condition, the organism (e.g., a birdlike creature called a *sorp*) underwent a catastrophic accident that resulted in many of its external features being altered, such that it now looked like a member of a different category (e.g., an insect) but still behaved like a member of its original category (birds). In the *essence* condition, the sorp underwent the same type of external change (i.e., it looked like an insect rather than a bird). But now it behaved like its new category rather than its old category (i.e., it behaved like an insect, not a bird), and was given a new name (e.g., a *doon*). So in one condition, there were *accidental* changes in the organism; in the other, there were *essential* changes in the organism.

After reading these stories, participants were given (1) a categorization task in which they were to rate the degree to which the sorp (or doon) fit into the category of bird on a scale from 1 to 10; and (2) a similarity-rating task in which they were to rate the similarity between sorps and birds (or the similarity between doons and birds) on a scale from 1 to 10. If the basis for categorization *is* similarity, then a measure of categorization should behave the same way as a measure of similarity. It should be influenced by the same variables, and in the same way. If some manipulation leads an organism to seem like a better member of a certain category, that manipulation should also lead the organism to be rated as more similar to members of the category. In the present experiment, changes in the accident and essence conditions should influence judgments of similarity and judgments of categorization in the same manner. Given that the basis for categorization is similarity to a prototype or exemplar, any manipulation that increases similarity ratings for an item should also make that item seem like a better member of the category.

The results were striking. Take a look at Figure 5.13. Presented are ratings of category membership in and similarity to birds, relative to a control group (who read only the description of the birdlike sorps). In the accident condition (in which the organism eventually looked like an insect but still behaved like a bird), the change lowered similarity ratings more than categorization ratings. So basically, in the case of an accidental change, participants saw the new organism as much less similar to birds

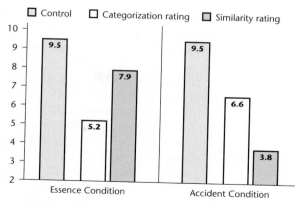

Effects of Changes on Categorizing and Similarity Ratings

Figure 5.13

Data from Rips (1989).

From Rips, L. J. (1989). Similarity, typicality, and categorization. In S. Vosniadu & A. Ortony (Eds.), *Similarity and analogical reasoning* (pp. 21–59). Cambridge, UK: Cambridge University Press. Reprinted by permission of Cambridge University Press.

than it had been. However, in terms of its category, it still seemed basically like a bird. In the essence condition (in which the organism eventually looked and behaved like an insect), the change lowered categorization ratings more than similarity ratings. Basically, in the case of an essential change, participants saw the new organism as still somewhat similar to birds. However, in terms of its category, it seemed less like a bird. The striking finding here is that similarity judgments and categorization judgments were influenced differently by the change manipulation.

This pattern should be getting more familiar to you now; it's yet another example of a dissociation. Different variables influenced the two judgment tasks in varying ways. Recall that a dissociation is a fairly strong piece of evidence that two tasks are based on different underlying processes. So basically, Rips's (1989) finding suggests that similarity judgments and categorization judgments are based on different underlying processes! This finding poses serious challenges to the prototype and exemplar approaches, which basically say that judgments of category membership and judgments of similarity are one and the same. Clearly, they aren't. However, it should be noted some recent evidence (Hampton, Estes, Simmons, 2007) suggests that the dissociation found by Rips depends on the particular task parameters involved in the categorization task. Regardless, these findings and others (e.g., Keil, 1989; Medin & Ortony, 1989) led to the ascendancy of essentialist approaches of categorization. These approaches propose that categorization entails what might be termed a *personal theory* about what a concept represents; that is, our views of categories are based on implicit theories about what makes a thing what it is—in other words, what is the *essence* of a bird?

Essentialist approaches do a better job of explaining the notion of *category coherence* than do the exemplar and prototype approaches. When asked to list examples of the category "weapons," how do disparate items such as guns, knives, missiles, candlesticks, and baseball bats all gain membership in this category? What is it about these objects that allow them to "hang together," or cohere, as members of the same concept? They certainly don't look similar, yet we have no trouble grouping them together. And conversely, what is it about two seemingly similar animals—a shark and a dolphin—that leads them to be placed in different categories (Ross & Spalding, 1994)? They look similar but we categorize them differently. According to an essentialist approach, a category is not the set of common features that objects share. So the fact that guns and knives don't look like each other and don't share an identifiable set of features doesn't matter; it's our idea about the essence of a weapon that must be similar. And our idea about the essence of a weapon is consistent with guns, knives, and baseball bats; consequently, they are placed in the same category. Also, the fact that dolphins and sharks share structural similarities doesn't matter. What matters is that our knowledge of dolphins and their essence (they're mammals) is not similar to our knowledge of sharks and their essence (they're fish). Based on these essential differences, the two do not cohere and consequently are categorized differently.

Stop&*Think* | REPRESENTING CONCEPTS

Ask two friends to tell you what they think about when they hear each category name:

    vegetable
    vehicle
    tool
    four-footed animal
    type of reading material

- Does it seem like a general prototype or a specific exemplar comes to mind?

- If it's a specific exemplar, why might this particular exemplar have been brought to mind? Was it seen recently? Was it appropriate to the context they're in?

- Was there any indication that they were using an essentialist approach? How so?

Biological Essentialism. As suggested by the results of the Rips (1989) study, essentialist approaches do a particularly good job of explaining our categorization of natural kind categories, which are inherently biological. A review by Medin and Atran (2004) ascribes special status to natural kind categories or, more generally, to our knowledge of the biological world. This everyday knowledge or intuition about living things and how they work is termed **folk biology,** which invokes the image of "common folk" discussing their knowledge. In fact, these investigators propose that knowledge of biological systems constitutes a cognitive module that has evolved in the service of adaptation to the environment. Recall that you read a similar argument about face recognition earlier in the chapter.

Research Theme
Evolution

    As noted by Medin and Atran, a biological knowledge system would certainly make evolutionary sense given that survival of humans and their ancestors no doubt depended on the ability to learn and reason about animals, plants, and other natural phenomena. This evolutionary claim is consistent with the fact that across all cultures of the world, people seem to think about biological entities in the same way, in terms of hierarchies of (i.e., different levels of categorization) (Atran, 1990). Even the gradation of these hierarchical categories (say, into fruit, apple, and Honey Crisp apple) seems to be the same across cultures, indicating that the levels into which categories are divided reflect a natural reality, rather than a cultural convenience (Berlin, 1992; Malt, 1995).

Research Theme
Culture

Bloom and Gelman (2008) cite a fascinating piece of evidence for the reality and universality of essence-based classification—the selection of the 14th Dalai Lama! As you may know, the new Dalai Lama is selected by Tibetan Buddhist officials upon the death of the previous Dalai Lama (from whom he is believed to have been reincarnated). Bloom and Gelman describe the accounts of the selection of the current Dalai Lama, then a 2-year old boy. Tibetan Buddhist officials tested the boy by having him make choices between pairs of items, one of which had belonged to the previous Dalai Lama, and a matched item that was inauthentic. The boy who was to become the 14th (and current) Dalai Lama made the correct choice on each of five choice trials, the last of which pitted a sleek and attractive drum against a rather dull alternative (which was the authentic one). Bloom and Gelman's (2008) point is not that the Tibetans made the right choice; rather, they highlight the implicit assumption underlying the whole procedure. They assumed that the belongings of the previous Dalai Lama were all imbued with essential properties that could only be reliably divined by a special child, one familiar with the essence—the boy the Tibetans believed (and still believe) to be the reincarnation of the 13th Dalai Lama.

Classification based on essential properties has clear and universal power. Prentice and Miller (2007) also speak to the power of essentialist categorization, albeit with some troubling overtones. They point to the tendency to essentialize human categories, citing the concept of *woman* as a prime example. There is a tendency to believe in some deeper, hidden, almost mysterious (i.e., essentialized) qualities that make women what they are. Of course, there is a biological reality to the categories of man and woman; they are both natural categories. But in Prentice and Miller's view, people's personal theories about the different essences of woman and man go well beyond these physical differences, and are perhaps more perception than reality.

The tendency to essentialize human categories is pervasive. Haslam, Rothschild, and Ernst (2000) had participants rate 40 different human categories (e.g., gender, race, sexual orientation, occupation, etc.) on a number of dimensions thought to relate to essentialism: the categories perceived degree of naturalness and stability, how discrete the boundaries are, how immutable (i.e., unchangeable) category membership is, and the necessity of features for the category members. Their results are summarized in Figure 5.14. Basically, the investigators were trying to get at people's views regarding which differences seem to go deep down, to the very nature (i.e., essence) of a person's being. Some categories were only weakly essentialized including those based on interests, appearance, and social class. Others, including gender, race, ethnicity, and disability were strongly essentialized. This implies that a person is more likely to be considered "categorically different" based on a difference in race, rather than a difference in music taste. Consider the sentence "You know, in spite of the extent to which people differ in terms of _____ (e.g., music taste, skin color) we're all basically

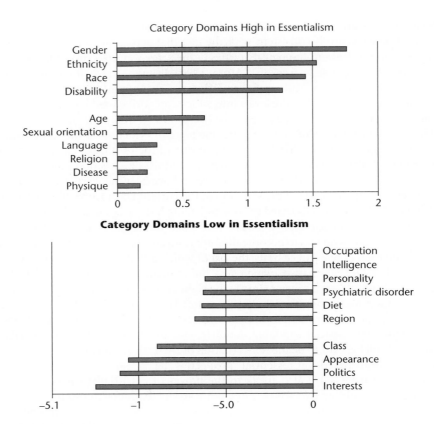

Figure 5.14
Do we see essential differences among fellow humans? On what dimensions?

the same." Haslam et al.'s findings indicate that our agreement with that statement would vary a great deal, depending on what filled in the blank.

As Prentice and Miller (2007) note, these findings on psychological essentialism would be just an interesting curiosity were it not for the implications. Perceived differences among individuals and groups can really matter to people, and have implications for how we perceive, approach, and evaluate others. For example, to the extent that we view different categories as having different underlying essences, we accentuate the differences between these categories (as well as the similarities within them). Bastian and Haslam (2006) showed that stronger essentialist beliefs were associated with a stronger endorsement of stereotypes. Clearly, an understanding of how people form psychological essences, and how these essences relate to cognitions and behaviors would seem to be an important endeavor.

The essentialist approach to categorization is not without its critics. Komatsu (1992) and Gabora, Rosch, Aerts (2008) summarize some of the problems with the view. Probably the most serious one is that it remains underspecified—the notions of "theory" and "essence" are both vague and ill-defined. It's not clear exactly what types of explanations and theories do and do not make up the essence for any given concept. A related problem noted by Komatsu (1992) is how to distinguish between *what one knows* about a concept and one's *representation* of a concept. For example, consider once again the concept dolphin. An explanation-based view of this concept might include that dolphins look like fish but aren't, that they're intelligent, that they're friendly enough so that you can swim with them (like Bridget did one summer), that *Flipper* was a 1960's show (badly remade in the 1990's) about a dolphin, and that Greg had a *Flipper* lunch box. But now we've blurred the line between our *concept* of a dolphin, and *everything we know* about dolphins. What's the difference? Where does one leave off and the other begin? Failure to draw this line clearly might render the notion of a concept meaningless for anything other than a descriptive term for what we know about something. "Concept" may cease to be a useful concept.

Stop&*Think* | THE GOLDEN OREO?

Both of your co-authors were taken aback when Nabisco introduced the "Golden Oreo." "Wait a minute," we thought, "aren't Oreos supposed to be deep brown, and devil's food chocolate flavored?!!" Basically, we were asking ourselves about the defining characteristics and/or the essence of an Oreo. We realized there could be (indeed, there are) all sorts of variations on favorite consumables. Consider all the varieties of M&M's—regular, peanut, peanut butter, cookies n' cream, pretzel (!). Are all of these M&M's?

Reflect on this important question by considering products that you know about, use, and eat. What is their essence or defining characteristics? How far can you push variations until you no longer have Oreos, M&M's, or whatever else could fill in the blank. You could also apply this to other favorites in completely different genres; for us baby boomers, the "Brady Bunch Movie" just wasn't the Brady Bunch without the cheesy 70s actors. Think of your favorite TV shows or movies—what is their essence? What character could they not do without, and why (aside from the obvious)?

Stop&*Review*

1. Describe the general idea behind a "semantic network."
2. True or false? The graded structure of categories cannot be accounted for by the classical view of categorization.
3. What are the prototype and exemplar approaches of categorization?

4. The essentialist approach of categorization
   a. seems to apply to children as well as to adults.
   b. states that categorization is based on similarity.
   c. would predict that similarity judgments and categorization judgments

should be affected by the same variables.

d. states that categorization is based on an item's outward appearance.

- One common way to describe the representation of categories and concepts is in terms of semantic networks. These networks can be assessed with the use of a category verification task and a feature verification task. Related concepts are conceptualized as being "closer" within this network relative to unrelated concepts. The spreading activation model is one example of a semantic network model. Concepts aid in understanding, predicting, and communicating about knowledge.

- Similarity-based approaches to categorization assume that categorization is a matter of judging the similarity between the target and a representation stored in long-term memory. According to the classical view, we compare targets to a set of features that defines the concept. The classical view is too rigid to account for the graded structure of categories and fuzzy boundaries between them.

- Another similarity-based approach, prototype matching, assumes that we compare objects to a best example from the category. Although this approach accounts for graded structure and fuzzy boundaries, it does not account for the variability of categories in context. The exemplar approach proposes that we think of concepts in terms of specific examples, and accounts better for the sensitivity of concepts to contextual factors.

- Some research shows that categorization and similarity judgments dissociate under certain conditions, which casts doubt on the view that categorization is based on similarity. According to essentialist approaches, concepts are represented in terms of their essence, or basic underlying nature.

CHAPTER OUTLINE

6

Basic Processes in Long-Term Memory: Encoding and Retrieving Information

Have you ever had the experience of studying hour upon hour, yet when faced with some of the test material for which you've put in all this time, it might as well be in Greek—you draw an absolute blank. How can this be? You studied and you never miss class!

You've no doubt had the experience of visiting an "old haunt"—a place where you used to hang out, like your high school, a club, or a family vacation spot. Memories come flowing back spontaneously in situations like these. Why do these memories pop back up in those circumstances but not in others? Do you have to be in the same, or at least a similar place for memories to come back? Should you be taking tests in the same place where you studied?

Have you ever had something running through your mind over and over—a song, maybe—but for the life of you, you can't figure out why? Is it a random thing, or did something happen earlier that prompted you to think of *that* particular song?

Have you ever experienced a profound sense of familiarity in some location or situation that you know you've never been in before (the often-experienced feeling of déjà vu)? The feeling of recollection is palpable, but you know it can't be an actual memory. What's going on?

Fundamental Issues and Distinctions

It would be difficult to overestimate the importance of memory. It serves as the cornerstone of cognition, informing and assisting every process in our cognitive arsenal. As discussed in Chapter 4, immediate memory is critical for online processing of incoming information. Another vital component of memory is our long-term memory. In previous chapters (and subsequent ones) the importance of long-term memory is readily apparent. Long-term memory forms the database for object recognition (Chapter 5), language (Chapters 9 and 10), decision making (Chapter 11), and problem solving (Chapter 12). Memory is also important from a personal standpoint; it houses our autobiographies, the personal histories that give us our sense of identity and place in the world (Chapter 7). In this chapter, we're going to take you through the basic workings of long-term memory, including the processes by which you manage to store and retrieve the countless bits of information that form the core of thinking.

As discussed in Chapter 4, some make a distinction between long-term memory and immediate memory. As you read toward the end of the chapter, this distinction has proven to be controversial. Whatever the resolution of the debate turns out to be, there is certainly enough evidence to justify using the distinction as a descriptive device. We will adopt this convention in our subsequent discussion.

In addition, the distinction certainly fits well with our conscious experience of memory. Clearly, memory exists both as a limited, immediate, "thinking about it right now" form as well as a more vast "warehouse of information" form that is largely removed from conscious awareness. Probably the most salient differences are the limitations (or lack thereof) of the respective systems. Immediate memory is quite limited in both duration and capacity. Information can be held (or, depending on your view, in the focus of attention), for only a limited period of time, and doing so requires mental rehearsal. There are ways to get around these limits, to be sure, but the limits are there. Contrast this with long-term memory, which is virtually limitless, in terms of both capacity and duration. Consider all of the important and inane information your friendly author Greg knows. He knows where he lives, how to drive a car, the lyrics to every Beatles song, what he did last night, and what he did on the Fourth of July in 1976. Information in long-term memory has the potential to last a lifetime. In addition, there is always room for more information—a testament to long-term memory's tremendous capacity.

Types of Long-Term Memory

According to the memory systems view (e.g., Schacter, 1989; Squire, 1993, 2004; Tulving, 1983, 2002), LTM is not a unitary entity. Rather, it is made up of a number of subsystems. According to Squire (2004) the major distinction is between two types of memory: declarative and procedural. **Declarative memory** is the long-term memory system responsible for retention of factual information about the world, as well as personally experienced episodes. Sometimes, knowledge based in the declarative system is informally described as "knowing that…" something is so. Bridget *knows that* during her senior year in college her school (Indiana University) won the NCAA basketball tournament, claiming the national championship, and she was watching the final game in her dorm room with friends. She also *knows that* the U.S. Declaration of Independence was signed on July 4, 1776.

Tulving (1972, 1983) suggests that these two declarative memories are examples of two distinct types: episodic memory and semantic memory. **Episodic memory** refers to one's memory for personally experienced events that include contextual elements like the time and place of the event's occurrence. **Semantic memory** refers to knowledge or information about the world that does not include contextual elements like the time or place the information was learned. Bridget's memory of watching the final game of the NCAA tournament is an episodic memory. She experienced it in a specific time and place (March, 1983 in her dorm room in Bloomington, Indiana). Bridget's knowing that the Declaration of Independence was signed on July 4, 1776, is a semantic memory. It's just something that she knows. She wasn't at the signing, so she has no personal memories of it.

Tulving (1983) outlines several other key differences between episodic and semantic memory (see Table 6.1). The retrieval of an episodic memory is typically associated with a recollective experience. Bridget's memory of the final game of the NCAA tournament is accompanied by a strong feeling of recollection, almost as if she can place herself there. Semantic memories feature no such recollective experience. They involve the simple retrieval of an isolated fact. Episodic memories are more vulnerable to forgetting. Many of the details of Bridget's watching IU win the national championship have faded over time. Semantic memories are relatively resistant to forgetting. Bridget will never forget that particular fact about the American Revolution. Episodic memories often include an affective (emotional) component. Seeing her team win the national championship was an exciting experience and is a positive memory. This contrasts sharply with semantic memories. Bridget has no emotional connection to the historical fact of the signing of the Declaration of Independence.

Table 6.1 **Contrasting Characteristics of Episodic and Semantic Memory**

Characteristic	Memory System	
	Episodic	Semantic
Likelihood of forgetting	High	Low
Usefulness	Low	High
Recollective experience	Present	Not present
Sensory component	Present	Not present
Presence of emotion	Present	Not present

Based on information in Tulving, E. (1983). *Elements of episodic memory.* New York: Oxford University Press.

As with the distinction between immediate memory and long-term memory, not all researchers agree that episodic and semantic memory represent two different memory systems; many believe the same memory system underlies both (recall the unitary view, discussed in Chapter 4). They point out that there may be as many similarities as differences in the two. Still, as with the immediate memory/long-term memory distinction, there does seem to be good intuitive and empirical evidence to use the distinction on a descriptive level, and most memory researchers accept the notion of separate memory systems as a given (e.g., Squire, 2004; Tulving, 2002).

In this chapter, we will be dealing primarily with episodic memory, discussing the processes that are used to encode and retrieve events. We should note that most of the research in this chapter is tightly controlled laboratory research, so the remembering done by participants (on the face of it) might not always bear a close resemblance to the way you remember every day. Most of the characteristics of episodic memory proposed by Tulving (1983) are more applicable to the everyday remembering (autobiographical memory), that we will discuss in Chapter 7. But in this chapter, we'll be discussing the basic laboratory work that serves as its foundation. This basic laboratory research still represents episodic memory—remembering a list of words that a cognitive researcher showed you is a personally experienced event that you will remember later.

Whereas declarative information can be characterized as "knowing that…" something is the case, **procedural memory** can be characterized as "knowing how" to do something. Procedural memory in contrast to declarative memory is difficult to verbalize. Imagine you're teaching someone to tie their shoe. (Really, try it.) Chances are you'd have a difficult time verbally describing the steps—so you'd probably demonstrate it by going through the motions. Examples of procedural knowledge include skills (tying your shoe, typing, swinging a golf club), and the formation of simple associations (like a classically conditioned taste aversion). As you'll see later in the chapter, the "recall" of skills based on procedural memory (i.e., the execution of skilled actions) can be easily dissociated from the recall of episodic and semantic memories. For example, the old saying "You never forget how to ride a bike" is more or less true, and this distinguishes procedural memory from declarative memories, particularly episodic memories.

A Descriptive Framework: Encoding, Storage, and Retrieval

When memory researchers discuss the processes involved in memory, they often appeal to a disarmingly simple and useful description of memory proposed by Melton (1963), who suggested that the processes of remembering can be characterized in terms of three stages: encoding, storage, and retrieval. **Encoding** refers to the processes involved in the acquisition of material. Encoding processes are what you engage in when you're studying material for your next test. You study the material repetitively, generate notes based on what you read, relate it to other material you already know, and/or form a silly picture of it in your head, all in the hope of remembering it later. **Storage** of information involves the formation of some type of memory representation, or *memory trace*. If you've encoded some event (like a class lecture) successfully, there should be some remnant of the study experience. (And to do well on an exam, it had better be a pretty big remnant!)

But simply having this stored remnant of experience is no guarantee that you're going to remember it. Memory depends critically on the final process in this sequence—retrieval. **Retrieval** refers to your ability to get something out of memory once it has been encoded and stored. Think of all the times you've been frustrated while you're taking a test, thinking, "I *know* this, but I just can't think of the answer right now!" This is a retrieval failure, and, unfortunately, professors don't give partial credit for retrieval failures (although you never know—check your syllabus).

The distinction between encoding, storage, and retrieval provides a useful thumbnail sketch for discussing how memory works. In this chapter, the focus will be on the processes of encoding and retrieval and how these processes interact. What about storage, you may ask? The term *storage* is used to refer to the state of information once it has been encoded; it doesn't really describe a process. *Encoding* is the term typically used to describe processes of study and retention and is really inseparable from the notion of storage. If something is processed effectively at encoding, then it will be stored. In this chapter, we'll examine exactly what comprises effective processing.

We're going to discuss encoding processes and retrieval processes separately, but discussing them in this way is mostly a matter of convenience. It turns out that remembering depends critically on the interaction between the two. You no doubt have some intuitive sense that this is the case. Do you study differently based on the type of test you're going to take? In other words, do you change how you encode based on how you'll have to retrieve? As you'll see, memory research has borne out that this intuitive strategy is based on solid empirical ground. The first major section of this chapter will deal with how various encoding factors influence memory. To enhance your understanding of these effects, you should be aware of some of the important retrieval distinctions we'll be referring to throughout our discussion of encoding.

LTM: Modes of Access and Use

Your intuition may suggest that long-term remembering involves reaching back into the past for some episode or piece of knowledge that you've learned. But as it turns out, that's only one way in which long-term memory can be queried. So let's discuss the various methods by which we can test memory.

Implicit vs. Explicit Memory Tests.   It seems sensible to assume that in order to remember information from your past you must consciously try to think back and retrieve it. But remembering does not have to be conscious. Memory researchers have drawn an important distinction between two ways in which information from the past can be retrieved. **Explicit memory tests** (or **direct memory tests**) involve conscious recollection of some specific event from the past. The first few decades of cognitive psychology research focused on explicit tests, and the first several sections of this chapter will focus on how encoding processes influence remembering in these sorts of situations. Sometimes, however, experiences and events have an influence on our behavior in the complete absence of conscious memory for that event. Tests that assess these indirect influences have been collectively termed **implicit memory tests** (or **indirect memory tests**).

To understand the difference between an implicit and explicit memory test let's consider a story from the French neuropsychologist Eduarde Claparede (1911/1951). Claparede had a patient who suffered from **amnesia,** or memory loss due to brain damage. One day, Claparede hid a pin in his hand and greeted his patient with a prickly handshake. The patient quickly forgot the incident. The next time the two met, the amnesic denied having met Claparede. But when Claparede held out his hand for the customary shake (this time without the pin!), the patient refused. When pressed for the reason, she insisted that she had the right to not shake hands. This is quite remarkable; the amnesic demonstrated that she both did and did not remember what had happened previously. In other words, the amnesic demonstrated a failure of memory when queried explicitly. That is, she completely failed to recollect the occasion of meeting Claparede. However evidence of that meeting was still evident in the amnesics' reaction to the handshake invitation, which constituted an implicit query of memory. When memory was tapped in this fashion, the patient showed that she remembered plenty. As you'll see, the distinction between explicit and implicit memory tests has been proven essential for describing how various encoding factors affect remembering. So let's take a look at the most common examples of these major classes of memory tests.

The most common explicit retrieval tests are free recall (or just recall), cued recall, and recognition. Suppose you're a participant in a memory experiment and you're presented with 48 words, followed by a memory test. If you're tested with **recall,** you are given little or nothing to work with in terms of hints, and your task is to come up with as many of the 48 items as you can. **Cued recall** is a little easier because you are provided with some hint (i.e., a cue) to help you retrieve the encoded words. The easiest retrieval task is **recognition,** in which you are presented with a large set of words that includes the previously present words and some new ones. Your task is to distinguish the two. This is the easiest memory test because you actually get to see the correct answers—you need only recognize them. Performance in all of these memory tests is gauged simply by accuracy—how many words a person correctly recognized or recalled. Recall (free and cued) and recognition are both explicit tests of memory because you have to consciously think back to the encoding episode to respond correctly.

Implicit memory tests are a little more complicated to conduct and assess. As in explicit memory tests, participants study some type of information, most commonly a word list. Later, their memory is tested, but the task is not presented as a "memory test." Participants are typically invited to complete some ostensibly unrelated word or puzzle task that is designed to reflect the influence of the information learned earlier. The most common implicit memory tests are word-fragment completion and word stem completion. In **word-fragment completion,** the participant is given a word in which some letters are there and some aren't, and their task is to come up with the appropriate word. (Think of the game show *Wh_ _l of F_rt_ne.*) In **word-stem completion,** the initial three letters of a word are presented, and the participant's task is to complete the stem with the first word that comes to mind.

As stated above, at the time of the implicit test there is no mention of the previously seen words. But presenting the word earlier makes it more likely that the person will come up with it later, either by successfully completing the word fragment with a previously seen word or by blurting out a previously seen word in response to a stem that could be completed by several possibilities. For example, if you saw the word

---

Table 6.2 A Word-Fragment Completion Study Example

Encoding	Retrieval
List A (studied):	
giraffe	
paper	g _ r _ f f _
tongue	p _ p _ r
chapel	_ o n _ u _
	c h _ _ e _
List B (unstudied):	
clock	
bottle	_ l o _ k
picture	b _ _ t l _
staple	p i _ _ u r _
	_ _ a p _ e

---

garlic in a list an hour ago, when you see the word stem *gar*_____, you're quite likely to respond "garlic" (rather than "garbage," "gargoyle," "garden," or some other nonpresented word).

Performance on an implicit memory test is typically measured in terms of **priming,** or the benefit in performance from previous exposure to a word. Let's get a little more specific with regard to the methodology used to assess priming on an implicit memory test (see Table 6.2). When using an implicit memory test, participants would encode a list of words (let's call it List A). Another list of words (List B) remains unstudied. Later, participants attempt to complete word fragments (or stems) for words from both lists. Another group of participants gets precisely the opposite arrangement: they study List B but don't study List A. Later, they attempt to complete the same set of word fragments (or stems). This arrangement may seem overly elaborate, but it allows the researcher to compare completion rates for the same words under both encoded and nonencoded conditions.

Now that you know how to methodologically implement an implicit memory test let's explain how priming is measured (see Table 6.2). Let's say you encode a list of 4 words and are tested later with 8 word fragments that includes the 4 studied words and 4 unstudied words. Let's say you successfully complete 3 of the 4 fragments with previously encoded words, or a proportion of .75. For the other 4 word fragments, you manage to complete only 1, or a proportion of .25. In this example, priming is .50—the proportion of completed word fragments (i.e., words remembered) increases by .5. And it's important to note that you may not be able to consciously recollect any of the words you saw; still, having seen them will help you complete a word fragment. So a memory benefit can occur from previous exposure to a word in the absence of conscious recollection of the word.

Prospective and Retrospective Tests of Memory.   Explicit memory tests involve remembering information from your past. These type of memory tests are collectively called **retrospective memory tests.** As a student, retrospective explicit memory tests are probably the most salient to you. You take numerous tests for previously encoded information every semester. Even the best student does not get 100% on every test so you also are painfully aware of the memory failures suffered on these types of tests. But if you ask your family or friends who are not currently in school to report their most bothersome memory failures, it probably wouldn't be a failure in a retrospective memory testing situation. Why don't you call or text one of these people and find out if we're right? You're probably thinking, I better do it now or I'll forget to do it.....And that thought represents the most common type of memory test—remembering to perform an action in the future (i.e., **prospective memory test**) and the potential for the most bothersome memory failure—forgetting to perform that intended action.

Let's contrast retrospective and prospective memory tests. Retrospective memory tests involve the retrieval of events that occurred in the past. In a prospective memory test situation the intention to act must be triggered and the action must be carried out. The intention to act can be triggered in one of two ways, according to Einstein and McDaniel (1990). Intentions to act can be triggered by some event; for example, when you see a friend, you have to remember to pay them back the $5 you borrowed for lunch yesterday. This is termed an *event-based* prospective memory test. Alternatively, intentions might be triggered by the mere passage of time; for example, you need to remember to turn off the lawn sprinkler an hour from now. This is termed a *time-based* prospective memory test.

These triggering situations highlight a fundamental difference between retrospective memory and prospective memory tests. In retrospective memory tests (e.g., free recall), retrieval is triggered by some external instruction that initiates a search of memory, such as, "Tell me all of the words that appeared on the previous list." In prospective memory tests there is no instruction to initiate the memory search; retrieval needs to be self-initiated. Suppose you see the friend to whom you owe $5. When you see them, no one tells you to give them the money. The idea must spontaneously occur to you. And once you realize that you have to give them some money, you must remember how much. This "half" of the prospective memory test involves retrospective remembering, as the content of the intended action (e.g., the amount of $5) must be recalled. So the unique feature of a prospective memory test seems to be the requirement of "remembering to remember," which is sometimes termed self-initiated retrieval. Later in the chapter, we'll talk more about retrieval, and the implications that self-initiation has for age-related memory deficits.

You probably noticed a similarity between the action slips we discussed in Chapter 3 and the foregoing discussion of failures on prospective memory tests. Indeed, within the categorization scheme of slips proposed by Norman (1981), prospective memory figures prominently. Loss of activation errors, in particular, represent failure in prospective memory, as we walk into the kitchen only to find that we have no idea why we're there. Errors like this represent a sort of "failure hybrid." In one sense, the attentional processes described in Chapter 4 have failed us as we lose an intention from immediate memory (or from the focus of awareness). Additionally, they represent a failure of retrospective memory; we stand empty-handed in the kitchen trying to recall the intention we formulated while sitting in front of the TV. We've already discussed some of the vagaries of attention, and the majority of this chapter will focus on retrospective remembering. We will examine prospective memory in a bit more depth later in the chapter.

Stop&*Review*

1. What's the difference between declarative and procedural memory?
2. Identify and define the three basic processes of long-term memory.
3. Identify the major difference between retrospective and prospective memory tests.

- Long-term memory is often subdivided into declarative memory (memory for factual information about the world and personally experienced episodes). Declarative memory can be further subdivided into episodic and semantic memories. Procedural memory involves memory for *how* to do things.

- There are three basic stages involved in memory: Encoding refers to the processes whereby events are taken in; storage refers to the retention of these events over time; retrieval refers to the processes whereby information is recalled.

- There are a number of ways to query long-term memory. Explicit tests of memory (often termed *direct*) require the conscious recollection of a specific event, while implicit tests of memory (often termed *indirect*) do not. Explicit test performance is measured by accuracy while implicit test performance is measured with priming. Retrospective memory tests involve remembering information from your past. Prospective memory test involves remembering to perform some event in the future.

Encoding Processes in Explicit Long-Term Remembering

It's obvious that your ability to remember something depends on what you do as the information is coming in. Think about the steps you take when you really want to remember something. What do you do to increase your chances of remembering it? In this section, we'll talk about some of the fundamental encoding factors that influence LTM. Keep in mind that the research discussed in this section deals primarily with explicit memory tests—memory tests that require conscious recollection. The rules may be different for implicit memory tests, as you'll see later.

Attention and Repetition

As you learned in Chapter 4, attention is the mechanism whereby we bring information into the focus of conscious awareness. So it should come as no surprise that attention plays a critical role in long-term memory. Quite simply, you're more likely to recollect something to which you paid attention. Think about sitting in class, listening to your professor. You're not going to recollect much of anything from the lecture if you're tuning in to the juicy gossip behind you instead of to what the professor is saying. A simple-minded explanation might be that attention leads to a longer-lasting and more retrievable memory trace. The role of attention is considerably more complex than this simple statement would imply, but there is little doubt that focused attention is necessary for explicit and detailed recollection of some event.

Another factor that affects retention is **repetition.** Material that is presented more than once is easier to remember. This principle is so fundamental that Crowder (1976) notes, "If any generalization is basic to the field of learning it is that an experience that occurs twice is more likely to be remembered than a single experience" (p. 264). But the picture gets a bit more complex when we consider the issue of exactly how material is repeated.

The Spacing Effect.   One important distinction involves how repetitions occur over time. **Massed repetition** involves repeated presentations that occur closely together in time, while **distributed repetition** involves repeated presentations spread out over time. Which do you think works better? The advantage of distributed repetitions over massed repetitions has been termed the **spacing effect,** and this effect has been found in numerous empirical investigations (Glenberg, 1974; Melton, 1970). Why should repetitions spaced out over time be better than repetitions that are crammed together? Researchers have proposed two likely explanations, both of which have some empirical support (Greene, 1992). These accounts place the locus of the spacing effect at different stages of the remembering process. The *deficient-processing view* focuses on encoding, suggesting that massed repetitions lead to deficient processing of the second presentation—you simply don't pay much attention to the later presentations relative to the first (Hintzman, Block, & Summers, 1973). As a result, you have only one fully encoded memory representation rather than many. The *encoding variability view* is similar in that it contends that massed presentations amount to little more than one presentation, but it places the locus of the effect at retrieval. According to this view, under massed presentation conditions, there is little or no variation in how the repeated events are encoded into memory, so the corresponding memory representations will be similar and relatively indiscriminable. This will make them more difficult to "find" in a memory search. When repetitions are distributed over time, each encoding will be relatively distinct from the others, so you're more likely to "stumble upon" one of them during your memory search.

The spacing effect is what researchers term a *robust phenomenon*—it's been found in many studies, using a variety of experimental contexts and tasks including the classroom (Seabrook, Brown, & Solity, 2005), so it's definitely relevant to how you study. If you're like many students, you cram more often than you should. Cramming—trying to learn material with massed repetition within a short time span—is a relatively ineffective study technique if your goal in college is to learn what is being taught (a sensible goal, given that you're investing a not-so-small fortune on it!).

The importance of spaced repetition is evident when one considers some research on the retention of information learned in school, which pretty much began with Bahrick's investigations of how we retain foreign language vocabulary. In these classic studies (Bahrick, 1979, 1984), the participants were individuals who had learned Spanish in either high school or college from 1 to 50 years earlier. Participants were administered various tests to assess their knowledge of Spanish, including reading comprehension, vocabulary recall and recognition, and grammar. A background questionnaire also was included to take stock of any important differences among participants other than age. These factors included the level of original language training, grades received, and the amount of rehearsal since the language was originally learned (i.e., continuing to read, write, or speak Spanish). Bahrick found that even after 25 years or more, participants still retained a fair amount of information. More important, however, this long-term retention was dependent on the degree of initial learning. Those with only a year of Spanish forgot everything relatively quickly. And not surprisingly, the people with more training showed better overall retention.

Bahrick and Hall (1991) arrive at a similar conclusion based on their assessment of students' retention of material from high school algebra. Participants in the study had all taken algebra, but only some of them had subsequently enrolled in college-level mathematics. As in the earlier studies (e.g., Bahrick, 1984), Bahrick and Hall took stock of important factors such as level of performance in high school algebra, subsequent rehearsals of the material, and scores on the Scholastic Aptitude Test (SAT). The results of this study were intriguing; although factors like SAT scores and grades did relate to overall levels of performance, they were relatively unimportant in predicting the maintenance of knowledge over time. The only good predictor of knowledge maintenance was the period of time over which the material was initially learned. Material learned over the course of a longer period persisted for decades; the same material learned over a shorter period vanished relatively quickly (Bahrick & Hall, 1991).

Appropriately enough, these conclusions also seem to apply to the very course for which you're reading this text! Conway, Cohen, and Stanhope (1991) examined retention of knowledge acquired in a cognitive psychology class taught over the course of one year at the Open University (located in England). The cognitive psychology course was highly structured, allowing for a systematic assessment of retention for different sorts of information, such as basic research methods, researcher names, theoretical concepts, and empirical findings. Particularly compelling to the authors was the sturdiness of what participants had learned about research methods. Retention of knowledge about general research methods showed no decline over the retention interval! Conway and colleagues offer a couple of reasons for the persistence of these particular concepts. First, the cognitive psychology course in question was a methods course, leading to more exposure to, and hands-on practice with, research methods. In addition, because research methods are covered in a number of psychology courses, they enjoy the benefit of spaced repetition. It's informative, at this point, to make a connection between the persistence of information learned about research methods and the Ebbinghausian notion of savings in relearning. You'll recall (from Chapter 1) that savings refers to the benefit we gain from having learned material previously. It's much easier to learn something in a second and third encounter, particularly if those encounters are sufficiently spaced out.

There are two factors that are critical in determining the effect of spaced repetitions on the long-term retention of studied information: the study interval (i.e., time between the repeated study sessions) and the retention interval (i.e., the time between the final study session and the final test of the studied information). Cepeda, Vuhl, Rohrer, Wixted (2008) conducted a massive study to determine the combination of study interval (SI) and retention interval (RI) that would maximize the amount of information retained over time. They tested 1354 participants on a set of 32 obscure facts (e.g., Q: What European country consumes the most spicy Mexican food? A: Norway), over a 1 year time interval, a massive undertaking facilitated by participant-testing via the internet, an increasingly common technique for modern-day researchers.

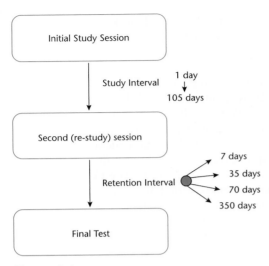

Figure 6.1

Outline of the procedure used in the Cepeda, Vuhl, Rohrer, & Wixted (2008) study.

The procedure for the experiment is presented in Figure 6.1. In the initial study session, participants were presented with the 32 facts in question form and were instructed to give an answer, even if it was a guess (as we imagine most of their answers were given the obscurity of the questions). After they guessed, the correct answer was given to them. They were repeatedly presented with each question until they got each of them correct. After varying study interval lengths ranging from 1 to 105 days (depending on the length of the retention interval), they participated in a second (re-study) session. The second session was identical to the first. Participants then took a final test after varying retention interval lengths (7 days, 35 days, 70 days or 350 days). This led to 26 conditions created by combining every retention interval with every possible study interval!! Needless to say, this study was truly an epic undertaking!

The researchers used their results to plot the impressive (perhaps daunting?!) function in Figure 6.2. This is a rare 3-D plot which allows for the conjoint consideration of three factors: study interval, retention interval, and recall. With regard to the study interval, spacing repetitions (study interval axis) helps recall to a point, but there came a point at which recall began to decline with more space between repetitions. The retention interval axis presents no surprises; memory declines rapidly as a function of increasing interval. The most interesting finding is the interaction between these two factors. The point at which the surface begins to

Figure 6.2

Proportion recall on a final test plotted as a function of study interval and retention interval as presented by Cepeda Vuhl, Rohrer, Wixted, and Pashler. (2008). The heavy white line represents optimal performance for each retention interval. Note that as retention interval increases, the study interval that produces optimal recall also increases. Typical educational practice is marked by the star; relatively short study intervals, and relatively short retention intervals. Note how this fails to optimize performance.

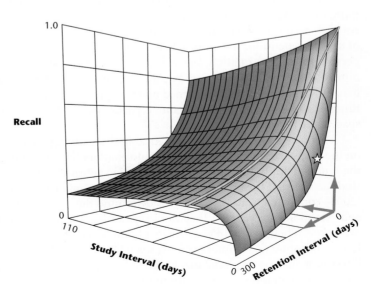

"curve" downward represents maximum recall. As you can see, as the retention interval increased, optimal recall occurred at increasingly longer study intervals; the best length of study interval (i.e., time between repeated study sessions) depends on how long you want to remember it. One principle is immediately apparent; if you want to remember something for a long time (on the order of years), a review after a fairly lengthy spacing period will provide a high return on the time investment. Unfortunately, this is definitely not accepted educational practice. Most often, the coverage of a given topic is compressed into a single week, and your studying of it is likely crammed into one, maybe two days within that week. That's going to put you in the least productive part of the curve (indicated by a star on figure), which features good immediate recall, but poor long-term recall.

Rehearsal

Well, you're probably a little disillusioned right now. What good is spacing when the optimal spacing needed to maximize retrieval won't even be possible when it comes to studying for college exams? Don't lose heart; there are still plenty of study strategies that will facilitate your learning. Space out your studying as much as possible but then follow the strategies we'll talk about next. These strategies should be used during those spaced-as-best-you-can study sessions.

In the previous section, we focused on how material should be presented and re-presented. We continue along a similar vein, but now we turn our attention to **rehearsal,** which is basically mental practice. It's easy to confuse the concepts of repetition and rehearsal because they are closely related. Repetition refers to the fact that an item is experienced more than once, whereas rehearsal refers to how that item is thought about internally. Let's consider the processes involved in the mental practice of information and how these processes relate to remembering.

Maintenance and Elaborative Rehearsal.
To a large extent, memory follows the old axiom "Practice makes perfect." Rehearsal is important for maintaining information in immediate memory and, according to some early models of memory (Atkinson & Shiffrin, 1968; Waugh & Norman, 1965), may be instrumental in encoding it permanently in LTM. The way we discussed rehearsal in Chapter 4 was through internally repeating the information over and over and over.... This definitely allows information to remain active in immediate memory (or in the focus of attention) but this type of simple rehearsal isn't as effective for storing information in LTM as you might think. An experiment by Craik and Watkins (1973) demonstrates how truly ineffective it can be. Participants were presented with lists of words, and their task was to keep track of the words that began with a specific letter (e.g., *p*). At the end of each list, participants were to report the last word that had begun with that letter. If you were a participant, you might be presented with *cherry, plow, tiger, desk, house.* After presentation of the list, your job would be to say "plow." How would you accomplish this fairly simple task? Probably by mentally repeating the word *plow* over and over until you got another *p* word or until you had to report the word *plow*, whichever came first. Consider this list: *tree, peach, carpet, table, igloo, garlic, bird, clock.* Your response would be *peach.* In this case, you would have

to repeat the word *peach* approximately twice as many times as the word *plow*. At the end of the experiment, when asked to recall all of the last *p* words from each list, you might think that the more time you spent rehearsing a *p* word, the more likely you'd be to remember it. It wasn't. Craik and Watkins varied the number of intervening items (and hence the amount of rehearsal) from 2 to 12 items, and found no difference in later recall.

The type of rehearsal employed in this situation is aptly termed **maintenance rehearsal,** because all you're doing is maintaining the item in consciousness, with little or no embellishment. Trying to memorize information from your class notes by simply repeating the information over and over is not a very effective technique. Certainly, repeating it once is better than not repeating it at all, but after one presentation there seems to be little additional memory benefit. So if you use maintenance rehearsal to study, one thorough exposure is as good as several. Based on your experience with college tests, you're probably thinking that one simple rehearsal would not be sufficient to pass most professors' tests.

But the story on maintenance rehearsal isn't quite so simple. Recall the earlier discussion about the importance of the interaction between the stages of encoding and retrieval. Whether or not you get any benefit from maintenance rehearsal depends on the retrieval task. While maintenance rehearsal is relatively ineffective in enhancing one's ability to recall information, it does lead to some improvement in the ability to recognize it. Successful recognition depends on the degree to which you've thoroughly processed an individual item, whereas recall depends more on making associations between the to-be-remembered items (Anderson & Bower, 1973; Gillund & Shiffrin, 1984). When you consider this, it's not difficult to see why maintenance rehearsal helps recognition but not recall. Repeating an individual item over and over will lead to more thorough processing of that individual item but will do little or nothing to build associations between items on a list (Nairne, 1983).

Let's consider the practical implications of these findings. In general, maintenance rehearsal is a relatively ineffective way to remember something. It helps in laboratory tests of recognition in which you have to answer the question, "Did you see this concept before?" But real-world memory situations are never this simple. Professors never ask, "Do you remember the term *rehearsal* from your reading?" If they did, everyone would get 100% on every test. You're more likely to be asked, "What's the difference between rehearsal and repetition?" Simply recognizing the word *rehearsal* isn't going to help you answer this question. So although maintenance rehearsal may be effective in certain laboratory settings, it is a relatively inefficient technique for committing information to long-term memory (Greene, 1992). There are much better uses for your study time. So read on....

A more effective alternative to maintenance rehearsal is **elaborative rehearsal.** This involves thinking about the meaning of the information that is to be remembered, as well as making associations between that information and information already stored in memory. An early study by Hyde and Jenkins (1969) demonstrates the effectiveness of this type of processing. Participants encoded single words by making a simple judgment about each one. They were to rate the pleasantness of the word, estimate the number of letters in the word, or determine whether the word had an *e*. Hyde and Jenkins were interested in how well the words themselves would be remembered. The results were clear-cut. Memory was much better when participants were required to judge the pleasantness of words relative to when they were noticing *e*'s or counting letters.

Consider the differences in these tasks. Judging the pleasantness of words requires that you think about what the word means and may even make you think about some associated information. For example, judging whether Jell-O is pleasant or unpleasant requires you to think about what Jell-O is and it even triggers a thought about the red-white-and-blue layered Jell-O salad you enjoy at family picnics on the Fourth of July. Counting the number of *e*'s in Jell-O would produce nothing like this. You would give the word cursory consideration but little quality thought.

One surprising aspect of this finding is that this advantage occurred in both incidental learning and intentional learning. Under **incidental learning** conditions, participants are not told that memory will be tested. Instead, they are under the impression that the encoding task is the sole focus of the experiment. Under **intentional learning** conditions, participants are explicitly told that they are participating in a memory experiment and that the encoded material will be tested later. Hyde and Jenkins found a memory advantage when participants were just reading words and making simple judgments about them, as long as the judgments made participants consider the meaning of the concept. It didn't even matter if participants were trying to remember the words. They just ended up doing so, because they gave the words quality processing. Given these findings, memory research began to focus on the effects of different types of processing on memory.

Stop&*Think Back* | MAINTAINING AND ELABORATING OR TOP DOWN*ING* AND BOTTOM UP*ING*?

The distinction between elaborative and maintenance rehearsal maps on in some ways to the distinction between top-down and bottom-up processing (discussed in Chapter 2). Can you figure out how? Relate it to studying—what type of rehearsal is especially effective in successfully encoding and retrieving information? Why might this be, in terms of top-down and bottom-up processing? (HINT: Think of the purpose of bottom-up and top-down processing, and which might map better onto the goals of studying.)

Levels of Processing

The notion that memory depends on how information is processed at encoding served as the foundation for Craik and Lockhart's (1972) landmark **levels-of-processing theory.** This theory served as an alternative to the modal model of memory. Recall that the modal model focused primarily on structural aspects of memory, proposing the existence of separate storage systems along with principles regulating the transfer of information between them. How the incoming information was processed was not ignored by this model, but it was not central.

Craik and Lockhart made processing the focus of their approach, proposing that how incoming information is processed is the critical determinant of whether that information is remembered (i.e. stored for the long term). According to their theory, analysis of incoming information proceeds from a shallow and superficial analysis of structural features to a more deep and thorough analysis of meaning. The primary determinant of whether information is remembered is how far processing gets on this continuum. Information that is processed to a deep level will be better remembered than information processed only to a shallow level. Craik and Tulving (1975) proposed that maintenance rehearsal has relatively little impact on later memory, because processing never gets beyond the superficial level. They proposed **elaborative rehearsal** as a superior alternative. During elaborative rehearsal, the analysis of incoming information proceeds to a deeper, more meaningful level.

Let's apply this analysis to the Hyde and Jenkins's (1969) study. According to the levels-of-processing approach, the different encoding tasks led participants to process information to different levels. Simply noting *e*'s or estimating the number of letters in a word can be accomplished with only a superficial level of analysis. Deciding whether a word is pleasant, however, requires more; you need to proceed all the way from encoding the physical features of the word to thinking of the word's meaning and if it is a pleasing concept. This determination relates to an obvious component of elaborative rehearsal—**elaboration** (Craik & Tulving, 1975), which basically refers to the degree to which information is specified, described, and/or related to other information in memory. The better elaborated a concept is at encoding, the more access routes you have to get to it at retrieval. A deep encoding task will probably lead you to think about associated information (like the information about Jell-O mentioned earlier). These associations can serve as routes to the information at retrieval. Conversely, a shallow encoding task does not lead to the production of such associates and hence produces a memory trace with relatively few (if any) retrieval routes. The more retrieval routes, the better the memory will be. Thinking about the meaning of an item and connecting it to information already in LTM leads to a more enduring and retrievable memory trace.

As fresh and popular as the levels-of-processing approach was when it was introduced, its vagueness was troublesome to many. For example, the word *mouse* is remembered better when it's presented with the question, "Is this an animal?" relative to when it's presented with the question, "Does this word rhyme with *house?*" Why? Because the first condition leads to a deeper level of processing. But how do we know that the first question leads to deeper processing than the second? There seems to be no clear answer other than "Because you remember it better." Depth of processing is used as an explanation for memory performance, and then memory performance is used to define depth of processing. This circular definition is really no definition at all. (You may remember the notion of a circular definition from our discussion of capacity in Chapter 3.) In order to avoid this circularity, we need something else (besides memory performance) that indicates a deep level of processing. Many of the effective encoding strategies we'll be discussing next could be considered the answer to this valid criticism of this approach.

Self-Reference

As we've seen, research on levels of processing has demonstrated that words processed deeply (i.e., in terms of their meaning) are remembered well. Later research by Rogers, Kuiper, and Kirker (1977) revealed an encoding condition that seems deeper than deep. In this experiment, participants encoded words (e.g., *happy*) with different types of encoding questions, as in the levels-of-processing studies, with one exception: the researchers added an encoding condition they termed "self-reference." Words in this condition (e.g., *generous*) were encoded with the question, "Does this term describe you?" The results demonstrated the standard levels-of-processing effect, with a twist: words that were self-referenced were remembered even better than those deeply processed. Over the last quarter-century, many studies have replicated and extended this basic **self-reference effect**, establishing it as a robust memory phenomenon (Symons & Johnson, 1997).

Why is relating information to yourself such an effective technique? In their review of studies on the self-reference effect, Symons and Johnson (1997) conclude that self-reference promotes good memory through elaboration (discussed previously in the context of elaborative rehearsal) and organization (which we'll be talking about in more depth in a minute). Because the self is such an elaborate, well-developed, and well-practiced network of knowledge, it offers incredible potential for both elaborative and organizational processing. The implications for your own memory are clear: Chances are that you'll increase the likelihood of remembering something to the degree that you can relate it to yourself. Processing in this way encourages both organization and elaboration of the incoming information, and this, in turn, makes it more likely that you'll remember it.

A study by Cunningham, Turk, Macdonald, and MacRae (2008) reveals another dimension of the self-reference effect, namely, how ownership affects memory. Cunningham et al. employed a clever procedure in which participants were assigned a blue or red shopping basket (the other was ostensibly assigned to another participant who was actually a confederate). The experimenter then showed the two participants a series of cards. Each card had a grocery item and a red or blue sticker on it. If the sticker matched the color of the participant's basket, they were told to imagine that they won that item. The experimenter randomly handed the card to the participant or the confederate to place in the appropriate basket. This experiment had two independent variables—ownership (whether the card ended up in one's own basket) and activity (whether the participant or the confederate put the card in the basket). The dependent variable was the number of grocery items correctly recognized at the end of the experiment and the reaction time to make the recognition decision.

The results are presented in Table 6.3. The major finding was that items were better remembered when they were "owned" by the participant than the confederate (there was no difference in memory for activity—who placed the card in the basket and there was no interaction between the two variables). In addition, recognition reaction times were quicker for self-owned than confederate-owned items, suggesting that the corresponding

Table 6.3 **Data from the Cunningham et al. (2008) Study on Ownership and Memory**

		Mover	
		Self	Other
Owner	Self	.67	.64
	Other	.59	.60

memory representations for owned items are especially salient. Cunningham et al. point out that it would be to one's advantage to have an especially good memory for items that are self-owned, given daily needs to visually apprehend, attend to, and remember items of personal importance.

Fitness-Relevant Processing

Research Theme
Evolution

The findings on ownership and memory highlight the importance of considering the *function* of memory and *why* it works the way it does. Remembering self-relevant information is useful and adaptive. Recent research by Nairne and colleagues (e.g., Nairne, Pandeirada, Gregory, & Van Arsdall, 2009; Nairne, Pandeirada, & Thompson, 2008) has fully embraced this perspective, investigating the relative benefits of various encoding tasks within an evolutionary framework. He begins with the straightforward and reasonable assumption that the processes involved in remembering were shaped by evolutionary pressures, which most likely "rewarded" individuals who were especially good at processing and retaining fitness-relevant information—survival of the fittest, hence the name, the fitness effect. To put it in caveperson-speak, person who remember tiger live more than person who not remember tiger.

Nairne, Thompson, and Pandeirada (2007) reasoned that processing information in terms of its survival value might tap into some sort of preferential processing and lead to better retention. To test their idea, Nairne et al. (2007) presented participants with a list of words. There were three conditions in the experiment. One group of participants performed a deep processing task by indicating how pleasant the word was (pleasantness condition). The second group rated each item in terms of how useful it would be to them if they were planning a move (moving condition). The third group was the group of interest. These participants were given a survival scenario in which they had to judge how useful each item would be to them in a situation in which their survival was in danger. The top row of Table 6.4 lists the specific instructions for each condition. The dependent variable was the percentage of words correctly recalled. The recall levels for each encoding condition are presented in their respective rows of Table 6.4. As you can see, processing a word in terms of its survival value led to better recall than the deep processing task (pleasantness) and the moving task.

Across these and other studies, survival processing has led to better memory than about a dozen different encoding conditions, all of which involve deep and meaningful processing. Even more astounding is what one might call the precision of the effect. Nairne, Pandeirada, Gregory, and Van Arsdall (2009) tested a "hunting" version of the survival scenario that had participants imagine they were responsible for hunting in order to feed the members of their tribe. They compared this condition to a nearly identically worded scenario that involved a hunting *contest*. Once again, the survival processing scenario led to superior memory. Clearly, there is something special about thinking in terms of the fitness relevance of incoming information. We seem to be tuned, perhaps through natural selection, to process and remember information that relates to our survival. Nairne proposes that researchers add a functionalist-evolutionary perspective on remembering to their tools of analysis; at the very least, framing memory questions within an evolutionary framework will lead to important new empirical questions and answers.

Table 6.4 Encoding Instructions for Each Condition of the Nairne (2007) Study on Survival Processing and Memory, and Recall Levels in Each Condition

	Pleasantness	Moving	Survival
Encoding Instructions	In this task, we are going to show you a list of words, and we would like you to rate the pleasantness of each word. Some of the words may be pleasant and others may not—it's up to you to decide.	In this task, we would like you to imagine that you are planning to move to a new home in a foreign land. Over the next few months, you'll need to locate and purchase a new home and transport your belongings. We are going to show you a list of words, and we would like you to rate how relevant each of these words would be for you in accomplishing this task. Some of the words may be relevant and others may not—it's up to you to decide.	In this task, we would like you to imagine that you are stranded in the grasslands of a foreign land, without any basic survival materials. Over the next few months, you'll need to find steady supplies of food and water and protect yourself from predators. We are going to show you a list of words, and we would like you to rate how relevant each of these words would be for you in this survival situation. Some of the words may be relevant and others may not—it's up to you to decide.
Recall	53%	52%	60%

Organization and Distinctiveness

In our discussion of levels of processing, we noted that the degree to which we think about the meaning of an event is important for memory. Conversely (or perhaps we should say, "In a complementary manner"), memory also depends on the degree to which individual events are organized or structured. The term **organization** can refer either to the characteristics of the incoming information (i.e., whether this information is structured in some way) or to the strategic orientation of the encoder (i.e., whether a person attempts to organize the incoming information).

The degree to which incoming information is structured exerts powerful effects on memory, as demonstrated in a study by Bower, Clark, Lesgold, and Winzenz (1969). It's extremely unusual for participants in a memory study to achieve perfect recall, but that is exactly what happened in this study. Bower and colleagues presented participants with four different lists of items to be encoded. Each set of items belonged to a particular category. For example, a list of items could belong to the category "minerals," and the subcategories "metals" and "stones." The experiment featured a very simple design. Participants in the organized condition saw the items organized into their respective taxonomic categories (e.g., "precious stones"), while participants in the unorganized condition were presented with the items in a random arrangement. Memory was tested with *multitrial free recall*. Participants attempted to learn the lists and then recall them; this learn-and-recall cycle was done three more times (four total cycles). The results were striking: participants in the organized condition recalled over 90% of the items by the second trial and were perfect on the final two trials. In contrast, the unorganized group never got up to 70% recall, even after studying the same lists four times.

In addition to the organizational structure inherent in the to-be-remembered information, deliberately imposing structure on incoming information also can be a powerful determinant of effective encoding. Such organization might be considered a close companion to chunking in immediate memory (discussed in Chapter 4). Recall that chunking refers to recoding information into meaningful groupings of information, thereby lightening the load of what must be recycled in immediate memory. Imposing organizational structure while encoding the information for later recall has a similar effect. The organizational scheme facilitates the rehearsal and/or formation of associations between the bits of information as they are being encoded. It also serves as a structure that can be used for later retrieval as we retrace the associations formed at encoding. How this facilitates retrieval makes sense if you think about it. Let's consider a frequently encountered situation in Bridget's life. She's looking for a particular ring to wear (the rose blush garnet ring that perfectly matches her outfit!). She is more likely to find it in an organized jewelry box (e.g., rings stored in groups by color of gemstone) than a disorganized jewelry box in which the rings are randomly grouped or worse yet thrown altogether in one compartment.

We are such resourceful information processors that we will use organization to aid our memory even when the to-be-remembered information lacks any type of organizational structure. Tulving (1962) was interested in the degree to which participants would impose their own organizational schemes on incoming information, so he used lists of words that had no inherent structure; that is, the list items were unrelated to one another. As in the Bower and colleagues (1969) study, memory was tested with multitrial free recall. Over the course of the first two trials, Tulving thought that participants would form idiosyncratic categories. They would think of certain words together and use this subjective organization to impose structure on the unstructured list. And, in keeping with the finding that organization helps memory, he hypothesized that people who formed these idiosyncratic categories (i.e., people who employed subjective organization) would recall more on the third recall trial than those who didn't. The results supported his hypothesis on. So, even when the to-be-remembered material does not possess an obvious organizational structure, we impose our own organization in order to help us recall the information.

Surprisingly, something that seems the complete opposite of organization also helps memory: distinctiveness. **Distinctiveness** refers to how well information is distinguished from other information in memory. According to this analysis, encoding an item in terms of what it means distinguishes the item better from its neighbors in memory, called relative to encoding an item in terms of how it sounds or looks. The more distinct an item, the easier it will be to find during retrieval. A classic demonstration of the effects of distinctiveness on memory, called the **von Restorff phenomenon** (von Restorff, 1933) was studied extensively in the early days of cognitive psychology. Early investigations of the phenomenon involved presenting a list of words in which one item "stuck out like a sore thumb" (e.g., in a different color); the "isolated" item was often particularly well remembered (Wallace, 1965).

Material-Appropriate Processing   You may be a little puzzled with the foregoing discussion. First we told you that retention depends on the degree to which you organize incoming information, imposing structure on it and seeing relationships. But, then we noted the importance of encoding information distinctively, differentiating it from other information. These two statements would seem to be at odds with one another; how can we make distinctions among items while at the same time draw relationships among them? The notion of **material-appropriate processing** (Hunt & Einstein, 1981; McDaniel & Einstein, 2005) provides an answer.

According to this framework, both ways of looking at information are critical for optimal memory performance. **Relational processing** describes the degree to which we process items in terms of their interrelationships and is aided to the degree that encoding information affords *organization*. **Individual-item processing** describes the degree to which we process items in terms of their *individual* characteristics and is aided by encoding that leads to distinctive processing. The key idea of the material-appropriate processing approach is that the type of processing that one should use in studying material for later retention depends on the nature of the material. If the material that one is trying to remember has a high degree of structure or is well organized, then the best type of processing would be individual-item (i.e., distinctive) processing. The converse is also true; if the material that one is trying to remember has little structure and is focused on specifics, then the best way to study it would be to use relational processing (i.e., organization). The processing strategy that one takes in approaching material they want to learn should be whatever strategy provides a complement to the information offered by that material.

You might assume that if the professor or textbook presents information in an organized manner then you don't need to focus on organization when you study. However, it's important to keep in mind that both types of processing are critical for good memory. When studying for a test you can't think about how the concepts go together (relational processing) unless you know what the individual concepts mean (individual item processing). So you should begin with the individual item processing to make sure you understand the concepts and then think about how each of these individual concepts relate to one another. In addition, no matter how organized your professor or textbook is, you should always try to rehearse that organization, and perhaps even add some of your own. Obviously, this will be easier with a professor who presents the material in an organized fashion. But also, keep in mind that you remember information better if you have ownership of it. Taking the time to organize the information presented by your professor or the textbook will give you "ownership" over the material, which should further enhance your memory for it.

Remembering Action

To this point, most of the research we've discussed has been pretty circumscribed in terms of method and materials. Most of the studies have involved memory for verbal materials, presented one word at a time. But what of memory for actions and activities? The issue of memory for action has enjoyed a surge of interest in recent years, another indication of the growing influence of a notion we discussed in Chapter 1—embodied cognition (Gibbs, 2006; Wilson, 2002), the notion that cognitive processes must be investigated within the context of the body's interaction with the environment. With the emergence of the embodied cognition approach over the past couple of decades, increasing attention

Research Theme
Embodied
Cognition

has been focused on how we remember actions, and how the act of remembering can be conceived of as an embodied activity. It's not that "the body remembers"—it's more that action is an integral component of daily events, so understanding the interplay between movement and memory is an important piece of the memory puzzle.

Enactment Effect.   Research reveals that people are quite good at remembering actions. This memory advantage has been termed the **enactment effect.** People are better at remembering action phrases like "hammer the nail" if they enact the activity, relative to conditions in which they simply read verbal descriptions. Most accounts of this effect propose that enacting an event results in a richer, more retrievable memory representation. Enacting an event brings in a motor component, not to mention richer visual and auditory components (e.g., Engelkamp & Zimmer, 1985).

It turns out that the mere *intention* to carry out an act leads to a similar memory advantage (Badets, Blandin, Bouquet, & Shea, 2006; Goschke & Kuhl, 1993). For example, Goschke and Kuhl (1993) asked participants to learn two procedural scripts. Each script consisted of five specific activities that served one goal (e.g., clearing a messy desk). After learning each of the scripts, participants were told that they would later have to perform one of them. This was done to activate an expectation or intention in the participants for later performance of the task. In the next phase of the experiment, participants were given single words and had to decide as quickly as possible whether each of the words had appeared in the earlier scripts. The interesting finding was that participants were quicker to respond to words taken from the scripts that they thought they would be performing than those they did not think they would be performing. This indicates that simply forming an intention to do something by thinking about it leads to increased memory activation of that activity.

Stop&*Think* | ENACTING ENACTMENT

The enactment effect is fairly easy to demonstrate. Set up two conditions, and test a couple of people in each. In one condition, read the phrases below and have them repeat the phrases out loud. In the other condition, read the phrases and have them do the activity described. The "control" condition (simply hearing the phrases) should be done in the presence of all the items mentioned as well, to control for effects of simply seeing toothpicks, pencils, etc.

After reading the phrases or having the participants enact the phrases, give them a distractor—talk to them about how great cognitive psych is—for a few minutes. Then, test recall by having the subjects write down the phrases.

Total Cost of Materials: 57¢
Demonstrating the Enactment Effect: Priceless
    Pick up the pencil.
    Bend the paper clip.
    Drink from the cup.
    Rip the paper.
    Kick the chair.
    Close the folder.
    Stack the books.

Actors' Memories. The beneficial effects of enactment may be one factor that lies behind the prodigious memory feats of actors. When you consider what actors must commit to memory—the scenes, the actions, the lines, the emotions—their skill in doing so cannot be underestimated. Interestingly, Noice and Noice (2006) note that actors themselves rarely mention memorization in discussing how they learn their lines; rather than trying to remember what the characters say, they actively experience and engage the character. It turns out that the stage is the perfect laboratory for investigating the relationship between embodiment and memory.

An actor using a line rather than rehearsing one.

In an analysis of how actors learn lines and roles, Noice and Noice (2006) used protocol analysis, interviewing actors for personal insights on their learning process. The analysis revealed two major phases in actors' processing. First, their protocols revealed that they do "memorize" in a sense; they spontaneously use most of the techniques discussed to this point, including elaboration (of their lines), self-reference and ownership (they become the character and the lines are "theirs"), and organization (grouping sets of lines that define the goals of a character). A second phase relates to the notion of embodiment. The lines and intentions of a character must be processed in terms of movement and emotion; Noice and Noice (2001) term this *active experiencing*. They provide the following example: when encoding the phrase *to intimidate,* the active experiencing technique would involve looking at and speaking to someone menacingly, as well as movement designed to intimidate (e.g., striding toward someone).

Noice and Noice (2001) investigated the memory benefits of active experiencing for the average college student. Their study involved pairs of participants memorizing the two parts of a two-person scene, in one of three encoding conditions. In a memorization condition, the pairs of participants worked together on memorizing their lines in anticipation of a memory test. In a partial active experiencing condition, participants practiced the lines as they read the dialogue in the play, complete with emotion. Full active experiencing involved reading and acting out the dialog and the scene, complete with appropriate movement. During the test phase, participants were given a script with their lines missing, and had to fill in the blanks. The dependent variable was verbatim accuracy in recalling their lines. The results are presented in Table 6.5.

As you can see, active experiencing was more effective than partial experiencing and memorization (there was no difference between the latter two conditions). Remember this study has been discussed in the context of the enactment effect. Actors were more

Table 6.5 Proportion of verbatim lines recalled in Noice and Noice (2001). Note the Advantage of Full-Active Experiencing in Remembering Speeches.

	Full Active Experiencing	Partial Active Experiencing	Memorization
Recall of Speeches (%)	31	23	18

likely to remember their lines when they engaged in active experiencing (rehearsing lines in the context of the movements required by the actor when saying the lines). This finding foreshadows a principle we'll be discussing later: the encoding specificity principle which emphasizes the overlap between encoding and retrieval conditions in determining later memory. According to Glenberg and Kaschak (2002) this strategy works because memories consist of the representations formed through lived experience, which includes sights, sounds, emotions, and movement. These experiences are most likely to be retrieved under conditions in which each component comes into play again.

Transfer-Appropriate Processing

All of the effective encoding strategies we just discussed were the result of the levels of processing theory that emphasized encoding as the primary determinant of memory. Often, but not always, research on encoding strategies does not focus much attention, if any, on retrieval. This makes sense on an intuitive level; encoding and retrieval are two separate phases of the memory process. But as we said earlier, this distinction is only a matter of convenience. Remembering depends critically on the interaction between the two. The importance of the interaction between encoding and retrieval was made abundantly clear in a study by Morris, Bransford, and Franks (1977) who proposed the notion of **transfer-appropriate processing** as an alternative to the levels-of-processing theory that was the dominant theory at the time. According to the notion of transfer-appropriate processing, no encoding task is inherently better than another in terms of leading to retrievable memory representations. What qualifies as memorable processing at encoding is defined by what is required at retrieval. In other words, the information gained in the study phase is going to have to transfer to the retrieval situation, so the processing performed at encoding should be appropriate for how it's going to be retrieved. That is, processing should be transfer-appropriate.

Morris, Bransford, and Franks (1977) claimed that the memory that results from a shallow encoding task (e.g., counting the number of e's in a word) might indeed be durable, but the typical memory test doesn't pick up on the information that was encoded (i.e., structural information about a word). According to this analysis, if the memory test *did* make use of this information, then a shallow processing task might actually lead to *better* performance than a deep processing task. The researchers tested their hypothesis in a clever series of experiments. In one experiment, participants encoded words either semantically (deep processing) by judging whether a word (e.g., *train*) fit in a sentence (e.g, "The _____ had a silver engine"), or phonologically (shallow processing) by judging whether a word (e.g., *eagle*) rhymed with a second word

Table 6.6 **Data from the Morris, Bransford, and Franks (1977) Study**

	Rhyme Recognition	Standard Recognition
Semantic Encoding	0.33	0.84
Rhyme Encoding	0.49	0.63

From Morris, D. C., Bransford, J. D., & Franks, J. J. (1977). Levels of processing versus transfer-appropriate processing. *Journal of Verbal Learning and Behavior, 16,* 519–533. Copyright 1977, Elsevier Science (USA). Reprinted by permission.

(e.g., *legal*). The dependent variable was memory accuracy on a traditional recognition test or a *rhyme-recognition test*. In the rhyme-recognition test, participants had to recognize words that rhymed with the words they'd encoded. For example, the word *regal* would appear on the recognition test, and participants would have to indicate if this word rhymed with one of the studied words.

According to the levels-of-processing approach, a more durable memory trace is created in the semantic condition, so participants in this condition should remember more words, regardless of the test. According to transfer-appropriate processing, both encoding conditions create durable memory traces, but ones that contain different information. Semantically encoded words should be better remembered on the typical recognition test, which requires access to the concepts represented by the words. Conversely, phonologically encoded words should be better remembered on the rhyme recognition test, which requires access to phonological information—that is, the spoken sound of the word. The results, displayed in Table 6.6, support the transfer-appropriate processing analysis, demonstrating what might be termed a *reverse levels-of-processing effect*. On the rhyme-recognition test, words processed less deeply were remembered better. What mattered the most was not the depth of processing but whether the encoding process was appropriate for the memory test. The practical implications for your studying are clear: Be sure that the memory trace you create for the material on an upcoming test is *appropriate* to the type of test you'll receive. In other words, the way you study should depend on the way you'll be tested.

The notion of transfer-appropriate processing was part of the shifting terrain of memory research, which was moving away from the simple analysis of encoding variables toward a focus on the *interaction* between encoding and retrieval. You'll read more about this later, but for now we will now turn our attention to retrieval processes in LTM. But before we do let's discuss the possibility that retrieval could be an effective encoding strategy. No that wasn't a typo, read on....

The Testing Effect.   Let's think about how you might study for your test over this chapter. Let's say you have four sessions in which you plan to read the textbook and study it (hopefully you'll spread these study sessions over as long a time period as possible). Obviously, you should utilize as many of the previously discussed encoding strategies as possible during these four study sessions. But here's another technique to add to your growing arsenal of study strategies. Let's say you read the chapter in the first session. During the final three sessions you should test yourself over the material rather

Table 6.7 Overview of Procedure for Roediger and Karpicke's (2006) Study of the Testing Effect

	Period 1	Period 2	Period 3	Period 4
SSSS	Study	Study	Study	Study
STTT	Study	Test	Test	Test

than simply rereading it (this would be simple maintenance rehearsal anyway, so you might as well try something else....even if testing yourself on the information doesn't feel very much like studying).

Roediger and Karpicke (2006) performed the laboratory analog to the hypothetical study sessions just described. Participants were presented with a scientific text passage to study. There were four 5-minute study periods. In the first period all participants read (i.e. studied) the text passage. But the task performed on the material over the next three sessions varied across two conditions (see Table 6.7).

In one condition (STTT, or "study, test, test, test"), participants read the text once and were tested on it (free recall) three separate times. They never reread the passage itself. In the other condition (SSSS, or "study, study, study, study"), the participants studied the passage four times. In both conditions, a final recall test was given 5 minutes or 1 week after session 4. In the final test, participants were told to recall the entire passage and write down as much of it as they could. The dependent variable was the number of main ideas recalled from the passage.

The results are presented in Figure 6.3, and represent a striking interaction between study condition and retention interval. When the final test was given after a short delay (five minutes), studying the passage four times led to a clear advantage in memory. However, the advantage was a short-lived one. When tests were given a week later, the pattern of results was the opposite! The group who had experienced repeated testing remembered much more than the groups who had repeatedly studied the material. Put another way, the two encoding conditions seemed to lead to markedly different forgetting rates. Participants who studied by repeatedly testing themselves forgot much less than those who had repeatedly read the material. It is almost as if the repeated testing was an inoculation against forgetting. It is important to remember that in the STTT condition, in which performance was the best, the participants only read the text passage one time yet they performed better than the group that read the passage 4 times!

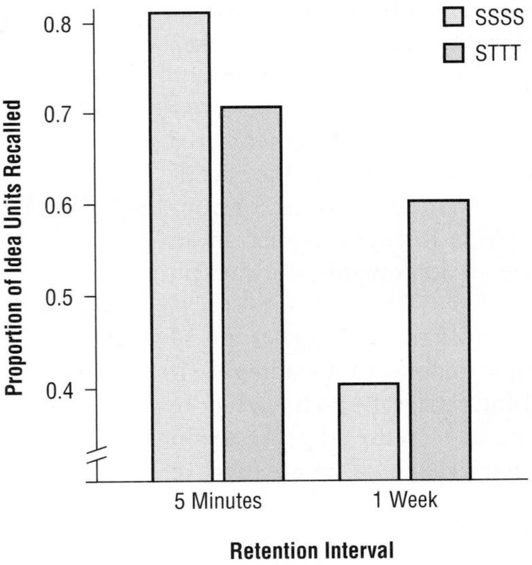

Figure 6.3
Results from Roediger and Karpicke's (2006) study of the effects of testing on retention.

From Roediger, H. L. & Karpicke, J. D. (2006). Test-enhanced learning: Taking memory tests improves long-term retention. *Psychological Science, 17*(3), 249–255. Blackwell Publishing. Reprinted with permission from the author.

The finding, termed the **testing effect** has been replicated several times (e.g., Butler & Roediger, 2007; McDaniel, Roediger, & McDermott, 2007). Simply reading and rereading material for class isn't going to do nearly as much good as reading followed by some type of repeated testing. The type of test seems to matter, too; McDaniel et al. (2007) found testing with short answer questions to be more beneficial to later recall than testing with multiple choice questions, particularly when feedback was provided soon after learning. Transfer-appropriate processing may be the reason for the testing effect. The reason testing yourself is such an effective encoding technique is because of the transfer-appropriateness of testing. What better preparation for a memory test could there be than....a memory test?! An interesting aside to the research just discussed would seem to speak to the utility and effectiveness of cumulative testing. Chances are you will be more likely to retain course-related information if the professor asks you repeatedly to retrieve the information over the entire semester in preparation for a cumulative final. So those instructors who give cumulative finals aren't being unreasonable they just want you to remember the material from their course!

Stop&*Think* | UGH! I HATE CUMULATIVE TESTS!

How common have cumulative tests been in your education, particularly in college? Think of concepts, facts, and theories you remember from your college classes. What classes are those concepts/facts/ theories from and was there a cumulative final in those classes? Reflect on how the style of testing in a given class has influenced your retention of information over time.

Stop&*Review*

1. True or false? Distributed repetition is more effective than massed repetition.
2. Describe three types of encoding tasks that are likely to lead to good retention.
3. What two types of processing combine to produce optimal memory?
4. Which memory principle underlies the testing effect?
   a. distributed repetition
   b. transfer-appropriate processing
   c. the enactment effect
   d. immediate memory

- Attention brings information into conscious awareness, enhancing the likelihood that the information will be stored for the long term. Repetition of information is more effective if distributed over time, rather than massed (i.e., the spacing effect). Maintenance rehearsal refers to simple mental repetition, while elaborative rehearsal involves making associations between the information to be remembered and other information stored in LTM and thinking about the meaning of the information. Elaborative rehearsal is more likely to result in long-term memory storage.

- The levels-of-processing approach emphasizes that how information is processed at encoding is the key determinant of memory. Processing that involves the analysis of meaning (i.e., deep processing) is more likely to lead to long-term storage than processing that involves a more superficial analysis (i.e., shallow processing). Material is also well-remembered if processed in terms of its survival value, or in terms of its relation to one's self.

• Material that is organized tends to be better remembered. Distinctive encodings (i.e., those that stand out from other events) are more likely to be remembered. According to the material-appropriate processing framework, relational processing (i.e., organization) and individual-item processing (i.e., distinctive encoding) combine to produce optimal memory. People are quite good at remembering actions, an example of the enactment effect. The beneficial effects of enactment are apparent from studies of actors' memories.

• Transfer-appropriate processing refers to the notion that memory is good to the extent that encoding processes are appropriate for the retrieval task. This principle may underlie the beneficial effects of memory testing, as shown in the testing effect.

Retrieval Processes in Long-Term Memory

Successful encoding and storage of information is necessary but not sufficient to guarantee later memory recall. Remembering also involves the processes of retrieval, whereby we regain access to encoded information. Of course, as mentioned early in the chapter, retrieval is not isolated from encoding and storage. The effectiveness of retrieval depends on the effectiveness of those two processes as well as on whatever reminders (i.e., **retrieval cues**) are present. This section will focus on the effectiveness of various retrieval cues and will consider how various retrieval tasks and situations interact with the encoding variables discussed earlier.

Availability and Accessibility

As mentioned earlier, the process of retrieval went relatively unnoticed in the early days of memory research as investigations focused on encoding and storage (Roediger & Guynn, 1996). Retrieval tasks were seen as a means to an end, namely, revealing the contents of storage. Failures to retrieve information were seen as failures of encoding (e.g., the material was not processed deeply enough) and/or storage (the material was lost due to disuse or interference). Retrieval itself was rarely varied and investigated systematically. However, early research by Endel Tulving (e.g., Tulving & Pearlstone, 1966) suggested that failure to remember information was not necessarily due to encoding or storage failure. Tulving thought it likely that a great deal of information was available in memory but was not accessible. You've experienced this distinction every time you've stared at a test question and the critical information fails to come to mind. The problem is not necessarily that the information isn't stored; the information may be there (i.e., it's available), but you can't get to it given the information (retrieval cues) in front of you (i.e., it's inaccessible). The problem is, this is still forgetting, and you're still going to lose points on the test. **Retrieval failure** is now widely recognized as a primary cause (perhaps *the* primary cause) of forgetting.

An investigation by Tulving and Pearlstone (1966) provides a simple illustration of the distinction between **availability** and **accessibility.** In this study, participants encoded categorized lists that contained two target words (e.g. garlic and parsley) from each of 24 categories. If you were a participant, you might be presented with "type of spice: garlic, parsley." Participants were instructed to remember the target words for a memory test. Some participants were tested with free recall. Under these conditions, participants recalled substantially less than half of the items. Tulving and Pearlstone suspected that this failure of recall was not necessarily a complete failure of memory. It was conceivable that all 48 encoded items were available in memory but that a blank piece of paper and instructions to recall the words were not good enough cues to allow access to the information. In other words, memory failure in this situation was due largely to problems in accessibility, or retrieval failure. To test this notion, the researchers had other participants take a cued-recall test. Tulving and Pearlstone provided these participants with the category names (i.e., type of spice) as retrieval cues. Incredibly, in this condition participants recalled nearly three-quarters of the words. Clearly, they had successfully encoded and stored the information. The locus of the problem had indeed been at retrieval. The information was available, and the right retrieval cues made it accessible.

Encoding Specificity

It's clear that retrieval cues are critical to remembering. This begs another question: What types of cues are most effective? One clue comes from those spontaneous memories (mentioned at the beginning of the chapter) that flood back to you when you visit a familiar location. It turns out that memory retrieval is aided by a cue to the extent that the cue helps reconstruct the encoding situation. In other words, memory depends on the amount of overlap between what's happening at retrieval and what happened at encoding. This fundamental retrieval principle is termed *encoding specificity.*

Let's consider a classic investigation by Thomson and Tulving (1970) that demonstrated the **encoding specificity principle.** Participants encoded weakly related word pairs, like *plant-bug,* in which the word *bug* was the word that had to be remembered (i.e., the target). After encoding a list of such pairs, a cued-recall test was given in which a cue was presented for each of the targets. Thomson and Tulving compared two retrieval conditions. In one condition, a strongly related word was presented to cue the target. For example, the participant would see *insect* as a cue for *bug.* In the other condition, the word from the original word pair (e.g., *plant*) was presented as a cue for *bug.* Intuitively, which word do you think would be a better cue for *bug*? It seems as though *insect* would be; it's a synonym for the target. But as it turns out, it was a relatively ineffective cue for recall relative to *plant.* Consider why this was the case in light of the encoding specificity principle. The event that has to be retrieved is encountering the pair *plant-bug.* The best retrieval cue will be one that helps reactivate that specific encoding situation, and *plant* is much more effective for this purpose because it was *part* of the encoding situation. If I wanted you simply to say the word *bug, insect* might be a good cue, but if I want you to remember an episode in which you saw the words *plant* and *bug* together, then *plant* is much more effective. By the way, this was part of the basis for Tulving's distinction between a memory system that stores episodes, complete with context (episodic memory), and one that stores contextless pieces of knowledge (semantic memory). The cue insect would trigger a semantic memory, but the cue plant cues the episode in which you encoded the word bug.

Habib & Nyberg (2007) used fMRI scanning to investigate the neural correlates of availability and accessibility. Participants were scanned during a three-phase procedure. The first phase involved encoding 60 pairs of words. They then received two memory tests. One involved responding to a presented cue by remembering the word that had been its partner during encoding (cued recall). For the second memory test, the researchers presented intact and recombined pairs from the originally encoded list. Participants had to determine whether each pair was intact or a recombination of words that had been previously presented (recognition test). A comparison of these conditions allowed for the assessment of words that were: (a) recalled and recognized (remembered), (b) not recalled, but recognized (available, or what the authors label as inaccessible), and (c) neither recalled nor recognized (forgotten). Measuring the brain activity during encoding allowed them to compare the brain activity when the memories for those words were subsequently remembered, forgotten, or temporarily forgotten (inaccessible).

Habib and Nyberg found that for words that were eventually remembered (recalled and recognized) both the medial temporal lobe (MTL) and left inferior frontal cortex (LIFC) were involved at encoding. However, activity in the MTL region distinguished inaccessible memories (not recalled but recognized) from those that were forgotten (neither recalled nor recognized) and activity in the LIFC distinguished words that were inaccessible from those that were remembered (recalled and recognized). This indicates that the medial temporal lobe is necessary for encoding information into memory but does not guarantee that it can be retrieved and the left inferior frontal cortex is necessary for retrieval. Interestingly, this activity was one of degree rather than kind. Memories that are inaccessible (i.e., can't be recalled but can be recognized) are associated with lower levels (not absence) of activity in the areas needed to successfully access (i.e., recall) the memory.

Extensions of Encoding Specificity: Context Dependency Effects. The Tulving and Pearlstone study indicates that the nature of retrieval cues is a critical determinant of memory. You might be wondering about the boundary conditions of this effect. Does it extend to the physical environment? Given that you learn much of the information from a course in a particular room, should you be in the same room when you're tested? Does the principle extend to how you feel? If you've had a couple of drinks and then meet some new friends, are you more likely to remember their names at the next party after you've had a couple of drinks? Evidence indicates that the encoding specificity principle is quite general. Studies manipulating physical context (e.g., Smith, 1979), presence or absence of music (e.g., Balch, Bowman, & Mohler, 1992), odor (e.g., Schab, 1990), drug or alcohol intake (e.g., Petersen, 1977), and mood (e.g., Eich & Metcalfe, 1989) at encoding and retrieval have all revealed **context-dependency effects.** That is, given a particular encoding context, memory is better when retrieval reinstates that context.

Table 6.8 **General Format of a Context-Dependency Study**

	Retrieval Condition A	Retrieval Condition B
Encoding Condition A	AA—match	AB—mismatch
Encoding Condition B	BA—mismatch	BB—match

The general structure of a context-dependency experiment is outlined in Table 6.8. These experiments generally involve four groups of participants. Some participants encode in context A and also take their memory test in context A. A second group of participants encodes in context A but is switched to context B for their memory test. A third group encodes in context B and is switched to context A for their memory test. Finally, a fourth group encodes in context B and is tested in context B. The prediction from the encoding specificity principle is that for a given encoding condition, memory will be better if the same context is reinstated at retrieval. So condition AA should be better than condition AB, and condition BB should be better than condition BA. It is important to point out that these comparisons are the only ones relevant to the encoding specificity principle. While it may seem reasonable to infer that AA should be better than BA and that BB should be better than AB, this can't be predicted by the encoding specificity principle. The encoding specificity principle states that *for a given encoding condition,* memory is best when the retrieval condition matches the encoding condition. A comparison between AA and BA involves different encoding conditions, and therefore would not represent the proper conditions to test this principle. This comparison would provide a test of the other encoding-retrieval overlap principle that we discussed earlier—transfer-appropriate processing. The prediction based on this principle is that for a given retrieval condition, memory is best when the encoding condition matches the retrieval condition. A comparison of BB to AB and AA to BA involves the same retrieval conditions and therefore is a test of the transfer-appropriate processing principle and *not* the encoding specificity principle. Regardless of which principle is being tested, the overriding message is that memory is best when encoding and retrieval conditions match.

If the physical environment in which an event occurs is truly part of the memory representation for the event, then a switch of environments between encoding and retrieval might result in poorer memory due to an encoding-retrieval mismatch. Godden and Baddeley (1975) tested this idea in a unique situation by having deep-sea divers participate in an underwater memory experiment. Divers encoded words in one of two conditions: on a beach or under several feet of water. Later, recall was tested in the environment in which divers had encoded the information or in the other environment. As you can see in Table 6.9 (on the next page) the results revealed a context-dependency effect. If divers had been on the beach during encoding, they were better off on the beach at retrieval. If they had been underwater during encoding, they were better off underwater during retrieval. Consider why this was the case. The divers' memory did not consist solely of the encoded words. It also included the physical environment in which the encoding had taken place. When this physical environment was presented as a cue at retrieval, memory was enhanced. This general finding has been found across a variety of experimental situations (Smith, 1988).

Table 6.9 Results of the Godden and Baddeley (1975) Study

		Retrieval Condition	
		Underwater	On Land
Encoding Condition	Underwater	32	22
	On Land	24	37

From Godden, D. R., & Baddeley, A. D. (1975). Context-dependent memory in two natural environments: On land and underwater. *British Journal of Psychology, 66,* 325–331. Copyright the British Journal of Psychology. Reprinted with the kind permission of the British Psychological Society.

Effects of Test Type.   A theme that should be increasingly obvious is that various memory phenomena depend on exactly how memory is tested. Therefore, it should come as no surprise that context-dependency effects vary with the type of memory test given. Research has shown that context-dependency effects are more likely to occur in free recall than in cued recall or recognition. For example, in the Godden and Baddeley (1975) underwater memory experiment, a context-dependency effect was not found when memory was tested with recognition. According to Eich (1980), the more direct the contact between the retrieval cue and the memory trace, the less likely it is that context will be needed to help retrieve the encoded episode. Cued recall and recognition both offer this direct contact and typically do not show context-dependency effects. Basically, you'll turn to context as a cue of last resort, only when better cues are unavailable. Smith (1988) proposed a similar notion, terming it the *outshining hypothesis.* Basically, it claims that context can be a useful cue for memory, but only when you need it. In recall, there are no retrieval cues, so context reinstatement provides some aid to the retrieval process. But in recognition, the retrieval cues are extremely strong (you get to see the item itself), so context reinstatement is not critical. In other words, on recognition tests, test items themselves "outshine" context as a cue.

Reality Check

Practical Implications.   What are the practical implications of this principle? Students often hear about these dependency effects and worry that perhaps they should eat, sleep, and (mostly) study in the room where they're going to be tested. The results are mixed on whether switching classrooms between study and test has any impact on performance. Metzger and colleagues (1979) found a negative effect of room switching, but other studies (e.g., Saufley, Otaka, & Bravaresco, 1986) have found no effect. There are a few reasons you needn't worry about taking a test in a different location than where you studied. First, most of the studies demonstrating context dependency use lists of unrelated words as the material to be remembered, which is hopefully not what you're learning in class (see the dean if you are!). Second, context almost certainly gets outshined by other more useful retrieval cues. Smith (1988) suggests that processing information in a meaningful way produces retrieval cues that are likely to outshine context. In other words, if you know the material well, you won't need to rely on the physical context for retrieval help. Also, many tests provide a great deal of cues (e.g., multiple-choice stems) that would outshine context at retrieval.

Although the effects of context dependency may be slight or nonexistent in many classroom situations, a study by Grant, Bredahl, Clay, Ferrie, Groves, McDorman, and Dark (1998) suggests that the principle should not be dismissed altogether. If you're like many students, you study under conditions of distraction. The iPod is playing music in your ear, the TV is on, your roommates are talking, or there's a buzz of activity at the library. But you're not tested in the presence of the TV, your iPod, your blabbing roommates, or the noisy library; you're tested in a completely silent room. Is there an effect of this mismatch of conditions (studying with background noise and activity and testing in silence)? To investigate this, Grant and colleagues followed the standard context dependency research design, manipulating the presence or absence of general background noise at both encoding and retrieval. They had participants encode a two-page article on psychoimmunology and tested them with a fill-in-the-blank exam followed by multiple-choice questions. In this study there were two independent variables, each with two levels: encoding environment (presence or absence of background noise) and retrieval environment (presence or absence of background noise). The dependent variable was test performance.

Mismatch between encoding and retrieval.

The results, shown in Table 6.10 (on the next page) are intriguing; there was no main effect of background noise at encoding. Participants who studied in the presence of background noise remembered just as much as participants who studied in the absence of background noise, which seems to support many a student's claim that studying with background noise, such as music, does not hurt memory. However, this main effect is mediated by an interaction: whether or not participants studied in the presence or absence of noise at encoding, they were better off in the same environment at retrieval. Consider the ramifications for test performance. Because tests are given in quiet conditions, studying should occur under quiet conditions, maximizing the encoding-retrieval match. So the next time you want to put those ear buds in your ears put your fingers instead!

Turn off the music while you're studying!

Table 6.10 **Results from Grant et al. (1998)**

a. Percentage correct on short-answer test

		Test Condition		
		Silent	Noisy	Row Mean
Study Condition	Silent	67	46	56.5
	Noisy	54	62	58.0
Column Mean		60.5	54.0	

b. Percentage correct on multiple-choice test

		Test Condition		
		Silent	Noisy	Row Mean
Study Condition	Silent	89	79	84
	Noisy	79	89	84
Column Mean		84	84	

From Grant, H. M., Bredahl, L. C., Clay, J., Ferrie, J., Groves, J. E., McDorman, T. A., & Dark, V. J. (1998). Context-dependent memory for meaningful material: Information for students. *Applied Cognitive Psychology, 12,* 617–623. Copyright 1998, John Wiley & Sons, Ltd. Reprinted by permission.

A Critique of the Encoding Specificity Principle.   Encoding specificity effects are so commonplace that the effects have been elevated to the level of a "principle," one of only a handful of cognitive psychology findings that could make that claim. However, Nairne (2002a) proposes that the basic tenet of encoding specificity—that successful memory depends on a match between retrieval and encoding circumstances—is a myth! According to Nairne, what determines successful memory performance is *cue distinctiveness,* or the effectiveness of a cue in singling out a specific memory representation. It just so happens that when encoding and retrieval overlap, you're more likely to have some cues that really are distinctive. But it is not the match between encoding and retrieval per se that leads to successful memory. So even circumstances in which there is almost no overlap between encoding and retrieval could produce good memory, if the minimal overlap is highly distinctive. So, according to Nairne (2002a),

Stop&*Think* | STUDY SKILLS COUNSELING

Imagine you have been asked to advise beginning students about how to prepare for college exams. Think of all the effective encoding and retrieval strategies discussed in this chapter and generate some tips for the new class.

- Which would you emphasize more: encoding or retrieval?

Of the factors shown to enhance memory:

- which would you emphasize as extremely important?

Which would you choose not to emphasize because they seem less important/relevant to studying for college exams?

the relationship between the encoding-retrieval match and successful memory performance is correlational, not causal. Having a rich set of retrieval cues increases both (1) encoding and retrieval overlap and (2) the chances of having highly distinctive cues. It is the highly distinctive cues that determine performance, rather than encoding and retrieval overlap. Nairne does not quibble with the practical implications of the encoding specificity principle, only the explanation of why an encoding-retrieval match is beneficial.

Aging and Retrieval

A central question in memory research, both retrospective and prospective, is how aging impacts remembering. Most of us have observed the cognitive decline that occurs with advancing age. Given the size of the aging baby boomer generation (of which your authors are card-carrying members), and the constant memory demands in terms of everyday retrospective and prospective tasks, understanding age differences in retrieval is a critical applied problem. Craik (1986) suggests that age-related deficits in remembering are larger to the extent that the memory task depends on **self-initiated retrieval,** or the degree to which individuals must rely on their own processing and memory representations to drive retrieval. Two of the explicit memory tests we've discussed thus far—recall and recognition—differ in the degree of self-initiated retrieval. Given the relative lack of cues in free recall (the only real cue is the instruction to recall a particular event or set of words), retrieval is largely self-driven. But in recognition, you are actually seeing the item; self initiation is less of factor in this test. Craik's view would predict larger age decrements in free recall than in recognition, and indeed, this is the obtained pattern (Craik & McCowd, 1987; Perlmutter, 1979).

Earlier in the chapter, we described the distinction between prospective and retrospective memory tests. As you might recall, one key difference between the two is that in a prospective memory test, retrieval is thought to be largely self-initiated, even more so than free recall. In free recall, a prompt is given to initiate recall. In prospective memory, however, there is no one tapping you on the shoulder telling you to take your meds or to go meet your classmates to work on a group project. *You* have to "remember to remember." Based on this, one might expect the same age-related decrements one sees in free recall, perhaps even to a greater degree. While it is true that deficits on prospective memory tests are often found in older participants (see Henry, MacLeod, Phillips, & Crawford, 2004 for a review), they are by no means consistently found. It turns out that the nature of memory differences between young and old is critically dependent on a number of variables that interact to produce different levels of performance. These variables include whether the prospective memory task is event-based or time-based, whether it's a laboratory task or a naturalistic task, whether reminders are used or not....it's quite the complex picture (McDaniel & Einstein, 2000).

One important distinction that seems to predict age-related decline in prospective memory tasks seems to be whether the ongoing activity or situation requires *focal processing* of the prospective memory cue. For example, when on vacation, I bring medications in a small pill container that I place in my toiletry kit. That kit ends up on the bathroom counter. The prospective memory task is remembering to take the medications before I go to bed, and the cue is the pill holder. If I simply go into the bathroom before bed to wash my face, the pill container is nonfocal, and the intention is unlikely to be activated. However, if I go into my toiletry kit looking for my toothbrush, the pill container is going to be focally processed, and is much more likely to trigger the intention automatically. Age-related deficits in prospective memory performance are more likely in situations where the prospective memory cue is nonfocal.

Stop&Review

1. What does it mean to say that a memory is available but inaccessible?
2. The encoding specificity principle indicates that retrieval will be best when
   a. retrieval conditions are different from those present at encoding.
   b. retrieval conditions match those present at encoding.
   c. multiple retrieval attempts are made.
   d. the person's mood at encoding matches their mood at retrieval.
3. True or false? If you test memory with recognition, you're more likely to find a context dependency effect than if you test it with recall.
4. Why is recall likely to lead to an age-related deficit in recall?

- Information stored in LTM (i.e., it's available) may not be remembered because the retrieval cues are insufficient (i.e., it's not accessible). Retrieval failure is a common cause of forgetting.

- According to the encoding specificity principle, a retrieval cue will be effective to the degree that it overlaps with the information provided at encoding. An example of this principle is that memory tends to be better when the context present at retrieval matches the context that was present at encoding (context-dependency effect). This applies to both external (i.e., physical surroundings) and internal (i.e., mood, body state) context.

- These context-dependency effects depend on how memory is tested. According to the outshining hypothesis, context-dependency effects are more likely to be found on free recall tests (few retrieval cues) than in cued-recall or recognition tests (more retrieval cues) because the presence of other retrieval cues tends to outshine the context cue.

- Age-related deficits in memory tend to occur for tests that require self-initiated retrieval, such as recall. On prospective memory tests, age-related deficits depend on the extent to which the task involves focal processing of the prospective memory cue.

Memory and Consciousness

In recent years, the question of how consciousness relates to memory has become a question of intense interest. This stands in stark contrast to 20 or 30 years ago, when the mystery of consciousness seemed too subjective to assess with the scientific method, and thus remained outside the realm of experimental psychology. The tide began to shift with research on implicit memory, which made it apparent that questions of consciousness could be addressed scientifically. Tulving's (1972, 1983) proposal of distinct memory systems also focused researchers' attention on questions of consciousness. As you'll recall, one of the major factors that distinguishes semantic (e.g., the Indianapolis football team is named the Colts) from episodic (e.g., watching the Colts win the 41st Superbowl) memories is that episodic retrieval is accompanied by an experience of recollection, or a *reliving* of the past experience. Tulving (1983) terms this "time-traveling" sense of memory **autonoetic consciousness.** This contrasts with the consciousness that accompanies retrieval from semantic memory. You may remember that when recalling a piece of information from semantic memory there is no sense of recollection or reliving. There is only a sense of familiarity with the fact, and the feeling that you just "know" it. Tulving termed this **noetic consciousness.**

Partially based on Tulving's distinction, dual-process theories of remembering have become popular. These approaches (e.g., Gardiner, 1988; Jacoby, 1991; Kelley & Jacoby, 2000; Mandler 1980) propose that recognition memory can be based on either or both of two types of information, which correspond to Tulving's consciousness dichotomy. Information can be recognized through a recollective process whereby we relive its encoding (and experience autonoetic consciousness), and/or through a familiarity-based process whereby we simply "know" the information was encountered before (noetic consciousness).

Remembering and Knowing

One of the more popular approaches for separating these two sources of information is to ask about one's state of awareness during the retrieval of a previous experience. This has been termed the **remember-know paradigm** (Gardiner, 1988). In this paradigm, participants are asked to recognize events (typically words) that occurred in an earlier list. For items that are recognized, another judgment is made: participants are asked whether they *remember* seeing the word or just *know* that they saw it earlier. A *remember* judgment means that participants can recall vividly the presentation of the word, basically reliving the experience. They can consciously recollect that the word was indeed presented (Rajaram, 1993). A *know* judgment means that although one knows that the word was part of the study list, they have no experience of recollection or reliving; the person just "knows" that the word appeared earlier. So if we "remember" that an event occurred, this reflects conscious and effortful retrieval. If we just "know" that an event occurred, this reflects nonconscious, automatic memory retrieval.

Research Theme
Metacognition

Research employing the remember-know paradigm has demonstrated a number of dissociations. Remember and know judgments are influenced by different variables. For example, both Gardiner (1988) and Rajaram (1993) found that a levels-of-processing manipulation had different effects on these two types of judgments. Rajaram (experiment 1) presented words (e.g., *cat*) to participants and had them generate either a rhyme associate (*bat*) or a semantic associate (*dog*). Memory was tested with recognition. If a word was recognized, participants also had to make a remember-know judgment. Based on what you've read about the levels-of-processing effect, you might correctly anticipate that participants better remembered words for which a semantic associate was provided.

Table 6.11 Data from Rajaram (1993, Experiment 1) Study

	Percent Correct Responses		
	Overall Recognition	Remember Judgments	Know Judgments
Shallow Processing	62	32	30
Deep Processing	86	66	20

From Rajaram, S. (1993). Remembering and knowing: Two means of access to the personal past. *Memory and Cognition, 21*, 89–102. Reprinted by permission of the Psychonomic Society, Inc.

So overall, there was a levels-of-processing effect. But when the conscious and nonconscious components of memory were teased apart, an interesting pattern emerged. The levels-of-processing effect was limited to remember judgments. In fact, as you can see in Table 6.11 the effect was reversed in know judgments.

Research employing the remember-know paradigm (see Gardiner & Richardson-Klavehn, 2000, for a review) has revealed that many of the encoding factors that improve performance in explicit memory tasks (i.e., recall and recognition) also influence *remember* judgments. These factors include attention (Gardiner & Parkin, 1990), picture presentation (Rajaram, 1993), and stimulus generation (Gardiner, 1988).

Research Theme
Emotion

Emotion and Memory.   Let's demonstrate how the dual-process view is used in an area of memory research that has recently generated a great deal of controversy in theoretical, empirical, and applied arenas: the effects of emotion on memory. This question will serve as a touchstone over the next couple of chapters, as we discuss the phenomenon of flashbulb memories and memory for trauma (Chapter 7), and the controversy over recovered memories of childhood sexual abuse (Chapter 8).

Intuitively, it would seem that emotional stimuli, particularly negative ones, like a shocking word, picture, or event, would be easily and vividly remembered. Considered within the remember-know paradigm, it would seem that emotional stimuli would be more likely remembered than known. In line with this prediction, a number of studies have shown remember judgments to be more likely for negative events than neutral ones (e.g., Kensinger & Corkin, 2003; Ochsner, 2000). Shirot, Delgado, and Phelps (2004) consider the neural correlates underlying remember judgments, and offer two plausible explanations for the enhanced "remembering" of negative events. It could be that highly emotional stimuli increase activity in hippocampal regions, enhancing memory *and* recollective experience. However, the plot thickens. Sometimes recollections of emotional events *seem* vivid and accurate, but this subjective sense of remembering is not a reliable indicator of memory accuracy (e.g., Ochsner, 2000; Talarico & Rubin, 2003).

To try and tease apart these two accounts and delineate the relationship between recollective experience and emotional (negative) stimuli, Shirot, Delgado, and Phelps (2004) used fMRI imaging to compare participants retrieval of emotional and neutral photographs. Participants were shown the images outside of the scanner, and then proceeded into the scanner to make remember and know judgments about the photos. Shirot et al. replicated previous findings, demonstrating enhanced recollective experience (as indicated by *remember* judgments) for negative photos relative to neutral ones. However, this subjective feeling of having seen the item did not correspond to memory accuracy. Negative and neutral photos were remembered at roughly the same rate. So it seems that our metacognition about the occurrence of negative stimuli does not translate into performance.

To bolster the conclusions derived from behavioral data, Shirot et al. (2004) also were able to establish distinct neural systems underlying the subjective sense of vivid recall of emotional material. The source of this subjective sense of remembering seems to be the amygdala, an almond-shaped structure in the lower forebrain thought to be linked to the processing of emotion (Glascher & Adolphs, 2003) that we'll be discussing in more detail in Chapter 8. So while the function of the amygdala may lead to a boost in memory confidence (i.e. a detailed recollection that an event occurred), this confidence far outweighs the boost in objective detail and quality of the memory (i.e., memory accuracy). This contrast between the subjective sense of recollection and objective accuracy will prove to be important in upcoming discussions of how emotion impacts (and sometimes distorts) our memories of the events that comprise our personal histories. As Shirot and Phelps note, the common assumption that a strong subjective sense of recollection for emotional stimuli is an indicator of memory accuracy may well be off the mark.

Implicit Memory

At the beginning of the chapter we discussed the distinction between explicit memory tests and implicit memory tests. As you'll recall, explicit memory tests require the conscious recollection of previously encoded information. And aside from our short discussion of implicit memory tests at the beginning of the chapter, we have been exclusively discussing explicit memory tests. But now we'll return to the topic of implicit memory tests which do not require conscious recollection of previously encoded information. Even if something isn't remembered explicitly, it may still have an impact on your attitudes, feelings, or behavior. In other words, you may "remember" something without really "remembering" it. Memory is reflected implicitly—as an improvement or change in some task that occurs even if the participant remembers nothing about the original event.

Here's an example of implicit memory from Greg's life. We were moving into our new house, carrying box after box into the house and up the stairs. Later that day, Greg found that a song was running through his head. He was whistling and humming it, and he had no idea why, much to his frustration (you know the feeling). The song was "Handle with Care" by the Traveling Wilburys (an 80's "supergroup" dinosaur band made up of dinosaur rock stars, two of whom are sadly no longer with us—George Harrison and Roy Orbison!). After thinking about it for a few hours, it finally came to him why he was whistling that song. Most of the boxes he had carried up the stairs earlier had "Handle with care" printed on the side, which in turn had led him to whistle that song. Although throughout the day he had no explicit memory of reading that phrase, his whistling of the tune was an implicit reflection of that event.

Schacter (1996) and Brown (2003, 2004) suggest that implicit memory may lie at the heart of **unconscious plagiarism.** In some instances, you come up with what you think is a brilliant idea—that is, until the friend you're describing it to informs you they had the same idea and discussed it with you three months ago. Your failure to recall that it was your friend's idea is a failure of explicit memory. Yet you do remember the encoding episode implicitly, as reflected by you generating the idea you encountered in an earlier conversation. Former Beatle George Harrison (and Traveling Wilburys' member) may have been an unwitting victim of this. The melody for Harrison's song "My Sweet Lord" sounded a little bit too much like "He's So Fine," an earlier hit by the Chiffons. Harrison acknowledged being aware of the song but denied copying it. The court found the similarity between the tunes too great to be an accident and ruled against Harrison. Interestingly, the actual ruling included language stating that in composing the song, Harrison must have been "subconsciously" primed by the earlier song (Schacter, 1996).

Reality Check

Schacter (1996) also suggests that implicit memory may lie at the heart of déjà vu experiences. Déjà vu occurs when we have the distinct impression or feeling that we've been in some place or had some experience before, when in reality we have not. These experiences are commonplace; in a review of the literature on déjà vu, Brown (2004) estimates that about two-thirds of individuals have had the experience at least once in their lifetimes, and most of these have had multiple experiences. He also notes that the experiences tend to be triggered by some physical context. This notion fits nicely with an analysis by Berrios (1995), who claims (in keeping with the encoding specificity principle) that some piece of a memory gets activated by a cue, but the entire memory is not retrieved. Instead, one is left with a feeling of familiarity that cannot be readily explained. Hence, déjà vu may be an implicit memory expression of the encoding specificity principle.

Dissociations Between Implicit and Explicit Tests of Memory.

Laboratory research on implicit memory tests began its rise to prominence in the 1960s, as researchers investigated memory functioning in amnesics (people with severely impaired memory function). For a while, it was believed that many amnesics lacked the ability to move things into long-term storage. This was based on the observation that amnesics demonstrated relatively normal immediate memory ability but suffered profound long-term memory deficits. So it seemed that immediate memory was intact but the mechanism whereby new information is transferred to long-term memory was nonfunctional (and, indeed, this dissociation was cited as evidence for a distinction between a short-term and a long-term memory store). But as it turned out, the story wasn't so simple. As you'll recall from Chapter 4 this explanation for the memory performance of amnesics has been called into question due to recent neuroscientific data. However, this belief fueled the research investigations into implicit memory tests; despite the inability of amnesics to consciously recollect previous events, the amnesics showed signs of long-term retention (as evidenced by the prickly handshake story discussed at the beginning of this chapter).

Let's consider an early investigation by Warrington and Weiskrantz (1970) that compared memory functioning in amnesics and nonamnesics. In one study, a list of words was presented, followed by an explicit memory test (recognition). Faced with this test, which required them to consciously think back to the earlier episode, amnesics were relatively lost, recognizing far fewer words than nonamnesics. This finding came as no surprise. But testing retrieval with an implicit test yielded some surprising results. When their memory was probed indirectly with word stems or word fragments, amnesics demonstrated priming, just like nonamnesics. Amnesics were better able to complete stems and fragments that corresponded to words they had seen earlier even though they could not consciously recollect many of those same words. Clearly, the words were represented in long-term memory but were simply not retrievable with explicit memory instructions. This general pattern—equal performance between nonamnesics and amnesics on implicit memory tests—has been replicated in countless investigations, and the investigation of nonconscious manifestations of memory has been one of the most active frontiers of memory research.

As demonstrated by the previous study, one of the most fascinating things about implicit memory tests is that they seem to follow a different set of rules than do explicit tests. Over the years, study after study has demonstrated dissociations between implicit and explicit tests. As you read in Chapter 1 and have seen several times, a dissociation occurs when some variable influences performance in different ways, depending on how performance is measured. The study by Warrington and Weiskrantz (1970) revealed dissociative effects of amnesia on memory. The ability to remember explicitly is impaired in amnesics, while remembering implicitly is unaffected.

Dissociations between implicit and explicit memory tests are not limited to remembering in amnesics. These intriguing patterns have been revealed in many studies of those with intact memories. Let's look at a classic study by Jacoby (1983), one of the first studies to show such a dissociation. In phase 1, Jacoby had participants encode common words in one of two different conditions. Let's say the target word was *cold*. In a *generate* condition, participants were visually presented with an opposite (hot-???) and had to generate the target: COLD. In a *read* condition, participants were visually presented with the target word alongside a row of x's (xxx-COLD). Note that in the generate condition, participants never actually saw the target word.

In phase 2, participants were given one of two different memory tests for the target words (e.g., *cold*). Half received a recognition test in which they had to determine whether each word was one of the targets from phase 1. This is an explicit test, because successful performance requires that participants consciously think back and recollect what happened in the initial encoding episode. The other half received a perceptual identification task in which words were presented for an extremely brief duration (about 30 ms). The only thing participants had to do was identify the word that had been presented. Performance on this task was measured in terms of priming, which we discussed at the beginning of the chapter. In this case, the identification rate for nontargets was subtracted from the identification rate for targets. The expectation, of course, was that having encountered a word during phase 1 would make the word easier to identify.

The results, presented in Table 6.12, represent a classic dissociation. As you can see, the encoding conditions had converse effects on the two memory tests. Recognition (explicit memory) performance for phase 1 targets was best for participants who had

Table 6.12 Results from Jacoby (1983), Demonstrating a Dissociation Between Implicit and Explicit Memory

		Encoding Condition	
		Generate	Read
Memory Test	Recognition (Explicit)	.71	.41
	Perceptual ID (Implicit)	.62	.83

generated the words in response to an opposite. Identification (implicit memory) performance for phase 1 targets was best for participants who had read the words in isolation. The dissociation between explicit and implicit memory tests demonstrated by Jacoby (1983) was only one of many. Early research comparing performance on explicit and implicit tests revealed many other dissociations involving classic encoding and storage variables like levels of processing, visual encoding, organization, and retention interval.

Accounts of Explicit-Implicit Dissociations.   What factors might underlie these dissociations, in which different measures of memory seem to be playing by different rules? And what might these rules be? Two explanatory frameworks have emerged. According to the *transfer-appropriate processing account* (e.g., Roediger, 1990), dissociations between implicit and explicit memory tests occur because these tests typically depend on different sorts of processing. Implicit tests such as word-fragment completion, word-stem completion, or the identification task used in Jacoby's (1983) study are *data driven* in that they rely on reading and perceptual operations for successful performance. Explicit tests such as free recall and recognition are *conceptually driven* in that they rely on elaboration and organization for successful performance. Performance on a given test will depend on how the material was processed at encoding. Successful performance will result if the encoding processes transfer to (i.e., are appropriate for) retrieval. Because implicit retrieval tends to be data driven, it will be aided by data-driven encoding processes. Explicit retrieval tends to be conceptually driven, so it will be aided by conceptually driven encoding processes.

Consider the dissociative effects of generation on implicit and explicit memory found by Jacoby (1983). According to the transfer-appropriate processing account, generating a target word in response to its opposite is a conceptually driven encoding process that will transfer better to a conceptually driven retrieval task like recognition. This explains why generated items were recognized better than read items; encoding and retrieval processes matched. Alternatively, reading is a largely perceptual (i.e., data-driven) process that should transfer well to a data-driven retrieval task like identification. Consistent with this prediction, priming in the identification task was higher for words that had been read, relative to words that had been generated. In sum, this account views the processing used at study and testing as the critical determinants of memory.

Let's consider the memory systems view of long-term memory that we briefly introduced at the beginning of the chapter. As you'll recall, the memory system view asserts that LTM is not a unitary entity. Rather, it is made up of a number of subsystems. At the beginning of this chapter, we talked about the distinction between memory for facts and events (declarative memory) and memory for skills and habits as well as priming (procedural memory). According to Squire (1993), these two types of LTM are mediated by different brain systems with different neurological underpinnings. Because performance on explicit (declarative memory) and implicit (procedural memory) tests is based in different systems, these tests are affected by different variables. The dissociation between conscious and nonconscious forms of memory in amnesics suggests that the brain systems underlying performance on these tests have been differentially affected by the associated brain damage. The structures associated with declarative memory have been damaged, but the structures underlying procedural memory have been spared.

So which explanation seems to provide a better account of what is currently known about memory? Although some researchers (e.g., Kelley & Lindsay, 1996; Tulving & Schacter, 1990) believe that the final answer may lie in some convergence of the two accounts, the notion that there are fundamentally different and discriminable memory systems seems to have carried the day (Squire, 2004). However, the complexities observed in decades of experiments comparing performance among various measures of memory have made it apparent that a simple two- or three-system view is not sufficient. Squire (1987, 2004) proposes the more complex grouping depicted in Figure 6.4. Note that the primary distinction in this organizational scheme is between declarative (verbal) memories and nondeclarative (i.e., nonverbal) memories.

The areas critical for the formation of declarative memories—episodic and semantic in Tulving's (1983, 2002) scheme—are medial temporal areas as well as structures in an area of the brain termed the *diencephalon*. The most critical structure in this area is the hippocampus, which appears to be important in indexing the "what, when, and where" of a given episode (Eichenbaum & Fortin, 2003). Recall that episodic memories in particular are distinguished by recollective detail of the sights, sounds, and other sensory details of the event. It's important to note that memories

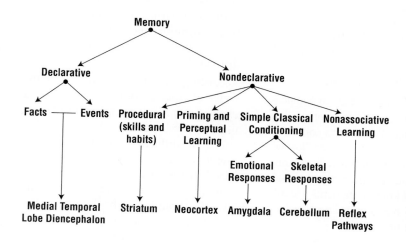

Figure 6.4
Memory systems.

From Squire, L. R. (2004). Memory systems of the brain: A brief history and current perspective. *Neurobiology of Learning and Memory, 82*(3), 171–177.

Copyright 2004 Elsevier. Reprinted with permission from Elsevier.

are not stored *in* the hippocampus, nor are they stored *in* any one area of the brain. As we discussed in Chapter 1, all knowledge—including the knowledge that comprises declarative memory—is thought to be represented in a distributed fashion across the brain. The retrieval of a given episode will involve the reactivation of areas that had been active during its encoding. The hippocampus is critical in the integration of these sensory details into a coherent episode that can be assembled during later recall. Squire (2004) describes declarative memory as our model of the world, and what we know to be true and false about it. For example, "Greg was born in Cincinnati, Ohio" is a true statement, based on information represented by the structures and processes of the declarative memory system.

Nondeclarative forms of memory don't involve the verbal processing of consciously recollected facts or episodes. Squire (2004) notes that, in contrast to declarative memory, nondeclarative memory is expressed in terms of performance rather than in propositions that can be deemed true or false. As such, it includes quite a hodgepodge of reactions and associations. Expressions of memory based in this system are as simple as a classically conditioned association (remember Pavlov's dogs?), an emotional response (a heart flutter upon seeing an old crush), or an increase in the ability to read a word or complete a word fragment (as described earlier in the chapter). Although these specific manifestations of nondeclarative memory are based in different systems within the brain, they all have two things in common: they are nonconscious and they are expressed only through changes in behavior.

Stop &*Review*

1. What's the difference between a "remember" judgment and a "know" judgment?
2. True or false? Dissociations between explicit and implicit memory tests are observed only in amnesic subjects.
3. Implicit is to explicit as
   a. declarative is to procedural.
   b. procedural is to declarative.
   c. free recall is to word-fragment completion.
   d. conscious is to unconscious.

• Recognition is thought to rely on two possible sources. When we "remember" that an event occurred, this reflects conscious and effortful retrieval. If we just "know" that an event occurred, this reflects nonconscious, automatic memory retrieval. Remember and know judgments are differentially sensitive to encoding variables such as levels of processing.

• Many variables seem to affect explicit and implicit memory tests differently. For example, amnesia tends to impact explicit remembering more than implicit remembering. Dissociations are also observed in nonamnesics with standard encoding variables (e.g., stimulus generation) influencing explicit and implicit memory differently.

• According to the memory systems view of dissociations, implicit and explicit memory tests rely on different memory systems, and thus are influenced by different variables. Implicit memory performance is thought to be based in the procedural memory system, and explicit memory performance is thought to be based in the declarative memory system.

CHAPTER OUTLINE

7

Autobiographical Memory: Recalling Important Events from Life

Why do people remember such precious little information from their early childhood? In fact, we're willing to bet that you remember not a thing from before you were age 3 or 4. A good deal of important stuff happens early in life, so why is memory for this period so poor?

Why is it that smells pack such a punch when it comes to memory? The smell of burning firewood reminds you of a great night around a campfire; the smell of baking cookies transports you to Christmases past. Is it really true that smells lead to more complete and vivid memories?

Did you ever wonder, as you relate the story of some event from your life, whether it actually is just a story? Obviously, the event happened to you in some form but it feels almost as if you're making it up, or reconstructing it as you tell it, rather than "grabbing it whole." What's going on?

Why do certain events seem as clear as if they happened yesterday? For most people, memory for the September 11 terrorist attacks probably seems like a crystal-clear moment, fixed forever in time. What gives rise to these memories, and do we ever forget something like that?

Everyday Memory

When we tell people that we teach psychology, this information elicits knowing glances or furrowed brows, or, worse yet, comments like, "Ohhhh...going to analyze me, huh?" We quickly inform these new acquaintances that no, we don't really care about their problems (in a clinical sense, at least); we do memory research. This triggers an entirely different (and at times, equally frustrating) set of questions and comments, such as, "Why do I have such a terrible memory for my childhood?" or "I'll never forget what I was doing when I heard that Princess Diana was killed" or "Why do I remember things differently than my spouse?" Why should we, as memory researchers, find these questions about memory frustrating? Because, until fairly recently, we haven't had very good answers to these questions. These questions are partially answered by material discussed in Chapter 6. But there is something unique about these questions, something that goes unaddressed by the material presented about memory to this point. These questions refer to one's personal experience and use of memory in an everyday context. As such, they aren't fully addressed by much of the memory research discussed thus far.

Neisser's Challenge: Ecological Validity and Memory Research

As you've no doubt noticed, cognitive psychology research is quite elegant: every confounding variable is anticipated and controlled, and each aspect of responding is carefully and precisely measured. To put it in terms of a concept introduced in Chapter 1, the *internal validity* of cognitive research is nothing short of impressive. Cognitive psychology no doubt owes behaviorism a debt of gratitude on this score; behaviorist challenges to the notion of scientifically analyzing mental processes (as defined by structuralists and functionalists) meant that any new approach to the study of cognition would have to live up to extremely high methodological standards. Cognitive psychology has more than answered the challenge.

But while saluting the incredible progress cognitive psychology has made in establishing an empirical base, many would say that it has come at a cost. Often, the *ecological validity* (also termed external validity) of cognitive psychology research has fallen well short of impressive. There exists a natural tension between the internal validity and the ecological validity of any research enterprise. You trade off one to get more of the other; more controlled is less natural, and vice versa. Take memory, for example; a great deal of the research in the first three decades of experimental work on memory fit a pretty standard pattern. Word lists carefully constructed to control for the effects of various extraneous variables were presented under precisely controlled conditions, and participant memory was tested with a number of standard laboratory memory tasks, like free recall or recognition. But one might argue that the number of words you can recall from a list of 48 concrete and abstract words presented for four seconds each doesn't tell you that much about why you can't remember events from your life that occurred before age 3. The emphasis in memory research (and cognition research in general) has always been on internal validity, often at the expense of ecological validity.

In an important address to cognitive psychologists in 1977, Ulric Neisser delivered a blistering critique of the memory research that had accumulated in the first quarter-century of cognition research, a critique that was directed at the emphasis on internal validity. According to Neisser (1978), "If X is an interesting or socially significant aspect of memory, then psychologists have hardly ever studied X" (p. 4). These were fighting words, to say the least. Neisser was basically saying that the first 30 years of memory research had been boring and trivial. Neisser went even further, claiming that although firm empirical generalizations about memory had indeed been made, most of these generalizations "are so obvious that every 10-year-old child knows them anyway" (p. 4). Extremely harsh words, perhaps, but many cognitive psychologists took them to heart. Since Neisser's address, there has been a veritable explosion of research on what might be considered "everyday" memory.

The explosion is evident in the number of citations found in the psychology research database PsychINFO, using the search terms "everyday memory" and "autobiographical memory." Up until 1986, only a few dozen psychology articles were directed at issues of everyday memory. Since then, there have been over 2500 investigations of these phenomena. Clearly, the investigation of how one remembers the events of their lives has become a central topic within the study of cognition.

Everyday Memory Research: Bankrupt? Not everyone jumped on Neisser's bandwagon. In an influential counter-critique, Banaji and Crowder (1989) decried what they termed the "bankruptcy of everyday memory," objecting strongly to most of Neisser's claims. They drew an analogy between the psychologist who conducts well-controlled basic laboratory research on memory and the chemist who does controlled experimentation on the properties of yeast in order to establish why bread dough rises. In their view, the precisely controlled experimentation of the chemist is a more sensible approach and is more likely to yield meaningful results than "loitering in professional bakeries and taking careful notes" (p. 1187). They add that memory psychologists should not be embarrassed or frustrated when faced with questions that can't really be answered by basic research. "What other science," they ask, "has established that its students should decide on the importance of questions by checking first with Aunt Martha?" (p. 1187). Banaji and Crowder argue that in everyday memory contexts (such as attempting to remember events from one's life), the uncontrolled factors are so numerous that generalizability of the results is limited, not increased. Banaji and Crowder assert that the emphasis on internal validity in investigations of memory is entirely appropriate and is likely to be the road to truly generalizable principles of memory function.

Striking a Middle Ground. Following Banaji and Crowder's (1989) critique, a number of researchers came to the defense of everyday memory research (e.g., Conway, 1991) and/or emphasized the value of both laboratory and everyday approaches (e.g., Loftus & Ketcham, 1991; Tulving, 1991). Tulving (1991) makes the important point that memory research is not a "zero-sum game" (i.e., someone must win, and someone must lose); forsaking everyday memory research for a basic laboratory approach, or vice versa, would be "throwing the baby out with the bath water." Both approaches can be quite valid and generalizable, and both approaches should be employed to discover the principles of memory function.

Since the opening salvos of the everyday memory debate, the dust has settled, and to no one's surprise, both laboratory and everyday approaches to the study of memory are still standing. And both approaches are probably the richer for the exchange. Laboratory psychologists are more sensitive to issues of ecological validity, and everyday memory researchers are more sensitive to issues of precision and control (i.e., internal validity). In this chapter, we'll review some of the discoveries that have been made by researchers investigating issues of everyday memory, so you'll be well informed in your conversations with "Aunt Martha."

Stop&Review

1. Discuss Neisser's criticism of traditional memory research.
2. What is the relationship between ecological and internal validity?
3. Which of the following accurately describes the current state of research in memory?
   a. Everyday approaches are the sole focus of memory research.
   b. Laboratory-based approaches are the sole focus of memory research.
   c. Both everyday approaches and laboratory-based approaches are used in memory research.
   d. Memory researchers are concerned with internal but not ecological validity.

- Neisser delivered a critique of this laboratory-based approach to memory research, claiming that it was boring, non-informative, and not very generalizable to everyday life. In answer to his challenge, recent years have witnessed an astounding increase in the number of studies devoted to the investigation of everyday memory.

- Traditional laboratory-based memory research is high in internal validity (experimental control), but often lacks ecological validity (generalizability to the real world). There is a tension between internal validity and ecological validity. You must trade off one to get more of the other.

- Not everyone agreed with Neisser's critique, arguing that controlled, laboratory-based memory research is more likely to yield meaningful and generalizable results than everyday memory research. Others argued that both approaches to memory research are valuable. Currently, both types of research programs are quite active.

Autobiographical Memory: Basic Issues and Methodology

The most popular topic of investigation within the realm of everyday memory has no doubt been autobiographical memory (AM), or memory for the experiences that comprise a person's life story, or *autobiography*. It's somewhat surprising that it took cognitive psychology so long to mine this important area of research. A person's past history is at the core of their identity. It shouldn't surprise you to learn, then, that autobiographical memories are as varied as the people who produce them. Given this level of complexity and individual variation, perhaps it isn't so surprising that it took cognitive psychology so long to explore this area. As you'll see, a host of variables affect the form and quality of autobiographical memories, including emotion, developmental stage, gender, and the cultural background of the rememberer.

Memories vs. Facts

On reviewing some of the early research on autobiographical memory, Conway (1990) provides a useful distinction between an **autobiographical memory** and an **autobiographical fact** (see also Brewer, 1986); the characteristics of each are presented in Table 7.1.

For your authors, an example of an autobiographical memory would be the events that took place on our wedding day. An example of an autobiographical fact would be the knowledge that the newest addition to our family was a sweet Maine Coon kitten (who is now a very large cat!). Both of these are autobiographical in the sense that they are part of our life story, but they are very different from each other. Both autobiographical memories and facts are high in self-reference; they are both closely related to our personal identity; and they both will likely last for years—we're not likely to forget our wedding day or the fact that we own a Maine Coon cat.

But that's where the similarities between autobiographical memories and facts end. Autobiographical memories feature an experience of remembering. When either of us thinks of our wedding day, a sort of "reliving" experience occurs: we can see, hear, and feel the sights, sounds, and emotions that occurred on that day. No such reliving experience occurs when we think of the fact that we have a Maine Coon cat. It's just something we know about our lives. Another difference is that autobiographical memories quite often feature an interpretation on the part of the rememberer. We each have our own interpretation of and reaction to the events of our wedding day. However, we have no personal spin on the fact that we own a Maine Coon cat; we just do. Related to this difference is the notion of veridicality: Are autobiographical memories and facts "true"? Consistent with the idea that autobiographical memories are often subject to interpretation, it should come as no surprise that their "truth" can be quite variable. Autobiographical facts fare much better on the dimension of truth; the facts that you know about your life are more or less "true," unless you're suffering some sort of psychopathological break with reality.

Table 7.1 Characteristics of Autobiographical Memories and Autobiographical Facts

	Autobiographical Memories	Autobiographical Facts
Experience of remembering	Always present	Rarely present
Personal interpretation	Frequent	Rare
Truthfulness	Variable	High
Context-specific sensory attributes	Always present	Rarely present
Self-reference	High	High
Duration of memory	Years	Years

From Conway, M. A. (1990). *Cognitive models of memory.* Cambridge, MA: MIT Press. Reprinted by permission.

An autobiographical memory (our wedding day) and an autobiographical fact (one of our cats is an orange Maine Coon with Buddhist leanings).

Let's consider the distinction between autobiographical memories and facts in light of another well-worn memory distinction: *episodic* and *semantic* memories (discussed in Chapter 6). Recall that episodic memories are memories for personally experienced events that can be tied to a specific time and place, while semantic memories refer to knowledge or information about the world that is not tied to any specific contextual information like time or place. Autobiographical memories would be considered episodic memories in that they are essentially relived personal experiences that are rich in contextual detail. Autobiographical facts would be considered semantic memories in that they refer to simple, context-free knowledge of one's own personal world.

Stop&*Think* | PERSONAL FACTS AND MEMORIES

In Chapter 6, you compared characteristics of episodic and semantic memories. Try the same exercise, this time for autobiographical memories and autobiographical facts:

- Generate an autobiographical memory and an autobiographical fact.

- Examine Table 7.1, summarizing the key distinctions between these two memory types.

- Assess the distinction by analyzing your examples. For each example, evaluate whether or not it fits the characteristics listed.

Linton (1975), in a self-study of her own memory, found that some memories undergo a transition from specific episodic memories (i.e., autobiographical memories) to more generic semantic memories (i.e., autobiographical facts). For example, think about your memories about college. When you started college, no doubt you remembered every day as its own distinct event (autobiographical memory) for about a week or so, after which you began to form more general semantic memories about the types of things that happen in college (autobiographical facts). This transition from specific-event memories to more general representations of repeated events is a common theme in much of the work on autobiographical memory. Our discussion in this chapter will focus primarily on autobiographical memories rather than autobiographical facts.

Methods of Investigation

Traditional studies of memory like the ones discussed in Chapter 6 are, in many ways, quite different from the ones we'll be discussing in this chapter. Typically, in these traditional sorts of studies, some type of material is presented during an encoding phase; then at some later point in time, memory for this information is tested, and the completeness and accuracy of the memory are assessed. Put another way, traditional modes of memory research focus on the memory *content*. What else would they focus on, you may be thinking? Recall from Chapter 1 our discussion of an increasing focus on first-person issues such as our own understanding of our cognitive processes, and the *subjective experience* and phenomenological qualities that characterize those experiences. It turns out that autobiographical memories are a treasure trove of these subjective qualities, which are central to our everyday experience of remembering.

Let's consider more closely the unique qualities of autobiographical remembering that make it a challenge to investigate empirically. First, whereas traditional memory research involves the controlled presentation of "events," this is certainly not the case for personal events. Events just happen when and how they happen, and are always out of the control of an experimenter. Second, accuracy of autobiographical memory can be difficult to assess. Who holds the right answer about what happened in the past? Even attempts to corroborate memories by talking to other people who experienced the same event are subject to that person's interpretations, biases, and just plain old forgetting.

Because there is no real way to control the events being remembered or to judge the accuracy of those memories, autobiographical memory researchers focus on aspects (both content-related and subjective) that can be assessed. These things include the age of the recalled memories, their vividness and detail, their emotional intensity, and how these characteristics differ systematically across different groups of people (men and women, young and old, East Asian and European). And, in spite of the difficulties involved, a number of studies have been successful in evaluating the accuracy of autobiographical memories.

Targeted Event Recall.   A number of methods have been developed to investigate the recall of life episodes. **Targeted event recall** requires the recall of specific events or well-defined periods from one's life and can allow for some assessment of memory accuracy. Often, corroborating information about the target event exists, either through the public record (in the case of memory for news events) or through family members (in the case of memory for major life events). However, evaluation of memory accuracy is limited by the completeness and accuracy of the corroborating source—be it public accounts or your Aunt Martha.

It turns out that the way in which you attempt to recall autobiographical events affects your subjective feelings about those memories. Lam and Buehler (2009) looked at the subjective experience of how distant or remote a given memory *feels*. You have no doubt considered this with regard to your own autobiography, having made observations like "feels like it was just yesterday" or "seems like that happened a lifetime ago" (well, you youngsters may not understand that one). As Lam and Buehler note, subjective distance is important. An embarrassing event that feels like it just happened may still arouse considerable angst (and consequently affect one's current self-assessment in the negative direction), but if the person has "put it behind them" the same event might seem trivial, even amusing.

To investigate the subjective temporal distance of memories, Lam and Buehler employed an interesting variation on the event recall technique. They varied whether participants recalled the events forward or backward. What was the reason for this manipulation? The researchers suspected that the subjective distance of a memory would depend upon how much the participant felt they had changed since the event, and this perception of self-change would vary, depending on whether recall occurred in a forward or backward direction. The forward direction would cause the rememberer to create a narrative story about how the person in the past event became the current person. Therefore, the most salient characteristic of the recollection would be change. Because change takes time, the participant will feel as if they are further away from the event (i.e., there would be more subjective distance).

Backward recall, on the other hand, would not focus on creating a narrative story; this progression would lead to a series of individual events that would seem somewhat unconnected. Think about a movie you've seen but imagine watching it in reverse. You would not see the development of the characters or the plot; you simply would be experiencing the events that happened to the characters. Eventually you would be able to "put it all together" and see how the person and the plot developed but while you were watching it, your focus would not be on that development. Well, the same might be true of your "life movie;" recalling it in reverse has the same effect as watching the movie in reverse. You focus on the individual events and not on your developmental change. Without the focus on how much change there has been, it "seems" as if there has been little change. Psychologically, little change means little time has passed. Consequently, the participant will feel closer to the event (i.e., less perceived distance).

Lam and Buehler (Experiment 4) asked participants to think of a target event—the day they were accepted into the university (Wilfrid Laurier University in Ontario Canada). In addition, they were asked to remember a series of events between that day and the day of the study. The key manipulation was the order in which they were asked to recall. One group was asked to recall the target event first, and then proceed through the rest of the events in chronological order. The other group was asked to begin recall with the most recent event and to proceed backward in chronological order through the events. For each event, they were to give a brief description of what they remembered. The subjective distance from the event was assessed by having participants mark an "X" on a 171 millimeter line that had *feels like yesterday* and *feels very far away* as anchors. Participants were also asked to provide a rating on a scale from 1 (not at all) to 9 (to a great extent) regarding how much they thought they had changed since the event.

Table 7.2 **Results from Lam and Buehler's (2009) Study on How People Experience the Distance of Memories as a Function of Recall Direction**

		Personally experienced "Distance from Memory"	Judgment of Self-Change
Recall Direction	Forward	108	7.25
	Backward	83	6.34

NOTE: The overall correlation between perceived distance and perceived change = .41

The results are presented in Table 7.2. Consistent with the predictions, participants felt closer to the target event when their 'trip down memory lane" had occurred in a backward fashion than a forward fashion, Backward recall was associated with events feeling more like yesterday than was forward recall. The ratings of perceived change were significantly correlated with subjective distance, which supports the contention that subjective distance is related to perceived change. Forward recallers viewed themselves as having changed to a greater degree than did backward recallers. The finding that the subjective experience of personal recollection can be influenced by the dynamics of recall is intriguing, and as Lam and Buehler (2009) indicate it has some important practical implications. For example a therapist working with a client might want to have them recall their progress by starting with recent successes, so that the client feels psychologically closer to those successes.

Diaries.   Most autobiographical memories recalled by the targeted event recall technique would be things that stand out in a person's life. The **diary technique** allows a broader range of memories to be sampled—both the mundane and the distinctive. In this technique, the participant keeps a running record of events that occur in daily life; in other words, an event diary is kept and at some point is used to query memory. In addition, the diary technique allows for firmer conclusions about memory accuracy. The remembered events can be verified as having occurred because they were recorded and dated as they occurred (or immediately after). Therefore, diary studies have been a primary vehicle for understanding the processes by which we date our autobiographical memories or place them correctly in time. In contrast to the Lam and Buehler (2009) study just discussed, research that uses diary studies is more interested in the objective assessment of when events occurred, and the common errors that are exhibited in dating events, rather than one's subjective sense of remembering. In addition, diary studies allow for the evaluation of the effectiveness of various types of cues in eliciting accurate autobiographical memories. We'll take up this issue later, in our discussion of autobiographical memory retrieval.

Cue Words.   One of the most popular techniques for eliciting autobiographical memories goes back quite a few years. The Galton-Crovitz technique (also termed the **cue-word technique**) was originally used by Sir Francis Galton, an early British psychometrician who was primarily responsible for introducing correlation as a statistical procedure.

The technique for cuing autobiographical memories was revived by Crovitz and Schiffman (1974). In the Galton-Crovitz technique, participants are presented with word cues and are asked to retrieve an autobiographical memory associated with each cue, write a short description of it and date the event. The use of this technique allows the researcher to assess something we're about to discuss in great detail: the autobiographical memory retention function—the distribution of autobiographical memories across the life span.

Stop&*Review*

1. Explain the difference between an autobiographical memory and an autobiographical fact.
2. Briefly describe the diary technique for investigating autobiographical memory.
3. True or false? The Galton-Crovitz cue word technique for investigating autobiographical memory allows researchers to assess the recall of events from different points in the life span.

• Autobiographical memory (a type of episo-dic memory) refers to one's memory for their life experiences. An autobiographical fact (a type of semantic memory) refers to a piece of general knowledge about oneself. Memory for events seems to undergo a transition from episodic to semantic. Initially, experiences are recalled as distinct episodes. With a great deal of repetition, memory for these events becomes general knowledge.

• A number of methods are used in the study of autobiographical memory. In the targeted event recall technique, specific questions about a particular event or period from one's life are asked. The diary technique requires the participant to record a number of events each day for a span of time, and memory for these events is tested later.

• In the Galton-Crovitz cue word technique, word cues are presented and participants must recall an autobiographical memory in response to each. This technique allows researchers to assess the autobiographical memory retention function, the distribution of personal memories from across the life span.

Recalling a Life: Developmental Aspects of Autobiographical Memory

Rubin, Wetzler, and Nebes (1986) used the Galton-Crovitz cue-word technique to investigate the shape of the memory function across the entire life span. Their analysis included participants ranging in age from 18 to 76. The complete memory function is presented in Figure 7.1.

What you see plotted is the number of memories recalled from each period of life, what has been termed the autobiographical retention function. Note the peaks and valleys of this function. These researchers observed that these patterns are indicative of three basic phenomena. First, there are very few memories from the early years of life and almost none before the age of about 3—a phenomenon typically termed **childhood amnesia.** Second, there is a disproportionately great number of memories from ages 10 to 30—a phenomenon termed the **reminiscence bump.** Third (and evident only for the older participants), there is a standard forgetting curve for information that occurs in the last 20 years. Most of the information recalled by older adults is for events that have happened recently. The specifics of this retention function have occupied autobiographical memory researchers' attention for the past 15 years.

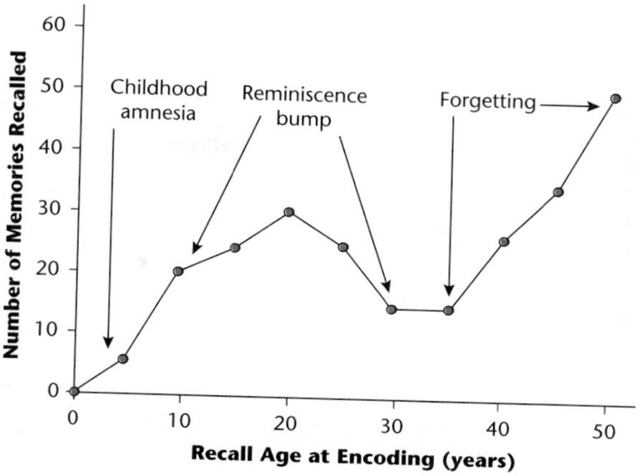

Figure 7.1

Autobiographical memories retrieved as a function of life period.

From Anderson, S. J., & Conway, M. A. (1997). Representations of autobiographical memories. In M. A. Conway (Ed.), *Cognitive models of memory* (pp. 217–246). Cambridge, MA: MIT Press. Reprinted with permission.

Childhood Amnesia

Look again at the first part of the retention function shown in Figure 7.1—memories for events from the first decade of life. What you see is a precipitous drop in the number of memories reported before the age of 10 and a complete lack of any memories before the age of 2 or 3. The paucity of memories from the first few years of life has been termed *childhood amnesia* (or, less commonly, *infantile amnesia*). This finding has been recorded by many researchers, using a variety of methods. Researchers often speak of "the emergence (or development of) autobiographical memory" or "the offset of childhood amnesia." These two phrases can be considered synonymous; they describe exactly the same process. As the amnesia of childhood is lifted, autobiographical memory emerges. We'll be using both of these phrases in our discussion.

Investigating memories for early childhood presents a formidable methodological challenge. One big problem is that there is no way to check on the accuracy of what is reported. In other words, when a participant remembers an event from their childhood, there are no guarantees that participants are truly remembering the events. Think of the big events you may remember from your childhood. Can you determine if these memories are real or not? Perhaps what you're remembering is someone else's description of the event or the pictures you've seen of it.

To avoid some of the pitfalls of faulty and subjective autobiographical recall, one research strategy involves asking participants about salient events from their childhood that can be corroborated, utilizing the targeted event recall technique discussed earlier. For example, Usher and Neisser (1993) asked participants to recall a number of critical events from their childhood that were documented and that could be checked with relatives and records. The events included birth of a sibling, a family move, the death of a family member, and a hospitalization. In addition, they were asked how frequently and recently they had rehearsed (i.e., thought about) the event and whether they had been exposed to pictures of it. Memory was tested with a set of questions asking basic information about each of the events.

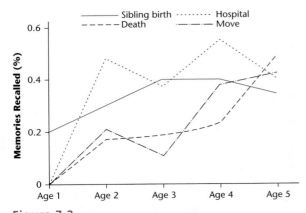

Figure 7.2

Results from Usher and Neisser (1993).

From Usher, J. A., & Neisser, U. (1993). Childhood amnesia and the beginnings of memory for four early life events. *Journal of Experimental Psychology: General, 122,* 155–165. Copyright 1993 by the American Psychological Association. Reprinted with permission.

The results are summarized in Figure 7.2. The figure plots recall scores for each of the events as a function of the age when it was experienced. The typical retention pattern for early childhood events was obtained: relatively poor memory before the age of 5. In addition, the offset of childhood amnesia occurred at different times, depending on the particular event. Memories for the birth of a sibling and hospitalization went further back than memories for a death or a family move. Hospitalization may be well remembered because it is such a distinctive, involving, and frightening event—a combination that makes the event unforgettable (Usher & Neisser, 1993). The birth of a sibling may be memorable because it becomes the first installment of a story that will be told again and again—in other words, the story receives a great deal of rehearsal. This explanation provides a preview of one explanation for autobiographical memory development that you'll be reading about shortly—an account that cites language development as a major factor.

You might imagine that there would be a relatively straightforward relationship between rehearsal of these salient events (in the form of family stories, photographs, etc.) and their later recall. Not so; the relationship is actually quite complex. The effect of rehearsal depended on the child's age at the time of the experience. If the child was three years old or younger at the time of the event, family stories and photographs actually led to fewer memories than if the child was 4 or 5; in this case, family stories and photographs tended to make the memories stronger. Usher and Neisser suggest that a two- or three-year-old's memory may be relatively fragile and that their memories may be easily confused with stories and photographs. The more of these that are present, the more obscured the actual memory becomes. But because a four- or five-year-old's memory may be less tenuous, these rehearsals are probably beneficial.

Stop&*Think* | CHILDHOOD AMNESIA

Generate the earliest childhood memory you can, and note the following things about it:

- How old were you when the event occurred?

- Is the memory an autobiographical fact or an autobiographical memory?

- How vivid is it?

- Is it positive or negative?

- To what degree has it been influenced by later rehearsals (retellings, pictures, etc.)?

- Can anyone corroborate your memory? Does their recollection match yours?

The Emergence of Autobiographical Memory.   At some level, the very existence of childhood amnesia is baffling. Many important and exciting things are happening during our first few of years of life. Why is it that we can't retain any of it? When do we start "writing our life stories" cognitively?

Brain Development.   One possible source of the memory deficits that characterize childhood amnesia is the immaturity of the developing infant brain. Perhaps the neurological structures that subserve the complex processing that leads to autobiographical memories are not fully developed; hence, early memories are not formed. In young organisms, the hippocampal areas of the forebrain, critical for the formation of new long-term memories, are underdeveloped (Nadel & Zola-Morgan, 1984; Squire, 1987). Also, the prefrontal cortex undergoes rapid development at around age 1, with a coincident improvement in the proficiency with which certain cognitive tasks are performed (e.g., Diamond & Doar, 1989). The development of a capacity for autobiographical memory would be limited to the extent that it is subserved by these brain areas. (Bauer, 2004, provides a useful and detailed overview of the establishment of explicit memory processes in the first two years of life.)

This physiological approach to explaining childhood amnesia also seems to fit with some findings about people who have suffered damage to the hippocampus. As discussed in Chapter 6, patients who have suffered such damage often show a dissociation in memory abilities. They are unable to effectively store (or perhaps retrieve) events that have been recently experienced, yet they show preserved ability to learn, and they retain many perceptual and cognitive skills (e.g., Squire & Zola-Morgan, 1988). This view contends that memory is not one thing but actually several different subsystems. (You'll remember this argument from Chapter 6 regarding the corresponding distinction between declarative and procedural memory.) So how might this apply to childhood amnesia? An early suggestion (Bachevalier & Mishkin, 1984; Schacter & Moscovitch, 1984) was that infant memory may obey a similar dissociation. Basically, infants have an early developing procedural system that allows them to succeed on relatively simple memory tasks—like forming associations between events and remembering how to perform tasks such as walking, talking, eating, and so on—and a later-developing declarative system that serves as the basis for more complex memories. This later-developing system serves as the basis for autobiographical memories.

Even if this distinction were correct (and many believe it to be, at best, oversimplified), it would explain childhood amnesia only for events that occur extremely early in life. As we've seen, childhood amnesia extends to ages 3 or 4. Neurological underdevelopment wouldn't be able to explain childhood amnesia for those events that occur relatively late in toddlerhood. Complicating the picture even more is that children themselves do not show childhood amnesia. In other words, little kids (ages 2 to 3) can remember things that happened when they were even littler kids (ages 1 to 2) (e.g., Bauer, 2004; Bauer, Wenner, Dropik, & Wewerka, 2000). Think about it—a three-year-old can relate something that happened when they were 18 months old, but when 20 years old, their retrieval of this event is extremely unlikely. The fact that they could retrieve it when they were three years old suggests that the basic brain "machinery" is in place, which casts doubt on a purely neurological account of childhood amnesia (see Bauer, 2007, for a review of neurodevelopmental research on recall in infancy).

Development of Language.   One of the more popular accounts for childhood amnesia cites the child's developing language skills as the critical factor in the emergence of autobiographical memory. In one of the early accounts, Pillemer and White (1989) suggest that autobiographical memory develops pretty much in lockstep with the development of language. In other words, children begin to remember events from their lives as soon as they are capable of describing these events with language. It makes sense, then, that the emergence of autobiographical memory would mirror the highlights in language development. Children make the most dramatic linguistic strides between ages 2 and 4 (at least in terms of verbal expression), so this is when they start verbally recounting their experiences; in other words, this is when they start developing autobiographical memory.

The importance of language in autobiographical memory has been found in a number of studies demonstrating consistent differences in *narrative style*—the way that families reminisce about, or narrate, past events (Fivush, 1991; Reese & Fivush, 1993). When conversing with their daughters, parents tend to adopt what is termed an *elaborative style;* this consists of long and richly detailed discussions of past events. When conversing with their sons, parents are more likely to adopt what is termed a *pragmatic style* which is more succinct and contains less detail and elaboration. The style of reminiscing influences the quality of childhood memories; children of elaborative parents have better elaborated accounts of past events than do children of pragmatic parents. Given that this difference between elaborative and pragmatic styles is linked to the sex of a child, it's not surprising that Davis (1999) found evidence for female superiority in autobiographical recall. This difference in narrative style could underlie one's ability to relate past events in great detail.

In fact, Nelson (1993) cites language as the critical factor in the development of autobiographical memory, claiming that autobiographical memory emerges as parents begin to engage in memory talk with their children. Parents play an active role in guiding and shaping a child's view of "what happened." They serve as "play-by-play announcers," pointing out what was important, how it happened, and why it happened. As events are discussed and recounted, the child begins to build a generic event memory for events that are often repeated (e.g., trips to the zoo) and an autobiographical memory system for unique events.

Memory talk.

Development of a Cognitive Self.   Not all believe that language is the critical variable in the emergence of autobiographical memory. Howe and Courage (1997; see also Howe, Courage, & Edison, 2003) believe that while language is critical to the expression of stored experiences, it is not the same thing as the stored experiences. In other words, the symbols used to express what happened yesterday are just that—symbols. Just because an 18-month-old child doesn't have the linguistic skill to tell the story of what happened yesterday doesn't mean they don't have a sophisticated notion of what happened yesterday. Language is the most powerful means for expressing experience, but it doesn't determine whether the event is remembered. So what is the critical factor in the offset of childhood amnesia according to these researchers?

According to Howe and Courage, the determining factor is a child's developing sense of self. A *sense of self* (or self-concept) refers to knowledge that one is a person with unique and recognizable characteristics, and that one thinks and knows things about the world and can serve as a causal agent. This developing sense of self becomes an important organizer of autobiographical experiences. Given that autobiographical memory is basically the knowledge of oneself and one's experience, it

One's development of a sense of self plays an important role in autobiographical memory.

makes sense that children don't really demonstrate autobiographical memory until they have a sense of themselves as independent entities. Howe and Courage view language as the mechanism by which autobiographical memories are "let out," not the basis for their development.

A study by Wang (2006) reveals the importance of cross-cultural differences in the development of self and the impact that these differences have on the offset of childhood amnesia and, more importantly, the content of early childhood memories. Wang compared the recall of early childhood events in Taiwanese and U.S. adults. Why these two particular groups? There is a large body of research revealing differences in the self-concept of individuals from these two cultures (Lu & Gilmour, 2007; Markus & Kitayama, 1991). Western cultures, in particular the U.S., place particular value on having an independent, and autonomous self, along with a strong emphasis on distinguishing oneself from others. Individuals are generally urged to "be your own person" and the like. Contrast this with an Eastern culture like Taiwan, which tends to emphasize interconnectedness and group identity. One's self is defined more by relationships and connections (e.g., with family, friends, and other social groups) than by individual autonomy. Given the emphasis on the self in Western cultures, these participants should have earlier memories (i.e., early offset of childhood amnesia) than participants from Eastern cultures. However, the most interesting prediction is that the nature of these early memories should vary as a function of culture. For Western cultures, early memories should feature personal autonomy whereas for Eastern cultures, early memories should focus on social or group relationships.

To test this hypothesis, Wang used the words self, mother, family, friend, and surroundings as cues and asked participants to relay their earliest memory associated with each cue. The primary dependent variables of interest were the age at the time of the remembered event, and the degree to which the memory reflected autonomy. Their results were exactly as predicted. U.S. had earlier childhood memories than did Taiwanese participants for all cue words and U.S. memories tended to reflect personal

Research Theme
Culture

Table 7.3 **Sample Childhood Memories Reported by U.S. and Taiwanese Participants from Wang (2006)**

Memory type	United States	Taiwan
Self	Preschool learning to tie my shoes on my own and playing with all those "skills games" with shapes and hand-eye coordination. I got a gold star and realized my friend didn't. So, myself was all I could appreciate for doing something on my own.	Ever since I was little, my relatives would compare me with my girl cousin. Everyone said that I was the more sensible one. My girl cousin and I were 4 months apart in age. Perhaps it's because of the influence of the environment, especially my mom!
Mother	My mother dressed me up as a queen for Purim at my preschool. She let me wear all her fake jewelry— very long beads & makeup. I wore a long white shirt as a dress with a belt & a paper crown. I was very happy when she walked into school with me.	My mom was always smiling. She was always working, and didn't have time to talk to me or listen to me. Even in my memory she was always busy walking around, and never stopped to take a rest.
Family	Going to Niagara Falls on a family trip. I was young so I still asked my parents if I got the shampoo out of my hair. My dad said I did. However, when we walked behind the falls in caves, my hair started to bubble because I didn't get it all out.	Grandpa, grandma, dad, mom, my little brother, and our family's puppy. The whole family was having breakfast in the dining room one morning. We had congee that day. I still remember the dishes: shredded pork, clam. . . .
Friend	In second grade, my best friend moved on my birthday. She called me on the phone to say goodbye, and I cried. My mother still made me practice the piano that night, and that made me angry and more upset.	In kindergarten, I had a pretty good relationship with a little girl who lived near my neighbor. Her family raised ducks for a living. Often, after school, we would play in the field behind her house or play hide and go seek in her house.
Surroundings	3 years old, lying on my "comfort blanket." The room had a carpet then (sky blue). My $1/2$ crib had all sorts of stuffed animals. It was mid afternoon and raining. Because the light was on. My brother and I were playing with blocks.	In the park, there were four or five different recycle bins. There were mothers and their children taking a walk and chatting. I was just about to go to preschool. We learned a children's song "Tiger Lady" at preschool.

autonomy, more than Taiwanese memories for all cue words (see Table 7.3 for memory examples).

This cultural difference does not imply that relationships are unimportant to Western cultures but demonstrates that the *relative* importance of relationships and personal autonomy varies between cultures, with Eastern cultures tending to emphasize the former over the latter. One relationship that Wang predicted would be important for both cultures is the mother-child relationship, because mothers tend to be the main care-givers in both cultures. One clear finding from Wang's study was that memories cued by the word *mother* led to especially early remembering, reflecting the centrality of the mother-child relationship within the developing autobiography of the individual.

A subsequent study by Jack, MacDonald, Reese, and Hayne (2009) provides the first prospective study of how the interaction between mother and child during early childhood affects autobiographical memory. Over the span of two years (while children were between age 2 and 4), mothers were asked to record natural conversations (on researcher-provided tape recorders) about six different events that had happened in the foregoing four months. The researchers were not present during the recordings, which took place at the time and place of the mothers' choosing. Once they had the tapes, the researchers recorded maternal elaborations (such as introducing a new topic, or talking about a different aspect of an event), and maternal repetitions (verbatim repetition or simple rephrasing of something the mother had already said). The investigators were interested in how these maternal reminiscing behaviors would be reflected in the children's memory for those events.

An impressive 10 years later, the researchers had the opportunity to interview most of the same dyads, and the children's (now adolescent's) recall of early childhood. Each adolescent was asked to recall their earliest childhood memory. Jack et al. then looked at the relationship between the age from which these early recollections came, and the ratio of maternal elaboration to maternal repetition. This measure reflected the degree to which the mother's talk about events was elaborative rather than simply repetitious (note the interesting connection to elaborative vs. maintenance rehearsal from Chapter 6). They found a strong negative correlation between maternal elaboration-repetition ratio and the age of the earliest memory. The adolescents with the earliest memories tended to be those who had enjoyed the most elaboration (relative to simple repetition) from their mother 10 years earlier. These findings and those of Wang (2006), along with a host of others (e.g., Davis, 1999; MacDonald, Uesiliana, & Hayne, 2000; Peterson, Peterson, Wang, & Hou, 2009; Wang & Ross, 2007) demonstrate the importance of cultural background and social relationships in the development and expression of the child's developing life story.

Social-Cognitive Development.   So you might feel a little confused about the most important factor in a child's emerging autobiography. There is compelling evidence for the central role of both self-concept and language in shaping it. Neurological development also plays some role. So which is correct? By now, we're sure it won't surprise you to hear that they all are! There is no doubt that the emergence of autobiographical memory involves a complex interplay between the developing brain, the use of language, and the child's developing sense of who they are (or indeed, *that* they are *someone*). Nelson and Fivush (2004) attempt to weave these disparate strands of explanation together in their *social-cognitive account* of the emergence of autobiographical memory. They place a particular emphasis on the notion of *emergence*. In their view, too much of the discussion on autobiographical remembering has focused on *the point* at which such remembering begins, implicitly making the assumption that there is such a point. Assuming there is some type of barrier to childhood memories that, once removed, allows for their formation is overly simplistic. Rather, autobiographical remembering is a complex ability that emerges as a number of abilities and contextual factors coalesce.

What are the factors critical to autobiographical memory development, according to the social-cognitive view? Obviously, the basic explicit memory abilities must be in place, and they seem to be by the time a child is 2 years of age (Bauer, 2004). Language then takes on a prominent role; over time, a developing understanding of *narrative* (i.e., the notion of a meaningful story) enables children to encode events in a richer and more complex manner than had been possible before. The child begins to encode episodes in their life as part of a coherent and meaningful story—the beginning story of their life. In addition, they're engaging in more *memory talk* with adults. As noted earlier in our discussion of the Davis (1999) study, this type of interaction is key in setting the stage for the ability to remember personal events.

Another important factor discussed by Nelson and Fivush is a developing consciousness about the past; children don't really have a sense of themselves across time (i.e., a sense that they have a past self that's connected to their present self) until they're about

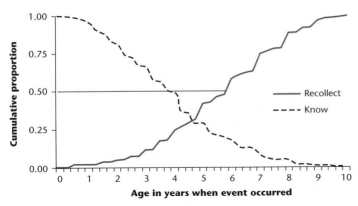

Figure 7.3

Multhaup, Johnson, and Tetrick's (2005) findings regarding the emergence of autobiographical memory.

four years old (Povinelli, Landry, Theall, Clark, & Castille, 1999). This sense of "extended consciousness" is critical to autobiographical memory. A related factor is what is commonly termed a *theory of mind,* which refers to a child's understanding that they have a unique set of beliefs, desires, and knowledge that is inaccessible to others.

So given the multitude of variables that form the basis for autobiographical remembering, and the fact that these all play out in different ways and at different developmental points for different individuals, it shouldn't surprise you that the precise point that marks the end of childhood amnesia is still under some dispute. Some researchers suggest ages as young as 2 to 2.5 (Eacott & Crawley, 1998; Usher & Neisser, 1998) and others suggest the age is closer to 5 (e.g., Wetzler & Sweeney, 1986). Multhaup, Johnson, and Tetrick (2005) attempt to explain these disparate results by having participants recall events from childhood and label them as either "know" memories or "recollect" memories (See Figure 7.3). For example, I *know* that I received a teal-colored tricycle for my 3rd birthday (I recall seeing a photograph of the event, but I don't really recollect the event). But I definitely *recollect* climbing around the gravel hills behind a shopping center in our neighborhood and putting a small gash in my hand. If this distinction sounds familiar, we're glad; you should recollect (or at least know) that you read about this distinction in Chapter 6 (the remember-know paradigm). Multhaup et al. suggest that our memories for childhood events gradually transition from known memories to recollected memories (See Figure 7.4). The point at which the majority of memories become recollect memories represents what the authors term the "wane of childhood amnesia." On average, it occurs at around 4.7 years, but there is considerable variability among individuals, which seems to fit quite nicely with the social-cognitive view of the emergence of autobiographical memory.

The Reminiscence Bump

What an odd title for a section! It sounds like a new dance that cognitive psychologists are doing. But actually, the reminiscence bump refers to another distinctive aspect of the retention function that people show for the memories from their lives. Namely, people recall a disproportionately greater number of memories for events that occur between the ages of 10 and 30 (see Figure 7.1, p. 269). Can you think of why this might be the case? Many of the events that occur in this period are "firsts," and many would be considered life milestones: first kiss, first date, first job, first year of college....the list goes on. These events serve as signposts in the stories of our lives. They're salient, distinctive, and important, so it's no wonder that they're well remembered.

This explanation sounds pretty reasonable until you consider some findings from a study by Rubin, Rahhal, and Poon (1998). These researchers reviewed evidence that demonstrates a reminiscence bump not only for personally experienced events (i.e., autobiographical memories), but also for autobiographical facts like the things that people prefer (e.g., movies, books, and music) as well as the events that people think are important or significant historically (like World War II or President Kennedy's assassination). For example, in a study by Holbrook and Schindler (1989) participants across a wide range of ages were asked to rate how much they enjoyed excerpts from songs that had been popular at different times from the 1930s to the 1980s. People showed a marked preference for songs that were popular when they were between the ages of 10 and 30. In a similar study, Larsen (1996) had older adults (average age 68) recall a particularly memorable reading experience. Books that were particularly memorable tended to have been read between the ages of 10 and 40. Schulster (1996) reported a similar effect for memorable films.

Not only do personal preferences seem to exhibit this "bump," but so do general semantic memories; things we learn in early adulthood are remembered best. Rubin, Rahhal, and Poon (1998) gave participants multiple-choice tests of their general knowledge for information learned at different times throughout their life span. These included questions about the Academy Awards, the World Series, and current events. As you can see in Figure 7.4, the reminiscence bump was evident. People knew much more about events that had happened in their early adulthood than during any other period. (Recent events were also remembered fairly well, as you can see.)

These authors suggest a variety of explanations for the reminiscence bump, any or all of which could play a role. First, it may be that the memory mechanisms described in Chapter 6 favor the retrieval of events from early adulthood because of their importance and distinctiveness (i.e., a cognitive-mechanisms account). According to this

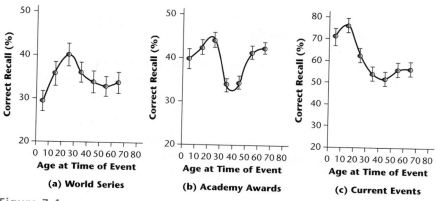

Figure 7.4

Results from Rubin, Rahall, and Poon (1998).

From Rubin, D. C., Rahhal, T. A., & Poon, L. W. (1998). Things learned in early adulthood are remembered best. *Memory and Cognition, 26,* 3–19. Reprinted by permission of the Psychonomic Society, Inc.

cognitive view, these events are thought of (i.e., rehearsed) often due to their importance and are not subject to much interference because of their distinctiveness. Another factor may be identity formation. As you know from experience, the period from adolescence to early adulthood is a critical time for the formation of an individual's identity (Erikson, 1950). So events that occur during this critical period will be the most defining ones, the ones that are recounted most often and incorporated into one's life story (i.e., an identity explanation account). A review by Habermas and Bluck (2000) fits nicely with this view. The article, cleverly titled "Getting a Life: The Emergence of the Life Story in Adolescence," points out that the cognitive tools a person needs to *construct* a coherent life story, as well as the social and motivational reasons one needs to *have* a life story, both develop during adolescence. It's no wonder, then, that both personally experienced events and general knowledge learned during this time are so memorable. This analysis provides an interesting parallel to the *cognitive self* explanation for the offset of childhood amnesia. Just as childhood events are encoded more memorably when we've developed a sense *that* we are, later life events are encoded more memorably when we've developed a sense of exactly *who* we are.

A final explanation appeals to neurological development as the source of the reminiscence bump (i.e., the peak functioning account). Because our cognitive abilities and brain function are at their peak in early adulthood, things experienced during this period are remembered best. A recent study provides some fairly strong evidence for this account. Janssen and Murre (2008) used the Internet to collect autobiographical memories. Almost 3500 visitors to their website (age 16–75) responded to 10 cue words with a specific personal event related to each. The events recalled did not have to be special in any way; just unique and personal. The investigators were interested in the lifespan distribution of the memories, the specific characteristics of those memories, and the role of novelty, emotionality, valence (positivity vs. negativity) in what was remembered. Novelty was assessed by having participants report whether the recalled event was a first-time occurrence. The subjective dimensions of emotionality, valence, and importance were assessed by having participants rate their memory on one of these three dimensions (one-third of the participants rated each dimension; the investigators wanted to avoid having the rating on one of the dimensions influence ratings on another).

You shouldn't be surprised to find out that the data revealed unmistakable evidence of a reminiscence bump. But you might be surprised to find out that the bump did not seem to be related to *any* of the memory-based factors mentioned previously—novelty, emotionality, valence, or importance! The memories were regular, unemotional, neutral and unimportant, all the things that should make them relatively unmemorable, yet they were memorable. Janssen and Murre speculate that this pattern may results from especially high-functioning encoding processes during adolescence, a view that is consistent with the "peak-functioning account" of the reminiscence bump, which claims that during adolescence, our cognitive and brain processes are working especially well.

So what about the (quite intuitive) accounts that focus on memory mechanisms? Janssen and Murre do attempt to reconcile these views with their findings. They propose that for older participants, some events (perhaps the more novel, emotional, and important events) are being rehearsed at the expense of the more mundane events, such that as we get older, these memories tend to "win out" and are remembered at the expense of the mundane ones. So while everyday events from the reminiscence period might enjoy an advantage while we're still relatively close to adolescence, this advantage tends to fade with increasing age. This explains the pattern of results typically found with the reminiscence bump. The identity formation and cognitive accounts may explain the different forgetting rates for mundane versus novel/emotional/important events.

An interesting side note relates to the relative role of brain development in explaining the offset of childhood amnesia and the reminiscence bump. Brain development seems to be necessary but not sufficient to explain why the amnesia of childhood lifts. However, brain development seems to be both necessary and sufficient to explain the reminiscence bump. Cognitive factors may explain why we remember the things we do from that period but neurological functioning may explain why we remember them in the first place.

Forgetting

Let's go back to our favorite figure—the retention function for autobiographical memory across the life span (Figure 7.1, p. 269). We've already discussed two of the three components that characterize this function—childhood amnesia and the reminiscence bump—now let's discuss the third characteristic: forgetting. For the period immediately preceding recall, there is a pretty standard forgetting curve: recent events are remembered fairly well, but recall falls off quickly for events that aren't as recent. Wagenaar (1986) found that memory dropped from nearly 75% correct to less than 33% correct over a four-year period. You'll note that this is the same pattern of forgetting found in countless studies of memory, beginning with Ebbinghaus's classic self-study (discussed in Chapter 1).

It's not too difficult to come up with some general reasons for autobiographical memory forgetting. As you've seen in Chapter 6, the causes of forgetting are many. Probably the most common cause of autobiographical forgetting is a simple lack of rehearsal; if events are not thought about or discussed (i.e., rehearsed), the corresponding memory representation will be, at best, transient and, at worst, nonexistent. There is also an incredible potential for interference between autobiographical episodes; one need only think of all of the events that have occurred over the past month and how hard it is to retrieve one event in the face of the others; most events don't really stand out. This relates to another likely cause of AM forgetting; many of the daily events in which we partake are routine; every day, we get up, eat breakfast, go to work or school, and so on. When events are this regular and routine, they blend together. Recall that Linton (1975) indicated that repeated episodes lose their individualized character, transitioning from autobiographical (episodic) memories to autobiographical facts (personalized semantic memories).

Earlier, you read about how differences in the cultural view of self might determine the characteristics of autobiographical memories. Recent research by Wang (2009) suggests that cultural differences also might produce variation in the specificity of those memories. According to Wang and Ross (2007) Euro-American cultures tend to remember specific episodes (autobiographical memories) whereas Asian and Asian-American cultures tend to remember generic memories (autobiographical facts). For example, a Euro-American might remember "getting a new toy" while an Asian American would remember "playing

Research Theme
Culture

with toys." Although this difference is phrased in terms of what is remembered, it could also be stated in terms of what is forgotten. Asian cultures tend to "forget" the individualized autobiographical memories remembering only the general autobiographical facts. According to Linton (1975) this is forgetting. When episodes lose their individual character, the "memory" is lost as the episode is transformed into a general "fact."

The typical explanation for this cultural difference focuses on post-encoding factors, positing that culture influences what is rehearsed. And as we learned in Chapter 6, if information is not rehearsed it is forgotten. Given the Western emphasis on autonomy, individuals are motivated to retain (i.e., rehearse) specific events with a focus on themselves as individuals. Conversely, the Eastern emphasis on relationships (rather than autonomy), motivates individuals to retain generic events, as these do not focus on the individual. According to this explanation, there is not much difference between Eastern and Western cultures in the type of information that's encoded; the difference lies in what type of information is rehearsed. Eastern cultures are not motivated to rehearse information about individual objects and events so this type of information is forgotten.

However, Wang (2009) points out that there is good reason to believe that cross-cultural differences stem from encoding (rather than rehearsal), making note of the growing literature demonstrating differences in perceptual tendencies among cultures. We discussed one of these differences in Chapter 2. Recall the differences between Western (U.K.) and African (the Himba) cultures in the global precedence effect. Perceptual differences between Eastern and Western cultures also were discussed in the context of face recognition in Chapter 5. As you'll recall, Eastern cultures tend to engage in holistic perceptual processing, leading them to focus on similarities and relationships among objects and events whereas Western cultures tend to engage in analytic processing, leading them to focus on the individual objects and events (Nisbett & Miyamoto, 2005; Norenzayan, Choi, & Peng, 2007). Given that what we perceive determines what we encode and subsequently what we remember or don't remember, it is possible that the cultural differences in memory specificity are due to differences *in what is encoded* rather than *what is forgotten* due to cultural differences in what is rehearsed. Therefore, the lack of specificity (i.e., facts rather than memories) in Asian-American memories doesn't represent forgetting at all. There are no individualized "memories" to transition to "facts"; the general autobiographical facts are all that is encoded.

The encoding and rehearsal views make different predictions about the rate at which memories are forgotten over time (i.e., the forgetting function) for each culture. If the cultural difference in memory for (or forgetting of) specific events is due to encoding differences, then recall of daily events will differ between Asian-American and Euro-American participants, but the difference should remain constant over the retention interval (i.e., events should be lost at the same rate over time). However, if cultural differences manifest themselves in how memories are rehearsed, then one might expect little difference at the point of encoding, but an increasingly large difference as the retention interval increases, and details are lost (i.e., as encoded information transitions from memory to fact).

To distinguish between these views, Wang (2009, Experiment 1) had Asian-American and Euro-American students keep diaries of detailed, important, and unique daily events that occurred each day for a week. They were instructed to write down these events at the end of the day, and not to include generic activities (e.g., "went to classes"). At the end of the week, the students turned in their diary and were given a surprise memory test in which they were to write down all of the events they had put in their diary. Finally, a week later they were asked to return to the lab, ostensibly to complete a payment form for the study. As you might guess, they were given another test on their diary entries.

The forgetting functions are shown in Figure 7.5. As expected, Euro-Americans re-membered more specific and unique episodes than did Asian Americans, replicating the effect found in other studies. But the relevant result for differentiating between the encoding and retrieval views was the forgetting function. As you can see, the rate of forgetting did not differ by culture. The Euro-American advantage remained the same (i.e., did not increase) throughout the retention interval

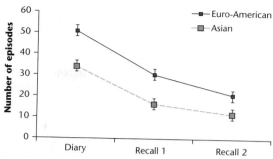

Figure 7.5

Wang's (2009) cross-cultural comparison of forgetting rates for specific autobiographical memories.

from immediate recall when the diary entries were first recorded, to final recall a week later. This pattern of results indicates that differences in how events are originally encoded underlie cross-cultural differences in memory specificity (facts vs. memories).

But a question remained: What leads to the cultural difference in encoding? A subsequent study (Experiment 3) addressed this question. Wang proposed that the difference between Eastern and Western cultures would lead to differences in how incoming information is organized and segmented. According to Zack and Swallow (2007) the segmentation and organization process makes autobiographical memories possible (as you'll recall from Chapter 6, organization is an important factor for the effective encoding of information). Therefore, differences in organization and segmentation will lead to differences in the type of information that is encoded.

Wang gave participants a fictional travel diary to read. They were asked to segment the diary into meaningful events by indicating when one meaningful event ended and another began. Perceptually, Western cultures tend to focus on specific objects and events. Conveying this type information should constitute relatively small segments of text; consistent with this prediction Euro-Americans segmented the text into a small number of discrete segments. For example, the following excerpt from the fictional diary was parsed into three small segments by Euro-Americans (segments indicated by a \):

> .....\Pete and I went to a play "The Wonderland" in the afternoon, \ and then had supper with the British wing of the family tonight. (At an Italian restaurant.) \ Except Pete was going to a football game. He is, for reasons none of us can understand, a passionate soccer fan and is going to take the Tube out to a distant suburb and sit quietly in the stands among drunken burly obscene men. \....

Eastern cultures, on the other hand, tend to focus on the relationship between objects or events. Conveying these relationships should require relatively large segments of text; consistent with this prediction Asian Americans parsed the incoming information into relatively large segments. For example, the previous excerpt was marked as only one segment by Asian Americans.

Based on these results, Wang concludes that the cultural difference in memory specificity between Asian Americans and Euro-Americans is the result of what they encode rather than what they forget (due to differences in what is rehearsed). However, encoding failure is viewed as a form of forgetting; you might be thinking the distinction is irrelevant. This is certainly not the case from a social psychological perspective. Given that forgetting has negative connotations, framing the issue in terms of what *is encoded* rather than what *is forgotten* is less likely to lead to negative evaluations of Eastern cultures. The way information is framed has important ramifications for cognitive processing, as you'll see in Chapter 11 when we discuss the effects of framing on the decision-making process.

Stop&*Review*

1. Describe the three basic components of the autobiographical memory function.

2. Two critical determinants of the emergence of autobiographical memory—language, and a sense of self—reach a critical stage of development at around age:
   a. 1
   b. 2
   c. 3
   d. 4

3. What is the most likely explanation for the reminiscence bump?

4. What accounts for the forgetting portion of the autobiographical memory function?

• Autobiographical memories retrieved thro-ughout the life span follow a predictable pattern, called the autobiographical memory function. First, there is a forgetting function, as many memories are retrieved from the last several years before the age of recall. Second, there is a disproportionate number of memories recalled between the ages of 10 and 30 (the reminiscence bump), and third, relatively few memories are recalled from early childhood, and none before the age of about 3 (childhood amnesia).

• Possible reasons for the lack of early memories and the eventual emergence of autobiographical memory include a lack of maturity of the brain before the age of 1. The most important factors in the emergence of autobiographical memory seem to be the large strides in language development and the development of the self that occur at around age two. The social-cognitive view assumes all of these factors are important in the offset of childhood amnesia and therefore can vary depending on the social or cultural context.

• There are several explanations for the reminiscence bump. The cognitive explanation account posits that the bump is due to the relative distinctiveness and salience of events that occur during the bump; the identity explanation account purports that the bump is due to the formation of our adult identity; and the peak function account asserts that the bump is a function of the our cognitive and brain functioning peaking during the bump. The latter explanation has received the most empirical support.

• Forgetting of autobiographical memories occurs as the joint result of lack of rehearsal and interference among memories. Memories that start as specific episodes often transform into more general autobiographical facts.

Autobiographical Memory Retrieval

While encoding failure may be at the heart of the cultural differences found in forgetting between Eastern and Western cultures, there is little doubt that much autobiographical memory forgetting is the result of retrieval failure. Information about our experiences is available but we need the right cue to access it (recall the availability/accessibility distinction discussed in Chapter 6). Everyone has had the experience of having "forgotten" memories come flooding back when revisiting some location, event, or person. This phenomenon is the autobiographical memory version of a context-dependency effect we talked about in Chapter 6. The representations of autobiographical memories are no doubt richly detailed and elaborated; these elaborations can serve to make the memory easier to access at retrieval, should the retrieval environment reactivate some of these elaborations.

Encoding Specificity in Autobiographical Memory

A context-dependency effect (discussed in Chapter 6) is an example of the powerful memory principle termed *encoding specificity*. According to this principle, memory will be successful to the degree that the cues present at retrieval match the way the event was encoded. Marian and Neisser (2000) developed an intriguing test of this idea for autobiographical memory. Their research participants were bilingual individuals who were fluent in Russian and English. Each was a student at a U.S. university and had emigrated from Russia approximately a decade earlier. So their autobiographical memories included events that occurred when they lived in Russia and events that had occurred since their arrival in the United States.

Research Theme
Culture

Marian and Neisser's method was disarmingly simple. They interviewed each participant using the Galton-Crovitz cue-word technique described at the beginning of the chapter to elicit autobiographical memories. Here's the catch: half of the cue words were presented in Russian, and half of the cue words were presented in English. Can you see where this is going? Marian and Neisser (in line with the encoding specificity principle) hypothesized that autobiographical memories would be especially accessible if the language of retrieval matched the language of encoding. So when participants were interviewed and presented with cue words in Russian, they should have recalled more "Russian memories" (defined as an event in which the only language used by anyone involved was Russian). The parallel prediction was made for the English interview and cue condition. The results, presented in Figure 7.6a, confirm the prediction.

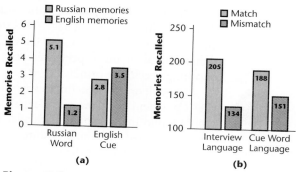

Figure 7.6

Results from Marian and Neisser (2000).

From Marian, V., & Neisser, U. (2000). Language-dependent recall of autobiographical memories. *Journal of Experimental Psychology: General, 129*, 361–368. Copyright 2000 by the American Psychological Association. Reprinted by permission.

Marian and Neisser explain their result by noting the inherently linguistic nature of autobiographical memories (discussed earlier in the context of the offset of childhood amnesia). Memories are not only expressed through language but also include language as a fundamental feature of the encoded event. When this salient feature is presented again at retrieval, the entire memory representation is more likely to become active. If you're particularly interested in experimental design, a thought may have occurred to you as you read about this study. The retrieval procedure used by Marian and Neisser involved the entire interview, which was conducted either in Russian or English. In addition, the cue words were presented in the corresponding language (e.g., in the Russian interview, Russian cue words were presented). This raises an interesting question: What was more important in producing the language-dependent recall—the Russian (or English) cue words or the ambience (or feeling) created by the Russian (or English) interview?

This question was tested in a second study in which Marian and Neisser separated the effects of cue word and interview ambience by adding two conditions to the mix. In addition to conditions in which they interviewed and cued in the same language, they added conditions in which the interviewing was done in one language while cues were presented in the other. For instance, the interaction with the participants might occur entirely in Russian except for the presentation of the cue words, which would occur in English. By adding these conditions, Marian and Neisser hoped to determine which aspect of the retrieval environment was more critical for recall.

The results are presented in the Figure 7.6b. This figure presents the number of autobiographical memories recalled by participants as a function of whether the language in which the memory had been encoded matched or didn't match the language of the cue word, and whether the language in which the memory had been encoded matched or didn't match the language of the interview. As you can see, a mismatch of either type led to lower levels of recall, but the effect of the interview (ambient) language seems to be the more important factor. Marian and Neisser explain this result by appealing to the notion of a *language mode*. As they point out, using a certain language doesn't just involve saying specific words; it involves a more general way of thinking that is specific to that language. This *state of mind* is distinctive and will likely serve as an effective cue if present at retrieval. The Marian and Neisser (2000) study reveals that retrieval of life experiences obeys a tried-and-true principle of memory—the encoding specificity principle.

Research Theme
Embodied
Cognition

Believe it or not, something as subtle as body posture can serve as an effective memory cue! Consistent with the encoding specificity principle, Dijkstra, Kaschak, and Zwaan (2007) found that assuming particular body positions aided in the recall of activities or events associated with those postures. For example, laying down served as an effective cue for recalling a trip to the dentist.

Casasanto and Dijkstra (2010) wondered whether this "embodied memory" effect might extend to motor movements that were irrelevant to the encoding of the original memory, but still related in a metaphorical sense. Do you think turning your thumb upward while recalling might lead you to recall positive memories, due to the match of body movement tone and encoded emotions from life events? This might sound a bit preposterous, but read on. Casasanto and Dijkstra (Experiment 2) gave participants a

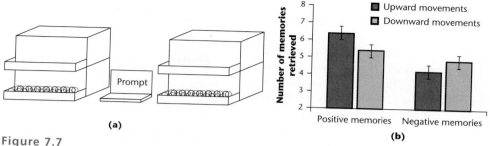

Figure 7.7

(a) Experimental apparatus used by Casasonto and Dijkstra (2010) and (b) positive and negative autobiographical recall as a function of type of movement.

rather strange combination of tasks, involving the setup depicted in Figure 7.7a. The flanking objects in the figure are pairs of boxes, stacked two high. The boxes differed in color; the boxes on top were red, and the ones on the bottom were blue (this arrangement was reversed for 1/2 of the participants). Marbles were placed in the top trays or (as pictured in Figure 7.7a) in the bottom trays.

Participants were required to think of an autobiographical memory in response to emotionally neutral prompts (e.g., "tell me about an event that happened yesterday") that were presented on a laptop computer at the center of the setup depicted in Figure 7.7a. While thinking of these memories, they also were required to move a marble for each beat of a metronome (every 2 seconds). In one block, participants moved marbles up (to the red box), while in the other, they moved them down (to the blue box). The instructions for the marble moving task used color words (e.g., blue, red) rather than position words (e.g., top, bottom) or motion words (e.g. up, down) in order to avoid any linguistic effect the words could have on the recall of positive and negative memories. Using color words in the instructions allowed them to assess whether movement alone would lead to an effect. After the marble task was completed, each cue was re-presented, and participants orally recounted the memory retrieved when the cue was presented (during the marble-moving task). After recall, both the participant and an independent rater coded the memories in terms of the valence (positive or negative).

The results are presented in Figure 7.7b. You can see a striking interaction between the valence of the memory and the direction of the marble movement. Incredibly, the small upward movements produced by transferring marbles to a higher platform were enough to somehow bias retrieval toward the recall of positive events, with the converse occurring in the context of downward movements. The authors cite their results as support for the notion of "metaphorical mental representations" that link cognitive processing and response processing (e.g., remembering and moving). Note the similarity between this view and the phenomenon of weak synesthesia, discussed in Chapter 2, in which there's a metaphorical connection between two different sensory systems (e.g., warm colors, which includes tactile and visual senses). This phenomenon indicates the integrated and embodied nature of cognitive processing in a fashion similar to the perceptual integration of perceptual experiences from different senses.

Stop&*Think* | THE POINT OF AUTOBIOGRAPHICAL MEMORY

Casasonto and Dijkstra (2010) found that body posture influences the type of memories retrieved. This exercise provides a test of this hypothesis. Get a few friends and test each of them in one of two conditions:

- Condition A: Have them (elbow resting on some surface) point their index finger straight up
- Condition B: Have them (arm at their side) point their index finger toward the ground

Explain to your "participants" that you're looking at the relationship between different gestures and remembering. Once they're in position, have them recall an autobiographical memory for each of the following cues:

- Event from yesterday
- Event from high school
- Event from childhood
- Event from college (prior to this year or semester)
- Event that involved you and a parent

Write down the memory in enough detail so that it will be recognized by your participant when you are finished. Have the participant review each memory, and rate it on a scale from 1 (very negative) to 5 (very positive). Look at the memories and ratings and assess whether they were consistent with the findings of Casasonto and Dijkstra (2010). Were the memories generated while pointing up any more positive than those generated when pointing down?

Effective Cues for Autobiographical Memories

As Casasonto and Dijkstra point out, encoding specificity doesn't provide a ready account for the marble-moving finding (unless the participants recalled a memory of moving marbles!). So effective cues for autobiographical remembering extend beyond the information that was originally encoded. So what other cues serve as useful triggers for autobiographical memories? Suppose your authors wanted to recall an episode from their first visit to the Minnesota Twins new outdoor baseball park. Of the following set of W questions (what? when? where? who?) used in a study by Wagenaar (1986), which do you think would serve as the best cues for memory retrieval?

> What comprised the memory (going to see the Minnesota Twins home opener)
> When the event occurred (April 12, 2010)
> Where it occurred (Target Stadium)
> Who was involved (Bridget and Greg)

Well, *what* do you think? "What" served as the best memory cue and the "when" cue was the least helpful. So the cue "seeing the Minnesota Twins home opener" will lead to quicker and better recall of that particular event than will "April 12, 2010."

The superiority of "what"-type cues also was demonstrated in the diary studies of Catal and Fitzgerald (2004) and Brewer (1988), who found that location ("where") and time ("when") were poor cues for retrieval, but actions ("what") were good cues for retrieval. Once again, this makes sense; in trying to remind a friend of an incident at a restaurant, it would be more effective to say, "Remember the time you won $150 playing pull tabs" than "Remember that time at Ol' Mexico?" This second cue will be relatively ineffective, particularly if going to Ol' Mexico is a repeated event. This result seems to indicate that the repetition of events leads to poor episodic memories (i.e., autobiographical memories), which replicates the result found in Linton's (1975) self-study indicating that event repetitions lead to a transition from specific episodic memories (i.e., autobiographical memories) to more general semantic memories (i.e., autobiographical facts).

Odors as Cues.   When we discuss autobiographical memories in class or with friends, the question of whether odors are especially strong memory cues invariably arises. Everyone has had the experience of a vivid memory leaping into consciousness in the presence of a distinctive odor. The most famous example of this is a literary one, from Marcel Proust's *Swann's Way* (1922/1960). In it, Proust speaks of a memory that vividly leapt to mind in response to a spot of tea that he had just sipped, which contained a

Target Field: The new home of the Minnesota Twins.

crumb of cake (a "petites madeleines"). This cue seemed to stimulate his memory even more profoundly than his palate. What he experienced was a momentary transformation of consciousness seemingly as stark as if he had traveled back to his childhood in a time machine.

This now-famous example from Proust provides some indication of the apparent power of odors to elicit memories that are especially vivid; this has been termed the *Proust phenomenon* (Chu & Downes, 2000). Proust's anecdote provides a powerful description of the power of olfactory cues. But anecdotes are poor evidence, so Chu and Downes (2000, 2002) set out to put the Proust phenomenon to the empirical test. Chu and Downes (2002) used a straightforward cuing procedure to compare the effectiveness of odors and verbal labels in eliciting autobiographical recall. They gave participants an odor-label cue (e.g., the word *ginger*), and asked them to recall an autobiographical memory. Once they had one in mind, they described it and rated it on a number of different scales including pleasantness, vividness, uniqueness, and personal significance. They were then asked to pursue the memory further, and this is where the critical comparison came in. Some of the participants were re-presented with the odor label, and were asked again to describe and rate the memory. Other participants were presented with the actual odor (ginger, in this example) and like

Reality Check

the other group, were asked to describe and rate the memory again. Chu and Downes (2002) were interested in how this second recall would differ from the first. The anecdotal evidence suggested that odors would prompt more vivid and detailed memories than the corresponding verbal cue.

It turns out that, as the authors quip in the title of their article, "Proust nose best." Odors did indeed turn out to be powerful cues for autobiographical memories. When the second recall was cued by the odor rather than a second presentation of the odor label, participant ratings of the personal nature of the memory, its vividness, and its pleasantness all increased significantly. When the second recall was cued by the odor label, rather than the actual odor, the ratings barely budged. In addition, the researchers measured recall detail by analyzing the words participants used to describe the memories in their verbal reports. This analysis provided converging evidence for the effectiveness of odors as cues; participants used more words to describe odor-cued memories relative to verbally cued memories (i.e., the odor label).

So why are odors such effective cues? Chu and Downes (2002) present a couple of possibilities. One involves the proximity of the sensory area for olfaction to mechanisms important to memory—more specifically, areas near the amygdala and hippocampus. Due to this proximity, Chu and Downes speculate that the olfactory areas may be especially likely to influence the memory-related processing of the amygdala. We'll discuss another possible reason for the effectiveness of odors as cues in the next section, as we consider a leading theory of autobiographical memory construction.

Models of Autobiographical Memory Retrieval

A couple of general models have been proposed as frameworks for how we encode, store, and access autobiographical memories. These models reflect two primary properties of autobiographical remembering: their distinctly episodic flavor (they involve a re-living and re-experiencing of the sensory and temporal characteristics of the original event), and the fact that these memories, to a large extent, are reconstructions rather than replicas.

The Self Memory System View.
At the beginning of the chapter, we discussed the differences between autobiographical memories and autobiographical facts and pointed out that autobiographical memories were examples of episodic memories, as discussed in Chapter 6. You'll recall that episodic memories are those that are accompanied by a "re-living" experience, complete with sights, sounds, smells, and other contextual elements from the original event. Conway (2009) turns that relationship on its head, and uses the notion of autobiographical memory as the basis for all episodic memory. With just a moment's consideration, it's obvious that he's correct in doing so; any event that we experience is an episode from our life and therefore an autobiographical memory. Even a list of 50 words encoded for a later recall test in a psych experiment (which we labeled as an episodic memory in Chapter 6) is something we personally experienced and hence an autobiographical memory.

According to his **self-memory system** view (Conway, 2009; Conway, 2005; Conway & Pleydell-Pierce, 2000; Conway, Singer, & Tagini, 2004) the heart of episodic (autobiographical) memory lies in what Conway terms the working self, which includes everything about who you are—your life story, your self-image, your goals and plans, even your attitudes and beliefs. According to this view, autobiographical memories are constructed rather than reproduced, the reconstruction guided by the working self. Hence, memories could be reconstructed differently as particular aspects of the working self changes (i.e., goals, beliefs, and attitudes change across the life span).

Autobiographical memories are constructed by accessing an autobiographical memory database. The autobiographical database is organized hierarchically. The first (most general) layer is *lifetime periods,* substantial slices of our lifetime that are characterized by specific goals, plans, or themes (e.g., the authors' years in graduate school at Purdue). Also, within a given lifetime period, autobiographical knowledge is organized into different thematic categories (e.g., academic experiences and relationships). The second layer of knowledge is *general events,* a specific representation of particular events that occurred over the weeks and months that make up each lifetime period. For example, Greg remembers all the times he shot pool at Locomotives, a local dive in West Lafayette, Indiana (and Bridget remembers watching him!). Knowledge at the general-event layer can be used to access information at the third layer of storage, *complex episodic memories.* These include the elements of episodic memories as discussed in Chapter 6, including sensory-perceptual details and other simpler components that can be used to construct a specific memory. For example, we remember the particular Friday afternoon happy hour when we met each other for the first time over a pitcher of Old Milwaukee Light (how romantic!). This type of cognitive organization should sound familiar. Do you recall the idea of levels of categorization (superordinate level, basic level, and subordinate level) discussed in Chapter 5? It seems that autobiographical memories are organized in much the same way.

The self-memory system model (in particular the notion of an autobiographical memory database from which we build memories) fits quite nicely with a number of findings from investigations of autobiographical memory. First, a study by Barsalou (1988) had participants generate specific memories of what they had done over their summer vacations. In spite of instructions to be specific, over 60% of the memories that the participants generated were general memories like, "I read a lot" or "We went to the beach." This suggests that rather than directly accessing specific memories, people sample from general knowledge of the period—specifically, the intermediate level (Conway, 1996). It's interesting to note here that this is the same level at which people tend to access categories—instead of thinking of "animals" (superordinate level) or "orange Maine Coon" (subordinate level), we think "cat" (basic—intermediate—level). Second, retrieval of autobiographical memories is typically a slow and effortful reconstruction

We tend to remember memories in terms of certain lifetime periods—for instance, your authors remember their years at Purdue.

rather than a rapid retrieval of facts. For example, it will take you longer to reconstruct what you did last June than it will to retrieve the colors of the rainbow or the 12 months of the year. Finally, the model's proposal that autobiographical memories are constructed "on the fly," and therefore can vary depending on the retrieval circumstances, is consistent with the fact that autobiographical memories can be variable across multiple recalls.

Stop&Think | RECONSTRUCTING AUTOBIOGRAPHICAL MEMORIES

Try and remember any event that relates to:

- Summer vacations
- Christmas
- Breakup of a friendship or romantic relationship
- Final exams

Take special note of the reconstruction process that you go through:

- Does this process match the autobiographical retrieval process as outlined by Conway?
- Was this reconstructive process rapid or slow?
- Do your memories seem to be hierarchically organized?

Let's return to the Chu and Downes (2002) finding that smell serves as an especially potent cue for autobiographical memory. One explanation for its potency relates to Conway's multiple levels of autobiographical knowledge and retrieval. According to Conway (1992), sensory cues such as smell are capable of bypassing the usual reconstructive process of autobiographical memory construction and making direct contact with information at the most specific level—event-specific knowledge. This is consistent with the fact that memories cued by smell don't seem reconstructed at all—they seem to present themselves immediately and completely to your conscious experience.

Stop&Think Back | LEVELS OF AUTOBIOGRAPHIZATION

As we note in our discussion, the levels of Conway's autobiographical memory model map onto the levels of categorization we discuss in Chapter 6. For example, animal-cat-Maine Coon, or tool-hammer-ball peen hammer. See how many examples of this type of "triplet" you can come up with for your own autobiographical memories. For example, one for Greg and Bridget would be "going out together"—"going to plays" and "going to see *Wicked*." Generate some similar examples, noting which level is easiest to generate.

The Basic-Systems View. Conway's model urges a re-consideration of episodic memories, simply re-casting them as examples of autobiographical remembering. However, the **basic systems view** (Rubin, 2005; 2006) claims that the episodic memories we form in laboratory experiments (i.e., rating a list of 50 words for their pleasantness) are qualitatively different from the autobiographical memories we form in daily living. They have no personal relevance, are unidimensional in terms of sensory experience, and have no sense of story, emotion, or other factors that define our personal recollections. Therefore, there needs to be different theoretical accounts to explain how each type of memory is constructed; the same mechanisms cannot explain both, as suggested by the self-memory system view.

The basic-systems view emphasizes the multi-dimensional makeup of autobiographical memory, proposing that autobiographical memory arises from the concurrent operation of several distinct brain systems. The systems proposed include each of the individual senses (i.e., vision, audition, touch, taste, and olfaction) and a spatial system that helps encode locations of people and objects. Also involved are the basic brain systems involved in emotion, and a narrative system that is used to provide causal coherence to the "story" that the events in our life comprise. Information from all of these systems is bound together by the explicit memory system we discussed in Chapter 6. It is important to note the basic systems view and the self-memory system view do have one thing in common: both assume a reconstruction process. The reconstructive nature of memory will be the focus of the next chapter.

Involuntary Autobiographical Memories

The research described in this chapter has dealt almost exclusively with effortful and *conscious* retrieval of autobiographical memories—cases in which people actively seek to reconstruct a memory from their past. But that's not always the way autobiographical memories are retrieved; quite often, memories enter consciousness without any effort or deliberate search. In fact, these unconsciously cued memories comprise a fair number of the autobiographical memories that we experience on a daily basis (e.g., Brewin, Christodoulides, & Hutchinson, 1996). But these memories have not been the focus of much investigation, for reasons that may be apparent: involuntary memories are just that—involuntary; therefore, neither the rememberer nor the experimenter can exert control over their appearance. This makes them difficult to study in a systematic manner. They have, however, long been of interest in a clinical setting; those who suffer from post-traumatic stress disorder (PTSD) often experience intrusive, frightening, involuntary recollections (Christiansen, 1992).

Much of the work on involuntary remembering has been conducted by Berntsen and colleagues (Berntsen, 1996; 1998; 2007; Berntsen & Hall, 2004; Berntsen & Rubin, 2002) using the diary method. These and other investigations have revealed a number of characteristics that seem to distinguish involuntary memories from voluntary ones. The most consistent finding is that involuntary memories tend to be for specific rather than general events (e.g., Ball & Little, 2006). This contrasts with research on voluntary autobiographical memories in which people often recall general memories (Barsalou, 1988; Linton, 1986) even when asked to provide specific ones. This voluntary retrieval is a slow and effortful process that takes about 10 seconds (e.g. Rubin, 1998). In contrast, the occasional voluntary retrieval of specific memories (Haque & Conway, 2001) is rapid (1–2 seconds) rather than slow. This fast retrieval of specific memories (which most involuntary memories are) seems to indicate that involuntary memories are retrieved in a qualitatively different way that avoids a lengthy reconstruction process. In addition, if the voluntary retrieval of specific memories is fast and involuntary memories tend to be specific, it seems logical to conclude that involuntary memory retrieval also is fast. It is important to note that this conclusion was based on logic, rather than empirical data, as it seemed impossible to obtain retrieval time for involuntary memories given their nature.

However, Schlageman and Kvavilashvili (2008) developed a clever procedure for comparing retrieval speed for both types of memories in a laboratory setting. Operating on the assumption that involuntary memories are often triggered by specific cues under conditions of diffuse attention, the experimenters created these conditions in their study. During the first phase, participants were given a vigilance task, which involved watching 800 trials on a computer display that showed a series of either horizontal or vertical lines. Their task was to press a key whenever they saw a display consisting of vertical lines. Trouble is, those lines only occurred on 15 of the 800 trials. The researchers were basically trying to induce our old friend from Chapter 4, mind wandering. And the researchers gave them something to which the mind could wander. On each trial of the detection task, they also were presented with a phrase that required no response; the phrases were however, designed to induce autobiographical remembering. Sample phrases included "sitting on a beach" and "missed opportunity." Participants were told to ignore the words. However, they were told that sometimes their mind would wander to thoughts unrelated to the detection task. If they experienced a memory in response to a cue, they were asked to click the mouse, which would suspend the vigilance task. Participants were to write down a description of the memory. A second phase, conducted a week later, served as the voluntary memory phase. The same participants were told that they were to focus on the phrase (these were the same phrases presented during the first phase) as it appeared on the screen, and they were to retrieve an autobiographical memory in response to each one. During both phases, participants filled out follow-up questionnaires to report on various characteristics of the retrieved memories.

The results indicated that involuntary memories were retrieved almost twice as fast as voluntary memories and involuntary memories were more likely to be specific than voluntary memories. These findings supported earlier empirical work using diary studies and the assumption that involuntary retrieval is a fast process. However, the authors concluded that the process of involuntary and voluntary retrieval was the same, not different. You might be thinking…the empirical findings supported the logical conclusions that led to the notion that there were two retrieval systems; so why did these researchers reach a different conclusion? They surmised that involuntary retrieval of mainly specific memories occurs on the order of 1 to 2 seconds; this matches the retrieval time for voluntary retrieval of specific memories in previous studies. This seems to indicate that the same process is used to retrieve specific memories, whether they be voluntary or involuntary. In addition, 20% of the involuntary memories were for general rather than specific events. So it seems that specific and general memories can be retrieved in voluntary and involuntary situations, further supporting the idea that the retrieval process must be comparable. This process must be reconstructive in nature because voluntary retrieval is typically slow, which is indicative of a reconstruction process; the difference between involuntary and voluntary retrieval lies in the way this reconstruction process occurs.

The authors appeal to the notion of spreading activation (discussed in Chapter 5) to account for this difference. In voluntary retrieval, the cue activates information in the hierarchical database and the spread of that activation is consciously directed by the rememberer. However, in involuntary retrieval, the spread of activation that results from an external event or stimulus activating information in the database, is automatic and occurs without conscious awareness. They further assert that in voluntary retrieval situations, participants only engage in an effortful search when this automatic activation fails to produce a memory. When successful, a specific memory is quickly reported, given the illusion that the memory was directly retrieved. If not successful, the effortful search begins and most likely will be terminated at the general events level due to any number of factors (time pressure, unwillingness to put in the requisite effort needed, etc.).

According to the authors, the interesting question, therefore, revolves around determining which aspects of an external stimulus will trigger the involuntary retrieval of a memory. One suggestion harkens back again to the encoding specificity principle; an exact match between the context of the cue and the central elements of the memory is needed for the retrieval of an involuntary memory. Another possibility is that some aspect of the memory was partially activated by a recent event, which primes the involuntary retrieval when the relevant cue is encountered. As you are now accustomed to hearing, the authors claim a combination of both factors may lead to involuntary memory retrieval.

Another factor may relate to the characteristics of the cue, itself. Schlagman and Kvavilashvili found that the emotionality of the cue phrase did lead to an intriguing difference between involuntary and voluntary memories. The proportion of memories elicited under voluntary conditions did not differ with the valence (positive, neutral, or negative) of the cue. However, involuntary memories were more likely to be elicited by negative cues than by any other type. This may indicate that involuntary memories are adaptive, and serve as some sort of warning mechanism that alerts us to upcoming situations that resemble dangerous circumstances from our past, a mechanism that would make evolutionary sense. This dovetails with the warning signal explanation for the intrusive and involuntary memories of those suffering from PTSD. These memories tend to be for events preceding the traumatic event. So, PTSD may be the abnormal and extreme result of a normally adaptive process. A final conclusion from this study is a methodological one—involuntary memories are indeed investigable in a controlled setting.

Research Theme
Emotion

Research Theme
Evolution

Stop&*Think* | WHAT POPS INTO YOUR HEAD?

For the next week or so, keep a diary of memories that seem to "pop into your head" for no apparent reason (i.e., involuntary memories). Jot a short description of each. After you've accumulated a number of memories, evaluate them in terms of the characteristics revealed in Berntsen's (1996) study.

- Do they tend to be recent?
- Do they tend to be positive?
- Do they tend to be specific rather than general?

Stop&*Review*

1. The most effective cue for retrieving an episode appears to be which of these "W questions"?
   a. what happened
   b. where something happened
   c. when something happened
   d. who was present
2. Name the three levels of the autobiographical memory database, according to the self-memory system model.
3. True or false? Involuntary memories are more likely to be elicited by positive cues than by negative ones.

- The reconstruction of autobiographical memories is subject to the encoding spe-cificity principle. Re-presenting linguistic context leads to enhanced recall of memories. Particular body motions or postures can also influence autobiographical remembering. The best cues for autobiographical memories tend to be hints about what happened in a specific episode, rather than where or when it happened, or with whom.

- Odors serve as effective cues for autobiographical memories. According to the self-memory system model of autobiographical memories, all episodic memories are examples of autobiographical memories and retrieval is based on three different levels of knowledge (lifetime periods, general events, and event-specific knowledge). According to the basic systems view, autobiographical memories and episodic memories are qualitatively different and therefore require different theoretical mechanisms to explain. Both theories assume a reconstructive process.

- Research on involuntary autobiographical memories reveals a number of distinguishing features. Methodologically, such research presents a challenge because involuntary autobiographical memories, by definition, are beyond experimental control. Research indicates that involuntary autobiographical memories are retrieved more quickly and automatically than voluntary ones, and that negative cues are more likely to elicit involuntary memories.

Emotion and Autobiographical Remembering

Research Theme
Emotion

Of all the influences on our life's memories, perhaps none is so evident as emotion. Many of the events we remember are emotionally charged: your first kiss; hearing a startling piece of news, good or bad; the time you won the spelling bee (actually, we both came in second—sniff); your favorite team winning the World Series or your college winning the NCAA basketball championship. The impact of emotion on autobiographical memories has been a focal point of investigation and, as we'll see, a source of some controversy. A number of studies have attempted to determine how we remember autobiographical experiences associated with particular emotions. In one early study, Robinson (1980) used the Galton-Crovitz cue word technique to retrieve memories in response to emotion-word prompts such as *angry*. The study revealed that emotional experiences are associated with shorter retrieval times than nonemotional experiences, implying that emotional events enjoy heightened accessibility in memory. Let's now turn to a discussion of the autobiographical memories that are among the most accessible ones you have.

Flashbulb Memories

No doubt one of the most interesting and well-documented forms of emotional memory is **flashbulb memory**—a detailed, vivid, and confidently held memory for the circumstances surrounding when you first heard some startling bit of news. Our parents will never forget what they were doing when they heard the news of John F. Kennedy's assassination; we'll never forget what we were doing when we heard about (or saw) the explosion of the space shuttle *Challenger*. And none of us will ever forget what we were doing when we heard that two airliners had hit and toppled the World Trade Center towers. Memories for when you heard the news of a surprising event are striking in their degree of detail and vividness, and therefore we'd swear to their accuracy. Indeed, the term *flashbulb* implies that the events are brief in duration, surprising, and lead to photograph-quality memories. As you'll see, there is some truth to these assertions.

Characteristics of Flashbulbs.   The defining research on flashbulb memories was reported by Brown and Kulik (1977). They asked adults to report their memory for when they heard about the assassinations of John F. Kennedy, Martin Luther King, Jr., and Malcolm X, among others. One of the most striking things to emerge from their investigation was the consistency in the types of information reported about these memories. The flashbulb memories that people reported tended to include five categories of information: *location* (where they heard), *activity* (what they were doing), *source* (who told them), *emotion* (how they felt emotionally when they heard), and *aftermath* (what they did next). Table 7.4 presents two accounts of the space shuttle *Challenger* explosion taken from an investigation by Neisser and Harsch (1992). Note that both accounts include each of the five components of a flashbulb memory.

Table 7.4 **Two Sample Accounts of the *Challenger* Explosion (from Neisser & Harsch, 1992)**

Flashbulb Account A

"When I first heard about the explosion I was sitting in my freshman dorm room with my roommate and we were watching TV. It came on a news flash and we were both totally shocked. I was really upset and I went upstairs to talk to a friend of mine and then I called my parents."

Flashbulb Account B

"I was in my religion class and some people walked in and started talking about [it]. I didn't know any details except that it had exploded and the schoolteacher's students had all been watching which I thought was so sad. Then after class I went to my room and watched the TV program talking about it and I got all the details from that."

From Neisser, U., & Harsch, N. (1992). Phantom flashbulbs: False recollections of hearing the news about *Challenger*. In E. Winograd & U. Neisser (Eds.), *Affect and accuracy in recall: Studies of "flashbulb" memories* (pp. 9–31). New York: Cambridge University Press. Reprinted by permission of Cambridge University Press.

What Produces a Flashbulb? What accounts for the seeming clarity, accuracy, and vividness of these memories? Early in the investigation of flashbulb memories, Brown and Kulik (1977) proposed that any event that is particularly surprising and consequential (such as the assassination of a leader) receives prioritized processing in the brain, almost as if the memory of the event was "seared in" by a special brain mechanism. This account is typically termed "Now Print!" Such a mechanism would have high adaptive value; an organism that can remember consequential past events is more likely to adapt to changing conditions. Brown and Kulik also proposed that the more consequential the event, the more rehearsal it receives. People think about the event frequently and relate it to others, which leads the memory to be more detailed.

This mechanism leads to one of the central questions about flashbulb memories—their accuracy. Subjectively, flashbulb memories seem so clear, but how accurate are they? And how do flashbulb memories hold up over time? Research has provided mixed results. Early studies indicated that such memories were highly accurate; Pillemer (1984) found that participants' memories for the 1982 assassination attempt on former president Ronald Reagan included many accurate details two months after the event and that seven months later, they had lost very little of that detail. But a number of studies of people's recollections for hearing about the space shuttle *Challenger* explosion gave researchers some pause. McCloskey, Wible, and Cohen (1988) found that these recollections were not astoundingly accurate; only a little over half of the accounts were consistent across two tests given one week and nine months later.

One of the most striking examples of inconsistency was provided by Neisser and Harsch (1992). Look back at the accounts of the space shuttle *Challenger* explosion in Table 7.4. We mentioned that these were two different accounts, but we left out the interesting fact that these accounts are from the same person. Neisser and Harsch found evidence for what they termed *phantom flashbulbs*. The day following the tragedy, the researchers gave a questionnaire to participants regarding the circumstances under which they first heard the news (account B). Two and a half years later, participants were once again given this questionnaire (account A). Much to Neisser and Harsch's surprise, there were many serious errors in reporting (although many accounts were correct as well). Even showing the participants their original (day-after) recall protocols failed to bring the memories back! And even when interviewed six months after this point in time, these erroneous accounts remained consistent. What mechanisms account for such striking inconsistencies and misplaced confidence?

One trend in the misremembrances was a phenomenon termed *TV priority* (Neisser & Harsch, 1992): many of the mistaken recollections were associated with participants having heard about the event on television. The researchers suggest that these mistakes likely arose in several ways. Participants no doubt watched a good deal of follow-up news reports on the tragedy; the image of the space shuttle going up in flames was widely and repeatedly broadcast; indeed, one still sees it occasionally replayed today. Perhaps most interesting of all, Neisser and Harsch propose that people have a schema for hearing about disaster news, a schema that includes having watched TV coverage. Given the prominence of TV in our culture, this is the avenue by which we most frequently hear about disasters. Therefore, it isn't surprising that a later reconstruction of how one first heard a piece of news would include a memory of having seen it on TV. For the events of

9/11, did you or a family member learn about the attacks by watching the plane hit the first tower of the World Trade Center? If so, this is an inaccurate reconstruction that is probably the result of TV priority. TV crews were not covering the event until AFTER the first tower was hit. (Note that footage of the first plane hitting the WTC was found days later but it was not available the day of the attacks). And no one is immune from the effects of TV priority; even George Bush said he saw the plane hit the first tower when he was asked about the events of that morning (Greenberg, 2004).

Another type of error observed was the *time slice error*—participants vividly recalled an occasion on which they heard about the event. And indeed, it may have been an instance of hearing about the event, but it wasn't the first instance. So participants remembered the wrong "slice" of time. This confusion about the source of an encoded event will take center stage in the next chapter as we discuss the reasons for distortions in our memories.

Based on studies like these, the current view on the formation of flashbulb memories is that for the most part, flashbulb memories can be accounted for by appealing to some of the well-known factors that have been shown in countless laboratory studies to influence memory: degree of rehearsal, distinctiveness, and salience or personal relevance. Each of these factors leads to well-formed memories of any event. But Schooler and Eich (2000) suggest that while these usual memory mechanisms can account for the formation of flashbulbs, the operation of these basic mechanisms is somehow supplemented and/or intensified by emotion. The nature of emotion's effect is still unclear; it may alter the initial encoding of the event, or it may enhance the likelihood that the event is rehearsed on a later occasion.

It is also important to note that even if flashbulbs are phenomenologically "special" in their seeming vividness and detail, they are not special in one respect: They involve the same reconstructive memory processes, and hence the distortion, that characterize any other memory. But even in the face of significant distortion, the degree of vividness and clarity that characterizes flashbulb memories does seem to distinguish them from other autobiographical memories. So in answer to the question, "Are flashbulbs a special type of memory?", most memory researchers would probably answer, "Yeah, sort of." Or perhaps with a little more attention to grammar, they'd say, "Flashbulb memories are 'special, but not that special'" (Christiansen, 1989).

Memories of 9/11.   Certainly some of the most powerful memories formed in the past decade or so are those related to the horrific events of September 11, 2001. Memories of the terrorist attacks on New York and Washington, D.C. would almost certainly qualify as flashbulb memories; people most likely remember information from all of the standard categories that define a flashbulb memory. But never have so many people felt so personally about a public event. The families of thousands of people were directly impacted by the attacks, and millions of people around the country (not to mention around the world) suffered from anxiety and stress in the attacks' wake. The tragedy also offered a rare opportunity to investigate a flashbulb memory that was likely shared by most everyone in the country. Indeed, the 10 years since the horrific attacks have seen a host of investigations (e.g., Fivush, Edwards, & Mennutti-Washburn, 2003; Kvavilashvili, Mirani, Schlagman, Foley, & Kornbrot, 2008; Pezdek, 2004; Schmidt, 2004; Talarico & Rubin, 2007) focusing on how people across the nation processed, remembered, and in some cases forgot the unforgettable events of that day.

Almost everyone will remember vividly the circumstances in which they heard about the tragic events of September 11, 2001.

Hirst and 15 of his colleagues (Hirst, et al. 2009) conducted an extensive investigation of memories for the events of September 11. The study represented a massive effort, with over 3000 participants from seven different cities across the country. Participants were recruited by setting up tables on the campuses of the collaborators or in local communities, and by word-of-mouth. Willing respondents were given a detailed survey to fill out. The survey included a series of questions about the participants' memory for how they found out about attacks (their flashbulb memory), memory for the events themselves (event memory), their confidence in the accuracy of these memories, and questions about their personal reactions to and feelings about the event. See Table 7.5 for examples of each type of question. The first survey was given one week after the attack. At two subsequent junctures (11 months and 35 months later), participants were again asked to fill out the same survey. Of primary interest to the investigators was a comparison between flashbulb memories and event memories, the degree to which these memories show forgetting, and the precise nature of the forgetting function for each type of memory.

Table 7.5 Sample of Different Types of Questions Asked in the Hirst et al. (2009) Study of Memory for the September 11, 2001 Terrorist Attacks

Flashbulb Memory Questions:
- How did you first learn about the attack (what was the source of the information)?
- What were you doing immediately before you became aware of the attack?

Event Memory Questions:
- How many airplanes were involved in the attack?
- Where was President Bush when the attack occurred?

Reactions and feelings questions:
- At this moment, how strongly or intensely do you feel sad about the attack?
- At this moment, how strongly or intensely do you feel angry about the event?

The results revealed a 43% loss in information in how participants heard about the event (i.e, flashbulb memory) in the three year span between the first and third survey. Most of that loss occurred in the first year (between the first and second survey). Interestingly, memory for their emotional reaction to hearing the news showed even more forgetting, with recall tumbling by 63% over the interval between the first and third surveys. The confidence ratings provided a sharp contrast with the memory data. Participants' confidence in their recall didn't deteriorate a bit; the confidence ratings remained the same across the three surveys. This replicates other findings (e.g., Talarico & Rubin, 2003) that indicate the most special quality of flashbulb memories is our unshakeable confidence in them. A second major question addressed by the study was memory for the actual events that occurred on 9/11 (i.e. event memory). The results were pretty similar to those found for the flashbulb memories. There was forgetting and most of it occurred between surveys 1 and 2.

What factors were associated with remembering and forgetting, and were these factors the same for flashbulb memories and event memories? To find out, Hirst et al. assessed the relationship between these types of memories and five factors: where participants lived, whether they were personally affected or inconvenienced by the events, their emotional reaction, media attention, and conversation. The forgetting pattern for flashbulb memories was unrelated to any of those factors. This was not the case for event memories, which were significantly impacted by *all* of these factors, except for emotion. The most noteworthy factors were media attention and ensuing conversation. Hirst et al. suggest that these two factors should be central to any account of event memories for flashbulb events; collectively, they and other memory researchers have labeled these sorts of factors *memory practices of a community,* or the ways in which a community processes and preserves its past.

Memory for Trauma

For many of us not directly involved or personally affected by the 9/11 attacks, the experience would not be said to reach the level of trauma. Certainly, the events of that day were surprising, shocking, angering, and anxiety-provoking. As we've seen, these factors led to the emotional reactions and unshakeable memories of that day that most of us have. But what of those who were fully immersed in the trauma of that day and its aftermath, such as the family members of those who died during the tragic chaos? How about victims of other traumatic circumstances, like a returning war veteran, a rape victim, or a witness to a murder? What are the characteristics of their memories for those deeply scarring events? Clear and unequivocal answers to these questions have proven to be elusive, and as you'll see in Chapter 8, at times extremely controversial.

Judging from the material we just discussed on flashbulb memories, and adding in your own intuition, you might guess that highly traumatic events are likely seared into memory, and extremely difficult to forget. It turns out that the answer is not so clear-cut. Memory for trauma seems to depend on a number of personal and situational variables that combine to form a somewhat unpredictable mix. There doesn't appear to be a one-size-fits-all answer to the question of how we recall trauma. Brewin (2007) outlines four areas of controversy in the literature. One of these questions is closely related to the present discussion of the role of emotion in autobiographical remembering, so we'll discuss it

Research Theme
Emotion

next. The other questions are more closely related to the processes of memory editing and distortion that we'll discuss in the next chapter.

Traumatic Event Memories: Fundamentally Different?   One central question regarding memories for personally experienced traumatic events is whether they're "special" or "unique." In other words, do traumatic experience memories differ in some fundamental way from the relatively mundane memories we've been discussing throughout the chapter? In reviewing the evidence, Brewin (2007) indicates that they don't seem to be any different from any other highly emotional memory. It is a difficult question to assess, to some degree; the only way to manipulate trauma in a memory study is to have participants view videotaped traumatic events which, needless to say, are a shadow of the real thing. There *does* seem to be important differences between the trauma memories voluntarily recalled by trauma victims in a research setting and the *involuntary* traumatic memories that are the hallmark of post-traumatic stress disorder (PTSD). These involuntary PTSD memories tend to be extremely distressing, without context (i.e., they "come out of nowhere") and involve an extensive reliving experience.

The jury is still out, though, on whether the differences are quantitative or qualitative. Brewin (2007) notes that PTSD memories might involve normal reactions to traumatic events, but the reactions have become extreme, and recovery never comes. If this is the case, then the same sets of processes might account for traumatic memories in everyone up to a point. However, others believe that there are qualitative differences between memory for traumatic events and those for "normal" events (van der Kolk & van der Holt, 1991). That is, they are based on fundamentally different mechanisms than everyday memories. We'll return to the "special mechanism" argument in Chapter 8, when we talk about the controversy over recovered memories of childhood sexual abuse.

Mood and Autobiographical Remembering

A second area of investigation that lies at the crossroads of emotion and memory is the relationship between mood and the types of memories people recall. If we're in a sad mood, do we recall sad experiences? Might such a link be at the root of psychological disorders like depression?

Research Theme
Emotion

Mood Dependence.   A great deal of the research on the interplay between mood and memory has focused on one phenomenon. **Mood-dependent memory** refers to the finding that retrieval of a previously encoded event is enhanced when the mood experienced at retrieval matches the mood that was present at encoding. Sound familiar? It should; the principle of mood dependency is conceptually quite similar to Tulving's encoding specificity principle, discussed in Chapter 6. This phenomenon would seem to have important ramifications for mood disorders. If one is depressed, does this lead to enhanced retrieval of negative autobiographical memories? And does this inclination, in turn, deepen depression?

Depression and Autobiographical Memory Recall.   The interplay between mood and memory has important implications for the treatment of depression. People often tend to recall events that are congruent with their current mood; as you might expect, people suffering from depression are likely to retrieve negative memories. Indeed, this is the case for both traditional laboratory materials, such as words and stories, and for autobiographical experiences (e.g., Williams & Scott, 1988). The bias also is evident in speed of retrieval; depressives are faster at retrieving negative events from memory and slower at retrieving positive events, relative to nondepressed controls. This *preferential treatment* for negative experiences can both worsen depression and impair one's attempt to overcome it.

Another possible reason for the dominance of negative autobiographical recall, and for its continuing hold on those suffering from depressive disorders, is a tendency for depressives to be overly general in autobiographical recall (Williams, Barnhofer, Crane, Hermans, Raes, & Watkins, 2007). For example, if asked to recall an academic failure from college, a nondepressed individual may recall that they really struggled on their midterm in biology. In contrast, in response to the same prompt, a depressed individual might remember that last semester was a complete disaster. Stated in terms of the self-memory system model of autobiographical memory, depressives recall events from the higher (more general) level of the autobiographical knowledge hierarchy.

Research indicates that the relative inability of depressed individuals to be specific in remembering past events leads to a number of memory deficits. For instance, lack of specificity in their remembering has been linked to their inability to solve present problems (Evans, Williams, O'Loughlin, & Howells, 1992). This makes sense; if people are unable to remember previous problems, along with the specifics of how the situations were resolved, then current problems will be more difficult to master. Lack of specificity in autobiographical memory also affects our perceptions of the future. Williams, Ellis, Tyers, Healy, Rose, and MacLeod (1996) found that suicidally depressed patients' lack of specificity about the past was associated with an inability to imagine future events. Based on this, depressed individuals will have trouble imagining in any specific and concrete way how things might get better in the future. This deficit in future problem solving makes depression that much harder to overcome.

Stop&*Review*

1. What is a flashbulb memory?
2. What are the five types of information typically included in a flashbulb memory?
3. True or false? The September 11 attacks were so jarring that flashbulb memories for that day are especially accurate.
4. Mood congruence refers to
   a. the fact that people tend to remember events when the retrieval mood is the same as the original encoding mood.
   b. the fact that people tend to retrieve events that match their current mood.
   c. the finding that depressed people tend to retrieve overly general memories.
   d. the general finding that mood and emotion influence autobiographical memory.

• Emotion has a number of powerful influences on autobiographical memory and is thought to play an important role in flashbulb memories, which are detailed, vivid, and confidently held memories for the circumstances when a person heard some startling bit of news.

- Flashbulb memories tend to include information about who told you about the event, where you were, what you were doing, how you felt, and what you did after you heard. Despite their vividness, these memories are subject to forgetting, as revealed by findings of phantom flashbulbs, and confident and vivid recall that is wholly inaccurate. Two explanations for these distortions is TV priority and time slice errors.

- Memories for the terrorist attacks of 9/11 include evidence of distortions, like any other memory. Memory for the flashbulb experience, events, and emotional reactions showed substantial decline over a three-year period but confidence in the accuracy of the memories did not.

- One question about memory for trauma (sill unanswered) is whether traumatic event memories are fundamentally different than other memories. Mood dependent memory refers to the fact that people tend to recall memories that match their current mood. Mood-congruent and overly general recall seem to play an important role in depression.

Functions of Autobiographical Memory

What is the importance of autobiographical memory? What are its functions? Bruce (1989) distinguishes between two senses of the word *function*. One sense is that of *adaptive significance*: Why would some set of memory processes have evolved in a particular way? Is there something adaptive about having strikingly vivid memories of newsworthy events, as in the case of flashbulb memories? Bruce also refers to another sense of function—*real-world usefulness*: What good is this type of memory to our daily living? Pillemer (1992, 1998) offers some compelling answers to these questions. According to his view, autobiographical memories serve three important functions: communicative, emotional, and directive.

Communicative Function

Autobiographical memory serves a *communicative function*. A significant part of the conversations we have with others involves telling them personal stories relevant to the topic at hand. Specific autobiographical memories are especially powerful in this regard. Relating details of personally experienced events makes our communications seem more truthful and believable and tends to make them more persuasive (Pillemer, 1992). Relating detailed autobiographical memories also allows us to connect emotionally with others in an intimate and immediate way. What would provoke a stronger reaction in you—a friend telling you that they came from a tough background, or the same friend telling you that her parents had divorced when she was 4, she had battled and overcome cancer when she was 10, and she was suspended in high school for underage drinking? Clearly, more detailed and personal memories offer you a greater sense of intimacy and a stronger connection with your friend. You will likely also feel empathetic and relate a similarly detailed and personal story of your own.

Emotional Function

According to Pillemer (1998), autobiographical memory also serves an important *emotional function* in that it helps us organize, reflect on, and think through important life events. Most approaches to psychotherapy place a good deal of emphasis on the connection between one's personal memories and one's psychological functioning. As you read earlier, the inability of many depressives to recall the specifics of memories deters their ability to solve current problems and to imagine a better future. According to some (e.g., Herman, 1992), recounting one's personal memories of trauma in detail is critical for recovery. But it's also important to note that the vivid reliving of trauma is not always associated with positive consequences, as in the case of post-traumatic stress disorder.

Directive Function

Finally, Pillemer (1998) notes what he terms the *directive functions* of autobiographical memory. Remembering personally experienced events in detail can help direct future behavior. For example, there may be important events from your life in which you really "learned your lesson"—when you mistakenly trusted someone, when you failed to plan ahead, when you were needlessly worried about something. Recollecting events of this sort can serve to change future behavior. Pillemer relates an especially relevant example, an English major's recollection in college that was critical in shaping her career aspirations:

> My first Shakespeare class would have to rank as one of my most influential experiences, since it started me on the life I'm following now (graduate school in Elizabethan literature). But the memory I have from that class is very small and tight. I remember the first day best. I was fascinated by the easy way [the professor] roamed through Shakespeare, by just the amount of knowledge that he had. He seemed to know everything. In fact, after class, I asked him if he could identify a quote I had found about fencing, "Keep up your bright swords, for the new dew will rust them." Immediately, he said "Othello, Act 1, Scene 2, I believe." Which turned out to be exactly right. I wanted to know a body of literature that well. I'm still working on it. (Pillemer, Picariello, Law, & Reichman, 1996, p. 330)

Clearly, this student's memory of this specific encounter with her English professor served an important directive function. One final point about the functions of memory outlined by Pillemer (1998; 2003): none of these functions is completely dependent on memory accuracy. In other words, for autobiographical memory to serve us in communication, in emotional adjustment, and in life direction, it isn't always critical that we remember events correctly. As Pillemer (2003) states, "From a functionalist perspective, it is permissible and often valuable to view personal event memory as a belief system rather than a mechanistic entity filled with traces that are objectively true or false (p. 19)." In other words, autobiographical memory serves us well, even if it's far from 100% accurate. And as you'll see in the next chapter, our memories typically fall well short of that level of accuracy.

Stop&*Think* | LIFE-SHAPERS AND LIFE-CHANGERS

Reflect on "stories" from your own life and how the events have served to define who you are or where you're going. You might cue your recall by attempting to retrieve memories with the general cue of "important episodes from my life story." Once you've generated some of these memories, assess them in terms of Pillemer's distinction among the three functions of autobiographical memories. Which function(s) do the specific episodes you retrieved serve?

Stop&*Review*

1. Describe the communicative function of autobiographical memory.
2. Describe the emotional function of autobiographical memory.
3. True of False? The functions of autobiographical memory don't depend on its accuracy.

• The communicative function of autobiographical memory is to allow for emotional connection with others, and to afford our communications with them more credibility and believability.

• The emotional function of autobiographical memory is to help us organize, reflect upon, and think through important life events.

• The directive function of autobiographical memory relates to the ways in which personal recollection can serve as life lessons, helping to direct our lives in certain ways. The functions of autobiographical memory don't really depend on memory accuracy.

CHAPTER OUTLINE

8

Malleability in Memory: Processes of Forgetting, Editing, and Distortion

How reliable are eyewitnesses to crimes, and how much stock should a jury put in their testimony? How common is it that people are wrongfully convicted because of mistaken testimony of an eyewitness?

Have you ever had a disagreement with a friend about how some event played itself out? The two of you are in pretty much complete disagreement, and with equal confidence. Both of you can't be right. How can memories that seem so real be mistaken?

It may seem obvious that we forget, given the incredible volume of information that we encounter every day. Forgetting may be annoying, but it probably seems like no big deal. It isn't like we create memories completely out of thin air...or do we? Can techniques like hypnosis help us get to "the truth"?

What happens to memories of traumatic or particularly painful experiences? Was Freud right? Do we manage to push memories of these experiences out of consciousness? Or are they impossible to get out of our minds? Can we forget things if we want to forget them?

One of the joys of having two memory researchers in the house is the fact that we each think our memories are better than the other's, which sets the stage for what we fondly call "memory fights." Memory fights highlight a fundamental principle of memory: it's not perfect; in fact, sometimes it's far from it. How we remember a person, place, or event depends on a host of factors, many of which we discussed in Chapter 6. Memory is not a simple process of rote retrieval or replay; rather, it's largely a matter of reconstruction. We remember (or reconstruct) past events with the help of fragmentary information, our own expectations and biases, and sometimes those of others.

The material in this chapter may seem a bit hard to accept, perhaps even a little threatening. It's hard for us to acknowledge that something that seems so real and tangible is actually a rather fragile reconstruction that is subject to a host of distortions. These so-called **memory distortions** have become a hot topic in memory research.

The Sins of Memory

Memory researcher Daniel Schacter puts an interesting spin on the processes by which memory fails, calling them the "seven sins of memory," which evokes an image of the biblical "seven deadly sins" (Schacter, 2001). Although the sins of memory may not be deadly, they certainly are frustrating. And as you'll see in our discussions of eyewitness memory and so-called recovered memories of child abuse, these "sins" can have tremendous ramifications. According to Schacter, the sins of memory include **transience,** or the loss of information from memory with the passage of time; **absentmindedness,** which refers to problems with the interface between attention and long-term memory; and **blocking,** which is a failure in retrieving information stored in long-term memory. Schacter classifies transience, absentmindedness, and blocking as *sins of omission*—failures to bring something to mind. These sins of omission have already been discussed: absentmindedness—the culprit responsible for action slips (Chapter 3); transience—forgetting (Chapter 6); blocking—cause of the tip of the tongue and nose phenomena (Chapter 5).

The remaining four sins are *sins of commission;* all of them involve the presence of unwanted or inaccurate memories (Schacter, 2001). **Persistence** refers to the continued (but unwanted) automatic retrieval of memories that we'd just as soon forget. This sin was at the root of the automatic memory retrieval seen in those suffering from PTSD (Chapter 7). In this chapter we will focus primarily on the three other sins of commission. **Misattribution** refers to a memory that is ascribed to the wrong source; you thought one of your friends said something when actually another friend did. **Suggestibility** occurs when someone is led to a false recollection, perhaps through leading questions or others' suggestions. The memory sin of **bias** refers to the influence of who we are—our beliefs, expectations, and desires—on what we remember.

Stop&*Think* | CONFESSING YOUR SINS

Attempt to spot the seven sins of memory, as discussed by Schacter (2001). You could do this in one of two contexts:

1. As you read the chapter, identify the sins (a) as sins of omission or commission and (b) as one of the specific types discussed by Schacter.

2. Keep a journal of memory errors. Log each memory error as a sin of omission or commission and then as one of Schacter's seven sins. Take note of when you are likely to fall victim to each sin and if any patterns emerge.

A classic investigation of reconstructive memory processes was conducted by Carmichael, Hogan, and Walters (1932). These investigators presented participants with ambiguous sketches, each of which could sensibly be interpreted as one of two objects. In Figure 8.1, the first sketch could be interpreted as a broom or a rifle; the second as barbells or eyeglasses; the third as the number 4 or 7. The twist was that participants were given different labels for the presented objects. Half of the participants were told that the pictures were of a broom, barbells, and the number 4; the other half were given the alternative labels—gun, eyeglasses, and the number 7. Later, memory was tested; participants were to draw the figures they had seen. The results revealed that the label had a striking effect on what participants remembered. In spite of the fact that all participants had seen identical sketches, their retrieval sketches were quite different, depending on the label they had received (see Figure 8.1). Gone were the ambiguous-looking sketches that could be interpreted in one of two ways. Participants' sketches depicted completely unambiguous renditions of the objects, renditions that were consistent with the encoded label. Participants who were given the label "broom" sketched a broom; those who were given the label "gun" sketched a gun. The label biased the way the object was encoded and, as result, the way the memory was reconstructed.

An application of Carmichael and colleagues' results isn't hard to come by. Take the "memory fights" we just mentioned. Quite often, people disagree about some sequence of events because they have different labels (i.e., a biased view) for what happened or

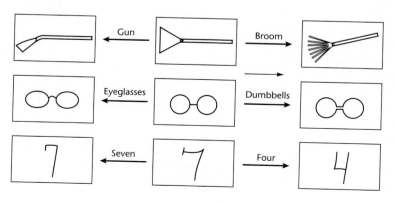

Figure 8.1

Figures presented by Carmichael et al. (1932), along with subjects' reproductions, given different labels for the items.

From Carmichael, L., Hogan, H. P., & Walters, A. A. (1932). An experimental psychology of the effect of language on the reproduction of visually perceived form. *Journal of Experimental Psychology, 15,* 73–86.

what was said. This (along with the results of the Carmichael study) is a clear example of the memory sin of bias (Schacter, 2001)—that is, when expectations and beliefs exert an undue influence on what is remembered.

Stop&*Review*

1. Which of these is considered a memory "sin of omission"?
   a. absentmindedness
   b. misattribution
   c. persistence
   d. suggestibility
2. Identify and define each sin of commission.

- Memory is a reconstructive process that is subject to a host of distortions. The memory sins of omission refer to errors in which information is absent or forgotten. These include blocking (failures to bring something to mind), transience (the loss of information from memory), and absentmindedness (problems with the interface between attention and long-term memory).

- The memory sins of commission refer to the presence of unwanted or inaccurate memories and include misattribution (memory that is ascribed to the wrong source), suggestibility (leading someone to a false recollection), bias (the influence of who we are on what we remember), and persistence (continued automatic retrieval of unwanted memories).

Eyewitness Memory

Although the early work of Carmichael and colleagues (1932) served (in part) as the foundation for later work on the reconstructive nature of memory, the results lay relatively fallow due to the tremendous influence of behaviorism. The fragility of eyewitness memory was empirically investigated by some early psychologists, such as Hugo Munsterberg (often cited as one of the forefathers of applied psychology), but because behaviorism held sway, research on the fallibility of memory in this domain ebbed. As the "cognitive revolution" took firm hold, things began to change, as researchers began to discover the vagaries of eyewitness memory and the consequent implications.

Reality Check

    Consider cases of wrongful conviction, which are increasingly coming to light, given advances in DNA technology. According to the Innocence Project (an organization whose main function is to exonerate via DNA testing those wrongly convicted of crimes), eyewitness misidentification is the single most important factor in producing wrongful convictions, having played a role in 77% of the cases overturned due to DNA evidence. So it would seem that the concern over the accuracy of eyewitness recollection is clearly well justified.

    Countless investigations have been conducted to determine exactly which factors affect the accuracy of eyewitness recollection. One helpful way to organize the findings from this work is by using the tried-and-true distinction between encoding and retrieval introduced in Chapter 6. You'll recall that *encoding* refers to the processes by which information is acquired and stored—that is, the processes through which a memory representation is formed. *Retrieval* refers to the collection of processes that allow us to recall the memory representation, or perhaps more correctly, *reconstruct* it. As stated in Chapter 6, distinguishing between encoding and retrieval factors is largely a matter of descriptive convenience; you can't really discuss one without considering the other. But for descriptive ease, we'll examine factors that are more intimately tied with encoding and storage, followed by those that are more likely to exert an influence on retrieval.

Encoding and Storage I: Event-Related Factors

You are about to read about a host of encoding factors that lead to problems in eyewitness accuracy. The heart of the problem is the difficulty we have in identifying an unfamiliar face after what usually amounts to a brief encounter during the commission of a crime. An intuitive inference you might make is that we are good at facial identification (how many of you have said "I never forget a face"?) and all of these soon-to-be-discussed factors disrupt an otherwise efficient and accurate process. Well let's just nip that inference in the bud. A distressing series of studies by Megreya and Burton (2008) indicates that all of the factors we are about to discuss exacerbate a problem we have even without any of the complicating factors. Faces are just plain hard to distinguish from one another when placed side by side! These researchers compared memory for faces presented live or in photos. The procedure was simple as can be. In the live condition, participants watched as targets walked to the front of the room, and stood there for 30 seconds, during which the participants were to encode the face. After a five-second blank period, a 10-photo array was presented, and participants were to choose the person who had just stood in front of them for 30 seconds. In the static condition, the same basic procedure was done using photos rather than a live presentation.

The results were surprising, to say the least. You would think that a 30 second exposure to a face would make it ridiculously easy to identify that face a mere five seconds later; recognition should be perfect. Guess again; overall accuracy was only about 66%, with a fair number of misses (failing to pick the person) and false alarms (picking the wrong person). As Megreva and Burton (2008) indicate, this is especially striking given that participants weren't subject to *any* of the factors we are about to discuss that have been shown to compromise eyewitness memory. This mediocre identification performance occurred under optimal conditions that would never be achieved in an actual forensic setting, so the implications of these findings are unsettling, to say the least. Now that we know the starting point in our ability to identify an unfamiliar face, let's discuss all of the factors that make it even more difficult.

Some of these factors are relatively straightforward, so we're not going to discuss them at length, but they do merit mention. The more obvious factors include the quality of the viewing conditions and the specific aspects of the event. Was it day or night? Were you a short or long distance away? What was your viewing angle? How long did the event last? Did you know you were witnessing a crime? Did the culprit wear a disguise? The influence of all of these factors is fairly intuitive. But the effects of the next variable we'll mention—emotional stress—isn't so intuitive.

Research Theme
Emotion

Stress and Trauma.   Towards the end of Chapter 7 we discussed the role of emotion in autobiographical memory for trauma. In our discussion we referred to an article by Brewin (2007), who outlined four areas of controversy in memory for trauma. We discussed one of those areas in Chapter 7 and we'll be discussing the other three in this chapter. The first of these controversies relates to the issue of whether memory for trauma is particularly good or bad. This question comes into clear focus when considering the effects of stress on event memory. Comparing the stress experienced by an eyewitness to a bank robbery to the stress experienced by someone in a POW camp might seem a bit like comparing a paper cut to open heart surgery. However, some of the same principles come into play in both situations; stress can disrupt or enhance memory, depending on the particular circumstances.

One way in which the effects of stress can manifest themselves in an eyewitness scenario is through a phenomenon termed **weapon focus.** The presence of a weapon can serve to focus one's attention quite narrowly, resulting in a lack of peripheral detail (e.g., the features of the perpetrator) in the memory representation, although the central detail (e.g., the weapon) is remembered quite well (Cutler, Penrod, & Martens, 1987; Kramer, Buckhout, & Eugenio, 1989). The central details of the event tend to be elaborated upon later as we "tell the story," further benefitting memory for central details. This general principle has been referred to as *memory narrowing* (Reisberg & Heuer, 2004) or *tunnel memory* (Safer, Christianson, Autry, & Osterlund, 1998). The weapon focus effect would seem to be as an instance of this. There is no doubt as to the centrality of a weapon when it appears in an event. It's no surprise then, that it becomes the most salient aspect of one's memory for that event.

As Brewin (2007) points out, the neat and tidy distinction between central and peripheral is not so clear in the context of trauma. Traumatic events involve varied experiences that can be extended over time. It is unclear which details would be considered "peripheral" and which would be "central." This is supported by some startling findings from a study by Morgan, Hazlett, Doran, Garrett, Hoyt, Thomas, Baranoski, and Southwick (2004), which offered a rare opportunity to do an experimentally controlled study of memory for a traumatically stressful event. To accomplish this, Morgan et al. received permission to test recruits in the U.S. Army's survival school training program. The program is extremely intense, and according to Morgan et al., provides a valid model for testing the effects of "threat-to-life" stress in humans. The training program involves two main phases: A classroom training program followed by an experiential immersion in a mock prisoner-of-war camp. During this phase, each participant is isolated and exposed to a variety of interrogation techniques that are designed to push the recruits to the limit. Physiological measures confirm the extreme stress experienced by recruits during this phase of training.

A frighteningly central detail.

Morgan et al. were interested in how the extreme stress experienced by the participants would impact memory for their interrogator. The investigators make note of previous findings for enhanced identification of central objects in emotional circumstances, however, in none of these studies had participants been exposed to circumstances that rose to the level of trauma, as would be experienced by participants in this survival camp. During interrogation, participants were in a room with an interrogator and a guard. In the high-stress condition, participants were physically confronted by the guard if they weren't complying satisfactorily with the interrogator. In the low-stress condition, no physical confrontation was involved, but the participant was intellectually challenged as the interrogator tried to trick him into a response. Participants took part in each condition, the order of which was counterbalanced. Participants were asked to identify the interrogator from each phase, under a number of different lineup conditions (we'll talk about lineups in more detail later), each with 15 faces to look at in order to ID the interrogator.

The staggering results are presented in Table 8.1, which plots two of the dependent variables. Not only did high stress not aid in memory for the face of the interrogator, it was highly detrimental. When under traumatic stress, participants did such a miserable job of encoding the face that they were both less likely to identify it (correct ID) and more likely to pick a wrong one (false positive). Think about how surprising this finding is; after being physically confronted by this person and subjected to 30 minutes of intense exposure, their memory for arguably the most central detail—the interrogator's face—was relatively poor. Clearly, the effects of emotion and trauma on memory mechanisms are incredibly complex, as alluded to in Chapters 6 and 7. So what could possibly account for *both* the narrowing of attention to one central detail as in weapon focus, and the *exclusion* of the central detail evident in the Morgan et al. study?

One possible resolution comes from Deffenbacher (1994), who observes that cognitive and bodily reactions to stress can vary widely as a function of the event, and the precise nature of this reaction is critical for determining the quality of the resulting memory. One critical factor is the attentional mode that is present when the event occurs. The *arousal mode* is engaged when the observer is physiologically relaxed and the task requires simple perceptual intake. In this mode, novel, surprising, and informative events receive the most attention, and will be remembered well. According to Deffenbacher, Bornstein, Penrod, & McGorty (2004), much of the research demonstrating the enhancement of central details in eyewitness memory would fit into this category.

The picture changes when we consider the second mode of attention, what Deffenbacher (1994) terms the *activation mode*. This mode is engaged when a person is

Table 8.1 **Results from the Morgan et al. study of identification memory in officers with intense military training. High stress conditions severely disrupt memory.**

	Correct Identifications	False Alarms
High Stress	.30	.56
Low Stress	.62	.38

experiencing high levels of both cognitive anxiety (worry) and physiological activation (bodily manifestations of anxiety). If physiological activation becomes too intense, it results in what Deffenbacher (1994) refers to as a catastrophic, discontinuous drop in performance. In other words, if someone is worried enough and is experiencing acute physiological arousal, their encoding of an event will suffer profoundly, even for the central details (Payne, Jackson, Ryan, Hoscheidt, Jacobs, & Nadel, 2006). This would account for the failure to recognize the interrogator's face in the high-stress condition of the Morgan et al. (2004) study. The most interesting aspect of this account is its prediction of a nonlinear relationship between physiological activation and memory under conditions of high cognitive anxiety. Under high levels of cognitive anxiety, increasing the physiological arousal will lead to increasingly good memory (as in the case with weapon focus), but only to a point, beyond which memory is severely impaired.

Another account of emotion's role in remembering is offered by Levine and Edelstein (2009), who propose that memory is indeed enhanced by a narrowing of attention that focuses one on central details. However, the rub is the operational definition of a central detail. According to Levine and Edelstein a stimulus is central if it relates to a person's goals. So the same detail might be central or peripheral, depending on the particular person's mindset. In the Morgan et al. study, the goal of the soldiers might have been to simply get through the experience, which would have essentially made any physical detail in the situation a peripheral one, not particularly likely to be remembered. When a gun is pointing at you, your goal is to avoid being shot, hence the gun becomes the central detail and is likely to be remembered.

Regardless of which view provides the most complete account of the effects of emotion on memory, it's clear that these effects are complex, nuanced, and dependent on a host of variables that all play an important role in determining whether an event will be remembered accurately. We'll return to this difficult question in our final section on the recovered memory controversy.

Other-Race Effect.   One of the more intriguing factors that can influence eyewitness accuracy involves an interaction between the race of the observer and the race of the observed. Research on face recognition (discussed in Chapter 5) demonstrates that people are better at recognizing faces of their own race relative to faces of other races (Behrman & Davey, 2001; Shapiro & Penrod, 1986). A meta-analytic review of 39 laboratory studies of the **other-race effect** by Meissner and Brigham (2001) indicates that the chance of mistaken identification is 1.5 times greater when the perpetrator is a different race than the witness. The extent of the other-race effect in real life cases is unknown but an estimate can be generated by examining DNA exoneration cases that involved cross-racial identification (gathered by the Innocence Project). A meta-analytic review of 77 mistaken eyewitness identifications by Scheck, Neufield, and Dwyer (2000) found that 35% of misidentifications were white witnesses misidentifying black suspects, whereas only 28% were cases of white witnesses misidentifying white suspects. Gross, Jacoby, Matheson, Montgomery, and Patil (2004) provide another piece of compelling evidence based on DNA exonerations. Between 1989 and 2003 just under half of the rape exonerations in which the race of both parties were known involved the conviction of a black man for raping a white woman. While interracial rape is uncommon (only about 10% of rapes involve a black man and white woman), problems in cross-racial identification no doubt play some role in these false convictions.

Encoding and Storage II: Post-Event Factors

One fact about memory that will become increasingly obvious over the course of this chapter is that memory is not some fixed entity. Memory is a reconstructive *process* and therefore malleable. This process can be profoundly influenced by what are termed *post-event factors*—events that occur after the originally encoded event.

Misinformation. The **misinformation effect** refers to the finding that misleading information presented between the encoding of an event and its subsequent recall influences a witness's memory. This corresponds to two of the memory sins discussed earlier. First, it reflects suggestibility—sometimes our recollections are unduly influenced by the prodding or expectations of others. Second, it's often an instance of misattribution, as witnesses get confused and misattributes the misinformation to the original event. By the way, this effect is also an example of a type of interference that we discussed in Chapter 4—retroactive interference. You'll recall that retroactive interference occurs when later information interferes with the ability to retain previously encoded information. This is precisely what happens with the misinformation effect. The misleading information works backward in time to distort memory for the original event.

The methodology used to investigate the misinformation effect is the granddaddy of paradigms for investigating memory distortion in eyewitness memory, having spurred over 30 years of research that is still going strong (see Loftus, 2005, for a review). This methodology is demonstrated in a classic study by Loftus, Miller, and Burns (1978). In the first phase of the study, participants viewed a series of color slides depicting an auto accident. For half of the participants, one of the slides depicted a car at a stop sign; for the other half, it was a yield sign. In the second phase of the experiment, 20 questions were asked about the slide sequence. Some participants were asked, "Did another car pass the red Datsun when it stopped at the yield sign?" and others were asked, "Did another car pass the red Datsun when it stopped at the stop sign?" So half the participants were misled, and the other half were given consistent information. A short time later, participants were given pairs of slides, and were asked to pick the one that came from the original series.

Participants given consistent information in the questionnaire chose correctly 75% of the time; those who were misled by the questionnaire chose correctly only 40% of the time. Loftus et al. concluded that the misleading information altered participants' versions of the events, leading to errant event recall. You may wonder whether small details such as those just discussed really matter; they seem fairly trivial. But, these details are anything but trivial and matter tremendously. A jury's perception of a defendant's guilt or innocence could turn on such a detail. If a witness remembers a mustache or a weapon when there was none, the wrong person may find themselves on the wrong side of prison bars.

Stop&*Think* | IMPLANT SOME MISINFORMATION

Be careful with this demonstration. See if you can implant a piece of misinformation. You'll want to take advantage of some of the memory principles you've read about. Pick an event that happened a while ago and one that you think your friends might be a little fuzzy on. Try and convince them of some detail that isn't true. (This, of course, assumes that you have a fairly good memory of the event in question!)

- Were you successful in your attempt?
- Why were you or weren't you?
- What was it about the original event (and/or the misinformation) that made it particularly malleable or nonmalleable?

Unconscious Transference. Sometimes previous exposure to someone, either through a photo array in a police station or through a chance encounter, can make that person seem familiar at a later point, sometimes with near-tragic consequences. In *Witness for the Defense*, Loftus and Ketcham (1991) relate the story of Howard Haupt, who was charged with the kidnapping and murder of a child in Las Vegas. The crimes had occurred near a hotel where Haupt had been a guest. Several witnesses saw a man luring the boy from the hotel's video arcade and walking with him through the hotel. Haupt was wrongly identified as that man. Two explanations for this possible misidentification are possible. One explanation is termed photo bias, which we will discuss later. The other explanation is termed **unconscious transference,** which occurs when witnesses fail to distinguish between a target person (i.e., a criminal) and another person encountered at a different time whose face is also familiar (Loftus, 1976). This may have been at play in the Haupt case; witnesses did see Howard Haupt at the hotel where the crime took place. The witnesses may have seen his face as well as the kidnapper's face and assumed that the two people were one and the same. Therefore, when presented with his face at a later point in time, they identified Haupt as the kidnapper. (Due in part to Loftus's testimony assailing the reliability of the eyewitness identifications, Haupt was acquitted of the charges.)

A recent analysis of unconscious transference by Davis, Loftus, Vanous, and Cucciare (2008) attributes the phenomenon, at least in part, to an old friend from Chapter 3—change blindness. As you know from the "gorilla study" (Simons & Chabris, 1999) people can fail to notice even salient changes in their environment. If people fail to notice a gorilla in the middle of a basketball game, it seems quite likely that they almost would be guaranteed to miss the much more subtle difference between the face of the perpetrator and the face of a suspect. You might be thinking, "Wait; these witnessing situations are completely different—the gorilla paradigm and the eyewitnessing paradigm are apples and oranges!" After all, the participants in the gorilla study weren't really looking at the gorilla, and were basically tricked into missing it. But in an eyewitness situation, a witness *is* looking (sometimes directly) at the perpetrator. But as we mentioned earlier, even looking directly at a face doesn't guarantee that a face will be identified, so these two attentional situations are actually more similar than you think.

Some studies of change blindness have used exactly this type of situation and shown that the finding extends beyond just gorillas walking through basketball games. For example, Levin, Simons, Angelone, and Chabris (2002) found that an actor with whom a person is directly interacting could change without the person noticing! Hard to believe, but true. Given that seeing is believing, check out the University of Illinois website by Dr. Daniel Simons for some rather unbelievable demonstrations of this exact scenario (http://viscog.beckman.illinois.edu/djs_lab/demos.html). Or maybe you could ask your professor to show some clips during class....

Davis, Loftus, Vanous, and Cucciare (2008) were interested in whether change blindness could play a role in producing the misidentification of an innocent suspect. This could occur through what Levin and Simons (2000) term illusions of continuity, whereby a perceiver misperceives continuity between two scenes or situations due to their own propensity to fill in gaps via top-down processing. Top down processing leads us to see what we *expect* to see; we expect to see continuity in the visual scene we're looking at, and so we do. But as change blindness indicates, this continuity is sometimes an illusion. Davis et al. contend that this analysis applies to the encoding of individuals during real-world crime situations. They provide the following example: Say you're in a convenience store and you see someone come in and go down the first aisle; subsequently, you see someone come out of the second aisle brandishing a gun and demanding money from the cashier. The illusion of continuity might lead you to believe it was the same person you saw walk down the first aisle. Such confusion would obviously have ramifications for the later identification.

In order to test this idea, Davis et al. (2008) showed participants a video of a staged crime involving a perpetrator, and two innocent bystanders. The scenario began with one of the innocent bystanders (the continuous innocent) entering an aisle and looking at products; when she reached the middle of the aisle, she passed behind a large stack of napkin boxes. At that point, the perpetrator emerged from behind the stack, and walked down the remainder of the aisle furtively, taking a bottle of wine. The camera then switched views to the produce section, where the other innocent bystander (the discontinuous innocent) was looking at oranges and then walked out of view. The dependent variable was accuracy at identifying the perpetrator in a lineup that contained the perpetrator, both innocents, and three nonencountered individuals who never appeared in the video. Based on change blindness research and the notion of the illusion of continuity, Davis et al. (2008) predicted that the participants would be more likely to misidentify the continuous innocent than the discontinuous innocent as the culprit.

Consistent with change blindness research discussed in Chapter 3, the majority of participants (60%) missed the switcheroo behind the napkin boxes. An even larger proportion (73%) misidentified an innocent person in the lineup test. This misidentification was more likely for those who did not notice the change than for those who did. Of primary interest for the illusion of continuity hypothesis was the relative probability of misidentifying the continuous and the discontinuous innocent. Davis et al. found that, of participants who missed the change event, 41% misidentified the continuous innocent, and only 23% misidentified the discontinuous innocent. This pattern was reversed in participants who noticed the change. Of these participants, only 10% misidentified the continuous innocent, and 25% misidentified the discontinuous innocent. Clearly, participants who missed the person-switching event behind the napkin boxes believed the person entering the aisle and the person emerging from behind the napkin boxes and stealing the wine were the same person.

Davis et al.'s (2008) results lead to a number of informative, albeit disconcerting, conclusions. Change detection and picking the correct person in the lineup proved to be exceedingly difficult for participants. Failures to detect change were associated with higher rates of misidentification, particularly of the continuous innocent. This supports the notion that unconscious transference had occurred. As you'll recall from a couple of pages back, unconscious transference occurs when witnesses fail to distinguish between a target person (i.e., a perpetrator) and another person encountered at a different time (an innocent bystander). In the Davis et al. study the time between encountering the perpetrator and the innocent bystander was a matter of seconds. Hence, confusion between the two was likely, still disturbing but maybe not all that surprising. But it's important to remember that the discontinuous innocent was misidentified 23% of the time, which was significantly higher than the number of nonencountered individuals who were misidentified (13%). This shows that even the discontinuous innocent was likely to be confused with the actual perpetrator (another victim of unconscious transference).

Photo Bias.   Perfect and Harris (2003) provide a specific example of unconscious transference known as **photo bias,** which refers to the increase in probability that a person will be recognized as the culprit due to previous exposure in a photo. Brown, Deffenbacher, and Sturgill (1977) were among the first to demonstrate this phenomenon. They had participants view two groups of five individuals labeled "criminals" for 25 seconds each; they were told that later they might be required to identify the individuals. After viewing the criminals, participants were exposed to 15 mug shot pictures. Some of the mug shots were of the original "criminals," and some were not. A week later, lineups were staged, and participants had to determine whether each included was one of the original 25 "criminals." There was a strong influence of mug shots on the selection of "noncriminals." Witnesses were more than twice as likely to incorrectly identify "noncriminals" who were included in the mug shots than "noncriminals" who were not viewed in the mug shots (20% vs. 8%). Obviously, presentation of the photos led participants to have a vague familiarity with the faces that was then wrongly attributed to the original "crime."

Let's reconsider the Haupt case and its relationship to the phenomenon of photo bias. There is one fact that we left out when we told the story—at first, witnesses saw Haupt's picture in a photo array, yet he was never chosen as the culprit (Loftus & Ketcham, 1991). Subsequently, each witness was taken to Haupt's place of work; he was viewed in isolation and, hence, was the only choice. In this context he was identified by several witnesses as the man seen walking with the boy at the hotel months earlier. The problem with this identification should be obvious—witnesses had seen Haupt in the photo array; therefore, he was a familiar face. Their later recognition of him may have resulted from the misattribution of this familiarity—they decided that, because he was familiar, he must have been the person walking with the victim. This explanation is particularly compelling when you consider that no one identified him as the kidnapper in the original photo array.

Retrieval Factors

Eyewitness accuracy (or inaccuracy, as you've seen) is not just a product of how events are encoded and stored. The way in which memory is queried also determines what will be remembered or at least what people are willing to report. Let's examine some of these factors.

Lineups. Attempting to remember a witnessed event can be likened to a recall test. Little or nothing in the way of cues is presented, and the person must provide an accurate summary of what they witnessed. Attempting to identify which of several people committed a crime can be likened to a recognition test. When presented with a lineup of people (via either a photo array or a live presentation), a variety of factors can affect whether a choice is made and whether that choice is accurate. In other words, eyewitness identification is influenced by the specifics of the retrieval environment (for a review, see Wells & Olson, 2003).

Let's consider four possible outcomes in a lineup situation. The first is a *correct rejection*—the culprit (the person who actually committed the crime) is not in the lineup, and the witness correctly states that the culprit is not there. The second is a *correct identification*—the culprit is in the lineup, and the witness correctly identifies the person. The third is an *identification failure*—the culprit is in the lineup, but the witness does not identify anyone in the lineup. This is clearly a negative outcome, because the criminal goes back on the street. The fourth is an *incorrect identification*—a person other than the culprit is chosen from the lineup. This outcome is doubly negative and highly undesirable; the real criminal is still free, and the wrong person is accused of the crime.

Given all of the encoding factors we just discussed you're probably thinking that an eyewitness has plenty of reason to lack confidence in their identification of a suspect from a lineup (but remember, they haven't read this chapter...). Despite the fact that uncertainty is called for in many circumstances, (and in spite of the fact that a witness might feel uncertain), innocents are often misidentified as culprits. For the dispassionate observer, it might seem puzzling why an unsure witness would make a choice from a lineup when they don't recognize (or are unsure that they recognize) the perpetrator. Why don't they just say "The person isn't there."? Wells (1984) explains that the choice in these situations is the likely result of *pressure* and *preference*. Faced with a lineup, how could a person *not* feel considerable pressure to make a positive ID? They witnessed the perpetrator, the police officers standing there expect a choice, and if they fail, the bad guy goes free. The witness who really doesn't know will likely form some sort of preference, because there will be a person in the lineup who looks more like the perpetrator than the others. This preference is a critical (mis)step that can lead to eventual misidentification. No one wants this outcome; the goal of a lineup is not to nab *someone*; the goal is to identify the person responsible for the crime.

The goal then, is to construct lineups in such a way as to maximize correct identifications and correct rejections and to minimize identification failures and incorrect identifications. Unfortunately, this ideal is often difficult to attain; due to the vagaries of memory, as well as the situational pressures of the identification scenario, mistakes occur. But tremendous progress has been made as the result of three decades of research on eyewitness identification.

In 1999, based largely on the research of cognitive psychologists, the U.S. Justice Department issued the first national guide for the collection and preservation of eyewitness evidence. As noted by Wells, Malpass, Lindsay, Fisher, Turtle, and Fulero (2000), psychological research (along with DNA-based exonerations and media pressure) played a large role in demonstrating the need for these guidelines and also provided the scientific foundation for their content. Several of the recommendations in these guidelines have become standard procedure in a number of jurisdictions, including the State of New Jersey, the State of North Carolina, Madison, Wisconsin, and our own home city of Minneapolis, Minnesota. In the following section, we discuss these main guidelines, along with some of the research and thinking that lies behind each. Most of the recommendations proposed relate to lineup structure and lineup instructions.

Lineup Structure. The makeup of a lineup should comprise a reasonable and fair memory test for the witness. It's in many ways like a multiple choice test. You no doubt have some intuitions about what makes a good multiple choice item ("good" as defined by a reasonable and fair test of what you know about a concept). A set of choices shouldn't draw you toward one particular response because it's obvious, and the lure responses (the nonanswers) should be feasible foils for a person who really doesn't know the answer.

Similar principles apply to lineups and photo arrays. Imagine a lineup in which the suspect is 20 years old and rather seedy looking and the other five members are 30-something professionals in suits. Of course, the seedy individual will stick out like a guilty thumb. In this case, the lineup size is not really six; it's one. The **functional size** of a lineup is a reflection of the probability that any one person might be selected based just on how they look. To assess functional size, Wells, Leippe, & Ostrom (1979) propose that one needs to look at nonwitnesses to the crime and who they choose from the lineup. If you think about it, someone who did not witness the crime should be equally likely to choose any of the people in the lineup as the culprit (just like a person with absolutely no exposure to course material should be equally likely to pick any alternative on a multiple choice test).

So what constitutes a "reasonable distractor"? Wells, Rydell, and Seelau (1993) compared lineups in which the distractors matched the appearance of the suspect to lineups in which the distractors matched the witness description of the culprit. Matching distractors in terms of suspect appearance has the potential to inadvertently provide information that witnesses may not have noticed, altering their memory for the culprit ala the misinformation effect (e.g., "Gee, all of these people have a big nose; I didn't really notice, but I guess my mugger must have had a big nose"). In contrast, matching to the witness description of the culprit may allow for the exoneration of a nonculprit who has a noticeable feature that was not part of the description (e.g., "Well, I know it can't be that guy, because that guy has kind of a big nose; my mugger didn't have a big nose"). Consistent with this analysis, Wells and colleagues found that when lineup distractors were matched in terms of the culprit's description rather than the suspect's appearance, the correct identification rate increased and the incorrect identification rate decreased.

Sequential vs. Simultaneous Lineups. Perhaps the most influential (and most contentious) change that has been recommended is the use of a sequential lineup, rather than the lineup you see in the movies and on TV. This type of lineup is termed a **simultaneous lineup** with lineup members presented at the same time, and the witness must choose one. A **sequential lineup** presentation is the rarer case; lineup members are presented one at a time, and the witness must decide whether each of the lineup members is or is not the culprit. Investigations of both modes of presentation have indicated that sequential line-ups are superior (Lindsay & Wells, 1985).

According to Wells (1993), sequential lineups are preferable to simultaneous ones due to the different strategies that the two invoke. Simultaneous lineups encourage wit-nesses to use a *relative judgment strategy* in which witnesses evaluate which of the lineup members most resembles the culprit they have in mind. Wells contends that this strategy encourages witnesses to pick someone. Sequential lineups, on the other hand, encourage an *absolute judgment strategy* in which witnesses are more likely to assess each individual in isolation, asking themselves, "Is this the one?" In addition to differences in judgment strategy employed, witnesses in a sequential lineup scenario are unaware of how many people are in the lineup; they never know if one more person might be coming and therefore will experience less pressure to pick someone.

Although research has borne out that sequential lineup procedures decrease the rate of false identification (Steblay, Dysart, Fulero, & Lindsay, 2001), there does appear to be a downside in that rates of correct identifications are also reduced. Ebbesen and Flowe (2002) contend that the reason for both of these outcomes is that sequential lineups raise the response criterion of the witness. You might remember the notion of response bias from our Chapter 2 discussion of perception. Response criterion basically refers to one's willingness to report the presence of a stimulus. In this case, it refers to the willingness of the witness to pick someone. Ebbesen and Flowe's account is that sequential lineups result in an across-the-board conservative tendency. Witnesses are less likely to identify *anyone* from the lineup even when the culprit is present.

In spite of the strenuous recommendation of sequential lineups by some (e.g Lindsay, Mansour, Beaudry, Leach, & Bertrand, 2009; Steblay, Dysart, Fulero, & Lindsay, 2001) and their adoption by many legal jurisdictions (some mentioned earlier), the issue of their superiority remains something of an empirical hot potato. The sequential over simultaneous advantage seems to be contingent on a variety of variables, including the position of suspects in the lineup (e.g., Carlson, Gronlund, & Clark, 2008), and the quality of the viewing situation in which a suspect was seen (e.g., Gronlund, Carlson, Dailey, & Goodsell, 2009). Given that sequential or simultaneous lineups can be shown to be superior under different circumstances, Gronlund et al. (2009) recommend a the-ory-driven approach to figuring out the actual mechanisms that underlie lineup choice in different conditions rather than the "which technique is better?" approach that has characterized much of the research.

Lineup Administration.   Other recommendations for ensuring lineup effectiveness and fairness relate to how the lineup test is presented to witnesses. These recommendations are aimed squarely at attempting to deal with the *pressure and preference* issue discussed ear-lier. To alleviate the pressure felt by unsure witnesses faced with a set of faces about which they're not confident, one recommendation is to be sure to instruct witnesses that the sus-pect may not be in the lineup. This simple modification eases the pressure on a witness, making a nonchoice more transparently acceptable. Another measure recommended to ease the pressure on eyewitnesses is to have the administrator of the lineup be "blind" as to the presence and identity of the suspect in the lineup. Just as an effective and unbiased researcher must be careful not to exert any influence on the participants of their study, an effective and unbiased investigator must not exert undue influence on an eyewitness making a choice. A double-blind procedure helps safeguard against this possibility.

Reality Check

Another important benefit that derives from the double-blind procedure relates to witness confidence. Researchers have revealed a number of facts about witness confidence that, considered together, are disturbing. First, the relationship between confidence and accuracy is not nearly as strong as you might think (Wells & Murray, 1984; Sporer, Penrod, Reed, & Cutler, 1995). In other words, the fact that a witness is confident is not a good indicator of their accuracy, but people think that it is (e.g., Wells, Olson, & Charman, 2002). Research reveals that juries tend to overbelieve witnesses, particularly confident ones (Cutler & Penrod, 1995). This exaggerated belief is even more disturbing in light of another finding—eyewitness confidence is malleable. When eyewitnesses are given confirmatory feedback about their eyewitness identification (e.g., "Yes, other people identified that person as well"), they become more confident about what they're reporting (e.g., Wells, Ferguson, & Lindsay, 1981; Wells & Luus, 1990). This brings us back to the importance of the double-blind procedure. If a lineup administrator is blind to the identity of the perpetrator, they cannot give the confidence-inflating feedback that proves to be so influential to juries.

But before you rush to the conclusion that confidence provides no information about witness accuracy, we need to present an empirically based qualification. A variable related to confidence—speed of identification—might be a useful diagnostic in assessing eyewitness identification. Imagine the confident witness who sizes up the photo array or live lineup and, within just a few seconds, has made a confident choice. You might think this identification is more reliable than that of the witness who hems and haws and takes a much longer time to decide. A host of studies have found just this type of relationship. The less time taken to make a choice, the more likely it is to be correct (e.g., Dunning & Perretta, 2002; Sporer, 1994; Sauerland & Sporer, 2009; Weber & Brewer, 2006). Information like this could prove useful to law enforcement personnel as they attempt to assess the accuracy of eyewitness identifications (Brewer & Wells, 2006).

Is a confident witness a more accurate one?

Interview Techniques. In Chapter 6, you learned that memory is critically dependent on the way in which memory is tested. Different results are obtained on recall and recognition tests as well as on implicit and explicit memory tests. It should come as no surprise, then, that the way in which an eyewitness is "tested" (i.e., interviewed) has important ramifications for the completeness and accuracy of their report.

Reality Check

Hypnosis. A popular assumption about memory is that everything is stored, and that given the right retrieval prompt or method, a memory will be "unlocked" and relayed accurately. You've already been presented with a good deal of evidence showing that this is simply not the case. A corollary to this common assumption is a belief that hypnosis can be used during retrieval as a way to reach and replay memories that are proving difficult to access. Research on hypnosis, however, provides no conclusive evidence that it reliably enhances memory (Smith, 1983). Hypnosis may lead to an increase in the amount of information reported, but this increase is for both correct detail and fabricated detail (termed **confabulation**). The heightened suggestibility associated with hypnosis makes the rememberer more willing to label something as a memory; it also makes one highly susceptible to the suggestions of others. There are several deleterious consequences of this suggestibility. First, requests for further information may be met with compliance, even if the witness doesn't have anything else to report. Second, the suggestions to which the witness does respond may well become incorporated in their memory for the event (i.e., the misinformation effect; see Scoboria, Mazzoni, Kirsch, & Milling, 2002). Third, hypnosis often involves instructions to imagine the target event. As you'll read later, the simple act of imagining how events may have occurred can lead a person to be less certain about whether they actually did occur (e.g., Hyman & Pentland, 1996). It is generally accepted that the use of hypnosis at retrieval is fraught with problems and should be avoided, particularly given that there's a better alternative: the cognitive interview.

You're getting verrrry sleepy.... and verrry likely to report false memories.

Cognitive Interview.   It's apparent that the reports and identifications offered by eyewitnesses can be distorted by a number of untoward influences. Concern over these influences led a group of researchers to develop the **cognitive interview technique** (Fisher & Geiselman, 1992). The cognitive interview has four primary features. First, there is an attempt to make the witness comfortable (e.g., by engaging in some relaxing and ice-breaking conversation at the beginning of the interview). Second, the witness is queried with *open-ended questions* (e.g., "Tell me what happened") that elicit answers with multiple pieces of information, rather than with *closed-ended questions* (e.g., "Where did the culprit put the money?") that elicit one specific piece of information and abbreviated answers. These latter types of questions are typical of police interviews. Third, the cognitive interview takes advantage of what we know about memory by implementing mnemonic instructions that can facilitate memory. For example, witnesses are encouraged to mentally reinstate the context of the encoded event (Dando, Wilcock, & Milne, 2009) and to try to recall the event from different perspectives and in different orders, using as many different retrieval pathways as possible (e.g., Anderson & Pichert, 1978). Both of these techniques take advantage of that tried-and-true principle from Chapter 6—encoding specificity (Tulving & Thomson, 1973).

A fourth feature of the cognitive interview is allowing witnesses some freedom in exactly how they describe events (e.g., using sketches).

The cognitive interview has become the preferred technique for interviewing witnesses to a crime (e.g., Wells, Malpass, Lindsay, Fisher, Turtle, & Fulero, 2000) and has met with good success. Compared to a standard police interview, the cognitive interview elicits anywhere from 35 to 75% more information, with no increase in confabulated information (e.g., Kohnken, Milne, Memon, & Bull, 1999).

Stop&Review

1. Describe the other-race effect.
2. Identify the post-event factors that can affect eyewitness accuracy.
3. The relationship between confidence and memory accuracy tends to be
   a. strong and positive.
   b. weak and positive.
   c. strong and negative.
   d. weak and negative.

- Eyewitness testimony is fallible and is affected by many factors that operate at encoding/storage, such as quality of viewing conditions and level of attention. Emotional stress can narrow the focus of attention and lead to decreased recall of (particularly) peripheral details. The other-race effect refers to increased difficulty in discriminating among faces of another race relative to faces of one's own race.

- A number of post-event factors can influence one's memory for an event.

Exposure to misinformation increases the chances of misremembering. Exposure to someone through a chance encounter (unconscious transference) or in a photo (photo bias) will make the person seem familiar and increase the chance of being misidentified as the culprit in a crime. A number of retrieval factors influence eyewitness memory, especially issues surrounding lineups—how they are constructed, how the distractors are chosen, and the functional size of the lineup.

- Other retrieval factors include hypnosis, which can increase recall, but at the expense of increased confabulation. A high level of confidence turns out to be, at best, a relatively weak indicator of memory accuracy, but witnesses who make a quick identification tend to be accurate. The cognitive interview technique implements principles of memory to enhance witness recall.

Illusory Memories

Research investigating the vagaries of eyewitness testimony leaves little doubt about the fragile nature of our reconstructions of previous events. It doesn't take much to tweak your memory for an event so that you remember seeing a Sprite can instead of a Coke can. Although this may seem somewhat disconcerting, maybe it's not surprising. But what may come as a surprise is the ease with which a memory can be created out of thin air.

Simple Events

Sometimes—more often than you might think—people can remember something that flat out did not happen. An ever-growing body of evidence studying the phenomenon of **illusory memories** (or **memory illusions** or **false memories**) has generally taken one of two basic tacks: one is a laboratory paradigm employing the basic list-learning approach discussed in Chapter 6. The other, partly in response to concerns of ecological validity, attempts to determine whether illusory memories can occur for everyday events like getting lost at a shopping mall.

The Deese-Roediger-McDermott (DRM) Paradigm.

Much of the recent focus on memory illusions stems from an investigation conducted by Roediger and McDermott (1995). These investigators scoured the periodical stacks in the library and then blew the dust off of a 1959 study by Deese, the subject of which was "particular verbal intrusions in list recall"—in other words, remembering words that had not occurred (i.e., intrusions) in presented lists. Participants saw lists of related words like *doze, rest,* and *snore* that all related to a theme word—in this case, *sleep.* But the theme word was never presented. In spite of this, it often was "remembered" by participants. Does this effect sound familiar? In our discussion of prototypes in Chapter 5, we reviewed a study by Posner, Goldsmith, and Welton (1967) that bears a striking resemblance to the Deese study. In the Posner study, participants were presented with dot patterns that were statistically generated distortions of a prototype. The parallel in the Deese study was words related to a particular theme. In the study by Posner and colleagues, the prototype itself was never presented, just as the theme word was never presented in the Deese study. In both studies participants tended to confidently confirm that they had seen the never-presented item. In the Posner and colleagues study, this was the prototype dot pattern; in the Deese study, it was the never-presented theme word.

Stop & *Think Back* | THE MEMORY DISTORTION FAMILY

Memory distortions bear a strong resemblance to prototypes, as we discuss in the text. Think about this relationship, and flip back to Chapter 5 to peruse the characteristics of prototypes (i.e., family resemblance, etc.). Think about what types of your personal memories are especially prone to converting into prototypes (in other words, you hang out with your friends at a particular place so often, that the memory becomes a "prototype," probably with some omissions and distortion). How do these memories exhibit "family resemblance" and the other characteristics of a prototype?

Roediger and McDermott (1995) replicated and extended the Deese study in an attempt to illuminate the nature of illusory memories. They adapted the Deese procedure in order to investigate false recognition as well as false recall. In Experiment 2, all participants were presented with a series of 15-word themed lists (a sample of the lists is presented in Table 8.2), followed by an immediate test of recall. After all lists had been

Table 8.2 **Themed Lists Used in the Illusory Memory Study of Roediger and McDermott (1995)**

Rough	Sleep	Slow	Soft
Smooth	bed	fast	hard
bumpy	rest	lethargic	light
road	awake	stop	pillow
tough	tired	listless	plush
sandpaper	dream	snail	loud
jagged	wake	cautious	cotton
ready	snooze	delay	fur
coarse	blanket	traffic	touch
uneven	doze	turtle	fluffy
riders	slumber	hesitant	feather
rugged	snore	speed	furry
sand	nap	quick	downy
boards	peace	sluggish	kitten
ground	yawn	wait	skin
gravel	drowsy	molasses	tender

From Roediger, H. L., & McDermott, K. B. (1995). Creating false memories: Remembering words not presented in lists. *Journal of Experimental Psychology: Learning, Memory, and Cognition, 21,* 803–814. Copyright 1995 by the American Psychological Association. Reprinted by permission.

presented, participants were given a recognition test that included the presented items and, more important, the nonpresented theme word for each of the lists. The recall and recognition results are presented in Figure 8.2. As you can see, illusory memories were quite common; the theme word was falsely recalled nearly half the time. Even more striking are the recognition results (the first two bars on the second graph); the theme word was falsely recognized at a level equivalent to correct recognition!

Roediger and McDermott (1995) were also interested in investigating the *metamemory* accompanying these false memories—that is, a person's phenomenological experience when recognizing a non-presented word. To do this they used the remember-know paradigm discussed in Chapter 6. Recall that in this procedure, participants are given an extra judgment task if they recognize an item as previously shown; they judge whether they remember the occurrence of the item (complete with contextual details) or simply know that the item occurred (but could recall no details of its

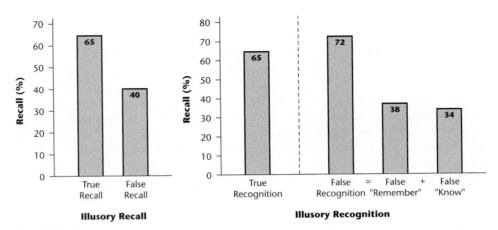

Figure 8.2

Results from Roediger and McDermott (1995).

From Roediger, H. L., & McDermott, K. B. (1995). Creating false memories: Remembering words not presented in lists. *Journal of Experimental Psychology: Learning, Memory, and Cognition, 21,* 803–814. Copyright 1995 by the American Psychological Association. Reprinted by permission.

presentation). Look again at Figure 8.2 (the last two bars on the second graph). Roediger and McDermott found that false recognition often was not simply a case of misattributed familiarity of the theme word. On more than half of the trials, participants remembered (i.e., consciously recollected) that the word had occurred, when it actually had not. In other words, they had created a fairly detailed memory of the word's occurrence. Since this initial investigation, the basic list-learning illusory memory effect has been obtained using a wide array of conditions (see Roediger & Gallo, 2004, for a review and synthesis).

Research Theme
Metacognition

Stop&*Think* | ILLUSORY MEMORIES

Recruit some of your friends and give them the lists in Table 8.2 (taken from Roediger & McDermott, 1995). You can either read the lists (without reading the theme word, of course) or present each of the items on separate index cards. After you've presented each of the lists, have your participants recall all of the items. Take note of how often they recalled the themed word (i.e., how many illusory memories occurred). Also note how the number of theme word intrusions compares with other types of intrusions.

True or False: Neural Processing and False Memories. Given that research into memory illusions is currently a hot topic, you shouldn't be surprised that it's been wedded to another hot topic—cognitive neuroscience. Over the last decade, researchers have been exploring the neural correlates and substrates of false remembering. One of the first such studies was done by Fabiani, Stadler, and Wessels (2000), who provide some intriguing evidence that while our behavior and our judgment may be fooled by the presentation of a new but highly familiar item, our brain isn't. Apparently, brain activity during true and false recognition reveals some telltale differences. Real experiences seem to leave a "sensory signature" that can be used to differentiate between true and false memories.

Fabiani et al. begin with the assumption (as do other cognitive neuroscientists) that retrieval of information from memory involves the reactivation of the sensory information that was present at encoding. Because false memories are not associated with a sensory event (after all, they didn't occur), this reactivation cannot occur. Therefore, differences in brain activity between true and false memories should be evident in regions of the brain associated with the sensory experience of encoding the event. Previous research by Gratton, Corballis, and Jain (1997) revealed a potential way to pick up on these differences. In this study, Gratton et al. found that when a stimulus was encoded predominantly by one hemisphere of the brain, the ERP (event-related potential) response evoked by the stimulus during recognition was larger on that same side of the brain. In other words, if the word was predominantly encoded by the left hemisphere at study, then a stronger ERP response occurred in the left hemisphere during recognition.

Fabiani et al. (2000) applied this reasoning to true and false recognition and the ERP responses associated with each. In the study phase, list items from the laboratory-based illusory memory paradigm were presented to participants. All words from a given associative list (e.g., the *sleep* list) were presented to the left or right of a fixation point (which meant they were processed primarily by the right or the left hemisphere, respectively). The encoding phase was followed by a recognition phase in which words were shown in the center of the display and ERP responses were recorded. Participants were to judge whether each item was *old* or *new*. The recognition list included words presented earlier, the theme words, and unrelated control words that had not been presented earlier. As is typically the case in investigations of illusory memory, participants demonstrated high levels of false recognition; theme words were called *old* as frequently as were presented items. More importantly, the ERP responses differentiated between true and false recognition. ERP responses for the recognition of words that had actually been presented were lateralized; that is, a greater ERP response occurred in the hemisphere that had encoded the word than in the hemisphere that had not encoded it. No such differentiation was found in the ERP responses associated with false recognition. In those cases, the pattern of ERP responses was the same in both hemispheres. Fabiani et al. conclude that although people often can't distinguish between true and false memories in terms of conscious decisions (i.e., a recognition judgment), brain activity does yield some telltale signs that allow for this discrimination. Such "signatures" of false remembering have been obtained in a host of studies since (e.g., Abe, Okuda, Suzuki, Sasaki, Matsuda, Mori, Tsukada, & Fujii 2008; Okado & Stark, 2005; Kim & Cabeza, 2007; Slotnick & Schacter, 2004).

Complex Events

So it seems that we can be convinced that a single word was presented on a list when in reality it was never presented. Big deal! The events we experience in everyday life are more complex than a simple list of words. Surely we can't be convinced that entire life episodes occurred when in fact they didn't—or can we? As it turns out, false recall and recognition are not limited to remembering a single word after presentation of its associates. Researchers have been able to induce participants into falsely remembering entire complex events that are as detailed in some cases as an authentic memory.

Memory Implantation.   One of the first investigations to demonstrate such wholesale false remembering was conducted by Loftus and Pickrell (1995). These investigators set out to determine whether they could induce participants to completely fabricate a memory. The participants were misled a bit; the study was ostensibly an investigation of childhood memories. With the help of a family member, the investigators discovered three actual experiences for which the participants were likely to have genuine memories. The twist was that a fabricated experience (getting lost in a shopping mall) was added. The participants were interviewed about all four events (three authentic, one not) and asked to write about the events in as much detail as they could remember. They then were interviewed twice about each of the events over the subsequent two weeks. During these interviews, family members "played along" with the researchers, attempting to draw out details about each of the events.

Most of the time, participants correctly reported that they recalled nothing about the fabricated event. But a significant proportion (25%) of the 24 participants

Have you ever been lost in a shopping mall? Are you sure?

generated a false memory. Participants' confidence in these memories and their level of detail wasn't quite as high as it was for memories of authentic events, but still, the memories were pretty convincing. How could an event that didn't happen become a fairly detailed and confidently held memory? Loftus, Feldman, and Dashiell (1995) offer some possibilities. Perhaps, unbeknownst to the family members, the person really had been lost, and the memory was authentic (this would have been true for Bridget; she was lost in a shopping mall as a child). A more likely possibility is that prompting and probing led participants to (implicitly) use a "getting lost" schema in imagining what it must have been like. Combining this schematic information with specific information about known locations (e.g., a local mall) could lead to a fairly detailed, but false, memory episode.

Routes to False Memory.   It should be getting increasingly clear that it's pretty easy to manipulate memory. Have you ever wondered whether something happened or you only imagined it? Has seeing a pictures or hearing a story made you question if you were remembering the photo/story about the event or the event itself?

Imagination.   As we pointed out in our earlier discussion of hypnosis, it turns out that simply imagining that an event occurred increases the likelihood of someone remembering that it really did occur. This phenomenon has been termed **imagination inflation.**

Table 8.3 **Have any of these events happened to you? Are you sure?**

Critical Events Presented to Participants

1. Got in trouble for calling 911
2. Had to go to the emergency room late at night
3. Found a $10 bill in a parking lot
4. Won a stuffed animal at a carnival game
5. Gave someone a haircut
6. Had a lifeguard pull you out of the water
7. Got stuck in a tree and had to have someone help you down
8. Broke a window with your hand

From Garry, M., Manning, C. G., Loftus, E. F., & Sherman, S. J. (1996). Imagination inflation: Imagining a childhood event inflates confidence that it occurred. *Psychonomic Bulletin and Review, 3,* 208–214. Reprinted by permission of the Psychonomic Society, Inc.

One of the first studies to demonstrate this phenomenon was conducted by Garry, Manning, Loftus, and Sherman (1996). These investigators employed a three-stage procedure to demonstrate the memorial power of imagination. First, participants were presented with events and were asked to rate the likelihood that these events had happened to them as children (see Table 8.3). Two weeks later, participants were asked to imagine that some of the low-likelihood events had really happened and to supply some detail about how the event might have played itself out. Finally, in a clever twist designed to get participants to rate the childhood events again, the experimenters acted panicked and explained to the participants that they had lost their original ratings. This allowed for a comparison of estimated event likelihood both pre- and post-imagination. This comparison yielded strong evidence of imagination inflation. When participants rated the events for a second time, their ratings of event likelihood increased (i.e., inflated), but only for the imagined events.

Imagination inflation is a subtle effect; imagining how a fictional event could have happened makes one a little less certain that it didn't happen. This effect demonstrates that simply imagining an event is enough to plant the seed of a memory. One interpretation of the findings is that when participants encountered the event in the second rating session, the events they had imagined seemed more familiar. However, this familiarity was misattributed to the possibility of a remote childhood memory rather than to the imagination session. In other words, participants failed to pin down the source of the familiarity. As you're about to see, failure to ascertain correctly the source of an event memory lies at the heart of memory distortion.

C'mon! You don't remember the hot air balloon ride when you were three??! How about that time you got lost in a shopping mall?

Pictures and Stories. Two cherished practices for reminiscing about past events are looking over photographs and telling stories. Your hunch may be that these can have the same contaminating effect on later memory that imagination does. That hunch would be correct.

Lindsay, Hagen, Read, Wade, and Garry (2004) were interested in the effects of viewing photographs on false remembering. Their investigation involved a bit of an elaborate setup, similar to the Loftus and Pickrell (1995) study. Parents of the college student participants (unbeknownst to the participants themselves) were interviewed and asked to give accounts of two real events that involved their children when they were in elementary school (each memory was to be from a different grade). They were also asked to provide their child's school picture from the same years as the events they recounted.

Then it was the now-grown children's turn to participate. The experimenter read each of the parent-provided stories, along with a pseudo-event (putting the toy slime in their teacher's desk) that had never happened (and the fact that it had never happened was verified by the parents). The oldest memory was the pseudo-event. Half of the participants were given the class picture that corresponded to the grade in which the event supposedly occurred, before the story was read. Participants were instructed to recall as much as they could, using mental reinstatement of context and imagery exercises. After this procedure, participants made a number of ratings including the degree to which their memory experience resembled reliving the event and their confidence that the event really occurred. At the end of the session, participants were told that the remainder of the experiment would focus on their ability to recall the oldest of the three memories (the pseudo-event). They were encouraged to think about it using the procedures that the experimenters had taught them, and were given copies of the narrative (and the photo, for those in the photo condition) to assist in their recall. One week later, they were brought back to the lab and were asked to recount the story of the pseudo-event and to make the same ratings.

Both interview sessions were tape-recorded and transcribed, and the transcriptions were coded by observers blind to the photo/no-photo manipulation. They were looking for evidence that participants were experiencing actual full-fledged memories for the pseudo-event, fragmented images of the pseudo-event, or no memories or images for the pseudo-event. The judges placed each recall of the pseudo-event into one of these three categories based on their review of the transcript. The results of this analysis are presented in Figure 8.3. As you can see, the proportion of participants reporting an actual memory for the pseudo-event was over twice as great in the photo condition,

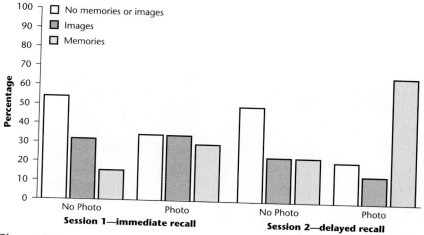

Figure 8.3

Results of the Lindsay, Hagen, Read, Wade, and Garry (2004) study.

Adapted from Lindsay, D. S., Hagen, L., Read, J. D., Wade, K. A., Garry, M. (2004). True photographs and false memories. *Psychological Science, 15*(3), 149–154. Published by Blackwell.

relative to the no-photo condition at immediate recall. After a week of looking at the photo and attempting to imagine the event, this difference became much more pronounced—the proportion of participants in the photo condition reporting an actual memory was nearly three times the proportion in the no-photo condition. In fact, nearly two-thirds of the participants in the photo condition reported having a memory of the pseudo-event! The ratings gathered from participants converged with these data, confirming the memory-inducing power of simply viewing a class photograph.

Based on these results, it might seem reasonable to assume that pictures are better than narratives at producing false memories but we can't conclude this because both conditions also included a narrative. There was no direct comparison of narrative-only and photo-only conditions.

However, a study by Garry and Wade (2005) did make this critical comparison, but with a twist. They used photos of a pseudo-event. A photo for an event that never happened? You may not have even questioned this, as most of you have grown up in the digital age. As Garry and Wade so aptly observe, the old adage "the camera never lies" is no longer true. The authors took a real photo of the participant with one or more family members and Photoshopped it into a hot air balloon ride photo! (see Figure 8.4). As in other studies, they relied on family members to provide the photos and to ensure that the participant had never taken a hot air balloon ride.

Participants were given a booklet that contained 3 events. The first two events were events actually experienced, and the last one was the pseudo-event (the balloon ride). Each event was presented as a narrative story or a photo. Participants were interviewed 3 times over the course of one week in a study ostensibly about childhood memories. In each interview the participants were asked to provide as much information as they could about each event. If they had no memory (as would be the case for the pseudo-event), they were asked to imagine themselves being in the hot air balloon. Similarly to Lindsay et al.'s study of pseudo-memories, recalls of the balloon ride was classified into one of three categories: experiencing actual full-fledged memories, images only, or no images.

Figure 8.4
Up, up, and away in my beautiful balloon…or maybe not.

The results indicated that more participants provided false information in the narrative condition than the photo condition at each interview. By the third interview 82% of participants in the narrative condition and 50% in the photo condition were providing false information about the balloon ride.

Garry and Wade explain the advantage of narratives over pictures in creating false memories by appealing to a three-step model of false memory development proposed by Mazzoni, Loftus, and Kirsch (2001). According to this model a person must first view the pseudo event as *plausible*, then *believe* the event happened to them, and finally *mistake* the internally generated information about the event as a real experience. The authors assert that photos and narratives accomplish the first two steps but diverge at step three. Narratives may make it easier to mistake the internalized story of the event as real experience because memories are story-like in nature. According to Garry and Wade "A narrative, whether true or false, flows with a purpose and tells a story. By contrast, a photograph is a snapshot of time, a memory atom. And, as the poet Muriel Rukeyser once observed, the universe is made of stories, not of atoms."

So an astute reader, such as yourself, might be wondering how this explanation fits with those of Lindsay et al. (2004) in which photos seemed to elicit more false memories than narratives. Recall that they compared photos plus narratives to narratives alone. It's possible that a photo plus a narrative made the event more *plausible* and/or *believable* than the narrative alone and consequently participants were more likely to *mistake* the pseudo-event as real. Or the fact that the Lindsay et al. study used a real photo rather than a fake one, may have enhanced all three stages, leading to more false memories. Regardless of the reason, narratives seem to be more effective than photos but *more* is a relative term; both are highly effective at false memory induction.

You may not find these studies all that distressing; it seems to have little practical significance. Most (if not all) photos are real, so why are these findings important? Given that several news organizations have been caught showing doctored photographs (e.g., Reuters and the LA Times, to name a couple), the ramifications for our perception and later recall of reality are serious. Garry, Strange, Berstein and Kinzett (2007) studied the effect of photos on memory for information in a news article (or should we say false memory for information not in a news article!). Participants read 4 newspaper articles under the guise that the study was on newspaper editing. They were to read each article and find errors (e.g., misspellings) and determine where in the article related photos should be placed. The third article was the one of interest. It was a story about a hurricane and the massive damage it caused, but there was no mention of personal injury or death (sidenote: data was collected prior to Hurricane Katrina). Half of the participants were

Can media images distort our memories?

given a photo before the hurricane and the other half were given a photo (from the same location) after the hurricane. A week after this session they were brought back for a surprise recognition test on information presented in the article. The test was incredibly easy (confirmed by 95% overall accuracy for the four articles). Half of the lures were unrelated to any of the four articles and the other half were thematically related (4 for each article). Two of the thematically related lures for the hurricane were about severe personal injury (e.g., a woman whose husband was seriously injured by flying debris and missing fisherman who were presumed dead).

The results showed that participants who saw the after photo falsely recalled the two lures about severe personal injury more than those who saw the before photo (32% vs. 9%, respectively). It is important to note that this effect was obtained with indirect, rather than direct misleading information (unlike the stop sign/yield sign study by Loftus, 1974) making it all that more surprising. Seeing a photo that portrayed nothing related to the lure information led about 1/3 of participants to falsely recall that information. This effect occurred when full attention was devoted to reading the article; yet this attention was unable to inoculate participants against a false recollection. In the real multitasking world, full attention is rarely focused on anything (e.g., reading the newspaper on the train to work) so it is fair to assume that this lack of attention should serve to exacerbate this effect. Combine this with the doctored photo literature and the evidence that news agencies have been caught using doctored photos, we have a false memory disaster waiting to happen. Lewandowsky, Stritzke, Oberauer, and Morales (2005) provide an example of such a disaster. They found that U.S. citizens were far more likely than German citizens to hold false memories for erroneous information, often cited in the press (but now known to be false) that supported the war in Iraq (e.g. memory that weapons of mass destruction were found).

Nash, Wadem, and Brewer (2009) attempted to explain what they term the *doctored-evidence effect*—the power of doctored evidence, including photographs, to distort memory. They examined three possible mechanisms that might account for the effect. The first is familiarity; real memories are accompanied by a strong sense of familiarity, so if an image or other information is associated with a strong subjective feeling of familiarity, this feeling might be misattributed to an actual memory. A second mechanism is imagination; real memories are rich with detail, so to the extent that doctored-evidence presents such detail (e.g., the hot air balloon study) the more likely it is that false remembering will occur. Finally, sources can lead to false remembering to the extent that they're credible. Evidence indicates that people accept misinformation more readily from credible sources, relative to non-credible ones (e.g., Echterhoff, Hirst, & Hussy, 2005). Therefore, a "doctored-evidence" effect would be more likely to occur to the extent that a source seems credible; this, of course, would apply to news media and other sources that have some type of authority. Unfortunately, in some cases, this credibility and authority is not warranted and as Garry et al. (2007) conclude at the end of their article "…in this era of 24 hour news, unabashedly biased news stations that choose their narratives and visual media accordingly might also alter our memories."

Collaboration and False Remembering.   Studies of illusory memories and imagination inflation involve compliance; participants are asked to imagine events that occurred, complete with the requisite detail. In some studies, family members are recruited to help "sell" the story. These conclusions point to another source of memory errors—the social context in which remembering occurs. Although this may seem self-evident to the layperson who has had plenty of experience reminiscing with friends, memory research has just recently begun to reflect the fact that remembering (and misremembering) is quite often a social enterprise (e.g., Weldon, 2000).

An unsettling demonstration of the role that social forces can play in false remembering comes from a study by Principe, Kanaya, Ceci, and Singh (2006). They were interested in how rumors might lead to false memories in preschoolers. The experimenters staged a magic show for four different groups of children, ages 3 to 5. During the show, the magician tried but failed to pull a rabbit from his hat. At this point, the four groups of preschoolers were exposed to different sources of information. In the *overheard* condition, the preschoolers were exposed to a conversation among adult confederates in which it was alleged (i.e., rumored) that the magician failed because the rabbit had escaped and was now eating carrots in one of the classrooms. In the *classmate* condition, the children did not hear the rumor firsthand, but were told about it by classmates who did hear it. In the *control* condition, the children neither heard the rumor nor were told about it. Finally, in the *witness* condition, children did not hear the rumor about the rabbit, but they did experience the event suggested by the rumor. That is, they actually witnessed a rabbit eating carrots in one of the classrooms. This group served as a baseline recall condition that would allow for a comparison between recall of the actual event and recall in the other conditions in which the event was not witnessed.

After the first phase involving the magic show, children were interviewed with either neutral (e.g., "Tell me about the day the rabbit visited your school") or suggestive ("What did the rabbit eat when he got loose in your school? Did he eat carrots or lettuce?"). Then, during a final interview, the children who had reported the rabbit incident in their initial interview were asked the critical question (i.e., the dependent variable)—whether they saw the rabbit "with their own eyes" or had simply heard about it from someone else.

The results can be seen in Table 8.4, which shows the proportion of children in each condition who answered the critical question in the affirmative—that yes, they had actually

Table 8.4 **The Proportion of Children Who Reported Seeing the Target Event in Principe, Kanaya, Ceci, and Singh (2006) as a Function of Rumor Condition and Type of Interview**

| | | Interview Type | |
		Neutral	Suggestive
Rumor Condition	Witness	1.0	.92
	Overheard	.38	.70
	Classmate	.68	.78
	Control	.00	.23

From Principe, G. F., Kanaya, T., Ceci, S. J., & Singh, M. (2006). Believing is seeing: How rumors can engender false memories in preschoolers. *Psychological Science, 17*(3), 243–248. Blackwell. Adapted with permission.

seen the rascally rabbit. In the witness condition, every child correctly reported that they had indeed seen the rabbit. The noteworthy findings are the alarmingly high levels of false reporting in the other three conditions, particularly in the suggestive interview condition. After this type of interview, nearly three-quarters of children reported that they had seen the event, when they had only overheard a rumor first- or secondhand. Even in the neutral interview condition, a good number of the children reported seeing the event. In addition, to showing the role of social interaction in remembering, these findings have important implications for the evaluation of children's memory reports.

A Practical (and Positive) Application.   All of this talk about false remembering and memory manipulation might have you a little unsettled, but just as magic (as discussed in Chapter 3) can take advantage of perceptual and attentional tendencies, the foibles of memory also can be exploited for positive ends. Let's discuss some memory magic reviewed by Bernstein and Loftus (2009). In a series of studies (Bernstein, Laney, Morris, & Loftus, 2005a, 2005b) these investigators and their colleagues have managed to use imagination inflation to manipulate food preferences. The general strategy of these studies was to convince participants (or at least get them to consider the possibility) that they had particular experiences with food in the distant past, and then to observe the changes in food preference that occur as result of these false beliefs.

For example, in a study humorously entitled "Asparagus: A love story," Laney, Morris, Bernstein, Wakefield, and Loftus (2008) attempted to get participants to change their attitude about asparagus through the implantation of a suggestion. In their experiment, participants were presented with a series of questionnaires for an experiment ostensibly on food preferences and personality. In reality, the researchers were interested in only a couple of questions on these questionnaires. In The Food History Questionnaire, the key item was: "Loved asparagus the first time you tried it," to which participants were to answer on a rating scale indicating the extent of agreement. In the questionnaire about restaurant preferences, the key item was a question asking how likely they were to order various menu items (asparagus was the item of interest).

A week later, participants came back and were given fake feedback supposedly generated from their responses to the questionnaires. The investigators really sold this story, telling participants that a computer program had generated a personality profile of their preferences, based on their responses. The profile contained 3 items about spinach, fried food, and sweets (you felt happy when a classmate brought sweets to school). For $1/2$ of the participants (the love group) it also included the critical statement which stated "You loved to eat cooked asparagus." The control group did not receive this statement. Both groups were asked to imagine some specifics about how they might have experienced the sweets statement and the love group did the same for the asparagus statement (i.e, where might they have eaten it, and with whom?). Finally, participants were given the food history questionnaire and the restaurant preference questionnaire a second time. The findings were quite intriguing; participants' attitudes about asparagus were influenced on both questionnaires. Apparently, the personality profile along with the subsequent imagination task, led participants to falsely believe that they had enjoyed asparagus as a child, and would enjoy it in the present. The implications for health psychology are obvious as maintaining a positive attitude about healthy foods is a critical aspect of a healthy life.

False Remembering: Theoretical Frameworks

A number of frameworks have been proposed to account for when and why false memories occur. These models focus on different aspects of the processes that underlie false remembering, and offer varied perspectives from which to view false memory phenomena. Let's take a look at each.

Fuzzy-Trace Theory.   Fuzzy trace theory (Brainerd & Reyna, 1995; Brainerd & Reyna, 2005) is based on the distinction between gist and verbatim information. You've no doubt heard these terms; getting the gist of something means understanding the main idea, whereas remembering something verbatim refers to remembering the exact words or form of a presented event or statement. **Fuzzy trace theory** states that we encode all events in both of these ways (i.e., as an exact replica, complete with details, and as a general idea). If we encoded the word "dog," the verbatim information would include the precise form of how the word was encoded—where, when, how, etc. The gist information would involve the activation of the general concept of a dog, and other related concepts like "pet" or "animal." The experiences of remembering that stem from verbatim and gist traces correspond to the remember-know distinction discussed in Chapter 6. Typically, the verbatim trace of an event would support recollective memory (i.e., the experience of "remembering"), whereas the gist trace of an event would support familiarity-based remembering (i.e., just "knowing" than an item occurred).

Memory performance depends on the retrieval of both verbatim and gist information. Verbatim retrieval will be good to the degree that verbatim traces are stronger than gist traces. If a single item (e.g., a word or sentence) is presented repeatedly, this will tend to strengthen the verbatim trace for that piece of information, and will be likely to result in recollective recall. However, if an item is presented only once, but in the context of many related items, the gist trace will be strengthened more than the verbatim trace. This might lead to phantom recollection, which occurs when a recovered gist trace is so strong that it inspires a subjective experience of remembering.

In the case of the DRM memory illusion, fuzzy trace theory would propose that when the critical (but nonpresented) lure is presented at retrieval, it strongly activates the gist traces that were encoded as a result of presentation of the other list items. This activation is so strong that the lure is mistakenly experienced as a recalled item. Similarly, the other memory illusions discussed, such as imagination inflation, occur because misleading or suggestive information increases the strength of gist information related to the target event. At retrieval, activation of these gist traces can lead to a strong (but false) subjective experience of recollection.

Constructive Memory Framework.   Daniel Schacter and his colleagues (Schacter, Norman, & Koutstaal, 1997; Schacter & Slotnick, 2004; Schacter & Addis, 2007) propose a **constructive memory framework** to explain the reconstructive nature of memory. According to this view, memory representations are collections of features that correspond to the different elements of an encoded experience (e.g., the sights, sounds, feelings, etc.), which are all processed in the areas of the brain responsible for those functions. Hence, a "memory" is not a localized trace; it's the reactivation of a pattern of activity distributed throughout the brain. Memory involves completing the pattern of these features.

Several processes must play themselves out correctly in order for an encoded event to be retrieved with some degree of integrity. Two of these processes occur during encoding. First, a *feature-binding process* occurs. All of the components of the encoded event—including the sights, the sounds, the people, and what they said—must somehow cohere into a unitized memory representation. Failure to bind the elements of an episode because of stress, emotion, lack of attention, or some other factor will result in disembodied memory fragments "floating around." Because of the disembodied nature of these fragments, their source is unclear. Second, the bound episodes must be kept separate from one another (*pattern separation*); otherwise, you'll confuse the sources of events. For example, if you repeatedly engage in the same activities or interact with the same friends at the same place, memory for these episodes will be difficult to separate; there are not enough unique features to differentiate the memories. Eventually, you may have just a memory of what generally happens when you and your friends go to your favorite hangout rather than a detailed memory of each occasion. This is similar to the issue discussed in Chapter 7 about autobiographical memory forgetting; autobiographical memories transition to autobiographical facts over time.

Three of the processes in the constructive memory framework operate at retrieval. Retrieval requires the use of a cue to get to the right memory—a process termed *focusing* (Norman & Schacter, 1996). A general retrieval cue like "hanging out with friends in the student union" wouldn't be very useful, because it fails to focus the memory search onto a unique episode. Something more distinctive about a particular episode (i.e., "the time the server spilled a cup of coffee on me") would better focus the memory search and hence serve as a more useful cue. This relates to the issue discussed in Chapter 7 about cue effectiveness in autobiographical memory retrieval. "What" was a better cue than other "W" words as it better helped to specify the specific autobiographical memory. The next process, called *pattern completion,* involves the successful reconstruction of the product from this focused search. But retrieval doesn't end here. After a pattern has been completed, a decision must be made. This stage, labeled *criterion setting,* involves deciding whether the completed pattern represents a valid memory. Criterion setting as the source of memory errors is evident in the effects of hypnosis on memory. The effects of hypnosis occur at retrieval, as the rememberer lowers the criterion for labeling a memory as valid. In hypnosis, criterion setting is influenced by the highly suggestible state of the rememberer.

Source Confusion. The last stage of the constructive memory framework could be considered to constitute what has been termed the source monitoring framework (Johnson, Hashtroudi, & Lindsey, 1993) which focuses on the processes whereby we monitor the origins of encoded information. In other words, memory (and memory failure) stems from our ability to nail down information about the source of events. The source monitoring framework proposes two stages: reality monitoring and source monitoring. The first and most fundamental stage is **reality monitoring**—the processes whereby we attribute an experienced memory to either a perceived external event or an internally generated event (i.e., imagined event).

In order to decide whether a memory is the product of encoding an actual event or an imagined event, people rely on a number of factors, such as whether the memory includes perceptual detail or semantic vividness—in other words, how fully fleshed out the memory is. The more perceptually salient the memory is, the more likely it will be judged a true memory rather than an imagined memory.

Ghetti (2008) provides a metamemory account of how we distinguish valid memories from the pretenders. This account focuses on a mechanism she terms the memorability-based strategy. Consider the following example: Did you ever fall and crack a tooth as a child? Your answer to this might be yes, because you know of or recollect the event clearly. Your answer may be no, because of a failure to recollect a specific episode in which this happened. But in the latter case, you can't be sure it *didn't* happen. In other words, there's some ambiguity about whether the event occurred or not.

Research Theme
Metacognition

According to Ghetti (2008), determining the nonoccurrence of an event involves a complex use of metamemory. Metamemory (a type of metacognition) is our understanding of the processes involved in remembering and forgetting. When using the memorability-based strategy in judging the actual occurrence of an event, we essentially evaluate whether the event we're considering should have been memorable ("Well, if that had happened, I certainly would have remembered it!"). If an event fails to reach an expected level of memorability, this would lead to its rejection as an authentic memory.

According to the source monitoring framework, if the memory is attributed to an externally perceived event, then the **source monitoring** stage is engaged to determine the source of the event (Did I hear this in class? On the news? From a friend?) The inability to distinguish between the source of event memories is termed **source confusion** and represents a failure of the source-monitoring process. Another way of putting it is that we often *misattribute* our memories to incorrect sources. Some researchers (e.g., Johnson, Nolde, & Leonardis, 1996) go so far as to suggest that all memory errors (except for errors of omission) stem from source confusion. Indeed, confusion over the source of memories has been a recurrent theme in this chapter.

Many, if not most, of the problems in eyewitness memory result from failures in the source monitoring stage. Let's reexamine two encoding factors—the misinformation effect and unconscious transference—in light of the notion of source confusion. After exposure to misinformation, witnesses fail to distinguish between the source of the misinformation and the source of the actual memory, blending them into one representation. The same blending process occurs in unconscious transference and photo bias; a bystander and a culprit are assumed to be the same person due to a failure to remember the source of the encounters.

The illusory memories for complex and simple events result from failures in reality monitoring. Participants fail to distinguish the internally generated target word (e.g., *sleep*) from the externally derived perceptual events (seeing the words *doze, rest, snore,* etc.). As Roediger and McDermott (1995) note, this failure is somewhat surprising, given that the illusory memories and the true memories differ in terms of the perceptual information they offer. The representations underlying illusory memories offer little or nothing in the way of perceptual characteristics, and so should be labeled as "internally generated" and hence false. But source confusion remains, and illusory memories occur.

The effects of imagination, photos, and narratives (i.e., stories) provide further examples of a failure in reality monitoring. As we noted in our discussion of imagination inflation, the participants in the Garry et al. (1996) study became a little less sure about the nonoccurrence of an imagined event. Imagined events seem to share many of the characteristics of remote memories (Johnson, Foley, Suengas, & Raye, 1988). Both are fairly diffuse, making it difficult to distinguish between them (Garry et al., 1996) to arrive at the correct reality-monitoring decision. This problem in reality monitoring made participants more willing to entertain the possibility that the imagined event was real. The same reasoning can be applied to the effects of narratives and photos. These devices lead to quite vivid imaginings of events, even providing precise detail from an external source (as opposed to simply an internal simulation of the event). Upon repeated recall, it becomes increasingly difficult to distinguish between memories of the narrative or photo and memories of the event.

Stop&*Review*

1. True or false? The false memories found by the DRM paradigm were more likely to be associated with familiarity-based judgments than with recollection-based judgments.
2. Describe the phenomenon of imagination inflation.
3. Identify and define the five stages of the constructive memory framework.

• Memory illusions involve the creation of a memory for an event that did not happen. High levels of false recall and false recognition have been found in the laboratory using the DRM paradigm, which involves presenting lists of words created around a non-presented theme word. False recognition tends to be based on recollection-based judgments rather than familiarity-based judgments. Some neuroscientific research indicates that it is possible to distinguish neurologically between real and illusory memories.

• False memories can induced for everyday events, such as being lost. Imagination inflation refers to the idea that imagining how an event may have occurred increases the feeling that it really did. False narratives and photos (especially doctored photos) are likely to induce false remembering. False remembering also is facilitated by the social context. False memories about liking healthy foods, which subsequently changes attitudes about that food, is a positive application of false memory implantation.

• Fuzzy trace theory proposes that gist (general information) and verbatim (exact information) traces are formed when an event is encoded. False memories are rooted in activation of gist traces. The constructive memory framework proposes that five stages are necessary for accurate memory reconstruction: feature binding, pattern separation, focusing, pattern completion, and criterion setting which can be conceived as two stages: reality monitoring and source monitoring. Failure in the source monitoring stage leads to source confusion, which is at the root of many memory failures.

The Recovered Memory Controversy

The issue of the accuracy and inaccuracy of memory lies at the heart of a fierce debate that raged throughout the 1990s and still provokes strong feelings today, although the deep divide may be closing a bit. At the center of the controversy lies the question of repressed, and subsequently recovered, memories that typically involve childhood sexual abuse. The early 1990s saw a rapidly growing number of these cases. These claims, coupled with research demonstrating the reconstructive nature of memory, have caused grave concern in the psychological community regarding the validity of recovered memories. The recovery of a *repressed memory* has the potential to completely devastate a family; that this devastation would occur as the result of a recovered memory that is false seems particularly tragic. In response to the increasing number of recovered memory cases, experimental and clinical researchers have intensified their investigations into the nature of illusory memories and the nature of memory for trauma (for reviews, see; Goodwin, Quas, & Ogle, 2009; Loftus & Davis, 2006; Brewin, 2007). Here, we once again take up the complex topics of how stress affects memory, and how memory for emotional and/or traumatic events differs from memory for "normal" ones. As you've seen in the last two chapters, there are no simple answers to these questions. And things certainly don't get simpler in the context of what some have termed the "repressed memory debate," which centers around the validity of the concept known as repression.

Reality Check

The notion of **repression** stems from Sigmund Freud's psychoanalytic approach to personality and psychotherapy. You're probably familiar with Freud's claims; the most relevant for present purposes is Freud's contention that traumatic memories are submerged in the unconscious. Although these repressed feelings and memories are unavailable to consciousness in any direct way, they do manifest themselves, most notably through problems in adjustment and behavior. Freud's notion of repression has become the centerpiece for some approaches to psychotherapy; these approaches champion the liberation of repressed memories as the road to recovery.

We will organize our discussion of the evidence for the validity of the recovered memory experience with three critical questions. Two of these are posed in Brewin's (2007) review of research on trauma and memory: Can memories of truly traumatic events be forgotten and then recalled later in life? and Are special mechanisms such as repression or dissociation required to account for forgetting of trauma? A final important question is added to the mix by Schooler (1994): Is it possible to fabricate false memories for traumatic experiences?

Memories for Traumatic Events: Forgotten, Then Recalled?

At the center of recovered memory claims is the idea that traumatic events are often forgotten for some period of time and then recalled later. The devil is in the details; what exactly is meant by "forgotten," "some period of time," and "recalled later"?

Retrospective Reports.
As the debate over the validity of repressed and recovered memories was heating up in the early 1990's, a number of researchers gathered retrospective

reports of abuse victims (e.g., Briere & Conte, 1993; Herman & Schatzow, 1987), and reported that clients often go through extended periods of time in which the abuse is forgotten. However, as Schooler (1994) and others note, this research is rife with problems in interpretation. First, the events cannot be definitively corroborated; neither can it be ascertained exactly how the respondents interpreted the questions. Also, the fact that abuse experiences were forgotten for a period of time does not necessarily mean that they were completely inaccessible.

Williams (1994) took a more direct route to corroborating cases of lost traumatic memories, finding individuals who had been admitted 17 years earlier to sexual abuse clinics and interviewing them about their current knowledge of the experience. Of the 129 women she managed to interview, a substantial portion (38%) had no memory of the incident for which they had been admitted. Although this finding does provide more compelling evidence for the forgetting of sex-related trauma than do the retrospective reports just discussed, it is subject to some interpretational limitations of its own. The majority of those who reported forgetting did recall other episodes of abuse; so the particular episode that was the subject of the research may simply have been confused with others (recall that a common cause of memory failure is source confusion). But compellingly, disregarding these individuals still left 12% who reported that they had never been sexually abused when they actually had been. So, while far from definitive regarding the reality of repressed then recovered memories as outlined by Freud, these studies do suggest that forgetting abuse and then recalling it later, is not an uncommon occurrence.

Corroborated Cases of Recovered Memories.   A primary reason why many are skeptical of claims of repressed then recovered memories is that they are nearly impossible to verify. The evidence is anecdotal, which many view as the weakest sort of evidence. Not only that, the anecdotes are usually uncorroborated. However, there are a number of corroborated cases that lend some valuable insight into the conditions associated with valid memory recovery (e.g., Gleaves, Smith, Butler, & Spiegel, 2004; Schooler, Bendiksen, & Ambadar, 1997).

Schooler et al. (1997) outline four such cases and note several themes that the memory recoveries seemed to have in common. First, the cues present in the recovery situation corresponded to elements of the originally encoded experience (consistent with the encoding specificity principle discussed in Chapter 6); that is, the memories were triggered by a retrieval cue that reinstated some aspect(s) of the encoded experience. Another aspect of corroborated cases of recovery was that they tended to occur very suddenly and were typically accompanied by extreme shock and emotion. Finally, if the memory was not always forgotten (i.e., it had been previously reported to others), there was evidence that the experience was interpreted differently at the time of "recovery" than it had been previously. In two of the corroborated cases, the rememberers were shocked to find out they had previously related the abuse incident to their husbands. That is, they believed they were completely unaware of the memory, but corroborating evidence demonstrated that they had previously been aware of it. Schooler and colleagues label this the "forgot-it-all-along effect," suggesting that because the recovered memory "packs such a punch," the rememberer assumes that it must have been completely forgotten. Recall that a feeling of familiarity is interpreted as evidence that an event is "old." In this case the stunning lack of familiarity is taken as evidence that the event had never been remembered, when perhaps it had.

This intriguing effect has now been empirically demonstrated in a variety of contexts (e.g., Joslyn, Loftus, McNoughton, & Powers, 2001; Merckelbach, Smeets, Geraerts, Jelicic, Bouwen, & Smeets, 2006), indicating that one's *lack* of memory can't even be taken as evidence that a memory is long forgotten. So how is this relevant to the recovered memory debate? As Geraerts, Arnold, Lindsay, Merckelbach, Jelicic, and Hauer (2006) note, it could be the case that abuse victims underestimate their prior recollections of the abuse, which leads to a false impression that they had repressed the memory. Indeed, Geraerts et al. found that the tendency to underestimate previous remembering (as in the forgot-it-all-along effect) was greater for individuals who had previously reported repressed memories of abuse, relative to individuals with continuous memories of their abuse and individuals with no history of abuse.

Differences in Recovery Experiences. The finding that the forgot-it-all-along experience was dependent on the individuals' previous experience of abuse—highlights an important point. Not everyone reports the same type of recovered memory experience. Some recovered memory experiences arise gradually, often as the result of extensive therapeutic work; others, as in the corroborated cases just described, seem to come out of the blue. And, of course, there are individuals who were abused that never forgot the abuse, recalling it all along.

In a self-report study, Geraerts et al. compared the relative rates of memory corroboration for these three groups. Their suspicion was that emerging recovered memory experiences in the context of therapy may have been the product of suggestive techniques, and hence more likely to be examples of false recall. They asked self-reported victims of childhood sexual abuse whether there was any corroboration for the abuse (e.g., a friend or family member who they told within a week of the abuse, another victim who had been abused by the same perpetrator, or an admission from the perpetrator). The results were striking, and were consistent with their hypothesis; the corroboration rate for two of the groups was statistically the same: those with continuous memories of the abuse (45%) and those who had recovered it suddenly (37%). However, *none* of those whose abuse memories emerged gradually within a therapeutic context had corroboration. While the authors are quick to caution that this does not mean those reports of abuse are necessarily false, it does suggest that memories obtained after suggestive therapy need to be interpreted carefully.

Remembering and Forgetting Trauma: Ordinary Forgetting or Special Mechanisms?

Another question critical to informing the debate over the validity of recovered memories of abuse is one highlighted by Brewin (2007) in his review of the trauma and memory debate. Are special mechanisms involved in remembering and forgetting trauma? The very notion of repression as described by Freud suggests such a mechanism, but as you've seen, the relationship between emotion, trauma, and memory is, in a word, complex. The Freudian notion of repression can be contrasted with an ordinary forgetting view that explains the forgetting of trauma in terms of normal memory mechanisms such as decay, interference, and lack of rehearsal. One ordinary mechanism that might account for the wholesale forgetting of childhood sexual abuse and its later emotional recall is described by McNally (2003). If the abusive acts were not accompanied by violence, they may not have been fully appreciated at the time. Only later, as an adult, would the person ascertain the gravity of what had happened. This realization would be experienced profoundly, but no special mechanism is necessary to explain the loss of the memory and its later retrieval.

So how does the evidence stack up? Can the laws of ordinary forgetting and remembering account for how people remember instances of trauma and childhood sexual abuse? The evidence reviewed by Brewin is mixed on this score. As one might expect, the ordinary forgetting view would predict (and it has been found) that memory for trauma including childhood sexual abuse should be quite vivid and unforgettable (Alexander, Quas, Goodman, Ghetti, Edelstein, Redlich, 2005; Andrews, Brewin, Ochera, Morton, Bekerian, & Davies, 2000; Schooler, 2001) and regularly relived by the victim. The ordinary forgetting view also would predict that the more upsetting the event, the better it should be remembered. Most research indicates that the opposite is the case. Traumatic experiences involving violence and threats of harm tend to be more poorly remembered than those less violent and threatening (e.g., Briere & Conte, 1993; Williams, 1994). In addition, some evidence (Edwards, Fivush, Anda, Felitti, & Nordenberg, 2001) indicates that those suffering repeated or severe physical and/or sexual abuse reported more forgetting than those less severely abused, inconsistent with what ordinary mechanisms would predict.

Brewin (2007) makes the important point that pitting an "ordinary forgetting view" against a repression view implies that repression is not ordinary forgetting. But there is plenty of evidence that people can suppress thoughts from consciousness and avoid thinking about them. This can be done so effectively that events could be forgotten for long periods of time. So "normal forgetting mechanisms" may, in a way, allow for repression of a sort.

If the special mechanism view is correct, what might the "special mechanisms" be, physiologically? Stressful events do seem to produce a complex pattern of effects on *explicit memory* (discussed in Chapter 6). As you read, explicit recall involves brain structures in and around the medial temporal lobe, including the amygdala and the hippocampus. Each area is responsible for different aspects of explicit memory. In addition, each area is affected in a characteristic manner by stressful events, with concomitant effects on explicit memory for those events. Nadel, Jacobs, and colleagues have investigated these effects extensively (e.g., Nadel & Jacobs, 1998; Payne, Jackson, Ryan, Hoscheidt, Jacobs, & Nadel, 2006; Payne, Nadel, Britton, & Jacobs, 2004; Ryan, Hoscheidt, Jacobs, & Nadel, 2005). Their research provides some basis for expecting both disruption and enhancement of different aspects of memory for the same stressful event.

High levels of stress enhance the functioning of the amygdala (essential for remembering emotionally charged events), but disrupt the functioning of the hippocampus (responsible for consolidating of each element of the memory into a coherent episode—Sapolsky, 2004). As a result, memory for stressful events demonstrate a predictable pattern of strength and weakness—memory in the form of feelings or mood states is enhanced, while memory in the form of a coherent episode is poor. This accounts for some of the oddities in the memories for traumatic events. For example, victims sometimes fail to recall the context of the event, but can vividly recall how they felt (the emotions surrounding the event). So the issue may be one of poor encoding rather than forgetting. Therefore, caution should be taken when considering the issue of "recovery." If the elements of the memory are not fully integrated at encoding, there is no coherent representation to retrieve.

Evidence From Clinical Populations.

As you've been reading, one research strategy has been to determine whether there is something unique or special about memory for trauma. A similar strategy has been used to determine whether there is something unique or special about the *people* who report and/or remember instances of childhood sexual abuse. For example, individuals that exhibit symptoms of dissociative disorders are unlikely to disclose documented abuse from childhood (Goodman, Ghetti, Quas, Edelstein, Alexander, & Redlich, 2003). In addition, these individuals are also better at forgetting trauma words than are those who have no dissociative tendencies (e.g., Moulds & Bryant, 2005). So there is at least some suggestion from the evidence that memory processes in clinical populations may differ in important ways from normal individuals.

False Memories for Traumatic Events?

Whether it is possible to create a false memory for a traumatic event is a tough question to answer directly. It would be unethical to attempt to implant false memories of traumatic events such as sexual abuse. But it is quite evident that we fairly easily can be convinced that something happened even though it really didn't. Clearly, under any circumstances, memory is a reconstructive enterprise. This is especially the case in the highly suggestive context that characterizes some therapeutic techniques.

Memory Work and Suggestive Influences in Therapy.

The research we've discussed on false memories has led to great concern about the risk of false memory creation in the therapeutic context, where some of the factors conducive to false remembering can be present. First, the therapeutic context itself is suggestive, as the client will tend to trust the expertise of the therapist and be open to therapeutic suggestion. In addition to the general suggestibility of this context, some therapeutic approaches involve what is sometimes termed *memory work*—elaborate attempts to retrieve memories using methods that include repeated imagining, hypnosis, and group attempts to retrieve memories. As you've read, imagining (Goff & Roediger, 1998; Hyman & Pentland, 1996), hypnosis (Scobria, Mazzoni, Kirsch, & Milling, 2002), and social conformity pressures (Roediger, Meade, & Bergman, 2001) are three factors that heighten the likelihood of forming illusory memories. By no means is anyone implying that these suggestive techniques are used by all therapists. But given the devastating potential of a false memory of childhood abuse, any usage of these techniques may be too much.

Self-Help Books and Checklists.

Suggestive influences also exist outside of the therapeutic context. Skeptics of recovered memories have expressed considerable concern about self-help books designed to aid in the recovery of childhood sexual abuse. These books were particularly popular in the early 1990's, coincident with the rash of claims and accusations. Many of these "recovery books" included checklists of symptoms that were meant to serve as indicators of previous abuse; however, these checklists were not derived or validated in any systematic manner, and the "symptoms" were so vague and nonspecific that they could apply to anyone:

Do you feel different from other people?...Do you have trouble feeling motivated?...Do you feel you have to be perfect?...Do you have trouble expressing your feelings?...Do you find that your relationships just don't work out?...Do you find yourself clinging to the people you care about? (Bass & Davis, 1988 p. 35)

People have a propensity to find themselves in vague descriptions like these—they ring "true" in the same way your horoscope does. The tendency for vague personality descriptions to seem intuitively valid is termed the Barnum effect. There probably isn't anyone reading this book right now that hasn't had at least one of the feelings mentioned at one time or another. Offering these sorts of descriptions with the suggestion that people who feel they fit them may have been abused is at best, reckless. Intriguingly, a study by Emery and Lilienfield (2004) revealed a moderately positive correlation between people's responses to Barnum-type self-descriptions and their responses to items from child sexual abuse checklists, indicating a general tendency to acquiesce to such items. In the same study, the investigators found that the sexual abuse checklists failed to distinguish between victims of childhood sexual abuse and nonvictims. While the barrage of self-help and recovery books has certainly declined over the years, there is no doubt about their role in fueling the repressed memory debate.

Converging Evidence of False Recovered Memories.

Although there is no direct experimental evidence of false trauma memories being implanted, there are several converging lines of evidence that suggest that this does occur (Schacter, Norman, & Koutstaal, 1997). First, many clinical practitioners have reported clients recovering memories of satanic ritual abuse (e.g., Wakefield & Underwager, 1994); however, these instances are never corroborated, and extensive investigations by law authorities continually fail to find evidence of satanic abuse (e.g., Nathan & Snedeker, 1995). Recovering memories of other experiences involving highly unlikely events (e.g., being abducted by aliens) would also seem to be evidence for memory implantation (Schacter, Norman, & Koutstaal, 1997). The reality of false memory implantation also is suggested by the existence of a significant number of retractors—individuals who recover memories of abuse but later recant their reports (e.g., Nelson & Simpson, 1994).

Finally, the research we've discussed throughout this chapter constitutes another line of evidence that memories can be implanted. Consider the range of events for which memories have been implanted or judgments of possible memories inflated: being lost in a mall (Loftus & Pickrell, 1995), spilling a punch bowl at a wedding reception (Hyman & Pentland, 1996), being hospitalized overnight (Hyman, Husband, & Billings, 1995), and witnessing demonic possession as a child (Mazzoni, Loftus, & Kirsch, 2001). Although these false memory experiences certainly are not on a par with sexual abuse, to dismiss their significance completely would seem foolhardy (Lindsay, 1998).

Answering the Questions

Let's look back at the three questions we used to frame the debate over the reality of recovered memories. As you can see, it's pretty clear from the preceding discussion that the answer to two of the questions we posed at the beginning is a qualified yes, Entire episodes of one's life can be completely forgotten for a period of time;. Also, there seems to be a significant number of recovered memory experiences that can be corroborated. On the other hand, it is just as clear that memories for entire events can be created, particularly in circumstances that involve imagining, hypnosis, and/or conformity pressures—all of which can be present in the therapeutic setting. The answer to the question of whether "special mechanisms" are necessary to explain the remembering and forgetting of trauma is less clear, and would likely produce both "yes" and "no" responses, depending on whom you ask and how terms are defined.

A New Solution to the Debate?
Given the (albeit qualified) affirmative answers to these questions, the issue becomes one of discrimination: How can we tell when a recovered memory experience is valid (i.e., the event really happened) and when it is not? McNally and Geraerts (2009) present what they term "a new solution to the recovered memory debate." They conclude in their review that the notion of repressed then recovered memories does not stand up to empirical scrutiny. However, they agree with the reality of "recovered" memories of sexual abuse.

In their view, what appear to be repressed then recovered memories are actually just discontinuous memories that can result from a number of different retrieval scenarios. In other words, there are indeed genuine recovered memories, but these cases fit one of several profiles: the event was not originally experienced as a trauma, but is in retrospect; the victim has no reminders for the abuse, so is able to forget it for long stretches of time; the victim actively suppresses memory for the abuse, dispelling it from their mind successfully; and the victim forgets a prior recollection they had of the abuse (the *forgot-it-all along effect* described earlier). McNally and Geraerts suggest a careful case-by-case consideration in considering the validity of recovered memory experiences. Bernstein and Loftus (2009) make a similar recommendation, noting that the determination of whether a particular memory is true or false should rely on the contents of the memory report itself.

The APA's Position.
In the midst of the most intense heat of the recovered memory controversy (in the mid 1990's), the American Psychological Association appointed a special working group to review the scientific literature on memory and abuse experiences and to identify future research and training needs relevant to evaluating recovered memory experiences. The working group was composed of prominent researchers and clinicians who represented a range of views on the reality of recovered memory experiences; their final report was published in 1998, and although that was some time ago and much more research has been done, the points of agreement and disagreement have not changed (see Table 8.5).

One reason that common ground has been so difficult to reach in the debate over recovered memories relates to the fundamental differences over what constitutes good evidence. The databases that clinicians and memory researchers rely on to make their arguments are quite different. Clinicians base much of their argument for the validity of recovered memories on their interactions with clients and other evidence in the form of

Table 8.5 **Points of Agreement and Disagreement from the APA Working Group on Memories of Childhood Sexual Abuse (APA, 1998)**

Points of Agreement	Points of Disagreement
• Controversies regarding adult recollections should not be allowed to obscure the fact that child sexual abuse is a complex and pervasive problem in America that has historically gone unacknowledged.	• How constructive is memory?
	• How accurately can events be recalled after extended delays, and what mechanisms that might underlie such remembering?
• Most people who were sexually abused as children remember all or part of what happened to them.	• Are memories of traumatic events "special"? How relevant is basic research on memory and development for understanding the recall of stressful events?
• It is possible for memories of abuse that have been forgotten for a long time to be remembered.	• What rules of evidence should guide hypothesis testing about the consequences of trauma and the nature of remembering?
• It is also possible to construct convincing pseudomemories for events that never occurred.	• How easy is it to create pseudomemories by suggestion, both within and outside of therapy? How often does it occur?
• There are gaps in our knowledge about the processes that lead to accurate and inaccurate recollections of childhood abuse.	• How easy is it to distinguish "real" memories and pseudomemories in the absence of external corroborative evidence?

case studies and interviews. But because these sources of data are descriptive and thus subject to various self-report biases, experimental psychologists are reluctant to draw definitive conclusions from them. But the database emphasized by memory researchers—the extensive data demonstrating our propensity toward illusory memories—leaves many clinicians unmoved. They point out that illusory memories are, in large part, laboratory contrivances that don't generalize to the real-world issue of how it is that we store and retrieve memories for trauma (e.g., Freyd & Gleaves, 1996; Pezdek, 2007; Pezdek & Lam, 2007; but see replies by Roediger & McDermott, 1996; Wade, Sharman, Garry, Memon, Mazzoni, & Merckelbach, 2007).

It does appear that since the polemics that characterized the opening salvos of the repressed memory debate, researchers have taken it upon themselves to tone down the rhetoric, collect data, and get a clearer view of how we process, remember, and forget traumatic events. Plotted in Figure 8.5 are the results of a PsycINFO search

Figure 8.5
Cumulative citations for articles focusing on "research" for emotional material and trauma (search keywords included memory, emotion, trauma and related) versus those focusing on the repressed memory "debate" (search keywords included repressed memory, controversy, debate).

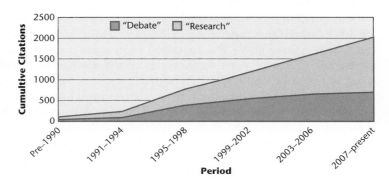

comparing the frequency of articles devoted to the "repressed memory debate" (abstracts that included recovered memory, repressed memory, and debate or controversy) to the frequency of articles devoted to investigating memory for emotional materials and trauma (abstracts that included "memory" "trauma" "traumatic experience" "emotion"). As you can see, articles devoted to "the debate" have leveled off in recent years, while research delineating the nature of memory for trauma continues to trend upward.

Stop&Review

1. True or false? There is no evidence that memories can be forgotten and recalled later.
2. Define the special mechanisms and ordinary forgetting view of repressed memories.
3. Describe one piece of evidence that indicates the possibility of implantation of false memories for traumatic events.
4. Why has it been difficult to establish the criteria for what constitutes a true and a false repressed memory?

• The existence of repressed and subsequently recovered memories has been an issue of much debate. Studies have revealed that it is possible to forget and later recall memories of sexual abuse. Corroborated memories of abuse seem to appear suddenly, in a context that reinstates some aspect of the abuse situation, and tend to be accompanied by great surprise. Recovery that occurs in a therapeutic context is more likely to be uncorroborated, and more subject to factors that lead to false remembering.

• The ordinary-forgetting view contends that forgetting traumatic memories can be explained in the same way as forgetting nontraumatic memories. The special mechanism view contends that encoding traumatic events is fundamentally different from encoding nontraumatic events. Trauma enhances functioning of the amygdala and disrupts hippocampus activity. Consequently, memory for feelings and images is enhanced; however, memory in the form of a coherent episode is poor.

• Research suggests that it is possible to implant false memories of traumatic events. One piece of evidence is the existence of retractors (individuals who recover memories of abuse but later recant their reports). Self-help books and therapeutic approaches that focus on memory recovery can provide a suggestive environment that may lead to the creation of memories of childhood sexual abuse.

• Current concern is focused on assessing the nature of recovered memory experiences. One view is that what appears to be repressed then recovered memories are simply memories that are discontinuous (i.e., forgotten for a period and recovered suddenly). Investigation of the nature of memory for trauma has intensified. Common ground between clinicians and experimental researchers has been difficult to find due to differing views on what constitutes good evidence.

9

Language I: Basic Issues and Speech Processing

Can animal communication be considered a form of language? Can we "grunt and squeak and squawk with the animals," as Dr. Dolittle aspired to do? You've probably heard or seen cases of chimps using sign language or other language-like systems—are they using and understanding language in the same way you are?

How in the world do infants learn language? They come into the world with no knowledge of it whatsoever, and by the time they're just a few years of age, they know hundreds of words and are stringing them together pretty accurately. What are some of the factors that underlie language learning and language use?

Why do people who speak a foreign language talk so fast? Why would anyone (in this case, your first author, in a conversation about baseball) ever hear, "The Mets beat Philly again" as "You must be silly again"?

You've no doubt embarrassed yourself with some type of speech error, or "Freudian slip," to use the better-known term. What factors underlie these slips of the tongue? Are they really windows into a person's unconscious mind?

Language: Basic Principles

Perhaps our most impressive and important cognitive achievement as human beings is language—the intricate symphony of representations and processes that allows us to communicate our thoughts to others. In fact, renowned linguist Steven Pinker, in titling his latest book on language *The Stuff of Thought*, gave language quite a lofty perch. He has a point. In many ways language is the culmination of all of our cognitive processes; in fact, it quite often serves as the means through which cognitive processes are revealed and, in Pinker's view is the very essence of cognitive processing.

The ease with which we acquire and use language is astounding, considering what is involved. We take our language ability for granted, rarely giving it a second thought. In this chapter, we'll take a closer look at some of the basic features of language. We'll also examine a number of the "instruments" in the "symphony"—the basic cognitive processes that we've discussed in earlier chapters, such as pattern recognition, immediate memory, and knowledge representation, all of which are critical to language.

Linguists and Psycholinguists

Cognitive psychologists certainly do not have a monopoly on the investigation of language. Cognition researchers investigate what would be termed *psycholinguistics*—the psychological processes involved in using language, as reflected in processes as varied as speech perception and reading and comprehending the ideas in this textbook. Psycholinguists also are interested in exactly how we execute our language abilities, or **linguistic performance.** Psycholinguistics is related to another field known simply as *linguistics.* Linguists would not be particularly interested in the exact mechanisms by which speech is perceived or misperceived, nor would they be interested in why a person said, "Oh my gooshness" instead of "My goodness!" (real-life speech error generated by one Bridget's students). These are psychological questions and issues of precisely how language plays itself out. Linguists would be interested in language in its pure form—the rules that define it and our knowledge of those rules. This (relatively) pure knowledge of language and its rules is termed **linguistic competence.** In the following pages, we will be concerned primarily with psycholinguistics and the cognitive processes that combine to allow for our seamless ability to speak, read, write, and understand.

Words and Rules

First, let's state what we mean by language. We'll begin with a relatively simple definition. **Language** can be defined as a set of symbols and principles for the combination of those symbols that allow for communication and comprehension. Let's again consult linguist Stephen Pinker (appropriately enough, this linguist has a way with words!) sums it up neatly in the title of his book on language: *Words and Rules* (emphasis added). Your ability to read and understand this textbook is based entirely on your knowledge of the words you're reading as well as your (mostly implicit) understanding of the rules that dictate how these words may be combined.

One obvious characteristic of language is that everything to which we refer is symbolized by a word. This is a simple, but stunning, fact when you consider the tens of thousands of these symbols that you know and the relative ease and speed with which you retrieve them; naming an everyday object takes well under one second. All the words a person knows comprise their **mental lexicon,** or mental dictionary. Your mental lexicon is a significant part of semantic memory, the general knowledge store that we introduced in Chapter 6. Each representation in the mental lexicon is thought to include more than just a representation of word meaning. It includes other information that we know about a word, such as its sound, its written form, and the roles it can take on in a sentence (e.g., noun, verb, etc.). We'll be returning to the mental lexicon at several points in this chapter.

Obviously, language doesn't consist simply of all the words we know thrown together in whatever grouping we please. If we were to say, "Walked me in cat front of the just," you would probably wonder whether we should be coauthoring a textbook. But if we were to simply rearrange these words—"the cat just walked in front of me"—you would have no confusion. Along with the words we use to represent objects, ideas, and actions are rules that govern how these symbols may be combined. The term commonly used to describe these rules is **grammar.** Although grammar is often used to describe the arrangement of words in sentences and words in paragraphs, it's actually a more general term referring to the rules for combining *any* unit of language, be it a sound, a word, or a sentence.

Design Features of Language

One framework that has proved useful in capturing some of the major characteristics of language was proposed by Hockett (1960), who delineated a number of **design features** shared by many (in some cases, all) languages. A complete list of these characteristics is presented in Table 9.1. In scanning the list, you might find that some of the design features seem to be more at the core of what language is. Think back to the distinction we made in Chapter 5 between characteristic features and defining features of a concept. This distinction can be loosely applied here. Certain design features of language seem to be more defining—that is, they seem to be central to what language truly is (Harley, 2008). Let's consider a few of these design features.

Language is not simply a group of sounds or marks on a piece of paper. These sounds and marks mean something. This aspect of language is termed **semanticity**—that is, the symbols of language refer to meaningful aspects of the real world. In addition, the symbols of language exhibit **arbitrariness**—that is, they (typically) in no way represent the concepts to which they refer. There's no reason that these particular shapes—C–A–T—should be used to denote a little four-legged furry thing that says "meow." This little furry thing could have just as easily been called a frog. Although this arbitrariness makes learning the symbols of language a formidable task, it also affords language tremendous power: theoretically, any symbol can be used to represent anything. Although arbitrariness is the general rule, there are exceptions. You may have noticed one such exception in the earlier sentence—*meow.* This word actually does bear some resemblance to the real-world features it represents. Also, some languages

Table 9.1 **Design Features of Human Languages**

Design Feature	Description
Vocal-auditory channel	Auditory reception of voice message
Rapid fading	Disappearance of message over time
Broadcast transmission and directional reception	Hearing of message by anyone within earshot; locating by direction
Interchangeability	Reproduction of linguistic message by the receiver
Total feedback	Complete understanding of what has just been said
Specialization	Communication is only purpose of speech transmission
Semanticity	Specific meanings of language sounds
Arbitrariness	Little or no connection between linguistic symbols and what they represent
Discreteness	Language symbols are categorical, not continuous
Displacement	Communication of ideas that are remote in space and time
Productivity	Infinite number of messages can be formed
Traditional transmission	Teaching and learning of "detailed conventions" of language
Reflectiveness	Thinking about and communication about language
Prevarication	Deceptive use of language
Duality of patterning	Combining the same limited number of linguistic symbols (i.e., simple sounds and letters) in different ways (e.g., *cat, act, tack*)

Adapted from Hockett, C. F. (1960). The origins of speech. *Scientific American, 203*, 89–96.

(American Sign Language, for one) do include symbols with a close correspondence to the named concept or feature.

Language has the power to transport us beyond the present place and moment. We can talk about what we're going to do tomorrow or what we did yesterday as easily as we can talk about things in the present. In other words, language allows for **displacement** in time. Language also allows for displacement of another sort—the creation of alternate realities through deception. In other words, we can lie. This design feature is termed **prevarication.** The flexibility of language is also evident in the design feature of **reflectiveness.** Language allows us to communicate about the very topic of language; in other words, we can use language to reflect on language, which is what we're doing in this chapter. Perhaps the most important design feature is **productivity.** From the vast array of symbols (words) available and rules for their combination, an infinite array of new messages can be formed. It's sort of mind-boggling when you consider that virtually every statement you utter is new; you've never said it exactly that way before. This versatility is the product of a productive system of words and rules.

Language in Nonhuman Animals

One philosophical and empirical question that has fueled much debate is whether non-human species are capable of language (see Hillix, 2007, for a detailed history and review of the evidence). There is no question that they are capable of communication—the exchange of information through some type of signal. Even the lowly insect is capable of

Stop&*Think Back* | THE ESSENTIAL FEATURES OF LANGUAGE

In Chapter 5, we talked about different approaches to explaining concepts (e.g., classical view, prototype view, exemplar view, and essentialist view). The classical view and essentialist view are especially appropriate for considering questions of what language truly is. Review the material on these two views of categorization, and then form (a) a definition of language that would fit the classical view of language, and (b) a description of the essence of language. Reflect on (a) and (b), and assess each of the examples of animal communication and "language" that we discussed. Based on this, do you believe animals have "language" as you've defined the concept with these views? By which view—classical or essentialist—do animals come closer to having true language?

---

basic information exchange. Von Frisch (1967) demonstrated that honeybees produce a complex dance that signals to other members of the hive the location of nectar. Many other species engage in various sorts of communication. For example, vervet monkeys use a variety of calls to warn other vervets of specific predatory dangers, such as the presence of snakes or eagles. These calls elicit specific predator-appropriate avoidance behaviors (Demers, 1988).

So, nonhuman species can communicate, but is this communication considered language? Your intuition is probably that it isn't, and most researchers would agree. Let's consider these nonhuman communication systems in relation to the design features of a language that were discussed at the beginning of this chapter. Semanticity is present to

Got language?

some extent. The dances of the honeybee and the warning cries of the vervet monkey might be considered "words" of a sort because they do mean something (e.g., "an eagle is approaching"). But animal language is not completely arbitrary. For example, the vervet warning sign for "an eagle is approaching" includes looking up, which does relate to the content of the message. Animal language systems are rigid and don't allow for change, so displacement (e.g., "an eagle will approach tomorrow") isn't possible. Nor do animal communication systems have the numerous symbols and rule systems that allow for endless novel combinations (productivity). The rigidity of animal language systems prevents prevarication—the deliberate misrepresentation of information (e.g., a wiseacre vervet issuing a snake warning when there is no danger)—as well as the ability to reflect on the communication system itself. Clearly, the built-in communication systems of honeybees, vervet monkeys, and the like fall well short of the design features that are at the heart of human language.

Language Training Projects.   Some research into the possibility of animal language has been directed at finding out whether nonhumans have the capability to learn and use systems of words and rules. A substantial number of these language training projects have been conducted over the past 40 years with a range of nonhuman species in order to determine whether language is or is not a uniquely human faculty. These projects have investigated the representational and communicative abilities of common chimpanzees (e.g., Gardner & Gardner, 1975; Premack, 1970; Premack & Premack, 1983; Terrace, Petitto, Sanders, & Bever, 1979), pygmy (bonobo) chimpanzees (Savage-Rumbaugh, Rumbaugh, & Boysen, 1980), sea lions (Gisiner & Schusterman, 1992), bottle-nosed dolphins (Herman, Kuczaj, & Holder, 1993), and African gray parrots (Pepperberg, 1999a, b; 2006).

The criteria applied to assess whether other species exhibit language essentially boil down to the two components of language described earlier: words and rules. First, do apes, parrots, and other animals learn to associate labels with objects in the world? Second, can these animals take the symbols they've learned and spontaneously combine them in unique and novel ways using rules? You do this every time you open your mouth or sit down at the computer to type something. Are nonhumans capable of this novel language generation? In a review of language training projects, Savage-Rumbaugh and Brakke (1996) provide a useful scheme for considering the successes of these training projects and the extent to which these successes might be labeled "language." The bottom-line conclusion that these authors reach is that however impressive the results of these training projects might be, they do not reveal that nonhumans use language (see Rivas, 2005, for an ape-signing review that reaches a similar conclusion; see also Premack, 2007 for a comparative analysis of human and animal cognition that includes a section on language). Still, their scheme provides a useful lens through which to examine exactly what language is, a lens that provides a complement to our discussion thus far.

Labeling: Is It Word Learning?   Let's take a look at whether nonhuman species are capable of mastering the first component of language: Can they learn to apply words to concepts? Almost all language training projects involve teaching the animal students labels for salient objects in their environment. For example, the Premacks (e.g., Premack & Premack, 1983) taught their chimpanzee, Sarah, to associate a set of plastic chips with objects in her environment. She was trained extensively on these "words" and was required to place the chips on a magnetized board in response to questions. Sarah was quite successful in learning and producing symbols in the appropriate context.

Similar (and quite astounding) successes have been reported by Pepperberg in her studies of African gray parrots, most notably her parrot Alex (Pepperberg, 1999a, b; 2006). In the training model, one trainer (trainer A) asks another (trainer B) to name an object (e.g., key). After trainer B does so successfully, trainer A asks Alex to do so. This procedure is repeated, with trainers A and B occasionally changing roles and with Alex being encouraged to participate. Another interesting aspect to the procedure is Alex's reward. Rather than getting some type of treat, Alex is simply given the thing that he named to grasp in his beak for a moment. The criterion for learning was 80% accuracy in naming an object or one of its properties. Using this method, Alex learned dozens of symbols, including object words (e.g., *paper* and *rock*), color words, and numbers. And another contestant has been entered into the animal language fray—none other than man's best friend, Fido (or Rover, or…pick your favorite dog name). Kaminski, Call, and Fischer (2004) report the case of Rico, a border collie who learned to label over 200 small toys with different labels, with a high degree of accuracy.

These results are quite impressive, but do they demonstrate linguistic ability? Some researchers (e.g., Markman & Abelev, 2004; Savage-Rumbaugh & Brakken, 1996) aren't convinced. Sarah, Alex, Rico, and others have succeeded in associating labels with objects, to be sure, but it's not clear whether the labels are truly *referential*. Think of how humans use words. If I tell you that I'm going to the library to get a book to read, the word *book* refers to the same (or very similar) concept in our respective heads. Note that I'm not holding up a book and saying "book." In the naming studies just described, the labels are not used in a referential manner. An object is simply held up, and the chimp, parrot, or border collie gives a label to what they've associated with it. There's no evidence that the label *is* the thing.

Language as Learning to Do as You Are Told.   Savage-Rumbaugh and Brakke (1996) discuss a second possible manifestation of language that has been observed in language training studies: appropriate responses to commands issued in some sort of artificial language. These research projects help to study the second component of language—rules. Appropriate responses to requests or commands generated from the rules of a language would indicate a capacity for grammar. Interestingly, sea mammals have been the subject of some of these studies—namely, the sea lions Rockie and Gertie (e.g., Schusterman & Krieger, 1988) and the bottle-nosed dolphins Ake and Phoenix (e.g., Herman, Richards, & Wolz, 1984). These studies have investigated whether these animals can respond appropriately to symbolic relations such as "fetch the hoop to the frisbee" or "surfboard basket tailtouch."

Although the ability to respond to these sorts of commands seems a bit more language-like than simply labeling objects, Savage-Rumbaugh and Brakke note that when compared to the language of children, these instances of communication fall short of language. The only reason the dolphins engaged in these interactions was to get a fish.

Outside of this context, they would have no reason to engage in the communication. In stark contrast, a child uses language in a much more intentional and deliberate way. If a child plays a new game and enjoys it, they are able to refer to the game later in a request to play it again. No such capacity is evident in these sea mammals. Savage-Rumbaugh and Brakke do note that the animals may be capable of more, but given the limits of the testing situation, their abilities fall well short of linguistic expression.

Language as Engaging in Social Routines.   Language involves the use of words and rules in spontaneous interactions with others. By its very nature, language is social; it involves intentional and referential communication between at least two people. To assess the ability of nonhumans to apply the words and rules of a language in this context, a number of researchers have conducted what Savage-Rumbaugh and Brakke (1996) refer to as *cross-fostering studies* (e.g., Gardner & Gardner, 1975; Terrace et al., 1979). In these studies, selected signs from American Sign Language (ASL) were taught to chimpanzees within the context of daily interactions. Communication occurred throughout the day, and the experimenters treated the chimpanzees' gesturing as intentional even if it wasn't, just as adults do with young children. Eventually, the chimpanzees (most notably the star pupil Washoe) started to produce symbols, just as small children start to produce words.

So, was Washoe learning language? In spite of the surface similarities between this training situation and a child learning language, there were some critical differences. To help the chimps learn the signs, the experimenters shaped their hands into the appropriate signs until the chimps "got it." Once the sign was learned, the chimps had to give it in order to gain access to certain desired activities (e.g., food or tickle games). Here, the signs served the same function as the labels learned by dolphins and sea lions: the signs are simply responses made to achieve a particular end. The animals aren't really communicating any type of idea or intention; their utterances seem limited to requests and are never used referentially (Rivas, 2005). So once again, we have evidence for successful labeling and manipulation of symbols but not for truly linguistic capabilities.

Kanzi and the Bonobos.   Although many, if not most, researchers would agree that the results discussed thus far fall well short of human language, some striking results have been found in investigations of the linguistic abilities of the pygmy chimpanzee, or bonobo. Kanzi is perhaps the most famous student in this breed, which has undergone extensive investigation by Savage-Rumbaugh and colleagues. Bonobos are more similar to humans (in terms of their social and sexual interactions) than are common chimpanzees (like Sarah and Washoe). Savage-Rumbaugh suspected this similarity might indicate a similarity in the development of communicative behavior.

The work of Savage-Rumbaugh and colleagues (e.g., Savage-Rumbaugh & Brakke, 1996; Savage-Rumbaugh, Rumbaugh, & Boysen, 1990) with Kanzi is noteworthy in a number of respects. First is the manner in which Kanzi learned; initially his learning was spontaneous. Trainers were teaching Kanzi's mother, Matata, to use a system of symbols, termed *lexigrams*. When Matata was separated from Kanzi for breeding purposes, the researchers were surprised to learn that he had picked up many of the lexigraphic signs. In subsequent investigations, the focus was squarely on Kanzi and his ability to learn and manipulate these lexigraphic symbols.

Lexigraphic symbols used in the bonobo language studies
of Savage-Rumbaugh and colleagues.
Courtesy of Language Research Center, Georgia State University.

Kanzi's learning was fast and spontaneous. It wasn't necessary to explicitly train him in the lexigraphic language. He learned simply through constant interaction and interchange with caretakers about the events and routines of each day. As they spoke, the caretakers would point to whatever symbols happened to be relevant. In addition to speaking and referring to lexigraphic symbols, caretakers also used informal gestures and a smattering of ASL signs. Another noteworthy difference in the study of Kanzi was that the human communication system was combined with Kanzi's physical environment. Rather than raising Kanzi as a human child and attempting to engage him in humanlike conversation about objects and activities chosen by humans (as had been done with Sarah and Washoe), the communication system was allowed to evolve during Kanzi's everyday adventures in his 55-acre playground. Finally, the work with Kanzi was noteworthy in the sheer volume of data recorded by the researchers. Using automated, rigorous, and consistent data-recording methods, Savage-Rumbaugh and colleagues amassed a corpus of over 13,000 utterances generated by Kanzi over a four-month period.

A painstaking analysis of the utterances generated by Kanzi indicated that he was quite capable of generating novel combinations of symbols. And these combinations weren't just random strings of symbols and gestures. It was clear that Kanzi made a distinction between types of words (nouns and verbs, basically) and was able to place these types in the appropriate slots of an utterance. Even more impressive, the analysis also indicated that Kanzi made up his own grammatical rules and used them consistently, a sign of the productivity that characterizes human language. In sum, work with Kanzi has yielded the most impressive evidence to date of language-like abilities in nonhumans. First, Kanzi learned the language spontaneously, in the absence of formal instruction, just as it is with human children. Second, the symbols Kanzi used seemed truly referential in nature. Third, Kanzi combined the symbols in a novel and rule-governed manner. And importantly, these utterances were not initiated by external events in the immediate context.

Some, the prominent linguists Noam Chomsky and Steven Pinker among them, remain unconvinced by the demonstrations offered in the preceding studies. As impressive and surprising as these nonhumans' abilities may be, they are not using language. This nativistic view of language holds that nonhuman animals are simply not equipped neurologically to learn a complex system of language; language is based in specific brain structures that have evolved only in humans. But still, there is heated debate. Opponents of Chomsky's view (e.g., Greenfield & Savage-Rumbaugh, 1990), referring to it as "creationist," point out that given the (99%) genetic similarity between humans and other primates, it would be surprising if there *wasn't* some degree of similarity in nonhuman primates' linguistic abilities (but this is an oversimplification; see Pinker, 1994, for a rejoinder to this genetic claim).

Assuming that human language is "special" and unique to humans begs a question: What is at the heart of its "specialness"? What makes language the truly astounding creative instrument that it is, and distinguishes it from the labeling and communicative behaviors of nonhuman animals? Hauser, Chomsky, and Fitch (2002) point to one particular characteristic, **recursion,** a decidedly difficult concept to define simply.

Let's start with what some apparently believe to be a funny joke about recursion: *In order to understand recursion, one must first understand recursion.*" In the context of language, recursion basically refers to embedding sentences within sentences; this can theoretically be done ad infinitum. Consider an example: "The student wrote the paper that the professor assigned, which was worth 25% of the semester grade, which was one of four grades that the student would receive at the end of the semester, which was his last semester at college."...You get the idea. According to Hauser et al., the universal grammar of human language that allows for recursion is *the* defining feature, and the only one that truly distinguishes it from animal communication systems.

By no stretch is Hauser et al.'s (2002) view shared by all researchers. Pinker and Jackendoff (2005) dispute the claim that recursion is the only distinguishing feature of human language. They argue that many nonrecursive aspects of language (many of which we will be discussing in this chapter) make human language special. And some tantalizing recent evidence suggests that recursion might not be unique to the human species. Gentner, Fenn, Margoliash, and Nusbaum (2006) reported evidence of recursive syntactic pattern learning by, of all things, starlings. So stay tuned; the animal language debate continues.

Levels of Analysis

As you may have already gathered, language is a topic that in some way or another encompasses all of the cognitive processes we've discussed so far in this chapter. Presenting a representative sample of this research is quite frankly a daunting task. Fortunately, the very nature of language provides a ready-made organizational rubric that we'll use to survey the field—its hierarchical structure. Language can be analyzed on a number of different levels each of which features its own set of methodologies, empirical findings, and theoretical issues. Another useful framework is the distinction between language reception (e.g., perception/recognition) and language production. Both language reception and language production can be analyzed at each level in the language hierarchy, and this is how we'll proceed in this chapter. Given space limitations, we will not be able to discuss both sets of processes at every level of analysis, but will do so when the distinction is critical to understand a particular level.

At a molecular level, language involves the analysis of the small bits of information that we know as letters and speech sounds. The next level in the hierarchy is comprised of words. Next, one must consider the syntactic and semantic rules that nonconsciously guide our ability to form sentences. The next level (and only relevant to speech) relates to the social context in which humans communicate with each other. In this chapter, we will scale the hierarchy in the context of spoken language. We'll turn to written language in Chapter 10.

Stop&Review

1. Distinguish between linguistics and psycholinguistics.

2. Name and define three design features of language.

3. True or false? Animal communication shows none of the design features of human language.

4. The most compelling evidence for the use of language by nonhuman animals comes from studies of:
   a. parrots.
   b. seals.
   c. bonobo chimps.
   d. dogs.

5. What is recursion?

- Psycholinguistics refers to the study of the processes involved in using language; psycholinguists are interested in the study of linguistic performance. Linguistics refers to the study of language in its pure form; linguists are interested in the study of linguistic competence. Language is defined by a set of symbols (i.e., words) and rules for their combination (i.e., grammar).

- Language is distinguished by a number of design features, which include semanticity (symbols have meaning), displacement (we can communicate about the future and past), prevarication (we can lie), reflectiveness (we can use language to talk about language), and productivity (we can generate infinite combinations from finite symbols).

- Animal communication does exhibit a few of the design features that characterize human language, but due to its lack of productivity, animal communication seems to fall well short of language. Although animals are able to learn labels or symbols for a wide array of objects and concepts, it is doubtful whether these labels are truly referential. Animals also fail to show evidence of using grammar intentionally or deliberately.

- The most impressive evidence of language-like abilities has been shown with Kanzi and other bonobo chimps. Trained with a cross-fostering technique that involved the spontaneous use of symbols in day-to-day interactions with his trainers, Kanzi generated a wide array of novel sign combinations that seemed to indicate a rudimentary use of grammar.

- Some argue that the defining feature of human language that separates human from animal language is recursion—or the ability of language to embed sentences and phrases within other sentences and phrases, theoretically without limit. Both language reception and language production can be addressed at a number of levels of analysis.

Phonology: The Sounds of Language

Understanding spoken language could be considered an exercise in auditory perception and pattern recognition. First, sounds must be registered in the auditory system (perception); subsequently, these sounds must activate representations of the corresponding concepts in semantic memory (pattern recognition).

A great deal of research has investigated the basic components of speech, how they are perceived, as well as how a given string of speech sounds is identified as a word. Recall the distinction between bottom-up and top-down processing discussed in Chapter 2. Bottom-up processing refers to the identification of a pattern based on the component data. But as you'll see, speech perception and recognition involve more than just the compilation of speech data. Understanding speech involves extensive top-down processing whereby we use everything but the data to aid in pattern recognition. Speech signals are quite often unclear or imperfect; therefore, we must rely on surrounding information or previous knowledge to disambiguate the signal.

Let's start with bottom-up processing and take a look at the "data" that comprise spoken language. **Phonology** refers to the analysis of basic speech sounds. Given that most of us have more experience working with visual language processing (processing written letters) than we do in analyzing basic speech sounds, let's start with a visual analogy. Consider the visual identification of the letter *A*. It always has the same component features (more or less) in approximately the same arrangement, regardless of the particular word in which it is embedded. But the sound of an /a/ (/ / indicate the sound, apart from its spelling) in a spoken word has different component features depending on the context. For example, the /a/ in *cat* is different when a person from the East Coast, the Deep South, or England says it, because each of these individuals speaks with a different accent. In order to understand this, we have to look at the actual physical sounds that make up words.

The acoustic structure of a speech signal can be viewed with the use of a *sound spectrograph,* which, when presented with a speech signal, yields a *sound spectrogram.* The spectrogram plots what are basically bursts of energy (sound waves of differing frequency) that result from speech. Sample sound spectrograms for several different words are presented in Figure 9.1 (on the next page). The vertical axis represents frequency, and the horizontal axis represents time. Intensity of the auditory signal is represented by the darkness of the frequency bands. The particular physical stimulus elicited by speech is different, depending on factors such as rate, stress, intonation, accent, and surrounding sounds.

Figure 9.1

Sound spectrograms for several different words.

From Denes, P. D., & Pinson, E. N. (1993). *The speech chain.* New York: Freeman. Copyright 1993 by W. H. Freeman and Company. Reprinted by permission.

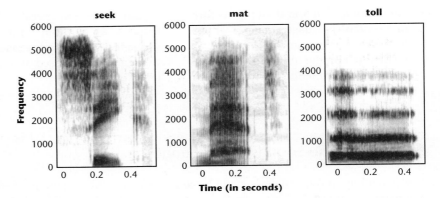

Phones and Phonemes

Because some variations in the speech signal are due to purely physical properties of the speech waveform, the smallest unit that we need to identify must be defined by the acoustic properties of a sound. This segment of speech is called a **phone.** For example, the /o/ in *boat* spoken by a Minnesotan is physically different from the /o/ in *boat* spoken by a New Yorker. The two sounds are phonetically different from each other; they represent two different phones. However, such phonetic (physical sound) differences do not change the meaning of a word: an *o* is an *o* no matter who says it. Therefore, we need another term—**phoneme**—to refer to categories of speech sounds that are clearly different and that change the meaning of a spoken signal. For example, the phonemes /b/ and /p/ are phonemically different from each other and yield quite different concepts when combined with the segment *-ig.* The phonemes of American English are listed in Table 9.2.

Table 9.2 **Phonetic Symbols**

The major consonants and vowels of English and their phonetic symbols.

Consonants				Vowels		Diphthongs	
p	pill	θ	thigh	j	beet	ay	bite
b	bill	ð	thy	I	bit	æw	about
m	mill	š	shallow	e	bait	ɔy	boy
t	till	ž	measure	ɛ	bet		
d	dill	č	chip	æ	bat		
n	nil	ǰ	gyp	u	boot		
k	kill	l	lip	U	put		
g	gill	r	rip	ʌ	but		
ŋ	sing	y	yet	o	boat		
f	fill	w	wet	ɔ	bought		
v	vat	M	whet	a	pot		
s	sip	h	hat	ə	sofa		
z	zip			‡	marry		

From *Psychology and Language: An Introduction to Psycholinguistics, 1st edition,* by H. Clark, E. V. Clark © 1977. Reprinted by permission of Brooks/Cole, an imprint of the Wadsworth Group, a division of Thomson Learning.

These phonemes can be categorized as consonants or vowels. It's important to note that the number of phonemes in a word doesn't necessarily correspond with the number of letters. Some phonemes are represented by a pair of letters (e.g., /sh/). Try to identify the number of phonemes in the word *boat*. Is it four? Or three? Remember that phonemes are sounds, and sounds don't necessarily correspond one to one with letters. Boat has three phonemes: /b/, /o/, and /t/.

Producing Phonemes. Speech sounds are a product of the vocal tract (see Figure 9.2), and can be described in terms of the movement of the structures within it. Differences among speech sounds result from differences in the way that airflow is or is not obstructed. Vowel phonemes involve a continuous flow of air through the vocal tract. Consonant phonemes involve some type of obstruction of the airflow (take note of this difference between vowels and consonants by making a few sounds of each type).

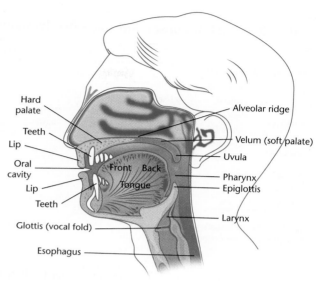

Figure 9.2
The vocal tract.

From Glucksberg, S., & Danks, J. H. (1975). *Experimental psycholinguistics: An introduction.* Hillsdale, NJ: Erlbaum. Reprinted by permission of Lawrence Erlbaum Associates.

Vowel phonemes (see Figure 9.3) are the product of differences in the position of the tongue vertically (high, mid, or low) and horizontally (front, central, or back). Say some different vowels and see how the placement of your tongue varies as you pronounce each one. Consonant phonemes differ along three dimensions. First, they differ in their place of articulation, which refers to the part(s) of the vocal tract used to make the sound. For example /p/ is termed bilabial, because it is articulated at the lips; /th/ is termed dental, because it is articulated with the teeth (try it yourself—it's fun!).

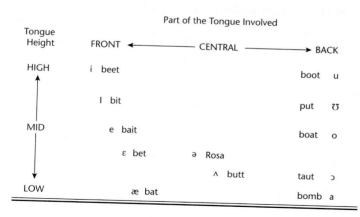

Figure 9.3
How American English vowels are produced.

From *Psychology and Language: An Introduction to Psycholinguistics, 1st edition,* by H. Clark and E. V. Clark © 1977. Reprinted by permission of Brooks/Cole, an imprint of the Wadsworth Group, a division of Thomson Learning.

Table 9.3 **English Consonants Classified by Manner and Place of Articulation**

Manner of Articulation		Place of Articulation						Glottal
					Alveolar			
Stops	Voiceless	P (*Pat*)			t (*tack*)		k (*cat*)	
	Voiced	b (*bat*)			d (*dig*)		g (*get*)	
Fricatives	Voiceless		f (*fat*)	θ (*thin*)	s (*sat*)	š (*fish*)		h (*hat*)
	Voiced		v (*vat*)	δ (*then*)	z (*zap*)	ž (*azure*)		
Affricatives	Voiceless					č (*church*)		
	Voiced					ǰ (*judge*)		
Nasals		m (*mat*)			n (*nat*)		η (*sing*)	
Liquids					l (*late*)	r (*rate*)		
Glides		w (*win*)				y (*yet*)		

From *Experimental psycolinguistics: An Introduction*, by S. Glucksberg and J.H. Danks. Copyright © 1975 by Lawrence Erlbaum Associates, Inc. Reprinted with permission.

Consonant phonemes also differ in their manner of articulation, which refers to exactly how the airflow is obstructed. For example, stop consonants (e.g., /t/) involve a complete disruption of airflow, whereas fricatives (e.g., /f/) involve only a partial disruption. Finally, consonant phonemes differ in voicing. Voicing relates to what the vocal cords do when the airflow disruption stops. If the vocal cords vibrate at this point, the phoneme is termed voiced. If the vocal cords vibrate after the disruption stops, it's termed voiceless. Voicing is a little difficult to grasp, but this demonstration might help. Put one hand in front of your lips and one hand on your throat (over your vocal cords). Now (really) slowly pronounce the /b/ sound—notice how your hand feels a puff of air at the same time your vocal cords vibrate—/b/ is a voiced consonant. Now slowly pronounce (exaggerate how slowly you pronounce it) the /p/ sound—notice how your hand feels the puff of air before the vocal cords vibrate—/p/ is a voiceless consonant. All of these features are combined to produce a given consonant (see Table 9.3).

Stop&*Think* | WHAT'S YOUR MOUTH DOING?

Take a look at look at the phonemes in Table 9.2 (p. 360) and the diagram of the vocal tract in Figure 9.2 (p. 361).

Do a little self-study of how your vocal tract produces phonemes. Sample some of the phonemes from Table 9.2 and enunciate them carefully. Take careful note of what every element of your vocal tract is doing (teeth, tongue, throat, vocal cords, etc.).

Phonemes also differ in what are termed **suprasegmental factors**—aspects of the speech signal such as rate, stress, and intonation—over and above the actual phonemes. In addition to differences produced by suprasegmental factors, any given phoneme within a word is affected by surrounding phonemes. The /a/ in *cat* sounds different from the /a/ in *bad,* because the /a/ is surrounded by different phonemes.

This is termed **coarticulation**; phonemes are, to some extent, articulated together (see Figure 9.4).

Perceiving Phonemes. In spite of coarticulation, we perceive more-or-less identical /a/ sounds in the words *cat* and *bad*. In other words the perception of phonemes is *invariant* across different contexts. Although coarticulation does make it a bit of a challenge to perceive phonemes as invariant, it does aid word recognition by hinting at what sounds are coming next. The words hill and hall feature a slightly different version of the /h/ phoneme because the subsequent phoneme is different in each word. This slight difference provides information about what is coming next, thereby facilitating recognition of later phonemes.

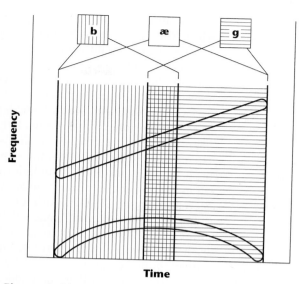

Figure 9.4

Coarticulation—the sound of each phoneme is influenced by surrounding phonemes.

In some ways, our perception of phonemes is analogous to the category formation process discussed in Chapter 5. The phoneme /p/ is like a category. We place all variants of the /p/ sound (e.g., /p/at, /p/e/t, /p/it, /p/ot, /p/ut) into one category labeled "/p/" just like we place various breeds of cats (Maine Coon, Tabby, Tuxedo, Siamese, Persian) into one category labeled 'cat." So it seems appropriate that the phenomenon allowing us to perceive invariance in phonemes in spite of their different acoustic properties is termed *categorical perception*. As you'll read later in the chapter characterizing phonemes as belonging to different categories may be a bit of an oversimplification, but, there is no doubt that phenomenonologically we don't discriminate between subtle shadings in the way a particular phoneme sounds.

The classic demonstration of categorical perception is a study by Liberman, Harris, Hoffman, and Griffith (1957), who used a speech synthesizer to produce and present speech sounds that differed along a continuum (*b–d–g*). In spite of the continuous variation in the speech signals presented, participants did not classify the sounds continuously. Rather, they placed the sounds into three distinct categories corresponding to the phonemes /b/, /d/, and /g/. They didn't hear *b*-ish *g*'s or *g*-ish *d*'s. As you'll see later in the chapter, some researchers have taken issue with this demonstration, and with the notion of categorical perception. We will return to this criticism when we discuss theories of speech perception.

Categorical perception would seem to ease the problems associated with coarticulation. Each phoneme represents a distinct category; any particular variation of one of these phonemes is still placed firmly into the appropriate category. Have you ever wondered why it is so hard to understand a nonnative speaker of English when they are trying to speak English? The reason involves categorical perception—their pronunciation of English phonemes is sometimes phonetically different enough that it doesn't fit within our English phoneme categories. So we have trouble deciphering the phonemes, which leads to trouble in figuring out the words, which leads to . . . well, you get the idea.

The occasional difficulties in understanding non-native speakers when they speak our native language occurs regardless of where we are born. Eventually we understand and produce the phonemes of our native language. This is truly amazing when you consider that the set of phonemes that defines a given language shows tremendous variation cross-linguistically. Some languages have phonemes and phonemic boundaries that are nonexistent in other languages. For example, native speakers of Japanese have trouble discerning between the phonemic segments /l/ and /r/ because in Japanese, these two belong to the same underlying category. The development of language-specific phoneme boundaries occurs early in infancy; evidence indicates that phonemic tuning is already under way as early as six months of age (e.g., Kuhl, Stevens, Hayashi, Deguchi, Kiritani & Iverson, 2006). And not only do infants seem to "tune in" to phonemic differences that are relevant to their language, they also seem to "tune out" differences that are not relevant (Bates, Devescovi, & Wulfeck, 2001). That is, there seems to be a process of suppression in speech perception that eliminates non-native phoneme contrasts from the perceptual repertoire. Some speculate that this *learned inhibition,* as Bates and colleagues (2001) term it, may be part of the reason that adults can't seem to learn a second language without an accent (McClelland, Thomas, McCandliss, & Fiez, 1999).

The Importance of Context.   Earlier in the chapter, we discussed the issues of bottom-up and top-down processing. Thus far, we have been discussing primarily bottom-up processing—the identification of a pattern based on the information that makes up the pattern (i.e., data in the form of speech sounds). But as we noted, speech perception also involves top-down processing—the use of context and/or previous knowledge to disambiguate a messy signal. A particularly compelling demonstration of the role of context comes from a classic series of studies by Warren and his colleagues (Warren, 1970, 1984; Warren & Sherman, 1974). Warren (1970) presented participants with one of these four sentences.

1. It was found that the *eel was on the axle.
2. It was found that the *eel was on the shoe.
3. It was found that the *eel was on the orange.
4. It was found that the *eel was on the table.

The presented sentences were completely identical except for the last word in the sentence. A coughing sound was spliced into the tape (at the point where the asterisk is) for each sentence. You can probably anticipate the result; participants restored the missing phoneme, but exactly which phoneme depended on the particular semantic context. This finding has been dubbed the **phonemic restoration effect.** It is important to note that the semantic context that allowed for the perception of the missing phoneme came four words *after* the cough that replaced it, demonstrating the power of top-down processing in phoneme perception.

Stop&Review

1. Distinguish between a phone and a phoneme.
2. What are the three dimensions that combine to produce consonant phonemes?
3. True or false? A given phoneme usually sounds quite different when presented in different contexts.
4. What is the phonemic restoration effect?

- Phonology refers to the analysis of the basic sounds of spoken language. A phone is an acoustically distinct sound. A phoneme is a category of speech sounds that change the meaning of a word.
- Vowel phonemes involve a continuous flow of air through the vocal tract and are the product of differences in the position of the tongue. Consonant phonemes involve some type of obstruction of the airflow in the vocal tract and are produced by varying three dimensions—

place of articulation, manner of articulation, and voicing.

- Phonemes also differ in suprasegmental factors, which refer to physical aspects such as rate, stress, and intonation. Coarticulation refers to the fact that the nature of phoneme transmission varies depending on neighboring phonemes. The invariance in perceiving phonemes in spite of their different acoustic properties is the result of categorical perception—our tendency to not discriminate between subtle shadings in the way a particular phoneme sounds.
- Context can aid in phoneme perception, an example of top-down processing. The phonemic restoration effect refers to the phenomenon in which missing phonemes are seamlessly replaced during phoneme perception, aided by semantic context.

Morphology: From Sounds to Words

If speech consisted only of sounds, this would be a very short chapter. But speech is made up of words that are combinations of phonemes. Perceiving and producing individual phonemes is necessary, but certainly not sufficient to allow for the production and comprehension of spoken communication. Sounds must be combined into meaningful units—words. So we need to ascend one more step in the language hierarchy and discuss the system of rules by which we combine phonemes into words and manipulate and change words to produce different shades of meaning. This level is termed **morphology.**

A **morpheme** is the smallest unit of language that carries meaning; it may refer to a single word (e.g., *tree*) or to a prefix or suffix that changes the precise meaning of the word (e.g., the *s* in *trees*). Word morphemes are termed **free morphemes** because they may stand alone; prefix or suffix morphemes are termed **bound morphemes** because they must accompany (i.e., they must be bound to) a free morpheme in order to have meaning. Let's consider the word *unprepared*. How many morphemes does this word have? It has three: *un* (bound morpheme; negates the verb); *prepare* (free morpheme; the verb); and *ed* (bound morpheme; indicates past tense).

Producing (or "Morphing") the Spoken Word

What happens when we change the form of a word? How does *mouse* become *mice*? How do we go from a *word* to a bunch of *words*? These important questions form the core of what Pinker and Ullman (2002) have termed "the past tense debate." Transforming *cook* to *cooked*, is a regular transformation (adding *-ed* to convey the action took place in the past); transforming *teach* to *taught* is an irregular transformation. Pinker (1991, 1997; Pinker & Ullman, 2002) proposes that making these transformations relies on two separate systems. First, for regular forms, we have a system of rules that is implemented to make the appropriate transformations. Second, for irregular forms we have an associative system whereby regular-irregular pairs (*teach-taught*) are simply committed to memory and used to retrieve each other.

There is a substantial amount of evidence supporting the two-system view. Pinker (1991) notes a number of dissociations that support the existence of two systems for morphing words. One interesting dissociation occurs in children as they learn the words and rules of language. At about age 3 or so, children begin to make mistakes termed **overregularizations**—the child extends a grammatical rule too far, treating an irregular form as regular (e.g., adding *-ed* to *go* to come up with the past tense *goed*). The funny thing is, *before* this point, children tend to use *correct* irregular forms (i.e., they say *went*, not *goed*). As children begin to apply the rules of language (e.g., adding *-ed* to indicate that an action took place in the past), they start making mistakes that they've never made before. As the child gets older, they get better at discerning when the rule applies, and when it doesn't, and add *-ed* (or not) accordingly. This rather odd sequence of doing it right, doing it wrong, and doing it right again suggests that two systems are at play, and occasionally in conflict (Pinker, 1991).

In addition, Ullman, Corkin, Coppola, Hickok, Growdon, Koroshetz, and Pinker (1997) found that different brain areas are active during the processing of regular and irregular word forms. Based on their findings, Ullman et al. propose that the associative mechanism used for irregular forms is a manifestation of the declarative memory system, while the rule-based mechanism used for regular forms is based in the procedural system. You'll remember these two memory systems from our discussion in Chapter 6. Recall that declarative memory refers to "knowing that..." something is the case and describes our knowledge of facts, while procedural memory refers to "knowing how..." to perform some skill or habit. In the present context, declarative knowledge refers to our "knowing that" *taught* is the irregular past tense of *teach*, while procedural knowledge refers to "knowing how" to add *-ed* to *cook* to convey the action occurred in the past.

Those on the other side of the debate are not convinced that that successful word morphing requires two distinct mechanisms, instead proposing a single mechanism view (see Haskell, MacDonald, & Seidenberg, 2003) and there is some neuroscientific data to support it. Desai, Conant, Waldron, and Binder (2006) did an fMRI study of the brain areas that were activated during generation of regular and irregular past-tense verbs, and observed similar patterns of activation for both, consistent with the idea that the generation of both forms is based on a common underlying system. As you've seen many times throughout this text, there is never a simple answer to issues of cognitive processing; there are usually empirical data to support each side of any debate. At present, the past-tense debate remains unresolved.

Perceiving the Spoken Word

Several theories for the recognition of spoken words have been proposed. A leading account of spoken word recognition is provided by the **cohort model** of Marslen-Wilson and colleagues (Gaskell & Marslen-Wilson, 2001; Marslen-Wilson & Welsh, 1978; Warren & Marslen-Wilson, 1988). According to this theory, speech perception starts with the first sound uttered by the speaker. With the appearance of that first phoneme, a cohort of possible matches is activated in long-term memory. Say the word in question was *boat;* according to the cohort model, the recognition process begins with the phoneme /b/, which activates *boat, bow, boast, bring, bug, bat*—any concept starting with that phoneme. But as you know, one phoneme is quickly followed by another (in this case, /o/). At that point, the cohort of possible matches is whittled down further—*bug, bat,* and *bring* would drop out as candidates. Eventually, the recognition process settles on the only candidate that remains standing.

The cohort model is supported by a number of findings. For example, it turns out that speed of recognition is strongly influenced by the number of words to which a target word is phonologically similar (e.g., Goldinger, Luce, & Pisoni, 1989). Another interesting finding comes from a study by Allopenna, Magnuson, and Tanenhaus (1998). In this study, participants were given spoken instructions that involved interacting with simple objects (e.g., "Pick up the beaker; now put it beneath the diamond"). Also present were distractor items that were selected to share a phonological cohort with the critical items. For example, distractors in the present case would include a *beetle* and a *speaker,* both phonologically similar to *beaker.* Eye movements were monitored as they followed these instructions. In line with the predictions of the cohort model, as participants were listening to the spoken instructions they glanced at the distractor item that began with the same phoneme as the critical item (i.e., upon hearing the first segment of *beaker,* they would glance at the *beetle*).

One problem with the cohort model is that it places special importance on discerning the initial phoneme of a given word. As you'll see, this is no mean feat; speech is so continuous that it can be difficult to discern where one word ends and the next one picks up. Other models of speech recognition (e.g., McClelland & Elman, 1986; Norris, 1994) loosen this sequential restriction of the cohort model but retain the notions of gradual and interactive (top-down and bottom-up) activation leading to word recognition.

One criticism of word recognition research is that it leaves some significant factors out of the equation. Note that in the cohort model, all that matters is the physical structure of the word (i.e., the sounds that make it up), and the phonological representation of this structure and its neighbors in semantic memory. But when we hear speech, it isn't some computer-generated monotone sequence of sounds. It's spoken by a human voice, either male or female, softly or loudly, excitedly or calmly, with rising pitch or falling pitch....you get the idea. Many of these factors fall under the general rubric of prosody, which refers to the rhythm, stress and intonation of speech.

Nygaard and Queen (2008) were interested in the role of *emotional prosody* (physical characteristics such as pitch and tone, that are associated with emotional speaking) in the recognition of individual words. More specifically, they were interested in whether participants would demonstrate a congruency effect—faster recognition of an

Research Theme
Emotion

emotionally valenced word (e.g., sad) when spoken in a tone that matched its valence (e.g., in a sad voice) rather than a mismatched tone. (e.g.,, in a happy voice). To answer this question, they had actors record happy words (e.g., *award*), sad words (e.g., *regret*), and neutral words (e.g., *handle*) in sad, happy, or neutral tones. Participants listened to the words being presented individually via headphones, and as each word was presented, they simply repeated it as quickly as possible. Naming latency was the dependent variable.

They found a congruency effect; words spoken in a tone that matched the word's valence were named more quickly than words spoken in a tone that mismatched the word's valence. The investigators interpret this result within the interactive top-down/bottom-up account mentioned earlier. They view emotional prosody as yet another top-down factor that can constrain vocal word recognition. Think about it; you're much more likely to hear the word regret said in a relatively somber tone, rather than a jovial tone. This tone will aid in your identification of the word regret.

Stop&*Think* | SAY IT WITH (OPPOSITE) FEELING!

Nygaard and Queen (2008) found that speech perception is facilitated when emotional prosody matches content. This exercise may seem odd, and will require some planning and acting, but it should prove informative. During the course of a conversation, deliberately mismatch the emotional prosody of what you're saying with the content. For example, you might express how stressed you are about an upcoming exam in a cheery, sunny voice. Conversely, you could say how excited you are for the weekend like Eeyore from Winnie the Pooh (i.e., in a sad tone). Observe the reactions you get. Do they notice? Were they thrown off? What conclusions do you have about the influence of emotional prosody-content match on comprehension?

Discerning Word Boundaries.   As you read in the section on phonology, the fact that individual sounds in a word run together poses a significant problem for the speech perception system. The same problem arises when we need to segment these sounds into words (i.e., locate word boundaries). Perceiving words is not a simple matter of identifying the blank spaces in the acoustic signal. Take a look at the spectrograph in Figure 9.5. You'll notice a pretty weak relationship between the breaks in the speech signal and the breaks between the words themselves. In other words, the "data" of the acoustic signal provide limited information regarding word boundaries. But you know from personal experience that understanding the component words of an utterance is (phenomenologically) a trivial matter. Mattys, White, and Melhorn (2005) desribe two tacks that researchers have taken in describing how listeners solve this segmentation problem. One is a bottom-up approach, the other a top-down approach.

Bottom-Up Factors.   A wide variety of factors present in the speech signal, itself, have been identified in facilitating the determination of word boundaries. One factor is

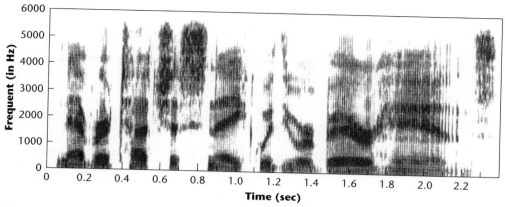

Figure 9.5

Speech spectrogram for the spoken sentence, "Never touch a snake with your bare hands." Note the lack of discernible boundaries.

From Liberman, A. M. (1970). The grammars of speech and language. *Cognitive Psychology, 1,* 301–323. Copyright, Elsevier Science (USA). Reprinted by permission.

phonotactic knowledge, which refers to sensitivity to the rules that govern phoneme (i.e., sound) combinations in different languages. For example, the phonemes /t/ and /zh/ are never combined in English. Similarly, the phoneme /h/ as in harp often starts a word but never ends one. Sensitivity to these types of constraints helps listeners discern words and word boundaries.

Another bottom-up factor is *metrical segmentation* (Cutler & Carter, 1987), which refers to the notion that the segmentation of words is dependent on the phonology of the particular language. For example, in English the important (content) words in a sentence are much more likely to start with a strong syllable (one that contains a short or long vowel sound, like the initial vowel sounds in eagle, candor, bacon), and end with a weak syllable (a schwa sound, like uh—the second vowel sounds in each of the aforementioned words). Based on this, our perceptual systems are "tuned" to detect word boundaries when a strong syllable is encountered (Vroomen, van Zon, & de Gelder, 1996). In line with this idea, Cutler and Butterfield (1992) found that listeners showed a strong tendency to mistakenly insert word boundaries before strong syllables, and to mistakenly delete word boundaries before weak syllables.

Using Statistical Probabilities to Determine Boundaries.   What may be the most powerful cue available for determining word boundaries is arguably the most subtle. Spoken language is a series of patterns to which we're exposed constantly. And if there's one thing the human brain is good at, it's detecting patterns. It turns out that there are plenty of statistical regularities embedded within speech than can be exploited by our perceptual systems in order to discern where words begin and end.

Some fascinating research by Saffran and colleagues (e.g., Saffran, Aslin, & Newport, 1996; Aslin, Saffran, & Newport, 1998) demonstrates that these statistical regularities can be exploited to discern word boundaries. Some syllable combinations are more likely to appear within a word, while other syllable combinations are more likely to appear between words than within them. For example, the syllables *pre* and *ty* are more likely to occur within a word than are *ty* and *ba*. Therefore, after extensive exposure to speech, when people here the string of syllables "prettybaby" they place the word boundary between the syllables *ty* and *ba* and hear "prettybaby." And, surprisingly, exposure to speech does not need to be that extensive in order to perceive this; infants are powerful little statisticians who pick up on these sorts of statistical properties of the speech signal quite easily.

In one of the initial studies demonstrating this provocative (and now firmly established) finding, Saffran, Aslin, and Newport (1996) presented infants with a continuous speech stream for two minutes. It was composed of four different three-syllable nonsense words strung together in random order. The infants heard something like *bidaku/padoti/golabu/bidaku* (slashes inserted to indicate experimenter-defined words). The stream was presented continuously, with no breaks whatsoever. The only cues to the experimenter-defined words were the differences in transitional probabilities between pairs of syllables within and between words. Some syllable pairs (*da* and *ku*) were more likely to occur within rather than between the experimenter-defined words, and some syllable pairs (*ku* and *pa*) were more likely to occur between rather than within the experimenter-defined words. For example, consider the string introduced above—*bidaku/padoti/golabu/bidaku*. The transitional probability for *da* and *ku* was 1.0. They *always* followed each other. This made daku a likely candidate to be a word. The transitional probability for *ku* and *pa* was only .33. This made paku more likely to represent a word boundary.

To find out whether the infants had learned the experimenter-defined "words" after this brief two-minute exposure, the infants were presented with two different types of test trials: (1) the previously defined "words" extracted from the two-minute stream or (2) new experimenter-defined words containing the same syllables but in new combinations. Infants could control their listening time by staring or not staring at a blinking light. If the infant stared at the light, the same sequence was continually presented. If the infant stopped staring at the light, a new sequence was presented.

Let's take a few minutes to describe this method. Infants prefer novelty and alter their behavior to gain access to novel events. So if the infants had picked up on the experimenter-defined "words" during the initial two-minute sequence, they should then prefer to listen to some other sequence during the test phase—that is, stimuli of type 2. If, on the other hand, they had not picked up on the experimenter-defined "words" and had essentially been listening to a string of syllables for two minutes, they should show no difference in preference for stimuli of type 1 or 2. Both are simply strings of the syllables they had heard earlier and are equally boring. Infants' listening times indicated a preference for novelty—that is, they preferred to listen to the type 2 stimuli (e.g., the same syllables, but in new combinations). This indicates that they recognized the type 1 stimuli as sequences they had heard before. During the two-minute encoding sequence, these infants had extracted the experimenter-defined "words!" Saffran, Aslin, and Newport underline how striking this finding is. Infants were able to pick up on word boundaries after only two minutes of exposure to a speech signal that had no cues—no pauses, no intonation, no variations in contour…nothing. This ability to pick up on phonemic boundaries effortlessly and automatically is astounding and has been replicated many times (e.g., Aslin, Saffran, & Newport, 1998; Maye, Weiss, & Aslin, 2008; McNealy, Mazziotta, & Dapretto, 2006; Pelluchi, Haye, & Saffran, 2009).

Top-Down Factors.   While there is no doubt that these bottom-up factors play a role in determining word boundaries, another approach flips the equation around, emphasizing that our knowledge of words in a given language helps us locate word boundaries. In order to understand this idea we'll consider a visual analog. Find the word boundaries in the following streams of letters.

THEDOGCHASEDTHECAT

This was relatively easy so it may have been difficult to see how your knowledge of the words in the sentence helped you form word boundaries. Now do this one:

IRANDOWNTHESTAIRS

Did you get confused at the beginning? Initially, your knowledge of words in the English language led you to segment the first four letters into one word. If "Iran" was not a familiar letter string in our language, you would have had no problem. But your knowledge of the language interfered with your ability to find the proper word boundaries. One more….find the word boundaries in the following letter stream:

THEREDONATEAKETTLEOFTENCHIPS

This one probably really stumped you. There are multiple interpretations: "There Don ate a kettle of ten chips"; "The red on a tea kettle often chips"; "There donate a kettle of ten chips." Your knowledge of the English language no doubt helped you (although, it still was difficult). But imagine if you were unfamiliar with the English language. In that case finding the word boundaries wouldn't just have been difficult; it almost would have been impossible.

Have you ever listened to a person engaged in the fluent speaking of a language other than English (that is, a language in which you are not fluent)? It sounds like they're talking a mile a minute, but really, this is a sort of illusion induced by your lack of familiarity with the language. Because you have only minimal (or no) knowledge of the words (i.e., no opportunity for top-down processing) in that language, finding the boundaries between words is nearly impossible. In many ways, it is like listening to the raw acoustic speech signal at the phonetic level that we discussed at the beginning of the chapter.

Mondegreens.   Even with knowledge of the statistical properties of words, and knowledge of the words within our own language, the perception of word boundaries remains a challenging perceptual task; misheard word boundaries have been dubbed **mondegreens.** The term was coined by American writer Sylvia Green in an article she wrote for the magazine *Harper's* entitled "The Death of Lady Mondegreen." It turns out that she had misheard the following rhyme that she remembered from childhood (from a 17th Century ballad):

Ye Highlands and ye Lowlands,
Oh, where have ye been?
They have slain the Earl O' Moray,
And Lady Mondegreen.

The final line is actually *and laid him on the green*. Once Sylvia Green realized this, she wryly declared "the death of Lady Mondegreen." No doubt her difficulties were caused by problems in top-down processing; there's not a lot of information or meaning in the verse so Green took her best shot at determining the word boundaries....but failed to find the right ones.

Song lyrics are fertile ground for mondegreens. (How many times have you heard someone say, "I can't understand the lyrics"?) We are not used to hearing language set to music; in some cases, it's almost like listening to a foreign language. One well-known musical mondegreen involves the butchering of a Jimi Hendrix classic in which one line of the song is heard as "'Scuse me while I kiss this guy." When the "data" for bottom-up processing are distorted or ambiguous (as they often are in sung lyrics), we apply our knowledge of words and make our best guess (which is often wrong). Top-down processing is playing a prominent role in the present example; "kissing a guy" fits with our previous knowledge a little better than "kissing the sky." Top-down processing could quite often lead to the successful resolution of ambiguous lyrics in a couple of ways. First, extensive experience with a given artist or type of music is likely to "fine-tune" our ability to process the "acoustic signals" produced. Second, knowing what someone is singing about—be it love, money, or the weather—is likely to aid recognition and segmentation.

It also turns out that our old friend bottom-up processing can aid us in the case of difficult-to-interpret lyrics. But in this case, it's not bottom-up processing of the speech signal, but of the accompanying visual stimulus—the facial and lip movements of the source! Massaro and Jesse (2009) found that when they presented a computer-generated "talking head" along with speech and sung lyrics, identification of the words was better than without the talking head. However, the effect was smaller for lyrics than for speech. So the distortion created by setting morphemes to music cannot be completely overcome by additional bottom-up information.

Stop&*Think* | ANNA LIZING MISS HURD LYRICS

Monitor your conversations in the coming weeks for mondegreens, or misheard speech.

1. Interview some friends to see if they have any examples of misheard song lyrics.

2. Look at the misheard speech and/or song lyrics, and evaluate the bottom-up and top-down factors that contribute to mishearing the segment.

The Mental Lexicon.   Our discussion of word recognition would not be complete without the discussion of its most breathtaking aspect, and arguably all of language: the incredible speed with which we access information about words. What are the processes that account for the fast and efficient retrieval of word information from semantic memory, our storehouse of general knowledge? Researchers commonly use the term mental lexicon to refer to our mental dictionary. The mental lexicon is really just another way of referring to the general knowledge represented in semantic memory (Chapter 6), albeit with a more linguistic bent. The process by which a concept is activated within the lexicon is termed lexical access. What factors influence our access to and recognition of words.

Factors Affecting Lexical Access.   One factor that affects lexical access is word frequency, which refers to how commonly a word occurs in one's day-to-day linguistic encounters. High-frequency words (e.g., house) are more easily and quickly accessed than low frequency words (e.g., bungalow). In a divided attention study that investigated lexical access, Foss (1969) had participants perform a phoneme monitoring task. They were to listen for a target phoneme (e.g., /g/) while attempting to comprehend a speech passage. The target phonemes immediately followed either low-frequency or high-frequency words within the passage. Detection times for the target phonemes were longer when the phonemes followed low-frequency words, relative to when they followed high-frequency words. Foss concluded that phoneme detection was slower in this condition due to the increased mental effort required for access to low-frequency words.

Another factor that affects lexical access is *lexical ambiguity*, which occurs when a word with two possible meanings (e.g., bank) is encountered. This raises several interesting questions with regard to lexical access. Do ambiguous words have two separate representations in semantic memory? Are both representations activated when the word is encountered, or only the one relevant to the particular context? An early study by Foss (1970) suggested that the first scenario is the case. The study used a phoneme monitoring task; participants listened for target phonemes, which appeared immediately after (a) words with only one possible meaning, or (b) words with two possible meanings. Foss found that participants were slower in detecting phonemes that followed ambiguous words, ostensibly because the ongoing disambiguation of the word delayed the detection of the subsequent phoneme. This suggests that all meanings of ambiguous words are activated, at least temporarily; context then leads to disambiguation of the word.

The Bilingual Lexicon.   Bilinguals, individuals fluent in two (or more) languages, make an interesting case for questions of lexical access. How are concepts represented in bilingual individuals? To put it in concrete terms, when a Spanish-English bilingual sees a cat or has to produce the word cat in either language, how many representations are activated? According to what Harley (2008) terms the *separate store approach* (e.g., Potter, So, von Eckardt, & Feldman, 1984), there are separate mental lexicons that correspond to a bilingual individual's two languages. The one that is accessed is the one that matches the language being used. Support for this approach comes from research by Kirsner and colleagues (e.g., Kirsner, Brown, Abrol, Chaddha, & Sharma,

1980; Kirsner, Milech, & Standen, 1983) revealing that priming in lexical decision tasks is not as strong when cross-language equivalents were used as primes, relative to when a word was repeated in the same language. In other words, "miedo" was not as good a prime for "fear" as was the word itself; "fear-fear" led to faster RT's than "miedo-fear." Note that there should be no difference between these conditions if both "fear" and "miedo" lead to the activation of one general (language nonspecific) representation.

In contrast, the *common stores approach* (Harley, 2008) proposes one common mental lexicon that is accessed through either language. This view would predict equivalent lexical access regardless of the language in which concepts are presented. For example, in an investigation of bilingual semantic memory, Caramazza and Brones (1980) had Spanish-English bilinguals decide whether a presented concept (e.g., cat or gato) was a member of a more general category (e.g., animal or sustantivo). In this study, it didn't matter whether or not the language of the presented word matched the language of the presented category name. This suggests that a general representation of the concept is being activated. This general activation facilitates either language's form of that concept.

A good deal of evidence supports the common-store view but it seems to depend on the nature of the lexical items, or on the nature of the bilingual individual. For example, if words are cross-linguistic cognates of one another (i.e., they have similar phonological properties in both languages like *flauta* and *flute*), they are more likely to be accessed via a common representation. Also, evidence suggests that late bilinguals (those who added a second language late in development) are more likely to have established separate lexicons for each language. Bilinguals who learned their languages concurrently, from early in life, are more likely to exhibit a common store (e.g., Silverberg & Samuel, 2004). Finally, it could be that bilinguals can choose to operate in a bilingual or unilingual mode, depending on task demands (e.g., Grosjean & Soares, 1986).

Entrance into the Mental Lexicon: Word Learning.   Earlier we discussed a study by Safran et al. (1996) that demonstrated how infants utilize the statistical regularities of phoneme placement within and between words to discern word boundaries. Although this is a critical aspect in learning words, it does not address how the child learns what the label for a word means. The attachment of meaning to linguistic information is a critical design feature of language—the feature of semanticity discussed at the beginning of the chapter. While it is amazing that infants can extract patterned sequences out of the speech they hear, it might be even more amazing that they are able to take those patterned sequences and apply them to objects. These associations between "patterned sequences" and "meanings" are the foundation for entry of these words in the mental lexicon.

Estes, Evans, and Alibali (2007) investigated whether infants could take newly learned sequences and apply them to objects. In the first phase of their experiment, they employed the Saffran et al. (1996) procedure in order to train the infants to hear experimenter-defined words. Recall that this involves the presentation of a continuous speech stream with syllable transition probabilities that encourage certain sequences to be extracted as words. In the second (habituation) phase, after infants had extracted the experimenter-defined words, they were presented with a word-labeling habituation task. In a standard habituation task, infants watch a video in which an object is

Table 9.4 **Looking times (sec) from the Estes et al. (2007) study; Infants were surprised only when there was a switch in the "word" condition.**

	Same	Switch
"Word" Condition	5.5	7.3
"Nonword" Condition	5.0	4.7

shown (and moved around a bit to keep their attention). At the same time its label is presented auditorily. Think of watching a screen with a stuffed bunny being waved around, and hearing a soothing voice saying "bunny!" This pairing is presented until the infants show *habituation*—basically, they get tired of it and look away. In the Estes et al. study they presented two different objects to infants, each paired with a label. For half of the infants (word condition), the labels for the two items were experimenter-defined words that they had learned during the first phase. For the other half of the infants (nonwords condition), the labels were "nonwords" (words not extracted in the first phase). For all infants, label-object pairings were presented to the point of habituation, as just described.

In the final phase, infants were presented with one of the objects from the habituation phase, either with its old label (*same* condition), or with the label for the other object in the pair (*switch* condition). If the word had been extracted in the first phase and then used as a label in the habituation phase (word condition), the infant should be surprised when a new label is presented in the switch condition. This surprise should lead the infant to spend more time gazing at that object in the switch than the same condition. However, when an object was labeled with a sequence not extracted in the first phase (i.e., a "nonword"), gaze time should be the same in the switch and same conditions. Both conditions involve the pairing of an object with a sound sequence that might as well be random noise. So the "switch" would not be surprising and gaze time should be the same. The results presented in Table 9.4 fit the prediction perfectly.

The gaze time data from the final phase revealed that the infants were surprised at the label change but only in the word condition. These results suggest that not only do infants extract patterned sequences out of a speech stream; they can readily associate these sequences with objects. These mechanisms are the very essence of word learning.

Stop&Review

1. Morphology refers to
   a. our ability to detect word boundaries in fluent speech.
   b. our tendency to fill in missing speech sounds.
   c. analysis of the meaningful units of a language.

2. What's the basic idea behind the cohort model of word recognition?
3. Name two bottom-up factors we use to segment words in speech.
4. What is a mondegreen?
5. True or false? Low-frequency words are more easily and quickly accessed from

the mental lexicon, relative to high-frequency words.

- Morphology refers to an analysis of the meaningful units of language. A morpheme is the smallest unit of language that carries meaning and may refer to a single word (free morpheme), a prefix or suffix (bound morphemes). The transformation of words may rely on two separate systems—one for regular forms and one for irregular forms.

- According to the cohort model of word recognition, spoken words are recognized by activating the entire set of possible words based on the word's initial sound, with a subsequent narrowing of the candidate set as more of the word is perceived. In addition to physical characteristics, word recognition depends on prosody, the physical dimensions of how a word is spoken.

- Identification of word boundaries is a perceptual challenge due to the weak relationship between breaks in the speech signal and breaks between words. Stress patterns of words and the rhythms of speech aid in this identification.

Phonotactic knowledge refers to implicit knowledge of rules that dictate phoneme combination. Word boundaries can also be identified via statistical regularities in the speech streams. All of these factors are bottom-up, in that they are part of the data of speech.

- The ambiguity of speech sequences leads to mondegreens (misheard word boundaries). When the speech signal is distorted or ambiguous, we apply our knowledge of words and make our best guess which is often wrong. The importance of top-down processing is also observed when we have difficulty parsing words in a foreign language because of a lack of familiarity.

- The process by which a concept is activated within the mental lexicon (our mental dictionary) is termed lexical access. High-frequency and nonambiguous words are more easily accessed than low frequency and ambiguous words. When an ambiguous word is encountered, both meanings are temporarily activated; context leads to disambiguation. Bilinguals seem to have a common semantic memory store underlying their two lexicons.

Syntax and Semantics: From Words to Sentences

So far we have talked about sound (phonology) and words (morphology). However, the essence of language lies not in individual sounds or even words, but in the combinations of particular words that we assemble to convey a thought. So we need to take one more step up the language hierarchy—combining words into sentences that convey a particular meaning.

Consider the following sentence: "The crowd booed the referee after his terrible call." It's clear that when we read (or listen), we implicitly understand not only the meaning of the individual words in the sentence, but also the structure of the sentence: the subject (*the crowd*), the object (*the referee*), and the connecting verb (*booed*). We understand each of these components and their interaction—the "who is doing what to whom," if you will. How do we arrive at this understanding? You no doubt have the intuition that it depends on a number of different factors: we must (1) successfully recognize each word in the sentence, (2) discern the grammatical structure of the sentence, and (3) form a representation of the meaning expressed by the sentence. In other words, sentence comprehension involves analysis at three levels in the language hierarchy: word (discussed early in this chapter), **syntax** (the set of rules that specify legal combinations of words within a given language), and **semantics** (the rules governing the effective transmission of meaning).

As you've seen in a number of places throughout the text, dissociations—cases in which one cognitive process is impacted by some variable while another is not, or is affected in the opposite fashion—provide evidence that the two processes may be based on fundamentally different mechanisms. This logic has been used to argue for the independence of syntactic and semantic processing in speech. The most commonly cited dissociation is between two types of aphasia: Broca's aphasia and Wernicke's aphasia. **Broca's aphasia,** associated with frontal lobe brain damage, tends to involve a breakdown of structure—speech is telegraphic and incorrectly structured. However, use of content words (i.e., nouns and verbs) is less affected. So there seems to be a loss in syntactic ability, with preserved semantic ability. **Wernicke's aphasia,** associated with temporal lobe brain damage, tends to involve a breakdown of semantic aspects of language. Those with Wernicke's aphasia speak with intact sentence structures, but distorted choice of content words. So there seems to be a loss of semantic ability with preserved syntactic ability. This dissociation is consistent with the view that syntactic and semantic processing are based on separate independent systems; if they were based on the same system, damage to one would mean damage to the other.

Transformational Grammar

A discussion of syntax and semantics begs mention of the most influential figure in linguistic history. You may remember from Chapter 1 that linguist Noam Chomsky's revolutionary ideas about the need for mental representations in order to understand language provided what may have been the most devastating blow to the behaviorist account of complex behavior. Chomsky argued convincingly that the breathtaking variety and creativity demonstrated by speakers of any language could not be accounted for by the simple mechanisms of imitation, positive reinforcement, and stimulus-response chaining. To Chomsky, it was inconceivable that such a simple, highly constrained mechanism could be at the root of language, with its infinite flexibility, novelty, and creativity.

One of Chomsky's main tenets is that language cannot be learned due to what he termed "the poverty of the stimulus." Children hear grammatical and ungrammatical sentences that aren't labeled as "grammatical" and "ungrammatical." and many of these grammatical mistakes are rarely, if ever made by an adult (e.g., "I goed to the bathroom"). And they typically receive no feedback concerning these errors. In addition, they say things that could have never been learned from an adult, because adults don't say them (e.g., "Look at the mouses"). So basically, with almost no direction, children learn language and learn it rapidly. Given that the learning environment provides no help (i.e., is an impoverished stimulus), language cannot possibly be learned solely on environmental input (although certainly environmental input is critical).

To Chomsky, this implied that children must be applying stored rules (rules that are represented physiologically from birth) to the symbols of language. These syntactic rules are at the heart of Chomsky's linguistic theory. According to Chomsky, we are born with an implicit sensitivity to sentence structure and the rules of syntax. When this implicit sensitivity is engaged by spoken language, it begins to develop rapidly in the absence of any formal "teaching." Chomsky's approach to how we engage in language is termed **transformational grammar.** And because these principles apply regardless of which particular language one is speaking about, Chomsky's approach is often termed **universal grammar.** Although the theory is not generally considered a complete model of language, it revolutionized the way language was viewed when it was first proposed and pretty much single-handedly established the field of psycholinguistics. So let's take a closer look at the key components of his theory.

Phrase Structure, Surface Structure and Deep Structure.   One component of his theory was the notion of *phrase structure.* This involves breaking a sentence down into its component phrases, termed **constituents.** Consider how you would break up the following sentence: "The engaging professor entertained the class." (No doubt this sentence describes your usual experiences in class!) Chances are you'd break the sentence into two major phrases, or constituents—a noun phrase ("the engaging professor") and a verb phrase ("entertained the class"). Each of these constituents can in turn be broken down into still smaller parts. The noun phrase consists of an article (*the*), an adjective (*engaging*), and a noun (*professor*); the verb phrase consists of a verb (*entertained*) and an object phrase (*the class*). Why the painstaking analysis of this sentence? We want to demonstrate the notion of phrase structure and to make it clear that we all have some intuitive notion of phrase structure rules—the rules that define the fundamental components of a sentence, the types of words that typically comprise these components, and the ways these words may be arranged.

The idea that we use phrase structure rules to generate and comprehend sentences seems plausible, but before long, this concept runs into problems. Consider the following sentence: "The shooting of the hunters was terrible." If you examine the sentence for a moment, you'll notice that the meaning is ambiguous. Does it mean that the hunters couldn't hit the broad side of a barn? Or could it be that somebody shot the hunters? Breaking the sentence down into its constituents doesn't help: "The shooting of the hunters"..."was terrible." The ambiguity remains. So a theory of grammar based only on phrase structure rules seems to lack something.

Based on the inadequacy of phrase structure in describing how a sentence like this can be formulated or understood, Chomsky had the critical insight that sentences must exist at two levels—both as an idea and as a concrete representation of that idea. He termed these **deep structure** and **surface structure,** respectively. The *deep structure* of a sentence conveys its meaning. The *surface structure* of a sentence is the particular ordering used to convey that meaning. The sentence "The shooting of the hunters was terrible" is an example of *deep-structure ambiguity;* in spite of the single surface structure, the sentence has two possible deep structures.

Two other scenarios make it apparent that phrase structure rules are insufficient for understanding language. Consider these sentences:

The professor is easy to please.
The professor is eager to please.

Although neither is necessarily true of any of your professors, note that describing the sentences in terms of phrase structure doesn't differentiate between them. Once again, the distinction between surface structure and deep structure is critical; while the surface structures are nearly identical the deep structures are radically different. Finally, consider these two sentences:

The professor graded the tests.
The tests were graded by the professor.

In this case, phrase structure rules make the sentences seem radically different; the noun phrase in one is the verb phrase in the other, and vice versa. But it's easy to see that these sentences are expressing identical ideas. In Chomsky's terms, these sentences have different surface structures but identical deep structures. According to the theory of transformational grammar, we use the rules of phrase structure to generate the underlying idea, or deep structure, of the sentence. Then we apply *transformational rules* to the deep structure to generate a surface structure that conveys the intended meaning.

Challenges to Chomsky.   As you may have gathered, Chomsky is a revered figure in the study of cognition and language. His theory (at least many of the assumptions underlying it) remained the dominant force in psycholinguistic research for years. His assumptions that language is universal, nonlearnable, and depends on rules that are with us from birth have been considered practically sacrosanct. But serious challenges to this view have been mounted on two fronts. One claims that language may not be so universal and the other that language may not be unlearnable.

(Non) Universal Grammar?   The first, and arguably more severe challenge focuses on the notion of universal grammar as introduced by Chomsky and proposed by other theorists (e.g., Jackendoff, 2002; Pinker & Jackendoff, 2005). The title of Evans and Levinson's (2009) epic review will give you a hint. It's titled "The myth of language universals." Their argument focuses on the breathtaking diversity of the world's languages, and based on that, the improbability that there are features that characterize *every single one* of them. To give full exposition to their argument would go way beyond the space we have here, but let's tantalize you with an example and some daunting math (and then maybe you'll go read the 63-page opus yourself!).

Research Theme
Culture

Evans and Levinson give the following example of a language that seems beyond comprehension, at least for English speakers. In the language of Bininj Gun-wok (Evans, 2003), a single word—*abanyawoihwarrgahmarneganjginjeng*—can represent what English would convey in the following sentence: "I cooked the wrong meat for them again." It is overwhelming to consider what this Bininj Gun-wok "word" and English sentence could possibly have in common (other than the meaning). And, according to the authors, given the way language research is going, there's not much chance we'll ever find out. Consider that some estimates place the total number of world languages at around 7,000, belonging to about 300 or 400 general groups. Evans and Levinson speculate that 500 years ago, prior to Western expansion, there were probably twice as many languages. Projecting backward through time, some (e.g., Pagel, 2000) make the argument that there have probably been as many as *half a million languages* spoken since languages first made their appearance. So the languages currently being spoken constitute (at least by this estimate) less than 2% of all of the languages that have ever been spoken. As if that weren't bad enough, modern psycholinguists only study about 10% of that 2%!!! Basing all of linguistics and psycholinguistics on this astoundingly narrow range of languages would be tantamount to us writing a 500-page cognitive psychology text based on our own subjective experiences.

Needless to say, Evans and Levinson (2009) believe an overhaul of the study of language is in order. This new approach should embrace the dizzying diversity of the world's languages. Far from daunting, they view it as:

> …a fundamental opportunity for cognitive science. It provides a natural laboratory of variation in a fundamental skill—7000 natural experiments in evolving communicative systems, and as many populations of experts with exotic expertise…We have a comparative psychology across species but not a proper comparative psychology inside our own species…. (p. 432)

Evans and Levinson's review appeared in the journal *Behavioral and Brain Sciences*, which is a unique forum in that other leading researchers in the field are invited to respond to the target article. As you might imagine, this particular review provoked some strong reactions from all directions. Needless to say, not everyone buys into the basic thesis laid out by the authors, and many were sharply critical of it.

Language heavyweights Pinker and Jackendoff (2009) acknowledge the linguistic diversity cited by Evans and Levinson, and the fact that it is too often ignored in modern psycholinguistic research. However, they reject the notion that no aspect of language can be considered universal. They point out that Evans and Levinson themselves acknowledge the existence of basic design features (i.e., semanticity—all languages convey meaning). With this acknowledgement, they are asserting the existence of language universals. Pinker and Jackendoff go on to critique Evans and Levinson on a number of grounds, and to defend their notion of universal grammar (UG). According to Pinker and Jackendoff, UG refers to a set of learning abilities that enable an individual to master any language. These abilities will manifest themselves no matter what the context, whether it be English or Bininj Gun-Wok. Pinker and Jackendoff further characterize UG as a toolkit, and readily admit that UG doesn't describe all possibilities for all languages; as they pithily put it, "….one builds structures *with* tools, not *from* tools."

Language: Not so Unlearnable?   A challenge to the unlearnability of language and the "poverty of the stimulus" argument has come from a recent approach that suggests that the structural aspects of language may be learnable. This challenge does not come from a return to a behavioristic approach but from the neural network approach to cognition.

Recall the connectionist approach to cognition that we discussed in Chapter 1. According to this approach, knowledge is embodied in distributed networks of excitatory and inhibitory connections between neuronlike units in the brain. These networks "learn" (i.e., are modified) through experience. Network connections are built up, solidified, and modified as we experience the world. According to the **constraint-based approach** to language (e.g., Chang, Dell, & Bock, 2006; Seidenberg, 1997), the gradual development and fine-tuning of neural networks during early linguistic experience play an important role in the rapid learning of language as well as in the cross-cultural consistency in the rate of language development.

Language is full of the probabilistic constraints that can be discovered by neural networks and exploited during the process of language learning. To get a better handle on the constraint-based approach, think back to the speech perception research that demonstrated infants' ability to compute word boundaries. With as little as two minutes of exposure to speech, infants could use the probability of syllable pairs occurring within and between experimenter-defined words to distinguish these words from similar words in which the syllables were rearranged. The same type of probabilistic constraints is present within sentences. Consider the following examples (from Seidenberg, 1997):

1. The plane left for the East Coast.
2. The plane left for the reporter was missing.
3. The note left for the reporter was missing.

What constraints are available for the processing of these sentences? It turns out there are several. First, the meaning of *plane* as a vehicle is much more likely than its other meanings. Also, the word *left* is used more often in the active form (as in sentence 1) than in the passive form (as in sentences 2 and 3). Also, the phrase "The plane left" imposes constraints on interpreting the relationships between the words; "plane" could not possibly be a modifier of "left," so "The plane left" cannot be a noun phrase. Another constraint is apparent in comparing sentences 2 and 3: sentence 3 is easier to comprehend, because it is much more plausible for a note to be left than it is for a plane to be left. In sentence 2, both senses of "The plane left" need to be considered, causing a temporary "hiccup" in comprehension. Constraints like these can be easily and rapidly learned by a neural network through repeated experience with linguistic strings (i.e., sentences). Combine this idea with the recent findings regarding infants' stunning abilities to do a probability analysis on a string of speech sounds in the space of two minutes, and you have the beginnings of a compelling argument for how language might be learned in the absence of any special grammar-learning module.

Not everyone is persuaded by the constraint-based approach. Pinker (2007) notes that while probabilistic constraints might allow infants to learn how syllables combine to form words, this does not generalize to their learning how words combine to form sentences. Words comprise a finite set of items, all of which can be deciphered and committed to memory. Sentences do not comprise a finite set of possibilities; they're an open-class (i.e., theoretically limitless) set and cannot all be committed to memory. Also, grammar doesn't just sequence words; it combines words hierarchically and relates them to a meaning. So learning how syllables are sequenced and learning how

Got prosody?

words are sequenced are different "computational" problems. What works for deciphering words won't work for comprehending and producing sentences.

It's also important to note that in many ways, the debate about language being learnable or innate (see Behme & Deacon, 2008 for a useful overview) oversimplifies matters. There is no doubt that the acquisition of language involves both sorts of mechanisms. As Yang (2004) notes, a human baby can learn language, but a kitten cannot. Therefore, there must be some biological substrate for language learning that the kitty lacks. And it is just as clear that this biological substrate alone does not lead to the emergence of language; sounds, words, and grammar all vary among languages, so it's quite obvious that they must be learned on the basis of linguistic experience.

Child Directed Speech. Intuitively, it seems obvious that this linguistic experience comes from listening to adult speakers. If you've ever spoken to a baby, you've no doubt altered the prosodic qualities of your speech. Recall that prosody refers to the rhythm, stress, and intonation of speech. In speaking to a baby you use an exaggerated, drawn out, sweet, and slow voice. The altered prosodic manner in which speech is delivered to infants has been dubbed **child directed speech** (a.k.a., infant directed speech, motherese, parentese, caretaker speech, and baby talk). Cross-cultural research shows that, relative to adult-directed speech, , child-directed speech (CDS) is higher in pitch with exaggerated "ups" and "downs," extended pauses, elongated vowels and a slower cadence (Fernald & Simon, 1984). In addition, infants show a marked preference for CDS over ADS (Fernald, 1985).

The altered prosody of CDS serves two functions: linguistic and emotional. Linguistic prosody refers to the fact that CDS facilitates language acquisition. CDS has been shown to help infants distinguish between noninformative, nonlinguistic sounds (e.g., sighs and laughs) and informative, linguistic sounds (Soderstrom, Blossom, Foygel, & Morgan, 2008). It also helps infants to segment the speech signal into words by isolating them through exaggerated pauses (Brent & Siskind, 2001; Soderstrom et al., 2008). Lastly, it has been shown to assist the infant in acquiring syntactic rules (Seidl, 2007).

As you learned earlier in the chapter, emotional prosody refers to the affective information conveyed in the tones and rhythms of language According to Scherer (1986), positive affect in speech captures attention and consequently aids development

Research Theme
Emotion

by focusing attention on an important aspect of the child's environment, a primary care-taker. Singh, Morgan, and Best, (2002) showed that positive affective speech, whether in the form of CDS or ADS (adult directed speech) is preferred by infants. The authors claim that given the "evolutionary primacy of affect, it seems reasonable that affective cues should guide infants' preference for speech."

Burnham, Kitamura, and Vollmer-Coona (2002) found that we talk to our pets (pet-directed speech or PDS) in a similar way as we talk to babies. But the similarity was tied to pitch and affect (indicated by intonation and rhythm) but not vowel hyper-articulation (exaggerated articulation of vowels—you are sooooo cuuuuuuute!). Vowel hyperarticulation is a linguistic prosodic feature unique to CDS; it facilitates the identification of a component (vowels) used to create words (Kuhl et al., 1997).. These results demonstrate that both linguistic and emotional prosody are important aspects of CDS. While children may prefer CDS because of its emotional prosody, it clearly provides information that aids in language acquisition.

An interesting study by Kempe, Shaeffler, and Thoresen (2010) investigated the rela-tionship between emotional and linguistic prosodic cues to syntax. In order to do this they varied the emotional relationship between the child and adult. They had mothers talk to their own child (high affect) or nonmothers talk to a child (low affect). Each woman was asked to convey to the child a syntactically ambiguous instruction (e.g., touch the cat with the spoon). The instruction was to represent one of the two possible mean-ings (see Figure 9.6 for each interpretation of the ambiguous instruction example). A pause between *cat* and *with* would be a prosodic indicator for the interpretation on the left side of Figure 9.5, while the absence of a pause would be a prosodic indication of the interpretation on the right side of Figure 9.6.

The results indicated that CDS prosody did exhibit linguistic cues to disambiguate the instruction but only for *nonmothers*. Mothers (speaking to their own child) tended to lengthen all pause durations (not just those between *cat* and *with*). Kempe et al, concluded that nonmothers use prosodic cues to syntactic structure in their CDS to maximize the

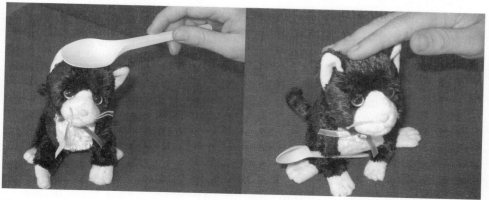

Figure 9.6

"Touch the cat with the spoon" stimuli from Kempe, Shaeffler, and Thoresen (2010).

Research Theme
Evolution

effectiveness of the communication. Emotional prosodic cues (e.g. exaggerated pauses) diminish the linguistic prosodic cues to syntax (an exaggerated pause in only one location). This demonstrates that the CDS of mothers may be dictated more by the need to forge an emotional bond with their child than the need to produce effective communication. This certainly would make evolutionary sense. The authors are careful to note that maternal CDS does not hinder language acquisition. In fact, many aspects clearly facilitate it (as mentioned earlier) but the acquisition of syntax may not be one of them. That aspect of language acquisition may be provided by the CDS of nonmaternal care-givers (e.g., fathers, siblings, babysitters). Therefore, their role needs to be further investigated in order to elucidate the role of CDS in language acquisition.

The evolutionary role of CDS is further supported (albeit in a completely different fashion) by Falk (2004) who proposes a provocative account on the evolution of language called the "put the baby down hypothesis." According to this hypothesis, CDS was an adaptation that served as a partial basis for present-day language expression. Her proposal is that early in the evolution of language, mothers would often have to put their babies down in order to carry out their daily tasks. To keep the babies content, they would engage in "prosodic," or song-like, vocalizations. This behavior would certainly have had selective value, and according to Falk, it formed a partial basis for the emergence of modern language.

Stop&*Review*

1. Distinguish between the surface structure and the deep structure of language.
2. True or false? The diversity of languages has caused linguistic researchers to completely abandon the idea of a universal grammar.
3. What is the basic idea behind the constraint-based view of language learning?

- Phrase structure is an important basis for understanding sentences, but it is incomplete. According to transformational grammar, a sentence exists as both a deep structure that represents meaning and a surface structure that conveys it. Sentences can have the same surface structure but different deep structures. Also, different surface structures may be associated with the same deep structure.
- The notion of universal grammar has recently seen serious challenges on two fronts. One is the claim that languages are much too diverse to suppose that the same underlying (i.e., universal) grammar can provide an account for all of them. Some leading theorists maintain the necessity of postulating a universal grammar.
- The other challenge is a constraint-based approach to grammar, which proposes that language is learnable via the same cognitive and brain mechanisms used for other tasks. Probabilistic constraints within language can be exploited by neural networks during the language-learning process. Child-directed speech (CDS) is one rich source of information that allows developing infants to pick up on words, word boundaries, and syntax. The prosody of CDS serves both a linguistic and an emotional function.

Pragmatics: The Social Aspects of Language

We are now ready to take the final step up the language hierarchy. When we consider the real-world contexts in which language is used, **pragmatics** is added to the mix of phonology, morphology, syntax, and semantics. Pragmatics refers to the practical knowledge we need to use language effectively during conversation. One aspect of conversing effectively is the need for coherence. Conversing is quite a challenge when things don't "hang together."

Conversational Structure

It is readily apparent (although seldom really noticed) that conversations have a fairly stable structure. If you consider the typical conversation in which you engage, you can probably come up with most of the notable characteristics that have been revealed by empirical research (e.g., Jaffe & Feldstein, 1970; Sacks, Schegloff, & Jefferson, 1974). First, conversations usually start with one of a number of standard greetings (Schegloff, 1972) like the unoriginal "Hey, how's it going?" in spite of the fact there are an infinite number of things that could be said. Try opening a conversation with something else, and observe the ensuing confusion. These stock openers elicit stock answers most of the time (e.g., "pretty good!"). In fact, if the stock answer isn't given, (e.g., Q: "What's up?" A: "Well, I've really been having a tough time lately.") it serves as a conversational "bump in the road." Another standard feature of conversations is *turn-taking*—the speakers alternate in what might be described as ABABAB fashion, conversational overlap is exceedingly rare. The veracity of this statement is evident by the frustrating delays in cell phone conversations that often lead to conversation partners talking over each other. The fact that we find this so annoying is evidence of the rarity in which it occurs in face-to-face language. However, you might also notice that individual styles of turn-taking vary widely. Some folks take long turns, while others tend to take shorter ones. Some (e.g., Jaffe & Feldstein, 1970) have suggested that the length of a turn is a fairly stable characteristic within a given individual's conversational interactions.

A number of standard signals indicate a change in turn—a head nod, a glance, a questioning tone. Sacks, Shegloff, and Jefferson (1974) propose three principles that (implicitly) guide turn-taking in conversations. The current speaker may choose the next speaker by directing a comment or question to a particular person. If this doesn't happen, then it is acceptable for any person to step into the conversational "gap." Or, the original speaker may simply continue talking. Sacks et al. suggest that these principles are ordered in terms of priority. The first is the most important, and the last is the least important. For example, if someone directs a question to you in conversation, and another person starts talking (i.e., initiates a turn) this would be conversationally inappropriate. The predictable rhythm of conversation, and the unwritten rules that seem to guide this rhythm, are an important source of coherence. Violation of these rhythms would lead to confusion, frustration, and misunderstanding.

In addition to the basic structural rules of a conversation, speakers seem to follow another set of rules when conversing. One might characterize these rules as comprising a sort of contract between speakers. Grice (1975) spelled out a number of characteristics that seem to define this contract. These "maxims," as they're termed, all support one overriding principle: *cooperation*. The four maxims are:

Quantity: Say as much as you need to, but not more.
Quality: Don't say things that you believe to be false; don't say things for which you lack evidence.
Relation: Be relevant to the topic at hand.
Manner: Be clear; avoid obscurity and ambiguity.

For an appreciation of how important these maxims are to our daily interactions, think of people you know who regularly violate them, and how others react to these people.

Stop&*Think* | BE A CONVERSATIONAL PAIN

To see how important the Gricean maxims of conversation are, deliberately violate them in the course of a conversation.

- Say too much, not enough, or fail to cooperate in some way.
- Observe the effects on the conversation.
- Be sure to "debrief" your conversational partners!

A simpler alternative is to think of the people with whom you regularly converse:

- Which of them violate the Gricean maxims?
- What impact do these violations have on their conversations?

Gender and Conversation

Based on your own experience, you probably know that conversations can be as varied as the people who are having them. Much research has investigated the factors that lead to this variation in conversation; a good deal of evidence points to differences in the ways that female and male speakers use language, and in the ways that they converse (Tannen, 1993). Pioneering work on these differences was done by Lakoff (1975), who enumerated a number of differences in the ways that women and men use language (It's important to note that Lakoff's work, while influential, was more of a sociological study, based largely on informal observation).

One difference noted by Lakoff (1975) is that women tend to be more polite than men. One indicator of this difference is that women tend to use *indirect requests*, in which the meaning communicated does not match the explicitly stated meaning of the request. For example, technically, the answer to the question "Do you know what time it is?" is "Yes" or "No," not "3:15." In spite of this, everyone expects the answer to this question to be a specific time. Indirect speech acts and indirect requests are considered polite ways of speaking and requesting, and are characteristic of women's speech. Lakoff (1975) noted a number of other characteristics of women's language. Women tend to employ more tag questions and hedges in conversation. *Tag questions* are questions placed at the end of a statement, as in "It's hot out today, *isn't it?*"

Hedges are qualifiers, like "kind of," or "could be." Another oft-observed difference in male and female conversational interaction is the incidence of interruption; male conversations tend to feature more interruption than female conversations. When men and women talk to each other, men are more likely to interrupt (Zimmerman & West, 1975).

Although most would agree that there are significant differences in the ways that women and men converse, not everyone would agree about what the differences indicate. Some claim that differences in conversational style reflect the relative differences in power between women and men; conversational differences are but one manifestation of deeply rooted cultural differences. Others contend that the conversational differences simply reflect differences in ways of interacting, rather than a lack of power in women relative to men. Some even argue that the differences aren't really that consistent. For example, a recent investigation by Mehl, Vazire, Ramírez-Esparza, Slatcher, and Pennebaker (2007) tested the commonly held belief that women are more talkative than men. As the authors point out, this is a deeply engrained assumption, complete with fantastic claims in the media. One famous and oft-cited claim is that women use 20,000 words for every 7,000 words uttered by man.

The claim of a 3:1 female to male conversational dominance had not been submitted to rigorous empirical test, so Mehl et al. set out to do so. They used a device termed an EAR (electronically activated recorder) to record natural conversation. The EAR is designed to track moment-to-moment interactions unobtrusively. It is a

Reality Check

Who's using more morphemes?

covert recording technique, and impossible to detect when it's activated or not activated. Mehl et al. collected data from nearly 400 individuals who wore the EAR during waking hours. The EAR was programmed to record for 30 seconds every 12.5 minutes. From those recordings, the researchers extrapolated the likely output for the day.

The results present a stark contrast to the mythical female dominance in talkativeness. On average, the number of words used by men and women in natural speech and conversation was strikingly similar. Mehl et al. acknowledge a number of limitations in their methodology, the most serious of which was the age and background of the participants, who were all college students in approximately the same age range. In addition, a limited number of participants wore the EAR (although it was a sample of 400). Nonetheless, the results are provocative in the contrast they provide to the assumptions made by the average person.

So it seems that gender differences in conversing may not be as prominent as generally believed, and that conversation may be as much a function of the situation in which it takes place as it is a function of speaker's gender. In addition, Thomson, Murachver, and Green (2001) note that speakers will change their language style so that it converges with the style of the person(s) to whom they are speaking. In other words, men talk more *like* women when they talk *to* women, and vice-versa. You may have observed this in your own experience; your talk molds itself to your conversational partner.

Stop&*Think* | INNOCENT EAVESDROPPING

Either in your daily conversations with friends, or by unobtrusively listening to the conversations of others, see if you notice any differences in the amount of time men and women talk in conversations. Did your anecdotal observations match the stereotype or the research?

Stop&*Review*

1. Define pragmatics.
2. True or false? Women use more words than men do in everyday speaking.

- Pragmatics refers to the practical knowledge we need to use language effectively, particularly in conversations. Conversations typically have a standard structure that includes a greeting, turn-taking, and little overlap. Conversation seems to be guided by unwritten rules based on the principle of cooperation termed Gricean maxims which inlude quantity, quality, relation, and manner.

- Some research indicates gender differences in conversation, although the precise nature and origin of the differences is a matter of debate. Contrary to popular belief, women and men seem to use about the same number of words in everyday speech.

Putting It All Together: Language Production and Perception

Now that we have discussed each component of language, we need to discuss some global issues. What are the theories that account for how we so effortlessly produce and perceive speech?

Speech Production

What are the processes involved in producing syntactically correct and semantically appropriate chains of speech? There is relatively little research in this area. Why? It's difficult to control what someone talks about or says. It is a spontaneous and generative product of what they're thinking, and it's difficult to control this spontaneity and generativity. Indeed, even if you could manage to control it, you would no longer be studying true language production as that is not the natural way in which we produce language. But the ever-resourceful cognitive psychologists have been able to amass enough empirical data to elucidate some of the main processes involved in speech production.

Stages of Speech Production.   One useful framework for research on speech production was proposed by Levelt and colleagues (Levelt, 1989; Levelt, Rolofs, & Meyer, 1999). This framework can be characterized as an information-processing approach in that it proposes four sequential steps in the production of language. The first step is *conceptualizing* what we want to say; the next step is *planning*, in which we formulate what is termed a *linguistic plan*—basically, organizing our thoughts in terms of language. The third step is *articulating* the linguistic plan. Finally, language production involves a process of *self-monitoring* in which we keep track of what we're saying and whether the message and tone are as intended. We should note here that this section will deal primarily with the *mechanics*, or basic processes, involved in the planning and production of speech.

Conceptualizing.   As you can imagine, some of the four processes proposed by Levelt and colleagues are easier to investigate than others. Not much research has been conducted on the conceptualization stage; this makes sense, for the reasons just discussed. There is no objective way to find out how ideas come together in anticipation of speech. Many believe that there is a sort of "mentalese"—a representational system distinct from language—from which linguistic expression proceeds, but there is little agreement on its form (Carroll, 1994). It seems obvious that this first stage of speaking exists, but it's hard to say much about it. Most research on language production has been done on the latter three stages.

Planning and Articulating.   Most of the research on language production has dealt with the processes by which we devise our linguistic plans and articulate them in speech. You might think that getting a handle on how people devise a linguistic plan would be nearly as difficult as figuring out how they conceptualize their thoughts. However, a rich

---

Table 9.5 **Categories of Speech Errors with Examples**

Type of Error	Example
Shift	He was dunk in prublic (drunk in public).
Exchange	Do you want water in your lemon (lemon in your water)?
Anticipation	Twitch on the television (switch on the television).
Perseveration	I haven't deleted the diles yet (deleted the files yet).
Addition	The girl's story is unbelievable (believable).
Deletion	Before I take the tape back I need to wind it (rewind it).
Substitution	Let's play some TV (watch some TV).
Blend	Oh, my gooshness (gosh/goodness).

---

source of data is available that has served as the primary database for research and theory on this stage of language production. This batadase—oops!…database—is slips of the tongue.

Slips of the Tongue.   You may do it several times a day: you get tongue-tied, you put the right word in the wrong slot of the sentence—in other words, you commit what psycholinguists term slips of the tongue. **Slips of the tongue** provide a valuable window into the processes involved in language production. They're also a close cousin of the action slips we discussed in Chapter 3. In fact, slips of the tongue are a type of action slip that we did not discuss, leaving it for discussion in this chapter. Systematic research into naturally occurring slips of the tongue has identified eight basic categories. Table 9.5 provides examples of each category, taken from the students in our cognitive psychology classes.

A **shift** occurs when one speech segment disappears from its appropriate location and appears somewhere else: "He was dunk in prublic." (The phoneme /r/ disappears from drunk and appears in public.) An **exchange** occurs when two segments change places (both segments disappear from their appropriate location): "Do you want water in your lemon?" (The words lemon and water switch places.) An **anticipation** occurs when a later segment replaces an earlier segment but does not disappear from its appropriate location. "Twitch on the television." (The later phoneme /t/ replaces the earlier phoneme /s/.) The opposite of an anticipation is a **perseveration,** in which an earlier segment replaces a later segment but does not disappear from its appropriate location: "I haven't deleted the diles yet." (The early phoneme /d/ replaces the later phoneme /f/.) A **deletion** refers to leaving something out: "I have to wind the tape." (The morpheme re is deleted from rewind). An **addition** refers to inserting something: "The girl's story is unbelievable." (The morpheme un is added to believable). A **substitution** occurs when an intruder replaces an intended segment: "Let's play some TV." (The word play replaces the word watch.) Finally, a **blend** occurs when two words combine into one, apparently because they are both being considered for selection. For example, one of Bridget's students came out with the unique exclamation of "My gooshness" (probably after having seen her grade on one of Bridget's killer tests), the second "word" of which represents a blend of goodness and gosh.

In looking at the samples of each type of error given in Table 9.5, you might notice that they can occur at any linguistic level, be it a sound (phoneme), a morpheme (e.g., suffixes or prefixes), or a word. And if an utterance contains a slip of the tongue, it tends to be at only one linguistic level; for example, you would switch a phoneme with another phoneme rather than a phoneme with a morpheme.

In addition to noting these eight categories of error that occur with some regularity, Garrett (1975) and Fromkin (1973) note several additional consistencies in slips of the tongue. Interacting elements within an utterance tend to come from similar positions within a word (switching the initial segments of two words rather than switching the end of one word with the beginning of another). They tend to be similar to one another (e.g., consonants switched with consonants) and receive the same sort of stress (i.e., emphasis, or accent) they would have if they had not interacted. In addition, the interaction seems too be based on phonological, rather than semantic similarity (e.g., saying "*Sesame Street* crackers" instead of "sesame seed crackers"). Slips of the tongue also seem to obey the rules of phonology: even when sounds are switched, the resulting errant "word" sounds like a word. For example, what slip would you expect from a combination of *slippery* and *slick*? If you said *slickery,* you're right; neither *slickpery* nor *slipkery* fit the rules of English morphology and therefore would not be the type of error we'd make.

A number of explanations for slips of the tongue have been proposed. These explanations differ in terms of the process involved in planning and articulation. Do these processes occur in a serial (step-by-step) or parallel (simultaneous) manner? And do these processes interact with one another? Serial accounts of linguistic planning have been proposed by Fromkin (1973) and Garrett (1988, 1992); their general structure is presented in Figure 9.7. Basically these models propose a number of substages within the broader stages of linguistic planning.

Stage 1—conceptualization, determination of stress patterns, determination of syntactical structure

Stage 2—content words and free morphemes added

| | student | prepare | | | test |

Stage 3—bound morphemes added

| | students | prepar*ed* | | | test |

Stage 4—function words added

| The | students | prepared | for | the | test |

Stage 5—overt articulation

Figure 9.7
Serial speech production accounts for the articulation of the idea of "The students prepared for the test."

Once we conceptualize what we want to say, we then determine the stress patterns and syntactic structure for our utterance. Then content words and free morphemes are added. (These are the words that convey the meaning of the sentence.) Next, bound morphemes (prefixes and suffixes) are added, followed by the addition of function words and overt articulation. Slips of the tongue occur at different levels of analysis. So the linguistic unit that "slips" tells us the stage of linguistic planning at which the error occurred. If a free morpheme or an entire word "slips," the error occurred at stage 2. A slip involving a bound morpheme occurred at stage 3. A phoneme level slip occurred at stage 5 when the phonemes are articulated to produce the final utterance.

One important assumption of these models is that the linguistic planning stages are independent of one another. Consistent with this assumption, many slips seem to occur at only one level of planning. Consider this classic slip of the tongue reported by Fromkin (1973): "a weekend for maniacs." The intended phrase was "a maniac for weekends." There are several interesting things about this error. First, the stress pattern of the sentence remained the same, as if that had been determined separately. The content words "weekend" and "maniac" switched places, but the *s* morpheme was stranded at the end of the sentence rather than moving with the word "maniac." This suggests the suffix *s* was added separately from the content word "weekend." Also, and perhaps most interesting, the sound generated for the stranded morpheme *s* fits the new context. An *s* at the end of weekends is a /z/ sound, but the *s* at the end of *maniac* is a "hissing" /s/ sound. When "weekend" and "maniac" switch places, the /s/ sound is adjusted to match its new context; this phenomenon is termed *accommodation*. Accommodation suggests that sounds are assembled after (and independently of) assembly of the words in the sentence. Other accounts of linguistic planning propose parallel processing. Speech production involves processes at a number of distinct levels (as just proposed), but these processes operate simultaneously (e.g., Bock, 2001; Dell, 1986; Dell, Chang, & Griffin, 1999; MacKay, 1987). Processing at each of these levels work in parallel, and may excite or inhibit processing within the same level as well as at other levels.

The study of slips of the tongue has a long and distinguished history within the discipline of psychology. No less than Sigmund Freud, the founder of psychoanalysis himself, investigated such slips of the tongue; they even bear his name—the so-called *Freudian slip*. Freud's view of these errors was decidedly different from those just described. Freud's interpretation of these sorts of errors was not in terms of the cognitive processes that lead to the errors, but in terms of what Freud viewed as the *unconscious motivation* for these errors. For Freud, slips of the tongue were a window into a person's fears, anxieties, or wishes. The person who goes into Dairy Queen and orders ice cream topped with "Reese's penis" (instead of "Reese's Pieces"—true story!) has done more than make a word error. According to Freud, this slip *means* something; it reflects something about the unconscious motivation that led to it (although for this particular example, we dare not go any further).

Reality Check

Is there any truth to Freud's claim? It seems unlikely that every slip of the tongue we make has a hidden meaning. But could unconscious thoughts play a role in slips of the tongue? Gathering naturally occurring slips would yield a biased sample and leave many questions unanswered. When someone commits a slip, it's anybody's guess as to why it occurred. However, if you can set up a situation in which slips are under experimental control, you have a more reliable way of assessing their causes.

Motley (1985) reports an intriguing series of studies assessing the Freudian account of slips of the tongue. Motley and Baars (1979) used a laboratory procedure that induced participants to make slips (e.g., saying "fluit fries" instead of "fruit flies"). Motley and Baars had participants read two-word phrases (like "fruit fly") silently; every so often, a buzzer sounded. On these occasions, participants were to read the presented pair out loud; of course, these trials were the ones of interest. Just to make errors a little more likely, the researchers preceded these spoken trials with a series of phrases that "primed the pump," so to speak. For example, to make the error "fluit fries" more likely to occur, the immediately preceding trials would be similar (e.g., "flag fright").

So where does hidden motivation come in? To engage participants in a given motivational frame, Motley and Baars varied the context in which the study was conducted. They preoccupied one group of participants with shock anxiety; these participants were hooked up to (bogus) electrodes and told they would be receiving an occasional electric shock during the procedure (although they never did). Another group was preoccupied with what might be called (for want of a better phrase) sexual anxiety; they were tested by "an attractive and provocatively dressed woman" (p. 118). A control condition was tested using an identical procedure but with neither environmental manipulation. The word pairs presented to participants, when rearranged, referred to either shock-related concerns (e.g., the pair *worst cottage* was presented so that the likely error was *cursed wattage)* or sex-related concerns (e.g., the pair *share boulders* was presented, with the likely error being *bare shoulders*—no, we're not kidding). The dependent variable was the number of slips committed.

The results were consistent with the Freudian view of slips of the tongue. As you can see in Figure 9.8, participants in the shock-anxiety condition were more likely to make

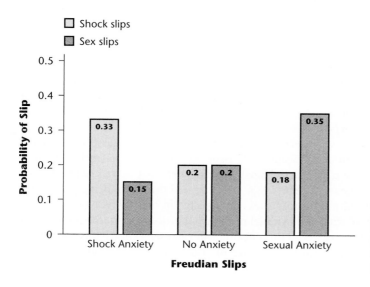

Figure 9.8

Results from Motley and Baars (1985).

From Motley, M. T. (1985). Slips of the tongue. *Scientific American, 253,* 116–127. Reprinted by permission.

shock-related errors than sex-related errors; the reverse pattern was found for participants (all men, by the way) in the sexual-anxiety condition. It is important to note that the number of shock-related slips in the sexual-anxiety condition (and the number of sex-related slips in the shock-anxiety condition) were not different from the number of slips made in the no-anxiety condition. This indicates that "anxiety" in general did not lead to more slips. An increase in the number of slips (relative to the control condition) was the result of the specific type of anxiety that led to a specific type of slip.

This humorous finding in no way discounts or qualifies what we've said about slips, the regularities they feature, or the possible underlying mechanisms. It simply adds another dimension to their explanation; in some cases, it seems that slips of the tongue can be made more likely by contextual variables, like what is currently occupying one's mind. But certainly, many (probably most) speech errors are more innocent, resulting from the mis-assemblage of linguistic units.

Stop&*Think* | FRIDIAN SLEUPS

Over the next week or so, monitor you own and other's conversations for speech errors.

- Take note of what was meant to be said.
- Identify the type it represents (following the classification scheme provided in Table 9.5, p. 390).
- Indicate the level (phoneme, morpheme, word) at which the slip occurred.
- For the serial account of linguistic planning, indicate the stage at which the slip occurred.

- Describe the circumstances in which the error occurred—when it occurred and what was happening (internally and externally).
- Based on what was happening internally could the slip be interpreted as a Freudian slip (i.e., motivated by unconscious thoughts)?

Self-Monitoring.   The final stage in Levelt's (1989) conceptualization of speech production is self-monitoring, which refers to the processes whereby we keep track of what we're saying and change it online if necessary. It's unclear whether we actually edit what we say before we say it, but there's no doubt (just think about it) that we regularly edit what we have already said. Often we engage in *self-repair*—we stop ourselves and correct what we've just said.

Levelt (1983) noted that self-repairs have a consistent structure. First, we interrupt ourselves when we detect an error. Second, we issue what might be termed an *editing expression,* like "um," "oh, wait," or "sorry." Finally, we "repair" what we've just said by saying such things as "er...I mean." Levelt (1983; 1989) termed this monitoring process the *perceptual-loop theory* of self-monitoring, and it is depicted in Figure 9.9. As you can see, the model includes both internal and external monitoring processes. Internal monitoring involves an inner speech version (recall this notion from Chapter 4) of what is about to be said. The external monitoring involves the act of listening to what you are actually

producing. This allows for two chances at repair; the internal mechanism may catch the
error, and if not, the external system will catch
it after the error is heard and comprehended.
One assumption is that potential errors are
more likely to slip through the monitoring
process to the degree that they're similar to
the intended utterance.

Slevc and Ferreira (2006) were interested
in how this internal checking process
operates. More specifically, they were interested in whether the internal monitoring
process is more sensitive to phonological or
semantic factors. That is, as we internally

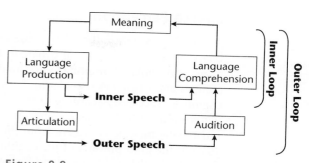

Figure 9.9

The perceptual-loop theory of self-monitoring (Levelt, 1983, 1989).

monitor our own speech production, are we more likely to be processing sound or
meaning? To address this, the researchers employed a stop-signal paradigm (e.g., Logan,
1984). In the stop signal paradigm, participants are required to respond to a series of
target stimuli. On some trials, after stimulus presentation but before a response is
made, the person receives a *stop-signal*, indicating that they should withhold their
response on that trial.

In the Slevc and Ferreira study, participants were presented with simple line
drawings of everyday objects (e.g., a couch) and they had to name the object as
quickly as possible. Sometimes the presentation of the picture was followed by the
corresponding word label (i.e., the printed word "couch") but in other cases, a different word was presented. The presentation of a different word was a "stop-signal" indicating that participants should withhold their response. The variable of interest was
the relationship between the stop-signal word and the target word. The stop-signal
word was either phonologically (e.g., "pouch") or semantically (e.g., 'sofa') related to
the target word.

The authors hypothesized that stopping should be more difficult in cases where the
stop-signal matches what is going on internally. If the internal monitoring process is
phonological (as might be predicted based on the material we discussed in Chapter 4), a
stop signal that was phonologically similar to the target word should make it more difficult to stop the response than a semantically similar stop signal. The converse would be
true if the internal monitoring process is semantic. The results provided clear support
for the notion that the internal monitoring process is largely phonological in nature.
Said in terms of the perceptual loop theory of self-monitoring, the inner speech that
goes on during the monitoring process is much like the inner speech we discussed in the
context of immediate memory—more sensitive to phonological characteristics than to
semantic ones. When a phonologically similar word was presented as a stop signal, it
basically "invited" the participant to say it given that they were in the process of phonological (rather than semantic) planning. In other words, speakers are especially sensitive
to the relationship between what they are planning to say and what they are hearing at
the same time.

Speech Perception

Attempting to explain the relative ease with which we are able perceive spoken language relates to a larger theoretical debate in language concerning the degree to which language is modular. A **modular view** holds that language is made up of a unique set of abilities and capacities that cannot be reduced to or explained solely in terms of other cognitive processes. According to this view, language is special. Correlaries to the modular view are that language is species-specific (only humans possess the module) and innate (the module is present from birth). The **nonmodular view** contends that language is the joint product of the cognitive processes we've been discussing throughout the text. The debate is largely a philosophical one; no experiment can provide a definitive answer to the question.

Debates about the modularity of cognitive processing is larger than language and is raging along many fronts in cognitive psychology (see Barrett & Kurzban, 2006). We have discussed this issue in several other chapters. In Chapter 5, we discussed the debate over the existence of a mechanism specialized for face recognition. In Chapter 4, we discussed the assertion of separate mechanisms that guide immediate and long-term forms of memory. In Chapter 6, we discussed the distinction between different memory systems underlying episodic and semantic memories. And earlier in this chapter, we discussed whether humans alone possess the ability to use language. We now turn to this issue in the context speech processing. Is there a speech perception module? To what degree is speech perception a special ability or just another instance of auditory perception? The tension between these two views has defined much of the theoretical and empirical work on speech perception.

Motor Theory of Speech Perception

The **motor theory of speech perception,** proposed by Liberman and colleagues (e.g., Liberman, Cooper, Shankweiler, & Studdert-Kennedy, 1967), is a modular view that posits a close link between the mechanisms we use to articulate speech and our perception of speech. Implicit knowledge about how speech sounds are articulated aids in our perception of those same sounds when we hear them. This approach is termed the *motor theory* because it contends that the basic representations we use for speech perception are the articulatory mechanisms that we use to produce the sounds when we speak. In other words, speech perception and speech production rely on the same specialized representations (Liberman & Whalen, 2000). Two other important principles follow that were previously discussed in this chapter. First, because only humans possess the mechanisms necessary for speech, only humans are capable of understanding speech. Second, speech perception is innate; infants are born with the representations that allow for speech perception and production.

The argument that speech perception involves a specialized module is consistent with a number of observations, most of which relate to the ease of speech perception in spite of a supposed lack of correspondence between the physical speech signal and the phonemes that need to be identified from within it (i.e., coarticulation) that we discussed earlier in the chapter. As you'll recall, the phoneme /a/ always has different phonetic features, depending on the context in which it's embedded, so there's really nothing for the perceptual system to "grab hold" of in order to identify it. Therefore, speech perception must rely on a special mechanism—**categorical perception.** Categorical perception is an important aid to speech perception, given the variability of a phoneme in different contexts. It is also unique in comparison to other forms of perception, which demonstrates that we are able to make relatively fine discriminations, not just categorical ones. Thus, speech perception does seem to be special.

Another argument for a specialized speech processor is the breathtaking speed apparently necessary for the perception of speech. Phonemes occur at a rate of around 10 to 20 per second. Our normal perceptual mechanisms are simply not capable of making so many discriminations in such a short period of time. To decode these rapid-fire speech stimuli, a special mechanism is needed.

Auditory Theory of Speech Perception

A nonmodular view of speech perception contends that speech perception is just another exercise in auditory perception and pattern recognition. The basic mechanisms that accomplish these tasks are the same ones we use to decode speech. No special mechanism is necessary (e.g., Massaro, 1994). And because other species have auditory systems similar to our own, the ability to perceive speech sounds should not be unique to humans. An early example of this approach is the **auditory theory of speech perception** (Miller, 1990), with a simple underlying contention: Speech perception is auditory perception, plain and simple. Massaro (1994) takes issue with many of the arguments typically used to argue for the special status of speech perception. Recall the argument that there are really no discernible physical features that defines a given phoneme because phonemes differ so widely with context. Massaro points out that this is a problem for speech perception only if the basic unit of perception is a phoneme, and there is good reason to believe that this isn't the case. If the perceptual units of analysis are syllables (which may involve as many as three or four phonemes in combination), the problem of invariance is not nearly as much of a problem. This also deflates another argument for the speech-is-special theory, the unmanageable speed of speech input. If the basic unit of speech perception is a cluster of phonemes, then we wouldn't need to process 10 to 20 units per second; it would be more like 5 to 10 units, which is more within the range of normal perceptual abilities.

Massaro also takes issue with the assumption that we perceive speech sounds categorically, contending that this assumption is simply wrong. As it turns out, categorical perception is more evident with consonants than with vowels (Repp, 1984). Also, research on how we perceive and recognize speech sounds has revealed that although people have the experience of categorical perception, we are actually capable of more fine-grained distinctions than previously thought.

In support of this contention, an article by Schouten, Gerrit, and von Hessen (2003) titled "The end of categorical perception as we know it" questions the very nature of the phenomenon, arguing that it's simply an artifact of the way the discrimination task was designed in the original study! Finally, the speech-is-special argument contends that the speech perception module exists only for humans, because the module is linked directly to the ability to speak. But some research indicates that nonhumans can perceive speech.

For example, Kleunder, Diehl, and Killeen (1987) found that quail (of all things!) were able to distinguish among different phonemic categories. So aspects of the auditory (speech) signal itself must provide information that allows for successful perception.

A Re-Assessment: Kind of Special?

Research Theme
Embodied
Cognition

Recently, there has been a flurry of theorizing about whether or not the nature of speech perception represents a specialized and unique processing system as proposed by the motor theory. One reason for the resurgence seems to be the notion of embodied cognition. If you haven't already made the connection, the motor theory is consistent with an embodied approach to cognition. From an embodiment perspective, it makes sense that understanding speech perception might involve the mechanisms we used to produce speech. A second reason relates to the discovery of **mirror neurons** that appear to react the same way when perceiving an act as they do when actually performing the act. These neurons are thought to provide a basis for the imitation and copying of actions simply by watching those actions. According to some, (e.g., Trout, 2003; Iacoboni, 2008) mirror neurons may provide the "common code" or link between speech perception and speech production that is proposed by the motor theory.

Fowler, Galantucci, and Turvey (2006) review how the main assumptions of the motor theory have fared in terms of its assumption that speech is special. As Fowler et al. note, this is difficult to assess, given the ambiguity of the term "special." At best, the evidence is mixed. One test for being special would necessitate that speech be the only perceptual stimulus that is directly tied to the motor system. Speech fails this test as other links between perception and action have been clearly demonstrated. The motor system is involved in a multitude of perceptual abilities and processes, not just speech. For example, you read in Chapter 2 about embodied perception, and the research that visual perception (e.g., of distance and slant) is critically tied to action.

Another sense in which speech might be special is that the stimulus for speech perception is different from other cases of audition. This relates to the claim that the object of speech perception isn't just the auditory stimulus but also the nature of the speech movements that produced the stimulus. Speech fails this test as well because this processing oddity is not unique to speech. For example, when we localize sounds, we're processing both the auditory stimulus itself, as well as aspects of its source.

A third sense of speech being "special" is that speech uses auditory perception mechanisms that are dedicated exclusively to speech, and to nothing else. The evidence for this is shaky at best; there do seem to be different brain mechanisms devoted to vocal vs. non-vocal sounds (e.g., Belin, Zatorre, Lafaille, Ahad, & Pike, 2000). However, the same brain mechanisms seem to underlie speech and nonspeech sounds (e.g., coughs, laughs).

In sum, Fowler et al. think speech is "special enough" in that its connection to the motor system warrants further investigation. However, they question the modular view inherent in the original formulation by Liberman and colleagues. They don't feel that the connection between speech perception and production warrants the need for a "special" mechanism to explain it.

Lotto and his colleagues (e.g., Holt & Lotto, 2008; Lotto, Hickok, & Holt, 2008; Lotto & Sullivan, 2008) contend that the only thing special about speech perception is its importance to everyday function. They further assert the necessity of subsuming the study of speech under a general (in Holt and Lotto's terms) *auditory cognitive science framework*. In their view (and as you may have gathered from our discussion to this point), the bases for distinguishing between speech and other auditory stimuli have weakened over the years, to the point that there is no doubt that general work on auditory perception can provide important insights about how we perceive speech, and vice-versa. That has not really happened due to the separation of speech as a separate and unique processing module. Holt and Lotto (2008) contend there is every reason *not* to believe in this sort of separation.

Stop&*Review*

1. Name and briefly describe the four stages in language production.
2. Which of these is not a type of speech slip?
   a. an anticipation
   b. a perseveration
   c. a blend
   d. a delay
3. True or false? Internal monitoring of speech seems to be phonological in nature.
4. True or false? The motor theory proposes that the same mechanisms underlie both speech perception and speech production.

- The four stages in language production are conceptualizing (determining what it is we want to say), planning (organizing our thoughts in terms of language), articulating (executing the linguistic plan), and self-monitoring (keeping track of content and tone).
- Slips of the tongue offer insight into the planning and articulation of speech. Slips of the tongue include shifts, exchanges, anticipations, perseverations, deletions, additions, substitutions, and blends. Slips can occur at any linguistic level—phoneme, morpheme, or word. A serial account of slips of the tongue proposes that after conceptualizing, we determine the syntactic structure for the utterance. Free morphemes, then bound morphemes and function words are added followed by overt articulation. There is evidence that slips of the tongue can be made due to motivational factors (i.e., Freudian slips) but it is the exception and not the rule.
- The final stage of speech production is self-monitoring. Often we engage in self-repair—we stop ourselves and correct what we've just said. Self-monitoring appears to be influenced more by phonological processing rather than semantic processing.
- According to the motor theory of speech perception, the same mechanisms and representations underlie speech production and speech perception and this mechanism is a separate and "special" mechanism. According to the auditory theory, speech perception is the product of "regular" auditory perceptual processes. Current evidence indicates that speech perception is most likely not an entirely separate module, and can be accounted for within an auditory perception framework.

10

Language II: Reading and Comprehending Text

Reading sometimes occurs so quickly and effortlessly that we barely notice it. But at other times, it's all we can do to make it through a page. What's going on when we read? What is the *best* way to teach little ones how to read?

You've probably heard that jmulbed wrods are as readable as normally printed words? Is this true? How do txt mssges affect our reading? What's going on in dyslexic readers? Are they just poor at reading comprehension? Can dyslexia be overcome?

When we read, there is so much that remains unsaid, but somehow, we manage to figure it all out. How is it that we're able to go beyond what's actually in print, and flesh out an entire plotline and miniworld when we read?

Sometimes when you read your textbook, it may seem like you really get it, but test performance indicates you didn't. What are some ways to improve judgment on this score? Speaking of reading improvement, what about speed reading; does it work?

In the last chapter we scaled the language hierarchy in the context of spoken communication. This chapter will make the same journey, but in the context of written communication. Let's take a closer look at the processes you are using right now as your read this textbook.

Mechanical Aspects of Reading

Just as speech perception involves the formulation of meaning from an inherently meaningless stimulus—air displacement in the form of sound waves—reading involves the formulation of meaning from little squiggles of different shapes, sizes, and spacings on a sheet of paper or similar medium. It's truly a wonder that we so quickly and effortlessly afford such a stimulus meaning. In the last four or five decades, a legion of researchers have amassed a great deal of information about the processes involved in reading and what happens when these processes go astray.

Top-Down and Bottom-Up Processes in Reading

Reading is basically an (albeit intricate) exercise in pattern recognition. A pattern of stimulation is encoded in the visual system, and a corresponding representation is activated in semantic memory. A theme you've encountered throughout the text is the fact that our mental processes involve a mix of bottom-up processing (building "up," starting with the sense data we take in) and top-down (working "down" from expectations and previous knowledge). Reading is no different; printed letters and words serve as the *data* that *drives* processing. But much of the processing in reading is driven by material not on the printed page, namely, our expectations and knowledge about what we're reading. Theoretical accounts of reading processes place varying degrees of emphasis on each, but there is no doubt that both are important, as you'll see throughout this chapter.

Eye Movements

The processing of information during reading starts at the point where the eyes take in the printed page. That being the case, the movements of the eyes across the printed page has been a primary focus of reading research. As you'll see, the consistencies in the speed and pattern of our eyes' trek through a written passage, along with the variables that influence these consistencies, can reveal much about the underlying mental processes.

Methodology.   It may strike you that eye movements must be a difficult thing to take stock of—after all, you can't gather much information from just staring at someone's eyes as they read (try it—you're likely to get a whap across the head!). But the ever-resourceful cognitive researcher has developed techniques for tracking eye movements. One method involves shining an (invisible) infrared beam onto the eye, which is then reflected back from the cornea or retina to a sensor. The method is relatively noninvasive—readers are free to do as they please—reread, slow down, speed up, and the eye movement tracking continues. However, we say *relatively* noninvasive because the reader whose eyes are being tracked does have to subject themselves to some minor contortions. So that the eye movements can be distinguished from head movements, the head has to be held in place; also, although we typically look down to read, the eye-movement set-up typically requires looking straight ahead. In spite of these differences, there doesn't seem to be any appreciable difference between comprehension in the two situations (Tinker, 1939)—thankfully for eye-movement researchers!

Saccades and Fixations.   If you think about how your eyes must move as you scan across a page of this book, you may think that your eyes scan smoothly across the page from left to right, then back again. This impression is mistaken. Your eyes actually move in a series of stops, pauses, and starts, termed saccades and fixations. **Saccades** are the discrete movements that our eyes make from one point to another when we're reading, taking in a visual scene, or searching for an object (Rayner, 1998); they occur continually. The saccades we make during reading are typically six to eight letters in length, and take about 20 ms. During saccades, we seem to take in little or no visual information, a phenomenon termed **saccadic suppression** (Matin, 1974); indeed, eye movements occur with such velocity that if we did take in information, it would probably register as a blur. It's not completely clear whether or not cognitive processing is suppressed during saccades; the empirical jury is still out on this issue.

In between saccades are **fixations,** in which the eyes pause briefly to take in information. Fixations typically last anywhere from 200 to 300 ms; the length depends on the nature of the reading task, be it silent reading, reading aloud, or reading music. Consecutive fixations in the same spot are sometimes labeled **gazes;** the summed duration of these gazes (i.e., **gaze duration**) is another dependent variable in the study of reading.

When vs. Where.   The investigation of eye movement patterns during reading has focused on two primary dimensions: when the eye movements occur (i.e., how long fixations are) and where they go (i.e., what determines the "landing spots" for eye movements). Look at Figure 10.1, which presents the pattern of fixations, gazes and saccades, along with the text that was being read (from Rayner & Pollatsek, 1989). You'll note a number of interesting characteristics of eye fixations and eye movements. First, some words are fixated twice, and some not at all. Notice how content words, like *devices* and *combustion* receive more gaze time than do function words like *and* and *that*; sometimes,

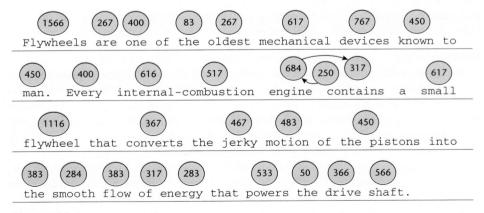

Figure 10.1

Length of eye fixations on words in a passage of text.

From Just, M. A., & Carpenter, P. A. (1987). *The psychology of reading and language comprehension.* Boston: Allyn and Bacon. Copyright 1987 by Pearson Education. Reprinted by permission of the publisher.

these function words are not fixated at all. About 80% of content words and only 40% of function words are fixated. Also, the more unfamiliar a word (e.g., flywheel), the longer the fixation. Overall, approximately 65% of the words in a given text are fixated; this proportion varies with content and with the characteristics of the reader. It is important to note that fixation is not a necessity for identification. We'll return to this question shortly in our discussion of perceptual span.

Drieghe, Rayner, and Pollatsek (2005) point out that the factors determining length of fixation time relate to how challenging the word is to process. One robust finding (e.g., Inhoff & Rayner, 1986; Schilling, Rayner, & Chumbley, 1998) is that words that are less frequently encountered in our day-to-day reading encounters (i.e., *penguin*, termed *low frequency words*) receive longer fixations than do words that we encounter at a much greater rate (i.e., *animals*, termed *high frequency words*). Other important factors include how predictable the word is from the context that precedes it. For example, consider the following sentence, taken from Rayner, Binder, Ashby, and Pollatsek (2001), in which the word winter or summer could be placed in the blank:

Near the end of the semester, students look forward to their _____ vacation.

In this context, the word *summer* will receive less fixation than will the word *winter*, because the word summer is more predictable from the context of the words leading up to it (at least for folks in the far-Northern Hemisphere, who deeply appreciate their summer vacations!). Another factor that influences length of fixation is the age at which a word is acquired; words known since you were a tyke (like "word") will be fixated for less time than words you learned later (like "tyke"), independent of the other factors we mentioned. In sum, the decision about when to move the eyes is determined by linguistic factors—aspects of what is being read. These factors also could be collectively referred to as top-down factors, because they show how reading is determined by previous knowledge and expectation.

The other important dimension that defines eye movements is where they move to—or, put another way, where they *land*. In contrast to fixation length, the landing spot for eye movements is determined primarily by lower-level (i.e., physical) characteristics of the information being taken in, like word length and word spacing. For example, the length of a saccade is determined jointly by the length of the word currently being fixated and the length of the word to the immediate right (e.g., O'Regan, 1980). Fixations for a given word seem to occur about 1/4 of the way into the word (in other words, our eyes would tend to jump to about the second "e" in *elephant*. The factors that determine the landing spots during reading can be classified as primarily bottom-up; that is, these factors tend to be physical aspects of the incoming "data."

Word Skipping.   Rayner (1998) estimates that about 30% of the words we take in during reading are skipped! In other words, we jump right over them without fixating. Interestingly, the probability of skipping words seems determined by both top-down and bottom-up factors as just outlined. We're more likely to completely skip words that are highly constrained (i.e., it's about the only word that would make sense, given the context; Balota, Pollatsek, & Raynor, 1985). In addition, not only do high frequency words like *animals* receive less fixation than low-frequency words like *penguin*; they're also more likely to be completely skipped (Rayner & Well, 1996). Bottom-up (i.e., visual or physical) aspects of stimuli also are important determinants of word-skipping. The variable that most strongly determines whether a word will be skipped is word length (Brysbaert & Vitu, 1998). Short words (e.g., an, the) are much more likely to be skipped, relative to longer words (e.g., flywheels, devices). This makes sense—shorter, more predictable words don't carry very much of the meaning in text, so spending too much time on them would be inefficient.

Stop&*Think* | READING FROM THE TOP DOWN

Have two of your friends read this passage:

In the previous chapter, we sketched some of the basics of language, such as its basic definition, major components, and fundamentals of speech perception. Although language is first and foremost a spoken medium, it takes only a moment's thought to consider its many different expressions. After all, we're not talking to you about cognitive psychology; we've written this text, and you're reading it—and not only that, but understanding it. After you learn about cognitive psychology, we're sure that you'll be so excited by it that you'll engage your classmates in conversation about it.

Tell one of your friends to count the number of *f*'s in this passage. Have the other friend count the number of *m*'s. There are 11 of each, but the *f*'s tend to be in shorter, more predictable words that are likely to be skipped during reading. See if your friend's letter counting fits this pattern.

Regressive Saccades.   You'll also notice that on occasion, the eyes move backward; these backward movements are termed **regressive saccades** and they constitute about 10 to 15% of all saccades. These occur when a reader makes too long of a saccade and has to backtrack, or if a word is particularly difficult to decipher. Regressive saccades may even occur *within* a word (Rayner, 1998). Good and poor readers differ in the "quality" of their regressive eye saccades. Good readers are better at regressing back to exactly where they encountered a problem; in contrast, poor readers must do more backtracking in order to zero in on where they had a problem (Murray & Kennedy, 1988). Based on the poorly placed eye movements of poor readers, you might be tempted to jump to the conclusion that poor reading is caused by inefficiency of eye movements. Indeed, this is what many reading specialists believed to be the case decades ago. As a result, many programs were designed to train eye movements in hopes of improving reading. Unfortunately, later research showed that inefficient eye saccades and fixation patterns were a *symptom* of poor reading, rather than the cause. As a result, these eye-movement training programs proved to be unsuccessful (Tinker, 1958).

Perceptual Span.   You may have noticed that when you read, your eyes basically "look ahead." The amount of text that the eyes can cover effectively to the right of any given fixation is termed **perceptual span.** For the English alphabet, perceptual span is about 3 characters to the left and 15 or so characters to the right of any given fixation (McConkie & Rayner, 1976). Interestingly, the characteristics of the perceptual span differ, depending on the writing system (i.e., the orthography) of the language in question. For Hebrew, which is read from right to left, the perceptual span is a mirror image of English; 3 characters to the right and about 15 to the left of fixation. Another interesting fact about the perceptual span is that it differs with the difficulty of the material (e.g., Henderson and Ferreira, 1990). It's quite likely that your perceptual span is different for reading this text than it is for reading your favorite novel (although it pains us to admit this).

How are we influenced by what falls slightly out of fixation but within the perceptual span? Such information is termed *parafoveal* (because it falls outside of the fovea—the point of central focus). Evidence indicates that **parafoveal information** aids in lexical access—in other words, getting the first few letters of the next word aids the word recognition process. Parafoveal information also allows the reader to detect word length, and where word boundaries are (a decidedly easier task than deciphering word boundaries in spoken language!) so the reader knows where to look next (e.g., Rayner & Morris, 1992). The detection of word length allows for the identification and skipping of short function words (Blanchard, Pollatsek, & Raynor, 1989), which in turn makes reading the fast and efficient process that it is in most circumstances.

Perhaps the single most important piece of parafoveal information is the blank space that separates one word from the next. It turns out that these are tremendous aids to reading; when they're deleted, reading is seriously impaired (e.g. Epelboim, Booth, & Steinman, 1994; Pollatsek & Rayner, 1982). Juhasz, White, Liversedge, and Rayner (2008) outline three reasons for the importance of blank spaces. First, blank spaces make words physically easier to see. Second, the spaces between words indicate the lengths of upcoming words, and are useful targets for the eyes. Third, blank spaces indicate the end of a given word (i.e., its word length), thus constraining the set of possible word candidates. For example, if the letters *el-* is followed shortly by a blank space, *elephant* can be eliminated as a word candidate; *elect* is more likely. Juhasz et al. (2008) suggest this last factor as the most important; spaces between upcoming words allows for the list of possible words to be whittled down, increasing the efficiency of reading. It might be difficult to wrap your mind around this finding (and the processes of reading in general) because reading is so rapid and efficient. As you'll be reading, this speed and efficiency indicates that a lot of processing is going on outside of consciousness.

Stop&*Review*

1. Distinguish between saccades and fixations.
2. Identify the two dimensions of interest in examining eye movements.
3. True or false? Perceptual span is longer for more difficult material.
4. The most important piece(s) of parafoveal information is (are):
   a. punctuation marks.
   b. blank spaces between words.
   c. last letters of words.
   d. first letters of words.

- Reading involves both bottom-up and top-down processing. When we read, our eyes move across the page in a series of jumps and pauses termed saccades and fixations. Saccades are 6 to 8 letters in length, and take about 20 ms. During saccades, little or no visual information is taken in (saccadic suppression). During fixations, we take in text information. Fixations typically last anywhere from 200 to 300 ms depending on the type of material or goal of the reading task.

- Two dimensions of interest in the investigation of eye movements are when they happen (fixation and gaze time) and where they go (landing spots). Fixation and gaze time are dictated largely by content. Content words are more likely to be fixated than are function words. Fixation times are also longer for unfamiliar and unpredictable words, relative to familiar and predictable ones. Landing spots for eye movements tend to be dictated by the physical aspects of a stimulus (e.g., word length).

- Eye movement research indicates that about 30% of words are skipped. Regressive (i.e., backward) saccades occur when words are difficult, and vary between readers; good readers' regressive saccades are more accurate. Perceptual span is about 3 characters to the left and 15 or so characters to the right of any given fixation for the English alphabet. Perceptual span is shorter the more difficult the material.

- Information falling outside of a fixation is termed parafoveal information, the most important type of which is the blank space between words, which makes words easier to see, signals word length and constrains the set of word possibilities.

Word Recognition

Now that you have a basic understanding of the mechanics of reading, let's take a step up in the language hierarchy. In the previous chapter, this involved moving from sounds to spoken words; here, we move from letters to written words. It's obvious that the look of a written word—its **orthography**—is an important factor in its visual recognition. The view that orthography provides the major route to word recognition is termed the **direct-access view.** Words are recognized by using the written label to access the appropriate semantic memory representation directly. Labeling this as the "direct" view implies that there must also be an "indirect view."

The **indirect-access** (or **phonological**) **view** of word recognition proposes that word recognition goes through the phonological representation of the word prior to the word's identification. In other words, *visual* recognition of the word *apple* as a sweet red thing you pick off trees in the fall, involves the activation of the word's sound. This view might remind you of the motor theory of speech perception from the last chapter—the view that the recognition of speech is aided by one's own knowledge and experience with the articulation of speech. Although it may seem a bit counter-intuitive, the indirect-access view has a good deal of support. It seems that even when we are silently looking at a printed word, the "road to recognition" goes through its phonological characteristics.

The ever-resourceful cognitive psychologist has come up with a novel way to investigate the issue of direct vs. indirect access, by analyzing the visual recognition of homophones.

Homophones are word pairs with the same component sounds, but different spellings and different meanings (e.g., reed and read). An early study (Van Orden, 1987) took advantage of the ambiguity of homophones to provide a test of phonologically-mediated access to semantic memory during word recognition. In this study (Experiment 1), participants were presented with a category verification task; a category name (e.g., flower) was followed by one of three types of stimuli: a member of the category (e.g., tulip), a homophone of a member of the category (e.g., rows, a "phonological replica" of rose), or a word orthographically similar to a member of the category (e.g., robs, which has orthography similar to rose). The task was to indicate if the word was a member of the category as quickly as possible. If access is direct, then "rows" and "robs" should both cause problems because they're visually similar to the label "rose." If identifying a word involves activation of a phonological code, however, then *rows* should activate two meanings (a line and a flower) because there are two meanings attached to the sound /roz/. Therefore, there should be a good deal of misclassification of "rows" and other homophones as member of the stated category (flower). In line with this prediction, participants made categorization mistakes nearly 20% of the time for homophones, but only 3% of the time for orthographically similar words; it's almost like homophones are "pseudomembers" of a category. This suggests strongly that word recognition involves access to sound.

More compelling evidence comes from research employing pseudohomophones. A pseudohomophone is a "made-up" word that sounds like a real word (e.g., "brane" for "brain.") Luo, Johnson, and Gallo (1998) tested whether pseudohomophones might show effects of semantic relatedness. In other words, would "chare" (mistakenly) be viewed as related to table because it sounds identical to "chair." If access to the mental lexicon were direct (i.e., not phonologically mediated), then you might expect that the pair "table-chare" would be easily classified as unrelated. If such access is mediated by phonology, however, then it is likely that such pairs would lead to more errors and/or a slower RT in judgments of semantic relatedness. The results are presented in Figure 10.2; as you can

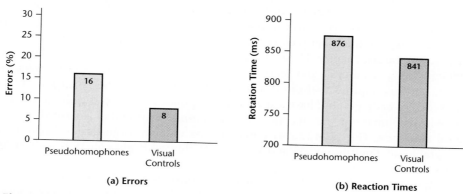

Figure 10.2

Results from Luo, Johnson, and Gallo (1998).

From Luo, C. R., Johnson, R. A., & Gallo, D. A. (1998). Automatic activation of phonological information in reading: Evidence from the semantic relatedness decision task. *Memory and Cognition, 26,* 833–843. Reprinted by permission of the Psychonomic Society, Inc.

see, pseudohomophones led to more errors and slower RT's, suggesting that access to the mental lexicon involves phonological information. Many researchers favor what is typically termed a **dual-route view** of word recognition, proposing that word recognition can proceed by either direct (visual-label only) or indirect (visual label + phonological representation) routes (see Van Orden & Kloos, 2005 for a review).

It would seem that the best way to determine whether phonological processing is a necessary part of word recognition would be to observe word recognition as a word is being recognized. If you'll recall, in Chapter 1 we introduced a neurophysiological research technique that allows a researcher to do just that—event-related potentials. Recall that ERPs are neural signals generated by the cortex in response to some stimulus, and they allow researchers to observe the neural substrates of cognitive processing and how they play out over time.

Ashby (2010) examined the role of phonological processing in visual word recognition using a simple procedure in which participants silently read target words that were preceded by a prime. The prime was a syllable of that word but in isolation was either phonologically congruent (e.g., BAS—priming BASKET) or incongruent (BAS—priming BASIN) with the target. Participants saw the prime followed by the target while ERPs were recorded.

The prediction was as simple as the procedure; if phonological processing is a critical stage of visual word recognition, then incongruent and congruent primes should produce different ERP responses. Ashby found the N100 (a negative deflection 100 msec after stimulus presentation) was significantly smaller in amplitude for words preceded by a congruent prime. In other words, primes prepared participants for the upcoming stimulus, essentially starting the processing, only if they were phonologically congruent with the target. This suggests that phonological processing is occurring as early as 100 msec after the presentation of a word for identification. These results and other similar neurophysiological evidence (e.g., Ashby, 2009) would seem to suggest that processing phonology is a critical aspect of word recognition. Word recognition, in turn, is critical for reading.

So while it makes complete sense that phonology is critical for speech, you may be surprised by its important role in reading. This similarity not withstanding, there are some sharp contrasts between reading and many of the principles of speech we discussed in the last chapter. These differences are outlined by Shaywitz and Shaywitz (2005). Speech is natural, and learned easily and rapidly, while reading must be taught. Reading requires that one realize that the letters and letter strings of a language (i.e., its orthography) have a specific correspondence to specific phonemes and phoneme combinations (i.e., its phonology or sound). This ability is termed phonological awareness. Goswami (2008) notes that even across languages as disparate in orthography as English, Greek, and Chinese, facility with phonology is critical for written word learning.

Pennington and Bishop (2009) reach similar conclusions, noting that printed word recognition is based on two component skills, phonological and orthographic coding. Phonological coding involves being able to apply the rules that connect speech sounds (i.e., phonemes) to their printed version, allowing the reader to pronounce words that have never been seen before. In addition to phonological coding, printed word recognition sometimes relies on purely orthographic coding, as in cases where there is a lack of correspondence between phonology and orthography (e.g., yacht).

Dyslexia

Reality Check

You're no doubt familiar with the reading problem termed **dyslexia** (often referred to researchers and specialists as **developmental dyslexia**), which involves severe reading difficulties (among them difficulties in word recognition). Those with dyslexia score in the normal range on traditional measures of intelligence and have normal comprehension ability. However, they have specific problems in printed word recognition, which results in slower (not poorer) reading comprehension. According to Lyon (2003), dyslexia is a specific neurobiological disorder that is characterized by accurate (but slow) word recognition accompanied by poor spelling and deficits in phonological decoding. That is, dyslexics have inordinate difficulties in mapping the sounds of words to their orthography (i.e., their printed form) and vice-versa. And as mentioned earlier, phonological recoding (i.e., indirect access) is critical to word recognition and consequently reading ability. It's not surprising, then, that dyslexics have difficulties in word recognition. Because word recognition can be based solely on orthography (i.e. direct access), this provides an alternative route to word recognition for those with dyslexia. But as indicated earlier, phonological recoding is the most efficient route to word recognition, so roadblocks on that route make word recognition difficult.

Shaywitz and Shaywitz (2005) offer the following example to demonstrate why dyslexia is a problem in word recognition and not comprehension. Say a person knows what an *apparition* is, and has no problems when they hear it. But when they're faced with the word in print and have to read it, their inability to map the orthography to the corresponding phonemes will block them from accessing the phonological representation of the word; basically they won't be able to "hear it in their head." Consequently they will be unable to access what the word means and it will seem like they do not comprehend the word, when in fact they do. A number of specific theories have been proposed to explain the reading difficulties encountered by dyslexics, but according to Shaywitz and Shaywitz (2005) there appears to be a strong consensus for a theoretical account based on phonology; the lack of phonological awareness is central to dyslexic deficits in reading (Ziegler & Goswami, 2005).

Dyslexia does not remit, nor is it something that a child "outgrows." As Shaywitz and Shaywitz (2005) note, over time dyslexics may develop strategies that help them compensate for their deficits and may become proficient in reading within a specific area of expertise or interest. However, the phonological deficits remain, and are likely to be revealed when looking at the fluency and automaticity of reading (Lefly & Pennington, 1991). This lack of fluency and automaticity has some serious ramifications in a number of applied settings, the most salient of which may be under timed testing situations. As noted, the comprehension of dyslexic individuals is equivalent to that of nondyslexic individuals, but the mapping between orthography and phonology that makes for quick and efficient reading is impaired. Therefore, dyslexic individuals need more time to arrive at the point of comprehension. This is the reasoning behind allowing individuals with dyslexia accommodations (most notably, extra time) on standardized tests such as the ACT and GRE.

Dyslexia and the Brain.   The foregoing discussion about deficits in phonological coding being the root problem in dyslexia has been borne out by neuroscientific data that has accumulated over the past couple of decades. As Goswami (2008) points out, the evidence is particularly compelling as it transcends languages and orthographies. That is, across cultures, dyslexics show similar deficits. The neurobiological "signature" of dyslexia seems to be impaired processing in posterior regions of the brain's left hemisphere, termed occipito-temporal regions, due to the fact that these critical regions straddle the temporal lobe (which includes the auditory cortex) and occipital lobe (which includes the visual cortex). This makes sense, as processes involved in printed word recognition involve both vision (orthography) and audition (phonology). Interestingly, neuro-imaging studies also suggest that individuals with dyslexia seem to develop compensatory strategies to deal with their reading deficits. Dyslexics show increased activity in anterior brain sites in the right hemisphere, and in an area termed the inferior frontal gyrus (Brunswick, McCrory, Price, Frith, & Frith, 1999; Frackowiak, Friston, Frith, Dolan, Price, & Zeki, 2004). These areas are important in sound articulation, and as Shaywitz and Shaywitz (2005) explain, are likely involved in helping a child with dyslexia become aware of the phonological (i.e., sound) structure of a word through articulatory movements such as forming the word with the lips, tongue and vocal apparatus. This would also be consistent with the accurate, yet slow and inefficient reading that can characterize dyslexic readers.

How Should Reading Be Taught?

Sounding it out?

As you've seen, cognitive researchers have amassed a wealth of data on the processes that underlie word recognition. So of course, their research findings provide a critical database that can be used to address an important educational question: What's the best method for teaching children to read? Educators have wrestled with this question for decades and several approaches have emerged. The *whole-word approach* involves the rote learning of words, which children eventually learn to recognize upon a quick glance. So basically, they're taught to apprehend "whole words" at a time; you might think of this as a top-down approach. The bottom-up rival to this approach is termed the **phonics approach,** and it involves sounding words out by noting the correspondence between the component letters and their sounds. This technique does run into problems when there is an irregular mapping of letters to sounds (which happens quite often in English).

Based on these types of problems with the phonics approach, some espouse a **whole-language approach.** This approach is in the spirit of the whole-word approach, but is even broader in its application of top-down elements. In this approach, young readers are given engaging things to read on their own, and are encouraged to guess at new or unfamiliar words by using illustrations, context, and storyline. They also are encouraged to make up their own stories. Basically, the aim of the whole-language approach is to make reading and reading instruction fun. The approach is almost anti-phonics; the mechanics of sound to letter mappings should not be taught explicitly, and a child should not be corrected when they mispronounce a word. According to the whole-language approach, they will eventually arrive at the correct usage and pronunciation of the words.

In a critical review of these three methods for reading instruction, Rayner, Foorman, Perfetti, Pesetsky, and Seidenberg (2001) provide ample evidence for a clear winner... the phonics approach. As you read earlier, a great deal of research indicates that reading involves access to the phonological representations of words. Rayner et al. point out that this is the case even for highly skilled readers. Therefore, it appears that learning these letter-to-sound correspondences is vitally important to reading instruction. The evidence supporting this assertion is overwhelming; recent reviews of the evidence by the National Reading Panel and the National Research Council clearly demonstrate the superiority of the phonics approach over the other two approaches in producing high levels of reading achievement (Rayner, Foorman, Perfetti, Pesetsky, & Seidenberg, 2002). Ashby and Rayner (2006) note that the whole-word and whole-language approach are not without their merit, and suggest that elements from these techniques might be effectively combined with the phonics approach.

But ultimately, phonics must be the foundation, as Rayner et al summarize: "...reading must be grounded in a firm understanding of the connections between letters and sounds. Instructors should recognize the ample evidence that youngsters who are directly taught phonics become better at reading, spelling and comprehension than those who must pick up all the confusing rules of English on their own. Educators who deny this reality are neglecting decades of research. They also are neglecting the needs of their students." (Rayner et al., 2002, p. 91).

Anglo-Centric Language Studies

You'll recall that in Chapter 9, after summarizing some basic conceptual and empirical work on language, we issued a caveat that generalizing from that work may be a stretch. The languages on which that work is based represent only a tiny subset of all languages. Share (2008) makes a similar argument about the study of the written word. He points out that research on reading is overwhelmingly biased toward the study of "Anglocentric" (i.e., English-centered) word orthography. This bias itself would be bad enough, but add to it the fact that English is sometimes just flat-out strange in its mapping of letters to sounds (think *kn* as in know, *pn* as in pneumonia, ps as in psychology, *cht as in yacht*...the list could go on), and you've got a real problem. Here's how Share puts it:

> ...the extreme ambiguity of English spelling-sound correspondence has confined reading science to an insular, Anglocentric research agenda addressing theoretical and applied issues with limited relevance for a universal science of reading. (p. 584)

Strong morphemes indeed; so, as in Chapter 9, all of the research you're reading about must be taken with a large grain (or a shaker full) of salt. It is incumbent upon reading scientists to move beyond English in their studies of the basic processes that underlie reading.

Research Theme
Culture

Some recent research has done just that. For example, some extremely intriguing questions arise in considering the processes that underlie reading in languages with a radically different structure than the alphabetic structure of Western languages. Consider Chinese, which is comprised of complex *characters* rather than letters and words. Bai, Yan, Zang, Liversedge, and Rayner (2008) review a number of noteworthy differences in Chinese that suggest that the corresponding reading processes might be quite different than in English. First, the characters that comprise written Chinese are all equally spaced from one another, and vary widely in complexity. Perhaps most problematic for Western readers, the characters don't neatly correspond to individual words. Chinese characters are more like morphemes, and words are often made up of multiple characters.

For example, 认知 心理学是乐趣 translates to "Cognitive psychology is fun." In no discernible way does this English translation map onto the Chinese character sequence. The idea is expressed by four English words of varying lengths with spaces between them, versus eight Chinese characters of more or less the same size with no spaces between them. Another observation about the Chinese written language adds to the intrigue. Among Chinese readers themselves, there exists ambiguity about how Chinese characters correspond to particular words. So not all Chinese readers would agree on how particular character(s) correspond to certain ideas in the sentence! For example, there might be disagreement on the particular character sequence that corresponds to "cognitive psychology."

Bai, Yan, Zang, Liversedge, and Rayner (2008) note some interesting implications of this ambiguity for assessing the importance of the word unit in Chinese. Do characters trump words or do words trump characters? Bai et al. (2008) tested this by introducing the spacing typically associated with written English into Chinese text to determine what effect it would have on eye movements, reading speed, and total reading time. They presented native Chinese speakers with a series of Chinese sentences in four different spacing conditions: Normal unspaced, as it would be presented in Chinese text; individual character spacing; word spacing (characters were combined and spaced such that each grouping corresponded to a word), and nonword spacing (characters were combined and spaced such that each grouping constituted a nonword). Can you come up with the critical predictions? If words are the fundamental unit of processing in Chinese character sequences, then presenting the characters grouped into words should facilitate processing. If characters are the fundamental unit, then word grouping should not facilitate (and might even interfere with) reading, due to readers' lack of familiarity with it.

The participants' task was to read each sentence; in some cases, a comprehension question followed the sentence and participants were to answer it. This was simply to assure that participants were actually reading the sentences. The researchers measured the eye movement patterns associated with processing in each condition. The results are presented in Table 10.1, which reports average reading speed (i.e., characters per minute) for sentences in each of the four conditions. As you can see, the normal Chinese text was the easiest for participants to read, but intriguingly, it was joined by the condition in which the

Table 10.1 Results from the Bai et al. (2008) study comparing the effects of spacing on reading Chinese characters. The English translation for the Chinese sentence is "The rapid development of science and technology brings great changes to society."

	Reading Speed (char per minute)
Normal Spacing 科学技术的飞速发展给社会带来了巨大的变化。	239
Single Character Spacing 科 学 技 术 的 飞 速 发 展 给 社 会 带 来 了 巨 大 的 变 化。	220
Word Spacing 科学 技术 的 飞速 发展 给 社会 带来 了 巨大的 变化。	239
Non Word Spacing 科 学技 术的飞 速发 展给 社 会带来 了巨 大的 变 化。	213

characters were grouped into word units. Both of these conditions led to better performance than the single character spacing condition and the nonword spacing condition.

What answers do these results suggest for the theoretical questions posed by the researchers? First, unlike in English, it was apparent that inserting spaces into Chinese text did not facilitate reading relative to normal unspaced text. The condition in which the characters all run into one another led to reading that was as good as if the words were separated by spaces. The other major question related to what serves as the more fundamental unit in Chinese—the character or the word. Bai et. al conclude that the word is actually a more fundamental unit in reading Chinese than is the character. The major piece of evidence they offer is that the condition in which each character was offset by a space was read more slowly than both the normal spacing and spaced word conditions. This study and others (e.g., Yan, Tian, Bai, and Rayner, 2006) provide compelling argument that words are the key psycholinguistic unit in reading. A *general* conclusion underlying *basic* reading processes; one that could not have been drawn if research had remained cloistered within Anglocentric orthography.

Reading Myths

Given the prevalence of reading and the ease with which we do it, it is probably not surprising that the average Joe or Jane (which you no longer are!) have some misconceptions about how we actually accomplish this feat. But by now you know that while cognitive processing, may seem effortless and easy, it can be profoundly complex. This disconnect between perception and reality can lead to oversimplifications and exaggerated claims. You have seen this throughout this book, and reading is no exception. Two claims relate most closely to issues of word recognition so we will discuss them next. The last one (speed reading) is relevant to the entire reading process so we will wait to discuss it until the end of the chapter.

Do We Rceoginze Wrods as a Wohle?   No, that heading you just read wasn't a typo—the misarrangement of the letters was deliberate. And the fact that you probably barely missed a beat in reading them is yet another testament to the power of top-down processing in word recognition. You may have seen this demonstration before; some years back, there was a report of a (as it turns out, apocryphal) study of word recognition being conducted at Cambridge University showing that jumbled words can be recognized easily (http://www.mrc-cbu.cam.ac.uk/people/matt.davis/Camabrigde/). We have seen this demonstration on posters/signs at craft fairs, novelty item shops/catalogs, and even at Jimmy John's sub shops! The proposed explanation in the "research article" was that only the first and last letters of a word need to be processed for word recognition to occur. While there is a "kernel" of truth in that statement, it is definitely a dramatic over-simplification, much like the left brain/right brain distinction discussed in Chapter 1. It's doubtful that we would recognize *ehnlpeat* as *elephant*, despite the fact that the first and last letters are in place.

Rayner, White, Johnson, and Liversedge (2006) add some important qualifications to the basic phenomenon of our sometimes-striking ability to recognize jumbled words. As it turns out, not all letter jumblings are created equal (as anyone who solves the daily newspaper puzzle, the Jumble, can attest!). Rayner and his colleagues assigned participants to one of four conditions, each of which required participants to read 80 sentences. In a control condition, the sentences were left intact. In the three experimental conditions, a few of the words in each sentence were transposed in one of three ways: internal letters only, beginning letters only, or ending letters only. Performance was measured by assessing fixations on the words (or wrods), and by a measure of how many words could be read in one minute.

The results, presented in Table 10.2, demonstrate that although jumbled words can be recognized, it comes at a cost. As you can see in the first column of the table, fixation times were longer for the words with transposed letters, particularly when

Table 10.2 **Results from the Rayner, White, Johnson, and Liversedge (2006) Jumbled-Word Study (Fixation Times per Word in Milliseconds and Reading Rates in Words per Minute for Each of the Transposition Conditions)**

Transposition Condition	Fixation Time (ms)	Reading Rate (wpm)
Normal text		
The boy could not solve the problem so he asked for help.	236	255
Internal letters transposed		
The boy could not slove the probelm so he asked for help.	244	227
Ending letters transposed		
The boy could not solev the problme so he asked for help.	246	189
Beginning letters transposed		
The boy could not oslve the rpoblem so he asked for help.	259	163

Adapted from Rayner, K., White, S. J., Johnson, R. L., & Liversedge, S. P. (2006). Raeding wrods with jubmled lettres: There is a cost. *Psychological Science, 17*(3), 192–193. Published by Blackwell, Inc. Adapted with permission from the author.

the transpositions involved beginning letters. An analysis of reading time (measured in words per minute) revealed a parallel effect, as depicted in the second column of Table 10.2. When transpositions were present, fewer words were read per minute, and the decreased rate varied systematically with the type of transposition. Internally transposed letters proved the least problematic, and initial-letter transposition was the most problematic. This finding was replicated in a recent study by White, Johnson, Liversedge, and Rayner (2008), who also found that transpositions within low frequency words were more costly to word recognition than transpositions in high-frequency words. Although these findings provide more evidence of the importance of top-down processing in word recognition, they also underscore the limits of such processing. Clearly, a word cannot be recognized solely based on context. Some data need to be present; the letters in a word and their respective positions are critical for word recognition (cf. Grainger & Whitney, 2004). While this explanation may not be pithy enough for a poster at Jimmy Johns sub shops, this explanation may impress your friends.

Stop&*Think* | REOGCNZIING JMULEBD WRODS

For this exercise, you'll do your own version of the jumbled-word study conducted by Rayner, White, Johnson, and Liversedge (2006). Recruit some friends, and test them in each of the four conditions presented below. Have them read each sentence in succession; tell them that some of the sentences may contain misspellings but that they should try to ignore them and read the sentences so that they make sense. Your dependent variable will be reading speed, in seconds. To obtain this, add together the times (in seconds) that it took each friend to read the three sentences (i.e., find one total time). Then, divide this time by the total number of words (35). How does the reading-time data compare to the pattern of results found by Rayner et al.?

Intact

John had three papers to write, so he spent most of the month in the library.

Psychology is the scientific study of mental processes and behavior.

Greg had his laptop computer stolen from the car.

Beginning Letters

John had three appers to rwite, so he psent most of the omnth in the ilbrary.

Psychology is the csientific study of emntal rpocesses and ebhavior.

Greg had his alptop ocmputer tsolen from the car.

Ending Letters

John had three papesr to wriet, so he spetn most of the monht in the librayr.

Psychology is the scientifci study of mentla processse and behaviro.

Greg had his laptpo computre stolne from the car.

Middle Letters

John had three paeprs to wrtie, so he spnet most of the motnh in the ilbrary.

Psychology is the sceintific study of mnetal procseses and beahvior.

Greg had his lpatop copmuter stloen from the car.

Reality Check

Text Messages.   Earlier, we discussed how Chinese characters are processed during reading. Now let's examine the processing of a type of text that for Greg, might as well be Chinese….lol. We're betting you didn't miss a beat in reading those last three letters; in fact, we're betting that for most of you, *lol* is essentially a word, due the omnipresence of the driving menace we discussed in Chapter 3, text messaging. Use of this mode of written communication has exploded over the past several years, and would seem to invite cognitive psychology research from a number of perspectives, including reading.

The abbreviated messages used by texters comprise what is termed short message service (SMS) and it is utilized in order to save time when constructing the message. Perea, Acha, and Carreiras (2009) summarize a number of strategies that are used in SMS. The first is orthographic abbreviation. Orthography refers to the physical makeup of a printed word—in other words, the letter sequence itself. Text messaging often involves abbreviations in which vowels are omitted, such as *pls* for *please*, and *wk* for *week*. The second strategy is phonetic respelling. Phonetics refers to the sounds of language, so this type of respelling involves substituting a symbol that captures the entire sound of a word, such as *b4* for *before*, or *c u later* for *see you later*.

There is no doubt that SMS saves time in constructing the message—but texting involves a receiver as well as a sender. So in order to know if SMS is an efficient shorthand, we need to look at receiver comprehension. To the average Joe or Jane, it may seem reasonable to assume that these SMS strategies should not affect comprehension. The orthographic abbreviations leave the first and last letters in place and the commonly-held view is that this is all we need (but you know now that this is false). The phonetic respelling creates a "word" that sounds exactly like the real word, so that shouldn't be a problem. Because word recognition is mediated by phonology, you probably think this intuition has some validity. Let's look at the empirical data and see if it supports the intuition, or the myth-busting conclusion about jumbled words.

Perea et al. (2009) constructed text messaging sentences that used primarily orthographic abbreviations or phonetic respellings and compared them to normal text. The procedure was quite similar to Bai et al. (2008) in that participants were asked to read each of the sentences, and answer comprehension questions that were presented on a random number of trials (to ensure that they read each sentence). The main measure of interest, again, was reading time. The results are presented in Table 10.3. As u cn c txt mssgng sux.

Reading times for the SMS (text-message style) sentences was woefully slower than those for normal text. In addition, specific measures of eye movements and fixations revealed that SMS words were less likely to be skipped, fixated longer, and featured more regressive saccades. Basically, they were incredibly hard to read and understand. So for you text messagers, all of the time you save by abbreviating, you lose in reading.

So jumbled words are hard to read, and phonetic respellings aren't aided by the phonological route involved in word recognition: two myths busted. You may not have been surprised by the former (after reading the last section) but you probably were surprised by

Table 10.3 **Rslts frm txt msgng stdy (Perea, Acha, & Carreiras, 2009)**

		Reading Time (sec)
Orthographic	SMS	2.17
	Normal Text	1.28
Phonetic	SMS	2.53
	Normal Text	1.40

the latter. If word recognition is mediated by phonology why are phonetic abbreviations so difficult to comprehend? Although word *identification* may be a critical component of reading *comprehension*, it certainly isn't the same as reading comprehension. Many other factors are involved in comprehension (as you'll read later in the section on discourse comprehension). Phonetic respellings basically are pseudohomophones, nonwords that sound like real words (sux, a nonword, sounds like the real word sucks) so let's look again at the research on these "words."

As you've seen, pseudohomophones have been empirically investigated, but only as a tool to examine the role of phonological processing in word recognition (as discussed earlier). One avenue of investigation has been to compare the processing of pseudoho-mophones to that of regular nonwords (e.g., frane) that do not sound like a real word (e.g, Seidenberg, Petersen, MacDonald and Plaut, 1996; Atchley, Halderman, Kwasny, and Buchanan, 2003). For example, we know that a pseudohomophone (e.g., roze) is named more quickly than a regular nonword (e.g. joze). *Roze* is phonologically similar to *rose* activating the lexical entry for the word *rose*. *Joze* does not activate any lexical entry and therefore is named more slowly than the psuedohomophone. However, this does not indicate anything about how the sentence, "The man gave his wife a beautiful red *roze*" would be comprehended in comparison to "The man gave his wife a beautiful red rose." There would have been no need to do this research; these words were never encountered in normal reading. The research on phonetic respellings in SMS seems to indicate the pseudohomophones reduce the overall comprehension of a sentence. Thanks to texting, pseudohomophones may become the focus of reading research rather than just an artificial and obscure stimulus used to support the idea of indirect access in word recognition.

Stop&Review

1. Contrast the direct-access view and in-direct access view to word recognition.
2. True or false? Dyslexia is characterized by poor text comprehension ability.
3. The most effective approach to teaching reading appears to be:
   a. the phonics approach.
   b. the whole-word approach.
   c. the whole-language approach.
4. True or false? Text messaging SMS is an effective form of written communication.

- Orthography refers to the printed structure of a word. According to the direct-access view, words are recognized by direct access to the word's representation. The indirect-access (phonological) view proposes that word recognition involves phonological activation. The dual route view proposes either route is possible. Phonological awareness refers to knowledge of relationships between orthography and phonology. Phonological access seems to be involved in word identification across all languages.

- Dyslexia is not an issue of poor text comprehension; it involves specific deficits in visual word recognition. Dyslexics show a lack of phonological awareness. Dyslexic deficits are characterized by abnormalities in brain function, including impaired functioning in the left hemisphere's temporal and occipital regions.

- Research on teaching reading indicates that the phonics approach (teaching letter to sound correspondence) is much more effective than the whole-word (rote learning of words) or whole-language approach (learning words largely via contextual elements like pictures and storyline).

- Reading research has been based almost exclusively on printed English. Reading of Chinese characters is sensitive to the word unit as well as the character unit. The popular notion that jumbled words are readily identifiable is oversimplified, as is the claim that text messaging SMS is an efficient form of printed communication.

Sentence Level Processing

It's clear that when we read, we implicitly understand not only the meaning of the individual words in the sentence, but also the structure of the sentence. Let's re-visit an example sentence from Chapter 9: "The crowd booed the referee after his terrible call." As we described in the previous chapter, without thinking, we understand the meanings of each word, as well as the sentence structure. We are able to segment the elements of the sentence into their component parts. In written communication this segmentation process is termed parsing.

Sentence Parsing

The identification of the component elements of a sentence and their grammatical relation to one another—a process termed **parsing**—is vital for language. Consider the following sentence.

She lasted about 10 minutes before throwing the textbook down and picking up the latest Mary Higgins Clark novel. She couldn't wait to see who committed the murder.

Consider that although you know that Mary Higgins Clark is a person, you mindlessly interpret her name here (appropriately) as a modifier for novel, and as part of the noun phrase "Mary Higgins Clark novel." Due to this immediate and accurate parsing, you don't even consider the possibility that the "she" in the following sentence refers to Mary Higgins Clark. It refers to the reader (in this case, Bridget, who is a big fan).

Parsing usually occurs so seamlessly that you don't even notice you're doing it. How is it accomplished? How are the components of a sentence recognized and combined? Does the syntactic (i.e., structural) analysis of a sentence have to finish before we compute the meaning of a sentence, or is meaning computed along with syntax?

The Importance of Syntax.   According to some views of sentence parsing, syntax is central. Word order serves the primary role in sentence comprehension. For example, sentences with a "noun-verb-noun" (i.e. subject-verb-object, or SVO) structure are quite common in English, so a running assumption of a reader would be that sentences fit this general structure; this assumption helps guide parsing.

One approach to parsing is termed the **garden-path approach** (e.g., Frazier & Fodor, 1978; Frazier & Rayner, 1982; Frazier, 1995) because it assumes that the reader follows a simple, word-by-word path through the sentence, attempting to fit each word within the assumed syntactic structure. Consider this sentence: "The professor argued the student's position passionately." If we (as English-speakers) parse this sentence according to the garden-path approach, we will assume that it fits a standard SVO (subject-verb-object) structure. You might imagine a representation of this sentence that includes two major segments corresponding to each of the sentence constituents—the noun phrase (*the professor*) and the verb phrase (*argued the student's case passionately*).

NP		VP	
NP	V	NP	Adv
The professor	*argued*	*the student's position*	*passionately*

According to the garden-path approach, as we read we assume the simplest syntactic structure, and then revise this assumption if it proves to be wrong. For example, when we read the sentence above, we make the simplest possible assumption about its syntax—we assume that the phrase *the student's position*, is the object of the just-encountered word "argued." This type of simplifying assumption makes sense when one considers the limited capacity and time pressures faced by the human information processor.

Let's get a little more specific—the garden-path approach assumes that we use two different heuristics, or rules of thumb, to parse a sentence. One heuristic is termed *minimal attachment*. This principle is that one does not assume that the syntax of the sentence is more complicated than it probably is. In the sentence above, we could assume that the phrase "the student's position" is the beginning of a sentence embedded within the main sentence as in the following: "The professor argued *the student's position was wrong.*" However, we do not make this assumption. Another way to look at it is that as readers, we are parsimonious (i.e., we make a minimal assumptions) about beginning new phrases. A second heuristic that converges on this interpretation of the sentence is *late closure*. According to the principle of late closure, we try and attach each word that we encounter to the phrase that is currently being processed. In this case, "the student's position" is assumed to be part of the verb phrase.

If our syntactic analysis proceeds down the garden path as just described, then we should have a problem with this sentence: "The professor argued the student's position was indefensible." Did you stumble over this sentence? Initially, it seems that the professor is arguing the student's position, but when the word "was" is encountered, the interpretation of the sentence must change. The professor is arguing *against* the student's position. This is termed a garden-path sentence.

Garden-path sentences provide strong evidence for the garden-path model of parsing proposed by Frazier and colleagues (e.g., Frazier & Fodor, 1978; Frazier & Rayner, 1982; Frazier, 1995). According to this model, when this sentence is read "the student's position" will be placed within the verb phrase that starts with "argued," because of the principles of minimal attachment and late closure. However, when the word "was" is encountered, this interpretation is rendered invalid; at this point, a new syntactic interpretation is constructed. Studies of on-line reading behavior confirm the difficulty readers have when they encounter garden-path sentences; these sentences are associated with longer reading times, longer fixations, and more regressive saccades (Frazier & Rayner, 1982). The difficulty in processing garden-path sentences seems quite general—even blind readers of Braille show regressive movements to cope with the ambiguity they create (Mousty & Bertelsen, 1992). The difficulty encountered in garden-path sentences supports the notion that our initial attempts at parsing are based on the principles of minimal attachment and late closure, and confirms our (quite sensible) English-speaking bias to read sentences as "subject-verb-object."

Stop&*Think* | SKIPPING UP THE GARDEN PATH

Badly worded headlines provide amusing examples of leading readers up the garden path. Consider the following examples:

- Prostitutes Appeal to Pope
- College Graduates Blind Senior Citizen
- Complaints about NBA Refs Growing Ugly

  Find some examples of garden-path sentences from newspapers or Internet sites. (There are, no doubt, Web sites explicitly devoted to these unfortunate headlines.) Analyze what you found by considering the following questions:

- How much effort did it take to "get" each interpretation of the headline/sentence?

- Which interpretation did you arrive at first?
- Was it easy to come up with the alternative?
- Was it difficult to figure out both interpretations?
- What parts of headlines/sentences (i.e., parts of speech) seem to be the most sensitive to misinterpretation?
- How did your general knowledge help you to disambiguate the headline/ sentence?

The Importance of Semantics.   The difficulty we encounter when presented with ambiguous language stimuli like garden-path sentences makes a second aspect of sentence processing evident. Obviously, understanding the standard S-V-O syntactic structure that serves as the basis for so much of communication in the English language is not enough for language understanding and production. If it was, you'd come up with sentences like "The hen polished the dictionary." As we said earlier, semantics refers to the manner in which we convey and understand the meaning of language.

One approach that highlights the importance of meaning is termed the **case grammar approach** (Fillmore, 1968). This approach contends that sentences are parsed through the assignment of words to various *case roles*. Case roles specify "who or what is doing what to whom or what" (tortured syntax indeed!). Consider the following example: "Jim shot the ball through the hoop." Rather than parsing the sentence into syntactic components like noun phrase and verb phrase, the case grammar approach assumes that the sentence is understood by parsing it into the roles played by each word in the sentence. In the sample sentence, Jim serves the case role of *agent*, the basketball serves the case role of *patient*, and the hoop serves the case role of *goal*. Understanding and producing sentences is an exercise in decomposing and composing the case role assignments for the words in the sentence, rather than their syntactic roles.

Which Takes Precedence: Syntax or Semantics?

The importance of both syntax and semantics in sentence parsing and understanding is a given. Psycholinguistic researchers are interested in the specifics of the interplay between syntax and semantics. Does one have primary importance? Does one affect the other, or do semantic and syntactic analyses proceed independently of one another? Do these analyses occur in parallel, or serially (e.g., syntax then semantics)?

According to what might be termed the **autonomous view,** the analyses of syntax and semantics proceed independently (i.e., *autonomously*) of one another. Sentence comprehension involves (in this precise order) computing the syntactic structure of the sentence followed by building a representation of the meaning being expressed in the sentence. The garden-path view of Frazier and colleagues, just discussed, is an example of this type of approach. This view has the flavor of the information processing approach, with its *serial* view of cognitive processing. An **interactionist view** of sentence comprehension (e.g., MacDonald, Perlmutter, & Seidenberg, 1994; Trueswell & Tanenhaus, 1994) would propose the same component processes but suggests that syntactic and semantic analyses occur in *parallel* (i.e., simultaneously). Furthermore, these processes *depend* upon each other. This view has more of a connectionistic flavor, in that it emphasizes parallel processing of different language modules.

Earlier, we discussed the garden-path model of sentence parsing which assumes that we follow one syntactic interpretation of a sentence until that interpretation leads up the wrong path, in which case we regroup and reinterpret. The garden-path approach is consistent with the autonomous view—sentence parsing is ultimately guided by syntactic structure. Semantic (i.e., meaning-based) factors do not exert their effect until later stages of sentence comprehension. In other words, syntactic analysis is primary and semantic analysis is, in some respects, secondary. If this is true then the syntactic analysis should proceed unaffected by meaning. However, if you think about it, the difficulty encountered in the processing of garden-path sentences could be viewed as either a syntactic *or* a semantic influence on parsing. After all, the juncture in the sentence that creates problems involves a change in meaning as well as a change in syntax. If there is an influence of semantic factors, then we might expect that the meaning of a sentence would influence whether or not the garden-path effect occurs.

A study addressing this general question was done by Pickering and Traxler (1998). They hypothesized that if semantic factors influence syntactic ones, then the difficulty induced by a garden-path sentence should be more severe when the initial interpretation makes sense than when it doesn't. In other words, silly sentences shouldn't be as likely to induce a garden-path effect. Consider these two sentences:

(a) *As the woman edited the magazine amused all the reporters.*

(b) *As the woman sailed the magazine amused all the reporters.*

Both of these are identical in terms of syntax, and both are garden-path sentences—and according to the garden-path principles of late closure and minimal attachment, the phrase "the magazine" should be placed with the verb in each sentence, leading to difficulties in comprehension for both.

But there is a critical difference between the initial parts of these two sentences—one is plausible (*as the woman edited the magazine*), and one is not plausible (*as the woman sailed the magazine*). Does this *semantic* difference in these syntactically identical sentences impact their comprehension of the sentence? Pickering and Traxler (1998) had participants read garden-path sentences that were either plausible or implausible to investigate the possibility of semantic effects in comprehension. Their results demonstrate stronger garden-path effects for plausible sentences. The semantic plausibility of the sentence induced more of a "commitment" from readers—once a particular semantic interpretation was made, encountering a syntactic change that caused the interpretation to be wrong created more problems in comprehending the sentence. If the sentence was not semantically plausible, the correct syntactic decision was usually made, reducing the difficulty normally seen in garden path sentences.

These results suggest that syntax does not necessarily have primacy over semantics in sentence processing (Wilson & Garnsey, 2009; Zhang, Yu, & Bohland, 2010). The cognitive struggle in which we seem to engage in when faced with the syntactic ambiguity of garden-path sentences can be compared to what happens when we're faced with lexical ambiguity (i.e., a word with two different meanings). You'll recall (from Chapter 9) that, somewhat surprisingly, all interpretations of a word are considered (however briefly) before context finally leads to the selection of the appropriate interpretation. The same general pattern seems to apply to garden-path sentences, at least to some degree; multiple interpretations are considered, and context biases one of them. This seems to support the interactionist view, which proposes that processing of both semantics and syntax likely proceeds in parallel (i.e. simultaneously) and interactively (the processing on each dimension influences the ongoing processing of the other).

Stop&*Review*

1. How does the garden path approach explain sentence comprehension?
2. True or false? Syntactic analysis and semantic analysis seem to proceed in a parallel fashion.

- Some approaches to sentence comprehension place primary emphasis on syntax. According to the garden path approach, we parse sentences according to syntactic rules, and test one interpretation at a time. Difficulty in the processing of garden-path sentences is consistent with this approach. Garden path sentences are associated with longer reading times, longer fixations, and more regressive saccades.

- Some approaches to sentence comprehension stress the importance of semantics. One example of this is the case grammar approach. According to this approach sentences are parsed by the assignment of words to various case roles that reflect the role of the concept within the given sentence. Evidence indicates that the processing of syntax and semantics occurs at least somewhat in parallel, each influencing the other.

Discourse Comprehension

All of the research we've discussed up to this point has a serious limitation—it's based primarily on how people process single sentences in isolation. But you almost never read single sentences in isolation; you read a flow of connected **discourse.** Simply put, discourse refers to linguistic output longer than a sentence. How does a reader understand a chain of sentences and paragraphs, keeping in mind and understanding the major themes? Research on the topic of **discourse comprehension** constitutes another major emphasis within the field of psycholinguistics.

Levels of Representation

When we read connected discourse, we obviously have some mental representation of it. Our representation of discourse exists at a number of different levels. Psychological work on discourse representation has concentrated on three of these, suggested in some classic work by van Dijk and Kintsch (1983). First, discourse may be represented as a **surface code,** which refers to its precise wording. Our representation of discourse does not include the surface code, except for the last few words read—more on this later. Discourse may also be represented as a **text base** which refers to the major facts and themes (i.e., the "stripped-down" meaning) of the discourse. Finally, our representation of discourse is thought to include a **situation model.** The situation model for a selection of discourse refers to the "world" it creates—this model is created from a combination of the places, settings, people, and events in the discourse and the background knowledge possessed by the reader.

In addition, it turns out that the situation model that we build during comprehension involves mentally simulating what's going on, perhaps even placing ourselves "in the action." Put another way, language comprehension can be embodied. Based on this notion, Ditman, Brunyé, Mahoney, and Taylor (2009) predict that during text comprehension, mentally simulating events from an actor's perspective will result in especially memorable situation models. Note that this predicted effect would be akin to the enactment effect we discussed in Chapter 6—carrying out an action results in better memory for a corresponding action phrase than does simply reading a verbal label.

Research Theme
Embodied Cognition

Ditman et al. constructed a series of three-sentence discourse scenarios that all had the same structure. The first sentence gave descriptive information about the main character (e.g., "I am a 44 year old college professor"). The second restated the same pronoun, along with an appropriate occupational activity (e.g., "I am working on a textbook"). The third reiterated the pronoun and the activity, along with a temporal marker (e.g., "Right now I am working on Chapter 10.") The critical independent variable was the personal pronoun used across the 3 sentences. The pronoun could either be "I," "You," or "He". The researchers expected the sentences associated with "You" to be the ones embodied by the participants (think of reading something that says "You are a college professor"; this would be the condition that should lead to embodiment.) Participants read 24 sequences of sentences, eight in each pronoun condition. After delays of either 10 minutes (Experiment 1) or 3 days (Experiment 2), participants received a recognition test in which each sentence was presented for a recognition judgment. Figure 10.3 presents sensitivity in recognition (the

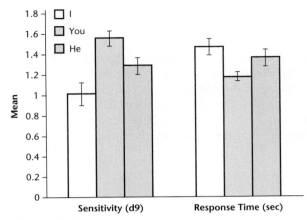

ability to discriminate old sentences from new ones) and recognition speed. As you can see, there was clear support for the hypothesis. Participants' memory for sentences that featured the pronoun *you* was especially good and response times for the recognition decisions for those sentences was especially fast. As stated earlier, this finding constitutes a text comprehension version of the enactment effect. It also has ramifications for those who write educational materials. Having readers imagine themselves at the center of the action may go a long way in getting them to form a rich and elaborated situation model (and memory trace) that will be easily retained at a later point in time.

Figure 10.3

Results from the Ditman et al. (2009) study showing embodiment in text comprehension.

Structure and Coherence

Comprehension of connected discourse depends on much more than the content of the individual sentences. Consider this story:

> The play wasn't very good. Greg bought a tyrannosaurus rex and some batteries. The mall was crowded. Bridget wondered about the airplane. Greg's feet were tired. Greg and Bridget ate dinner. Ann told Bridget to come over around 1:00. Greg relaxed and watched some college football. Jim had no problem putting it together.

Did you follow that? Probably not—it's a pretty poor description of what we did this weekend (sounds like an exciting life, doesn't it?), and it's not very easy to follow—the events aren't in any apparent order, and there's no connection between the individual ideas expressed in each sentence. This lack of connection is a lack of what is typically termed **local structure**— explicit and/or implicit connections between individual sentences. Discourse that has some local structure is much easier to understand and remember. Now consider this passage.

> If the balloons popped, the sound wouldn't be able to carry far since everything would be too far away from the correct floor. A closed window would also prevent the sound from carrying, since most buildings tend to be well insulated. Since the whole operation depends on the steady flow of electricity, a break in the middle of the wire would also cause problems. Of course, the fellow could shout, but the human voice is not loud enough to carry that far. An additional problem is that a string could break on the instrument. Then there could be no accompaniment to the message. It is clear that the best situation would involve less distance. Then there would be fewer potential problems. With face-to-face contact, the least number of things could go wrong.

Here, the individual sentences seem to hang together better; there does seem to be some local structure. But still, the passage is difficult to get a handle on, this time because it lacks a broader context, or what is termed global structure. **Global structure** refers to the general knowledge that we bring to bear on what we're reading. The lack of context for this passage prevents it from enjoying any global structure. As is the case with the first passage, we're not likely to understand or remember much about it, unless perhaps we see a picture that provides some idea of what's going on (see Figure 10.4). Both local and global structure relate to a more general principle—**coherence.** Connected discourse should hang together, or cohere, both in terms of a sentence-to-sentence flow, and in terms of broader themes. Global structure leads to global coherence; local structure leads to local coherence. What is it about the structure of connected discourse, and our processing of it, that produces coherence, thus benefitting understanding and memory?

Anaphoric Reference.   One important source of coherence in discourse is anaphoric reference. **Anaphoric reference** occurs when a current expression refers to something encountered earlier in the text. For example:

> Greg was anxious to get to the music store to buy the latest CD by <u>his</u> favorite group. He figured that <u>it</u> was likely to sell out the first day <u>it</u> was on sale. He left for the store; the traffic was terrible, and it took him 30 minutes to get <u>there</u>.

In this sentence, "his" refers back to Greg, "it" refers back to the CD store (twice, in fact), and "there" refers to the music store's location (there are a few more; can you identify the others?). The referring expression is called an **anaphor** (e.g. his), and the corresponding events are termed **antecedents** (e.g., Greg). Although it doesn't seem to require much thought to make the connection, such connections are vital for a text to maintain coherence. When one encounters an anaphoric reference in discourse, they must make the connection back to the antecedent. Based on this, you may be able to intuit one variable that puts a strain on anaphoric reference (and thus works against coherence)—the amount of separation between the anaphor and its antecedent. If "he" refers to a person five or six sentences back, the connection is not likely to be made, and the text will lose coherence.

Figure 10.4

Does this help you interpret the passage (see previous page)?

From Bransford, J. D., & Johnson, M. K. (1972). Contextual prerequisites for understanding: Some investigations of comprehension and recall. *Journal of Verbal Learning and Verbal Behavior, 11,* 717–726. Reprinted by permission of Lawrence Erlbaum Associates.

The effects of delay on the ability to make anaphoric reference makes one fact of comprehension apparent—comprehension is critically dependent on immediate memory. You'll recall that immediate memory allows for the processing of information currently in conscious awareness. As such, it plays an important role as we integrate the elements of what we're reading with what we've just read, as well as with our general knowledge. In the case of anaphoric reference, the reader must retain in immediate memory the major players in the discourse (mainly subjects and objects of sentences), and integrate these with the appropriate anaphora. The more distant the connection between ideas in the text and their corresponding anaphora, the greater the strain on immediate memory. Indeed, in an extensive meta-analytic review, Daneman and Merikle (1996) found that immediate memory span (discussed in Chapter 4) serves as a good predictor of text comprehension.

A number of factors influence the accessibility of the antecedents that need to be retrieved when anaphora are encountered. An antecedent is retrieved more easily if it occurs frequently throughout a text (Crawley, 1986), if it has occurred recently (von Eckardt & Potter, 1985), or if it has received *first mention* (i.e., whether the antecedent was one of the first concepts mentioned in a text; Gernsbacher, 1989). The latter two findings provide an interesting parallel to the effects of primacy and recency in (discussed in Chapter 4). You'll recall that words occurring early and late in a list are the easiest to recall.

Given and New Information.   Another factor that allows us to maintain coherence as we read or listen to discourse is termed the **given-new contract** (Clark and Haviland, 1977). The given-new contract refers to an implicit "agreement" between a writer and a reader (or between a speaker and a listener). This implicit agreement means that all discourse includes information that is assumed to be known by the reader, (termed **given information**—you could think of it as background information), and information that is assumed to be unknown (termed **new information**). For example, consider the following sentence: "My cognitive psychology professor gives really challenging exams." When you read this sentence, the given information is what you already assume—that your cognitive psychology professor gives exams. The new information is what you probably didn't know—that those exams are really challenging.

Clark and Haviland (1977) propose three components in following the given-new contract. First, a reader must determine what information in a sentence is given, and what is new; next, the reader must figure out what the "given" information refers back to earlier in the text. Finally, the "new" information must also be linked to that part of the text. The implicit agreement to use given information and supplement it with new information is present in all forms of discourse, including spoken.

Inferences.   In a given piece of discourse, not everything is explicitly stated: "After the storm, the sun came out, and the leprechaun started searching for the gold." (If you remember that sentence from Chapter 1, we're really impressed). We repeat it here to demonstrate how easily inferences are made during reading. Chances are your processing of this sentence went well beyond the explicitly stated facts. You may have "read between the lines," and inferred that the leprechaun will be in search of a rainbow, and that the gold he finds will be in a pot. And if you're Irish (like Bridget) you may have inferred he was drinking a Harp Lager during his search! These facts are not explicitly stated, but chances are good they would be part of your representation of the sentence. **Inferences** are conclusions drawn by a reader that are not explicitly stated in the discourse. Our ability to combine the information in the text with our world knowledge provides another important source of coherence for the reader.

A classic study by Kintsch (1974) demonstrates that inferences, just like explicit statements, are part of the text representation. In this study, readers were presented with texts that included information about events that were either explicitly stated or simply implied. For example,

Did you make all of these inferences?

(a1) *A carelessly discarded burning cigarette started a fire.*

(a2) *The fire destroyed many acres of virgin forest.*

(b1) *A burning cigarette was carelessly discarded*

(b2) *The fire destroyed many acres of virgin forest.*

In version (a), the fact that the cigarette started a fire is explicitly stated; in version (b), it is only implied. After reading the text containing the target sentence, participants were given a sentence verification task in which they were to confirm or deny the truth of certain sentences based on what they read. Some of the sentences were explicitly stated (e.g., "The fire destroyed many acres of virgin forest) and some where implied (e.g., "A cigarette started a fire"). Reaction time to make this decision was recorded. The sentence verification task was used to see if the implied information was inferred and had become part of the discourse representation. Kintsch also varied the delay between when the passage was read and when the sentence verification task occurred. Some participants were tested immediately, others after 15 minutes had passed.

Take a look at the results, depicted in Figure 10.5. As you can see, a fairly striking interaction was found; when the sentence verification task occurred immediately after the text was read, participants were quicker to verify the explicitly presented facts than they were to verify the facts that had simply been implied. But something interesting happened after a short delay—in this condition, there was no difference in verification time between explicitly stated facts and implied facts. Apparently, information resulting from an inference became (after a short delay) just as prominent in the discourse representation as explicitly stated facts.

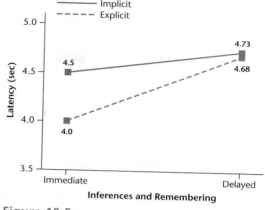

Figure 10.5

Results from Kintsch's (1974) study of inferences in reading. After a brief delay, implied facts (ostensibly inferred by the participants) are verified as quickly as are explicitly stated facts.

From Kintsch, W. (1974). *The representation of meaning in memory.* Hillsdale, NJ: Erlbaum. Reprinted by permission of Lawrence Erlbaum Associates.

Types of Inferences.   Psychologists make a distinction between bridging inferences and elaborative inferences. A **bridging inference** is a relation constructed to connect two sentences or ideas that are not connected explicitly. Consider the following sentences:

Hank was learning to be a better dancer.
The instructor was very patient.

Although it isn't explicitly stated, we assume that "the instructor" is a dance instructor teaching Hank. Our inference serves as a *bridge* that connects the second sentence to the first. Bridging inferences are also called **backward inferences;** they allow us to connect material currently being encountered backwards, to earlier material. Bridging inferences add a great deal of coherence to a text. Consider a case where a bridging inference is unlikely:

Hank was learning to be a better dancer.
The pilot was very patient.

These two sentences don't cohere at all; our previous knowledge doesn't support an inference between "pilots" and "learning to be a better dancer." Our ability to use previous knowledge to bridge gaps in written text is critical for our ability to maintain a coherent representation.

An important type of bridging inference is a **causal inference,** in which readers figure out what must have prompted an event about which they have just read. Consider the following passage:

> As Keisha rode her bike at breakneck speed, a squirrel ran out in the road. Seconds later, Keisha found herself and her bike lying in a ditch at the side of the road.

There is little doubt that you now have the idea that Keisha wrecked her bike trying to avoid the squirrel that ran out in the road. If so, you made a causal inference—nothing in the sentence explicitly stated that this is what happened, but it's hard not to make the inference. You'll note that this is a backwards inference, from Keisha lying in a ditch back to what must have happened immediately before.

Elaborative inferences involve adding extra information to one's representation of a text; the information is useful, but not necessary for coherence (Singer, 1990). For example, if you read the sentence: "Hank was learning to be a better dancer," you might infer that he was taking dance lessons, a sensible assumption, but not explicitly stated. Elaborative inferences are also termed **forward inferences,** because in making them, we move beyond (or forward from) the text. The distinction between bridging and elaborative inferences seems to be a valuable one, as indicated in a study by Singer (1980). In this study, participants read one of these three sentences—one explicitly stating a piece of information, one requiring a bridging inference, and one in which an elaborative inference could be made (the critical item here is *ball*).

(a) *The pitcher threw the ball to first base. The runner was halfway to second.* (explicit)

(b) *The pitcher threw to first base. The ball sailed into right field.* (*bridging* inference: ball)

(c) *The pitcher threw to first base. The runner was halfway to second.* (*elaborative* inference: ball)

Note that for passage (b), an inference tying "ball" back to throw must be made to maintain coherence. A bridging inference is not necessary for coherence in the case of passages (c). However, an elaborative inference is possible.

After reading (a), (b), or (c), participants were to verify if a sentence was true based on the passage

(d) *The pitcher threw a ball.*

as quickly as possible. The results are presented in Figure 10.6. As you can see, sentence (d) was verified most quickly in conditions (a) and (b). This makes sense for sentence (a), because it explicitly mentions the ball. But it's surprising for sentence (b), which doesn't. In fact, making

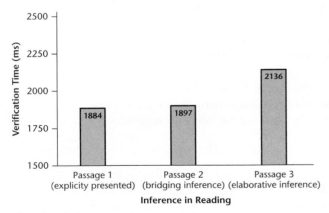

Figure 10.6

Results from Singer's (1980) study of inferences. A sentence that led to a bridging inference was as effective as explicitly presenting the same information, as indicated by the verification times.

From Singer, M. (1980). The role of case-filling inferences in the coherence of brief passages. *Discourse Processes, 3,* 185–201. Reprinted by permission of Lawrence Erlbaum Associates.

the bridging inference in sentence (b) seemed to be just as good as actually reading it, basically replicating Kintsch (1974). Singer concluded that the bridging inference was made at encoding, and became part of the representation. Participants who saw sentence (c) took significantly longer to verify (d). This indicates that the inference was not made until they had actually read the question—that is, at retrieval, rather than encoding. The inference required in sentence (c) is an elaborative inference. It is not necessary for coherence, so is not made at encoding.

A particularly compelling demonstration of elaborative inferencing comes from a classic study by Sulin and Dooling (1974). They presented participants with passages like the following:

> Gerald Martin strove to undermine the existing government to satisfy his political ambitions. Many of the people of his country supported his efforts. Current political problems made it relatively easy for Martin to take over. Certain groups remained loyal to the old government and gave Martin trouble. He confronted these groups directly and so silenced them. He became a ruthless, uncontrollable dictator. The ultimate effect of his rule was the downfall of his country. (p. 256)

Some of the participants read the passage exactly as above; others read it with the name Adolph Hitler substituted for Gerald Martin. Can you see where this is going? Participants who read the paragraph ostensibly about Hitler went beyond the information presented, and made elaborative inferences. For example, these participants were likely to remember that a statement about hatred of Jews had occurred in the passage, when it actually had not. Participants made elaborative inferences based on their knowledge of Hitler; these inferences, although sensible, were inaccurate. The sensible inferences that we make while reading are at the root of many of the memory distortions we discussed in Chapter 8.

When Are Inferences Made?   One of the central questions in research on inferences concerns how often they are made, and with what degree of effort. Do we make inferences whenever we have the chance, or are they made more selectively, only under certain circumstances? Related to this question is the issue of attention's role—is forming an inference an automatic, effortless process that occurs in the absence of any conscious strategy, or is forming an inference a strategic and effortful process?

According to what might be termed the *constructivist view* of text processing, we are constantly making inferences whenever we can, combining our knowledge with the information in the text to form a rather elaborate working model of the text. Text comprehension is characterized as an intelligent and strategic search for meaning (e.g., Graesser, Singer, & Trabasso, 1994). We actively seek to build a relationship between the various elements in the text (the actors, their actions, and other events); whenever an inference is offered by the elements of a text, that inference is drawn. This is closely aligned with the idea of top-down processing; we use context and world knowledge in the text comprehension process.

The constructivist view contends that the formation of inferences is an active, searching process. In contrast, the *minimalist view* championed primarily by McKoon and Ratcliff (1992) contends that making inferences is an automatic, memory-driven process that is engaged only under a *minimal* number of circumstances. Our "default setting" in reading is *not to* constantly search for and make all of the inferences that are possible. McKoon and Ratcliff make use of the distinction between local and global coherence, and claim that inferences are made primarily to maintain local coherence. Therefore, we infer to connect segments of the text that occur in close proximity. We do not regularly make inferences to connect remote ideas. This is more closely aligned with bottom-up processing than top-down processing. We stick closely to the data (i.e., the information explicitly presented in text) whenever possible. We engage in a top-down search for connections only when the data themselves are insufficient for comprehension.

However, McKoon and Ratcliff do acknowledge that many inferences are made as a result of motivated strategies on the part of the reader—in other words, the reader who is motivated and has specific goals and strategies in mind will look for connections and find them. Bridget's experience with reading Mary Higgins-Clark mystery novels reflects this type of motivation. According to Bridget the joy of reading a mystery novel is trying to figure out "whodunit." In order to do this she is motivated to make connections between what she is currently reading and information that was presented earlier in the book. Inferences are constantly and automatically made on-line, but only in the limited set of circumstances just outlined.

By this point in the text, we suspect that you've made the inference that when two theories are pitted against one another, positing different sets of mechanisms, the answer regarding which view is correct is almost always "it depends on the situation," or essentially "both." Such is the case with the constructivist and minimalist views of inferences during sentence comprehension. As Gueraud and O'Brien (2005) note, if we are to make the eminently reasonable assumption that text comprehension requires both top-down and bottom-up processes, then the processes proposed by each of the approaches come into play under different circumstances.

Stop&*Review*

1. Identify the three levels of discourse comprehension.
2. Define anaphoric reference, and state how it relates to coherence.
3. When do we make inferences according to
   a. the constructivist view and
   b. the minimalist view?

- Discourse comprehension refers to the comprehension of linguistic material longer than a sentence. It can be represented at three different levels, termed surface code, textbase, and situation model. Situation models can show an enactment effect, demonstrating the embodiment of language. Coherence is important for discourse comprehension at both a sentence to sentence (local) and entire passage (global) level.

- One source of coherence is anaphoric reference, when current information makes reference to earlier information. The amount of separation between the anaphor and its antecedent disrupts coherence. The ability to make anaphoric reference is dependent on immediate memory. Frequency of occurrence and first mention influence antecedent accessibility. Coherence is also aided by the given-new contract, an implicit understanding that new information is being presented in the context of common backround (i.e., given) information.

- Inferences involve going beyond the information provided in a text. Bridging inferences involve drawing conclusions that tie new material back to older material, and are important for maintaining coherence. Elaborative inferences involve drawing conclusions that add to the detail of a text representation, but are not necessary for coherence. According to the constructivist view of inferences, we constantly and automatically draw inferences as we read a text. According to the minimalist view of inferences, inferences are made primarily to preserve local coherence.

Discourse Memory and Representation

Now that we've discussed some of the processes involved in the initial reading and coding of discourse, let's turn to the processes whereby we store it for the long term. You'll note some parallels between these findings and models that we'll discuss, and the two concepts discussed in Chapter 6: episodic and semantic memory.

Memory for Discourse

Much of the work on discourse comprehension has focused on our memory for connected discourse. As you know from the chapter on memory distortions (Chapter 8), memory is perhaps better characterized as a storyteller, rather than some sort of recording device. Much of the work supporting that conclusion comes from research on memory for discourse. In fact, what may be the most-cited study of memory distortion was actually a study on discourse memory. Take a short break from this reading, and read the following story.

> One night two young men from Egulac went down to the river to hunt seals, and while they were there, it became foggy and calm. Then they heard war-cries, and they thought: "Maybe this is a war-party." They escaped to the shore and hid behind a log.
>
> Now canoes came up, and they heard the noise of the paddles, and saw one canoe coming up to them, There were five men in the canoe, and they said:
>
> What do you think? We wish to take you along. We are going up the river to make war on the people."
>
> One of the young men said: "I have no arrows."
>
> "Arrows are in the canoe," they said.
>
> "I will not go along. I might be killed. My relatives do not know where I have gone. But you," he said, "may go with them."
>
> So one of the young men went, but the other returned home.
>
> And the warriors went on up the river to a town on the other side of Kalama. The people came down to the water, and they began to fight, and many were killed. But presently the young man heard one of the warriors say, "Quick, let us go home: that Indian has been hit." Now he thought: "Oh, they are ghosts." He did not feel sick, but they said he had been shot.

So the canoes went back to Egulac, and the young man went ashore to his house, and made a fire. And he told everybody and said: "Behold I accompanied the ghosts, and we went to fight. Many of our fellows were killed, and many of those who attacked us were killed. They said I was hit, and I did not feel sick."

He told it all, and then he became quiet. When the sun rose he fell down. Something black came out of his mouth. His face became contorted. The people jumped up and cried. He was dead.

Kind of leaves you scratching your head, doesn't it? The story is one that we alluded to in Chapter 1—you'll recall Frederick Bartlett and his classic research on memory. One theme of his research was the reconstructive nature of story memory, and one of his most famous stories was the one you just read, titled *War of the Ghosts*. Now that it's been a few seconds since you read it, close your book and try to recall it in as much detail as you can.

Stop&*Think* | WAR OF THE INFERENCES

Look at your recall of the "War of the Ghosts" story. If you haven't read it and tested your recall, do it now. Does your recall show any evidence of inferences you must have made while reading the story? In other words, if you recalled something that was not in the story, did the errant recall result from an inference you may have made while reading the story?

Gist vs. Verbatim Information.   You probably found it pretty difficult to recall, and impossible to recall word-for-word. So did Bartlett's (1932) participants. Details that were hard to fathom, or that didn't make much sense would be omitted, or distorted to be more consistent with participant knowledge. Sensible details that weren't part of the original story were sometimes added. A sample recall is given in Table 10.4; compare it with your own and see if you made the same mistakes as Barlett's participants approximately 70 years ago. We'll return to Bartlett's study a little later when we discuss models of discourse representation.

Table 10.4 **One sample recall from Bartlett's (1932) study. Compare it with the original story.**

Two Indians were out fishing for seals in the Bay of Manapan, when along came five other Indians in a war canoe. They were going fighting.

"Come with us," said the five to the two, "and fight."

"I cannot come," was the answer of the one, "for I have an old mother at home who is dependent on me." The other said he could not come, because he had no arms. "That is no difficulty," the others replied, "for we have plenty in the canoe with us"; so he got into the canoe and went with them.

In a fight soon afterwards this Indian received a mortal wound. Finding that his hour was coming, he cried out that he was about to die. "Nonsense," said one of the others, "you will not die." But he did.

From Bartlett, F. (1932). *Remembering: A study in experimental and social psychology.* New York: Macmillan.

Your experience, along with the findings of Bartlett, reflects one of the most well-worn distinctions in discourse memory: gist vs. verbatim recall. **Gist information** refers to the basic ideas or main points of a piece of discourse, while **verbatim information** refers to exact wording. Consistent with the picture of memory that emerged from Chapter 8 (memory distortions), we're much better at recalling gist than we are at verbatim recall. In fact, you'll recall that one of the theories of memory distortion we discussed in Chapter 8 was fuzzy-trace theory, which uses the distinction between gist and verbatim traces in accounting for forgetting and memory editing. Although we do remember many things verbatim (e.g., songs, poems, prayers), these are the exception rather than the rule. Virtually everything we read or hear is almost immediately distilled into its essence, or gist.

The speed with which this occurs was revealed in a classic study by Sachs (1967). She presented participants with a passage about the invention of the telescope:

> There is an interesting story about the telescope. In Holland, a man named Lippershey was an eyeglass maker. One day his children were playing with some lenses. They discovered that things seemed very close if two lenses were about a foot apart. Lippershey began experiments and his "spyglass" attracted much attention. <u>He sent a letter about it to Galileo, the great Italian scientist</u> (T1). Galileo at once realized the importance of the discovery and set out to build an instrument of his own. He used an old organ pipe with one lens curved out and the other curved in. On the first clear night he pointed the glass towards the sky. He was amazed to find the empty dark spaces filled with brightly gleaming stars! (T2). Night after night Galileo climbed to a high tower, sweeping the sky with his telescope. One night he saw Jupiter, and to his great surprise discovered with it three bright stars, two to the east and one to the west. On the next night, however, all were to the west. A few nights later there were four little stars. (T3)

At one of three different points in the passage (marked T1, T2, and T3 above), Sachs queried readers' memory for the underlined sentence. She did so with a recognition test in which she gave one of three types of sentences: the exact target sentence (e.g., <u>He sent a letter about it to Galileo, the great Italian scientist</u>), a transformed version of the sentence that retained the meaning (A letter was sent about it to Galileo, the great Italian scientist.), or a sentence that retained some of the words, but changed the meaning (Galileo, the great Italian scientist, sent him a letter about it.). Participants were to determine whether the test sentence was identical to a sentence from the passage.

The results, presented in Figure 10.7, provide a demonstration of the transition from verbatim to gist memory (the graph shows the

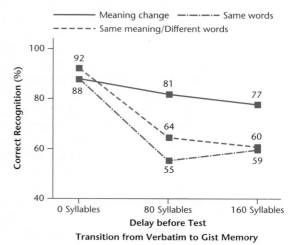

Figure 10.7

Results from Sachs's (1967) study of verbatim and gist memory. As more time passed between reading and test, participants were less likely to remember the exact wording of the sentence but still were quite likely to remember the gist of the sentence.

From Sachs, J. (1967). Recognition memory for syntactic and semantic aspects of connected discourse. *Perception and Psychophysics, 2*, 437–442. Reprinted by permission of the Psychonomic Society, Inc.

number of correct responses on a recognition test; a correct response could be "yes" or "no," depending on the type of sentence presented). At T1, immediately after the presentation of the target sentence, participants showed near-perfect discrimination, saying "yes" to the sentence containing the same words or "no" to the sentence that maintained the same meaning but used different words. When recognition of the target sentence was tested later in the passage (at T2 and T3), performance dropped sharply in the conditions where participants had to notice a change in the verbatim form of the sentence that maintained the sentence's meaning (i.e., gist). Because the sentence retained the meaning of the target sentence, the two were difficult to discriminate. But look at the condition where the test sentence changed the meaning of the original sentence; here, participants were not fooled—they realized it was different. This classic finding provided an elegant demonstration of how readers quickly collapse the verbatim structure of what they read, while maintaining the gist of what it meant.

In general, the last statement is true. But as you have come to expect, cognitive psychology is never that simple. There is some intriguing evidence that suggests that verbatim structure might not be so collapsed after all. Consider the phenomenon of **syntactic persistence** (e.g., Pickering & Ferreira, 2008), which refers to a tendency to use syntactic structures that one has recently heard. Ferreira, Bock, Wilson, and Cohen (2008) provide the following example. If a person hears or says something with a particular syntactic structure, like "The governess made a pot of tea for the princess," they will be more likely than not to re-use that same syntactic structure in describing an unrelated idea (e.g., "The boy is handing the paintbrush to a man" rather than "the boy handed the man the paintbrush"). Using or hearing a syntactic structure once primes a person to use it again, an indication that syntax is retained in some form.

Now if you have retained some of the ideas from earlier in the text in some form, you may be experiencing some conceptual persistence, because what Ferreira et al. are talking about is an implicit memory test. Their contention is that syntactic persistence is a form of priming—a benefit in performance due to earlier exposure to some information. As you recall from Chapter 6, amnesics, while showing a deficit on explicit memory tests (e.g., recall) they show no deficits on implicit memory tests (e.g., word fragment completion measured by priming). If the syntactic persistence effect reflects implicit memory testing, amnesics, who would have little to no explicit memory for a recently heard or used syntactic structure, should still exhibit this effect.

Ferreira et al. conducted a study to test this idea. They employed a clever procedure that would allow them to assess syntactic persistence and at the same time, assess memory for the sentences themselves. In their study, participants (both amnesics and normals) took part in a task that was ostensibly a test of sentence and picture memory. In the first phase, they were presented with a series of sentences that had varying syntactic structures. In a second phase, they were presented with pictured events that they were to describe with a sentence (syntactic persistence would be indicated by their repeating a syntactic structure from the first phase). Finally, they were presented with a series of sentences, some of which had been presented during phase one, and some of which were new (this was the explicit memory test). They repeated each sentence and then assessed whether they had encountered it during phase one.

Ferreira et al. found precisely what they predicted. First, syntactic persistence was evident. Experience with a syntactic structure during the sentence reading task significantly increased the probability that the same structure would be produced later as the participants named pictures. Perhaps even more importantly, both amnesics and normals demonstrated a high a level of persistence. The complementary finding of the typical implicit/explicit memory test dissociation also was obtained; amnesics' memory for which sentences they had encountered earlier in the experiment was quite poor, relative to that of normals.

Models of Discourse Comprehension

Reading and remembering a selection of discourse requires the formation of some internal representation. What is the nature of this representation? A number of proposals have been offered to describe how discourse is represented.

Schemas and Scripts.   One of the most ubiquitous explanations for how we come to understand and remember discourse is based on the notion of schemata, or **schemas.** Based on his participants' sketchy yet sensible recall of *War of the Ghosts*, Bartlett (1932) proposed that recall was based on some generalized form of knowledge representation. A schema refers to the general knowledge we possess about some person, place, or event. Schemas make new information easy to assimilate, understand, and remember. For example, your notions about war (guns, fighting, killing), and ghosts (mysterious, magical) may well have guided your encoding and your retrieval of *War of the Ghosts*.

Four processes are thought to underlie the use of schemas in understanding discourse (Alba & Hasher, 1983). First, the important parts of the incoming message need to be selected and attended. The second stage of schema use is the abstraction of meaning from what we're reading, and a disposal of the verbatim details. This process was highlighted in the gist vs. verbatim memory study conducted by Sachs (1967). Third, the appropriate schema needs to be activated; recall the "balloon" passage that we discussed in the section on discourse comprehension (see page 425). This passage was near-impossible to understand, because the general knowledge you needed to understand it was inactive. Once we gave you the picture depicting the situation, the meaning became clear. Finally, the information taken in and the information activated to comprehend it must be integrated into a single unified representation.

A special type of schema is a **script,** which is a generalized knowledge representation of routine activities, such as going to a restaurant. Scripts include information about the typical objects, situations, and activities encountered in conjunction with certain activities. Schank and Abelson (1977) proposed that the information represented in scripts is essential to our understanding of discourse. Scripts do seem to be psychologically "real;" Bower, Black, and Turner (1979) had participants list activities commonly associated with certain situations, such as going to a restaurant or attending a lecture. Their responses showed a striking level of consistency. Just as people tend to mention "apple" when you ask them to give an example of fruit, they tend to say "take notes," when asked for things that happen at a lecture. Schemas and scripts have much the same characteristics as the concepts that we discussed in Chapter 5, such as proto-typical members and graded structure.

Further support for the notion of scripts and their role in discourse comprehension comes from Bower, Black, and Turner (1979). According to Schank and Abelson's (1977) original conceptualization of scripts, elements of a story that are irrelevant to the major theme or purpose of a script will not be well-encoded or remembered. Also distracting events—ones that are salient, but not consistent with the theme of a script—should be particularly well-encoded and well-remembered because of their distinctiveness. In accordance with these hypotheses, Bower et al. found that participants were unlikely to recall script-irrelevant details, such as the color of the waiter's shoes, but were very likely to recall distracting and salient events that stood out from the scripts, such as the waiter spilling water on the restaurant guests.

Research also indicates that the use of scripts is an important element in the coherent representation of text. Walker and Yekovich (1987) found that central elements of scripts (such as "taking notes" for attending a lecture) were comprehended faster than were more peripheral elements (such as "falling asleep"), even if the central elements had not been explicitly presented. In other words, when we encounter a script-typical concept, it's much easier to find the antecedent and make the bridging inference that's necessary for coherence.

Although there is no doubt that the notions of schemas and scripts have been an important driving force in research on discourse representation, they have been found wanting by many. The concepts are quite general and vague, and really serve more as simple descriptions of the characteristics of discourse comprehension and memory, rather than explanations. Schema- and script-based theories don't provide very precise accounts of how we make inferences, or how we connect anaphors to their antecedents.

Stop&*Think Back* | SCRIPTING MEMORY DISTORTIONS

Enlist a few friends as participants and ask them to generate the first five elements that come to mind when they think of the following situations:

- Going home for the holidays
- First day of a college class
- Going to a movie with friends
- Finals week
- Graduation

Do you see any commonality among the responses for each script? Which seem to have consistent scripts? If any do not, why might that be the case?

How do scripts relate to memory? How might they lead to memory distortions? To what type(s) of "memory sin(s)" discussed in Chapter 8 are scripts likely to lead? What other memory distortion phenomena and theories can be related to scripts?

Story Grammars. Some researchers (e.g., Mandler, 1987; Rumelhart, 1975; Thorndyke, 1977) took the notion of sentence grammar and applied it to how we encode and understand longer pieces of discourse. Just as sentences have standard elements (e.g., subject, object, etc.) so do stories—they have settings, plots, themes, and resolutions—these elements comprise what is termed a **story grammar.** You might think of a story grammar as a schema that represents the developments typically encountered as we read a story (Carroll, 1994). The story-grammar approach to comprehension proposes that we understand stories by parsing them into their components, much like we do sentences. Our representation of discourse consists of episodes that correspond to the important elements of a story (e.g., the beginning, some important development, and a conclusion). The notion that we remember discourse as a series of story-grammar based episodes has received some empirical support. Episodes seem to be important defining units in our representation of stories. Recall of episodes in a story tends to be all-or-none, almost as if each episode were encoded as one "chunk" of information (e.g., Glenn, 1978). Also, the length of one episode doesn't seem to affect the ability to remember another episode, suggesting that they're processed as partially independent "chunks."

Although the story-grammar approach has enjoyed some success, it suffers from the same lack of definition that characterizes the schema-based approach. In contrast to the well-defined syntactic components of a sentence (e.g., nouns, verbs, etc), it's not easy to state definitively what the corresponding components are for stories. Similarly, the notion of an episode is not easy to define precisely. Story grammars and schemas serve as useful descriptions of some of the processes of discourse comprehension, but fall short of providing a comprehensive *explanation* of how we comprehend text.

The Construction-Integration Model.   Perhaps the most influential theory of discourse comprehension was proposed by Kintsch and van Dijk (1978), and later revised by Kintsch (1988; 1998). The basic idea underlying the theory is that the major ideas from discourse are encoded and represented as propositions (true or false statements about the relationships between events), which are expressed primarily in terms of *arguments* and *predicates*. The argument is usually the focus of the proposition (i.e.,what the proposition is about). The predicate is the information given about the argument. Some sentences might consist of a single proposition:

The dog ran.

ARGUMENT: DOG   *PREDICATE:* RUN

or, as is more often the case, a series of two or more propositions.

The frightened dog ran from the massive cat.

There are several relationships expressed in this sentence, hence a number of propositions.

ARGUMENT: DOG   *PREDICATE:* RUN

ARGUMENT: DOG   *PREDICATE:* FRIGHTENED

ARGUMENT: CAT   *PREDICATE:* MASSIVE

Breaking a complex sentence into a series of propositions essentially boils down to a "re-write" in terms of simple sentences, like:

The dog ran

The dog was frightened

(The dog ran) away from a cat.

The cat was massive.

Another important point about the propositional encoding of text is that the encoding is *hierarchical*, with the most important propositions (representing the major theme or events of a text) at the top of the hierarchy and more tangential propositions (representing relatively unimportant details from the text) at the bottom. According to the Kintsch and van Dijk model (and later versions of it; e.g., Kintsch 1988, 1998) as we read discourse, we *construct* a *network* of hierarchically-related propositions, and *integrate* this network with our world knowledge. The model has been dubbed the **construction-integration model** of comprehension.

The notion of immediate memory plays an important role in this conceptualization of comprehension. Because of the well-known limits on immediate memory, we are limited in our ability to consider propositions concurrently as we are reading; typically, we encode discourse in "cycles" of 6 to 12 propositions (note the connection to the "magic number" that describes immediate memory span for unrelated items we discussed in Chapter 4). Given this selectivity, what determines the contents of immediate memory? The propositions most likely to be held in immediate memory at any given point are those that are high up in the hierarchy (i.e., the most important, or central, propositions), and those that have occurred recently. When propositions overlap (i.e., immediate memory load is low), processing of text is relatively easy, because all of the propositions are in immediate memory concurrently. More stress is placed on the limited capacity of immediate memory when a proposition does not overlap with its current contents. In these cases, we must search for an earlier antecedent and perhaps make a bridging inference to a distant point in the text; comprehension is more difficult as a result.

A number of research findings support the basic tenets of this approach. For example, Kintsch and Keenan (1973) estimated the time taken to read a passage, and found a strong relationship between this measure and the number of propositions in the text. This is to be expected if we encode texts in terms of propositions; immediate memory limits would be felt more severely (and reading would slow), as the number of propositions increased. The notion of a propositional hierarchy is also supported by a **levels effect** in discourse memory. This refers to the oft-replicated finding that information from higher levels of a text-representation hierarchy are more likely to be recalled than information from lower levels (e.g., McKoon, 1977; van Dijk & Kintsch, 1978).

The propositional network model has a distinctly bottom-up flavor. According to the propositional approach, we build a text representation "from the bottom up." In contrast, schema-based theories propose that we come to a representation of the text "from the top-down," by imposing schematic knowledge on the incoming information. It is important to note however, the importance of world knowledge in both approaches.

Structure Building.   A relatively straightforward, yet compelling view of text comprehension has been proposed by Gernsbacher (1991, 1997). She terms her approach the structure-building framework. According to the **structure-building framework,** comprehension is all about building *structures*, or coherent mental representations of the information in the text. Three subprocesses comprise structure building. The first process is termed *laying a foundation* and occurs whenever a new topic is introduced. The fact that readers tend to slow down when taking in the first sentence of a paragraph, even if that sentence isn't the topic sentence (Gernsbacher & Hargreaves, 1988), suggests that readers are laying a foundation for later material. This foundation-laying process is driven by what Gernsbacher terms *first mention*. A host of studies have demonstrated that the first participant mentioned in a sentence or passage of text is easier to access later than participants mentioned later. For example, in this sentence

> *The student asked the professor a question.*

verifying that the phrase "the student" occurred in the sentence turns out to be faster than if the actors in the sentence are reversed (e.g., The professor asked the student a question). In the former case, the student serves as the foundation for the representation of that particular sentence. This finding, termed the **advantage of first mention,** holds true for both spoken and written comprehension (e.g., McDonald & MacWhinney, 1995), and also cross-linguistically (e.g., Carreiras, Gernsbacher, & Villa, 1995).

The advantage of first mention seems to conflict with another well-established finding in text comprehension, the **advantage of clause recency.** The later a clause is in a sentence, the easier it is to recall (e.g., von Eckardt & Potter, 1985). Upon closer examination, the two don't really conflict—the advantage of first mention occurs if the test stimulus is presented after a bit of a delay. The advantage of clause recency occurs if the test stimulus is presented immediately. The idea of first mention and clause recency is another example of the notions of primacy and recency discussed in Chapter 4.

The second process in structure building is *mapping*. Once a foundation has been laid, the comprehender maps on subsequent information. Mapping involves using world knowledge and linguistic knowledge to relate new information to information already encoded. In other words, cues that provide for coherence of a text (e.g., anaphoric reference and inferencing) are used in the process of mapping. If the incoming material is unrelated to the current foundation, then a new structure is begun, and a new foundation laid. This is the third process in the structure-building framework—*shifting*. Shifting also occurs when an overt cue such as "on the other hand," or "later that same day," is encountered. The existence of this process is indicated by the finding that cues to a new story episode (i.e., a change in scene) slow down comprehension (Gernsbacher, 1989).

To help accomplish the subprocesses involved in structure building, Gernsbacher (1991; 1997) proposes two general mechanisms: suppression and enhancement. These mechanisms are not unique to language—they're also used in other domains of cognition. *Suppression* involves (in Gernsbacher's words) a "fine tuning" of the activation of a word's meanings. Recall our discussion of lexical ambiguity in the previous chapter. Evidence indicates that multiple meanings of a word are activated simultaneously, yet the inappropriate ones are quickly weeded out (fine-tuned) out and inhibited. This process is guided by suppression. *Enhancement* is the converse of suppression, and involves processes that increase the accessibility of information in memory. For example, given the semantic and syntactic constraints of a given sentence, certain concepts become enhanced, and more accessible to comprehension and production. The structure-building approach is an intuitively appealing framework, and it provides an extremely useful framework for analyzing broad aspects of text comprehension. In addition, some of its more specific assumptions have received good empirical support.

Later research has attempted to extend the model by investigating individual differences in structure building. For example, Callendar and McDaniel (2007) were interested in how different types of text adjuncts might assist high and low-structure builders. Allow us to define some terms here. A text adjunct is a feature of a text that's designed to aid in your text comprehension. Our book—the one you're reading this very moment—features a number of text adjuncts, including the Stop and Think! and Stop and Review exercises. It's reasonable to assume that the effectiveness of these text adjuncts might differ across individuals; for some, they might be highly effective and for others, not so much. (You probably have your own thoughts about how useful they are for you, but as you'll soon read, your sense of your own comprehension leaves something to be desired). Callendar and McDaniel were interested in whether the effectiveness of text adjuncts would differ as a function of a person's skill in structure building.

As you've seen, structure building involves laying a foundation with information that is encountered, and continuously mapping new information into this existing structure. If new information cannot be mapped onto the existing structure, the reader starts building a new substructure. This cycle continues until the person has developed a structure of the entire text. According to Gernsbacher (1990), poor structure builders have trouble inhibiting irrelevant information, and as a result, they shift their attention too much, which results in building too many substructures. Therefore, they don't end up with a very coherent structure of the text. Note the interesting similarity here between the poor structure builders, and the person with poor working memory (WM) span (as discussed in Chapter 4). Recall that WM span is predictive of the ability to control attention.

Callender and McDaniel investigated the usefulness of what they termed *embedded questions.* These were fact-based questions embedded in the text that queried readers about things they had just read. These would be akin to the Stop and Review questions we pose after each major section of a chapter. Their expectation was that, because low structure builders have trouble highlighting important information and ignoring irrelevant information, embedded questions would serve as anchors of a sort, highlighting important information. High structure builders, who are good at identifying important and unimportant points, will derive little or no benefit from these questions. The embedded questions aren't adding much beyond what they already know based on their superior structure building. The researchers divided participants into high- and low-structure builders by giving a standardized test designed to assess skill in structure building.

Participants in the experiment were presented with a chapter from a social psychology text in one of two study conditions. One group read the text with embedded questions presented every couple of pages throughout the chapter. Another group simply read the text, but to control for the extra time likely spent by the embedded questions group, the control group read the text twice. Participants received a multiple choice test

Table 10.5 **Results from Callender and McDaniel (2007), Showing the Effects of Embedded Questions in Text on Comprehension for Low and High Structure Builders**

	Low Structure Builders		High Structure Builders	
	Read Twice	Embedded Q's	Read Twice	Embedded Q's
Target Questions	.54	.75	.84	.83
Related Questions	.46	.68	.68	.75

with two types of items. *Target questions* asked about concepts that had been the subject of the embedded questions. *Related questions* asked about concepts related to those concepts. The results are presented in Table 10.5, and fit nicely with Callender and McDaniel's predictions. As you can see, embedded questions were a big help, but only for the low structure builders. Low structure builders who read with the embedded questions performed about 20% better than low structure builders who simply read the text twice. The high structure builders did better overall (demonstrating the usefulness of the structure-building measure itself), and were not helped by the embedded questions. These findings are in the spirit of the encoding-retrieval interactions we talked about in Chapter 6. You'll recall that there is no "one size fits all" best encoding method. The best type of encoding depends on the nature of the retrieval test. Callender and McDaniel's results indicate that the best type of reading and testing style for maximizing comprehension depends on the reader.

Metacomprehension

Before we end the section on discourse, let's look at one final issue—one that's critical to your performance as a student. When you close this book and put it aside for the night (if you can...it is a page-turner, isn't it?), how well will you be able to judge how well you know it—in other words, do you know if you know it? This is an extremely important question, because as you no doubt realize from personal experience, the answer to the question determines whether you choose to keep on studying, or engage in alternative (perhaps more fun) activities.

Research Theme
Metacognition

The term **metacomprehension** is used to describe a person's knowledge about what they do and don't understand from a text they've read. The news isn't good; people have pretty poor metacomprehension skills. In an extensive series of studies, Maki (1998) reported a meager correlation of .27 between what participants thought they knew from short texts and what they actually did know. So people don't seem to be very good judges of their own comprehension. The implications for mastering class material are a bit disturbing—feeling like you "really know this stuff" doesn't tell you whether you actually do. This conclusion is disheartening and somewhat surprising. Are people really that bad at judging what they've learned? Follow-up research has addressed this question on two fronts. First, research has attempted to test a variety of methods for assessing metacomprehension; second, research has attempted to discover ways in which metacomprehension might be improved.

One problem with previous methods for assessing metacomprehension, according to Dunlosky and Lipko (2007), is that they required participants to make global judgments of what they knew from the targeted texts. Imagine being asked to provide a 1 to 10 rating of how well you know the material in this chapter. This isn't a very sensitive measure, because there may be things from the chapter that you comprehended extremely well, and other information that went right over your head. How can feelings about individual sections and topics be mentally averaged into one number that accurately captures metacomprehension? Another problem is that participants may be limited in their ability to estimate their level of knowledge about a text if they don't even really understand the text to begin with. Later studies of metacomprehension have attempted to deal with these issues and allow for more informative and useful assessments of comprehension.

One technique has been to encourage readers to engage in activities during processing of texts that encourage them to monitor their own learning more thoroughly. One simple technique is re-reading; it turns out that simply reading a text passage twice substantially improves judgments of metacomprehension (Rawson, Dunlosky, & Thiede, 2000). In a similar vein, Thiede and his colleagues (Thiede & Anderson, 2003; Thiede, Dunlosky, Griffin, & Wiley, 2005) have found that having participants generate key terms, or summarize what they have read also improved metacomprehension judgments substantially.

A final method shown to improve metacomprehension is to decrease the *grain size* of estimation. Consider the following example from Dunlosky & Lipko (2007). When participants are asked how well they understand a relatively "large" topic (i.e., how well do you understand reading comprehension), their estimates are not as accurate as when they are asked a more "bite-sized" (i.e., smaller-grained) portion of the topic (i.e., how well do you understand the garden path approach to sentence parsing?). An intriguing qualification to this result was added to the picture by Dunlosky, Rawson, and Middleton (2005). They compared estimates of comprehension that were made either before or after participants attempted to recall definitions of important terms. They found that estimates of comprehension that were made after attempted recall were more accurate (correlation between judgment and comprehension of .73) than estimates of comprehension that were made in the absence of this attempted recall (correlation between judgment and comprehension of .57). Basically, if participants made comprehension judgments after having tested themselves, their estimates were more accurate than if they hadn't tested themselves. Recall from Chapter 6 how testing oneself is a useful method for enhancing retention (i.e., the testing effect). Here is yet another benefit of testing yourself—a considerable improvement in metacomprehension accuracy.

So what's the lesson for you as you study? Well, metacomprehension judgments will be pretty uninformative if all you do is read the text. So if you read a chapter once, and then sit back and make a judgment about how well you've comprehended what you've read, the judgment is likely to be pretty useless. Simply rereading the text will improve the judgment. Better yet, testing yourself on what you've just read by summarizing it or generating key points will greatly improve the accuracy of your comprehension judgments as well as your retention of the that material. In addition, it's better to assess your comprehension of individual terms and concepts, rather than making global judgments of how well you understand an entire chapter.

Speed Reading?

A chapter on reading would not be complete without mention of the popular notion of *speed reading*. This seems like an appropriate topic on which to end the chapter, as a proper analysis of the claims about speed reading require an understanding of every topic discussed in this chapter: the mechanical aspects of the reading process, text comprehension, and long-term retention of text material. We armed you with necessary tools, so let's evaluate the efficacy of speed reading.

The claims of speed reading proponents sound pretty fantastic. Double your reading speed and improve your comprehension and retention of the material. One method we found on the internet even made the preposterous claim of 25,000 words per minute! Is there any possible truth to the claims? Or does it smack of late night hokum? The short answer is no and yes, respectively. But we'll give you the long answer (but it won't be so long if it only takes you 30 seconds to read the next couple of pages!).

According to those who champion the methods of speed reading, the typical reading speed of 250 to 350 words per minute can be increased to thousands of words per minute with some relatively simple mechanical changes in reading. One claim is that the brain does not process things to maximal efficiency—it "wastes time" with too many saccades (similar to the baseless claim that we use only 10% of our brain, discussed in Chapter 1). Also, the inner speech that typically accompanies reading is seen as an unnecessary drag on the system. So the goals of speed reading are to increase the information taken in during each eye fixation (thus cutting down on the number of movements) and to eliminate inner speech. Some evidence suggests that speed readers are indeed reading very differently than normal readers (Llewellyn, 1962; McClaughlin, 1969). These studies found that speed readers fixate for about the same length of time as normal readers, but they fixate only once per line. Even stranger, the speed readers in these studies read down the left-hand page and *up* the right-hand page! That is, they read the right-hand page in the reverse order. These mechanical changes are purported to facilitate comprehension and improve retention of the material.

Rigorous empirical tests of speed reading are few and far between, which should probably tell you something about the reality of the phenomenon. Not only that, much, if not most, of the *evidence* is anecdotal, or based on self-report testimonials; as you know, anecdotes are poor evidence. And even the anecdotes aren't completely supportive of speed reading effectiveness (Carver, 1971). The methodologically sound research that has been done fails to support the fantastic claims. According to Just and Carpenter (1987), many studies of speed reading fail to measure what was remembered from the material read, others use tests with easy multiple choice questions, and still others fail to test an appropriate control group.

One of the only studies to provide a thorough and internally valid empirical test of speed reading was conducted by Just, Carpenter, and Masson (1982); as you can infer from the date (an elaborative inference not a bridging inference), this study pretty much slammed the empirical door on the issue. In their study, speed readers were compared with two control groups—normal readers and normal readers who were instructed to *skim*. Figure 10.8 shows a sample of the saccades made by each type of reader. The readers

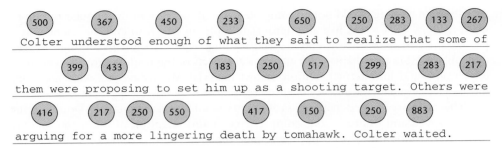

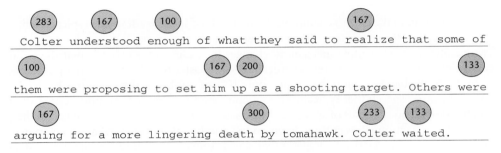

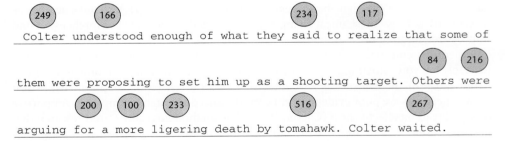

Figure 10.8

Eye fixations of normal readers, speed readers, and skimmers.

From Just, M. A., & Carpenter, P. A. (1987). *The psychology of reading and language comprehension.* Boston: Allyn and Bacon. Copyright 1987 by Pearson Education. Reprinted by permission of the publisher.

were tested for their comprehension of the general idea (or gist) of the passage, as well as for their memory for the details. The results demonstrated that all readers did fairly well on the general information questions. However, on the detailed information questions, normal readers performed better.

Speed readers seem to show the reading equivalent of a speed-accuracy. Reaction time and accuracy often trade off in performance situations; if people are trying to be especially fast, their accuracy is likely to suffer. The same is true of speed reading; people are trying to blaze through a reading passage, then their *accuracy* (in the form of memory for and comprehension of the passage) is likely to suffer. You've probably suffered this fate yourself as a result of skimming. Although you may have gone through the "mechanics" of reading some material for your class, it's almost like you haven't read it at all. Why? Because the essence of reading is not perceptual processing—the essence of reading is understanding or comprehension.

Stop&*Review*

1. True or false? Gist memory for discourse is much better than verbatim memory.
2. What is the basic unit of discourse representation, according to construction-integration theory?
3. Outline the basic processes proposed by structure building theory.
4. What is metacomprehension? Give one method for improving it.
5. True or false? Speed reading is no better than skimming in promoting comprehension.

- Memory for the gist of a text tends to be quite good, while memory for verbatim details is quite poor. The transition from a verbatim to gist representation occurs immediately as a passage is encoded. People do show implicit memory for verbatim aspects (i.e., the syntax) of what they read. The notion of schemas/scripts provides a useful descriptive model of discourse comprehension and memory. According to the story grammar approach, we represent discourse in terms of the important elements of the story.

- According to the construction-integration approach, we represent discourse in terms of propositions, or relations between objects and events. Consistent with this view, comprehension of discourse is closely related to the number of propositions in a text. The account is also supported by a levels effect, the finding that higher-level propositions are easier to recall than lower level ones.

- According to the structure-building approach, the representation of discourse involves laying a foundation for new ideas, mapping on subsequent information, and shifting to a new foundation upon a change in topic. Research reveals that the effectiveness of certain text aids depends on the reader's structure-building ability.

- Metacomprehension, a person's knowledge about what they understand from a text they've read, is sometimes poor, but does depend on how it is measured, and can be improved simply by rereading material, or by testing oneself on specific ideas from the material.

- In spite of strong claims, evidence indicates that speed reading is ineffective in promoting comprehension. Speed readers do fairly well in their understanding of the general idea of a passage but fail to grasp the details. This same pattern characterizes readers who "skim" rather than read.

11

Judgments and Decisions: Using Information to Make Choices

Sometimes you make decisions quickly, based on an intuition or hunch. Other times you make decisions after a long and laborious process of weighing and considering alternatives. How do these modes of reasoning differ? Which one is better, or more likely to lead to a rational choice?

Sometimes it seems that people go on hot streaks or cold streaks. What underlies these streaks? Are they even real? People seem pretty confident in their beliefs about them; does this confidence tell us anything? How does confidence in judgment relate to actual judgment?

We often make snap judgments about people. What lies behind the quick and intuitive judgments we make about others? Are the judgments fair? How might they relate to judgment practices like racial profiling?

"I could have told you that would happen." You hear it all the time, and you've probably said it yourself. The counter to this mundane claim is, "Yeah, well, hindsight is 20/20." Do our hindsight judgments and views of events reflect what we really would have thought or said beforehand, in foresight?

Fundamental Concepts

Consider the following evaluations:

> If you don't manage your time effectively, then you aren't going to do well in your classes.
> My roommate is bombing all of his classes.
> He's not very good at time management.

> All my professors are cool.
> Cool people wouldn't get worked up about extending a paper deadline.
> So my professor shouldn't have a problem with giving the class an extra week.

> There's been a "pop" quiz every other Monday for two months.
> It's Sunday night, two weeks after the last quiz.
> I'd better get ready for a quiz tomorrow.

> Boy, that guy is sure a tall drink of water.
> He's at least 6' 6".
> He must be a basketball player.

> Should I buy that brand of new truck?
> The consumer magazines rave about it, but a friend of my brother's bought one, and it was a real lemon.
> I'd better not.

Each of these seemingly simple evaluations is actually quite complex at its core. Each involves making certain assumptions and arriving at a conclusion. For some, there is incomplete or missing information; others entail an educated guess. In other words, each scenario involves one of the processes we'll be discussing next: reasoning, judgment, or decision making. Each of these complex cognitive processes is based on the simpler processes that we have discussed in previous chapters. Think about it (hopefully, after reading this text, you've grown fond of that phrase). In each case, your attention is required to take in the information; pattern recognition helps you to identify the elements within each scenario; immediate memory allows you to consider the alternatives; long-term memory serves as the database from which you build your assumptions; and language allows you to express and process each of the assertions.

The major difference among reasoning, judgment, and decision making relates primarily to what each requires. **Reasoning** involves the evaluation of a conclusion based solely on given information. Decision making and judgment require you to go beyond the information given. With **judgment,** you apply reasoning processes about given information, but you must use the given information to arrive at a conclusion (rather than simply evaluate a given conclusion). The pop quiz example involves judgment; you discern a pattern in particular events and form a conclusion (i.e., "Pop quizzes occur every two weeks"). Unlike the first two examples, you must go beyond the information given. **Decision making** involves an even further progression beyond the given information—to situations that involve uncertainty or risk. In decision making, you must evaluate given information, arrive at a judgment, and, based on this judgment, make a choice among several possible alternatives.

This is "risky," because it involves a considerable amount of guesswork. Decision-making situations often provide limited information or require a degree of knowledge or computational skill that is well beyond the range of what humans can do. Take the car-buying scenario from earlier; there's no possible way you can know every fact about every car, and there is no easy way to combine what information you have to arrive at the correct choice. Indeed, in this case, it's not even clear what the correct choice would be! So in cases of decision making, we stray well beyond the given information into uncertain territory.

The Focus on Errors

As you'll see, the emphasis in research on reasoning, judgment, and decision making has been on the mistakes people make. In fact, after reading about all of the ways in which these processes go wrong, you may think that people are idiots. Quite the contrary; errors are the price we pay for quick and efficient processing. So why the emphasis on error? One reason, noted by Nobel Prize-winning psychologist Daniel Kahneman (1991), is informativeness. The conditions under which our thinking fails reveal important aspects of cognitive processing. You've seen a number of examples of this throughout the text; theories of memory have been richly informed by the phenomena of memory distortion (Chapter 8); the nature of automaticity is revealed by our susceptibility to action slips (Chapter 4). Along the same lines, the patterns of error that are evident in reasoning, judgment, and decision making inform us about how these processes typically operate.

The fact that so much research focuses on errors begs a question: How exactly do we know that a given chain of reasoning, judgment, or decision making is in error? What is the benchmark against which we compare people's thinking in order to evaluate whether the thinking was accurate or proper? This question relates to a distinction researchers make between two approaches to the study of reasoning, judgment, and decision making. One approach, termed a **normative approach,** describes how we *ought* to think in a given situation. As you'll see, we often fall short of this ideal, so researchers have developed what is termed a **descriptive approach.** This approach, as the label would imply, describes how we actually *do* think.

Let's consider an example that allows for a comparison of the approaches. Suppose a woman told you she has 10 children—all boys. Suppose you were asked to estimate the probability of her having a girl in her next pregnancy. What would be your answer? According to a normative analysis, your answer should be 50/50. But people often overestimate the probability of the next child being a girl. They look at the long run of boys, and because this seems so unusual and unlikely, they think that it is especially likely that the situation will "return to normal" (in other words, become half boys and half girls). One descriptive model of judgment claims that people use a principle termed *representativeness.* (We'll discuss this principle in more detail later; here, we'll keep it simple.) In this example, people will see 10 boys in a row as very nonrepresentative of what should happen in 10 pregnancies. For this sequence to be representative there should be as many boys as girls; therefore, a girl being born next will be seen as especially likely. Although this judgment violates the principles of basic probability (which serve as the normative model here), people often make it. As you'll see, normative models of reasoning, judgment, and decision making are not always a reasonable standard against which to compare human thought.

People aren't calculators and few are statisticians, so they usually don't have all of the information they need to follow a normative model.

Bounded Rationality.   You're going to see throughout this chapter that people violate normative models of reasoning, judgment, and decision making. Does this mean that human beings are irrational? As we'll see, there is no one simple answer to this question. Adherence to or deviance from rational thought and behavior depends on a variety of factors, not to mention exactly how we define *rational*. Baron (1999) contends that rationality is not necessarily the same as accuracy (getting the "right" answer), and that irrationality is not necessarily the same as error (getting the "wrong" answer). By Baron's analysis, rationality involves choosing the methods that help us attain our goals, whatever those may be. We can reason well but still have a decision work out badly; conversely, we can reason badly yet still luck into a good outcome.

There is no dispute over the notion that our powers of reason are limited (a notion often dubbed **bounded rationality**). However, there are some profound differences of interpretation when it comes to how one should view bounded rationality. In many ways, these differing views represent a version of the glass as half empty/half full debate. As stated earlier, historically most of the research evidence on these processes has seen the glass as half empty. It's focused on errors, which have become an oft-used vehicle to examine what's *wrong* with the human reasoner, judger, or decision maker, and how conclusions, judgments, and decisions might differ from the "rational" standard. The more recent approach (championed by Gigerenzer and colleagues) has been to view the cognitive processing used by human thinkers in these situations as "simple heuristics that make us smart" (Gigerenzer & Todd, 1999; Gigerenzer, 2008). The approaches you're going to read about in the coming pages are not signs of stupid humans making mistake after mistake; rather, they are signs of extremely well-adapted humans making the best decisions possible given cognitive limitations and contextual demands. We'll examine Gigerenzer's view in more detail a bit later.

It's interesting to note that this debate is symptomatic of a wider trend in psychological theory and research. For nearly a century, many would claim that psychology has accentuated the negative aspects of human mental processes and behavior. From clinical psychologists' focus on psychopathology to social psychologists' emphasis on the dark side of human behavior as evidenced by studies of social influence to cognitive psychologists' emphasis on errant cognitions such as memory distortion and reasoning errors, it's clear that human failings have fascinated psychologists. The current trend in the field is to investigate positive aspects of human behavior—what humans do right. The entire field of *positive psychology* is a testament to this emerging trend (also, see Krueger & Funder, 2004, for an extensive discussion of this issue within the field of social psychology).

Dual-Process Views

Currently, many researchers studying reasoning, judgment, and decision making adopt what is typically termed a *dual-process view* (e.g., Evans, 2008; Sloman, 1996; Stanovich, 2004; Stanovich & West, 2000). According to this view, the human thinker operates in one of two modes, depending on the particular nature of the situation: the heuristic

Table 11.1 **Comparison of System 1 vs. System 2 reasoning processes (based on Evans, 2008)**

System 1	System 2 (Analytic)
Unconscious (Heuristic)	Conscious
Automatic	Controlled
Rapid	Slow
Nonverbal	Linked to language
Capacity-Free	Capacity-Limited
Shared with Animals	Animals Don't Have
Evolutionarily Old	Evolutionarily New

mode and the analytic mode. See Table 11.1 for a comparison of each mode's features. In many ways, this distinction is similar to the automatic-controlled distinction we discussed in Chapter 3. In the *heuristic mode* (also called *System 1*), the processes used for thinking operate quickly and without much deliberation—that is, automatically. Heuristics are shortcuts or rules of thumb that we use in cases in which limitations in time or information compromise one's ability to arrive at an optimal judgment or decision. We'll be discussing heuristics in some depth in this chapter as well as the next one (problem solving) as heuristics are often used to solve problems. The heuristic mode of thinking is fast and efficient, and is based on previous experiences and beliefs (i.e., top-down processing). The heuristic mode of thinking actually doesn't sound much like "thinking" in the colloquial sense. The colloquial term that might apply to the heuristic mode of thinking is *intuition,* which, in contrast to its mystical connotations, has recently found firm empirical footing in the experimental psychology literature.

The heuristic mode contrasts powerfully with what is termed an analytic mode of thought (also termed *System 2*). In this mode, thinking is relatively slow, deliberate, and controlled. In addition, the analytic mode is more cognitively demanding than the heuristic mode; that is, it demands a good deal of immediate memory capacity. Because of this demand and the fact that capacity is limited, we often reason and make judgments and decisions in the heuristic mode, as you'll see throughout this chapter. The dual-process view has proven to be quite effective as an organizational tool for describing two important dimensions of thinking. In fact, Evans (2008) contends that the postulation of dual reasoning processes has become "axiomatic." However, some researchers have criticized it as overly vague, and have begun to propose newer, more complex models (e.g., Frank, Cohen, & Sanfey, 2009).

Stop&*Review*

1. Distinguish among reasoning, judgment, and decision making.
2. Normative is to descriptive as
   a. how we do think is to how we ought to think.
   b. how we ought to think is to how we do think.
   c. reasoning is to judgment.
   d. judgment is to reasoning.

3. What are the two processes in the dual-process view of reasoning?

- Reasoning involves evaluating conclusions based solely on given information. Judgment involves the application of reasoning processes to given information and the use of this information to arrive at a conclusion. Decision making involves evaluating given information, making a judgment, and choosing among several possible alternatives based on this analysis.

- Research on thinking emphasizes error because analyzing the types of mistakes people make and when they make them can be quite informative with regard to typical cognitive processing. The normative approach describes how we *ought* to think, given objective standards of rationality. The descriptive approach describes how we *do* think in actual situations.

- Researchers now conceptualize bounded rationality as part of an adaptive approach to reasoning, judgment, and decision making given limited capacity and contextual demands. The dual-process view contends that thinking operates in two modes. System 1 is in an automatic, low-demand heuristic mode and System 2 is a controlled, high-cognitive-demand analytic mode.

Reasoning

As stated a bit earlier, reasoning involves arriving at a conclusion based on some given information. One primary difference between forms of reasoning relates to whether general assertions are considered in order to arrive at specific conclusions, or whether specific conclusions are reviewed to arrive at a more general principle. These two forms of reasoning are labeled (respectively) *deductive* and *inductive*.

Deductive Reasoning

Determining if a specific conclusion is valid based on general principles or assertions (i.e., **premises**) is termed **deductive reasoning.** Think about the way psychology experiments are conducted. Let's say you want to do a study about memory encoding and retrieval. First, you would review the literature to examine the theories concerning the relationship between these two concepts. Then you would find the encoding specificity principle, which states that retrieval is best when the conditions at retrieval match those at encoding; this is your *general premise*. From this general premise, you would make a *specific prediction* (conclusion) about what should happen when you vary the mood of people at encoding and retrieval: people will retrieve more information if their mood during retrieval is the same as their mood at encoding. In this example, you would go from a general principle (encoding specificity) and make a specific conclusion (about mood) based on that principle. Two forms of deductive reasoning have received a great deal of attention from cognitive researchers: syllogistic reasoning and conditional reasoning (see Evans, 2002, for a review).

Syllogistic Reasoning.   The first type of deductive reasoning is called **syllogistic reasoning.** Consider the following *syllogism* (no doubt a familiar sight if you've had a logic course):

> All students are bright.
> All bright people complete assigned work on time.
> Therefore, all students complete assigned work on time.

Syllogisms consist of two premises and a conclusion. The premises and conclusion may begin with a *universal quantifier* (*all*) or a *particular quantifier* (*some*). In addition, the terms within a syllogism may be stated positively ("All A are B") or negatively ("All A are not B"). Syllogisms are either valid or invalid—that is, the conclusion either does or does not hold, given the premises.

There is an important difference between the validity of an argument and the truth value of an argument. When we speak of an argument being *valid,* we're just saying that the conclusion does follow from the premises. However (and this is important), it says nothing about whether the premises themselves are true. The truth value of an argument depends on *both* validity of the argument form *and* the truth of the premises. Consider this argument:

> All professors are comedians.
> All comedians are funny.
> Therefore, all professors are funny.

This argument is valid in form; the conclusion does follow from the premises. However, the truth (or soundness) of the argument also depends on the truth of the premises. You could take issue with either premise; if either premise is false, then the argument is not true (i.e., it is not sound).

Confused? You're not alone. People are quite often bedeviled by these sorts of reasoning problems, and consequently they make predictable errors. Try your hand at this one (from Sternberg & Ben-Zeev, 2001):

> 1. All A are B.
>   All C are B.
>   Therefore, all A are C.

Is this conclusion valid, based on the premises? No, it isn't, although many judge that it is (Wilkins, 1928). What underlies these reasoning errors? One account that applies to the present example is that the premises of syllogisms, in combination, create a sort of "atmosphere" or context that extends to the conclusion. In both examples, the premises begin with the same qualifier, which tends to invite the validation of a conclusion that also begins with that qualifier. This is termed an **atmosphere effect.**

Conditional Reasoning: Minding Your P's and Q's.   The second form of deductive reasoning is called **conditional reasoning** (or **if-then reasoning**) and involves evaluating whether a particular conclusion is valid given that certain conditions (premises) hold. For example, consider the following premises (1) and (2) and the conclusion (3):

1. If someone likes Winnie the Pooh, then they're a sensitive person.

2. Mary likes Winnie the Pooh.

3. Therefore, Mary is a sensitive person.

The *conditional statement* (1) provides the rule that is expressed in an *if-then* format: if P (some sort of antecedent condition), then Q (some sort of consequent condition).

So is this a valid conclusion, based on the premises? Yes, given that sensitive people like Winnie the Pooh and given that Mary likes Winnie the Pooh, one can validly conclude that Mary is a sensitive person. Notice that the evaluation of a conclusion is in terms of validity, not truth. (See our earlier example about professors being funny!) It may not be true that people who like Winnie the Pooh are sensitive, but this is irrelevant to determining the validity of the conclusion. In conditional-reasoning tasks, like syllogistic-reasoning tasks, the goal is to determine only whether the conclusion can be derived logically from the premises.

Let's try another version of the reasoning problem. Once again, let's assess whether conclusion (3) is valid—that is, does it flow logically from premises (1) and (2)?

1. If someone likes Winnie the Pooh, then they're a sensitive person.

2. Mary is a sensitive person.

3. Therefore, Mary likes Winnie the Pooh.

It seems, on the face of it, that the conclusion (3) is valid: Winnie the Pooh and sensitivity go together. But in reality, the conclusion is invalid. It could be that Mary is a sensitive person who couldn't care less about Winnie the Pooh. There are many reasons besides liking Winnie the Pooh that can indicate a person's sensitivity. People fall prey fairly easily to validating these sorts of erroneous conclusions.

In actuality, conditional-reasoning conclusions can be evaluated quite easily if one applies a set of logical rules. Consider again the argument form of conditional-reasoning problems. Line 1 gives the if (antecedent)–then (consequent) contingency—that is, "If someone likes Winnie the Pooh, then they are a sensitive person." Line 2 either affirms or denies either the antecedent ("Mary does or does not like Winnie the Pooh") or the consequent ("Mary is or is not a sensitive person"). This creates four different argument forms, which are outlined in Table 11.2.

Two of the forms have already been discussed. The first example is termed *affirming the antecedent* (antecedent: if a person likes Winnie the Pooh is affirmed: Mary likes Winnie the Pooh). When the antecedent is affirmed, the conclusion (Mary is a sensitive person) is valid. In logic lingo, this argument form is termed *modus ponens*. It is valid to

---

Table 11.2 **Conditional-Reasoning Forms**

Condition statement

If a person likes Winnie the Pooh, then they're a sensitive person.

(Antecedent)   *(Consequent)*

Four conditional-reasoning scenarios

	Affirm	Deny
Antecedent	Mary likes Winnie the Pooh. Therefore, Mary is a sensitive person.	Mary does not like Winnie the Pooh. Therefore, Mary is not a sensitive person.
Consequent	Mary is a sensitive person. Therefore, Mary likes Winnie the Pooh.	Mary is not a sensitive person. Therefore, Mary does not like Winnie the Pooh.

conclude that Mary is a sensitive person, because the conditional statement gives us that rule: if a person likes Winnie the Pooh, then they're a sensitive person. It is stated that Mary likes Winnie the Pooh; therefore, she must be a sensitive person. The second example we discussed was (can you guess?) *affirming the consequent* (consequent: then they're a sensitive person is affirmed: Mary is a sensitive person). When the consequent is affirmed the conclusion (Mary likes Winnie the Pooh) is invalid. It does not necessarily follow that Mary likes Winnie the Pooh given that she is a sensitive person. The conditional statement does not say anything about what sensitive people will like or will not like. It tells only what it means if a person likes Winnie the Pooh.

The other two argument forms involve denying each part of the conditional statement. One is *denying the antecedent* (antecedent: if a person likes Winnie the Pooh is denied: Mary does not like Winnie the Pooh). When the antecedent is denied the conclusion (Mary is not a sensitive person) is invalid. If she does not like Winnie the Pooh, this does not necessarily mean that she is not a sensitive person. There are many other correlates of sensitivity; liking Winnie the Pooh is just one of them. The final one is *denying the consequent* (consequent: then they're a sensitive person is denied: Mary is not sensitive). When the consequent is denied the conclusion (Mary does not like Winnie the Pooh) is valid. Logicians call this modus tollens. If Mary is not sensitive, it is valid to conclude that she does not like Winnie the Pooh. According to the conditional statement, liking Winnie the Pooh means the person is sensitive. Given that we know that Mary is not sensitive, she must not like Winnie the Pooh.

Deductive Reasoning Biases and Errors.   As you might imagine, people run into a fair amount of difficulty when judging the validity of conclusions derived from if-then statements. No one walks around with a card in their pocket describing the valid and invalid argument forms. So what types of errors are common in these sorts of reasoning tasks? One tendency people have is to interpret the initial conditional statement as *biconditional*—thinking that "If p, then q" also means "If q, then p" (Wyer & Srull, 1989). In the previous problem, people would tend to think that "If someone likes Winnie the Pooh, then they're a sensitive person" also means "If someone is a sensitive person, then they like Winnie the Pooh." But conditional statements don't work that way. By assuming that the if-then statement is biconditional, we are essentially assuming that p can be an antecedent or a consequent. If we affirm p, this leads to a valid conclusion only if p is an antecedent. If we make the biconditional assumption and assume that p can also be the consequent, then affirming p leads to an invalid conclusion (see Table 11.3).

Table 11.3 **Affirming the antecedent leads to a valid conclusion. However, affirming the consequent leads to an invalid conclusion.**

Conditional statement	Biconditional assumption
If a person likes Winnie the Pooh (antecedent), then they're a sensitive person (consequent).	If a someone is a sensitive person (antecedent), then *they like Winnie the Pooh* (consequent).
Affirm: Mary likes Winnie the Pooh.	*Affirm:* Mary likes Winnie the Pooh.
Conclusion is valid, affirming the antecedent.	Conclusion is invalid, affirming the consequent.

Stop&*Think* | I LOVE LOGIC

Read the following reasoning problems and determine which conclusions are valid. Answers are below.

1. Some politicians are dishonest people. All dishonest people are untrustworthy. Therefore, some politicians are untrustworthy.
2. All college students are curious. All curious people read books. Therefore, all college students read books.
3. If I do really well on my GREs, then I'll get into graduate school. I got into graduate school. Therefore, I did well on my GREs.
4. If the tickets for the rock concert are under $50, then I will go to the concert. I did not go to the concert. Therefore, the tickets for the concert were not under $50.

- Which types of reasoning are represented by these problems?
- How did the problems differ in terms of difficulty? What factors led to differences in difficulty?

1. valid
2. valid
3. invalid (affirming the consequent)
4. valid (denying the consequent)

One of the most investigated conditional-reasoning tasks is the Wason Selection Task (WST). The classic version of this task is depicted in Figure 11.1. The reasoner must determine which of the four cards needs to be turned over in order to determine whether the following if-then statement holds: if a card has a vowel on one side, then it must have an even number on the opposite side. Can you figure out which cards should be turned over? If you had a logic guide (as we mentioned earlier), you would realize that to test this conditional rule, you need to apply modus ponens and modus tollens. In other words, you would need to turn over the E card (affirming the antecedent "if vowel"), and the 7 card (denying the consequent "then even number"). However, people rarely choose this combination of cards; in fact, they choose these particular cards less than 10% of the time (Sternberg, 2001). The most common choices are to turn over the E and the 6 cards (nearly half choose 6, which amounts to the error of affirming the consequent) or only the E card. (About 33% choose this option.)

Why does this task pose such difficulty? One reason is the biconditional thinking discussed above: "If p, then q" is often misinterpreted to imply "If q, then p." As a result, the WST if-then statement is inappropriately interpreted as also meaning "If a card has an even number on one side, it must have a vowel on the other." Based on this invalid assumption, it seems that the 6 card must be turned over (applying the valid rule of affirming the antecedent).

If a card has a vowel on one side, then it must have an even number on the other side.

Figure 11.1

Wason Selection Task

From Wason, P. C., & Johnson-Laird, P. N. (1970). A conflict between selection and evaluating information in an inferential task. *British Journal of Psychology, 68,* 325–331. Copyright 1970, the British Journal of Psychology. Reprinted with kind permission of the British Psychological Society.

But the if-then statement is not biconditional. Turning over the 6 card demonstrates the error of affirming the consequent.

The selection tendencies revealed on the WST have been cited as evidence for a confirmatory bias in reasoning. **Confirmatory bias** refers to our tendency to seek out or notice evidence that is consistent with a particular hypothesis rather than evidence that would be inconsistent with the hypothesis. Once again, consider the selection task "If vowel, then even number." What would support, or help confirm, the validity of this rule? Answer: a vowel with an even number on the other side. What cards are most commonly turned over? Answer: even numbers and vowels. If you'd thought in terms of disconfirmation—what should not be the case, given the rule—you'd have realized that odd numbers are never with vowels. Thinking along these lines would more likely lead one to (correctly) turn over the *E* and 7 cards.

Confirmation bias represents a pervasive tendency in reasoning. Nickerson (1998) describes confirmation bias as an "inappropriate bolstering of hypotheses or beliefs whose truth is in question" (p. 175). MacPherson and Stanovich (2007) note this inappropriate bolstering can be driven either by one's own prior opinions or by one's world knowledge. In other words, a person often has trouble separating their opinions and their own knowledge (i.e., top-down processing) from the information processing they must engage in when they reason their way to some view or conclusion.

Myside Bias.   **Myside bias** is a type of confirmation bias that refers to a tendency to be overly swayed by a prior opinion on a topic, failing to give enough weight to evidence or arguments to the contrary. For example, in watching a political debate, both sides frequently claim that their candidate "won" the debate, because during the debate, they were busy gathering evidence for "their side," ignoring points made by the opponent. MacPherson and Stanovich (2007) were interested in how instructions might affect individuals' tendencies to exhibit this bias. If people were explicitly told to put aside their opinion and consider evidence on both sides of an issue, might this affect their reasoning? In their study, they presented participants with two different topic statements about which students were likely to have strong opinions. One statement was about tuition costs, and claimed that students should be funding their own education to a greater extent rather than having funding come from taxes. The other statement argued that (music) file sharing among individuals via the internet should be OK.

To examine myside bias, the researchers had the participants generate arguments relevant to each statement, in response to instructions of two different types. In the decontextualizing condition, participants were told to generate arguments both for and against the views expressed, and were urged to set aside their personal opinions on the topic. A control group was told simply to generate opinions about the topic. The degree of myside bias was assessed by calculating the difference between the number of otherside and myside arguments. (In an initial phase of the study, the researchers had ascertained the participants' true opinion on each of the topics by embedding a couple of questions in an ostensibly unrelated questionnaire; this allowed them to classify each argument as a myside or otherside argument). The results present a bad news/good news scenario. The bad news is that there was clear evidence of a myside bias. Participants generated significantly more arguments in favor of their own position than in favor of the opposing side. The good news is that this tendency was significantly moderated by instructions. When participants were sensitized by the instructions to set their opinions aside and consider both sides of an argument, they were able to do so.

Belief Bias.   Another form of confirmation bias is the **belief bias,** which occurs when what people know to be true interferes with their ability to assess argument validity. Rather than evaluating the validity of the argument form, people can be swayed by the believability of the premises. Consider the following example from Macpherson & Stanovich (2007):

> All flowers have petals.
> Roses have petals.
> Therefore, all roses are flowers.

Previous knowledge quickly and easily leads you to accept the premises, and invites you to accept the conclusion. However, the task is to determine whether the conclusion follows logically from the premise. The truth or falsity of the statement all *roses are flowers* is irrelevant. Indeed, in this example, all *roses are flowers* is invalid. Consider the converse case:

> All students are kangaroos.
> All kangaroos are musically inclined.
> Therefore, all students are musically inclined.

Here, based on world knowledge, the premises seem preposterous, and the conclusion sounds implausible at best. And yet, this is a valid syllogism. Macpherson and Stanovich (2007) also investigated the effects of instructions on the belief bias effect, and found that sensitizing participants to the difference between validity and believability decreased the bias to a small extent. So although sensitization can improve reasoning performance, biases remain.

Biases most likely remain because the processes of reasoning aren't under complete conscious control. Here, we re-visit the distinction between the two modes of thinking discussed earlier, heuristic and analytic. The myside and belief biases are circumstances in which the two modes of operation are both influencing performance, and are essentially in conflict (Evans, 2003; 2008). The quick, heuristic, intuitive mode of reasoning is influenced by the believability of the conclusion—does it seem reasonable or not, based on my opinion, or based on what I know? Meanwhile, the slower analytic mode is trudging along, attempting to evaluate the validity of the conclusion given the premises. But because this mode takes more immediate memory capacity than the heuristic mode, it is often abandoned. In line with this analysis, immediate memory capacity is negatively correlated with susceptibility to the belief-bias effect (Stanovich & West, 1997) and with deductive reasoning in general (Copeland & Radvansky, 2004). Evidence seems to indicate fairly strongly that conscious and analytic (i.e., System 2) processing is critical to valid reasoning.

Stop&*Think Back* | CONFIRMATORY ATTENTION

Confirmatory bias isn't just a reasoning phenomenon; it has its basis in perception and attention (Chapters 2 and 3). Think of some ways in which this might be true. What are some beliefs and expectations you have about the people, places, and events you experience every day, and how might perception and attention be altered or tuned as a result? How does top-down processing relate to confirmatory bias? Are there other perceptual and/or attentional phenomena that you can think of that might lead to confirmation bias?

Rules or Models?   Explanations for how we reason deductively generally fall into one of two camps. One view might be termed a "strict" or rule-based account (Rips, 1994). This view contends that people possess the representational equivalent of logic rules (a mental version of the ones discussed earlier). These rules are then applied to the premises to determine if the conclusion is valid. A contrasting view is the mental models view of Johnson-Laird and colleagues (e.g., Bauer & Johnson-Laird, 1993; Johnson-Laird & Byrne, 2002). According to this approach, we first form a mental model based on the information in the premises and our own previous experience (i.e., top-down processing). Next, we search for a mental model in which the premises would be true but the stated conclusion would be false. If we find such a model, we deem the conclusion invalid; if we don't find such a model, we deem the conclusion valid. Currently, the jury is still out regarding whether a rule-based account or a mental models account provides a better explanation for deductive reasoning. It may well be that people rely on both sorts of processes (e.g., Oberauer, 2006; Smith, Langston, & Nisbett, 1992).

Inductive Reasoning

The flip side of the reasoning coin is **inductive reasoning.** Rather than working from general premises to arrive at a specific conclusion, we take the opposite tack, moving from specific pieces of data or information, and working toward a general conclusion. Think about theory development in psychology. Based on the results of specific empirical investigations, researchers will develop a general theory that explains each specific finding. Unlike deductive reasoning, in which conclusions can be labeled *valid* or *invalid* with absolute certainty, inductive reasoning leads to uncertain conclusions that vary in their strength.

For an everyday example of inductive reasoning, consider the following:

Professor X gets upset when asked if she'll issue a paper extension.
Professor Y won't accept late papers.
Professor Z takes 20% off each day a paper is late.

You might (correctly) induce from these specific pieces of data that professors find late papers unacceptable. Note the differences between this type of inductive reasoning and deductive reasoning. If this were a deductive-reasoning situation, you would be given the general principle—"Professors find late papers unacceptable"—and would need to determine if the specific statements about Professors X, Y, and Z follow from that general principle. In the above inductive-reasoning example, you are inferring the general principle ("Professors find late papers unacceptable") based on specific pieces of information about Professors X, Y, and Z. Deductive reasoning moves from general to specific, while inductive reasoning moves from specific to general.

Bisanz, Bisanz, and Korpan (1994) describe some characteristics that seem to typify inductive reasoning. First, the product of inductive reasoning (the general principle) is not necessarily correct. Suppose you assume that professors won't accept late papers or extend paper deadlines, you may miss an opportunity to get an extension. This characteristic of inductive reasoning provides a sharp contrast to deductive reasoning, in which the validity of a conclusion is inherent in the premises. Inductive arguments are evaluated in terms of their strength rather than in terms of their validity; in other words, how solid the conclusion is based on the evidence. Second, as Rips (1990) points out, with inductive reasoning, there is a need for constraint on the conclusions reached. If there were no constraints, you could come up with some pretty wild conclusions based on the evidence. For example, given the pieces of evidence from Professors X, Y, and Z, you could induce that people whose last names are letters of the alphabet don't like late papers. As you can see, constraint is needed in order to avoid unreasonable conclusions.

Confirmatory Bias Revisited.

Earlier we discussed Wason's Selection Task, which reveals people's tendency to seek out information consistent with a given hypothesis in deductive reasoning. The same effect can be found for inductive reasoning. A classic study investigated the confirmation bias within the context of social cognition—the information processing we perform about other people. Snyder and Swann (1978) had participants simulate the role of an interviewer whose task it was to discover whether an interviewee was extroverted (outgoing) or introverted (shy). The participants were given a suggested set of questions to ask the interviewee and were instructed to use the questions they thought would be the most diagnostic—in other words, the ones that would definitively determine whether the person was extroverted or not. Note how this situation involved inductive reasoning; the interviewers were to use specific information derived from the answers to the questions to arrive at a general conclusion (i.e., that the person was or was not extroverted).

Rather than seeking out information that might have been incongruent with what they were thinking, the interviewers tended to ask questions that were congruent with their hypothesis. If they expected an extrovert, then they asked questions that would reveal extroversion (e.g., "What are some reasons you like parties?"). Any answer would serve only to bolster the interviewer's already-held idea. Interviewers tended not to ask questions that would be inconsistent with extroversion and reveal contrary evidence. Nickerson (1998) provides a wide-ranging review of confirmatory bias and its role in real-world reasoning.

Inductive Reasoning in Categorization.   Inductive reasoning is pervasive; it underlies some of the processes we've discussed in other chapters. For example, the processes of categorization and concept formation are, by their very nature, inductive. As you learned in Chapter 5, forming a concept or category involves making a connection between specific instances that seem similar in some manner; in other words, concept formation and categorization involve deriving a general principle (i.e., a category) from specific examples (i.e., the members of the category). Inductive reasoning provides another window through which to view the phenomenon known as the *typicality effect* (which you read about in Chapter 5)—the finding that some members of a category are more readily identified as such. Rips (1974) extended these findings beyond simple judgments of category membership to inferences induced from knowledge about category members. Consider the following inductive arguments:

1. Robins are susceptible to disease A.
   Therefore, all birds are susceptible to disease A.

2. Turkeys are susceptible to disease B.
   Therefore, all birds are susceptible to disease B.

Participants rated argument 1 as more likely to be true, because robins are seen as more typical birds than turkeys. The typicality effect seems to carry over to reasoning about unknown properties; inferences from typical category members are "safer bets."

Another interesting phenomenon observed in inductive reasoning about categories might be termed a *diversity effect* (Rips, 1974). Which of the following inductive arguments seems stronger?

1. Robins are susceptible to disease Y.
   Sparrows are susceptible to disease Y.
   Therefore, all birds are susceptible to disease Y.

2. Cardinals are susceptible to disease Z.
   Turkeys are susceptible to disease Z.
   Therefore, all birds are susceptible to disease Z.

In this case, people tend to rate the second argument as stronger because cardinals and turkeys represent a more diverse set of birds relative to robins and sparrows. Because of this diversity, the conclusion seems more warranted and more likely to be true.

Spacing and Induction.   As mentioned earlier, determining category membership involves inductive reasoning. In addition knowledge about category membership (e.g., that animal is a dog) is an example of semantic memory. In Chapter 6, we discussed why spacing (i.e., distributing) repetitions of material you want to remember results in better episodic memory for the event. But what about semantic memory? Is it also improved by spacing repetitions of material? Suppose little Jimmy (4 years old) is trying to figure out what a *dog* is. Will it be better if Jimmy and his dad run into 12 dogs in a row at the park, with dad labeling each one as "dog"? Or would it be better if during a once monthly walk in a park, little Jimmy sees one dog each time, with it being labeled as "dog" by his dad? Intuitively, it seems that in this case (i.e., learning what a dog *is*) it would be better to have the massed repetitions, rather than the spaced ones. It seems that spacing out the repetitions would prevent Jimmy from honing in on what makes a dog a dog, and then connecting those characteristics to the next dog he sees.

Kornell and Bjork (2008) note that the intuition behind the analysis is so sensible that it's never been put to the psychological test. Therefore, they decided to investigate this issue, asking (from their article title), "is spacing the enemy of induction?" Data addressing this question are surprisingly sparse, perhaps given the power of the intuition. To find out whether massed repetition enhances induction (and what pattern of massing would maximize induction), Kornell and Bjork presented photographs of 72 paintings, 6 by each of 12 artists. For each participant the work of six artists was presented in blocked fashion; all six artworks were presented in a row. The works for the other six artists were spaced by varying intervals. After encoding, participants were presented with 48 test trials in which never-before-seen work from each of the artists was presented, and participants were to respond with one of the 12 artist names. The results surprised the researchers; counter-intuitively, *spaced* repetition of an artists' work was more likely to lead to successful induction, as indicated by participant's accuracy in identifying the proper artist for the new works. And it wasn't really even that close; spaced repetition led to performance of over 60%, while performance in massed repetition was just over 40%.

The results also revealed a striking failure of metacognition. In addition to asking the participants to identify the artists for the test paintings, the researchers also asked them which condition they thought led to more effective learning. The results are plotted in Figure 11.2. Each participant is classified in terms of repetition outcome: (1) massed > spaced, (2) spaced > massed, or (3) massed = spaced. The figure plots the number of participants who obtained each these outcomes as a function of their subjective intuition about which outcome was most likely. As you can see from height of each of the individual bars, most people (an overwhelming majority, in fact) felt that massed repetition had served them best. But now look at the divisions *within* each bar, which shows the number who achieved each outcome. As you can see, regardless of what they may have thought or felt, most participants were helped by spaced repetitions more than massed repetitions.

The authors note that their counterintuitive result has important implications for both education and metacognition. Clearly, spaced repetitions are effective in situations that go well beyond episodic list learning, in spite of intuitions to the contrary. In addition, the results underscore the need for accurate metacognition. The intuitive sense that massed repetition would aid in the acquisition of general concepts would certainly bias educators and students in their approaches to teaching and learning, so both should take heed.

Research Theme
Metacognition

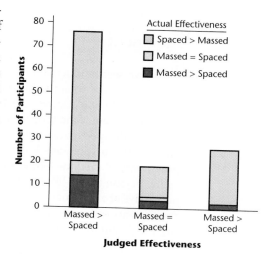

Figure 11.2

Perceived vs. actual effectiveness of spacing in learning; data from Kornell & Bjork (2008).

Stop&*Review*

1. Distinguish between syllogistic reasoning and conditional reasoning.
2. Describe two biases that occur in reasoning.
3. True or false? Spacing repeated presentations improves induction:

- Deductive reasoning involves determining whether a conclusion is valid based on premises. Syllogistic reasoning involves deciding whether two premises necessitate a conclusion. The atmosphere effect occurs when quantifiers combine to form an atmosphere, resulting in inaccurate assessments of argument validity. Conditional reasoning involves evaluating whether a particular conclusion is valid given that certain conditions hold.

- People often wrongly assume that conditional statements are actually biconditional (*If p then q* also means *If q then p*). Confirmatory bias refers to our tendency to seek evidence that affirms our hypotheses. One type, myside bias, refers to our tendency to be swayed by our personal opinion on a topic. Another confirmation bias is belief bias, when our world knowledge interferes with judgments of validity. These biases represent a conflict between System 1 and System 2 thinking.

- The rule-based account of reasoning contends that people possess the mental representational equivalent of logic rules. The mental models view contends that we base reasoning on models we build based on premises and our own previous experience. Inductive reasoning involves using specific information to arrive at a general conclusion, and is important to categorization. Contrary to intuition, evidence indicates that induction of new categories is more likely to occur under conditions of spaced learning, rather than massed.

Judgment

As you've seen, inductive reasoning involves arriving at general conclusions based on specific pieces of what might be called "data." Judgment is an extension of inductive reasoning. Hastie and Dawes (2001) define judgment as "the human ability to infer, estimate, and predict the character of unknown events" (p. 48). Judgment is a process of making educated guesses, based on (sometimes quite severely) limited information along with our previous knowledge, expectations, and beliefs. We make these sorts of judgments all the time. For example, when a friend tells you that there's this really interesting person they'd like to fix you up with, you're very likely to gather some initial data and arrive at a judgment. Your impression will differ depending on whether the person's major is art or business. Right or wrong, this information is likely to lead you to strikingly different inferences (i.e., judgments) about this individual.

Much of the research on judgment has been conducted by social psychologists. Indeed, much of the work in social cognition (the study of how we process information about other people) is concerned with the factors that underlie our judgments of others (such as our hypothetical art or business major). Stereotypes—the set of beliefs that we hold about members of certain groups—are largely based on the processes of judgment.

Even though judgments can be overly broad or outright wrong, it seems necessary for us to make them. In almost every situation requiring a judgment, we usually don't have all of the information we need to arrive at an accurate conclusion. Even if we did, we do not possess the computational power required to successfully combine the information. So we make educated guesses using the heuristic mode discussed earlier in this chapter. As you read the following sections, keep in mind the contrasting views of heuristics posed earlier in the chapter. The dominant view has been to perceive heuristics as examples of suboptimal thinking tools that are employed by the overloaded thinker, leading to errors and biases in judgment. The alternative, proposed by Gigerenzer and colleagues, is that heuristics are "fast and frugal" approaches to thinking that have evolved as an effective tool to deal with everyday situations that require cognitive processing.

The Availability Heuristic

Scan the names in Table 11.4 and then come back to the reading. There were a total of 21 names. Try to estimate the number of first names that began with *J*, began with *C*, and began with *B*. Do you have your estimates? You may have guessed that there were more names that began with *J* than with the other letters. If so, you fell victim to what is termed the *availability heuristic*. The **availability heuristic** indicates that we base our estimates of likelihood, or probability, on the ease with which we can think of examples. In this case, the names that begin with *J* are relatively well known, while those names that begin with *C* or *B* are not. Therefore, *J* names seem more numerous because it is easier to remember famous rather than nonfamous names.

Consider why you would need such a heuristic in this situation. Given the characteristics of human attention and memory, it's simply not possible to memorize 21 names with a brief glimpse. Therefore, you rely on a fairly sensible strategy: when asked about the names, you try to think of as many names as you can and see with what letter those names begin. In other words, you turn to the information that is available in memory. The problem, as you saw in detail in Chapter 8, is that memory is not always the most reliable database. When the availability heuristic is applied, systematic biases in memory can lead to systematic biases in judgment. Just because something seems like a common occurrence doesn't mean that it is. So availability in memory is not always the best basis for judgment; it is affected by a host of factors that can distort our judgment.

Table 11.4 **Availability and Frequency Estimation**

Jimmy Stewart	Jack Bauer	J. K. Rowling
Bob Smitson	Joe Mauer	Chris Baines
Joe Biden	Beth Feynman	Jackie Robinson
Charlie Horton	Bobbi Castel	Cory Lidle
Cecil Patterson	Barbara Edison	Claude Shelet
Bill Arnold	Jennifer Aniston	Bruce Thomas
Charley Tifton	Joan Crawford	Bess Severson

Table 11.5 **Availability and Judgment**

A. Tornadoes	A. Motor vehicle accidents
B. Extreme cold	B. Stroke
A. Homicide	A. Food poisoning
B. Stomach cancer	B. Smallpox vaccination
A. All cancers	A. Floods
B. Heart disease	B. Asthma

From Lichtenstein, S. (1978). Judged frequency of lethal events. *Journal of Experimental Psychology: Human Learning and Memory, 4,* 551–578. Copyright 1978 by the American Psychological Association. Reprinted by permission.

Biased Encoding. Something may be easier to get out of memory because it is overrepresented in memory. Why might this occur? Consider the exercise you just did. Because the names that start with *J* are more familiar than the other names, you were much more likely to have encoded them successfully. So your memory retrieval is biased because the information you've stored is biased.

Another study, conducted by Lichtenstein, Slovic, Fischhoff, Layman, and Comb (1978) on the cheery subject of causes of death, provides another example. Before we talk about the study, try it yourself. Look at the causes-of-death pairs listed in Table 11.5. For each pair, decide which of the two results in more deaths. If you're like the participants in this study, you overestimated the frequency of some causes of death and underestimated others. For example, at the time this study was conducted, there were more deaths from stomach cancer than from homicide, more from asthma than from flood, more from stroke than from motor vehicle accidents, and more from extreme cold than from tornadoes. But the participants in the study tended to make the opposite estimates, overestimating the number of deaths caused by homicides, floods, auto accidents, and tornadoes and underestimating the number of deaths caused by stomach cancer, asthma, stroke, and extreme cold. When faced with this estimation task, the only possible way to do it is to sample memory for examples. In this case, however, you're likely to come up with a biased sample, because the first member of each cause-of-death pair (e.g., floods) is "front-page news." The very nature of such events is dramatic, and therefore deaths from such causes are more likely to be reported on the evening news and in magazines and newspapers. The second member of each pair (e.g., asthma) is undramatic. (When was the last time your newspaper reported someone dying of asthma?) The bias in reporting of these types of death leads to a biased knowledge base.

Your authors' personal experience in teaching in different geographic locales provide an example of the effects of a biased knowledge base. (Keep in mind that this example is anecdotal and subject to our own processes of memory distortion!) We began our teaching careers in Indiana, where tornadoes are probably the most serious weather hazard; in other words, they're front-page news. Hoosiers hear a great deal about tornadoes and encode lots of information about the damage they wreak. We now teach in Minnesota, where the extreme cold is front-page news. Minnesotans are exposed to conditions of extreme cold for several months every year and thus are likely to encode information about this hazard. In line with the experiential differences between our two populations of students, when we've asked students to compare tornadoes and extreme cold as causes of death, Indiana students were clearly biased toward saying "tornadoes." But since our move to Minnesota, we've heard more people claim "extreme cold" as the more common cause of death. Once again, the information that is encoded in memory exerts an influence on our judgments; differences or biases in encoding lead to differences or biases in judgment.

Which causes more deaths?

The media no doubt serve as one source of encoding-based availability biases. Vivid news reports of certain types of events lead us to overestimate those events' frequency and likelihood. For example, as Hastie and Dawes (2001) point out, when a former psychiatric patient commits a crime, the fact that they were formerly in treatment is often mentioned in the news report. But how often do we hear the negative case— "Harold Smith, who has never received psychiatric treatment, was arrested for murder today"? Therefore, being a former psychiatric patient and committing a crime are vividly connected. These biases in reporting can lead to biases in people's knowledge database. Many researchers would contend that the media's vivid reporting is at the root of many public anxieties, such as the safety of drinking water, the likelihood of school shootings, and the chances of a plane crash. This is not to say

Does vivid media coverage lead people to worry too much about certain events?

that these issues are of no concern, but that there is little doubt that vivid and intense reports may increase their prominence in memory in disproportion to their actual danger.

Biased Retrieval.   The availability heuristic leads us astray when our memory contains a biased sample of information. Availability can also lead us astray if the sampling process itself is biased. Try the following demonstration, based on Tversky and Kahneman (1973), and estimate whether there are more of number 1 or number 2:

1. six-letter words that have the letter *n* as the fifth letter

2. words that fit the pattern __ __ __ *ing*

Participants in Tversky and Kahneman's study estimated that words of type 2 were much more likely than words of type 1. Can you see why this is a rather silly answer and why the answer must be type 1? The set of words defined by type 1 includes every single word that fits type 2—that is, words that fit type 2 are six letters long with the fifth letter being *n!* Therefore, there have to be more words that fit category 1. But making this judgment requires a person to sample memory, and people generate a biased sample because it's easier to think of words that end in -*ing* than it is to think of words that have *n* as the fifth letter. Note that the problem here is not one of encoding; the information stored in memory really does have more words with *n* as the fifth letter than words that fit the pattern __ __ __ *ing*. The problem here is one of retrieval; being asked to think of examples of words that end in -*ing* serves as a more precise, hence easier-to-use, retrieval cue.

Another instance of a retrieval-based bias in the use of the availability heuristic related to recency. One of the most tried-and-true principles of memory research (going all the way back to Ebbinghaus's ubiquitous forgetting curve, discussed in Chapter 1) is that more recent events are easier to retrieve than more remote events. Therefore, the availability heuristic can lead us to overestimate the frequency of events because of their recency. Consider again the news reports of tragedies such as the hijackings on September 11, 2001. In addition to being selectively encoded into memory (as described earlier), these events also affect our judgment more when they've occurred recently and their aftermath is fresh in our minds. Therefore, people probably felt that the likelihood of being a victim of a terrorist attack was greater immediately after the World Trade Center disaster than it was prior to the attacks. In reality, the probability may be less, because of the heightened security that resulted from that disaster.

Another availability-related result of the September 11 terrorist attacks was a drastically reduced willingness to fly, due to what some term **dread risk** (Slovic, 1987). Dread risk refers to our tendency to avoid situations in which many people may be killed at the same time while simultaneously being relatively impervious to risky situations in which the same number of deaths are spread out over a longer period of time. But avoiding dread risk results in a cruel irony, as noted by Myers (2001); the fear of getting on to a plane that swept the country after the 9/11 attacks no doubt caused people to drive rather than fly. (Greg actually decided to drive rather than fly to see his family in Cincinnati in October 2001.) This led to an elevated number of traffic fatalities. This speculation was confirmed by a later analysis of traffic accident data by Gigerenzer (2004). In the three months of 2001 after the 9/11 attacks, the number of fatal traffic accidents was greatly elevated, relative to baseline rates from other years during the same period. So, indeed, the September 11 attacks may have led to a second toll of lives due to the impact of raw emotions on people's judgments and subsequent decisions.

Stop&*Think* | ASSESSING AVAILABILITY

Consider the following question: Do you think there are more words in the English language that start with the letter *k* or that have *k* as the third letter? Now answer these questions:

- How did you arrive at your answer?
- Which of the judgment heuristics came into play?

Find two friends to be "research subjects." Vary the conditions under which you give them this problem. For one friend, have them answer quickly. Tell the other to take as much time as needed to think about it. These two different conditions correspond to the dual modes of reasoning discussed earlier. What would you expect under these two conditions?

Illusory Correlations.   Everyone has heard claims or stories like the following:

> I know a couple who had just given up trying to get pregnant, started to look into adoption, and then bam! They got pregnant!

Because of the vividness of some examples like the above, people see relationships where none likely exist. To know if starting adoption proceedings really is associated with an increase in the chances of getting pregnant, one needs to know four different pieces of information: (1) how frequently people who can't conceive start adoption and get pregnant, (2) how frequently people who can't conceive start adoption and do not get pregnant, (3) how frequently people who can conceive start adoption and get pregnant, and (4) how frequently people who can conceive start adoption and do not get pregnant (see Table 11.6). All four pieces of data allow for an assessment of whether the circumstance (i.e., getting pregnant after starting adoption proceedings) occurs an inordinate number of times. Of course, people can't readily bring to mind all four pieces of information; they tend to rely on only the first piece, which essentially boils down to noticing coincidences. When one notices primarily (or only) coincidences, two events will seem to be linked even when they're not. This perception is termed **illusory correlation.**

One well-known example of an illusory correlation is the "Madden jinx," which goes something like this: if an athlete appears on the cover of the well-known football video

Table 11.6 **Influence of Coincidental Events**

Our tendency to notice distinctive coincidences causes us to be overly influenced by coincidental evidence.

	Get Pregnant	Don't Get Pregnant
Start adoption proceedings	Distinctive coincidence	Nonevent
Don't start adoption proceedings	Nonevent	Nonevent

game, then they are doomed to suffer some calamity soon after—a season-ending injury, an awful performance slump, or personal problems. Of course, the correlation between appearing on the cover of *Madden* and having some calamity occur is nonexistent; but people notice when such an appearance is followed by some bad event, and they don't notice other combinations of events, such as someone appearing on the cover and continuing to excel. This also is an example of the statistical principle termed *regression to the mean.* Sometimes an athlete performs below their average, sometimes above their average, but most of the time their performance hovers right around their average. (That's why it's called the average!) After performing far above or below their average, performance will tend to *regress toward the average.* Football players appear on the cover of *Madden* only when they perform well above average. So of course, their performance will tend to move back (i.e., regress) toward their mean level of performance.

It's important to note that (as with all of the judgment heuristics) the availability heuristic can be quite useful. If, based on thinking of examples from memory, you conclude that your professor is going to be a trifle annoyed (or worse) when you hand in a late paper, this is most likely an accurate judgment. Use of the availability heuristic tends to get us into trouble only when there are especially memorable examples that seem to carry the weight of a thousand.

The Recognition Heuristic

Reasoning is adaptive; we simply cannot consider all of the data, nor do we have access to it. In fact, sometimes a *lack of data* can be informative! Such is the case with another memory-based judgment tool termed the **recognition heuristic** (e.g., Goldstein & Gigerenzer, 2002). The recognition heuristic is often used when we're faced with two alternatives—one that's recognizable and one that's not. Under these conditions, we tend to infer that the recognizable alternative has the higher value on whatever criterion is of interest. Let's look at a concrete example from a study by Gigerenzer and Hoffrege (1995). In one study, they asked Americans and Germans to pick which city had the higher population: San Diego or San Antonio. Nearly two-thirds of Americans correctly picked San Diego; obviously, fewer Germans would answer correctly, right? Guess again; *all* of the Germans correctly surmised that San Diego was the more populous city. According to the researchers, the Germans used their having heard of San Diego to infer that it must be more noteworthy in terms of the criterion characteristic, in this case, population.

The Representativeness Heuristic

We've all made judgments based on similarity. For example, we see an unusually tall person, say, 6' 8", and we assume that anybody so tall must play basketball. But think about it. Most people, even tall people, don't play basketball. So why do we make such judgments? When trying to place a person in a particular category (e.g., basketball player), we have a tendency to base our judgment on the similarity between the person and the stereotype we hold about that category. If you met Greg, you'd soon realize that he's a long-suffering fan of the Cincinnati Bengals professional football team. Given that, you might brand him a sports fan, and assume that he also likes the Cincinnati Reds (you'd be correct). Judgments like this rely on what is termed the **representativeness heuristic** whereby we assess the degree to which the object represents (is similar to) our basic idea (or stereotype) of that object.

Ignoring Base Rates.

Let's consider a classic demonstration of this heuristic from a study by Kahneman and Tversky (1973, p. 241). Participants were given the following instructions:

> A panel of psychologists have interviewed and administered personality tests to 30 engineers and 70 lawyers, all successful in their fields. Based on this information, thumbnail descriptions for each of these individuals have been written. For each description, please indicate the probability that the person described is an engineer, from 1 to 100.

Participants were then given the following description:

> Jack is a 45-year-old man. He is married and has 4 children. He is generally conservative, careful, and ambitious. He shows no interest in political and social issues and spends most of his time on his many hobbies, which include home carpentry, sailing, and mathematical puzzles.

Probabilities would dictate that an engineer would be pulled from the 100 names about 30% of the time, because 30% is the proportion of engineers in this sample. This type of statistical information is termed *base rate*—the rate of occurrence of a particular category in the population or sample (i.e., how often a certain event tends to occur). Consider this example: The base rate of professional football players in the general population is quite low. The base rate of males in the general population is relatively high. If you select somebody out of the population at random, you're very unlikely to pick a professional football player. However, you're about 50% likely to pick a male. Now consider the engineer-lawyer problem above. Given that there are 30 engineers in the sample, the probability that a randomly drawn name is an engineer is 30/100, or 30%. Indeed, when participants were asked to estimate the probabilities without the personality description that is the guess they made. But the description, which just happened to fit their stereotype of an engineer, overruled this base-rate information, leading participants to overestimate the probability (50%) that Jack was an engineer.

Use of the representativeness heuristic, and the concomitant tendency to ignore base rates may relate to the use of the controversial practice known as racial profiling. Racial profiling involves the assumption that a certain type of criminal (i.e., a drug dealer) fits a certain profile; in many cases, the profile includes race as a prominent component. For example, in racial profiling, the "typical" or "average" drug dealer is often assumed to be young, black, and male. As is the case with the biased use of the representativeness heuristic (just discussed), use of the heuristic in this situation leads to judgment errors. Operating on the basis of this profile, police will be especially prone to detain and question individuals that fit, or represent, this profile. Just as we expect that 10 pregnancies should result in a mixture of boys and girls, so do we tend to expect criminals to fit a particular racial profile. Just as in the engineer-lawyer example, this expectation leads to biases in judgment and in subsequent behavior.

Reality Check

This was empirically demonstrated by a study by Harris (1999) on traffic patterns and traffic stops. In this study, more than 5,000 cars on a state highway were observed over the course of about two days, and the race of the driver was noted (this was possible in 97% of the cases). Also recorded was the number of drivers who were actually violating traffic laws

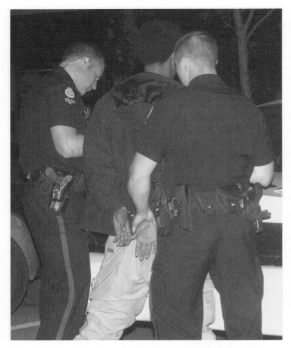

Overreliance on the representativeness heuristic?

at the time they were observed. Table 11.7a presents the number of drivers overall, as well as the number of violators, as a function of racial group. Note that the percentage of violators per racial group is a rough estimate of the base rate of individuals who could potentially be pulled over; as you can see, 74% were white and 18% were African-American. Now look at Table 11.7b, which presents the number of motorists stopped in an 18-month period along the same stretch of highway. Over this time span, 823 motorists were stopped and searched. Just going by the base rate, you would expect that 609 (74%) of these motorists would be white. However, the traffic stops show that 600 (73%) of the motorists were African-American. So although the base rate suggests that whites would be much more likely to violate traffic laws (and hence eligible to be stopped), actual behavior deviated strikingly from this baseline. The representativeness heuristic is strongly implicated as the culprit.

The Conjunction Fallacy. Base rates aren't the only type of information people ignore when they make probability judgments. In their classic investigation of judgment heuristics, Tversky and Kahneman (1983, p. 299) presented the following problem to participants:

> Linda is 31 years old; she's single, outspoken, and very bright. She majored in philosophy. As a student, she was deeply consumed with issues of discrimination and social justice, and participated in anti-nuclear demonstrations.

Based on this information about Linda, participants were asked to decide whether it was more likely that she was (1) a bank teller or (2) a bank teller who was active in the feminist movement. Which do you think? If you said 2, you agreed with the vast majority of

Table 11.7 Profiling as an Instance of the Representativeness Heuristic

Harris's (1999) observational study revealed that although African-Americans comprise a small minority of drivers who are committing traffic violations, they comprise the majority of drivers who are actually pulled over.

	Caucasian	African-American	Other Minorities
(a) Drivers observed	4,314 (76%)	973 (17%)	241 (4%)
Offenders observed	4,000 (74%)	938 (18%)	232 (4%)
	Caucasian	African-American	Other Minorities
(b) Drivers searched (out of 823)	162 (19.7%)	600 (73%)	61 (7.3%)

From Harris, D. A. (1999). *Driving while black: Racial profiling on our nation's highways.* ACLU Report. Washington, DC: ACLU. Reprinted by permission of the author and the American Civil Liberties Union.

Tversky and Kahneman's participants. If you think about it, there's no possible way that 2 could be more likely than 1, because 1 includes 2! If you think about the universe of bank tellers, you can imagine that some subset of them would consider themselves feminist bank tellers; so the chances of Linda being a feminist bank teller have to be smaller than (or at the very least the same as) the probability of her being a bank teller. Figure 11.3 makes this apparent.

Another way to look at it is that being a bank teller and a feminist is the conjunction of two events. The probability of a conjunction between two independent events is the probability of one multiplied by the probability of the other. Because probabilities are always less than 1, conjunctions always have to be less likely than either event considered alone. For example, if the probability of event 1 is 0.5 and the probability of event 2 is 0.5, the probability of the conjunction of event 1 and event 2 is 0.25 (less than the 0.5 probability of either event in isolation). Failure to use this knowledge in the Linda problem is termed the **conjunction fallacy.** The conjunction fallacy is another compelling demonstration of the power of stereotypes. Because Linda fits the stereotype (i.e., is representative) of a liberal individual, we assume that she has to be a feminist, and we use this information as the basis for our judgment.

Not everyone buys the conjunction fallacy and Kahneman and Tversky's interpretation of it. In fact, there are a number of general criticisms of the approach to judgment taken in these studies. One of these has already been discussed—what many see as the "half-empty" view of judgment that is implicit in the approach, which compares judgment to an ideal or rational standard. Another objection to the research program of Kahneman and Tversky relates to their methodology. Many researchers have claimed that the scenarios presented to participants in these judgment tasks were a bit odd in their structure, and there was often more than one *rational construal,* or reasonable way of viewing the problem. Therefore, what appears to be an "irrational" judgment when compared with an ideal or normative standard might be perfectly rational when considered within the context of the participant's construal of the problem. Actually, these complaints have been lodged against each of the research paradigms discussed throughout this chapter, but we'll discuss the objection in the context of the conjunction fallacy, because this is the task that has perhaps been most roundly criticized (Stanovich, 1999). In fact, Margolis (1987) goes as far as to say that "many critics have insisted that in fact it is Kahneman and Tversky, not their participants, who have failed to grasp the logic of the problem" (p. 158).

Follow-up analysis of and research on the conjunction fallacy seems to indicate that the critics have a point. As Stanovich (1999) notes, people may not be likely to apply a probability analysis to the conjunction fallacy. Rather, the question has some subtle linguistic cues and implications that are likely to lead to certain inferences on the part of the participant. The participant's answer may be the result of these linguistic influences rather than a failure to understand probabilities. Hilton (1995) points out that when participants read "Linda is a bank teller" and also read "Linda is a bank teller and active in the feminist movement," they take "Linda is a bank teller" as implying that "Linda is a

Figure 11.3

Is it more likely that Linda is a bank teller or that she is a bank teller and a feminist?

bank teller and not active in the feminist movement." Given that both options include "Linda is a bank teller" and that the second option includes additional information about the feminist movement, it is reasonable to infer that the first option also includes information about the feminist movement (albeit implicitly). If this is the interpretation, then the choice commonly made by participants seems rational rather than irrational. This task-construal analysis of the conjunction "fallacy" (as well as of other judgment tasks) implies that what looks like irrationality and rash judgment is actually adaptive by making the most of our limited capacity, given the demands of the situation.

Misperception of Event Clusters.   When a given event has two different ways of working out, such as a coin flip, people tend to misconstrue what a random sequence should look like. That is, they tend to underestimate the number of streaks, or clusters of like events, that would occur in a truly random sequence. For example, look at the following two coin-flip sequences (where H is heads, and T is tails) and judge which is more likely:

H T H T T H T H H H T H T

H H H H H H T T T T T T

If you think that the first sequence is a more likely outcome, you're incorrect—but not alone (Tversky & Kahneman, 1974). Each sequence has an equally low probability of occurring—namely $(^1/_2)^{12}$. But because the first sequence represents how we picture the outcome of 12 coin flips, it's perceived as more likely. Runs of like events (six heads, then six tails) are perceived as extremely unlikely.

Reality Check

The Hot Hand.   The tendency to misperceive event clusters as indicating nonrandomness may underlie what sports fans term a "hot hand." This pet phrase of sports announcers refers to situations in which it seems a player can do no wrong; for example, in basketball, a player has made six straight shots. While in the midst of these streaks, players are often said to be "in the zone" or "white hot." A study by Gilovich, Vallone, and Tversky (1983) suggests that the player's shots are nothing more than a random sequence dictated by the player's overall shooting percentage. These researchers were interested in whether there was any truth to the claim that players get "hot," and they investigated this by looking at the official shooting statistics of the 1983 Philadelphia 76ers (the only team to keep shot-by-shot records). If a hot-hand phenomenon exists, then the probability of making any particular shot should be higher, given that some number of immediately previous shots have been made. In other words, the probability of making any given shot should be higher if the player is hot, and this "heat" should carry over to subsequent shots.

The study indicated that there was no relationship between making a basket and having made any number of previous baskets. A shooter is just as likely to make a shot after having missed the previous three baskets, as they are if they'd made each previous shot. There was no support for the idea of a hot hand. So although clusters of events seem unlikely, they do arise, even within completely random sequences. In an interesting corollary to these conclusions, Carlson and Shu (2007) present a good deal of evidence (the analysis of which is beyond our scope here) that *three* consecutive events of the same type is the critical number that seems to signal to someone that a streak is under-way (Bar-Eli, Avugos, & Robb, 2006).

   Some recent research on the hot hand phenomenon casts it in a considerably more posi-tive light (e.g., Burns, 2004; Wilke & Barrett, 2009), as an adaptation which leads to desirable behavioral outcomes. For example, Wilke and Barrett (2009) propose that people have evolved a tendency to view things as occurring in "clumps" (i.e., streaks) rather than randomly. Our cognitive "default" isn't the perception of randomness; it's the perception of patterns or streaks. People's inability to per-ceive true randomness is no surprise; in fact, Wilke and Barrett contend that it would be surprising if they *could* per-ceive it. They make the compelling argument that in our an-cestral environment, important events were likely to have been patterned rather than random. The most relevant con-text is foraging (i.e., searching for food); plants and animals were likely to exhibit a degree of (in the author's terms) clumpiness, tending to occur in relatively close proximity in space or time. Therefore, perceiving this clumpiness would have been adaptive. The hot hand perception might be viewed as a leftover indicator of this tendency.

Research Theme
Evolution

Is there such a thing as a "hot hand"?

   Wilke and Barrett tested their hypotheses in a series of investigations in which they compared Western partici-pants (students at UCLA) to participants from a horticul-tural/hunter tribe, the Shuar of Amazonian Ecuador. All participants were presented with foraging games in which they experienced a sequence of 100 events (i.e., a series of hits and misses) within a particular foraging context. They compared natural foraging contexts such as fruits and nests to artificial sequences like coin flips. One of the nat-ural foraging scenarios was searching for fruits. The par-ticipants' task was, after the presentation of each event in a sequence, to guess what the next event would turn out to be (e.g., a "hit" meant "piece of fruit"; "miss" meant "no piece of fruit"). Foraging sequences were all structured to have 50 misses and 50 hits. Based on the participants' for-aging choices across the 100 trials, the researchers calculated an alternation probability, as an index of how often the participant thought the present trial would repeat the result of the previous trial (i.e., a low alternation probability would indicate that the participant expected the same result, or, put another way, expected the streak to continue).

Research Theme
Culture

   Compellingly, the results revealed a "hot hand" in both the Shuar and the UCLA students for the fruit foraging; alternation probabilities were well under 50%, indicating that participants believed current streaks would continue. Also compelling is that the Shuar showed the hot hand tendency for coin flips to a greater extent than did the UCLA students. The authors cite this as evidence for their hypothesis as well; the default tendency to perceive "clumps" dictates that they should be perceived in any context. This tendency was reduced in the UCLA students, who are familiar with coin flips as a method of randomization, so would be less likely to perceive streaks. Based on the finding of hot hand perception across domains and across cultures, Wilke and Barrett conclude that the tendency is an evolved default, rather than a learned misperception.

Reality Check

The Gambler's Fallacy. The representativeness heuristic, and its relation to the misperception of event clusters, also underlies what Tversky and Kahneman and (1971) term the **gambler's fallacy.** This refers to the belief that after a run of bad luck (or a run of a certain type of outcome), a change is "due" to occur. Because a run of events seems so unlikely, people believe that a return to normalcy is likely to occur. This misperception leads to people's prolonged stays at the blackjack table despite a nasty losing streak as a winning streak is often thought to be right around the corner. But in this situation, future events (i.e., better card hands) have nothing to do with whether you've won or lost previously. Nonetheless, people often overestimate the probability of winning after a losing streak and continue to play.

My luck *has to* change...doesn't it?

The Anchoring and Adjustment Heuristic

In many cases of judgment, people start with an idea, or standard, in mind. Say you were guessing how much money the average college student makes from working part time over the course of the school year. As we've seen, there's no way you can possibly know or calculate this value, so you do the next best thing: you use a rule of thumb to help educate your guess. If you are a working college student, you might recall that you earn $8.10 per hour and work 15 hours a week at your job. Based on this knowledge, you may estimate that the average working college student makes around $100 to $150 a week. Although the information from your own work experience is helpful to start the estimation process, it may exert too much influence, essentially "anchoring" your judgment. That is, our initial estimate or first impression tends to make us overly biased toward it. The heuristic involved in these judgments is termed **anchoring and adjustment.** We often make an initial estimate, based on previous knowledge or presented information, and then make adjustments to that initial anchor to arrive at a final judgment. But just as an anchor holds a ship in place, your initial estimate can hold your guess in place, and you can fail to make sufficient adjustments.

Bridget experienced the anchoring and adjustment heuristic in our recent vacation to Colorado. We ate at an Italian restaurant in Winter Park that had one-dollar bills on the ceiling, walls, and every table. We both scanned the area and came up with our estimates of the total amount of money. When Bridget first contemplated the question, she thought the answer was about 20,000 dollars. Greg (perhaps under the influence of too much Chianti), blurted out "5000 dollars." After Greg's guess, Bridget vocalized her (now revised) estimate. Greg's (miserable) guess of 5,000 dollars anchored Bridget's guess all the way down to 10,000 dollars (the actual amount was 25,000).

The effect of the anchoring and adjustment heuristic in the previous example is quite innocuous, even cute, but an everyday context in which the heuristic can prove costly is credit card payments. If you've fallen under the spell of those little plastic cards that seemingly get you stuff for free—that is until the mail comes a few weeks later. Can you think of where anchoring enters the picture? Say you owe $700 on your credit card. How much do they demand you pay? Probably about $30; this is the minimum payment. Now, because you pay interest on the amount that sits on your credit card, it's best to pay as much as you can. The credit card company certainly doesn't want you to; the more you have on the bill, and the longer you have it there, the more money they make. And they may have a secret weapon in doing so: The minimum payment, which serves as an anchor, weighing down your payment (Stewart, 2009). You use the minimum payment as the starting point for how much

Anchors aweigh! Pay off those credit cards!

you will pay. The lower the minimum payment the less you'll pay and the more money the credit card company will make.

The Spotlight Effect.

Gilovich and colleagues (Gilovich, Krueger, & Medvec, 2002; Gilovich, Medvec, & Savitsky, 2000) cite anchoring and adjustment as the underlying cause of what they term the **spotlight effect.** The spotlight effect refers to our tendency to believe that others notice our actions and appearance more than they actually do—in other words, we believe that the "social spotlight" shines more brightly on us than it actually does. In three of their studies, these researchers had participants don a T-shirt that was embarrassing (Barry Manilow or Vanilla Ice) and then enter a room where other people were assembled and stay for a few minutes. Afterward, the participants were asked to estimate how many of the people assembled in the room had noticed their T-shirt. The results clearly demonstrated the spotlight effect: participants guessed that about twice as many people noticed their T-shirt as actually did. The result was even stronger in a later study when participants were asked to wear a nonembarrassing (perhaps even cool) T-shirt of their choice (with Martin Luther King, Jr., Bob Marley, or Jerry Seinfeld); the result was the same: participants thought everyone had noticed their T-shirt, but few did.

So how is this an example of anchoring and adjustment? The researchers suspected that participants would be overly aware of and self-conscious about their T-shirt and that this intense self-awareness would serve as an anchor, leading to overestimates of how many other people noticed it. They tested this idea in a disarmingly simple manner. After participants estimated the number of people who had noticed their T-shirts, the experimenters asked participants if they had considered any other number. The researchers' logic was simple: If participants' guesses were based on the very high anchor of their own self-consciousness, then their initial estimate likely would be even higher than their final estimate. The results from these two experiments supported this anchoring-and-adjustment interpretation.

Biased Evaluation of Our Judgments

We've seen that people employ some reasonable-sounding judgment heuristics in situations in which information, computational power, or both are lacking. We've also seen that people overly rely on heuristics, which sometimes leads to biased judgments. Sometimes we're not so good at estimating how much we know or when we knew it. We now turn to a couple of biases of this sort.

Hindsight Bias. "I could have told you that was going to happen." Who hasn't heard (or offered) this little gem of wisdom? People always seem to be sure after something has occurred that they knew things would work out just that way. This tendency is termed **hindsight bias** (and sometimes, quite descriptively, the *I-knew-it-all-along effect*).

A good example of an everyday situation that may be powerfully influenced by the hindsight bias is civil litigation. Civil suits involve disputes in which a plaintiff claims that they are the victim of some type of harm caused by the defendant. The purpose of the suit is to determine whether the plaintiff is entitled to some type of monetary compensation. When a jury or judge has to make a determination about liability, they are required to judge whether the defendant could have foreseen what was going to happen and acted accordingly. But, as described, people often fall victim to a hindsight bias. Therefore, they're likely to believe that they could have foreseen the events that led to the plaintiff's injury and therefore the defendant should have seen it coming, too (see Harley, 2007, for a review of the hindsight bias within a legal context).

A study by Hastie, Schkade, and Payne (1999) provides a dramatic demonstration of the hindsight bias in the context of a civil case with a plaintiff seeking punitive damages. The scenario they used was based on an actual case of a California train derailment and a resulting toxic herbicide spill. The case was presented in two slightly different ways. In the foresight condition, participants were told that there was a potentially dangerous situation developing along mountainous railroad tracks in California and that the National Transportation Safety Board (NTSB) had deemed the situation unsafe and ordered the railroad to stop operations. Expert testimony supporting the NTSB finding was also presented. Participants were told that the railroad had appealed the NTSB order and were to evaluate whether the appeal should be upheld. In other words, participants had to demonstrate foresight, judging how likely it would be that an accident would occur.

In the hindsight condition, participants were given the same information, with one important addition: there had already been a train derailment with an associated toxic spill. Instead of ruling on an appeal of the NTSB order, participants were instructed to decide whether punitive damages against the railroad were in order. These participants were susceptible to hindsight bias; they knew an accident had occurred and they were asked to judge whether the railroad should have seen it coming. The procedure required that all participants give an overall probability of an accident. The question in the foresight condition was "Estimate the probability that a serious accident will happen." The question in the hindsight condition was "*Ignoring what you now know,* what probability *would you have estimated* for

Was this accident foreseeable?

a serious accident happening?" (emphasis added). In addition to this overall judgment, participants in both conditions were asked to judge various elements of liability.

The results demonstrated a striking hindsight bias. The average probability estimate for the occurrence of an accident was 0.34 in foresight and 0.59 in hindsight; indeed, hindsight participants were fairly certain that they could have predicted the accident. Judgments on the elements of liability are presented in Table 11.8. Hindsight participants rated the railroad company more harshly for each of these elements (except maliciousness, which was not statistically significant but was in the predicted direction). Notice that the exact same rating questions were presented to the foresight and hindsight participants. All questions related generally to the core issue of whether the company should have foreseen the accident. The hindsight participants were overwhelmingly more likely to say yes, based on knowledge they had gained after the fact. Hastie, Schkade, and Payne contend that this type of hindsight bias is nearly inevitable when people are asked to reason about the causes and precursors to everyday events; this is pretty much what happens when juries or judges in civil trials consider punitive damages. To ameliorate the effects of hindsight bias, the authors offer a number of suggestions, including taking the question of punitive damages out of the hands of jurors and placing it in the hands of experts who might be less likely to fall victim to hindsight bias, given their extensive knowledge in the particular area.

The hindsight bias is robust, and has been demonstrated across a variety of contexts and experimental paradigms, so much so that some wonder whether everyone is discussing the same phenomenon when they mention "hindsight bias." Actually, Blank, Nestler, von Collani, and Fischer (2008) suggest there are three different hindsight biases, phenomenonologically unique (that is, all associated with different subjective feelings and

Table 11.8 **"They Should Have Seen It Coming"**

Judgments on Elements of Liability	Foresight Condition	Hindsight Condition
Defendant was (would be) reckless.	2.89	5.12
Risk was (is) foreseeable.	3.40	5.52
Defendant is (would be) liable for accident.	3.50	6.08
Defendant disregarded (is disregarding) grave risk.	3.36	5.59
Defendant was (is being) malicious.	1.80	2.12

Note: 1 = definitely "no"; 10 = definitely "yes."

From Hastie, R., Schkade, D. A., & Payne, J. W. (1999). Juror judgments in civil cases: Hindsight effects on judgments of liability for punitive damages. *Law and Human Behavior, 23,* 445–470. Reprinted by permission of Kluwer Academic/Plenum Publishers.

experiences). The first type of hindsight bias is what they term an *impression of necessity.* This form of hindsight bias refers to an increase in an event's perceived inevitability after it has already occurred. After an event happens, it seems like it was bound to happen. A second type of hindsight bias is the *"I knew it all along"* or "I told you so" effect we described earlier, a feeling that we would have been able to predict an event that has occurred. A third type of hindsight bias is *memory distortion.* After receiving feedback about some outcome, people's memory for how likely they felt the outcome was, will be distorted in favor of the outcome. For example, if I ask you today (July 2) what you think the probability is that the Minnesota Twins baseball team will win their division, you may say 60%. In October, if they won the division, you might misremember that your judgment of the probability was 80%; if they lost the division, you may misremember that your judgment of the probability was 40%. According to Blank et al., these are three different senses of hindsight bias that may occur in isolation from one another, or in any combination, depending on the particular nature of the individual and the task.

Metacognition

Miscalibration of Confidence.   The fact that we overestimate the extent to which we knew something was going to happen demonstrates insensitivity to what we knew and when we knew it. This general lack of sensitivity is also revealed by the finding that we have a general tendency to be overconfident (or, in some circumstances, underconfident) about what we know. In other words, we are not very good at calibrating our confidence. If confidence were perfectly calibrated to what we know, then our confidence would match our knowledge. If we were 50% sure about some set of facts, then we would get 50% of them correct. If we were 100% sure about another set of facts, then we would get all of them correct.

Many studies have investigated confidence calibration and revealed it to be "off" in a fairly systematic manner. For example, Fischhoff, Slovic, and Lichtenstein (1977) had people answer general knowledge questions (e.g., "Is absinthe a type of liqueur or a type of precious stone?") and rate their confidence that they had given a correct answer. If participants were completely guessing, their confidence rating should have been 50%. Also, if confidence was well calibrated, then the average confidence value should have matched the average percentage correct. The researchers found that participants tended to be overconfident; for questions about which they were 100% confident, they managed to get only 75% or so correct. This **miscalibration of confidence** seems to be most serious in cases when we're extremely confident; it seems that people who are "absolutely sure" are the ones most likely to be wrong. It's important to note that although overconfidence is common, it is not always the rule. In cases in which answers are rather easy to arrive at, we are actually a little underconfident. For instance, having taken a test that was fairly easy, you may be a little cautious in your estimation of how you did, perhaps to avoid "getting your hopes up." In this type of situation, people are a little too cautious in their estimates. (By the way, absinthe is a liqueur.)

Plous (1993) notes the potentially grave consequences of overconfidence, citing a study by Bedau and Radelet (1987) on wrongful convictions for capital crimes. This study revealed 350 documented instances of innocent defendants being wrongfully convicted. Plous points out that this is an example of overconfidence. The standard of proof in a criminal trial is a volume of evidence that would suggest that a defendant is "guilty beyond a reasonable doubt." Obviously, the convictions of these innocent individuals were instances of overconfident juries that failed to find reasonable doubt when there was some to be found.

Stop&*Think* | CONFIDENCE CALIBRATION

Your task here is to set a 90% confidence interval for each answer. In other words, your answer will be a range within which you're 90% sure the answer falls. Try to set your ranges so that they're not too narrow (overconfident) or too wide (underconfident).

I am 90% confident the answer falls between:
1. Estimated number of tigers (all types) in the wild as of 2007 _____ and _____
2. Year in which the first professional baseball team was established
3. Highest recorded temperature in Oslo, Norway _____ and _____
4. Length of the Amazon River _____ and _____
5. Average salary in 2007 for an NBA player _____ and _____
6. Population of Dublin as of 2006 census _____ and _____
7. Estimated number of civilian casualties in World War I _____ and _____
8. Year in which Genghis Khan was born _____ and _____
9. Approximation gestation period of a giant panda _____ and _____
10. Number of nations that belong to the UN _____ and _____

If your confidence is well calibrated to your accuracy, you should be correct on 90% or more of your intervals (answers below).

- Did you show good calibration of confidence?
- Was your range too narrow (showing overconfidence)?
- Was your range too wide (demonstrating underconfidence)?
- What is your explanation?

1. 6000 2. 1869 3. 95 degrees Fahrenheit; 35 Celsius 4. 4195 mi/6712 km 5. $5.2 million 6. 505,000 7. 10 million 8. 1162 9. 145 days 10. 192 nations.

Just like hindsight bias, it seems that overconfidence is used too generally with several distinct phenomena grouped under the same umbrella. As coincidence would have it, just as there are three senses of hindsight bias, there would appear to be three different manifestations of overconfidence. Moore and Healy (2008) label the first variety *overestimation*; an example of this would be you walking away from a test thinking you aced it, when in actuality, you earned a B. Overconfidence is demonstrated in an overestimation of your own performance (then when you get the score back, you probably show one of the three senses of hindsight bias!). The second type is termed *overplacement*; an example of this would be guessing that you're one of the best two or three students in a class, when actually, you're no better than tenth. Overconfidence is demonstrated by the overplacement of your performance relative to the performance of others. The third type of overconfidence is termed overprecision; an example is believing that you definitely got the right answer on an exam question, when in fact you missed some of it. Overconfidence is demonstrated by excessive certainty in your accuracy.

Stop&*Review*

1. What are heuristics, and why are they used?
2. Define the availability heuristic.
3. When people make judgments based on representativeness, they're basing their judgments on
   a. recency in memory.
   b. similarity.
   c. their first impressions.
   d. what they thought they knew before.
4. Describe the spotlight effect and what heuristic seems to be implicated.
5. What is the hindsight bias?

- The processes of judgment involve arriving at some conclusion about unknown events. Because of limits in capacity and information, we rely on heuristics, "shortcuts" that allow us to make quick judgments.

- The availability heuristic is the tendency to make judgments based on how easily an example can be brought to mind. Biases in the encoding and retrieval of events can lead to biased application of the availability heuristic. An illusory correlation is made when the vividness of an example causes someone to see a relationship between events when none exists. The recognition heuristic is the tendency to choose a familiar alternative over an unfamiliar one when asked to pick which is greater on some dimension.

- The representativeness heuristic involves making judgments based on the similarity between an event or person and our stereotype of it/them. This heuristic can lead to a tendency to ignore basic principles of probability which results in the conjunction fallacy (the belief that two events are more likely than just one of the events). The conjunction fallacy (and other thinking biases) might sometimes be attributable not to irrationality but to alternative construals that participants might have of the problems.

- People tend to misperceive event clusters as nonrandom, leading to a fallacious belief in a "hot hand" and the gambler's fallacy. Perceiving events in clusters seems to have some adaptive value. The anchoring-and-adjustment heuristic occurs when a person makes an initial estimate and then fails to make sufficient adjustments to arrive at their final estimate. Anchoring and adjustment seem to underlie the spotlight effect, our tendency to believe that others notice our actions and appearance more than they actually do.

- Judgments about our own judgments are also suspect. The hindsight bias refers to our tendency, after an event has happened, to inflate the degree to which we knew that something was going to happen. There are several different interpretations of the hindsight bias. Miscalibration of confidence refers to the fact that the confidence we have in our judgments is not always a good indicator of our judgments' accuracy. Overconfidence can be manifested in multiple ways.

Decision Making

Despite the limitations that we're subject to in making judgments, they form an important part of the database for the process of decision making. For example, consider the following conversation:

> *Person A:* If there's a good chance that Tom will be at the party, then I think we should go. What do you think the chances are he'll go?
> *Person B:* Oh, I'm pretty sure he'll be there.
> *Person A:* OK, then let's go.

In this situation, the decision (going to the party) is based on the judgment of another event happening (whether Tom will be there). But decision making goes beyond this judgment to include a choice between alternatives: Do you go to the party or stay home? The fact that decision making involves choice introduces another element to the thinking mix—that of risk, or uncertainty. When you choose among a number of alternatives, there is always a chance that your choice will be the wrong one.

Expected Utility: A Normative Approach

The study of simple choice and decision making has a long history. Economists always have been interested in the factors involved in choice and what type of model describes rational choice behavior. One of the most well-established theories of decision making is **expected utility theory.** This theory states that when faced with some type of uncertain choice, we make our decisions based on two factors—the expected utility of the outcomes and their respective probability. Utility refers to whatever end a person would like to achieve, be it happiness, money, or something else. Baron (1999) suggests that *good* might be a better word to use; utility refers to the amount of good that comes out of a decision (Broome, 1991). So we weigh the good that might come out of each alternative against the costs of that alternative. We also assess the probability of each alternative occurring. Whichever alternative provides the best combination of "good" and "likelihood of occurring" will be the one we choose. Consider these choices:

Flip a coin; if it turns up heads, you get $40.
Roll the dice; if it comes up 4, you get $50.

Most people would probably choose the first option because it seems like a better combination of good and probability. You stand to get $10 less than if you choose the second option, but the probability of winning in the first option is much greater. This greater probability offsets the slight difference in monetary value.

Violations of Expected Utility.   Expected utility theory provides a normative description of decision making—that is, it lays out the ways human beings would choose among alternatives if humans were perfectly rational decision makers. Given that expected utility theory provides a view of the ideal decision maker, it serves as a useful baseline against which actual decision making can be compared. So what should the ideal decision maker do and not do? Let's look at one of the normative predictions made by expected utility theory. According to the principle, our choices should show *invariance*; that is, a decision maker's choices should not depend on the way a choice is presented. (In other words, a preference should be invariant across different sorts of situations.) If I prefer choice A over choice B in situation 1, then I should prefer choice A over choice B in situation 14 (as long as A and B are identical in the two situations).

As you'll see, it's quite easy to get people to violate the assumption of invariance. People often do switch their preferences of one outcome over another, based only on how these outcomes are presented, thereby demonstrating *irrationality*. Consider the **preference reversals** shown in a classic series of studies by Lichtenstein and Slovic (1971, 1973). Their general procedure involved having participants look at two different gambles and decide (1) which gamble they would like to play and (2) how much the gamble was worth. Try this for yourself. Look at the choices in Table 11.9. First, imagine which gamble you would choose; then for each pair, imagine that you "own" the gamble and are trying to sell it—how much will you charge? You would think that a rational person would be consistent. If they preferred one gamble over the other, they also should say it was worth more and set a higher price for it. (Is this what you did?) Lichtenstein and Slovic expected otherwise; they thought that the choice of which gamble to play would be influenced by the probability of winning, whereas the choice of the selling price for the gamble would depend on the potential dollar amount to be won. Think about why this preference reversal is irrational. If participants think that one gamble should go for a higher price than the other gamble, why didn't they choose it? And this result is not limited to questionnaires about theoretical choices given within a laboratory setting.

Table 11.9 **Sample choices in preference reversal experiments.**

1. 80% chance to win $4.00
    20% chance to lose $.50
	4. 10% chance to win $40.00
	    90% chance to lose $1.00

2. 95% chance to win $3.00
    5% chance to lose $2.00
	5. 50% chance to win $6.50
	    50% chance to lose $1.00

3. 99% chance to win $4.00
    1% chance to lose $1.00
	6. 33% chance to win $16.00
	    67% chance to lose $2.00

From Lichtenstein, S., & Slovic, P. (1971). Reversals of preference between bids and choices in gambling choices. *Journal of Experimental Psychology, 89,* 46–55. Copyright 1971 by the American Psychological Association. Reprinted by permission.

Lichtenstein and Slovic (1973) found exactly the same results when they conducted the study in a Las Vegas casino (in which the sample included a number of card dealers!).

The preference reversal phenomenon is only one of a number of phenomena that demonstrate the inadequacy of expected utility as a descriptive model of decision making. The expected utility model fails to provide a good description of how we make choices in many circumstances because it assumes too much; humans rarely, if ever, have all of the information necessary to make a decision. Even if we did, we would lack the ability to combine and weigh the information accurately. Also, expected utility proposes that we base our decisions on expected consequences, but there is no real way to foresee consequences with any certainty. Expected utility is still one of the most common yardsticks by which the rationality of human decision making is measured, but psychologists have attempted to develop descriptive models of how we actually do make decisions in order to accommodate "irrationality."

Prospect Theory: A Descriptive Approach

One popular alternative to expected utility theory is Kahneman and Tversky's (1979) prospect theory. **Prospect theory** is a descriptive model of decision making that attempts to describe how we make decisions and why our decisions violate the expected utility model. According to prospect theory, decisions are not valued based on the absolute value of the end result, as proposed by expected utility; instead, we value decisions based on the amount of gain or loss from what we have right now. Another important feature of the model is that it proposes that gains and losses are on different scales of value. Figure 11.4 plots the value that we place on gains and losses. Gains are to the right of center, and losses are to the left. Note that the value we attach to gains increases more slowly as a function of the size of the gain than does the (negative) value we place on losses as a function of the size of the loss. We feel losses more acutely than we feel gains; the psychological pain associated with losing $50 is greater than the psychological pleasure of gaining $50. Prospect theory predicts that people will be especially averse to loss and will show differences in preference depending on how alternatives are presented, or framed.

Framing. Prospect theory predicts that our preferences will change whenever our reference point (i.e., what we have right now) changes. This means that decisions can be influenced by how information is presented. If information is presented in terms of a positive "gain frame" (emphasizing the certainty of what we have right now), we will be more likely to avoid risk (i.e., risk averse), and pick the surer bet. However, if the same information is presented in a negative "loss frame" (emphasizing what we might

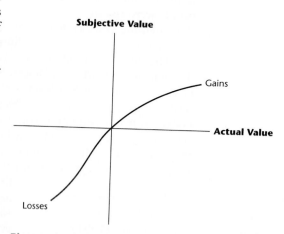

Figure 11.4

Hypothetical value function proposed in prospect theory.

From Kahneman, D., & Tversky, A. (1984). Choices, values, and frames. *American Psychologist, 39,* 341–350. Copyright 1984 by the American Psychologial Association. Reprinted by permission.

lose if we make a particular decision), we will be more likely to take a risk (i.e., risk prone) to avoid this loss. **Framing** is the term used to describe the effects on decisions based on how a scenario is presented.

Consider the results of a classic study by Tversky and Kahneman (1981, p. 453). Participants were presented with this scenario and two choices:

Imagine that the U.S. is preparing for the outbreak of an unusual Asian disease, which is expected to kill 600 people. Two alternative programs for combating the disease have been proposed. Assume that the exact scientific estimate of the consequences of the program is as follows:
If program A is adopted, 200 people will be saved.
If program B is adopted, there is a 1/3 probability that 600 people will be saved, and a 2/3 probability that no one will be saved.

Other participants were presented with exactly the same problem but different choices:

If program C is adopted, 400 people will die.
If program D is adopted, there is a 1/3 probability that nobody will die, and a 2/3 probability that 600 people will die.

If you look closely, you'll note something a little peculiar: the choice between A and B is exactly the same as the choice between C and D, but they're worded differently. The first choice is presented in terms of what is to be gained, while the second is presented in terms of what is to be lost.

Table 11.10 shows the proportion of participants who picked the nonrisky options (A and C) and risky options (B and D) alternatives as a function of how the alternatives were presented. As you can see, when the alternatives were presented in a gain frame, people were *risk averse*—unwilling to take a risk and preferring the "sure" alternative. But when the exact same choices were reworded and presented in a loss frame, people were *risk prone*—much more willing to take a risk to avoid loss.

The effects of framing are relevant to our everyday decisions. Studies of medical decision making (McNeil, Pauker, Sox, & Tversky, 1986), decisions about health-related behaviors (Rothman & Salovey, 1997), and decisions about the continuation of romantic relationships (Boon & Griffin, 1996) have all shown influences of framing. As we've seen, one of the major assumptions of Prospect Theory is an asymmetry in the valuation of positive and negative outcomes (i.e., gains and losses). Negative outcomes pack more of a punch than positive ones. In a recent extension of the theory, Caruso, Gilbert, and Wilson (2008) propose another cognitive asymmetry that has ramifications for how we make decisions. In their view, the value of outcomes also differs with regard to *time*; they propose that people experience a *temporal value asymmetry* in thinking about future events and past events. Specifically, people place more value on the future than they do on the past.

They relate a story from the philosopher Seneca the Younger that may help demonstrate the point. Seneca suggested that fearing death is irrational, because the time that people will lose when they die (i.e., the time in

Table 11.10 Results from Kahneman and Tversky (1981)

		Type of Frame	
		Gains	Losses
Choice Made	Risky	.28	.78
	Nonrisky	.72	.22

the future beyond the point of death) is no more valuable than the time that we didn't get because we weren't born earlier. They quote Seneca who asserts, "If anyone pities the dead, he must also pity those who have not yet been born." It's quite likely that you're not buying it, due to what Caruso et al. contend is your tendency to care about and value the future more than the past. Why might this be? Caruso et al. suggest that the future is less certain and more changeable than the past, leading people to (rationally) value the future more.

To test for the reality of a temporal-value asymmetry, Caruso, et al. had participants answer a survey about their upcoming winter break. Half of the participants (future condition) took the survey a couple of weeks before the break, and the other half took it a couple of weeks after the end of their break. The survey asked the destination of travel, who they were visiting (or had visited), and how much they had enjoyed (or would enjoy) the trip on a 0 to 6 scale. In addition, they were asked how much they would pay (or would have paid) for the opportunity to extend their trip. The results neatly supported the notion of a temporal value asymmetry. Participants considering the past trip rated it as less enjoyable than those considering their future trip. In addition, participants who were considering their future trip were willing to spend more to extend it ($113 vs. $91), indicating that they placed more value on the time than those reflecting on their past trip. This pattern was obtained in each of five studies, all posing different valuation scenarios.

Caruso et al. contend that the temporal value asymmetry calls for some serious reconsideration of prospect theory and the framing phenomenon. The Kahneman and Tversky framing scenarios are always framed as occurring at a single point in time. The present results make it clear that the subjective value experienced for a particular gain or loss scenario will depend critically on a time dimension as well. The pleasure and pain associated with gains and losses will be further moderated by whether these experiences are already past, or loom in the future.

Risky Decision Making in the Brain.

A number of studies have investigated the brain areas thought to be involved in decision making (e.g., Gonzalez, Dana, Koshino, & Just, 2005; Sanfey, Loewenstein, McClure, & Cohen, 2006; Trepel, Fox, & Poldrack, 2005). An fMRI study by Gonzalez, Dana, Koshino, and Just (2005) was designed to reveal a possible interaction between the frame in which a problem is presented and the amount of effort expended in arriving at a decision. Brain activity was monitored as participants made decisions within standard framing scenarios that resembled the "Asian disease problem." The behavioral results replicated the standard finding nicely. In a gain frame, a sure thing was preferred to a risk while in a loss frame, the risk was preferred to the sure thing.

The brain-imaging results proved intriguing and indicated differences in cognitive effort between the two conditions. Overall, much of the brain activity occurred in frontal and parietal regions, indicating the involvement of immediate memory and, to some extent, mental imagery. But especially intriguing were the differences in relative amounts of brain activity between framing conditions. When things were framed in terms of gains, brain-imaging results indicated that the brain was considerably less active when faced with the certain alternative, relative to when it was faced with the risky alternative. The converse relationship was shown when choices were framed in terms of losses. In this case, the brain was considerably less active when faced with the risky alternative, relative to when it was faced with the certain alternative. These findings present an intriguing parallel to the oft-replicated behavioral result, and suggest that another consideration in decision making is the desire to minimize cognitive effort.

Psychological Accounting.   The research on framing indicates that we make different choices depending on how the alternatives are worded or framed. Kahneman and Tversky (1981, p. 457) demonstrate a similar effect in people's consideration of the outcomes of their decisions. According to the *psychological accounting principle,* people will make different decisions depending on how the outcome is felt or perceived. Consider the following scenarios:

1. *Imagine that you have decided to see a play for which admission is $10 a ticket. As you enter the theater, you discover that you have lost a $10 bill. Would you still pay $10 for a ticket to the play?*

2. *Imagine that you have decided to see a play for which admission is $10 a ticket. As you enter the theater, you discover that you have lost the ticket. The seat was not marked, and the ticket cannot be recovered. Would you pay $10 for a ticket to the play?*

In these scenarios, what is being manipulated is not the cost or benefit; it's the way that participants are likely to think about the extra $10 that needs to be spent. Kahneman and Tversky (1981) term this a *difference in psychological accounting.* In both scenarios, an extra 10 bucks needs to be shelled out. In which scenario does this seem more painful? In Kahneman and Tversky's study, participants were less willing to purchase a ticket in scenario 2. Why should this be? In that scenario, $10 has already been invested for the play, so spending another $10 seems an unattractive alternative. In scenario 1, we simply have lost $10, money that could have been spent for anything. So it seems that we are less averse to losing money from our general "psychological account" than we are from our "play account," which has already been tapped for the $10 play ticket. But this distinction is a little silly. In both scenarios, we're out $20, and we get to see a play, so there should be no difference in our willingness to spend 10 more dollars.

Sunk Costs.   Another interesting variation on the notion of psychological accounting relates to what has been termed the **sunk-cost effect.** This effect was demonstrated by Arkes and Blumer (1985). In one experiment, participants were to imagine that they had purchased tickets for two different ski trips: one ticket (for a ski trip to Wisconsin) cost $50, while the other ticket (for a ski trip to Michigan) cost $100. The scenario made it clear that the trip to Wisconsin was preferable because it would be more enjoyable. Then a complication arose: the two trips were on the same weekend, and the tickets were nonrefundable. Which trip would you choose to go on? Most participants chose the Michigan trip even though the Wisconsin trip was touted as being more enjoyable. Why? Because, according to their "psychological accounting," not going to Michigan would waste more money. Keep in mind, however, that the costs were already "sunk." Participants were out $150 no matter what. But because more money was invested in the Michigan trip, participants felt that they had to follow through on this particular investment. When people have invested more time, effort, or money into a given situation, they feel more compelled to go ahead with it, sometimes "throwing good money after bad."(Garland, 1990).

Emotions and Decision Making

Research Theme
Emotion

The framing and psychological accounting effects just discussed underscore the role that *emotion* and subjective feelings can play in decision making. Positive and negative outcomes *feel* different to us, with predictable implications for the decisions we make. In other words, *emotion* is an important determinant of decision making, and can have a sizable impact on choices and decisions. In addition, emotion can serve as the basis for decisions; according to dual-process approaches, emotion is associated with System 1, the decision-making system thought to operate unconsciously and automatically. Do we ever pay a price for this automatic decision making under conditions of emotion and stress?

This question was addressed in a study by Porcelli and Delgado (2009), who investigated the effects of acute stress on framing effects in decision making. Participants were presented with trials that included a choice between two gambles that involved winning money (gain domain) and other trials involved a choice between two gambles that involved losing money (loss frame). To induce stress, the researchers used a cold pressor task, which involves sticking your arm in ice-cold water for an extended period of time (in this case, 2 minutes). Imagine fishing around in the bottom of a cooler full of Miller Lite for the last Guiness. Greg would leave his arm in there for at least five minutes under those circumstances! Participants made their decisions under stress (hands in the ice cold water) or no stress (hands in room temperature water). Porcelli and Delgado were interested in how exposure to acute stress would influence their choices.

The results are presented in Table 11.11. The left-hand table presents the choice behavior of participants in the no stress condition, and the pattern should look familiar. What you see is precisely the same interaction that was obtained by Tversky and Kahneman (1981). In gains domain, participants were more likely to make conservative choices than risky choices. The converse was true in the loss domain, where risky choices were more likely. The right-hand table presents the choice behavior of those exposed to the cold pressor task. Once again, the pattern is the same, but, as you can see, it is greatly accentuated. The tendency to be risk-averse in the gains frame and risk taking in the loss frame were intensified. Porcelli and Delgado explain that these are automatic (i.e., System 1) tendencies, and when acute stress is introduced, there is even more reliance on System 1; acute stress interferes with the processes of System 2 (which require conscious attention and effort)

How about if you took your hand out of that nasty ice water and got a nice long backrub, or maybe just a comforting touch on the shoulder. How would this affect your willingness to take risks? This turns out to be the key independent variable in a study by Levav and Argo (2010). These researchers were interested in the relationship between the

Table 11.11 **Data from Porcelli & Delgado (2009); Proportion of Risky and Non-Risky Choices as a Function of Frame and Stress Level**

NO STRESS		Type of Frame			STRESS		Type of Frame	
		Gains	Losses				Gains	Losses
Choice Made	Risky	.42	.61		Choice Made	Risky	.33	.66
	Non-Risky	.58	.41			Non-Risky	.67	.35

Table 11.12 **Data from Levav & Argo (2010); Amount (out of $5) Invested in a Risky Fund**

	Type of Touch		
	None	Handshake	Shoulder
Male Toucher	2.59	2.18	2.63
Female Toucher	1.05	2.04	3.44

emotional security associated with physical contact, and the tendency for risk-taking behavior. They set the stage for their study by discussing the large body of literature (both human and animal) that emphasizes the role of physical contact in leading to attachment, feelings of security, and exploratory behavior. They extend these findings to the decision-making domain and speculate that the security associated with simple contact might increase risk taking. The authors go even further, suggesting that a situation that involves a maternal touch would increase risk taking.

To test this notion, Levav and Argo (Experiment 2) manipulated two of the stranger independent variables you've read about in the text: type of touch and gender of toucher. Participants were tested by either a male or female experimenter (i.e., the toucher), and as they were being instructed in the task, either received no touch, a handshake, or a touch on the shoulder. The task involved the participant receiving $5 at the start of the experiment, and then deciding how to allocate their $5, given two different investment opportunities, one risky and one safe. Any money not invested in the risky option was automatically invested in the safe option, so not investing was not an option. To up the stakes a bit, they were told to imagine that each $1 represented $100. The results are presented in Table 11.12, which shows the amount (out of the $5 given to participants at the start of the experiment) of money invested in the risky option. The lesson?.... beware of overly friendly female stockbrokers. Believe it or not, something as subtle as a touch on the shoulder led to increased financial risk taking. The results revealed an interaction between type of touch and gender of the toucher. Financial risk taking was unaffected by any interaction with a male experimenter. However, risk taking was increased by physical contact with a female experimenter and only in the condition where it was a touch on the shoulder. Here we have yet another manifestation of the influence of emotion on decision making, demonstrating the complexity of the underlying processes.

Decision Making: Biases or Adaptive Tools?

The topics discussed in this chapter have been profoundly influenced by (perhaps even defined by) the Kahneman and Tversky (KT) research program. And in large part, this research program would be in absolute agreement with what Gigerenzer proposes regarding fast and frugal heuristics. But the two views clearly have different starting points (captured by the half-empty/half-full analogy discussed earlier). The KT research program was designed to answer questions like "Why does our judgment *fall short of* optimization?" How is our decision making *biased*? What underlies cognitive *errors* and *illusions*? Note that the emphasized terms in each question underscore the KT emphasis on error and limitation. Gigerenzer's motivating questions are more of the "Given cognitive limitations, how do we manage to make *good decisions*" and "How is it that we are able to tailor our reasoning and decision strategies effectively to particular environmental demands?"

Gigerenzer (2008) contends that heuristics get a bad rap. His view of heuristics is that they comprise an "adaptive toolbox", an evolved set of procedures and strategies that we use for the judgment and decision problems we face on an everyday basis. You may recall from Chapter 1 our discussion of the ecological approach to cognition, which emphasizes how cognition plays itself out in everyday contexts. Gigerenzer's adaptive toolkit is most definitely an ecological approach. He views heuristic processing as the joint product of the thinker (who he would agree has bounded rationality), and the demands of the environment. Given this combination of cognitive boundaries and situational demands, we have evolved effective tools that for the most part, succeed in helping us adapt to circumstances by making good choices and decisions. He labels these tools as "fast and frugal" heuristics; they're fast in the answers they produce, and frugal in the amount of information processing they require. In addition, one could easily make the argument that KT's judgment scenarios are not ecologically valid. Many of the biases shown by this research program occur in response to specific (and as we've seen, sometimes obscurely worded) verbal scenarios.

Research Theme
Evolution

An array of misconceptions about bounded rationality and the use of heuristics have developed (Gigerenzer, 2008) due to the manner in which the study of judgment evolved. One is that heuristics provide second-best results. Another is that heuristics are necessary only because of cognitive limitations; Gigerenzer contends that a combination of environmental demands and cognitive limitations necessitate the use of heuristics. Another misconception is that people rely on heuristics only for minor decisions, or for situations of little importance. Finally, Gigerenzer criticizes the implicit notion that more information and computation are always better than heuristics (i.e., heuristics are viewed as a "shortcut" alternative to more accurate approaches). This sells heuristics short; heuristics are strategies that work, because they have evolved to be applicable to specific problems that cannot be solved purely through logic or probability analysis (i.e., normative approaches). A fruitful direction for decision-making research would be a systematic study of different heuristics and the environments in which they work.

Improving Decision Making

At several points throughout the chapter, we've discussed differing views on whether the reasoning, judgment, and decision making glass is half-empty or half-full. One point that all would agree on is that we want to get more into the glass. So what does the research on these topics have to tell us about improving our abilities? Milkman, Chugh, and Bazerman (2009) stress the need for work in this area. First, they point out that errors are costly, and are likely to get costlier. Consider one example—the mortgage meltdown that led to the serious recession/near depression in 2008. Clearly, this was a situation that was rife with bad reasoning, judgment, and decisions. Suboptimal decisions impede us in potentially every area of life. And as the world continues to grow in industrial and technological complexity, so will the cognitive challenges. Combine this with our tendencies to overload ourselves with external stimulation and information, and you've got bad decisions and choices waiting to happen.

Most of Milkman et al.'s (2009) suggestions are posed within the dual-process framework discussed earlier, and they seem particularly concerned with a reliance on System 1 (the emotional, intuitive, unconscious mode) in situations that call for conscious and deliberate consideration. The authors propose a number of methods for encouraging the careful analysis that characterizes System 2. First, they suggest taking an outsider's perspective. Better yet, ask an outsider for an opinion on the available choices. Another option for engaging System 2 is to consider the opposite of the choices you are about to make. Conscious decision-making processes also can be engaged by having groups rather than individuals make decisions, by training people in mathematical or statistical reasoning, and/or by holding people more accountable for decisions. In sum, Milkman et al. (2009) propose that any change in decision context that makes a person "stop and think" is advisable in order to oppose the impulsivity and short-sightedness that can characterize System 1 processes.

Another way to deal with a possible overreliance on System 1 decision-making processes is to set up situations in such a way that System 1 thinking actually leads to the desirable outcome. In other words, set decision-making scenarios up in such a way that the automatic response is the optimizing response. Thaler and Sunstein (2008) and others label this *choice architecture*—building choice scenarios to optimize the value of choices. For example, upon hiring in some companies, you have an option of putting extra money into a retirement account, but you have to actively make that choice by checking a box and filling in some extra information. System 1 decision-making processes would tend to push you toward just going with the default option (no extra retirement funds, and/or consider it later). But with a different choice architecture, System 1 can be tricked. Suppose the company made the extra money withdrawal the default, and you had to actively opt out of the option by checking a box. In this case, you'd have System 1 working for you ("Oh, just go with the status quo," which in this case is beneficial). Engineering choices in this way have been shown to improve employee retirement savings (e.g., Benartzi & Thaler, 2007). Milkman et al. conclude that the key to improving decision making lies in delineating the situations that are appropriately served by System 1 and System 2 reasoning processes.

Stop&*Review*

1. On what do we base our choices, according to expected utility theory?
2. True or false? According to prospect theory, gains carry more psychological weight than losses.
3. Describe the sunk-cost effect.
4. Attempts to improve decision making generally focus on giving System 1 processes a bigger role in the process.

• Decision making involves choosing among alternatives that have different costs, benefits, and consequences. Expected utility theory, a normative approach to decision making, contends that choices are based on the attractiveness of consequences and the probability of the consequence. The outcome with the best combination is chosen. Choices should not vary with how choices are presented. Preference reversals indicate that they do.

- Prospect theory, a descriptive model, assumes that people make decisions based on what they have right now and interpret gains and losses on different scales, losses being more psychologically powerful. This theory predicts the framing effect, whereby people are risk averse when faced with certain gains, and risk prone when faced with certain losses. People also seem to value future events more so than past events.

- According to the psychological accounting principle, people make different decisions depending on how they feel about each outcome. The sunk-cost effect states that people overuse the resources already invested in a particular course of action as a decision criterion. Emotions influence choices and decisions. Stress can lead to increased reliance on System 1 (automatic) thinking processes. Feelings of emotional security have been shown to lead to increased financial risk taking.

- Some current researchers are critical of the Kahneman and Tversky framework for describing heuristics, feeling that it tends to equate heuristics with bias and error. Newer approaches view heuristics as effective and adaptive approaches to solving real-world problems. Attempts to improve decision making generally focus on engaging System 2 (conscious reasoning) and avoiding an overreliance on System 1.

12

Problems and Goals: Using Information to Arrive at Solutions

Have you ever been faced with a really tough problem, one that seems nearly insurmountable—perhaps the mound of tests and assignments facing you right now? What are the basic processes that people engage in as they attempt to arrive at solutions to problems? What obstacles tend to get in their way, and how might these obstacles be overcome?

What's happening when you get stuck in a mental rut? In these cases, it sometimes seems helpful to take a break and walk away from the problem. This seems to be exactly when the solution pops into your head. Does taking a break help problem solving, and if so, why?

How does one get to be an expert? Is it possible for anyone to become an expert at anything? If someone becomes an expert in a particular domain, does this have implications for their performance in other domains? Are there any drawbacks to expertise?

Some people just seem to have brilliant, creative minds. What exactly *is* creativity? What underlies creativity? Are people born with the ability to be creative? Can anyone be creative?

What Is a Problem?

Chances are, you've got a big problem facing you. More than likely, you're approaching the end of your semester, and you have to engage in quite a balancing act. You no doubt have papers to write, presentations to give, and/or exams for which to study. Oh, and let's not forget about the 30 hours a week that you're working and the fact that you need to maintain a B average in order to keep your scholarship, or a C average to maintain your parents' support, or (fill in the appropriate constraint here). Grappling with this complex scenario involves the processes that a cognitive psychologist would term **problem solving.** Problem solving is a fitting chapter on which to end a book on cognitive psychology. It is truly the ultimate in cognition, as it involves every one of the processes discussed thus far, combining to serve an extremely complex entity: a problem.

A **problem** consists of several basic components: an **initial state** (the situation at the beginning of the problem), a **goal state** (the solution to the problem), a set of *rules* (or constraints) that must be followed, and usually, a set of *obstacles* that must be overcome. In the present example, the initial state is you, in a panic, staring at a blank computer screen, trying to get a start on your first paper. The goal state is finished research papers and sterling performance (OK, B-level performance) on several finals, which will result in a happy trip home for semester break. The rules and obstacles are numerous. The research paper topics are difficult, and many of the sources you've found are not in the school's library. You have only two weeks to finish everything. You're working at Starbucks, and they just asked you to work extra hours because of heavy business lately…shall we go on? *Problem solving* seems a most apt term.

Well-Defined and Ill-Defined Problems

The problems we face every day, from the morning crossword puzzle to retrieving our keys from a locked car, can be classified along a continuum from well defined to ill defined. **Well-defined problems** are clear and structured; the initial state, goal state, and constraints are all understood, and once you reach a solution, it's easily assessed. Solving an anagram (unscrambling letters to form a word) is an extremely well-defined problem. The initial state of this problem is the set of scrambled letters; the goal state is a word; the constraints are to use only the letters provided. Once you arrive at a solution, it's clear whether you're right or wrong. In contrast to well-defined problems, an **ill-defined problem** is fuzzy and abstract. One of the term papers you have to write is a good example of an ill-defined problem. You're not quite sure where you're starting, where you need to get to, or what the constraints are. The topic is up to you, the length is up to you, and you're not 100% sure "what the professor wants." In addition, once you've come up with a solution, you're really not sure if it's a good one. You may think the paper is good, but you're not the one grading it. Needless to say, ill-defined problems tend to present more of a challenge to the solver than well-defined ones.

Routine and Nonroutine Problems

Problems also vary in terms of how familiar we are with the procedures they involve. A **routine problem** is one that can be solved by applying well-practiced procedures. Consider the task of writing a psychology research paper. For a senior psychology major, this may be a fairly routine problem, consisting of individual tasks that have been performed many times: identifying a topic, searching the library, and organizing the paper. But a first-time psychology student, taking their first course in research methods, would likely find this problem decidedly nonroutine, having never identified a research topic, searched research literature, or organized a research paper. As you might expect, people tend to find more challenge in a **nonroutine problem** than in a routine one.

Consider the relation between how routine a problem is and whether the problem is well or ill defined. You might imagine that as the procedures involved in solving problems become more routine, people have an easier time giving the problem some definition. Let's turn back to the psychology student writing a research paper. For the senior psychology major, four years of psychology classes have made the procedures involved in writing a research paper increasingly routine. As a result, the student has an easier time conceptualizing and proceeding with the assignment (i.e., the problem is more well defined). For our beginning student, all of the subtasks involved in writing a research paper are nonroutine. So, this student will have a more difficult time *defining the problem* (i.e., the problem is more ill-defined).

Problem-Solving Research: Some Methodological Challenges

In many ways, problem solving is the culmination of all of the processes that make up our cognitive arsenal. Completing all of your end-of-semester assignments requires perception (to take in the problem information), pattern recognition (to recognize words in the paper guidelines and on the final exams), attention and immediate memory (to hold the information in conscious awareness when necessary), language (to understand the exam items), and decision making (to decide which solution options to follow and when to follow them).

As a result of this complexity, problem solving often occurs over a much longer time interval than many of the cognitive processes previously discussed in the text (such as naming a word or remembering a string of digits). The time required to solve a problem presents a challenge to researchers. Often, participants can be presented with only one problem within a reasonable time frame (which precludes the study of many everyday problems!). Therefore, assessing problem solving in terms of accuracy rate (as is the practice in many other domains of cognitive psychology) provides a rather gross estimate of problem-solving proficiency. Measuring solution times provides some useful information but doesn't shed much light on the nature of the processing that occurs during problem solving. Take a look at the country dance problem below:

> One Saturday night at a local country dance, 40 people, 20 men and 20 women showed up to dance. The dance was a "contra dance," in which men and women face each other in lines. From 8:00 to 10:00 P.M. there were 20 heterosexual couples (consisting of one man and one woman each; i.e., two women or two men cannot dance together) dancing on the floor. At 10:00 P.M., however, 2 women left, leaving 38 people to dance. Could the dance caller make arrangements so that the remaining people could all dance together at the same time in 19 heterosexual couples? The dance caller must remain a caller only and cannot take a partner. Answer yes or no, and give the reasoning behind your answer.

This problem may take someone a few moments to solve and the solution is a yes or no answer, with a brief justification. In reality, almost everyone solves this problem (the correct answer is no), and they solve it fairly quickly. But the fact that 95% of people solve a given problem in an average of 30 seconds tells us nothing about exactly how the problem was solved.

Verbal Protocols.   In order to gain a window into the processes of problem solving, researchers have made extensive use of verbal protocols. **Verbal protocols** are reports generated by problem solvers as they "think out loud" during the solution process. Verbal protocols might be considered a close cousin of the introspective technique employed in the early days of psychology by the structuralists (discussed in Chapter 1). Recall that the structuralists attempted to gain insight into the components of conscious experience by asking people to introspect and report on a variety of perceptual experiences. Whereas structuralist introspections provided rather static descriptions of the contents of awareness for relatively short and discrete periods of time, verbal protocols attempt to give a more dynamic view of cognitive processing as it occurs over a longer span of time.

As is the case with introspective reports of any type, verbal protocols have a number of potentially serious limitations. First, not everyone has the verbal ability required to reflect accurately on what they're thinking. Second, there is no way to assess the accuracy of a verbal report; indeed, it may be that the most important processes cannot be verbalized at all. Finally, the mere act of thinking out loud may interfere with or change the very nature of the thought processes being described. In the years since introspection was reintroduced as a legitimate means of gathering data about thought processes, debate has raged over its validity. Some (e.g., Nisbett & Wilson, 1977) argue that the interpretational difficulties associated with verbal protocols render them essentially useless as a means of analyzing higher thought processes. Others (e.g., Ericsson & Simon, 1980, 1984) have demonstrated that in most cases, verbalizing cognitive processing has a minimal influence on performance and for some (e.g., Locke, 2009) a return to the use of introspective techniques is long overdue. In spite of their potential problems, verbal protocols have proved valuable to problem-solving researchers, and no doubt their use will continue.

Stop&*Think* | THINKING OUT LOUD

Pick out some everyday problem (like choosing the courses you have to take next semester, or planning a birthday party), and spend about 15 minutes solving it. Here's the catch: Think out loud while you're doing it.

1. Collect your own verbal protocol.

2. Observe the sorts of processes your mind seems to go through as you're "talking it out."

3. Reflect on your own protocol and how it demonstrates problem-solving principles.

The Varied Nature of Problems.   The complexity of problem solving presents another challenge to researchers. The term *problem* can apply to a breathtakingly diverse set of circumstances, from solving math problems to writing a term paper, to figuring out an alternative route home during rush-hour traffic. Getting problem solving into the cognitive psychology laboratory can be a challenging task indeed. In most studies, researchers use fairly short, discrete, circumscribed sorts of problems—much like the brainteasers and puzzles you

1. Tower of Hanoi Problem

   The rings must be rearranged so that the pyramid on the far left peg ends up on the far right peg. The following constraints must be observed:

   A larger ring can never be above a smaller one.

   Only one ring can be moved at a time.

2. "KIGVIN"

   Rearrange the letters to form another word.

3. Think of as many uses for a brick as you can.

4. "All professors are caring people" and "All caring people are good"; would you accept the conclusion that "All professors are good"?

5. Take a look at the following number sequence:

   8, 5, 4, 1, 7, 6, 10, 0

   What is the next number in the sequence?

1. Transformation 2. Arrangement 3. Divergent 4. Deduction 5. Induction

Figure 12.1

Some sample problems from studies of problem solving. Can you identify each type?

see in newspapers, magazines, and puzzle books. This makes the investigation of problem solving more tractable. It is assumed that the basic processes used for these sorts of problems are the same ones we employ when we face complex problems like planning a wedding.

Mayer (1992) provides some order to the diversity by distinguishing between five sorts of problems. **Transformation problems** present the solver with a goal state; the solver must find the proper strategies, or "moves," that will eventually transform the initial state into the goal state. **Arrangement problems** involve presentation of all the necessary elements to solve the problem; the solver must figure out how the elements are to be arranged. In *induction problems,* the solver is given a series of examples and must figure out the pattern or rule that relates them. In **deduction problems,** premises or conditions are given, and the solver must determine whether a conclusion fits these premises. Actually, deduction and induction are forms of everyday reasoning and were discussed in Chapter 11. Finally, **divergent problems** require the solver to generate as many solutions as possible to a given problem. It's important to note that many of the complex problems we face every day are actually sets of problems that may involve aspects of any or all of these five problem types. Now that you have read about each of these problem types, examine the problems presented in Figure 12.1. Try to determine the type of problem that each represents.

Stop&*Think Back* | PROBLEM SOLVING FROM THE BOTTOM, UP AND TOP, DOWN

Reflect on the types of problems we present throughout the first part of the chapter, and how solving might involve both the processing of data, as well as your own knowledge and expectations. Take the sample problems and explicitly list the bottom-up information and the top-down factors (discussed in Chapter 2) that allow for solution. Which type of information seems more important to solving the problem. When you encounter difficulties in solving these problems, do you think it's more related to bottom-up processing or top-down processing?

Stop&*Review*

1. Name the main components of a problem.
2. List two differences between an ill-defined problem and a well-defined problem.
3. What are verbal protocols, and why are they employed in problem-solving research?
4. Identify and define the five types of problems.

- A problem consists of an initial state (the situation at the beginning of the problem), a goal state (the solution to the problem), a set of rules (or constraints) to follow, and a set of obstacles that must be overcome.

- Problems range from well defined (clear and structured, solution easily assessed) to ill defined (fuzzy and abstract, solution not easily assessed). Problems also vary along a continuum from routine (involving well-practiced procedures) to nonroutine (involving less familiar procedures).

- Revealing the nature of problem-solving processes presents a methodological challenge to researchers due to the time and complexity involved. Reaction time and accuracy are limited in the information they provide about problem solving. Therefore, problem-solving researchers often use verbal protocols—verbal reports generated by problem solvers during the solution process.

- Problem types include transformation (solver must transform the initial state into the goal), arrangement (solver must figure out how the presented problem elements are to be arranged), induction (solver must figure out the rule that relates the presented examples), deduction (premises given and solver must determine if a conclusion follows), and divergent (solver generates as many solutions to a given problem as possible).

Approaches to the Study of Problem Solving

The study of problem solving has a surprisingly rich and varied history. Believe it or not, some of the earliest work on problem solving was conducted with a veritable menagerie of animal subjects, including rats, cats, monkeys, and those titans of cognition, goldfish (Dewsbury, 2000). In many ways, the evolution of problem-solving research mirrors the evolution of cognitive psychology in general, as outlined in Chapter 1. The key players in the debate over the processes underlying problem solving have been behaviorists, Gestalt psychologists, and cognitive psychologists.

Behaviorism: Problem Solving as Associative Learning

One of the first systematic studies of problem solving was conducted by E. L. Thorndike in the late 1800s. Thorndike was interested in the basic processes involved in learning. His participants were cats, which he placed in a predicament that cats most definitely do not enjoy. He put cats in what he termed "puzzle boxes," that were basically homemade enclosures. This posed a problem for his feline subjects because (as anyone who has taken a yowling cat to the vet can attest) cats hate being confined. Phrased in terms of the problem components, the initial state was being confined; the goal state was to be outside of the confining enclosure. The constraint was basically the enclosure itself and the fact that its construction prevented escape. Thorndike was interested in whether the ability to solve this confinement problem would appear through some sort of sudden "insight," or gradually through a process of trial and error.

Take a look at Figure 12.2, which shows the puzzle box along with the solution times for a sample cat, graphed over a series of trials. The cats basically learned through trial and error. When first placed in the box, the cats behaved more or less randomly—meowing, scratching, and pawing in a vain attempt to escape their predicament. But as you can see in the figure, over the course of many trials, they eventually figured out how to escape, finally learning the response well enough to quickly escape whenever placed in the situation.

Thorndike described this learning process with what he termed the **law of effect**. According to the law of effect, if a response leads to a satisfying outcome, the connection between the response and the situation in which it took place (in this case, the puzzle box) will be strengthened. If a response leads to a nonsatisfying outcome, this connection will be weakened. Over the course of many experiences in the box, consider what happens: Ineffective responses like crying and scratching will weaken and disappear, while more effective responses that get the cat closer to escape will increase. So eventually, the cat will engage only in those effective responses and quickly exit the box. Behaviorists believe that, contrary to what you might think intuitively, problem solving is essentially a "mindless" process whereby learned responses automatically play themselves out. As you might recall from Chapter 1, this stimulus-response account was preferred by behaviorists for all varieties of behavior, not just problem solving.

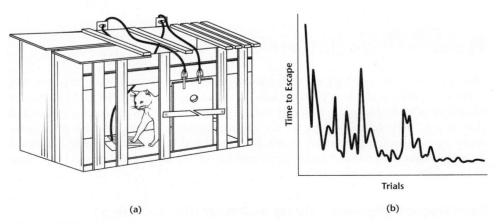

(a)   (b)

Figure 12.2
A rendition of Thorndike's puzzle box and idealized response data showing trial-and-error learning.

Gestalt Psychology: Problem Solving as Insight

Gestalt psychologists have a radically different (and decidedly more cognitive) view of problem solving. Recall from Chapter 1 the basic tenets of the Gestalt approach: the mind has an inherent tendency to organize incoming information, and these organizational processes are the defining feature of cognition. So, rather than a mindless playing out of associations that gradually build up over time, problem solving involves a restructuring or reorganization of problem elements that results in a sudden realization of the solution.

A little help, please? There's no banana in sight.

Consider the work of the pioneering Gestalt psychologist Wolfgang Kohler, who conducted extensive investigations of problem solving in apes (Kohler, 1925). In one task, an ape was put in a pen with some crates, and something desirable (like a banana) was suspended from the ceiling, just out of reach. The solution to this problem was to drag the crates over and use them as steps to reach the banana. What interested Kohler was the manner in which apes seemed to be solving this problem (and other ones like it). Contrary to the gradual trial-and-error process observed by Thorndike, Kohler noticed that apes sat for a while as if they were pondering the problem; then all of a sudden they would jump up, push the crates to the appropriate spot, stack them, and fetch their treat. What led to this sudden solution? For Gestalt psychologists, problem solving involves a process of restructuring whereby problem elements are suddenly reorganized and seen in a new way. The sudden and successful restructuring of problem elements is termed **insight,** and this is a major focus of the Gestalt approach.

Contrasting the Behaviorist and Gestalt Views.   The Gestalt approach characterizes problem solving as a process of apprehending relationships between problem elements, and failures in problem solving as failures to correctly or completely encode these relationships. This view contrasts sharply with the behaviorist characterization of problem solving as the mindless execution of a well-learned response. A behaviorist would have explained the apes' behavior as a series of simple responses learned through association. Over the course of many experiences in acquiring food that was difficult to attain, the apes formed a dominant response of stacking and standing on objects in order to do so, much as Thorndike's cats learned appropriate escape responses after many trials of confinement.

Both the behaviorist and the Gestalt approaches to problem solving are compelling in some ways but deficient in others. The appeal of the behaviorist approach is its precision and simplicity. Many seemingly complex behaviors can be characterized as sets of simple responses that are based on a straightforward association mechanism. But as discussed in Chapter 1, the behaviorists are limited in what they can explain via a simple stimulus-response (S-R) association mechanism. This analysis seems to apply fairly well to the behavior of Thorndike's cats but fails to explain more novel and creative behavior. The Gestalt approach has the converse set of strengths and limitations. To its credit, it attempts to explain novel and creative behavior in terms of mental representations, but to its detriment, it is imprecise and vague. Gestalt psychologists have never provided really satisfactory (i.e., testable) definitions for concepts like "insight" and "restructuring of problem elements." The notion of insight was (and still is, to some researchers) problematic in that it's circularly defined. Insight is said to have occurred when a person suddenly arrives at a solution that had previously been difficult to reach. But when asked for an explanation of how the problem was solved, the explanation is...insight. You can't use insight as both the phenomenon to be explained *and* as the explanation.

Let's finish our evaluation of these two approaches by applying them to your end-of-semester problem. You have to fit writing research papers and studying for several final exams into the space of two weeks. It's hard to imagine your solution to this problem as the triggering of a series of associations that have been built up through experience. Behavior in this situation is much too complex and unpredictable to be adequately explained in such simple terms. But it's also hard to imagine that you're going to sit in your room and then all of a sudden, in a burst of insight, exclaim, "I know exactly how to successfully write these papers and ace these exams!" A view with the precision of behaviorism but also some room for the novel and creative problem-solving demanded by everyday situations seems necessary. The stage was set for the cognitive psychologist to take the best of each approach and integrate them within the emerging information-processing paradigm, which emerged in the 1950's as the dominant paradigm for exploring problem solving.

Cognitive Psychology: Problem Solving as Information Processing

You'll recall from Chapter 1 that one of the major factors in the emergence of cognitive psychology was the development of the computer, which served notice that intelligent behavior (of a sort) was not the exclusive province of human beings. Early cognitive psychologists (e.g., Newell, Shaw, & Simon, 1958) felt that computer programs might serve as useful tools for modeling human problem solving. Just as a computer solves problems by executing programs that use information stored in some type of database, humans solve problems by applying mental processes to representations in memory. So, if you design a computer program that can solve a reasoning problem, you've essentially proposed a possible theory for how humans do the same.

The General Problem Solver. Newell and Simon (1972) originated the conceptualization of problem solving as a step-by-step progression from an initial state to a goal state. They did so within the framework of a computer program termed the **General Problem Solver (GPS),** which they proposed as a general model of human problem solving—one that can be applied to any problem. Basically, the GPS approach to problem solving attempts to minimize the "distance" between an initial state and a goal state by breaking the problem down into a series of subgoals. This **subgoal analysis** is accomplished through the application of **operators,** which is basically a fancy word for problem-solving techniques. These techniques are applied (at a microlevel) to reduce the difference between the current state and the current subgoal state and (at a macrolevel) to reduce the difference between the initial state and the final goal state. Consider the following sets of subgoals (with nested set of subgoals in parentheses) for your end-of-semester problem.

Subgoal 1

Study for cognitive psych exam (read the book, outline notes, meet with study group)

Subgoal 2

Study for physics exam (read the book, meet with prof to discuss unclear points, highlight important passages in reading)

Subgoal 3

Finalize paper topic for psychology (check with prof about topic, go to library, see if there are enough relevant resources)

Another important aspect of GPS is the notion of problem space. **Problem space** refers to the problem solver's mental representation of the initial state, the final goal state, all possible intermediate (subgoal) states, and the operators that can be applied to reach each subgoal and the final goal state. Hence, the problem-solving process is essentially an excursion through problem space. Note the features that define GPS as an information-processing model. First, information in the external world (e.g., the problem information) is transformed into an internal (mental) representation. Then, in a sequential fashion, various mental operations are applied to this representation to transform it into other representations that are closer and closer to the goal state. This general information-processing framework has served as the model for modern problem-solving research. Given this, it should come as no surprise that problem solving is usually characterized as a step-like progression through a series of stages.

Stop&*Review*

1. To which of these concepts would a behaviorist NOT make reference when explaining problem solving?
   a. responses
   b. behavior
   c. insight
   d. learning
2. True or false? Insight involves the restructuring of problem elements.
3. Describe the basic idea behind the General Problem Solver.

- Behaviorists viewed problem solving as a learning process that can be described in terms of the law of effect. Problem solving is viewed as the formation of increasingly complex chains of stimulus-response connections.

- The Gestalt psychologists viewed problem solving as a process whereby the elements of a problem must be restructured. Often, problem restructuring results in a sudden insight regarding problem solution.

- The information-processing approach views problem solving as a stage-like progression from starting state to goal state. One of the first attempts to model this process was within the framework of a computer program termed *General Problem Solver*. GPS models view problem solving as successive reductions in "distance" between an initial state and a goal state by breaking a problem into a series of subgoals (subgoal analysis).

Problem Representation

As stated, problem solving involves a process of converting presented information into some type of internal mental representation. Within the framework of GPS, **problem representation** involves correctly specifying the problem space—in other words, correctly identifying the initial state as well as the operators that may be applied within the constraints of the problem. The process of problem representation may seem automatic or trivial in some respects, but it is a critical component of successful problem solving. And the ways in which problems can be represented are as varied as problems themselves.

Let's look at a few examples. As you read each one, try to solve it, taking note of the particular manner in which you represent the problem.

1. Once there was a monk who lived in a monastery at the foot of a mountain. Every year, the monk made a pilgrimage to the top of the mountain to fast and pray. He would start out on the mountain path at 6 a.m., climbing and resting as the spirit struck him, but making sure that he reached the shrine at exactly 6 p.m. that evening. He then prayed and fasted all night. At exactly 6 a.m. the next day, he began to descend the mountain path, resting here and there along the way, but making sure that he reached his monastery by 6 p.m. of that day. Prove that there must be a spot along the path that the monk will pass at exactly the same time on the two days.

2. A man bought a white horse for $60 and then sold it for $70. Then he bought it back for $80 and sold it for $90. What was his net gain (or net loss) in the horse business?

Clearly, these two problems would lead the problem solver to form different problem representations. The problem about the monk (based on Duncker, 1945) leads the problem solver to form a visual representation of the monk ascending and descending the mountain. The horse-trading problem leads the problem solver to form an arithmetic representation, given that the solver must add and subtract the appropriate numbers to come up with a solution.

Not only will these problems lead to different representations, but the ability to solve the problems depends critically on the exact nature of the representation. Take the monk problem: one possible representation is to form two separate visualizations—one of the monk ascending and another of him descending. A much more effective representation is to imagine these two excursions superimposed; it immediately becomes apparent that there must be a point of intersection. This point would be the critical spot in the path (see Figure 12.3).

Figure 12.3
The monk problem proves to be much more manageable when represented appropriately. Visualization makes it apparent that the ascent up the mountain and the descent down the mountain must intersect at some point.

The horse-trading problem was used in a study by Maier and Burke (1967), who found that less than 40% of participants could successfully solve it. Did you? The answer is $20. The key to an easy solution, once again, is problem representation. Consider this similar problem:

A man bought a white horse for $60 and then sold it for $70. Then he bought a black horse for $80 and sold it for $90. What was his net gain (or net loss) in the horse business?

This problem seems similar to problem 2 above. But it's not just similar; it's pretty much identical. When presented this way, as two separate transactions involving different horses instead of a continuous pair of transactions involving the same horse, everyone gets the solution. Clearly, the manner in which the problem solver mentally "sets up" the problem has powerful implications for whether it is solved.

Rigidity in Problem Representation

The initial representation of a problem is critical to its eventual solution. Failure in representation might result from a number of factors: the problem elements may not have received sufficient attention; the problem elements may not have been understood; or previous experience with similar problems may have led to encoding the problem elements in a rigid manner. Let's consider the following induction problem previously presented in Figure 12.1 (p. 496).

Take a look again at the number sequence from that figure: 8, 5, 4, 1, 7, 6, 10, 0. Now, attempt to figure out the rule that generated the sequence. This challenging problem is not what it seems to be. In an attempt to identify some pattern in these differences, you no doubt attempted to calculate the difference between each consecutive pair of numbers in this way: "Let's see, 8 and 5 differ by 3, 5 and 4 differ by 1, 4 and 1 differ by 3...." If you followed this line of reasoning, you could add and subtract all day and still not come up with the correct solution. The key to the problem lies in viewing the numbers as words rather than as numerical values. Does this hint help? The numbers in the sequence are arranged alphabetically. However, given that in your experience, most number sequences are arranged numerically, not alphabetically, you no doubt struggled quite a bit with this problem.

Mental Set. This tendency to rely on habits and procedures used in the past is termed **mental set.** A mental set can interfere with your ability to solve everyday problems. An anecdote from our life provides an (embarrassing for Bridget) example of mental set. We drove to a restaurant for dinner, and Bridget was delayed in exiting the car because she was looking for something in her purse. Greg, unaware of this, locked the door with the remote lock

Is there another way to unlock the car door and my mental set?

control. After finding what she needed, Bridget attempted to unlock the car with the automatic lock button in the car, but for some reason it didn't work. So she sat there, unable to figure out how to get out of the car. After letting her wait long enough to maximize his own amusement, Greg pointed to the lock and motioned for her to lift it. Bridget had used the automatic locking control so regularly that it was the only option in her mind at that moment—reflecting her mental set.

Mental set tends to affect the representation phase of problem solving, as past experience leads to an inappropriate representation of the problem. For Bridget, her past experience with the car led her to represent the problem of unlocking the car in only one way (with the automatic lock control). In the number sequence problem, your tendency to view digits numerically instead of in terms of verbal labels most likely prevented you from solving the problem. Consider if the problem had been presented in this way: eight, five, four, one, seven, six, ten, zero. Chances are, the correct solution would have come to you more easily. People seem to make unnecessary assumptions or follow habits acquired through past experience that impede the problem-solving process.

Functional Fixedness.   A close cousin of mental set is termed **functional fixedness** which refers to people's tendency to view objects in a narrow, fixed sense—that is, in terms of the typical functions of the object. We witnessed a clever and practical example of overcoming functional fixedness to solve an important and vexing problem often experienced at the movies: never having butter on the popcorn at the bottom the bucket! In many Minneapolis theaters, you put your own butter on your popcorn via a dispenser. What a great idea; you can put as much or as little on as you want! But all the butter ends up on top, which presents a seemingly insoluble problem. One possible solution is to ask for an empty bucket and putting half the popcorn in each bucket and buttering each half. This seemed cumbersome and annoying (and likely to create a problem for the concessionaire!). Then we saw a clever problem solver take a straw and attach it to the butter spigot. Then she put the popcorn bucket under the spigot so that straw was inserted deep into the popcorn bucket, and turned on the butter dispenser; butter flowed through the straw and into the middle of the popcorn Problem solved! (It really does work.) This solution is also a good example of creativity, which we will discuss later in the chapter.

The previous example is anecdotal, and it seems that functional fixedness might be a difficult thing to investigate in a controlled fashion. So, how has functional fixedness been investigated in the lab? Consider one of the classics of problem-solving research—Duncker's candle problem (see Figure 12.4). In this classic experiment, Duncker presented participants with a number of objects, including the following critical materials: matches, tacks, boxes, and candles. The problem was to attach the candles to the wall and light them.

In order to influence the solvers' problem representations, Duncker presented the materials in one of three conditions (see Figure 12.4). In the functional fixedness condition, the boxes were each filled with one of the three critical materials: candles, matches, and tacks. In the first control condition, the boxes sat empty, alongside the other materials. In a second control condition, the boxes contained materials not critical to the solution, like buttons. The correct solution is to tack the boxes to the wall and use them as candleholders, placing a

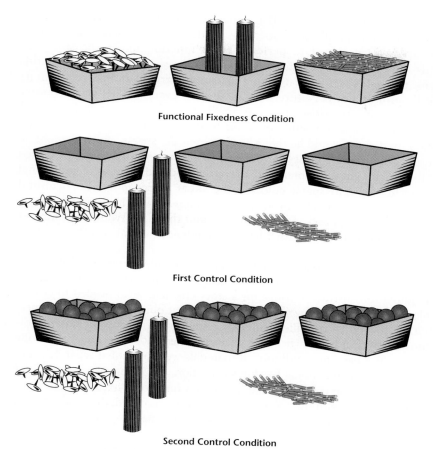

Figure 12.4
Three conditions of
Duncker's candle problem.

Adapted from Duncker, K. (1945).
On problem solving. *Psychological
Monographs, 58,* 1–112.
Copyright 1945 by the American
Psychological Association.

Functional Fixedness Condition

First Control Condition

Second Control Condition

candle in each box, which can then be safely lit. The key to solving this problem is to view the boxes as boxes, not as boxes of matches, tacks, or candles. Note that this is an issue of problem representation. In the first control condition, all of the participants successfully solved the problem. But in the functional fixedness and second control conditions (in which the boxes were narrowly perceived as containers for the objects they were holding), less than one-third of the participants successfully solved the problem.

Stop&*Think* | MENTAL RUTS

Try and think of times when you were absolutely stuck on some type of problem.

1. Describe the circumstances.

2. Note how you were able to overcome whatever obstacle(s) blocked your way.

3. Classify your examples as (a) mental set or (b) functional fixedness.

German and Barrett (2005) note that functional fixedness has typically been demonstrated in technologically sophisticated cultures that have seemingly endless numbers of "artifacts" designed to perform every function under the sun—can openers, bottle stoppers, lint rollers, fondue forks, olive trays, cat litter scoops, . . . this could go on for pages. It could be that having such a (as German and Barrett term it) "technologically promiscuous" culture leads us to view every artifact we encounter in terms of a narrowly prescribed function, making us more prone to functional fixedness (seriously, what else would you *want* to use a cat litter scoop for?). The complementary prediction would be that a "technologically sparse" culture might be more able to discern alternative uses for objects, given that culture's less proscribed technology. To test this idea, German and Barrett conducted a study of functional fixedness in a technologically sparse culture—the Shuar of Ecuador, a horticultural and hunting society with relatively few artifacts; the ones they do have are fairly simple and nonspecialized (e.g., axes, pots, fishhooks, and the like). Would this simpler approach to objects be associated with a lessened tendency to fixate on the function of an object?

The task presented by the researchers involved using provided props to solve a problem posed by a simple story. Participants (adolescent and young adults from Shuar villages) were required to construct a bridge for a story character who needed to cross a river. The objects they were given were a spoon (the target object, and the only object long enough to do the job), a cup filled with rice, a smaller plastic cup, an eraser, a lollipop stick, and a small clear ball. Participants were presented with these materials in one of two conditions. In a baseline condition, all materials were presented separately and next to one another. In the functional fixedness condition, the spoon was in the cup of rice. This latter condition was considered the "prime" for functional fixedness. The solution was to bridge the river with the spoon. Two times were recorded: the time it took a participant to select the spoon, and the time it took a participant to use it to solve the problem successfully.

The results indicated that the Shuar, just like their technologically promiscuous counterparts in more modernized cultures, were susceptible to functional fixedness. In the functional fixedness condition, it took participants much longer to (a) select and (b) use the spoon as the solution (33 and 45 seconds, respectively), relative to the baseline condition (25 and 20 seconds, respectively). Priming the function of the spoon made it more difficult for participants to use the spoon in an atypical manner. German and Barrett surmise that even in a technologically sparse culture, representations of concepts (e.g., spoons) in semantic memory must have design information—what the object is intended for—as a core property.

It's important to note that thinking of things in the same old way is not always a bad thing. As noted by Bransford and Stein (1993), most situations in life require that we think conventionally as opposed to nonconventionally. Conventional, everyday thinking (because it tends to rely on processes that have become automatic, as discussed in Chapter 3) tends to be quick and require little conscious effort, allowing us to do other things at the same time. The best-case scenario for effective problem solving may be to balance conventional and nonconventional thinking, sticking with the basics unless the circumstances demand a more creative solution.

Individual Differences in Problem Representation

Reality Check

G – R – E Do those three letters, said in that order, make the hair on the back of your neck stand up? If you're on the grad school track, it's quite possible that they do. One reason for this is the quantitative portion of the exam, which has long been the bain of existence for aspiring graduate students. Evidence reveals some consistent differences between women and men on the quantitative portion of the GRE, with women scoring, on average, any where from 70 to 100 points lower than men (ETS, 2009). While much has been written about what might underlie these differences, we're going to limit our discussion to a couple of factors that relate to the topic at hand—problem representation.

A good deal of social psychological research over the past couple of decades has pointed to the power of stereotypes to drive cognitive performance, largely in a negative way. Take the stereotype that women aren't as good as men are at math. This might be the underlying reason for the difference we just mentioned, right? Well, no...sex differences in math are infinitely more complex than that simple statement implies; indeed, depending on what you mean by "mathematical abilities," that statement is flat-out wrong. Not only that, even when sex differences are found on math-related tasks, one of the factors that leads to them might be the anxiety created by the stereotype! **Stereotype threat** occurs when a member of a negatively stereotyped group feels that the stereotype might be used to judge their behavior, thus resulting in a negative judgment that will propagate the stereotype. The anxiety caused by this feeling undermines performance.

To assess the possible influence of stereotype threat on math performance, Quinn and Spencer (2001) had men and women solve either math word problems or numeric/algebraic equivalents of the word problems. Sample problems of each type are given in Table 12.1 (a). The mathematical knowledge necessary to solve these problems was equivalent in both conditions; however, the word problem condition required participants to transform the problem into its proper mathematical *representation*. In this condition, Quinn and Spencer (2001) believed stereotype threat would have its effect. Stereotype threat produces anxiety, which in turn undermines the ability to accurately represent the

Table 12.1 **Results from Quinn and Spencer (2001)**

(a) Solution Rates for Word Problems and Numeric Equivalents

	Women	Men
A sporting goods store sold 64 Frisbees in one week, some for $3.00 and the rest for $4.00 each. If receipts from Frisbee sales for the week totaled $204, what is the fewest number of $4.00 Frisbees that could have been sold?	.08	.20
$3(64 - x) + 4(x) = 204 \qquad x = ?$ (a) 24 (b) 12 (c) 8 (d) 4 (e) 2	.38	.40

(b) Solution Rate and Failure Rate as a Function of Stereotype Threat

	SOLUTION %		FAILURE %	
	High Stereotype Threat	**Low Stereotype Threat**	**High Stereotype Threat**	**Low Stereotype Threat**
Women	26	39	14	4
Men	45	34	2	9

problem. The results are presented in Table 12.1 (a). Men outperformed women on word problems only; on the more straightforward numeric/algebraic problems, men and women did not differ. Apparently, women had the mathematical ability to solve the problem but, ostensibly due to stereotype threat, ran into interference in conditions that required an involved stage of problem representation.

In order to test this assumption, the authors manipulated the level of stereotype threat in the situation. Participants in a low-stereotype-threat condition were told that the test had been shown previously to be gender fair, yielding equivalent performance between men and women. Participants in the high-threat conditions were not given this information. The results are presented in Table 12.1 (b). In the high-stereotype-threat condition, men outperformed women; in the low-stereotype-threat condition, there were no sex-related differences.

To bolster their assertion that stereotype threat led to difficulties in problem representation, participants in the second experiment were recorded while solving the problems. (Remember the verbal protocol procedure we discussed earlier?) The number of problems in which participants could not determine a strategy (i.e., proper problem representation) to solve the problem (i.e., a "failure rate") was assessed. Look one more time at Table 12.1 (b). In the high-stereotype-threat condition, women had higher failure rates than men. In the low-threat condition, these failure rates were equivalent. It appears that when stereotype threat is reduced, women perform equally as well as men, quite possibly because an obstacle to successful problem representation was removed. Complementary evidence (Schmader & Johns, 2003 Schmader, 2010) indicates that the effect of stereotype threat on problem solving may be rooted in executive control, as discussed in Chapter 4; the priming of a stereotype leads to resource-demanding processing that interferes with finding a problem representation, and ultimately, problem solution.

Stereotype Threat Meets Mental Set.   Earlier, we made the point that mental set isn't always a bad thing; as a matter of fact, it's often advantageous to approach problems in a well-learned and customary way. It turns out that stereotype threat isn't always a bad thing, either! Jamieson and Harkins (2009) investigated what they term the *mere effort* account of stereotype threat. According to this account, stereotype threat can be negative or positive depending on the problem solving strategy the solver brings to the situation; the authors call this the prepotent response. Stereotype threat motivates a person to perform well in order to avoid perpetuating the negative stereotype. This leads to stronger reliance on the prepotent response than when not under stereotype threat. This is only a problem if the prepotent response is wrong (i.e., will not lead to the correct problem solution). If the prepotent response is correct, then performance will be enhanced. To test their hypothesis, they needed to compare items associated with different prepotent responses. So they went to our friend, the quantitative portion of the GRE. The test presents two types of problems: *solve* problems and *compare* problems. *Solve* problems are those that can be figured out with a conventional application of an equation or formula. *Comparison* problems require that a test-taker use logic and estimation to arrive at the solution. See Table 12.2 for an example of each type of problem. Previous research on how people solve math problems (e.g., Gallagher, De Lisi, Holst, McGillicuddy-De Lisi, Morely, & Cahalan, 2000) strongly suggests that people's prepotent response to solving

Table 12.2 Sample *Solve* and *Comparison* Problems and Results from Jamieson & Harkins's (2009) Study of Stereotype Threat; Number of Problems Solved Correctly in Each Condition

Solve Type

If the total surface area of a cube is 24, what is the volume of the cube?

a. 8   b. 24   c. 64   d. $48\sqrt{6}$ e. 216

Comparison Type

$n = (7)(19^3)$

Column A	Column B
The number of distinct positive factors of n	10
a. Column A is greater	b. Column B is greater
c. quantities are equal	d. can't be determined

	Stereotype Threat	No Stereotype Threat
Men	4.64	4.88
Women	5.22	4.26

	Stereotype Threat	No Stereotype Threat
Men	4.94	4.84
Women	2.17	4.69

any type of math problem is to apply an equation. For the solve problem this response is correct, but for the comparison problem, it's an inappropriate strategy.

Have you thought of the connection to mental set implied by the title of this section? Prepotent responses are basically mental sets. So what Jamieson and Harkins are saying is that when people experience stereotype threat, it reinforces the use of a mental set, which if appropriate for the circumstances should aid in performance. So in their study, they presented women with both *solve* and *comparison* GRE math problems, under conditions of stereotype threat (in which participants were informed that the math test was associated with gender differences) or no stereotype threat (participants were informed that the test yielded no gender differences). The investigators predicted that stereotype threat would improve performance for the solve problems, where the mental set of calculation and applying formulas is appropriate, However, when that mental set is inappropriate (i.e., for comparison problems), stereotype threat should disrupt performance. The results are presented in Table 12.2, and support the researchers' hypothesis. As predicted, stereotype threat aided performance in cases where their mental set (i.e., their prepotent response) was the appropriate one.

There also are other circumstances in which stereotypes lead to advantages in performance. For example, consider the case of a positive stereotype, such as the one that characterizes Asians as more accomplished math problem solvers than their Western counterparts; might this stereotype enhance Asians' performance on math tasks? Evidence would indicate that this indeed is the case. Asian-Americans who are primed by the math stereotype do better than those who are unprimed (Shih, Ambady, Richeson, Fujita, & Gray, 2002). And it's not just a difference in cultural sensitivity to stereotypes in general. Shih, Pittinsky, and Trahan (2006) tested Asian-American women on verbal tasks (a situation in which the stereotype is negative), and showed that priming a negative stereotype about verbal skills had detrimental effects on performance. So it would seem that the specific impact of stereotypes on cognition (adaptive or maladaptive) depends on the particular task as well as on the stereotypes.

Stop&*Review*

1. What processes are involved in problem representation?
2. Define (a) mental set and (b) functional fixedness.

- Cognitive psychologists have explored the various stages of the problem-solving process. Problem representation involves correctly identifying the initial state as well as the operators that may be applied within the constraints of the problem. The initial problem representation is critical to the eventual solution to a problem. Failure to represent a problem correctly is likely to hinder finding a solution.

- Rigidity in the representation phase can be seen in cases of mental set (the tendency to rely on habits and procedures used in the past) and functional fixedness (the tendency to view objects in terms of their typical functions). Problem representation can also be hindered by stereotype threat (which occurs when a member of a negatively stereotyped group feels that the stereotype will be used to judge their behavior). Stereotype threat can be mitigated by relying on a mental set (if the mental set is a procedure that could lead to a successful solution).

Problem Solution

Once a problem has been successfully transformed from externally presented information into an internal representation, the next phase of the problem-solving process involves searching for, testing, and evaluating problem solutions. Within the context of Newell and Simon's (1972) information-processing approach, problem solution amounts to traveling through the problem space. Two general approaches to this excursion are through algorithms and through heuristics; each approach has different implications for exactly how the problem space is traversed.

Algorithms

An **algorithm** is basically a set of rules that can be applied systematically to solve certain types of problems. A mathematical formula is a good example of an algorithm. Suppose I were to tell you that the two shorter sides of a right triangle had lengths of 3 inches and 4 inches. You could easily apply a well-known algorithm (the Pythagorean theorem) to calculate the length of the hypotenuse (5 inches). Algorithms are very powerful problem-solving techniques; applied correctly, an algorithm will always lead to the correct solution, if one exists. But it's not a perfect world; algorithms are seldom if ever used to solve problems on a day-to-day basis.

For human problem solvers, algorithms are often unfeasible, for a couple of reasons. The Pythagorean theorem is easy enough to apply, but consider a more difficult problem. Suppose someone asked you to solve the word anagram *kigvin* (an arrangement problem previously presented in Figure 12.1 on page 496). You could solve this problem algorithmically by systematically working through every possible letter combination, but you would have to consider hundreds of possibilities. Think of it in terms of problem space; obviously, hundreds of possible sequences comprise this extremely large problem space. The exhaustive nature of algorithms makes them overly tedious and quite impractical, at least for humans. On the other hand, computers are well suited to algorithmic problem solving because they are well suited for what algorithms require: speed, power, and reliable application. A second factor that limits the usefulness of algorithms is that algorithms don't exist for most of the problems we face on a daily basis. Alas, life is not a right triangle. There is no algorithm for deciding on a major or a career, for figuring out how to complete two papers and study for three finals over the space of two weeks, or for deciding how to be happy in life. These very complex and ill-defined problems demand a more flexible, dynamic approach.

Heuristics

Given the strengths (flexibility) and limitations (computing power) of the human problem solver, along with the fact that most problems are ill defined and have relatively large problem spaces, heuristic problem solving is much more effective. **Heuristics** are general strategies, or rules of thumb, that can be applied to various problems. Heuristics serve as "shortcuts" through problem space. Take another look at the anagram *kigvin*. Immediately, you reject certain possibilities because of your morphological knowledge of the English language (discussed in Chapter 9). For example, no English words start with *gk* or *vg* or *ikn,* so these would not be explicitly considered. While the algorithmic approach entails the consideration of every possible solution, the strength of the heuristic approach is that the trip through problem space is faster; the solutions come more quickly. But unlike algorithms, heuristics do not guarantee a correct solution. (By the way, the solution is *viking.*)

Specific heuristics exist for specific problem domains. One of our favorite card games is euchre, the object of which is to win tricks by playing high cards or trump cards. When dealt a hand in euchre (or any card game, for that matter), you certainly can't consider every possible play of the cards in preparation for your bid (although it seems like some people do!). Instead, you do a quick heuristic evaluation of your hand. If you have at least two cards that are pretty certain to win a trick, then a bid is a good risk. In addition to situation-specific heuristics, a number of general-purpose heuristics exist that can be applied to a wide array of problems.

Quick heuristic solution to this Euchre problem: BID!!

Stop&*Think* | YOUR OWN HEURISTICS

Consider the personal problem solving you do every day.

- Are there any everyday problems for which you use algorithms?
- What types of problems do these tend to be?

You no doubt use heuristics a great deal.

1. Generate a list of strategies, or shortcuts, you use to solve everyday problems.
2. List the heuristics you use in your favorite game or sport to make it more likely you'll succeed.

Means-End Analysis.   The General Problem Solver developed by Newell and Simon utilizes the heuristic known as means-end analysis. **Means-end analysis** involves breaking a problem into smaller subgoals in which accomplishing each subgoal moves the solver closer to the final goal—the problem's solution. As the term means-end analysis implies, the solver systematically attempts to devise means to get to each of the subgoal's ends. Means-end analysis can be an effective way to solve a transformation problem, which involves moving from the initial state to the goal state through a series of transformations. For example, your problem of writing some papers and studying for several final exams isn't going to be solved overnight. It's going to be manageable only if you break it up into a series of subgoals and systematically accomplish each. As you do, you will slowly but surely reach your goal.

Analogies.   Before you read on, take a look at the following problem (termed the mutilated checkerboard problem) and try to come up with a solution.

> You are given a checkerboard and 32 dominoes. Each domino covers adjacent squares on the board. Thus, 32 dominoes can cover all 64 squares of the checkerboard. Now suppose two squares are cut off at diagonally opposite corners of the board. If possible, show how you would place 31 dominoes on the board so that all 62 of the remaining squares are covered. If you think it is impossible, give a proof of why.

Can you solve it? Chances are, you didn't; this is a fairly difficult problem. Did the problem ring any bells? Remind you of anything else you've read recently? It turns out that this problem is analogous to the country dance problem discussed earlier and presented near the beginning of the chapter. As in that problem, the key to the solution lies in realizing that it is going to be impossible to pair off each of the black-and-white combinations of the checkerboard if two squares of the same color are removed, just as it is impossible to form man-woman dance partnerings if there is not an equal number of men and women.

The connection between these problems is an example of an analogous relationship. The use of **analogies**—problems that have already been solved as aids for representing and solving a current problem—is potentially one of the most powerful heuristics. Have you ever said, "Hey, this is just like the time when...."? If so, you've been thinking in terms of an analogy. The use of analogies in problem solving has been investigated extensively by problem-solving researchers (much more than any of the other heuristics), and the news isn't too good. Research indicates that problem solvers are unlikely to use analogies to aid in problem solving unless the problem solvers are practically "hit over the head" with the connections between problems. This is why you may not have realized the connection between the mutilated checkerboard and country dance problems. But, as you'll see, there are conditions that encourage the successful application of analogies.

Duncker (the problem-solving pioneer who developed the candle problem discussed in the section on functional fixedness) developed what has become known as the radiation problem. Take a few minutes and see if you can solve it.

Suppose you are a doctor faced with a patient who has a malignant tumor in his stomach. It is impossible to operate on the tumor, but unless the tumor is destroyed, the patient will die. There is a kind of ray that can be used to destroy the tumor. If the rays reach the tumor all at once at a sufficiently high intensity, the tumor will be destroyed. Unfortunately, at this intensity, the healthy tissue that the rays pass through on the way to the tumor will also be destroyed. At lower intensities, the rays are harmless to healthy tissue, but they will not affect the tumor either. What type of procedure might be used to destroy the tumor with the rays and at the same time avoid destroying the healthy tissue?

Did you figure it out? The correct solution is to aim many radiation beams (at sufficiently weak intensity to avoid damage) at the tumor from different angles. Hence, the tumor receives the summed energy of the radiation (and is destroyed), while the surrounding tissue is unharmed. In a classic series of studies, Gick and Holyoak (1980, 1983) utilized the radiation problem (Duncker, 1945) to investigate whether an analogous problem might help solvers succeed at finding a solution to it.

In their initial series of investigations on whether analogies might aid in problem solving, Gick and Holyoak (1980) presented participants with one of several stories analogous to the radiation problem. For example, in the commander problem, a military commander is trying to capture the military headquarters of an opposing force. The headquarters are located on an island connected to the surrounding area by several bridges. A bridge can accommodate only a few tanks, which will not be enough for a successful attack. Therefore, the military commander conducts the attack by sending a few tanks across each bridge; this results in enough tanks arriving at the island for a successful attack. After looking over this initial story (the *source problem*) under the guise of a story-comprehension task, participants were given the radiation problem (the *target problem*). Some participants were given only the target problem; in this condition, 10% came up with the convergence solution. Some participants were instructed to memorize the source problem and then try to solve the target problem. In this condition, 30% of participants came up with the convergence solution. A comparison of these two conditions indicates that 20% of participants spontaneously noticed the analogous relationship and used it.

In a follow-up series of investigations, Gick and Holyoak (1983) set out to determine the conditions under which analogical transfer would occur. They attempted to get solvers to notice and use analogies under three different conditions. In the analogy-plus-general-principle condition, participants received an analogous problem plus an extra passage that basically stated the underlying principle (or, in Gick and Holyoak's terms, the underlying *schema*)—namely, that simultaneously applying small forces from different locations is as effective as applying one large force from the same location. In the analogy-plus-diagram condition, participants received an analogous problem plus a diagram (multiple arrows converging on one location) that sketched out the underlying schema. Alternatively, in the analogy-plus-another-analogous-problem condition, the participants received two analogous problems and were asked to find the relationship between them. Which of these three conditions (if any) do you think would be most likely to lead to the transfer of the analogy?

Figure 12.5 summarizes the results from experiments that tested these different conditions. Each pair of bars represents a comparison between one of the three conditions just discussed to an analogy-alone condition in which the participants received just one analogous problem. As you can see, only one of the analogy hints was successful. Providing a diagram (analogy-plus-diagram condition) or a statement of the general principle underlying the problem (analogy-plus-general-principle condition) did not help participants to spontaneously recognize and use the analogy. However, when participants read and related two analogous stories (analogy-plus-another-analogous-problem condition), they were able to use the knowledge in the new problem.

Gick and Holyoak explain that in this condition, solvers were able to map the connections between the two different problems. This mapping process is a defining feature of analogical reasoning and is a critical determinant of whether an analogous problem is going to be an aid. Gick and Holyoak term this mapping process *schema induction*. A schema is a mental representation of facts and procedures that apply to a specific object or situation. In this context, a schema is a mental representation of the underlying principles that multiple problems share. Once this schema is formed, the problem solver can make use of it in solving analogous problems. This finding is another example of a concept we discussed in Chapter 6, transfer appropriate processing. In the analogous-problem-plus-another-analogous problem condition, participants attempted to find the relationship between the two problems. Given that this is the process required for analogical transfer, doing this in the first phase appropriately transfers to the process required in the second phase (using the underlying principle to solve the new problem).

Let's examine the steps that are necessary for analogies to succeed as problem-solving techniques. Some researchers (e.g., Novick & Holyoak, 1991) summarize the role of analogy by describing three processes that might be termed *noticing, mapping,* and *schema development.* First, the problem solver must *notice* that a relationship exists between the two problems in question. Next, the solver must be able to *map* the

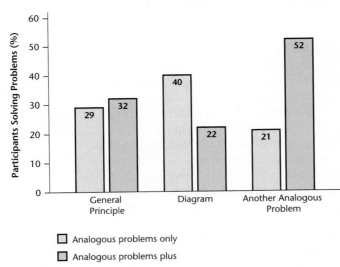

Figure 12.5

Results from Gick and Holyoak (1983).

From Gick, M. L., & Holyoak, K. J. (1983). Schema induction and analogical transfer. *Cognitive Psychology, 15,* 1–38. Copyright 1983, Elsevier Science (USA). Reprinted by permission.

key elements of the two problems (e.g., that the tumor in the radiation problem can be represented as the military headquarters in the commander problem). Finally, the solver must arrive at a general *schema* underlying the problems that will allow for the solution of the target problem (i.e., the convergence schema).

A good deal of research (e.g., Holyoak & Koh, 1987; Ross, 1987) reveals that the first stage, where a relationship must be noticed, is a major culprit for the failures in analogical problem solving. Why is this the case? It's basically a failure of memory; the current problem fails to trigger the memory of other problems that may be helpful. A hint (i.e., retrieval cue) to use the related problem leads the solver to use it. But in most everyday cases of problem solving, there's no one to provide hints about other analogous problems. So what factors promote the spontaneous recognition and retrieval of a related problem? One answer to this question relates to the types of features the two problem situations may or may not share.

Surface vs. Structural Features.   Our ability to notice, map, and develop schemata depends on the particular *type of similarity*. Researchers generally distinguish between the *surface features* and the *structural features* of problems (e.g., Gentner, 1989). **Surface features** are the specific elements of the problem. If two problems share surface similarity, this means that the parts of the problems look similar. A fiasco that occurred while printing the first draft of this very chapter serves as a good example. One of our printers (the newer one) decided to start munching paper as it printed, and it shut down. As we flailed around, looking for the printer manual to get instructions on clearing a paper jam from the new printer, we realized (via analogy) that this printer probably would work like our old printer. Paper jams on our old printer were cleared by opening up the back of the printer. Sure enough, the same principle applied to the new printer. The two problems shared surface features; we noticed the relationship, and the problem was solved.

Structural features are the underlying relationships among the surface features of the two problems. If two problems are structurally similar, they may look quite different on the surface but have underlying similarities in terms of their relationships. Does this sound familiar? Remember the distinction we made in Chapter 9 between surface structure and deep structure? Two sentences could have different surface structures (i.e., look similar) but have the same deep structures (i.e., mean the same thing). For example, "The dog chased the cat" and "The cat was chased by the dog" have different structures but the same meaning (i.e., deep structures).

Think about the radiation and commander problems. These problems are completely different in terms of their surface features: military attack versus cancer. Yet in terms of structural features, they are pretty much the same. Both require the use of many smaller forces applied simultaneously from different directions. In spite of the fundamental (structural) similarity between the radiation and commander problems, their dissimilarity on the surface is likely to prevent you from making a connection between the two. Simply put, in many circumstances, structural similarity is not enough to cue your memory regarding previous problems; the reminder must be more obvious.

Speaking of reminders, recall our earlier discussion of verbal protocols—think-out-loud reports that help researchers get a handle on the processes underlying problem solving. Might these serve another purpose? You might have the intuition, or even the personal experience, that "talking through" a problem helps you solve it. This has been found to be true in many circumstances of learning and problem solving (e.g., Chi, 1996). Could thinking through a problem out loud lead one to stumble upon the connections that might unlock a problem solution?

Lane and Schooler (2004) investigated the effects of verbalizing on the apprehension and retrieval of analogies by having participants read 16 short scenarios. A few minutes later, they were asked to read eight more test scenarios. For each of these new scenarios they had to decide which of the original scenarios seemed most analogous. It turns out that each of these eight scenarios was indeed related to two of the original scenarios; each of these test scenarios had been designed to bear a superficial relationship (surface similarity) with one of the encoded scenarios and a deeper relationship (structural similarity) with another of the encoded scenarios. Half of the participants "thought out loud" during this retrieval task, while the other half worked silently. Table 12.3 presents the results. As you can see, verbalizing seemed to have converse effects on the discovery of different sorts of analogies. Verbalizing seemed to encourage participants to see superficial analogies (surface similarity) at the expense of deeper analogies (structural similarity). Lane and Schooler explain these results by proposing that the requirement of verbalization leads one to focus on superficial similarities because these are easier to talk about. Basically, verbalization biases people toward verbalizable processes.

Even though a good deal of research indicates that people aren't too good at picking up on analogies unless the relationship is pretty obvious (Gick & Holyoak, 1980, 1983; Hayes & Simon, 1977), a study by Blanchette and Dunbar (2000) provides a hopeful assessment of analogy use. The seeming ineffectiveness of structural similarity for analogy use is deceiving; some research suggests that it might be (at least in part) an artifact of the cognitive psychology laboratory. Several studies of real-world problem solving indicate that the analogies people use are based on structural features, not surface ones (e.g., Dunbar, 1995). In their study, Blanchette and Dunbar had participants produce their own analogies to various target problems, and the characteristics of these generated analogies were evaluated. The results indicated that when analogies were produced by participants, the analogies shared structural similarity, rather than surface similarity, with the target problem. This finding indicates that people in everyday circumstances may actually be more sensitive to structural similarity than had been suggested by earlier research and consequently the use of analogies may be more beneficial in everyday problem solving than laboratory investigations would indicate.

This conclusion is bolstered by some data collected by Markman, Taylor, and Gentner (2007). They point out a simple, yet apparently serious, limitation of most (if not all) research on the effectiveness of analogy in aiding problem solving. These studies present the

Table 12.3 **Number of Analogous Problems Identified in Lane and Schooler's (2004) Study**

	Surface Similarity	Structural Similarity
Verbalization	3.8	1.0
No verbalization	1.9	2.3

source problem and the subsequent analogical problems in written form. Markman et al. contend that there is good reason to expect people to be more sensitive to structural relationships among problems in the case of *spoken* presentation (i.e., listening to the problem). Given that the success of an analogy depends on problems solvers remembering an analogous problem, their study focused specifically on memory rather than problem solving.

Recall the concept of anaphoric reference from Chapter 10; anaphoric reference connects an anaphor (e.g., he) with its referent (e.g., a man mentioned earlier in the paragraph). Research shows that an anaphor is comprehended more efficiently when listening (spoken form) than when reading (written form). The authors extended this to memory in general in order to test their hypothesis. They wanted to see if previously presented proverbs (e.g., the swiftest steed can stumble) would be retrieved better with proverb cues that were superficially (surface features) similar (e.g., a rough steed needs a rough bridle) or structurally similar (e.g., the greatest master is wrong from time to time). They also varied whether the proverbs were presented in spoken or written form. Consistent with their prediction, when the cue proverb and original proverb shared structural features, participants were more likely to remember the original proverb in the listening than reading condition. When they shared superficial (surface) features, there was no difference between the listening and reading conditions. Given that analogical transfer requires the problem solver to notice (remember) analogous problems, studying problems in written form may underestimate the use of analogies to solve problems.

Another set of findings cast the use of analogy in a more positive light than the early returns indicated. Once again, the key factor seems to be the manner in which the problems are presented. You've read a number of examples throughout the text about cognitive processes being embodied, and the important role that action plays in cognition. Problem solving is no different; it seems that analogical reasoning can be beneficially influenced through action. Catrombone, Craig, and Nersessian (2006) speculated that *kinesthetic information*—information that arises from body movement—could play a key role in encoding the structural features of a problem, setting the stage for later analogical retrieval. In order to test this idea, the researchers used the Duncker radiation and General problems. Recall that the key principle in eliminating the tumor (in the radiation problem) and overtaking the enemy (in the General problem) was the idea of convergent forces—the sum of smaller lines of attack approaching from varied directions would produce the required force to eliminate the tumor or overtake the enemy.

Research Theme
Embodied
Cognition

Catrombone, Craig, and Nersessian had all participants encode the *General* problem followed by three "retrieval" phases. In the first phase participants were told to recall the *General* problem in one of three modes. In the *verbal* condition, participants were asked to recall the story from memory. In the *visual* condition, participants were asked to recall the story from memory while at the same time drawing a sketch of what had happened in the story. The key condition was the *enactment* condition. Participants in this condition were asked to recall the story while manipulating blocks to help describe what had happened. In the second phase, all participants were presented with the radiation problem for eight minutes and were told to come up with as many solutions to the problem as possible. Finally, in the third phase, participants were told to start fresh, and attempt to come up with a solution to the problem based on the story they had read earlier.

Table 12.4 **Results from Catrambone, Craig, & Nersessian (2006); Proportion of Participants in Each Condition Who Produced the Analogous (Convergence) Solution**

		Second Phase	Third Phase
ENCODING CONDITION	**Enactment**	.52	.91
	Sketch	.27	.85
	Verbal	.19	.86

The results are presented in Table 12.4. The effectiveness of enactment is apparent. While nearly everyone solved the problem eventually (third phase), participants in the enactment condition were much more likely than participants in the nonenactment conditions to solve the problem in the second phase when no explicit direction was given to use the initial story (i.e., the *General* problem). Remember in this situation, people are unlikely to make the analogical transfer but those in the enactment condition did. Nonenacting participants were not likely to come up with the solution without being explicitly told to use the initial story (third phase). The effectiveness of the enactment condition in producing a spontaneous solution to the radiation problem is yet another demonstration of the key role of action and embodiment in cognitive processing.

Problem Solution: Dual Processes Revisited.   The contrast we drew earlier between algorithms and heuristics may have reminded you of an analogous distinction from the last chapter. But, maybe not, given the seeming ineffectiveness of analogies without the appropriate hints! Here's a hint: the distinction between algorithms and heuristics is another example of a dual-process view of thinking. At first blush, it may strike you that heuristics (fast and efficient) are akin to System 1 processes (automatic and unconscious), while algorithms (slow and inefficient, yet effective) are akin to System 2 processes (analytic and conscious). But closer consideration makes it apparent that the mapping isn't perfect. Both algorithms and heuristics can involve System 1 or System 2 processing. Well-practiced algorithms such as multiplication tables or other problem solving abilities that develop with extensive practice (as we'll see in the section on expertise) are probably best characterized as System 1. Other algorithms, such as closely following a new recipe, are best characterized as System 2. Similarly, heuristics can be quick and efficient System 1 processes (as when you glance at a black-jack hand and decide that you shouldn't hit on 19) or slow and deliberative System 2 processes (as when you attempt to solve a problem using an analogous one). Is one type of processing—algorithms or heuristics—better? Well, as we stated earlier, given limits in processing capacity, and the imperfect and limited information available to us in any given situation, heuristics no doubt serve us best most of the time. How about System 1 versus Sytem 2 processing? Is one better than the other? If you've been paying attention throughout the text, you can probably anticipate the answer; either one, depending on the situation!

Pretz (2008) compared these two modes of processing. She calls them intuition (System 1) and analytic (System 2), and was interested in how they might be applied to complex problems faced by college students. Her goal was to see how the problem solving mode might interact with the experience level of the problem solver. Her hypothesis was that when faced with ill-defined problems that can characterize college life, deliberative analysis (i.e., System 2) won't be that helpful, because ill-defined problems are hard to represent, difficult to break down, and not amenable to conscious analysis. In these cases, holistic, intuitive thought—thinking with your gut—might better serve your purposes. She also reasoned that the best problem-solving method should interact with experience. The more knowledge one has in a given domain, the more information they have to work with. As you'll recall, when this happens problems tend to be perceived as well-defined. The limitations associated with less knowledge will lead a person to rely on intuition or gut feelings to arrive at a solution.

Pretz used the College Student Tacit Knowledge Inventory as their measure of problem solving. A sample item from the test is presented in Table 12.5. As you can see, the test presents problem scenarios, along with possible courses of action, which the test taker rates in terms of appropriateness or likely effectiveness. According to her analysis, the best mode of processing for solving this problem would depend on one's level of knowledge and experience. People with more college experience, and more experience interacting with professors, will be well served by thinking the scenario out and weighing alternatives carefully (i.e., analytic mode). Those with relatively little college experience on the other hand, will likely tie themselves in knots trying to reason their way to the best solution when they use this mode because of their limited range of knowledge

---

Table 12.5 Sample Item from the College Student Tacit Knowledge Inventory Used in the Peretz (2008) Study

You have decided to apply for an internship during the upcoming break, and want to ask one of your professors for a letter of recommendation. The professor you have in mind is teaching a fairly large class, and he does not know you very well. One day you run into him in the coffee shop, where he is sitting with what you assume are his kids. Given this situation, rate the quality of the following options:

1	2	3	4	5	6	7
----+----	----+----	----+----	----+----	----+----	----+----	----+----
Extremely Bad	Very Bad	Somewhat Bad	Neither Bad Nor Good	Somewhat Good	Very Good	Extremely Good

3.20 a) You decide that this is a good time to talk to him about the letter.

5.51 b) You go up and greet him, reminding him of your name and what class you are in.

4.13 c) You greet him and then start chatting with his kids.

3.69 d) You nod but do not talk to him.

3.19 e) You pretend you have not seen him. He probably does not want to deal with students outside of his workplace.

2.93 f) You ask if you can sit down with him and his kids and talk about different things.

5.12 g) You greet him and ask for an appointment with him the following day.

2.44 h) You greet him and offer to buy him and his kids coffee or sodas.

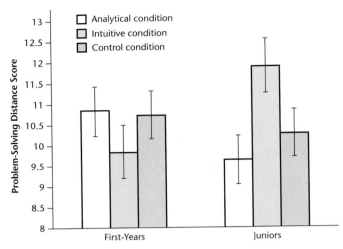

Figure 12.6

Problem solving performance from Pretz (2008). A lower score means better performance; heights of bars indicate distance from consensus solution.

and experience. Therefore, they should be better off using the intuition mode to solve the problem.

Pretz presented these scenarios to first-year and third year students. Each student did so after receiving one of two sets of detailed instructions, emphasizing analysis or intuition. The *analytic* instructions were designed to maximize use of System 2, or deliberative, conscious strategizing. Participants in this condition were encouraged to use a four-step method for analyzing the problem. The steps included defining the problem, identifying relevant information, deciding how to use resources to solve the problem, and evaluating the possible solutions and consequences. Participants receiving the *intuition* instructions were told simply to imagine the situation vividly, think about it holistically, to trust their gut and intuition, and to incubate (take a break from the question and come back to it). A control group was told simply to solve the problem in any way that felt comfortable to them.

The results are presented in Figure 12.6 and provide clear support for Pretz's hypothesis. The figure plots the distance of a person's solution ratings from the consensus solution. So a high score indicates poor performance; the solution deviates from what the majority of people think is appropriate. As you can see, the best problem solving strategy depended on whether the participant was an overwhelmed first year student or a seasoned junior. The first-year students most likely would have been overwhelmed by the analysis instructions, not to mention underequipped in terms of knowledge and experience, so they were best served by reading the choices and going with their gut. Conversely, students with more experience and knowledge were better served by considering their experiences and their knowledge via the analysis instructions (and System 2).

Stop&*Review*

1. Which of the following is FALSE about algorithms?
   a. They involve a systematic application of rules.
   b. They involve the random application of rules.
   c. They guarantee a solution.
   d. They are most useful in everyday problem-solving situations.

2. True or false? Heuristics are generally preferable to algorithms.

3. What is an analogy? What steps are necessary for people to notice and use analogies?

4. When do people tend to successfully use analogies?

- Algorithms involve the systematic and exhaustive application of rules for specific types of problems. Algorithms guarantee a solution if correctly applied. For human problem solvers, algorithms are limited in their usefulness because their exhaustive nature makes their use tedious. Also, algorithms do not exist for most everyday problems.

- Heuristics are rules of thumb. They're generally preferable to algorithms because they tend to be more efficient. Heuristics include means-end analysis (breaking a problem into smaller subgoals) and the use of analogies (the application of previous solution procedures to current problems).

- Research indicates that people often fail to spontaneously make the critical connections between analogous problems. The steps necessary to make the connection are *noticing* that a relationship exists, *mapping* problem elements, and *schema development*, detecting a general principle that underlies the problems. Many failures in analogical problem solving occur in the noticing stage.

- Making the connection between two analogous problems is more likely if the two problems share surface features than if they share structural features (the underlying relationships). However, in everyday situations, people may actually be more sensitive to structural similarity than laboratory research would indicate. Physically acting out problem solutions or listening to problem analogs rather than reading them seems to aid analogical problem solving.

Experts: Masters of Representation and Solution

The previous study showed that problem solving success depended on the match between a problem solver's experience and the nature of the problem situation. One of the most investigated topics within problem research is the effects of extensive experience—that is, expertise.

Expertise can be defined as exceptional knowledge and/or performance in some specific problem domain. For some time, it was commonly believed that the exceptional performance of an expert reflected some innate capacity or talent. Since the advent of cognitive psychology in the 1950s, however, this view has given way to what might be termed an *information-processing account* of expertise (Ericsson & Charness, 1994). Rather than viewing expert performance as the product of innate capacities, many researchers now view it as an outgrowth of learning and repetition over the course of years that produces an extensive body of knowledge and an extremely well-learned set of skills. One estimate is that expertise involves approximately 10 years of continuous exposure to a given domain, comprising thousands of hours of practice (Ericsson & Charness, 1994). For the past 50 years, researchers have investigated differences in the cognitive processing of experts and novices in various domains (e.g. bridge, football, ballet, serving tables, medical diagnosis).

Expert Advantages

The core of problem solving is memory—the long-term memory that allows for the storage of domain-related general knowledge and specific episodes and the immediate memory that allows for quick and efficient online processing of problem information. To some extent, experts might be considered *skilled memorizers* (Deakin & Allard, 1991); in fact, one popular framework for explaining expertise effects in problem solving is termed *skilled-memory theory* (Ericsson & Polson, 1988). According to this framework, there are a number of fundamental differences between experts and novices, all to the advantage of experts. First, the semantic networks that we talked about in Chapter 5 are much more richly elaborated in experts, which leads to a second advantage enjoyed by experts, information is more easily and quickly encoded into long-term memory by experts than novices. In addition, the speed of this encoding improves with practice. Third, experts have quicker and more direct access to long-term memory.

Stop&*Think* | ANALYZING YOUR EXPERTISE

Below are some of the advantages that experts have over novices:

- richer semantic networks
- faster retrieval from memory
- faster encoding into memory

Consider some area of your "personal expertise"; it can be anything—a game you're good at, a skill you've developed at work, athletic performance.

1. Reflect on how your expertise demonstrates these characteristics.
2. Compare your performance in your domain with that of a novice.

A groundbreaking investigation of expert memory was conducted by de Groot (1946/1978), who investigated memory in chess players of varying skill levels by presenting them with brief glimpses of meaningful board positions and then having them reconstruct the boards. Perhaps not surprisingly, recall differed as a function of expertise, with the best players recalling the boards almost perfectly.

Another classic study by Chase and Simon (1973) replicated de Groot's findings but included an encoding condition in which the chess pieces were randomly rearranged to find out whether the advantage enjoyed by experts was a general one (good immediate memory overall) or a specific one (exceptionally good immediate memory for chess game configurations the experts had seen before). For the most part, expertise seems to be domain specific; There is some evidence that the transfer of expertise is possible, particularly if the transfer domain bears some similarity to the original domain. For example, Jessup (2009) found knowledge of baseball could transfer to learning about the somewhat similar game of cricket. (See Kimball & Holyoak, 2000, for a brief review of other evidence for the transfer of expertise.)

Consistent with this view, expert chess players remembered game configurations better than novices but they demonstrated no superiority in memory for random board configurations. Chase and Simon explained the superiority in the former condition by appealing to the notion of chunking in immediate memory (discussed in Chapter 4). According to this account, experts can instantly recognize game board configurations based on their extensive knowledge and experience base. The superior pattern recognition ability of experts has been shown in contexts other than chess, including video games (Sims & Mayer, 2002) and Scrabble (Halpern & Wai, 2007).

As a result of this prodigious pattern recognition ability, experts can easily and quickly chunk pieces, and these chunks become increasingly larger and more complex; each of the 7 ± 2 (the magical number) chunks in memory contains more information. Later evidence has demonstrated that the superior memory exhibited by the experts in these studies is not an exclusive function of immediate memory, because it doesn't seem subject to many of the limits you read about in Chapter 4. For example, Charness (1976) found that expert memory for chess positions was not diminished by delay, even with an interfering task. Also, Gobet and Simon (1996) found that chess masters who quickly glimpsed at several game boards were able to process more chunks than the typical view of immediate memory would allow. Ericsson and Kintsch (1995) propose the idea of **long-term working memory** to explain expert advantages in online processing. Basically, this theory states that experts can bypass the limits of immediate memory by using the information in immediate memory to directly access LTM; in essence, immediate memory serves as a retrieval cue for information in LTM. If you remember the content from Chapter 4 you might be thinking that this sounds like a theory that would fit well within the unitary view of memory. According to this view, it might be more reasonable to think of long-term working memory as simply the domain-specific activation of long term memory that is currently in consciousness. Regardless of how you conceptualize its locus, it would seem that the prodigious memory of experts is at the heart of their advantage (Ericsson & Roring, 2008).

Aside from the general advantages in the power and efficiency of memory within their domain area, expert problem solvers also use general strategies that differ from those of novices. For example, Chi, Feltovich, and Glaser (1981) found that experts tend to search problem space in a forward fashion, reasoning from givens toward the goal. Novices, on the other hand, tend to think about the goal and reason backward about the steps that will lead there. For example, forward search characterizes the play of chess grandmasters (Chabris & Hearst, 2003). Also, experts are much better at picking up on structural features of problems, whereas novices are more likely to focus on surface features (Hogan & Rabinowitz, 2009; Novick, 1988). Given what you've learned about analogy, you've probably inferred (correctly) that experts are more likely to recognize analogous problems or situations when faced with a new problem or situation (within their area of expertise).

Another perspective on expertise is proposed by Lemaire and Siegler (1995), who conceptualize differences between novices and experts in terms of strategy use. Their *Adaptive Strategy Model* proposes four "layers" of difference, the first being *strategy existence*. Although experts and novices may have some strategies in common, experts have many more at their disposal. A second layer is *strategy base rate*, which refers to the notion that experts in a given domain know which strategies tend to work in general, and are biased toward selecting those strategies. The third layer is *strategy choice*, which refers to experts' advantage in discerning which strategies should be chosen for a specific circumstance.

Finally, *strategy execution* refers to the expert advantage over the novice in actually carrying out the strategy, in terms of speed and accuracy. The Adaptive Strategy Model has been quite successful as an account of problem solving across a wide variety of domains, from something as simple and well defined as children learning multiplication (Lemaire & Siegler, 1995) to something as complex and ill defined as platoon leadership in the Army (Schunn, McGregor, & Saner, 2005).

Expertise Advantages vs. Age-Related Deficits.   In Chapter 6, we briefly discussed age-related deficits in cognition. If you'll recall, elderly individuals have difficulties in self-initiated retrieval, or memory tasks that require them to initiate memory retrieval and processing. It turns out that age-related declines are observed on a number of cognitive tasks, including those that involve inhibitory processes, multitasking, and spatial abilities (e.g., Craik & Salthouse, 2008). But it's also true that there are age-related *inclines* in experience! In other words, the older you get, the more expertise you have in various domains. So can this expertise overcome, or at least mitigate, age-related deficits?

Nunes and Kramer (2009) investigated this question with an interesting, important, and stressed group of professionals: air-traffic controllers. As the researchers note, the question is a pressing one; air-traffic control (ATC) is a profession that is facing severe worldwide staffing shortages. The ramifications are potentially serious, as fewer air traffic controllers means less controlled airspace. One source of the shortage is relatively early mandatory retirement ages (for example, 56 in the U.S.) which were imposed due to the fear of age-related decrements in performance. Nunes and Kramer note that some of the evidence that formed the basis for the retirement mandate is suspect. One important reason is that the tasks used to reveal age-related decrements don't map well onto the types of tasks performed by air traffic controllers. As a result, the benefits gained from expertise in air traffic control aren't tapped in these tests, putting the older (but more experienced) controller at an unfair disadvantage.

Nunes and Kramer set out to test older and younger air traffic controllers (along with a control group of older individuals) in various cognitive tasks, some of which involved activities that would benefit from ATC experience, and some not. The expectation would be that on non-ATC tasks, the performance of older individuals (ATCers included) would show deficits relative to younger individuals. However, on ATC-related tasks, the age-related deficits of ATCers should be mitigated. In other words, their performance should look more like young ATCers than older adults. The investigators gave all participants basic cognitive tests that measured immediate memory capacity, inductive reasoning, processing speed, and two tasks of executive control that seemed related to ATC performance: task switching and inhibitory control.

They also gave a set of computer simulation tasks that replicated specific ATC functions. Two of these ATC tasks resembled the basic cognitive processing tasks just described. *Conflict detection* involved making judgments about whether two aircraft depicted on a display would conflict with each other at some future point. *Conflict resolution* took this task further, requiring that participants resolve the conflict with an appropriate response.

The other two tasks were more complex, dynamic, and representative of an ATC situation. *Vectoring* involved sequencing aircraft within corridors around an airport, and *airspace management*, which involved managing the flow of air traffic within airspace that was growing increasingly crowded. Nunes and Kramer were interested in whether experienced air-traffic controllers would show what they termed *experience-related sparing* of abilities. Basically, would the experience and expertise associated with being an air-traffic controller mitigate the young-old performance deficits? To find out, they compared the performance differences observed in young and old non-controllers to the differences observed in young and old controllers.

The researchers found partial support for their hypothesis. As expected, there were age-related declines on each of the basic cognitive tasks assessed. Older participants performed worse than younger participants on all basic cognitive tasks. However, this age deficit was much less pronounced (that is, there was experience-based sparing of abilities) for two tasks that assessed executive control (and seemingly related to ATC performance (inhibitory control and task switching). On the two simpler ATC tasks (conflict detection and conflict resolution), there was no experience-related sparing. But interestingly, on the more complex and representative tasks there was. In both vectoring and airspace management, age-related deficits were substantially reduced by experience. Nunes and Kramer argue that the older experts were able to rely on their domain-specific experience to mitigate some of the detrimental effects of cognitive aging, and argue that perhaps the policy of mandatory retirement for air-traffic controllers of a particular age should be reexamined.

Expert Disadvantages: Costs of Expertise

Although experts enjoy tremendous advantages in processing (primarily within their own domains), there is what might be considered a "downside" to expertise. For example, in the Chase and Simon (1973) study, novices were actually a little better at recall of randomly arranged chess pieces. Also, some studies of medical expertise (e.g., Rikers, Schmidt, & Boshuizen, 2000; Schmidt & Boshuizen, 1993) have revealed that those at an intermediate level of knowledge (e.g., residents in a teaching hospital) actually remember more information about specific patient cases than do experts (e.g., experienced physicians); this has been termed the **intermediate effect.** Rikers et al. (2000) offer an "encapsulation hypothesis" to account for the intermediate effect, proposing that medical experts chunk case information into higher-level summarizing concepts, and then tend to recall these concepts rather than the specific case information, almost as if System 1 (automatic and unconscious processing) is operating a little too efficiently. A study by Wimmers, Schmidt, Verkoeijen, and van de Wiel (2005) suggests that when experts are required to more explicitly elaborate on the cases they are encoding, the expected expert advantage emerges. This underscores a principle discussed in Chapter 6—the importance of both organizational and distinctive processing for memory. This seems to be true for both the novice and the expert (Rawson & Vanderschelde, 2008).

In a rather dramatically titled article "The Dark Side of Expertise" (Stephen King meets cognitive psychology?) Castel, McCabe, Roediger, and Heitman (2007) wanted to determine whether the knowledge base and organizational tendencies of the expert might lead them down the road to memory distortion. Recall from Chapter 8 the Deese-Roediger-McDermott paradigm for investigating illusory memories, in which lists of related words are presented, often leading to the misremembering of a central theme word that is never presented. The false memory is ostensibly due to the internal generation of the target word, and the failure to realize that it had been internally generated rather than presented. Using similar logic, Castel et al. (2007) reasoned that experts, given the combination of a rich and often-activated knowledge base and a tendency toward organizational processing, would be more likely to falsely recall items related to their area of expertise.

They conducted a simple experiment in which people high and low in knowledge of American football were presented with lists of animal names (e.g., bengals, colts) that also happened to be American NFL football team names. The thought was that the high-knowledge participants would encode them as football teams, whereas the low-knowledge participants would encode them simply as animals. A control list of words expected to yield no difference in memory between high- and low-football knowledge groups (body parts) was also presented. Castel et al. suspected that experts would correctly recall more of the animal names (which to them were football team names, and in their area of expertise). However, they also expected that they would falsely recall animal names (that were names of football teams not on the list) than the low-knowledge groups. The results were precisely in line with these predictions. There were no differences (either in correct or false recall) for the recall of body parts, but football experts were more likely to recall—both correctly and falsely—the animal names. Thus, the "dark side" of expertise refers to the heightened likelihood of memory distortion in the expert, a finding akin to the intermediate effect. Experts sometimes seem to not only gloss over the details, but add some as well.

Expert Mental Set?   Earlier, in our discussion of expert advantages in problem solving, we made a strong argument for the flexibility of the expert, discussing their exceptional knowledge base, their ability to apply a multitude of strategies. But our discussion in the last section might also lead you to believe that experts aren't all that flexible, and tend to rely on mindless strategies or routines (i.e, mental sets) that are mostly effective, but sometimes not. Their extensive practice routinizes their behavior, so it would seem reasonable to expect that operating on autopilot in this way might lead to mental set, and perhaps subpar performance. Bilalic, MacLeod, and Gobet (2008) tested chess players at varying levels of expertise, from merely skillful players to super experts (players with exceptional levels of experience, expertise, and skill). They put them in game situations where they were confronted with a game problem that could be solved with one of two moves. One possible move represented a nonoptimal but very familiar solution, while the other move was optimal, but unusual and unfamiliar. Mental set would be indicated by going with the nonoptimal familiar move. Interestingly, the less skilled experts demonstrated mental set, picking the nonoptimal move that was familiar to them. However, the super experts were able to recognize the unusual and optimizing move. Bilalic et al. (2008) conclude that mental set in experts is both a reality and a myth. It depends on the level of expertise. If expertise is extensive enough, mental sets are likely to be avoided.

Stop&*Review*

1. Define expertise.
2. What are the memory advantages of experts, relative to novices.
3. In what way can experts be at a disadvantage in problem-solving?

Expertise (exceptional knowledge and/or performance in some specific problem domain) is due to learning and repetition over years that produce an extensive body of knowledge and an extremely well-learned set of skills.

According to skilled-memory theory, knowledge networks are more richly elaborated in experts. Experts have quicker and more direct access to long-term memory and more quickly and easily encode infor-

mation into long-term memory. Expert memory skills are limited to the domain of expertise, but can generalize to similar domains.

Experts seem able to bypass the limits of working memory by using WM information to access LTM directly. Processing advantages of experts come at the expense of memory for detail. The intermediate effect indicates that people with intermediate knowledge are better at detail retention. The tendency to think within an area of expertise can serve as a mental set but can be avoided in those with extremely high levels of expertise.

Insight and Creativity

Based on an extensive analysis of several cases in which great thinkers made significant breakthroughs, Wallas (1926) proposed that the processes leading up to a creative breakthrough can be described in terms of four stages. In the first stage of *preparation,* the solver gathers information and makes initial attempts at problem solution. This initial stage corresponds roughly to the problem-representation phase of processing discussed earlier. Often, these attempts are stymied, leading to a period of **incubation,** which might be described as productive inactivity. You may have had the experience that when you were trying to solve a problem, putting it aside for a time seemed to allow for a breakthrough. We'll examine the empirical evidence for this experience later. After the incubation period, the problem solver arrives at a critical insight—an important realization or understanding that leads to what Wallas termed *illumination.* Ever see a cartoon where a lightbulb appears over a character's head? A solution to a problem has occurred suddenly, probably with a tangible "Aha!" feeling for the solver. The final stage comprising creative thought is *verification,* in which the problem solver assesses whether the solution will actually work.

The Wallas framework provides a useful description of problem solving but is, by no means, an accepted theory. It was based on Wallas's introspections about the creative process and case studies on the introspections of creative individuals. Although too vague to really test, the theory has provided fodder for two of the more intriguing questions in problem-solving research. First,  Aha!

what is the nature of the ubiquitous experience we term *insight?* Do solutions to problems really appear out of nowhere? Second, if sudden breakthroughs in problem solving are a reality, can these be encouraged by a period of incubation?

Insight

One problem-solving phenomenon that has been a topic of extensive debate and investigation since the beginning of research on problem solving is the notion of insight. As we discussed earlier, *insight* involves the sudden realization of a problem's solution (or of a key idea necessary to the solution). The debate over the nature (or the very existence) of insight goes back to the Gestalt views of problem solving. Gestalt psychologists believe that the key to problem solution lies in a restructuring of the problem elements, which, if successful, leads to a sudden realization of the problem's solution. This sudden realization is insight. The notion of insight is controversial; many theorists believe that problem solving is an incremental process of getting closer and closer to a solution rather than a sudden realization. Another problem is that insight (until relatively recently) never has been clearly defined or experimentally demonstrated by Gestalt psychologists.

Even if insight is a reality, it would not apply to every problem. Many researchers (Gilhooly & Murphy, 2005) make a distinction between noninsight and insight problems (which can be seen as loosely analogous to the earlier distinction between ill-defined and well-defined problems). **Noninsight problems** are those that are likely solved through incremental, or "grind out the solution," processes. They require analytical, step-by-step processing—like the problems in logic, arithmetic, chess, and the like. The transformation problem called the Tower of Hanoi (previously presented in Figure 12.1 on page 496) is an example of a noninsight problem—no simple breakthrough is going to give you the answer. **Insight problems** are those in which the solution appears suddenly. Here are a couple of problems of each type:

Insight Problems

Water lilies double in area every 24 hours. At the beginning of summer, there is one water lily on the lake. It takes 60 days for the lake to become completely covered with water lilies. On which day is the lake half-covered?

A prisoner was attempting to escape from a tower. He found in his cell a rope which was half long enough to permit him to reach the ground safely. He divided the rope in half, and tied the two parts together and escaped. How could he have done this?

Noninsight Problems

Three people play a game in which one person loses and two people win each round. The one who loses must double the amount of money that each of the players has at that time. The three players agree to play three games. At the end of the three games, each player has lost one game, and each person has $8. What was the original stake of each player?

Next week I am going to have lunch with my friend, visit the new art gallery, go to the social security office, and have my teeth checked at the dentist. My friend cannot meet me on Wednesday; the social security office is closed weekends; the dentist has office hours only on Tuesday, Friday, and Saturday; the art gallery is closed Tuesday, Thursday, and weekends. What day can I do everything I planned?

Two of the key assumptions about insight problem solving are (1) that it involves a mistaken assumption that, once removed, will clear the way to a successful solution of the problem, and (2) that the solver is hit with the solution suddenly, "out of the blue," and has what might be termed an "Aha!" experience. Let's take a look at some research that has addressed these fundamental assumptions.

Removal of a Mistaken Assumption?   The notion of insight was an integral part of much of the early work on problem solving, but as many researchers have noted (e.g., Weisberg & Alba, 1981), the concept is vaguely defined, and until the 1980s had not really been put to the empirical test. This may have been due in part to the intuitive appeal of the idea. But intuitive appeal and common sense are poor bases for knowledge. However, since the 1980s, insight has become one of the most hotly researched topics in problem solving. Many of these studies (e.g., Lung & Dominowski, 1985; MacGregor, Ormerod, & Chronicle, 2001; Weisberg & Alba, 1981) employed what is possibly the most thoroughly investigated insight problem, the *nine-dot problem*—in which participants must connect all the dots with one continuous line. This problem (surprisingly difficult for most) and its solution are presented in Figure 12.7.

Some research in this area has focused on the notion that the difficulty of insight problems is that they involve one key—but errant—perception or assumption that if removed, would lead to an easy solution. You'll recall that earlier in the chapter we discussed Duncker's candle problem and the assumption that the difficulty in solving it stems from a would-be solver's failure to perceive the box of tacks in a different manner (i.e., as a candleholder). In the nine-dot problem, the mental set is the assumption that one must stay within the boundary created by the nine dots. According to the notion of insight, removing this mental set should reveal an easy solution. A review of the research on the nine-dot problem by Kershaw and Ohlsson (2004) takes issue with this assumption. They contend that the difficulty with insight problems—the reason that they can't be solved with a simple hint about a faulty mental set—is that they're overdetermined. That is, they have multiple causes and sources of difficulty, rather than just one.

According to Kershaw and Ohlsson, three sources of difficulty are evident in the nine-dot problem (as well as in

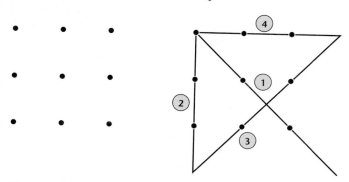

Figure 12.7

The nine-dot problem and solution.

From Weisberg, R. W., & Alba, J. W. (1981). An examination of the alleged role of "fixation" in the solution of several "insight" problems. *Journal of Experimental Psychology: General, 110,* 169–192. Copyright 1981 by the American Psychology Association. Reprinted by permission.

many other insight problems). *Perceptual factors* relate to the Gestalt organizational principles mentioned in Chapter 2—figure-ground, proximity, similarity, and the like. These affordances, or ways of initially seeing problems, can have a dramatic impact on our ability to successfully break through to a solution. *Process factors* relate to the information-processing demands of the problem, like the size of the problem space and the complexity of the solution. Finally, *knowledge factors* involve prior knowledge that a solver brings to bear on a problem. This is often where mental set can interfere, as a problem solver repeatedly tries ineffective approaches because of prior success with them in other contexts. Any combination of these factors (i.e., not just one of them) might come into play as people try to solve an insight problem and find themselves at an impasse.

Research Theme
Metacognition

The "Aha!" Experience.   Another defining feature of the insight experience is a sudden and tangible feeling of discovery, usually described as an "Aha!" experience. The issue of what someone is thinking as they think relates to metacognition. Metacognition refers to a person's knowledge of their own thought processes. In a series of clever experiments, Metcalfe (Metcalfe, 1986a; Metcalfe & Weibe, 1987) investigated the metacognition of problem solvers faced with different sorts of problems. Metcalfe and Weibe (1987) developed one of the more interesting dependent variables in cognitive psychology—*ratings of warmth* collected from problem solvers during their problem-solving attempts. You know the old "hot and cold" game when you're looking for something? If the hider tells you you're cold, you're nowhere near the hidden object; if you're hot, you're practically on top of it.

Metcalfe and Weibe adapted this game to problem solving by having participants rate how warm they were with regard to the solution of a problem. Their reasoning was as follows: if insight involves sudden realization of the solution, solvers who are working on an insight problem should have no clue whether they're close to a solution or not, and their warmth ratings should reflect this. They should report little warmth throughout the problem-solving interval until a solution finally appears. With a noninsight problem, however, the metacognition should be different: participants should realize that they're getting closer and closer to a solution, given the grind-it-out nature of a noninsight problem. To test their hypothesis, Metcalfe and Weibe (1987, experiment 2) presented participants with noninsight problems and insight problems like the ones previously introduced. They were allowed four minutes for each problem, and within that interval, they were to rate their warmth every 15 seconds by making a mark on a scale. In addition to rating warmth, solvers were asked to judge whether or not they would be able to solve each of the problems.

The results revealed some interesting differences in the metacognitive processes underlying the solution of insight and noninsight problems. Simply put, metacognition was not nearly as good for the insight problems. Let's take a look at the warmth ratings. These were incremental for the noninsight problems, increasing gradually throughout the solution interval. Participants felt as if they were nearing a solution when they really were near a solution. For the insight problems, however, the warmth ratings didn't really increase at all throughout the solution interval until the problem was solved. So participants had no idea if and when they were approaching a solution. The other metacognitive judgment ("Will I be able to solve this problem?") paralleled the warmth ratings. For the noninsight problems, participants were decent judges of whether they would be able to solve the problems. However, for the insight problems, participants were relatively poor judges of solution probability. They demonstrated overconfidence, underestimating how difficult the problems were.

The results from both metacognitive judgments indicate a fundamental difference between insight and noninsight problems. Participants' metacognitions about noninsight problems were more accurate and more predictive of actual performance. Metacognitions about insight problems tended to be unrelated (or even negatively related; see Metcalfe and Wiebe, 1987) to the probability of eventual solution. Metcalfe and Wiebe (1987) suggest that the processes underlying the solution of insight and noninsight problems may be fundamentally different and that the pattern of warmth ratings observed during a solution can be used as an indicator of whether a problem involves insight, thereby avoiding the circularity problem in defining insight. In a critique of the metacognitive studies of insight, Weisberg (1992) lodges a number of objections to these conclusions. He acknowledges the subjective "Aha!" experience produced by some problems but points out that this does not necessarily mean that the problems are solved suddenly, as the Gestalt position suggests. It may be that step-by-step processes are involved but that the solver is unaware of them.

Intuition as Insight.   In the past decade or so, research attention has shifted from the phenomenological differences (i.e., differences in subjective experience) between insight and noninsight problems to more subtle problem-solving processes that lie outside of conscious awareness. The issue of whether insight problem solving involves special, unconscious processes—like a sudden restructuring of problem elements or removal of some mistaken information—still stirs controversy in the field. Certainly, insight problems do seem unique phenomenologically—that is, in terms of the conscious experience that a problem solver has. Insight problem solving feels like an all-or-none process that occurs suddenly. But, as we just mentioned, an alternative conceptualization is that insight problem solving (like noninsight problem solving) is really more gradual, but the gradual progress is not open to conscious awareness. One analysis of insight problem solving along these lines was proposed by Bowers, Regehr, Balthazard, and Parker (1990), who proposed a two-stage model of insight (which they term *intuition*). In stage 1, the *guiding stage,* mnemonic networks relevant to the problem are activated, and this activation begins to spread. In essence, the problem solver is working on the problem unconsciously; the results of this unconscious processing may serve as a basis for a hunch or intuition regarding the solution. In stage 2 (the *integrative stage*), the buildup of activation reaches enough strength to break through into conscious awareness. This transition from stage 1 to stage 2 is insight.

A good deal of evidence now supports this basic outline of insight problem solving. Much of this evidence comes from research by Kounios, Beeman, Bowden, and colleagues (Bowden & Beeman, 1998; Bowden, Jung-Beeman, Fleck, & Kounios, 2005; Kounios & Beeman, 2009, Kounios, Fleck, Green, Payne, Stevenson, Bowden, & Jung-Beeman, 2008).

In one of their earlier articles, appropriately entitled "Getting the Right Idea," Bowden and Beeman (1998) begin with the assumption that insight problems involve more creative thought than noninsight problems, because insight problems require unusual interpretations and arrangements of problem elements. In other words, insight problems involve venturing into unexplored problem space. As you've seen in a number of places throughout the text, one of the major questions addressed by cognitive neuro-scientists is the relative role of each brain hemisphere in accomplishing various cognitive tasks. As we noted in Chapter 1, the distinction between the left and right hemispheres is quite often overgeneralized in the popular press, with the left hemisphere labeled as the constrained "logical" hemisphere and the right as the unfettered "creative" hemisphere. Although this is undoubtedly an oversimplification, evidence does suggest that the right hemisphere plays the more important role in insight problem solving, which Bowden and Beeman take to be tantamount to creativity.

In order to investigate the relative roles of the left and right hemispheres in insight problem solving, the researchers combined the logic of priming (which we discussed in many previous chapters) with an insight problem called the Remote Associates Test (RAT). In the RAT, problem solvers look at three apparently unrelated words and gener-ate one word that ties the triplet together. For example, if presented with *apple, family, house,* the remote associate is *tree* (apple *tree,* family *tree,* and *tree*house). The relation-ships among the items are designed to be difficult to ascertain upon a quick glance. Their logic was as follows: if the solution to an insight problem is associated to a greater degree with right-hemisphere activation, then solution-related concepts should show more priming when presented to the right hemisphere than when presented to the left hemisphere.

In their study, participants were presented with a word triad for 15 seconds during which participants attempted to come up with the solution word. After they had gener-ated the solution, or after time had run out, the screen was erased, and then a target word was presented for pronunciation. On half of the trials, this target word was the solution word for the RAT. On the other half, the target word was a nonsolution word (a word that did not relate the three words together). Pronunciation time was the measure of interest.

Critical to note here is exactly where the target word was presented. Sometimes it was presented left of fixation (i.e., to the right hemisphere) and sometimes right of fixa-tion (i.e., to the left hemisphere). The researchers reasoned that if the right hemisphere is more involved when solving insight problems, then pronunciation times should reveal more priming (i.e., faster pronunciation times for solution than nonsolution words) when presented to the right hemisphere. Why? Because the increased activation of the right hemisphere when solving (or attempting to solve) a problem should translate into an enhanced ability to say the solution word relative to saying the nonsolution word.

The results are shown in Figure 12.8. What you see are priming scores. These scores were calculated by taking pronunciation times for nonsolution words (which boils down to basic word-naming RT) and subtracting the reaction times for solution words. Remember—the solution words were those on which participants had actively been working, so no doubt this "active work" served to speed up identification. The figure plots this increase in response speed.

First, take a look at the solved-problem condition—here you see a priming effect in the reading of solution words, regardless of which hemisphere they were presented to; however, there was significantly more priming for words presented to the *right hemisphere* than there was for words presented to the left hemisphere, indicating greater activation in the right hemisphere.

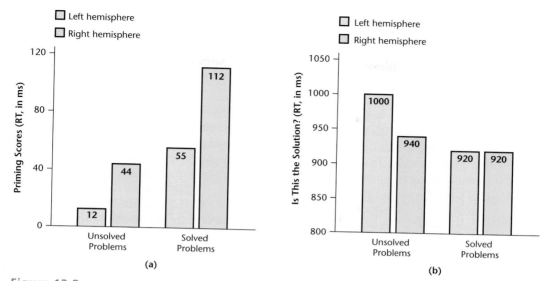

Figure 12.8

Results from Bowden and Beeman's (1998) study of hemispheric activation during insight problem solving.

From Bowden, E. M., & Beeman, M. J. (1998). Getting the right idea: Semantic activation in the right hemisphere may help solve insight problems. *Psychological Science, 9,* 435–440. Copyright 1998 by Blackwell, Inc. Reprinted by permission.

Now look at the unsolved problems, which offer an even more compelling picture. In this condition, participants looked at the three words, but were unable to generate the solution word. In this situation, a priming effect was found *only* for words presented to the right hemisphere (the small priming effect in the left hemisphere was not significantly greater than 0). This indicates that when a solution has not yet been consciously reached, the right hemisphere "knows what's coming," and is speeded up in naming the solution word. The left hemisphere doesn't know what's coming, and is not speeded up.

In a follow-up study, Bowden and Beeman used exactly the same procedure but changed the required response. After presentation of the target word, participants had to make a simple yes or no response—yes if the word *was* the solution word, or no if it wasn't. The results are presented in Figure 12.8b. A cautionary note about reading this half of the figure; since RT is the variable plotted here, the speed up in processing enjoyed by the right hemisphere is indicated by *lowered* response times (rather than an *increase* in priming score, as indicated in the left panel).

Not surprisingly, there was no difference between the right and left hemispheres for solved problems. Given that the solution had already been figured out, saying yes or no was trivially easy for either hemisphere. More interesting is the unsolved problem data. In this situation, participants were still engaged in solution processes. As you can see, the right hemisphere was much faster than the left hemisphere at classifying whether the presented word was the solution or not, indicating that only the right hemisphere was "aware" of the solution.

Subsequent research (e.g., Bowden & Jung-Beeman, 2003; Bowden, Jung-Beeman, Fleck, & Kounios, 2005, Kounios and Beenman, 2009) has clarified and extended this analysis of how problem solving occurs in the brain. For example, Kounios and Beeman (2009) review the evidence from their research which links the occurrence of insight (or as they term it, "the AHA! Moment") to a number of distinct neural signatures. First, brain-imaging results from fMRI scans revealed increased activity in a right-hemisphere area termed the *anterior superior temporal gyrus* while solving insight problems. In addition, EEG recordings made while solving insight problems revealed a sudden burst of neural activity in this same region immediately *preceding* the solution (i.e., "the AHA! Moment").

This work also has revealed some interesting differences between the brain activity underlying the two problem solving modes (i.e., the approach taken in order to solve the problem) discussed throughout the chapter. Pretz (2008) labeled these two modes as intuition and analytic. Kounis and colleagues refer to them as intuition and insightful problem solving. These researchers found differences in the brain activity underlying insightful and analytic problem solving that occur even *before* the problems are presented!

Kounios, Frymiare, Bowden, Fleck, Subramanian, Parrish, and Jung-Beeman, (2006) assessed patterns of neural activity prior to problem presentation in conditions where problems were to be solved in the insight mode (i.e., go with your gut) and compared these patterns to brain activity associated with the presentation of the same problems in conditions where the problems were to solved in an analytic mode (i.e. take your time and think it out). Prior to insight problem solving, the active areas of note were both right and left temporal areas, and also the mid-frontal cortex. These areas are associated with the processing of lexical and semantic information (i.e., information about words and their meanings). In contrast, prior to analytic problem solving, there was increased activity in the visual cortex. Kounios et al. have an interesting proposal; they suggest that prior to insight problem solving, it's almost as if attention is "directed inward," toward priming the word associations that would be important in solving the task. Prior to analytic problem solving, attention was "directed outward" to concentrating on the visual presentation of the stimulus.

Research Theme
Emotion

Research linking emotion to problem solving suggests an interesting connection between positive and negative emotion and the use of insight vs. analytic processes to solve problems. For example, Subramaniam, Kounios, Parrish, and Jung-Beeman (2009) found that the preparatory activity associated with instructions to use an insight mode was enhanced when participants were in a positive mood, and that more insight problems were solved by participants in these positive moods, relative to participants in less positive moods.

A recent review by Andrews and Thomson (2009) provides an interesting interpretation of the negative effect of mood when using the insight mode of problem solving. According to their analysis, the clinical state of depression is actually a set of adaptations that allows for complex problem solving to occur. They propose an *analytic rumination hypothesis*, which proposes that depression is designed to enhance problem solving by giving prioritized access to the problem at hand (e.g., a difficult relationship), reducing one's desire to engage in other more enjoyable activities, and inhibiting physical activity. These three consequences of a depressed state allow for focus on the problem(s) at hand and avoidance of potential distractions. So those who are in a sad mood would not naturally use the insight mode and so when asked to do so their performance is hindered (i.e., fewer problems solved) relative to those in a positive mood.

Taken together, the findings of Subramaniam et al, (2009) and Andrews and Thomson (2009) findings suggest a relationship between mood and the operation of the dual-process reasoning system discussed in the last chapter. Positive moods may encourage the use of System 1 processes (fast, unconscious, automatic—intuition or insight problem solving modes) while negative moods might enhance the System 2 processes (slow, conscious—analytic problem solving mode) that get us to slow down and think deliberatively.

Does Incubation Lead to Insight? One of the more controversial notions within the study of problem solving is *incubation,* or the idea that taking a break in problem solving leads to a quicker solution than does continuing effort. The idea is that the break allows for the elements of the problem to be reorganized or for unconscious processes to continue to work on the problem (perhaps as described earlier) and that this unconscious processing will not take place if conscious work on the problem continues. The anecdotal evidence for incubation is strong; everyday problem solvers, including scientists, artists, and writers, often observe that some critical realization or breakthrough occurs only after a period of frustration and setting the problem aside (Wallas, 1926). However, anecdotal evidence is viewed skeptically by scientists. As intuitive as it seems, this phenomenon has proved to be elusive quarry for problem-solving researchers, who, more often than not, have failed to find replicable incubation effects (e.g., Dominowski & Jenrick, 1972; Olton, 1979; Olton & Johnson, 1976).

Reality Check

Smith (1995) suggests that incubation effects do occur, but only under specific circumstances—namely, when a problem is doable and when the solver is blocked in some way from the solution. The incubation period allows the interfering information to be forgotten, clearing the way for a solution. This effect was nicely demonstrated in a study by Smith and Blankenship (1991). In this study, participants attempted to solve rebus problems—word puzzles in which pictures and words are used to indicate a common phrase. See if you can figure out the following sample rebus problems (the answers will be given a bit later, rather than just below!):

(a) **YOU JUST ME**

(b) **R|E|A|D|I|N|G**

(c) **FLY NIGHT**

In their experiment, Smith and Blankenship had participants solve rebus problems; for some, they provided a pair of misleading cue words. For example, for rebus (c), *paper* and *over* were presented as misleading cues; do those hints help you? Probably not, because they're misleading. They suggest two compound words that are not correct solutions (i.e., *flypaper* and *overnight*). By the way, the correct solutions are *just between you and me*, *reading between the lines*, and *fly by night*. Then the researchers retested unsolved rebuses either immediately or after varying periods of incubation. After attempting to solve the rebus again, participants were asked to recall the cue word that went along with it originally. Consistent with Smith's (1995) analysis, longer break periods were associated with higher probabilities of solution. Memory for the misleading cues provides a possible explanation; memory for the misleading cues decreased as incubation time increased. Apparently, as the misleading cue was forgotten, the problem became more solvable. Vul and Pashler (2007) replicated this basic effect, arguing that incubation effects are also the likely product of forgetting an inappropriate solution or approach (they term this explanation *fixation forgetting*).

Smith (1995) provides a framework in which to interpret these results. According to Smith incubation is basically the encoding specificity principle in reverse. If you'll recall from Chapter 6, the *encoding specificity principle* states that retrieval will be effective to the degree that retrieval conditions match encoding conditions. The *contextual view* of incubation states that when problem solving is stymied, a solution will come more easily if there is a contextual change from the previous situation. Essentially, staying in the same situation continually reinstates the circumstances in which the failure to find a solution was first encountered, increasing the likelihood that the failure will continue. Changing the environment prevents this reinstatement, making success more likely. Smith provides some anecdotal support for this idea, noting that a number of famous cases of incubation followed by insight took place when the problem solver was in a completely different environment than usual.

One example of a decidedly different environment in which incubation might lead to a problem-solving breakthrough is...sleep! You must agree that sleep is categorically different from the waking state in many ways. But as you know, the brain is far from inactive during sleep, and there is many an anecdote of thinkers having some type of creative breakthrough during sleep. For example, Kekule's discovery of the structure of the organic compound benzene seems to have resulted from a special process like sudden restructuring or insight that reportedly occurred after he had dreamed about snakes biting each other's tails. Recent empirical research seems to bear out the anecdotal suggestion that sleep aids in creative insights (see Wagner, Gais, Haider, Verleger, & Born, 2004).

A recent review of incubation effects in problem solving (Sio & Ormerod, 2009) does indeed find consistent enough evidence to establish the phenomenon as real. However, their conclusion includes a major qualification; there are multiple varieties of incubation, and incubation is problem specific. They urge the investigation of a wide variety of problem situations, and suggest there may be individual differences in incubation, as well as interactions between other cognitive processes (e.g., immediate memory) and the processes that underlie incubation.

Creativity

When someone has an insight, demonstrating the ability to hurdle over the problem-solving obstacles that block us mere mortals, what do we say about them? It's quite likely that we would comment on their **creativity.** Creative individuals are able to think "outside the box"—to come up with new ideas, view old problems from a fresh perspective, and connect seemingly disparate problem situations. Because creativity might seem like the pinnacle of thought in many ways, it might surprise you to learn that it hadn't received much attention in psychology until J. P. Guilford issued a wake-up call in his presidential address at the 1950 meeting of the American Psychological Association. The last couple of decades or so have witnessed a considerable surge in research into the creative process, from a breathtakingly diverse range of perspectives. And according to leading researchers on creativity (e.g., Hennessey & Amabile, 2010; Runco, 2004), it's a good thing, because the understanding of creativity is of paramount importance today, as technological advances occur in the blink of an eye, and the world becomes increasingly complex.

What Is Creativity?   Everyone would agree that something called creativity exists, but defining it seems to be a real challenge. In fact, creativity researchers themselves seem to have trouble doing it. Plucker, Beghetto, and Dow (2004) sampled 90 articles from various disciplines interested in creativity (e.g., psychology, business, and education, among others), and found that less than half of them even defined the term! Experts on creativity generally agree that creative solutions have two components—novelty and appropriateness (Hennessey & Amabile, 2010; Lubart, 1994; Sternberg, 2004). Creative solutions are novel, different from previous solutions, and usually unexpected. Yet surprise and originality alone do not make a problem solution creative. The solution must also satisfy the constraints of the problem at hand; it must fulfill a need and be sensible and useful. Let's think back to your end-of-semester problem. One "solution" to the problem might be to fake your death. That way, you wouldn't need to hand in the assignments or take the tests. Although it certainly fulfills the criterion of novelty, this solution is entirely inappropriate, failing to fit within the problem constraints. It would be considered aberrant rather than creative.

One tact researchers have taken in defining creativity is to examine the the impact of the creative products on others. This approach has led researchers to propose what has been termed (we're not kidding) *Big-C* creativity and *little-c* creativity. Big-C creativity is also termed *eminent creativity*, and would be exemplified by people whose creative efforts have ripple effects with major impact on others—think Nobel prize winners, artists, inventors, and the like. Almost none of us show eminent creativity. But most of us show little-c creativity, which refers to what might be termed *everyday creativity*. Anytime you proudly think about some minor thing "Gee, I'm glad I thought of that"; it was probably a creative idea, with a little-c. Beghetto and Kauffman (2007) add another c to the mix, which they call *mini-c*. They define mini-c as "the novel and personally meaningful interpretation of experiences, actions, and events (p. 73)." It's basically a person learning from their own experiences. This type of creativity also has been termed personal creativity, and only can be assessed intrapersonally (i.e., by the person themself).

Recently, Kaufmann and Beghetto (2009) proposed what they term the 4-c model of creativity. They round out the previous list of creativity types (Big-C, little-c, and mini-c) by proposing a fourth type called *Pro-C*. Pro-C refers to the professional development and expertise that might not reach Big-C, but is an advancement nonetheless. They give the example of musicians. Few would

Wynton Marsalis: Creativity with a Big-C

disagree that Wynton Marsalis exhibits Big-C. However, there seemed to be a need for another type of creativity that would distinguish the high school music teacher who plays in a popular local band from their trumpet student, who might be the best in the class. The distinction between these two individuals doesn't seem to be captured by Big-C, little-c or mini-c. The teacher has achieved some professional success within the domain of music expertise but not at the level of Big-C. Pro-C is the label Kaufman and Beghetto (2009) apply in this situation. In the following discussion, the principles we'll cover apply most readily to little-c and not Pro-C or mini-c but some of the elements of Big-C also will be apparent.

One useful framework for describing and investigating creativity was originally proposed by Rhodes (1961/1987), who suggested that creativity can be informed by a focus on several dimensions, which he labeled *person, process, press,* and *product*.

Person. First, there is evidence that creativity, to some extent, is related to aspects of the *person,* or personality . Creative persons are thought to exhibit a number of personality characteristics, including broad interests, appreciation of complexity, tolerance of ambiguity, self-confidence, independence, and sensible risk taking (Barron & Harrington, 1981; Feist, 1999). In addition, creative individuals seem to have a high degree of intrinsic motivation for their fields (Amabile, 1990). Runco (2004) adds other important characteristics that define creative people: flexibility and reactivity. The creative individual must be flexible and able to react effectively to changes in technology, circumstances, and opportunity.

Reality Check

Simonton (2000) also notes some developmental aspects of creativity, characterizing it as a constantly developing ability rather than a static attribute present at birth, and waiting to emerge. According to Simonton's review (and perhaps counter to intuition), creativity is not always the product of a particularly *comfortable* environment. In fact, a person's potential to exhibit creativity seems dependent on having had a diverse set of life experiences, which then enhance an individual's ability to take fresh perspectives. Creative potential also depends on a person having faced sufficiently challenging life experiences, which helps develop the ability to persevere (Simonton, 1994). Such perseverance is important for creative problem solving, which, by definition, includes numerous obstacles. It's useful at this point to note the correlational nature of this personality data. It's not clear whether creativity is the *product* of or the *cause* of this type of personality. It also could be that some third variable leads to the emergence of someone with propensities toward creativity and these particular personality characteristics.

Process. Creativity also can refer to a specific set of *processes*. Two contradictory ideas about cognitive processing in creativity have been proffered—one view asserts that creativity involves special processes and abilities, like the quick ability to restructure problem information and to connect seemingly remote possibilities. Conversely, another view contends that creative thinking is the product of the garden-variety cognitive processing that we've discussed throughout the text, such as attention and memory. So which view is closer to the truth? The **creative cognition approach** (Smith, 2003; Smith, Ward, & Finke, 1994) argues that the probable answer is that creative thinking can be the result of *either* type of process, or of both. It seems fitting that we end this book (just a few pages to go) with a constant theme found in cognitive psychology: when conflicting theories exist to explain a particular phenomenon, the correct answer is that either or both could be correct.

What specific cognitive processes seem to be important? You've no doubt picked up on some of them in our foregoing survey of problem solving. Two that seem especially important are attention and memory. That might seem obvious, so let's get a little more specific. Attentional deployment seems to be important in creativity. More specifically, wide and diffuse attentional deployment seems to be associated with creative problem solving (Martindale & Greenough, 1973; Wallach, 1970). Memory in the form of general knowledge is also vital. Recall the discussion of expertise earlier in the chapter; experts have a larger knowledge base from which to work, enhancing their chances of producing a creative solution, relative to a novice in the area. However, as you read earlier, expertise also can inhibit problem solving.

Sternberg and Davidson (1983; Davidson, 1995) cite three processes as important in reaching creative insights. *Selective encoding* involves distinguishing between relevant and irrelevant information in the domain of expertise. Creative individuals are better at distinguishing useful information from red herrings. *Selective combination* involves going beyond discovering and encoding information to the combination of that information in new and productive ways. Finally, *selective comparison* involves relating new information to old information in novel ways. The processes involved in applying analogies from one problem to another could be considered a process of selective comparison.

Press.   Odd word choice—but Rhodes needed a "p" word, so it made the list. Press refers to the notion that creative behavior does not occur in a vacuum, that it's subject to various contextual factures and external pressures (maybe they felt removing the -ure was creative!). Simonton (2000) makes a similar point. Creative acts also are products of interpersonal, disciplinary, and sociocultural environments. Research on creativity indicates a sensitivity to a number of interpersonal factors. For example, some evidence (e.g., Amabile, 1996) indicates that being evaluated by others can decrease creativity. The popular notion of *brainstorming* refers to the supposed creative benefit of generating ideas in groups. Unfortunately, research evidence fails to support a relationship between brainstorming and creativity. Still, the technique enjoys great popularity in corporate settings. Another social component of creativity is the disciplinary environment in which it takes place, in part because experts in a given area define what is deemed creative. Finally, creativity is partially dependent on the sociocultural milieu in which one's work is conducted. According to Simonton, cultural diversity enhances creativity; a civilization's creativity tends to thrive when it opens itself up to alien influences through immigration or foreign study.

Product.   The final approach to creativity in the Rhodes (1961/1987) scheme is *product*, which refers to the outcome yielded by the creative process, be it a painting, poem, design, or new technology. Quite often, this approach is applied to case analyses of famously creative individuals like Picasso, Freud, Einstein, or da Vinci. The analysis of creativity from this perspective is a challenge, as its evaluation requires some type of objective standard. One such standard is productivity; some of the most creative individuals exhibited incredibly productive periods. Analyses of these "bursts of creativity" no doubt lend some insights into the creative process (Simonton, 1994). However, productivity is a narrow window on the creative process—although productivity and creativity may be associated, *more* doesn't always mean *better*. Another problem with using famous cases to illuminate creative processes is that it's limited in generalizability and applicability. The factors that made Einstein a brilliant and creative thinker were no doubt fairly unique to his abilities and life experiences and as we said earlier, Big-C is not the same as little-c or Pro-C.

A Taxonomy of Creative Processes and Products.   Dietrich (2004) proposes a useful scheme that imposes some order on the disparate research into creativity. In addition, he sketches the brain systems that are implicated in each of creativity's various manifestations. Although his neuropsychological analysis is beyond the scope of our discussion here, his taxonomy does provide an interesting framework for thinking about creativity.

Dietrich's scheme is captured by the simple matrix pictured in Figure 12.9. As you can see, Dietrich characterizes creative insights as a product of two distinct dimensions: processing mode and knowledge domain. *Processing mode* refers to whether creative insight emerges as the result of a deliberate and effortful search (i.e., System 2 or analytic problem solving mode) or whether it emerges spontaneously as an unexpected flash of insight (i.e., System 1 or intuition). *Knowledge domain* refers to the nature of the creative insight. Is it characterized more by a cognitive or emotional breakthrough?

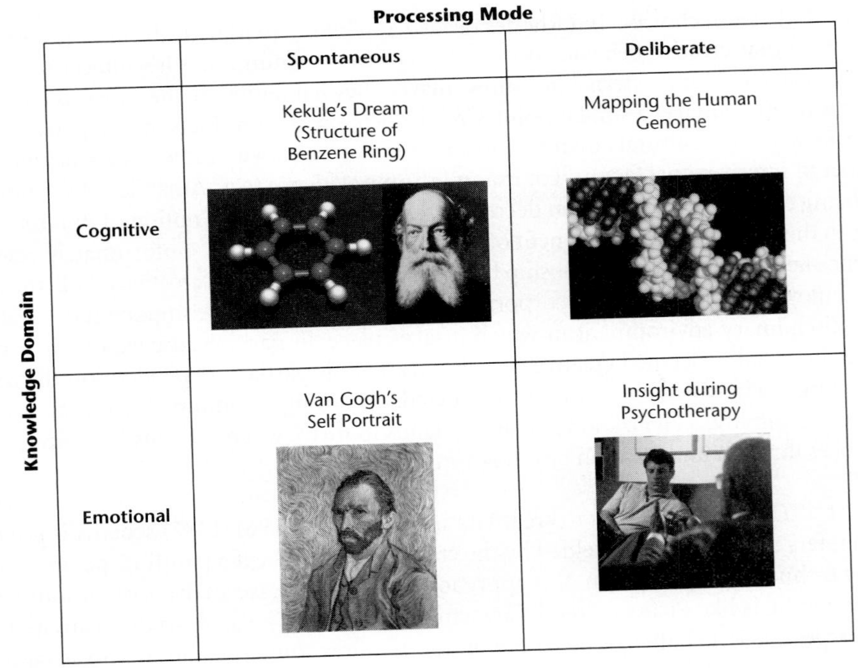

Figure 12.9

Four types of creative processes/products proposed by Dietrich (2004).

From Dietrich, A. (2004). The cognitive neuroscience of creativity. *Psychonomic Bulletin & Review, 11*(6), 1011–1026. Published by the Psychonomic Society. Adapted with permission.

Dietrich makes a point of emphasizing that the two key dimensions are continua, rather than dichotomies. A given creative product won't necessarily fall neatly into one of the four bins pictured. According to Dietrich, examples of *deliberate-cognitive* creativity would include the deliberate piecing together of the DNA structure and the systematic approach to inventing seen in Thomas Edison's work. *Spontaneous-cognitive* creativity would include Kekule's discovery of the structure of benzene (briefly mentioned earlier in the chapter) and Newton's supposed realization of the principle of gravity upon seeing an apple fall to the ground. *Deliberate-emotional* creativity would be exemplified by the insight of a psychotherapy client who has just had an emotional breakthrough. Finally, *spontaneous-emotional* creativity would involve the intense emotional experiences that are often said to lead to artistic creation. So what of the relationship between these dimensions of creativity, and the two main c's of creativity (Big and little) we discussed at the beginning of the section? There would seem to be no necessary correlation between the two approaches. Both eminent creativity (Big-C) and everyday creativity (little-c) could be manifested in any of the four categories sketched above.

Stop&Review

1. The illumination phase of problem solving is synonymous with
   a. insight.
   b. incubation.
   c. problem representation.
   d. creativity.
2. Describe the major difference between noninsight and insight problems.
3. What is incubation?
4. Identify the four types of creativity.

- Wallas proposes a four-stage model of problem solving. In the preparation stage, the solver gathers information. This is followed by a period of incubation (productive inactivity), which leads to illumination or insight (sudden realization of a problem's solution); the solution is checked in a verification phase.

- Noninsight problems are solved through incremental processes; insight problems are those in which the solution appears suddenly. Research has cast some doubt on the assumption that insight involves an "all-or-none" breakthrough, although metacognitive research verifies that people do have an "Aha!" experience as they arrive at the solution to an insight problem. The moments preceding insight, as well as the "aha" moment, have identifiable neural correlates.

- Although findings are somewhat inconsistent, it does appear that incubation (taking a break from problem solving) can enhance problem solving, but a problem's solution can be preceded by unconscious activation of problem-related concepts. One view of incubation states that a contextual change from the solution-blocking situation increases the likelihood of finding a solution.

- Creative problem solving is viewed as the product of a number of disparate influences, including aspects of the person, cognitive processing, and the particular context and pressures at play. Eminent creativity (Big-C) can be distinguished from little-c (everyday creativity), and also from personal (mini-C) and professional creativity (Pro-C).

References

Abe, N., Okuda, J., Suzuki, M., Sasaki, H., Matsuda, T., Mori, E., et al. (2008). Neural correlates of true memory, false memory, and deception. *Cerebral Cortex, 18*, 2811–2819.

Acheson, D. J., Postle, & Macdonald, M. C. (2010). The interaction of concreteness and phonological similarity in verbal working memory. *Journal of Experimental Psychology. Learning, Memory, and Cognition, 36,* 17–36.

Alais, D. & Burr, D. (2004). The ventriloquist effect results from near-optimal bimodal integration. *Current Biology, 14*, 257–262.

Alba, J.W. & Hasher, L. (1983). Is memory schematic? *Psychological Bulletin, 93*, 203–231.

Alexander, K.W., Quas, J. A., Goodman, G. S., Ghetti, S. G., Edelstein, R. S., Redlich, A. D. (2005). Traumatic impact predicts long-term memory for documented child sexual abuse. *Psychological Science, 16*, 33–40.

Alley, T. R., & Greene, M. E. (2008). The relative and perceived impact of irrelevant speech, vocal music and non-vocal music on working memory. *Current Psychology, 27*, 277–289.

Allopenna, P. D., Magnuson, J. S., & Tanenhaus, M. K. (1998). Tracking the time course of spoken word recognition using eye movements: Evidence for continuous mapping models. *Journal of Memory and Language, 38*, 419–439.

Amabile, T. M. (1990). Within you, without you: The social psychology of creativity, and beyond. In M. A. Runco & R. S. Albert (Eds.), *Theories of Creativity.* Newbury Park, CA: Sage.

Amabile, T. M. (1996). *Creativity in context.* Boulder, CO: Westview Press.

Anderson, J. R. (1982). Acquisition of cognitive skill. *Psychological Review, 89,* 369–406.

Anderson J.R. (1983). Retrieval of information from long-term memory. *Science* 220, 25–30

Anderson, J. R., & Bower, G. H. (1973). Human associative memory. Washington, DC: Winston.

Anderson, R. C., Pichert, J. W. (1978). Recall of previously unrecallable information following a shift in perspective. *Journal of Verbal Learning & Verbal Behavior, 17*, 1–12.

Andrade, J. (2009). What Does Doodling do? *Applied Cognitive Psychology*, 24, 100–106.

Andrews, B., Brewin, C. R., Ochera, J., Morton, J., Bekerian, D. A., Davies, G. M., (2000). The process of memory recovery among adults in therapy. *British Journal of Clinical Psychology, 39*, 11–26.

Andrews, P. W., & Thomson, J. A. (2009). The bright side of being blue: depression as an adaptation for analyzing complex problems. *Psychological Review, 116*, 620–654.

Argyle M,, & Cook, M. (1976) Gaze and mutual gaze. Cambridge, England: Cambridge University Press.

Arkes, H. R., & Blumer, C. (1985). The psychology of sunk cost. *Organizational Behavior and Human Decision Processes, 35,* 124–140.

Ashby, J. (2010). Phonology is fundamental in skilled reading: Evidence from ERPs. *Psychonomic Bulletin & Review, 17*, 95–100.

Ashby J, & Rayner K (2006). Literacy development: Insights from research on skilled reading In *Handbook of early literacy research*, Volume 2, (p. 52–63) D. Dickinson, S. Neuman (Eds), New York: Guilford Press.

Ashby, J., Rayner, K., & Clifton, C. (2005). Eye movements of highly skilled and average readers: Differential effects of frequency and predictability. *Quarterly Journal of Experimental Psychology, 58A*, 1065–1086.

Ashby, J., Sanders, L. D., & Kingston, J. (2009). Skilled readers begin processing phonological features by 80 ms: Evidence from ERPs. *Biological Psychology, 80*, 84–94.

Ashcraft, M. H. (1992). Cognitive arithmetic: A review of data and theory. *Cognition, 44,* 75–106.

Aslin, R. N., Saffran, J. R., & Newport, E. L. (1998). Computation of conditional probability statistics by 8-month-old infants. *Psychological Science* 9, 321–324.

Atchley RA, Halderman L, Kwasny K, & Buchanan L. (2003). The processing of pseudohomophones by adults with a history of developmental language disabilities. *Brain and Cognition, 53*, 139–144.

Atchley, R., & Kwasny, K. M. (2003). Using event-related potentials to examine hemispheric differences in semantic processing. *Brain and Cognition, 53*, 133–138.

Atkinson, R. C., & Shiffrin, R. M. (1968). Human memory: A proposed system and its control processes. In W. K. Spence & J. T. Spence (Eds.), *The psychology of learning and motivation,* Vol. 2: *Advances in learning and theory* (pp. 89–195). New York: Academic Press.

Atkinson, R. C., & Shiffrin, R. M. (1971). The control of short-term memory. *Scientific American, 224*, 82–90.

Atran, S. (1990). *Cognitive foundations of natural history.* New York: Cambridge University Press.

Auvray, M., Gallace, A., Hartcher-O'Brien, J., Tan, H. Z., & Spence, C. (2008). Tactile and visual distractors induce change blindness for tactile stimuli presented on the fingertips. *Brain Research, 1213*, 111–119.

Bachevalier, J., & Mishkin, M. (1984). An early and a late developing system for learning and retention in infant monkeys. *Behavioral Neuroscience, 98*, 70–77.

Baddeley, A. D. (1966). Short-term memory for word sequences as a function of acoustic, semantic, and formal similarity. *Quarterly Journal of Experimental Psychology, 18, 362–365.*

Baddeley, A. D. (1986). *Working memory.* Oxford: Oxford University Press.

Baddeley, A. D. (1993). Working memory or working attention? In A. Baddeley & L. Weiskrantz (Eds.), *Attention: Selection, awareness, and control: A tribute to Donald Broadbent* (pp. 152–170). Glouchestershire, UK: Clarendon Press.

Baddeley, A. (1996). The fractionation of working memory. *Proceedings of the National Academy of Sciences, 93*, 13468–13472.

Baddeley, A. D. (2000b). Short-term working memory. In E. Tulving & F. I. M. Craik (Eds.), *The Oxford handbook of memory* (pp. 77–92). New York: Oxford University Press.

Baddeley, A. D. (2002). Is Working Memory Still Working? *European Psychologist, 7,* 85–97.

Baddeley, A. D. (2007). *Working memory: Thought and action.* Oxford, England: Oxford University Press.

Baddeley, A. D., Lewis, V., & Vallar, G. (1984). Exploring the articulatory loop. *Quarterly Journal of Experimental Psychology, 36,* 233–252.

Baddeley, A. D., Thompson, N., & Buchanan, M. (1975). Word length and the structure of short-term memory. *Journal of Verbal Learning and Verbal Behavior, 14,* 575–589.

Badets, A., Blandin, Y., Bouquet, C. A., & Shea, C. H. (2006). The intention superiority effect in motor skill learning. *Journal of Experimental Psychology: Learning, Memory, and Cognition, 32,* 491–505.

Bahrick, H. P. (1979). Maintenance of knowledge: Questions about memory we forgot to ask. *Journal of Experimental Psychology: General, 108,* 296–308.

Bahrick, H. P. (1984). Semantic memory content in permastore: Fifty years of memory for Spanish learned in school. *Journal of Experimental Psychology: General, 113,* 1–29.

Bahrick, H. P., & Hall, L. K. (1991). Lifetime maintenance of high school mathematics content. *Journal of Experimental Psychology: General, 120,* 20–33.

Bai, X., Yan, G., Liversedge, S. P., Zang, C., & Rayner, K. (2008). Reading spaced and unspaced Chinese text: Evidence from eye movements. *Journal of Experimental Psychology. Human Perception and Performance, 34,* 1277–1287.

Balch, W. R., Bowman, K., & Mohler, L. A. (1992). Music-dependent memory in immediate and delayed word recall. *Memory and Cognition, 20,* 21–28.

Ball, C. T., & Little, J. C. (2006). A comparison of involuntary auto-biographical memory retrievals. *Applied Cognitive Psychology, 20,* 1167–1179.

Balota, D. A., Pollatsek, A., & Rayner, K. (1985). The interaction of contextual constraints and parafoveal visual information in reading. *Cognitive Psychology, 17,* 364–390.

Banaji, M. R., & Crowder, R. G. (1989). The bankruptcy of everyday memory. *American Psychologist, 44,* 1185–1193.

Banich, M. T. (2009). Executive function: The search for an integrated account. *Psychological Science, 18,* 89–94.

Bar-Eli, M., Avugos, S., & Raab, M. (2006). Twenty years of "hot hand" research: Review and critique. *Psychology of Sport and Exercise, 7,* 525–553.

Bargary, G., Barnett, K. J., Mitchell, K. J., & Newell, F. N. (2009). Colored-speech synaesthesia is triggered by multisensory, not unisensory, perception. *Psychological Science, 20,* 529–533.

Baron, J. (1999). *Thinking and deciding* (3rd ed.). New York: Cambridge University Press.

Baron-Cohen, S., Burt, L., Smith-Laittan, F., & Harrison, J. (1996). Synaesthesia: Prevalence and familiarity. *Perception, 25,* 1073–1080.

Barrett, H. C., & Kurzban, R. (2006). Modularity in cognition: Framing the debate. *Psychological Review, 113,* 628–647.

Barron, F., & Harrington, D. M. (1981). Creativity, intelligence, and personality. *Annual Review of Psychology, 32,* 439–476.

Barsalou, L. W. (1983). Ad hoc categories. *Memory and Cognition, 11,* 211–227.

Barsalou, L. W. (1988). The content and organization of autobiographical memories. In U. Neisser & E. Winograd (Eds.), *Remembering reconsidered: Ecological and traditional approaches to the study of cognition* (pp. 193–243). New York: Cambridge University Press.

Bartlett, F. C. (1932). *Remembering: A study in experimental and social psychology.* New York: Macmillan.

Bass, E., & Davis, L. (1988). *The courage to heal: A guide for women survivors of childhood sexual abuse.* New York: Harper and Row.

Bastian, B., & Haslam, N. (2006). Psychological essentialism and stereotype endorsement. *Journal of Experimental Social Psychology, 42,* 228–235.

Bates, E., Devescovi, A., & Wulfeck, B. (2001). Psycholinguistics: A cross-language perspective. *Annual Review of Psychology, 52,* 369–396.

Bauer, M. I., & Johnson-Laird, P. N. (1993). How diagrams can improve reasoning. *Psychological Science, 4,* 372–378.

Bauer, P. J. (2004). Getting explicit memory off the ground: Steps toward construction of a neuro-developmental account of changes in the first two years of life. *Developmental Review, 24,* 347–373.

Bauer, P. J. (2007). Recall in infancy. *Psychological Science, 16,* 142–146.

Bauer, P. J., Wenner, J. A., Dropik, P. L., & Wewerka, S. S. (2000). Pa-rameters of remembering and forgetting in the transition from infancy to early childhood. *Monographs of the Society for Research in Child Development, 65.*

Bechtel, W. (2002). Aligning multiple research techniques in cognitive neuroscience: Why is it important? *Philosophy of Science, 69,* S48–S58.

Bedau, H. A., & Radelet, M. L. (1987). Miscarriages of justice in potentially capital cases. *Stanford Law Review, 40,* 21–179.

Beghetto, R. A., & Kaufman, J. C. (2007). Toward a broader conception of creativity: A case for mini-c creativity. *Psychology of Aesthetics, Creativity, and the Arts, 1,* 73–79.

Behrman, B. W., & Davey, S. L. (2001). Eyewitness identification in actual criminal cases: An archival analysis. *Law and Human Behavior, 25,* 475–491.

Behrmann, M. (2000). The mind's eye mapped onto the brain's matter. *Current Directions in Psychological Science, 9,* 50–54.

Belin, P., Zatorre, R. J., Lafaille, P., Ahad, P., & Pike, B. (2000). Voice-selective areas in human auditory cortex. *Nature, 403,* 309–312.

Beluggi, U., Klima, E. S., & Siple, P. (1974). Remembering in signs. *Cognition, 3,* 83–125.

Benartzi, S., & Thaler, R.H. (2007). Heuristics and biases in retirement savings behavior. *Journal of Economic Perspectives, 21,* 81–104.

Berlin, B. (1992). *Ethnobiological classification.* Princeton, NJ: Princeton University Press.

Berman, M. G., Jonides, J., & Kaplan, S. (2008). The cognitive benefits of interacting with nature. *Psychological Science, 19,* 1207–1212.

Bermeitinger, C., Goelz, R., Johr, N., Neumann, M., Ecker, U. K., Doerr, R. (2009). The hidden persuaders break into the tired brain. *Journal of Experimental Social Psychology, 45,* 320–326.

Bernstein, D. M., & Loftus, E. F. (2009). The consequences of false memories for food preferences and choices. *Psychological Science, 4,* 135–139.

Bernstein, D. M., Laney, C., Morris, E. K., & Loftus, E. F. (2005a). False beliefs about fattening foods can have healthy consequences. *Proceedings of the National Academy of Sciences, 102,* 13724–13731.

Bernstein, D. M., Laney, C., Morris, E. K., & Loftus, E. F. (2005b). False memories about food can lead to food avoidance. *Social Cognition, 23,* 11–14.

Bernstein, D. M., & Loftus, E. F. (2009). How to tell if a particular memory is true or false. *Perspectives on Psychological Science, 4,* 370–374.

Berntsen, D. (1996). Involuntary biographical memories. *Applied Cognitive Psychology, 10,* 435–454.

Berntsen, D. (1998). Voluntary and involuntary access to autobiographical memory. *Applied Cognitive Psychology, 6,* 113–141.

Berntsen, D. (2007). Involuntary autobiographical memories: Speculations, findings and an attempt to integrate them. In J. Mace (Ed.), *Involuntary memory.* Oxford: Blackwell.

Berntsen, D., & Hall, N. M. (2004). The episodic nature of involuntary autobiographical memories. *Memory & Cognition, 32,* 789–803.

Berntsen, D., & Rubin, D. C. (2002). Emotionally charged autobiographical memories across the life span: The recall of happy, sad, traumatic and involuntary memories. *Psychology and Aging. 17,* 636–652

Berrios, G. E. (1995). Deja vu in France during the 19th century: A conceptual history. *Comprehensive Psychiatry, 36,* 123–129.

Bertelson, P. (1999). Ventriloquism: A case of crossmodal perceptual grouping. In G. Aschersleben, T. Bachmann, & J. Müsseler (Eds.), *Cognitive contributions to the perception of spatial and temporal events. Advances in psychology, 129,* (347–362). Amsterdam, Netherlands: North-Holland/ Elsevier Science Publishers.

Besner, D., Stolz, J. A., & Boutilier, C. (1997). The Stroop effect and the myth of automaticity. *Psychonomic Bulletin and Review, 4,* 221–225.

Biederman, I. (1987). Recognition-by-components: A theory of human image understanding. *Psychological Review, 94,* 115–147.

Biederman, I., & Cooper, E. E. (1991). Priming contour-deleted images: Evidence for intermediate representations in visual object recognition. *Cognitive Psychology, 23,* 393–419.

Biederman, I., & Gerhardstein, P. C. (1993). Recognizing depth-rotated objects: Evidence and conditions for three-dimensional viewpoint invariance. *Journal of Experimental Psychology: Learning, Memory, and Cognition, 19,* 1162–1182.

Bilalić, M., McLeod, P., & Gobet, F. (2008). Inflexibility of experts— reality or myth? Quantifying the Einstellung effect in chess masters. *Cognitive Psychology, 56,* 73–102.

Bisanz, T., Bisanz, M., & Korpan, J. (1994). Inductive reasoning. In R. J. Sternberg (Ed.), *Thinking and problem solving* (pp. 179–213). New York: Academic Press.

Bisiach, E., & Luzzatti, C. (1978). Unilateral neglect of representational space. *Cortex, 14,* 129–133.

Blais, C., Jack, R. E., Scheepers, C., Fiset, D., & Caldara, R. (2008). Culture shapes how we look at faces. PLoS One, 3, e3022.

Blanchard, I., Pollatsek, A., & Rayner, K. (1989). The acquisition of parafoveal word information in reading. *Perception and Psychophysics, 46,* 85–94.

Blanchette, I., & Dunbar, K. (2000). How analogies are generated: The roles of structural and superficial similarity. *Memory and Cognition, 28,* 108–124.

Blank, H., Nestler, S., von Collani, G., & Fischer, V. (2008). How many hindsight biases are there? *Cognition, 106,* 1408–1440.

Block, N. (1995). On a confusion about a question of consciousness. *Behavioral and Brain Sciences, 18,* 227–287.

Bloom, P. & Gelman, S. A. (2008). Psychological essentialism in selecting the 14th Dalai Lama. *Trends in Cognitive Science, 12,* 243.

Bock, J. K. (2001). Language production. In R. A. Wilson & F. C. Keil (Eds.) *The MIT encyclopedia of the cognitive sciences.* Cambridge, MA: MIT Press.

Boduroglu, A., Shah, P., & Nisbett, R. E. (2009). Cultural differences in allocation of attention in visual information processing. *Journal of Cross-Cultural Psychology, 40,* 349–360.

Boon, S. D., & Griffin, D. W. (1996). The construction of risk in relationships: The role of framing in decisions about intimate relationships. *Personal Relationships, 3,* 293–306.

Bowden, E. M., & Beeman, M. J. (1998). Getting the right idea: Semantic activation in the right hemisphere may help solve insight problems. *Psychological Science, 9,* 435–440.

Bowden, E. M., & Jung-Beeman, M. (2003). Aha! Insight experience correlates with solution activation in the right hemisphere. *Psychonomic Bulletin & Review, 10*, 730–737.

Bowden, E. M., Jung-Beeman, M., Fleck, J., & Kounios, J. (2005). New approaches to demystifying insight. *Trends in Cognitive Sciences, 9*, 322–328.

Bower, G. H., Black, J. B., & Turner, T. J. (1979). Scripts in memory for text. *Cognitive Psychology, 11*, 177–120.

Bower, G. H., Clark, M. C., Lesgold, A. M., & Winzenz, D. (1969). Hierarchical schemes in recall of categorized word lists. *Journal of Verbal Learning and Verbal Behavior, 8*, 323–343.

Bowers, K. S., Regehr, G., Balthazard, C., & Parker, K. (1990). Intuition in the context of discovery. *Cognitive Psychology, 22*, 72–110.

Brainerd, C. J., & Reyna, V. F. (2005). The science of false memory. New York: Oxford University Press.

Brannon, L. A., & Brock, T. C. (1994). Test of schema correspondence theory of persuasion: Effects of matching an appeal to actual, ideal, and product "selves." In E. M. Clark, T. C. Brock, & D. W. Stewart (Eds.), *Attention, attitude, and affect in response to advertising* (p. 169–188) Hillsdale, NJ: Erlbaum.

Bransford, J. D., & Stein, B. S. (1993). *The IDEAL problem solver* (2nd ed.). New York: Freeman.

Brédart, S., Brennen, T., Delchambre, M., McNeill, A., & Burton, A. M. (2005). Naming very familiar people: When retrieving names is faster than retrieving semantic biographical information. *British Journal of Psychology, 96*, 205–214.

Bregman, A. S. (1990). *Auditory scene analysis: The perceptual organization of sound.* Cambridge, MA: MIT Press.

Behme, C., & Deacon, S. H. (2008). Language learning in infancy: Does the empirical evidence support a domain-specific language-acquisition device? *Philosophical Psychology, 21*, 641–671.

Brent, M. R., & Siskind, J. M. (2001). The role of exposure to isolated words in early vocabulary development. *Cognition, 81*, B33–B44.

Brewer, N., & Wells, G. L. (2006). The confidence-accuracy relationship in eyewitness identification: Effects of lineup instructions, foil similarity, and target-absent base rates. *Journal of Experimental Psychology: Applied, 12*, 11–30.

Brewer, W. (1986). What is autobiographical memory? In D. C. Rubin (Ed.), *Autobiographical memory* (pp. 25–49). Cambridge, UK: Cambridge University Press.

Brewer, W. F. (1988). Memory for randomly sampled autobiographical events. In U. Neisser & E. Winograd (Eds.), *Remembering reconsidered: Ecological and traditional approaches to the study of memory* (Emory Symposia in Cognition, vol. 2, pp. 21–90). Cambridge, UK: Cambridge University Press.

Brewer, N., & Wells, G. L. (2006). The confidence-accuracy relationship in eyewitness identification: Effects of lineup instructions, foil similarity, and target-absent base rates. *Journal of Experimental Psychology: Applied, 12*, 11–30.

Brewin, C. R., Christodoulides, J., & Hutchinson, G. (1996). Intrusive thoughts and intrusive memories in a nonclinical sample. *Cognition and Emotion, 10*, 107–112.

Brewin, C. R. (2007). Autobiographical memory for trauma: update on four controversies. *Memory, 15*, 227–248.

Briere, J., & Conte, J. (1993). Self-reported amnesia for abuse in adults molested as children. *Journal of Traumatic Stress, 6*, 21–31.

Broadbent, D. A. (1958). *Perception and communication.* London: Pergamon Press.

Brooks, L. R. (1968). Spatial and verbal components of the act of recall. *Canadian Journal of Psychology, 22*, 349–366.

Brooks, L. R. (1978). Nonanalytic concept formation and memory for instances. In E. Rosch & B. B. Lloyd (Eds.), *Cognition and categorization* (pp. 169–211). Hillsdale, NJ: Erlbaum.

Brooks, L. R. (1987). Decentralized control of categorization: The role of prior processing episodes. In U. Neisser (Ed.), *Concepts and conceptual development: The ecological and intellectual factors in categorization* (pp. 141–174). Cambridge, UK: Cambridge University Press.

Broome, J. (1991). *Weighing goods: Equality, uncertainty and time.* Oxford: Basil Blackwell.

Brown, A. S. (2003). A review of the déjà vu experience. *Psychological Bulletin, 129*, 394–413.

Brown, A. S. (2004). The déjà vu illusion. *Current Directions in Psychological Science, 13*, 256–259.

Brown, E., Deffenbacher, K., & Sturgill, W. (1977). Memory for faces and the circumstances of encounter. *Journal of Applied Psychology, 62*, 311–318.

Brown, J. (1958). Some tests of the decay theory of immediate memory. *Quarterly Journal of Experimental Psychology, 10*, 12–21.

Brown, R., & Kulik, J. (1977). Flashbulb memories. *Cognition, 5*, 73–99.

Bruce, D. (1989). Functional explanations of memory. In L. W. Poon, D. C. Rubin & B. A. Wilson (Eds.), *Everyday cognition in adulthood and late life* (p. 44–58). Cambridge: Cambridge University Press.

Bruce, V., & Young, A. W. (1986). Understanding face recognition. *British Journal of Psychology, 77*, 305–327.

Bruner, J. (1990). *Acts of meaning.* Cambridge, MA: Harvard University Press.

Bruner, J. (1996). *The culture of education.* Cambridge, MA: Harvard University Press.

Bruner, J. S., Goodnow, J. J., & Austin, G. A. (1956). *A study of thinking.* New York: Wiley.

Brunswick, N., E. McCrory, C. J. Price, C. D. Frith, & U. Frith. (1999). Explicit and implicit processing of words and pseudowords by adult developmental dyslexics: A search for Wernicke's Wortschatz. *Brain, 122*, 1901–17.

Brysbaert, M., & Vitu, F. (1998). Word skipping: Implications for theories of eye movement control in reading. In G. Underwood (Ed.), *Eye guidance in reading and scene perception* (pp. 125–147). Amsterdam: Elsevier Science.

Buchsbaum, B. R., & D'Esposito, M. (2008). The search for the phonological store: From loop to convolution. *Journal of Cognitive Neuroscience, 20*, 762–78.

Bunge S. A., & Souza M. J. (2009). Executive function and higher-order cognition: Neuroimaging. In L. R. Squire (Ed.) *Encyclopedia of Neuroscience, Volume 4*, (p. 111–116). Oxford: Academic Press.

Bunting, M. F., Conway, A. R. A., & Heitz, R. P. (2004). Individual differences in the fan effect and working memory capacity. *Journal of Memory and Language, 51*, 604–622.

Burnham, D., Kitamura C., & Vollmer-Conna U. (2002). What's New Pussycat? On talking to babies and animals. Science, *296*, 1435.

Burns, B. D. (2004). Heuristics as beliefs and as behaviors: The adaptiveness of the "hot hand." *Cognitive Psychology, 48*, 295–331.

Burton, M. A., & Bruce, V. (1992). I recognize your face, but I can't remember your name: A simple explanation? *British Journal of Psychology, 83*, 45–60.

Butler, A. C., & Roediger, H. L. (2007). Testing improves long-term retention in a simulated classroom setting. *European Journal of Cognitive Psychology, 19*, 514–527.

Cacciari, C. (2008). Crossing the senses in metaphorical language. In R. Gibbs (Ed.) *Cambridge Handbook of Metaphor and Thought*, (pp. 425–446). New York, NY: Cambridge University Press.

Calderwood, L., & Burton, A. M. (2006). Children and adults recall the names of highly familiar faces faster than semantic information.

British Journal of Psychology, 441–454.

Callender, A. A., & McDaniel, M. A. (2007). The benefits of embedded question adjuncts for low and high structure builders. *Journal of Educational Psychology, 99*, 339–348.

Calvert, G. A., Bullmore, E. T., & Brammer, R. (1997). Activation of auditory cortex during silent lipreading. *Science, 276*, 593–596.

Campbell, R., & Dodd, B. (1980). Hearing by eye. *Quarterly Journal of Experimental Psychology, 32*, 85–99.

Caramazza, A., & Brones., I. (1980). Semantic classification by bilinguals. *Canadian Journal of Psychology, 34*, 77–81.

Carlson, C. A., Gronlund, S. D., & Clark, S. E. (2008). Lineup composition, suspect position, and the sequential lineup advantage, *Journal of Experimental Psychology: Applied, 14*, 118–128.

Carlson, K. A., & Shu, S. (2007). The rule of three: How the third event signals the emergence of a streak. *Social Psychology, 104*, 113–121.

Carmichael, L., Hogan, H. P., & Walters, A. A. (1932). An experimental psychology of the effect of language on the reproduction of visually perceived form. *Journal of Experimental Psychology, 15*, 73–86.

Carreiras, M., Gernsbacher, M. A., & Villa, V. (1995). The advantage of first mention in Spanish. *Psychonomic Bulletin and Review, 2*, 124–129.

Carrier, M., & Pashler, H. (1992). The influence of retrieval on retention. *Memory and Cognition, 20*, 633–642.

Carroll, D. W. (1994). *Psychology of language* (2nd ed.). Pacific Grove, CA: Brooks/Cole.

Caruso, E. M., Gilbert, D. T., & Wilson, T. D. (2008). A wrinkle in time. *Psychological Science, 19*, 796–801.

Carver, R. P. (1971). Pupil dilation and its relationship to information processing during reading and listening. *Journal of Applied Psychology, 55*, 126–134.

Casasanto, D., & Dijkstra, K. (2010). Motor action and emotional memory. *Cognition, 115*, 179–85.

Castel, A. D., Mccabe, D. P., Roediger, H. L., & Heitman, J. L. (2007). The dark side of expertise. *Psychological Science, 18*, 3–5.

Castles, A., & Coltheart, M. (2004). Is there a causal link from phonological awareness to success in learning to read? *Cognition, 91*, 77–111

Catal, L. L., & Fitzgerald, J. M. (2004). Autobiographical memory in two older adults over a twenty-year retention interval. *Memory & Cognition, 32*, 311–323.

Catrambone, R., Craig, D. L., & Nersessian, N. J. (2006). The role of perceptually represented structure in analogical problem solving. *Memory & Cognition, 34*, 1126–1132.

Cave, K. R., & Bichot, N. P. (1999). Visuospatial attention: Beyond a spotlight model. *Psychonomic Bulletin & Review, 6*, 204–223.

Cepeda, N. J., Vul, E., Rohrer, D., Wixted, J. T., & Pashler, H. (2008). Spacing effects in learning. *Psychological Science, 19*, 1095–1102.

Chabris, C. F., & Hearst, E. S. (2003). Visualization, pattern recognition, and forward search: Effects of playing speed and sight of the position on grandmaster chess errors. *Cognitive Science, 27*, 637–648.

Chang, F., Dell, G. S., & Bock, K. (2006). Becoming syntactic. *Psychological Review, 113*, 234–272.

Charness, N. (1976). Memory for chess positions: Resistance to interference. *Journal of Experimental Psychology: Human Learning and Memory, 2*, 641–653.

Chase, K., & Ericsson, W. G. (1982). Exceptional memory. *American Scientist, 70*, 607–615.

Chase, W. G., & Simon, H. A. (1973). Perception in chess. *Cognitive Psychology, 4*, 55–81.

Chatterjee, A. (2005). A madness to the methods in cognitive neuroscience? *Journal of Cognitive Neuroscience, 17*, 847–849.

Cheesman, J., & Merikle, P. M. (1984). Priming with and without awareness. *Perception & Psychophysics, 36,* 387–395.

Cherry, E. C. (1953). Some experiments on the recognition of speech, with one and with two ears. *Journal of the Acoustical Society of America, 25,* 975–979.

Chi, M. T. H. (1996). Constructing self-explanations and scaffolded explanations in tutoring. *Applied Cognitive Psychology, 10,* 33–49.

Chi, M. T. H., Feltovich, P. J., & Glaser, R. (1981). Categorization and representation of physics problems by experts and novices. *Cognitive Science, 5,* 121–152.

Chisholm, S., Caird, J. K., & Lockhart, J. (2008). The effects of practice with MP3 players on driving performance. *Accident Analysis and Prevention, 40,* 704–713.

Chomsky, N. (1957). *Syntactic structures.* The Hague: Mouton.

Chomsky, N. (1959). Review of Skinner's *Verbal Behavior. Language, 35,* 26–58.

Chomsky, N. (1986). *Knowledge of language: Its nature, origin, and use.* New York: Praeger.

Christiansen, S.-A. (1989). Flashbulb memories: Special, but not so special. *Memory and Cognition, 17,* 435–443.

Christiansen, S.-A. (1992). Emotional stress and eyewitness memory: A critical review. *Psychological Bulletin, 112,* 284–309.

Chu, S., & Downes, J. J. (2000). Long live Proust: The odour-cued autobiographical memory bump. *Cognition, 75,* B41–B50.

Chu, S. and Downes, J. J. (2002) Proust nose best: odors are better cues of autobiographical memory. *Memory and Cognition., 30,* 511–518.

Claparede, E. (1951). Recognition and "me-ness." In D. Rapaport (Ed.), *Organization and pathology of thought* (pp. 58–75). New York: Columbia University Press. (Reprinted from *Archives de Psychologie,* 1911, *11,* 79–90.)

Clark, H. H., & Haviland, S. E. (1977). Comprehension and the given-new contract. In R. O. Freedle (Ed.), *Discourse production and comprehension.* Norwood: Ablex.

Clement S., Demany L., & Semal, C. (1999). Memory for pitch versus memory for loudness. *Journal of the Acoustical Society of America, 106,* 2805–2811.

Clifasefi, S. L., Takarangi, M. K., & Bergman, J. S. (2006). Blind drunk: the effects of alcohol on inattentional blindness. *Applied Cognitive Psychology, 20*(5), 697–704.

Cole, J. (1995). *Pride and a daily marathon.* Cambridge, MA: MIT Press.

Cole, N. S. (1997). *The ETS gender study: How females and males perform in educational settings.* Princeton, NJ: Educational Testing Services.

Colegate, R. L., Hoffman, J. E., & Eriksen, C. W. (1973). Selective encoding from multielement visual displays. *Perception & Psychophysics, 14,* 217–224.

Collins, A. M., & Loftus, E. F. (1975). A spreading-activation theory of semantic processing. *Psychological Review, 82,* 407–428.

Collins, A. M., & Quillian, M. R. (1969). Retrieval time from semantic memory. *Journal of Verbal Learning and Verbal Behavior, 8,* 240–247.

Collins, A. M., & Quillian, M. R. (1970). Does category size affect reaction time? *Journal of Verbal Learning and Verbal Behavior, 9,* 432–438

Coltheart, M. (2001). Assumptions and methods in cognitive neuropsychology. In B. Rapp (Ed.) *Handbook of Cognitive Neuropsychology,* (3–22). New York: Psychology Press.

Coltheart, M., Rastle, K., Perry, C., Langdon, R., & Ziegler, J. (2001). DRC: A dual route cascaded model of visual word recognition and reading aloud. *Psychological Review, 108,* 204–256.

Coltheart, V. (1993). Effects of phonological similarity and concurrent irrelevant articulation on short-term memory recall of repeated

and novel lists. *Memory and Cognition, 21,* 539–545.

Conrad, C. (1972). Cognitive economy in semantic memory. *Journal of Experimental Psychology, 92,* 149–154.

Conrad, R. (1964). Acoustic confusions in immediate memory. *British Journal of Psychology, 55,* 75–84.

Conrad, R., & Hull, A. J. (1968). Input modality and the serial position curve in short-term memory. *Psychonomic Science, 10,* 135–136.

Costantini M, & Haggard P. (2007). The rubber hand illusion: Sensitivity and reference frame for body ownership. *Consciousness and Cognition, 16,* 229–40.

Conway, M. (1992). A model of autobiographical memory. In M. A. Conway, D. C. Rubin, H. Spinnler and W. A.Wagenaar, (Eds), Theoretical perspectives on autobiographical memory, (pp.167–194) Kluwer, Dordrecht.

Conway, A. R. A., Cowan, N., & Bunting, M. F. (2001). The cocktail party phenomenon revisited: The importance of WM capacity. *Psychonomic Bulletin & Review, 8,* 331–335.

Conway, M. A. (2009). Episodic memories. Neuropsychologia, 47, 2305–2313.

Conway, M. A. (1990). *Autobiographical memory: An introduction.* Buckingham, UK: Open University Press.

Conway, M. A. (1991). In defense of everyday memory. *American Psychologist, 46,* 19–26.

Conway, M. A. (1997). Introduction: Models and data. In M. A. Conway (Ed.), *Cognitive models of memory.* Cambridge, MA: MIT Press.

Conway, M. A. (2005). Memory and the self. *Journal of Memory and Language, 53,* 594–628.

Conway, M. A., & Bekerian, D. A. (1987). Organization in autobiographical memory. *Memory and Cognition, 15,* 119–132.

Conway, M. A., Cohen, G., & Stanhope, N. (1991). On the very long-term retention of knowledge acquired through formal education: Twelve years of cognitive psychology. *Journal of Experimental Psychology: General, 120,* 395–409.

Conway, M. A., & Pleydell-Pearce, C. W. 2001. The construction of autobiographical memories in the self memory system. *Psychological Review, 107,* 261–288.

Conway, M. A., Pleydell-Pearce, C. W., & Whitecross, S. E. (2001). The neuroanatomy of autobiographical memory: A slow cortical potential study of autobiographical memory retrieval. *Journal of Memory and Language, 45,* 493–524.

Conway, M. A., Singer, J. A., & Tagini, A. (2004). The self and autobiographical memory: Correspondence and coherence. *Social Cognition, 22,* 495–537.

Conway, M. A., Turk, D. J., Miller, S. L., Logan, J., Nebes, R. D., Meltzer, C., & Becker, J. T. (1999). A positron emission tomography (PET) study of autobiographical memory retrieval. *Memory, 7,* 679–702.

Cooper, J. M., Strayer, D. L., & City, S. L. (2008). Effects of simulator practice and real-world experience on cell-phone related driver distraction. *Human Factors, 50,* 893–902.

Cooper, R. P., & Shallice, T. (2006). Hierarchical schemas and goals in the control of sequential behavior. *Psychological Review, 113,* 887–916.

Copeland, D. E., & Radvansky, G. A. (2004). Working memory and syllogistic reasoning. *Quarterly Journal of Experimental Psychology, 57,* 1437–1457.

Corkin, S. (1968) Acquisition of motor skill after bilateral medial temporal-lobe excision. Neuropsychologia, 6, 255–265.

Cornoldi, D., & de Beni, R. (1991). Memory for discourse: Loci mnemonics and the oral presentation effect. *Applied Cognitive Psychology, 5,* 511–518.

Correa-Chávez, M., Rogoff, B., & Arauz, R. M. (2005). Cultural patterns in attending to two events at once. *Child Development, 76,* 664–678.

Corteen, R. S., & Wood, B. (1972). Autonomic responses to shock-associated words in an unattended channel. *Journal of Experimental Psychology, 94,* 308–313.

Cosmides, L. (1989). The logic of social exchange: Has natural selection shaped how humans reason? Studies with the Wason selection task. *Cognition, 31,* 187–276.

Costello, P., Jiang, Y., Baartman, B., McGlennen, K., & He, S. (2009). Semantic and subword priming during binocular suppression. *Consciousness and Cognition, 18,* 375–82.

Courtois, C. A. (1997). Delayed memories of child sexual abuse: Critique of the controversy and clinical guidelines. In M. Conway (Ed.), *Recovered memories and false memories* (pp. 206–229). Oxford: Oxford University Press.

Cowan, N. (1988). Evolving conceptions of memory storage, selective attention, and their mutual constraints within the human information-processing system. *Psychological Bulletin, 104,* 163–191.

Cowan, N. (1995). *Attention and memory: An integrated framework.* New York: Oxford University Press.

Cowan, N. (2001). The magical number 4 in short-term memory: A reconsideration of mental storage capacity. *Behavioral and Brain Sciences, 24,* 87–185.

Craik, F. I. M. (1986). A functional account of age differences in memory. In F. Klix & H. Hagendorf (Eds.), *Human memory and cognitive capabilities: Mechanisms and performances* (pp. 409–422). Amsterdam: Elsevier-North-Holland.

Craik, F. I. M., & Lockhart, R. S. (1972). Levels of processing: A framework for memory research. *Journal of Verbal Learning and Verbal Behavior, 11,* 671–684.

Craik, F. I. M., & McDowd, J. M. (1987). Age differences in recall and recognition. *Journal of Experimental Psychology: Learning, Memory, and Cognition, 13,* 474–479.

Craik, F. I. M., & Salthouse, T. A. (2008). *The handbook of aging and cognition* (3rd ed.). New York: Psychology Press.

Craik, F. I. M., & Tulving, E. (1975). Depth of processing and the retention of words in episodic memory. *Journal of Experimental Psychology: General, 104,* 268–294.

Craik, F. I. M., & Watkins, M. J. (1973). The role of rehearsal in short-term memory. *Journal of Verbal Learning and Verbal Behavior, 12,* 599–607.

Crawley, R. (1986). Some factors influencing the comprehension of pronouns in texts. In C. Clifton (Ed.) (p. 613–620). *Proceedings of the Eighth Annual Conference of the Cognitive Science Society.* Hillsdale, NJ, Erlbaum.

Crovitz, H. F., & Schiffman, H. (1974). Frequency of episodic memories as a function of their age. *Bulletin of the Psychonomic Society, 4,* 517–518.

Crowder, R. G. (1976). *Principles of learning and memory.* Hillsdale, NJ: Erlbaum.

Cunningham, S. J., Turk, D. J., Macdonald, L. M., & Neil Macrae, C. (2008). Yours or mine? Ownership and memory. *Consciousness and Cognition, 17,* 312–318.

Cutler, A., & Butterfield, S. (1992). Rhythmic cues to speech segmentation: Evidence from juncture misperception. *Journal of Memory and Language, 31,* 218–236.

Cutler, A., & Carter, D. M. (1987). The predominance of strong initial syllables in the English vocabulary. *Computer Speech and Language, 2,* 133–142.

Cutler, B. L., & Penrod, S. D. (1989). Moderators of the confidence-accuracy relationship in face recognition: The roles of information-processing and base rates. *Applied Cognitive Psychology, 3,* 95–107.

Cutler, B. L., & Penrod, S. D. (1995). *Mistaken identification: Eyewitnesses, psychology, and the law*. New York: Cambridge University Press.

Cutler, B. L., Penrod, S. D., & Martens, T. K. (1987). Improving the reliability of eyewitness identifications: Putting context into context. *Journal of Applied Psychology, 72,* 629–637.

Dade L. A., Zatorre R. J., Evans A. C., & Jones-Gottman, M. (2001). Working memory in another dimension: Functional imaging of human olfactory working memory. *Neuroimage 14,* 650–660.

Dando, C., Wilcock, R., & Milne, R. (2009). The cognitive interview: The efficay of a modified mental reinstatement of context procedure for frontline police investigators *Applied Cognitive Psychology, 23,* 138–147.

Daneman, M., & Merikle, P. M. (1996). Working memory and language comprehension: A meta-analysis. *Psychonomic Bulletin and Review, 3,* 422–433.

Darwin, C. J., Turvey, M. T., & Crowder, R. G. (1973). An auditory analogue of the Sperling partial-report procedure. *Cognitive Psychology, 3,* 255–267.

Davenport, J. L., & Potter, M. C. (2004). Scene consistency in object and background perception. *Psychological Science, 15,* 559–564.

Davidoff, J., Fonteneau, E., & Fagot, J. (2008). Local and global processing: Observations from a remote culture. *Cognition, 108,* 702–709.

Davidson, J. E. (1995). The suddenness of insight. In R. J. Sternberg & J. E. Davidson (Eds.), *The nature of insight* (pp. 125–155). Cambridge, MA: MIT Press.

Davis, P. J. (1999). Gender differences in autobiographical memory for emotional experiences. *Journal of Personality and Social Psychology, 76,* 498–510.

Davies, G., & Hine, S. (2007). Change blindness and eyewitness testimony. *The Journal of Psychology, 141,* 423–34.

Davis, D., Loftus, E. F., Vanous, S., & Cucciare, M. (2008). 'Unconscious transference' can be an instance of 'change blindness'. *Applied Cognitive Psychology, 22,* 605–623.

Davoli, C. C., & Abrams, R. A. (2009). Reaching out with the imagination. *Psychological Science, 20,* 293–295.

Deakin, J. M., & Allard, F. (1991). Skilled memory in expert figure skaters. *Memory and Cognition, 19,* 79–86.

Deese, J. (1959). On the prediction of occurrence of particular verbal intrusions in immediate recall. *Journal of Experimental Psychology, 58,* 17–22.

Deffenbacher, K. A. (1980). Eyewitness accuracy and confidence: Can we infer anything about their relationship? *Law and Human Behavior, 4,* 243–260.

Deffenbacher, K. A. (1994). Effects of arousal on everyday memory. *Human Performance, 7,* 141–161.

Deffenbacher, K. A., Bornstein, B. H., Penrod, S., & McGorty, E. K. (2004). A meta-analytic review of the effects of high stress on eyewitness memory. *Law and Human Behavior, 28,* 687–706.

De Fockert, J., Davidoff, J., Fagot, J., Parron, C., & Goldstein, J. (2007). More accurate size contrast judgments in the Ebbinghaus illusion by a remote culture. *Journal of Experimental Psychology: Human Perception and Performance, 33,* 738–742.

de Groot, A. D. (1978). *Thought and choice in chess.* The Hague, Netherlands: Mouton. (Original work published 1946).

Dell, G. S. (1986). A spreading-activation theory of retrieval in sentence production. *Psychological Review, 93,* 283–321.

Dell, G. S., Chang, F., & Griffin, Z. M. (1999). Connectionist models of language production: Lexical access and grammatical encoding. *Cognitive Science, 23,* 517–542.

Della Sala, S., Gray, C., Baddeley, A., Allamano, N., & Wilson, L. (1999). Pattern span: A tool for unwelding visuo-spatial memory. *Neuropsychologia, 37,* 1189–1199.

Demers, R. A. (1988). Linguistics and animal communication. In F. J. Newmeyer (Ed.), *Language: Psychological and biological aspects* (pp. 314–345). Cambridge, UK: Cambridge University Press.

Demers, R. A. 1988. Linguistics and animal communication. In F. Newmeyer (Ed.), *Linguistics: The Cambridge Survey.* (314–335). Cambridge: Cambridge University Press.

Dempster, F. N. (1992). The rise and fall of the inhibitory mechanism: Toward a unified theory of cognitive development and aging. Developmental Review, *12,* 45–75.

Denes, P. B., & Pinson, E. N. (1993). The Speech Chain. Murray Hill, NJ: Bell Telephone.

Desai R, Conant L, Waldron E, Binder JR (2006). The effects of phonological complexity and task difficulty on past tense processing: An fMRI study. Journal *of Cognitive Neuroscience, 18,* 278–297.

Desor, J. A., & Beauchamp, G. K. (1974). The human capacity to transmit olfactory information. *Perception & Psychophysics, 16,* 551–556.

Deutsch, J., & Deutsch, D. (1963). Attention: Some theoretical considerations. *Psychological Review, 70,* 80–90.

Dewsbury, D. A. (2000). Comparative cognition in the 1930's. *Psychonomic Bulletin and Review, 7,* 267–283.

Diamond, A., Barnett, W. S., Thomas, J., & Munro, S. (2007). Preschool program improves cognitive control. *Science, 318,* 1387–1388.

Diamond, A., & Doar, B. (1989). The performance of human infants on a measure of frontal cortex function, the delayed response task. *Developmental Psychobiology, 22,* 271–294.

Diamond, R., & Carey, S. (1986). Why faces are and are not special: An effect of expertise. *Journal of Experimental Psychology: General, 115,* 107–117.

Diehl, R. L., Lotto, A. J., & Holt, L. L. (2004). Speech perception. *Annual Review of Psychology, 55,* 149–179.

Dietrich, A. (2004). The cognitive neuroscience of creativity. *Psychonomic Bulletin & Review, 11,* 1011–1026.

Dijksterhuis, A., Aarts, H., & Smith, P. (2005). The power of the subliminal: On subliminal persuasion and other potential applications. In R. Hassin, J. Uleman, & J. Bargh, *The new unconscious* (p. 77–106). New York, NY: Oxford University Press.

Dijkstra, K., Kaschak, M. P., & Zwaan, R. A. (2007). Body posture facilitates retrieval of autobiographical memories. *Cognition, 102,* 139–49.

Di Lollo, V. (1980). Temporal integration in visual memory. *Journal of Experimental Psychology: General, 109,* 75–97.

Ditman, T., Brunyé, T. T., Mahoney, C. R., & Taylor, H. A. (2009). Simulating an enactment effect: Pronouns guide action simulation during narrative comprehension. *Cognition, 115,* 172–178.

Dodson, C. S., & Hege, A. C. G. (2005). Speeded retrieval abolishes the false-memory suppression effect: Evidence for the distinctiveness heuristic. *Psychonomic Bulletin & Review, 12,* 726–731.

Dodson, C. S., & Schacter, D. L. (2001a). "If I had said it, I would have remembered it": Reducing false memories with a distinctiveness heuristic. *Psychonomic Bulletin and Review, 8,* 155–161.

Dodson, C. S., & Schacter, D. L. (2001b). Memory distortion. In B. Rapp (Ed.), *The handbook of cognitive neuropsychology: What deficits reveal about the human mind*(pp. 445–463). New York: Psychology Press.

Dominowski, R. L., & Jenrick, R. (1972). Effects of hints and interpolated activity on solution of an insight problem. *Psychonomic Science, 26,* 335–338.

Dornburg, C. C., & McDaniel, M. A. (2006). The cognitive interview enhances long-term free recall of older adults. *Psychology and Aging, 21,* 196–200.

Drews, F. A., Pasupathi, M., & Strayer, D. L. (2008). Passenger and cell phone conversations in simulated driving. *Journal of Experimental Psychology. Applied, 14,* 392–400.

Drews, F. A., Yazdani, H., Godfrey, C. N., & Cooper, J. M., Strayer, D. L., (2009). Text messaging during simulated driving. *Human Factors, 51,* 762–770.

Drieghe, D., Rayner, K., & Pollatsek, A. (2005). Word skipping during reading revisited. *Journal of Experimental Psychology:Human Perception and Performance, 31,* 954–969.

Driver, J. (2001). A selective review of selective attention research from the past century. *British Journal of Psychology, 92,* 53–78.

Dror, I. E., & Kosslyn, S. M. (1994). Mental imagery and aging. *Psychology and Aging, 9,* 90–102.

Druckman, D., & Bjork, R. A. (1991). *In the mind's eye: Enhancing human performance.* Washington, DC: National Academy Press.

Dunbar, K. (1995). How scientists really reason: Scientific reasoning in real-world laboratories. In R. J. Sternberg & J. E. Davidson (Eds.), *The nature of insight* (pp. 369–395). Cambridge, MA: MIT Press.

Duncker, K. (1945). On problem solving. *Psychological Monographs, 58,* 1–112.

Duncan, J. (1984). Selective attention and the organization of visual information. *Journal of Experimental Psychology: General, 113,* 501–517.

Dunlosky, J., & Lipko, A. R. (2007). A brief history and how to improve its accuracy. *Psychological Science, 16,* 228–232.

Dunlosky, J., Rawson, K. A., & Middleton, E. (2005). What constrains the accuracy of metacomprehension judgments? Testing the transfer-appropriate-monitoring and accessibility hypotheses. *Journal of Memory and Language, 52,* 551–565.

Dunning, D., & Perretta, S. (2002). Automaticity and eyewitness accuracy: A 10- to 12-second rule for distinguishing accurate from inaccurate positive identifications. *Journal of Applied Psychology, 87,* 951–962.

Durgin, F. H., Evans, L., Dunphy, N., Klostermann, S., & Simmons, K. (2007). Rubber hands feel the touch of light. *Psychological Science, 18,* 152–157.

Eacott, M. J. & Crawley, R. A. (1998). The offset of childhood amnesia: Memory for events that occurred before age 3. *Journal of Experimental Psychology: General, 127,* 22–33.

Easterbrook, J. A. (1959). The effect of emotion on cue utilization and the organization of behavior. *Psychological Review, 66,* 183–201.

Ebbesen, D. B., & Flowe, H. D. (2002). Simultaneous v. sequential lineups: What do we really know? Retrieved June 2, 2005, from http://www.psy.ucsd.edu/~eebbesen/SimSeq.htm.

Echterhoff, G., Hirst, W. & Hussy, W. (2005). How eyewitnesses resist misinformation: Social postwarnings and the monitoring of memory characteristics. *Memory & Cognition, 33,* 770–782.

Edelman, S., & Bülthoff, H. H. (1992). Orientation dependence in the recognition of familiar and novel views of three-dimensional objects. *Vision Research, 32,* 2385–2400.

Edwards, V. J., Fivush, R., Anda, R. F., Felitti, V. J., & Nordenberg, D. F. (2001). Autobiographical disturbances in childhood abuse survivors. In J. Freyd & A. DePrince (Eds.), *Trauma and Cognitive Science: A Meeting of Minds, Science and Human Experience* (pp. 247–263). Binghamton, NY: The Haworth Trauma and Maltreatment Press.

Egly, R., Driver, J., and Rafal, R. D. (1994). Shifting visual attention between objects and locations: Evidence from normal and parietal lesion subjects. *Journal of Experimental Psychology: General, 123,* 161–177.

Ehrsson H. H., Holmes N. P., Passingham R. E. (2005). Touching a rubber hand: feeling of body ownership is associated with activity in multisensory brain areas. *Journal of Neuroscience, 25*, 10564–10573.

Ehrsson, H. H., Rosén, B., Stockselius, A., Ragnö, C., Köhler, P., & Lundborg, G. (2008). Upper limb amputees can be induced to experience a rubber hand as their own. *Brain, 13*, 3443–3452.

Eich, E. (1980). The cue-dependent nature of state-dependent retrieval. *Memory and Cognition, 8*, 157–173.

Eich, E. (1984). Memory for unattended events: Remembering with and without awareness. *Memory and Cognition, 12*, 105–111.

Eich, E., & Metcalfe, J. (1989). Mood-dependent memory for internal vs. external events. *Journal of Experimental Psychology: Learning, Memory, and Cognition, 15*, 443–455.

Eichenbaum, H., & Fortin, N. (2003). Episodic memory and the hippocampus: It's about time. *Current Directions in Psychological Science, 12*, 53–57.

Einstein, G. O., & McDaniel, M. A. (1990). Normal aging and prospective memory. *Journal of Experimental Psychology: Learning, Memory, and Cognition, 16*, 717–726.

Einstein, G. O., McDaniel, M. A., Richardson, S. L., Guynn, M. J., & Cunfer, B. (1995). Aging and prospective memory: Examining the influences of self-initiated retrieval processes. *Journal of Experimental Psychology: Learning, Memory, and Cognition, 21*, 996–1007.

Ellis, A. W. (1984). *Reading, writing, and dyslexia: A cognitive analysis.* London: Erlbaum.

Emery, C. L., & Lilienfeld, S. O. (2004). The validity of childhood sexual abuse checklists in the popular psychology literature: A Barnum effect? *Professional Psychology: Research and Practice, 35*, 268–274.

Emmorey, K. (2002) Language, Cognition, and the Brain: Insights from Sign Language Research. Erlbaum, Mahwah, NJ.

Engelkamp, J., & Zimmer, H. D. (1985). Motor programs and their relation to semantic memory. *German Journal of Psychology, 9*, 239–254.

Engle, R. (2002). Working memory capacity as executive attention. *Current Directions in Psychological Science, 11*, 19–23.

Engle, R. W., & Kane, M. J. (2004). Executive attention, working memory capacity, and a two-factor theory of cognitive control. In B. H. Ross, (Ed.), *The psychology of learning and motivation: Advances in research and theory* (Vol. 44, pp. 145–199). New York: Elsevier Science.

Epelboim, J., Booth, J. R., & Steinman, R. M. (1994). Reading unspaced text: Implications for theories of reading eye movements. *Vision Research, 34*, 1735–1766.

Epley, N., & Whitchurch, E. (2008). Mirror, mirror on the wall: Enhancement in self-recognition. *Personality and Social Psychology Bulletin, 34*, 1159–1170.

Erickson, R. P. (1982). Studies on the perception of taste: Do primaries exist? *Physiology and Behavior, 28*, 57–62.

Erickson, R. P., Priolo, C. V., Warwick, Z. S., & Schiffman, S. S. (1990). Synthesis of tastes other than the "primaries": Implications for neural coding theories and the concept of suppression. *Chemical Senses, 15*, 495–504.

Ericsson, K. A. (1985). Memory skill. *Canadian Journal of Psychology, 39*, 188–231.

Ericsson, K. A., & Charness, N. (1994). Expert performance: Its structure and acquisition. *American Psychologist, 49*, 725–747.

Ericsson, K. A., Chase, W. G., & Faloon, S. (1980). Acquisition of a memory skill. *Science, 208*, 1181–1182.

Ericsson, K. A., & Kintsch, W. (1995). Long-term working memory. *Psychological Review, 102*, 211–245.

Ericsson, K. A., & Polson, P. G. (1988). An experimental analysis of the mechanisms of a memory skill. *Journal of Experimental Psychology: Learning, Memory, & Cognition, 14*, 305–316.

Ericsson, K. A., & Roring, R. (2007). Memory as a fully integrated aspect of skilled and expert performance. In A. S. Benjamin & B. H. Ross (Eds.) *Skill and Strategy in Memory Use* (p. 351–380). San Diego, CA: Academic Press.

Ericsson, K. A., & Simon, H. E. (1980). Verbal reports as data. *Psychological Review, 87*, 215–251.

Ericsson, K. A., & Simon, H. E. (1984). *Protocol analysis.* Cambridge, MA: MIT Press.

Eriksen, B. A., & Eriksen, C. W. (1974). Effects of noise letters upon the identification of a target letter in a nonsearch task. *Perception & Psychophysics, 16*, 143–149.

Eriksen, C. W., & Murphy, T. D. (1987). Movement of attentional focus across the visual field: A critical look at the evidence. *Perception & Psychophysics, 42*, 299–305.

Eriksen, C. W., & Yeh, Y. (1985). Allocation of attention in the visual field. *Journal of Experimental Psychology: Human Perception and Performance, 11*, 583–597.

Erikson, E. H. (1950). Growth and crises of the healthy personality. *Symposium on the Healthy Personality.* 91–146.

Estes, K. G., Evans, J. L., Alibali, M. W., & Saffran, J. R. (2007). Can infants map meaning to newly segmented words? *Psychological Science, 18*, 254–260.

Evans, G. W., & Schamberg, M. A. (2009). Childhood poverty, chronic stress, and adult working memory. *Proceedings of the National Academy of Science, 106*, 6545–6549.

Evans, J. B. T. (2002). Logic and human reasoning: An assessment of the deduction paradigm. *Psychological Bulletin, 128*, 978–996.

Evans, J. B. T. (2003). In two minds: Dual-process accounts of reasoning. *Trends in Cognitive Sciences, 7*, 454–459.

Evans, J. B. T. (2008). Dual-processing accounts of reasoning, judgment, and social cognition. *Annual Review of Psychology, 59*, 255–78.

Evans, M. A., Shedden, J. M., Hevenor, S. J., & Hahn, M. C. (2000). The effect of variability of unattended information on global and local processing: Evidence for lateralization at early stages of processing. *Neuropsychologia, 38*, 225–239.

Evans, J., Williams, J. M. G., O'Loughlin, S., & Howells, K. (1992). Autobiographical memory and problem-solving strategies of parasuicide patients. *Psychological Medicine, 22*, 399–405.

Evans, N. (2003). Bininj Gun-wok: A pan-dialectal grammar of Mayali, Kunwinjku and Kune. 2 vols. Pacific Linguistics. [arNE]

Evans, N., & Levinson, S. C. (2009). The myth of language universal: Language diversity and its importance for cognitive science. *The Behavioral and Brain Sciences, 32*, 429–448.

Fabiani, D., Stadler, R., & Wessels, F. (2000). True but not false memories produce a sensory signature in human lateralized brain potentials. *Journal of Cognitive Neuroscience, 12*, 941–949.

Falk, D. (2004). Prelinguistic evolution in early hominids: Whence motherese? *Behavioral and Brain Sciences, 27*, 491–541.

Farah, M. J. (1992). Patterns of co-occurrence among the associative agnosias: Implications for visual object representation. *Cognitive Neuropsychology, 8*, 1–19.

Farah, M. J. (1996). Is face recognition 'special'? Evidence from neuropsychology. Behavioral Brain Research, 76, 181–189.

Feinberg, T. E., & Keenan, J. P. (2005). Where in the brain is the self? *Consciousness and Cognition, 14*, 661–78.

Feist, G. J. (1999). The influence of personality on artistic and scientific creativity. In R. J. Sternberg (Ed.), *Handbook of creativity*

(pp. 273–296). New York: Cambridge University Press.

Fernald, A. (1985). Four-month-old infants prefer to listen to motherese. *Infant Behavior and Development, 8*, 181–195.

Fernald, A., & Simon, T. (1984). Expanded intonation contours in mothers' speech to newborns. *Developmental Psychology, 20*, 104–113.

Ferreira, V. S., Bock, K., Wilson, M. P., & Cohen, N. J. (2008). Memory for syntax despite amnesia. *Psychological Science 19*, 940–946.

Fillmore, C. J. (1968). The case for case. In E. Bach & R. T. Harms (Eds.), *Universals of linguistic form* (pp. 101–190). New York: Holt, Rinehart, & Winston.

Fink, G. R., Markowitsch, H. J., & Reinkemeier, M. (1996). Cerebral representation of one's own past: Neural networks involved in autobiographical memory. *Journal of Neuroscience, 16*, 4275–4282.

Fischhoff, B., Slovic, P., & Lichtenstein, S. (1977). Knowing with certainty: The appropriateness of extreme confidence. *Journal of Experimental Psychology: Human Perception and Performance, 4*, 552–564.

Fisher, R. P., & Geiselman, R. E. (1992). *Memory-enhancing techniques for investigative interviewing: The cognitive interview*. Springfield, IL: Thomas.

Fivush, R. (1991). Gender and emotion in mother/child conversations about the past. *Journal of Narrative and Life History, 1*, 325–341.

Fivush, R., Edwards, V. J., & Mennuti-Washburn, J. (2003). Narratives of 9/11: relations among personal involvement, narrative content and memory of the emotional impact over time. *Applied Cognitive Psychology, 17*, 1099–1111.

Fivush, R., Gray, J. T., & Fromhoff, F. A. (1987). Two-year-olds talk about the past. *Cognitive Development, 2*, 393–409.

Fleck, M. S., & Mitroff, S. R. (2007). Rare targets are rarely missed in

correctable search. *Psychological Science, 18*, 943–947.

Foss, D. J. (1969). Decision processes during sentence comprehension: Effects of lexical item difficulty and position upon decision times. *Journal of Verbal Learning and Verbal Behavior, 8*, 457–462.

Foss, D. J. (1970). Some effects of ambiguity upon sentence comprehension. *Journal of Verbal Learning and Verbal Behavior, 9*, 699–706.

Fowlkes, C. C., Martin, D. R., & Malik, J. (2007). Local figure–ground cues are valid for natural images. *Journal of Vision, 7*, 1–9.

Frackowiak, R., Friston, K., Frith, C., Dolan, R., Price, C., Zeki, S. (2004). *Human brain function* (2nd Ed.). San Diego, CA: Academic Press/Elsevier Science.

Frank, M. J., Cohen, M. X. and Sanfey, A. G. (2009). Multiple systems in decision making: A neurocomputational perspective. *Current Directions in Psychological Science, 18*, 73–77.

Frantz, R. (2003). Herbert Simon. Artificial intelligence as a framework for understanding intuition. *Journal of Economic Psychology, 24*, 265–277.

Frazier, L. (1995). Constraint satisfaction as a theory of sentence processing. *Journal of Psycholinguistics, 34*, 437–476.

Frazier, L. & Clifton, C. (1996). *Construal*. Cambridge MA: MIT Press.

Frazier, L. & Fodor, J.D. (1978) The sausage machine: A new two-stage parsing model. *Cognition, 6*, 291–325.

Frazier, L., & Rayner, K. (1982). Making and correcting errors during sentence comprehension: Eye movements in the analysis of structurally ambiguous sentences. *Cognitive Psychology, 14*, 178–210.

Freyd, J. J., Gleaves, D. H. (1996). "Remembering" words not presented in lists: Relevance to the current recovered/false memory controversy. *Journal of Experimental*

Psychology: Learning, Memory, and Cognition, 22, 811–813., *22,* 811–8.

Friederici, A. D. (1983). Children's sensitivity to function words during sentence comprehension. *Linguistics, 21,* 717–739.

Fromkin, V. A. (1973). *Speech errors as linguistic evidence.* The Hague: Mouton.

Gabora, L., Rosch, E., Aerts, D. (2008). Toward an ecological theory of concepts. *Ecological Psychology, 20,* 84–116.

Galantucci, B., Fowler, C. A., & Turvey, M. (2006). The motor theory of speech perception reviewed. *Psychonomic Bulletin & Review, 13,* 361–377.

Gallagher, A. M., De Lisi, R., Holst, P. C., McGillicuddy-De Lisi, A. V., Morely, M., & Cahalan, C. (2000). Gender differences in advanced mathematical problem solving. *Journal of Experimental Child Psychology, 75,* 165–190.

Galpin, A., Underwood, G., & Crundall, D. (2009). Change blindness in driving scenes. *Transportation Research Part F: Traffic Psychology and Behaviour, 12,* 179–185.

Garavan, H. (1998). Serial attention within working memory. *Memory and Cognition, 26,* 263–276.

Gardiner, J. M. (1988). Functional aspects of recollective experience. *Memory and Cognition, 16,* 309–313.

Gardiner, J. M., & Parkin, A. J. (1990). Attention and recollective experience in recognition memory. *Memory and Cognition, 18,* 579–583.

Gardiner, J. M., & Richardson-Klavehn, A. (2000). Remembering and knowing. In E. Tulving & F. I. M. Craik (Eds.), *The Oxford handbook of memory* (pp. 229–244). New York: Oxford University Press.

Gardner, B. T., & Gardner, R. A. (1975). Evidence for sentence constituents in the early utterances of child and chimpanzee. *Journal of Experimental Psychology: General, 104,* 244–267.

Gardner, H. (1983). *Frames of mind: A theory of multiple intelligence.* New York: Basic Books.

Gardner, H. (1985). *The mind's new science: A history of the cognitive revolution.* New York: Basic Books.

Garland, H. (1990). Throwing good money after bad: The effect of sunk costs on decisions to escalate commitment to an ongoing project. *Journal of Applied Psychology, 75,* 728–731.

Garrett, M. F. (1975). The analysis of sentence production. In G. Bower (Ed.), *The psychology of learning and motivation: Advances in research and theory* (Vol. 9). New York: Academic Press.

Garrett, M. F. (1988). Processes in language production. In F. J. Newmeyer (Ed.), *Language: Psychological and biological aspects* (pp. 69–96). Cambridge: Cambridge University Press.

Garrett, M. F. (1992). Disorders of lexical selection. *Cognition, 42,* 143–180.

Garry, M., Manning, C. G., Loftus, E. F., & Sherman, S. J. (1996). Imagination inflation: Imagining a childhood event inflates confidence that it occurred. *Psychonomic Bulletin and Review, 3,* 208–214.

Garry, M., Strange, D., Bernstein, D. M., & Kinzett, T. (2007). Photographs can distort memory for the news. *Applied Cognitive Psychology, 21,* 995–1004.

Garry, M., & Wade, K. A. (2005). Actually, a picture is worth less than 45 words: Narratives produce more false memories than photographs do. *Psychonomic Bulletin & Review, 12,* 359–366.

Gaskell, M. G., & Marslen-Wilson, W. D. (2001). Lexical ambiguity resolution and spoken word recognition: Bridging the gap. *Journal of Memory and Language, 44,* 325–349.

Gauthier, I., & Bukach, C. (2007). Should we reject the expertise hypothesis? *Cognition, 103,* 322–330.

Gauthier, I., & Curby, K. M. (2005). A perceptual traffic jam on highway N170: Interference between car and face expertise. *Current Directions in Psychological Science, 14,* 30–33.

Gauthier, I., Curran, T., Curby, K. M., & Collins, D. (2003). Perceptual interference supports a non-modular account of face processing. *Nature Neuroscience, 6,* 428–432.

Gauthier, I., Skudlarski, P., Gore, J. C., & Anderson, A. W. (2000). Expertise for cars and birds recruits brain areas involved in face recognition. *Nature Neuroscience, 3,* 191–197.

Gazzaniga, M. S. (1985). *The social brain.* New York: Basic Books.

Gazzaniga, M. S. (1998). *The mind's past.* Berkeley, CA: University of California Press.

Gazzaniga, M. S., Ivry, R. B., & Mangun, G. R. (2002). *Cognitive neuroscience: The biology of the mind.* New York: Norton.

Gazzaniga, M. S., & Smylie, C. S. (1984). Dissociation of language and cognition. *Brain, 107,* 145–153.

Gelman, S. A. (2003). *The essential child: Origins of essentialism in everyday thought.* New York: Oxford University Press.

Gelman, S. A. (2004). Psychological essentialism in children. *Trends in Cognitive Sciences, 8,* 404–409.

Gelman, S. A., & Wellman, H. M. (1991). Insides and essences: Early understandings of the nonobvious. *Cognition, 38,* 213–244.

Gentner, D. (1989). The mechanisms of analogical learning. In S. Vosniadou & A. Ortony (Eds.), *Similarity and analogical reasoning* (pp. 199–241). New York: Cambridge University Press.

Gentner, T. Q., Fenn, K. M., Margoliash, D., & Nusbaum, H. C. (2006). Recursive syntactic pattern learning by songbirds. *Nature, 440,* 1204–1207.

Geraerts, E., Arnold, M. M., Lindsay, D. S., Merckelbach, H., Jelicic, M., & Hauer, B. (2006). Forgetting of prior remembering in persons reporting recovered memories of childhood sexual abuse. *Psychological Science, 17,* 1002–1008.

German, T. P., & Barrett, H. C. (2005). Functional fixedness in a technologically sparse culture. *Psychological Science, 16*, 1–5.

Gernsbacher, M. A. (1989). Mechanisms that improve referential access. *Cognition, 32*, 99–156.

Gernsbacher. M. A. (1990). *Language comprehension as structure building.* Hillsdale, NJ: Erlbaum.

Gernsbacher, M. A. (1997). Two decades of structure building. *Discourse Processes, 23*, 365–204.

Gernsbacher, M. A., & Hargreaves. (1988). Accessing sentence participants: The advantage of first mention. *Journal of Memory and Language, 27*, 699–717.

Ghetti, S. (2008). Rejection of false events in childhood. *Psychological Science, 17*, 16–20.

Gibbs, R. W. (2006). *Embodiment and cognitive science.* New York: Cambridge University Press.

Gibson, J. J. (1966). The problem of temporal order in sensation and perception. *Journal of Psychology, 62*, 141–149.

Gibson, J. J. (1987). *The perception of the visual world.* New York: Houghton-Mifflin.

Gick, M. L., & Holyoak, K. J. (1980). Analogical problem solving. *Cognitive Psychology, 12*, 306–335.

Gick, M. L., & Holyoak, K. J. (1983). Schema induction and analogical transfer. *Cognitive Psychology, 15*, 1–38.

Gigerenzer, G. (2004). Dread risk, September 11, and fatal traffic accidents. *Psychological Science, 15*, 286–287.

Gigerenzer, G. (2008). Why heuristics work. *Psychological Science, 3*, 20–29.

Gigerenzer, G., & Hoffrage, U. (1995). How to improve Bayesian reasoning without instruction. Frequency formats. *Psychological Review, 102*, 684–704.

Gigerenzer, G., & Todd, P. M. (1999). *Simple heuristics that make us smart. Evolution and cognition.* New York: Oxford University Press.

Gilhooly, K. J., & Murphy, P. (2005). Differentiating insight from non-insight problems. *Thinking & Reasoning, 11*, 279–302.

Gilinsky, A. S., & Judd, B. B. (1994). Working memory and bias in reasoning across the life span. *Psychology and Aging, 9*, 356–371.

Gillund, G., & Shiffrin, R. M. (1984). A retrieval model for both recognition and recall. *Psychological Review, 91*, 1–67.

Gilovich, T., Kruger, J., & Medvec, V. H. (2002). The spotlight effect revisited: Overestimating the manifest variability of our actions and appearance. *Journal of Experimental Social Psychology, 38*, 93–99.

Gilovich, T., Medvec, V., & Savitsky, K. (2000). The spotlight effect in social judgment: An egocentric bias in the estimates of the salience of one's own actions and appearance. *Journal of Personality and Social Psychology, 75*, 332–346.

Gilovich, T., Vallone, R., & Tversky, A. (1983). The hot hand in basketball: On the misperception of random sequences. *Cognitive Psychology, 17*, 295–314.

Gisiner, R., & Schusterman, R. J. (1992). Sequence, syntax, and semantics: Responses of a language-trained sea lion (Zalophus Californianus) to novel sign combinations. *Journal of Comparative Psychology, 106*, 78–91.

Glanzer, M., & Cunitz, A. R. (1966). Two storage mechanisms in free recall. *Journal of Verbal Learning & Verbal Behavior, 5*, 351–360.

Glascher, J., Adolphs, R. (2003). Processing of the arousal of subliminal and supraliminal emotional stimuli by the human amygdala. *Journal of Neuroscience, 23*, 10274–10282.

Gleaves, D. H., Smith, S. M., Butler, L. D., & Spiegel, D. (2004). False and recovered memories in the laboratory and clinic: A review of experimental and clinical evidence. *Clinical Psychology: Science and Practice, 11*, 3–28.

Glenberg, A. M. (1974). Influences of retrieval processes on the spacing effect in free recall. *Journal of Experimental Psychology: Human Learning and Memory, 3*, 282–294.

Glenberg, A. M., & Kaschak, M. P. (2002). Grounding language in action. *Psychonomic Bulletin & Review, 9*, 558–565.

Glenn, C. G. (1978). The role of episodic structure and of story length in children's recall of simple stories. *Journal of Verbal Learning and Verbal Behavior, 17*, 229–247.

Gobet, F., & Simon, H. A. (1996). Recall of rapidly presented random chess positions is a function of skill. *Psychonomic Bulletin and Review, 3*, 159–163.

Godden, D. R., & Baddeley, A. D. (1975). Context-dependent memory in two natural environments: On land and underwater. *British Journal of Psychology, 66*, 325–331.

Goel, V., Gold, B., Kapur, S., & Houle, S. (1998). Neuroanatomical correlates of human reasoning. *Journal of Cognitive Neuroscience, 10*, 293–302.

Goff, L. M., & Roediger, H. L. (1998). Imagination inflation for action events: Repeated imaginings lead to illusory recollections. *Memory and Cognition, 26*, 20–33.

Goldinger, S. D., Luce, P. A., & Pisoni, D. B. (1989). Priming lexical neighbors of spoken words: Effects of competition and inhibition. *Journal of Memory and Language, 28*, 501–518.

Goldstein, D. G., & Gigerenzer, G. (2002). Models of ecological rationality: The recognition heuristic. *Psychological Review, 109*, 75–90.

Goldstone, R. L., & Kersten, A. (2003). Concepts and categorization. In A. F. Healy & R. W. Proctor (Eds.), *Handbook of psychology: Experimental psychology* (Vol. 4, pp. 599–621). Hoboken, NJ: John Wiley & Sons, Inc.

Gonzalez, C., Dana, J., Koshino, H., & Just, M. (2005). The framing effect and risky decisions: Examining cognitive functions with fMRI. *Journal of Economic Psychology, 26*, 1–20.

Goodman G. S., Ghetti S, Quas J. A., Edelstein R. S., Alexander K. W., (2003). A prospective study of memory for child sexual abuse: new findings relevant to the repressed-memory controversy. *Psychological Science, 14,* 113–18.

Goodman, G. S., Quas, J. A., Batterman-Faunce, J. M., Riddlesberger, M. M., & Kuhn, J. (1994). Predictors of accurate and inaccurate memories of traumatic events experienced in childhood. *Consciousness and Cognition, 3,* 269–294.

Goodman, G. S., Quas, J. a., & Ogle, C. M. (2010). Child maltreatment and memory. *Annual Review of Psychology, 61,* 325–51.

Goschke, T., & Kuhl, J. (1993). Representation of intentions: Persisting activation in memory. *Journal of Experimental Psychology: Learning, Memory, and Cognition, 19,* 1211–1226.

Goswami, U. (2008). Reading, dyslexia and the brain. *Educational Research, 50,* 135–148.

Graesser, A. C., Singer, M., & Trabasso, T. (1994). Constructing inferences during narrative text comprehension. *Psychological Review, 101,* 371–95.

Graham, S. A., Kilbreath, C. S., & Welder, A. N. (2004). Thirteen-month-olds rely on shared labels and shape similarity for inductive inferences. *Child Development, 75,* 409–427.

Grainger, J., & Whitney, C. (2004). Does the huamn mnid raed wrods as a wlohe? *Trends in Cognitive Sciences, 8,* 58–59.

Grant, H. M., Bredahl, L. C., Clay, J., Ferrie, J., Groves, J. E., McDorman, T. A., & Dark, V. J. (1998). Context-dependent memory for meaningful material: Information for students. *Applied Cognitive Psychology, 12,* 617–623.

Gratton, G., Corballis, P. M., & Jain, S. (1997). Hemispheric organization of visual memories. *Journal of Cognitive Neuroscience, 9,* 92–104.

Greenberg, D. L. (2004). President Bush's false [flashbulb] memory of 9/11/01. *Applied Cognitive Psychology, 18,* 363–370.

Greene, R. L. (1992). *Human memory: Paradigms and paradoxes.* Hillsdale, NJ: Erlbaum.

Greenfield, P. M., & Savage-Rumbaugh, E. S. (1990). Grammatical combination in *Pan paniscus:* Processes of learning and invention in the evolution and development of language. In S. T. Parker & K. R. Gibson (Eds.), *"Language" and intelligence in monkeys and apes: Comparative developmental perspectives* (pp. 540–578). Cambridge: Cambridge University Press.

Greenwald, A. G., Spangenberg, E. R., Pratkanis, A. R., & Eskenazi, J. (1991). Double-blind tests of subliminal self-help audiotapes. *Psychological Science, 2,* 119–122.

Gregg, M. K., & Samuel, A. G. (2008). Change deafness and the organizational properties of sounds. *Journal of Experimental Psychology. Human Perception and Performance, 34,* 974–91.

Grice, H. P. (1975). Logic and conversation. In P. Cole & J. L. Morgan (Eds.), *Syntax and semantics:* Vol. 3: *Speech acts* (pp. 41–58). New York: Seminar Press.

Griggs, R. A., & Cox, G. R. (1982). The elusive thematic-materials effect in Wason's selection task. *British Journal of Psychology, 73,* 407–420.

Groeger, J. A. (1999). Expectancy and control: Perceptual and cognitive aspects of the driving task. In P. A. Hancock (Ed.), *Human performance and ergonomics* (p. 243–264). San Diego, CA: Academic Press.

Gronlund, S. D., Carlson, C. A., Dailey, S. B., & Goodsell, C. A. (2009). Robustness of the sequential lineup advantage. *Journal of Experimental Psychology. Applied, 15,* 140–152.

Grosjean, F.. & Soares, C. (1986). Processing mixed language: Some preliminary findings. In J. Vaid (Ed.), *Language processing in bilinguals: Psychoiinguistic and neuropsychological perspectives* (pp. 145–179). Hillsdale, NJ: Erlbaum.

Gross, S. R., Jacoby, K., Matheson, D. J., Montgomery, N., & Patil, S. (2004). Exonerations in the United States 1989 through 2003. *The Journal of Criminal Law and Criminology, 95,* 523–560.

Gruneberg, M. M., Smith, R. L., & Winfrow, P. (1973). An investigation into response blockaging. *Acta Psychologica, 37,* 187–196.

Gueraud, S., & O'Brien, E. (2005). Components of comprehension: A convergence between memory-based processes and explanation-based processes. *Discourse Processes, 39,* 123–124.

Habermas, T., & Bluck, S. (2000). Getting a life: The emergence of the life story in adolescence. *Psychological Bulletin, 126,* 748–769.

Habib, R., & Nyberg, L. (2007). Neural correlates of availability and accessibility in memory. *Cerebral Cortex, 18,* 1720–1726.

Hahne, A., Eckstein, K., & Friederici, A. D. (2004). Brain signatures of syntactic and semantic processes during children's language development. *Journal of Cognitive Neuroscience, 16,* 1302–1318.

Halpern, D. F., & Wai, J. (2007). The world of competitive Scrabble: Novice and expert differences in visuospatial and verbal abilities, *13,* 79–94.

Hampton, J. A. (1993). Conjunctions of visually-based categories: Overextension and compensation. *Journal of Experimental Psychology: Learning, Memory, and Cognition, 22,* 378–396.

Hampton, J. A., Estes, Z., & Simmons, S. (2007). Metamorphosis: Essence, appearance, and behavior in the categorization of natural kinds. *Memory & Cognition, 35,* 1785–1800.

Hanley, J. R., & Cowell, E. S. (1988). The effects of different types of retrieval cues on the recall of names of famous faces. *Memory and Cognition, 16,* 545–555.

Hanson, V. L. (1982). Short-term recall by deaf signers of American Sign

Language: Implications of encoding strategy for order recall. *Journal of Experimental Psychology: Learning, Memory, and Cognition, 8,* 572–583.

Haque, S., & Conway, M. A. (2001). Sampling the process of autobiographical memory construction. *European Journal of Cognitive Psychology, 13,* 529–547.

Harley, E. M. (2007). Hindsight bias in legal decision making. *Social Cognition, 25,* 48–63.

Harley, T. A. (2008). *The psychology of language: From data to theory.* (3rd Ed) East Sussex, UK: Taylor & Francis.

Harris, D. A. (1999). Driving while black: Racial profiling on our nation's highways. Washington, DC: American Civil Liberties Union.

Harris J. A., Miniussi, C., Harris I. M., & Diamond, M. E. (2002). Transient storage of a tactile memory trace in primary somatosensory cortex. *Journal of Neuroscience, 22,* 8720–8725.

Harris, J. E. (1980). Memory aids people use: Two interview studies. *Memory and Cognition, 8,* 31–38.

Harrison, J. E., & Baron-Cohen, S. (1997). Synaesthesia: A review of psychological theories. In J. E. Harris & S. Baron-Cohen (Eds.), *Synaesthesia: Classic and contemporary readings.* (pp. 109–122). Oxford: Blackwell.

Hartley, A. A. (1992). Attention. In F. I. M. Craik & T. A. Salthouse (Eds.), *The handbook of aging and cognition* (pp. 3–49). Hillsdale, NJ: Erlbaum.

Harvey, A. G. (2005). Unwanted intrusive thoughts in insomnia. In D. A. Clark (Ed.), *Intrusive thoughts in clinical disorders: Theory, research, and treatment* (pp. 86–118). New York: Guilford Press.

Hashtroudi, S., Johnson, M. K., & Chrosniak, L. D. (1989). Aging and source monitoring. *Psychology and Aging, 4,* 106–112.

Haskell, T. R., MacDonald, M. C., & Seidenberg, M. S. (2003). Language learning and innateness: Some

implications of compounds research. *Cognitive Psychology, 47,* 119–163.

Haslam, N., Rothschild, L., & Ernst, D. (2000). Essentialist beliefs about social categories. *British Journal of Social Psychology, 39,* 113–127.

Hastie, R., & Dawes, R. M. (2001). *Rational choice in an uncertain world: The psychology of judgment and decision making.* London: Sage.

Hastie, R., Schkade, D. A., & Payne, J. W. (1999). Juror judgments in civil cases: Hindsight effects on judgments of liability for punitive damages. *Law and Human Behavior, 23,* 445–470.

Hauser, M. D., Chomsky, N., & Fitch, W. T. (2002). The faculty of language: What is it, who has it, and how did it evolve? *Science, 298,* 1569–1579.

Haxby, J. V., Hoffman, E. A., & Gobbini, M. I. (2002). Human neural systems for face recognition and social communication. *Biological Psychiatry, 51,* 59–67.

Hayes, J. R., & Simon, H. A. (1977). Psychological differences among problem isomorphs. In N. J. Castellan, D. B. Pisoni, & J. R. Potts (Eds.), *Cognitive theory.* Hillsdale, NJ: Erlbaum.

Hayward, W. G. (2003). After the viewpoint debate: Where next in object recognition? *Trends in Cognitive Sciences, 7,* 425–427.

Hayward, W. G., & Tarr, M. J. (1997). Testing conditions for viewpoint invariance in object recognition. *Journal of Experimental Psychology: Human Perception and Performance, 23,* 1511–1521.

Hebb, D. O. (1949). *The organization of behavior: A neuropsychological theory.* London: Wiley.

Henderson, J. M., & Ferreira, F. (1990). Effects of foveal processing difficulty on the perceptual span in reading: Implications for attention and eye movement control. *Journal of Experimental Psychology: Learning, Memory, and Cognition, 16,* 417–429.

Hennessey, B. A., & Amabile, T. M. (2010). Creativity. *Annual Review of Psychology, 61,* 569–598.

Henry, J. D., MacLeod, M. S., Phillips, L. H., & Crawford, J. R. (2004). A meta-analytic review of prospective memory and aging. *Psychology and Aging, 19,* 27–39.

Herlitz, A., Nilsson, L. G., & Backman, L. (1997). Gender differences in episodic memory. *Memory & Cognition, 25,* 801–811.

Herman, J. L., & Schatzow, E. (1987). Recovery and verification of memories of childhood sexual trauma. *Psychoanalytic Psychology, 4,* 1–14.

Herman, J. S. (1992). *Trauma and recovery.* New York: Basic Books.

Herman, L. M., Kuczaj, S. A., & Holder, M. D. (1993). Response to anomalous gestural sequences by a language-trained dolphin: Evidence for processing of semantic relations and syntactic information. *Journal of Experimental Psychology: General, 122,* 184–194.

Herman, L. M., Richards, D. G., & Wolz, J. P. (1984). Comprehension of sentences by bottlenosed dolphins. *Cognition, 16,* 129–219.

Herman, J. L. & Schatzow, E. (1987). Recovery and verification of memories of childhood sexual trauma. *Psychoanalytic Psychology, 4,* 1–14.

Herz, R. S., & Cupchik, G. C. (1992). An experimental characterization of odor-evoked memories in humans. *Chemical Senses, 17,* 519–528.

Hester, R., & Garavan, H. (2005). Working memory and executive function: The influence of content and load on the control of attention. *Memory & cognition, 33,* 221–233.

Hillix, W. A. (2007). The past, present, and possible futures of animal language research. In D. A. Washburn (Ed.), *Primate perspectives on behavior and cognition* (pp. 223–234). Washington, DC: American Psychological Association.

Hilton, D. J. (1995). The social context of reasoning: Conversational inference and rational judgment. *Psychological Bulletin, 118,* 248–271.

Hintzman, D. L. (1986). "Schema abstraction" in a multiple-trace memory model. *Psychological Review, 93,* 411–428.

Hintzman, D. L., Block, R. A., & Summers, J. J. (1973). Modality tags and memory for repetitions: Locus of the spacing effect. *Journal of Verbal Learning and Verbal Behavior, 12,* 229–238.

Hirst, W., Phelps, E. A., Buckner, R. L., Budson, A. E., Cuc, A., Gabrieli, J. D., et al. (2009). Long-term memory for the terrorist attack of September 11: flashbulb memories, event memories, and the factors that influence their retention. *Journal of experimental psychology. General, 138,* 161–76.

Hitch, G. J., & Baddeley, A. D. (1976).Verbal reasoning and working memory. *Quarterly Journal of Experimental Psychology, 28,* 603–621.

Hockett, C. F. (1960). The origin of speech. *Scientific American, 203,* 89–96.

Hogan, R. M., & Kintsch, W. (1971). Differential effects of study and test trials on long-term recognition and recall. *Journal of Verbal Learning and Verbal Behavior, 10,* 562–567.

Hogan, T. M., & Rabinowitz, M. (2009). Teacher expertise and the development of a problem representation. *Educational Psychology, 2,* 153–169.

Hogarth, R. M. (2005). Deciding analytically or trusting your intuition? The advantages and disadvantages of analytic and intuitive thought. In T. Betsch & S. Haberstroh (Eds.), *The routines of decision making* (pp. 67–82). Mahwah, NJ: Lawrence Erlbaum Associates Publishers.

Holbrook, M. E., & Schindler, R. M. (1989). Some exploratory findings on the development of musical tastes. *Journal of Consumer Research, 16,* 119–124.

Hollingworth, A., & Henderson, J. M. (1998). Does consistent scene context facilitate object perception? *Journal of Experimental Psychology: General, 127,* 398–415.

Holt, L. L., & Lotto, A. J. (2008). Speech perception within an auditory cognitive science framework. *Current Directions in Psychological Science, 17,* 42–46.

Holyoak, K. J., & Koh, K. (1987). Surface and structural similarity in analogical transfer. *Memory and Cognition, 15,* 332–340.

Hosey, L. A., Peynircioğlu, Z. F., & Rabinovitz, B. E. (2009). Feeling of knowing for names in response to faces. *Acta psychologica, 130,* 214–224.

Hötting, K., & Röder, B. (2004). Hearing cheats touch, but less in congenitally blind than in sighted individuals. *Psychological Science, 15,* 60–64.

Howe, M. L., & Courage, M. L. (1993). On resolving the enigma of childhood amnesia. *Psychological Bulletin, 113,* 305–326.

Howe, M. L., & Courage, M. L. (1997). The emergence and early development of autobiographical memory. *Psychological Review, 104,* 499–523.

Howe, M. L., Courage, M. L., & Edison, S. C. (2003). When autobiographical memory begins. *Developmental Review, 23,* 471–494.

Howe, M. L., Courage, M. L., & Peterson, C. (1994). How can I remember when "I" wasn't there: Long-term retention of traumatic experience and the emergence of the cognitive self. *Consciousness and Cognition, 3,* 327–355.

Hsee, C. K., & Rottenstreich, Y. (2004). Music, pandas, and muggers: On the affective psychology of value. *Journal of Experimental Psychology: General, 133,* 23–30.

Hull, C. (1943). Principles of Behavior. New York : Appleton-Century-Crofts

Hulme, C., Roodenrys, S., Brown, G., & Mercer, R. (1995). The role of long-term memory mechanisms in memory span. *British Journal of Psychology, 86,* 527–536.

Hunt, R. R., & Einstein, G. O. (1981). Relational and item-specific information in memory. *Journal of Verbal Learning and Verbal Behavior, 20,* 497–514.

Hyde, T. S., & Jenkins, J. J. (1969). Differential effects of incidental tasks on the organization of recall of a list of highly associated words. *Journal of Experimental Psychology, 82,* 472–481.

Hyman, I. E., Husband, T. H., & Billings, F. J. (1995). False memories of childhood experiences. *Applied Cognitive Psychology, 9,* 181–197.

Hyman, I. E., & Pentland, J. (1996). The role of imagination in the creation of false childhood memories. *Journal of Memory and Language, 35,* 101–117.

Iacoboni, M. (2008) The role of premotor cortex in speech perception: evidence from fMRI and rTMS. *Journal of Physiology, 102,* 31–34

Inhoff, A. W., & Rayner, K. (1986). Parafoveal word processing during eye fixations in reading: Effects of word frequency. *Perception & Psychophysics, 40,* 431–439.

Ishak, S., Adolph, K. E., & Lin, G. C. (2008). Perceiving affordances for fitting through apertures. *Journal of Experimental Psychology. Human Perception and Performance, 34,* 1501–14.

Iverson, P. (1995). Auditory stream segregation by musical timbre: Effects of static and dynamic acoustic attributes. *Journal of Experimental Psychology: Human Perception and Performance, 21,* 751–763.

Jack, F., Macdonald, S., Reese, E., & Hayne, H. (2009). Maternal reminiscing style during early childhood predicts the age of adolescents' earliest memories. *Memory, 80,* 496–505.

Jackendoff, R. (2002) *Foundations of language: Brain, meaning, grammar, evolution.* New York, NY: Oxford University Press.

Jackendoff, R. & Pinker, S. (2005). The nature of the language faculty and its implications for evolution of language (Reply to Fitch, Hauser, & Chomsky) *Cognition, 97,* 211–225.

Jacoby, L. L. (1983). Remembering the data: Analyzing interactive processes in reading. *Journal of Verbal Learning and Verbal Behavior, 22,* 485–508.

Jacoby, L. L. (1991). A process dissociation framework: Separating automatic from intentional uses of memory. *Journal of Memory and Language, 30,* 513–541.

Jaffe, J., & Feldstein, S. (1970). *Rhythms of dialogue.* New York: Academic Press.

James, W. (1890). *The principles of psychology.* New York: Holt.

Jamieson, J. P., & Harkins, S. G. (2009). The effect of stereotype threat on the solving of quantitative GRE problems: A mere effort interpretation. *Personality and Social Psychology Bulletin, 35,* 1301–14.

Janssen, S. M., & Murre, J. M. (2008). Reminiscence bump in autobiographical memory: Unexplained by novelty, emotionality, valence, or importance of personal events. *Quarterly Journal of Experimental Psychology,* 1847–1860.

Jennings, J. M., & Jacoby, L. L. (1993). Automatic versus intentional uses of memory: Aging, attention, and control. *Psychology and Aging, 8,* 283–293.

Jessup, R. K. (2009). Transfer of high domain knowledge to a similar domain. *The American Journal of Psychology, 122,* 63–73.

Jonides, J., Lewis, R. L., Nee, D. E., Lustig, C., Berman, M. G., Sledge Moore, K., et al. (2008). The mind and brain of short-term memory. *Annual Review of Psychology. 59,* 193–224.

Johnson, M. K. (1988). Reality monitoring: An experimental phenomenological approach. *Journal of Experimental Psychology: General, 117,* 390–394.

Johnson, M. K., Foley, M. A., Suengas, A. G., & Raye, C. L. (1988). Phenomenal characteristics of memories for perceived and imagined autobiographical events. *Journal of Experimental Psychology: General, 117,* 371–376.

Johnson, M. K., Hashtroudi, S. & Lindsay, D. S. (1993). Source monitoring. *Psychological Bulletin, 114,* 3–28

Johnson, M. K., Nolde, S. F., & Leonardis, D. M. (1996). Emotional focus and source monitoring. *Journal of Memory and Language, 35,* 135–156.

Johnson, R., Jr. (1984). P300: a model of the variables controlling its amplitude. *Annals of the New York Academy of Sciences, 425,* 223–229.

Johnson-Laird, P. N., & Byrne, R. M. (2002). Conditionals: A theory of meaning, pragmatics, and inference. *Psychological Review, 109,* 646–678.

Johnston, W. A., & Heinz, S. P. (1978). Flexibility and capacity demands of attention. *Journal of Experimental Psychology: General, 107,* 420–435.

Jones, D. M., Hughes, R. W., & Macken, W. J. (2007). Commentary on Baddeley and Larsen (2007). The phonological store abandoned. *Quarterly journal of experimental psychology, 60,* 505–511.

Jones, D. M., Macken, W. J., & Nicholls, A. P. (2004). The phonological store of working memory: is it phonological and is it a store? *Journal of Experimental Psychology. Learning, Memory, and Cognition, 30,* 656–74.

Jones, G. V., & Langford, S. (1987). Phonological blocking in the tip of the tongue state. *Cognition, 26,* 115–122.

Jonides, J., Lacey, S. C., & Nee, D. E. (2005). Processes of working memory in mind and brain. *Current Directions in Psychological Science, 14,* 2–5.

Jonides, J., Lewis, R. L., Nee, D. E., Lustig, C., Berman, M. G., Sledge Moore, K., (2008). The Mind and Brain of Short-Term Memory. *Annual Review of Psychology.*

Jonides, J., & Smith, E. E. (1997). The architecture of working memory. In M. D. Rugg (Ed.), *Cognitive neuroscience. Studies in cognition* (pp. 243–276). Cambridge, MA: MIT Press.

Jönsson, F. U., Olsson, M. J. (2003). Olfactory metacognition. *Chemical Senses, 28,* 651–658.

Joslyn, S., Loftus, E., McNoughton, A., & Powers, J. (2001). Memory for memory. *Memory & Cognition, 29,* 789–797.

Juhasz, B. J., White, S. J., Liversedge, S. P., & Rayner, K. (2008). Eye movements and the use of parafoveal word length information in reading. *Journal of Experimental Psychology. Human Perception and Performance, 34,* 1560–1579.

Jusczyk, P. W. (1997). *The discovery of spoken language.* Cambridge, MA: MIT Press.

Just, M. A., & Carpenter, P. A. (1987). *The psychology of reading and language comprehension.* Boston: Allyn and Bacon.

Just, M. A., & Carpenter, P. A. (1992). A capacity theory of comprehension: Individual differences in working memory. *Psychological Review, 99,* 122–149.

Just, M. A., Carpenter, P. A., & Masson, M. E. J. (1982). *What eye fixations tell us about speed reading and skimming* (Technical report). Pittsburgh: Carnegie-Mellon University.

Kadosh, R. C., & Henik, A. (2008). Can synesthesia research inform cognitive science? *Trends in Cognitive Sciences, 11,* 177–184.

Kahneman, D. (1973). Attention and effort. Englewood Cliffs, NJ: Prentice-Hall.

Kahneman, D. (1991). Judgment and decision making: A personal view. *Psychological Science, 2,* 142–145.

Kahneman, D. & Tversky, A. (1973). On the psychology of prediction. *Psychological Review, 80,* 237–257.

Kahneman, D.; Tversky, A. (1979). Prospect theory: An analysis of decisions under risk. *Econometrica, 47,* 313–327

Kahneman, D., & Tversky, A. (1984). Choices, values, and frames. *American Psychologist, 39,* 341–350.

Kako, E. (1999). Elements of syntax in the systems of three language-trained animals. *Animal Learning and Behavior, 27*, 1–14.

Kaminski, J., Call, J., & Fischer, J. (2004). Word learning in a domestic dog: Evidence for "fast mapping." *Science, 304,* 1682–1683.

Kane, M. J., & Engle, R. W. (2000). WM capacity, proactive interference, and divided attention: Limits on long-term memory retrieval. *Journal of Experimental Psychology: Learning, Memory, and Cognition, 26,* 336–358.

Kane, M. J., & Engle, R. W. (2003). Working-memory capacity and the control of attention: The contributions of goal neglect, response com-petition, and task set to Stroop interference. *Journal of Experimental Psychology: General, 132,* 47–70.

Kane, M. J., Poole, B. J., Tuholski, S. W., Engle, R. W. (2006). Working memory capacity and the top-down control of visual search: Exploring the boundaries of "executive attention." *Journal of Experimental Psychology: Learning, Memory, and Cognition, 32,* 749–777.

Kanwisher, N. (2006). What's in a face? *Science, 311,* 617–618.

Kanwisher, N., McDermott, J., & Chun, M. M. (1997). The fusiform face area: A module in human extrastri-ate cortex specialized for face perception. *Journal of Neuroscience, 17,* 4302–4311.

Kaplan, S. (1995). The restorative bene-fits of nature: Toward an integrative framework. *Journal of Environmental Psychology, 15,* 169–182.

Kaplan, S. (2001). Meditation, restora-tion, and the management of mental fatigue. *Environment and Behavior, 33,* 480–506.

Kapur, S., Craik, F. I. M., Tulving, E., Wilson, A. A., Houle, S., & Brown, G. M. (1994). Neuroanatomical correlates of encoding in episodic memory: Levels of processing effects. *Proceedings of the National Academy of Sciences USA, 91,* 2008–2111.

Karremans, J., Stroebe, W., & Claus, J. (2006). Beyond Vicary's fantasies: The impact of subliminal priming and brand choice. *Journal of Experimental Social Psychology, 42,* 792–798.

Kass, R. E., & Raftery, A. E. (1995). Bayes factors. *Journal of the American Statistical Association, 90,* 773–795.

Kaufman, E. L., Lord, M.W., Reese, T.W., & Volkmann, J. (1949). The discrimination of visual number. *American Journal of Psychology, 62,* 498–525.

Kaufman, J. C., & Beghetto, R. A. (2009). Beyond big and little: The four c model of creativity. *Review of General Psychology, 13,* 1–12.

Keenan, J. P., Freund, S., Hamilton, R. H., Ganis, G., & Pascual-Leone, A. (2000). Hand-response differences in a self-face recognition task. *Neuropsychologia, 38,* 1047–1053.

Keenan, J. P., Gallup, G. G., & Falk, D. (2003). *The face in the mirror: The search for the origins of consciousness.* New York, NY: HarperCollins/Ecco.

Keenan, J. P., & Gorman, J. (2007). The causal role of the right hemisphere in self-awareness: It is the brain that is selective. *Cortex, 43,* 1074–1082.

Keenan, J. P., McCutcheon, B., Freund, S., Gallup, G. G., Sanders, G., & Pascual-Leone, A. (1999). Left-hand advantage in a self-face recognition task. *Neuropsychologia, 37,* 1421–1425.

Keenan, J. P., Wheeler, M. A., Gallup, G. G., & Pascual-Leone, J. (2000). Self-recognition and the right pre-frontal cortex. *Trends in Cognitive Sciences, 4,* 338–344.

Keil, F. (1989). *Concepts, kinds and cog-nitive development.* Cambridge, MA: MIT Press.

Kellogg, R. T. (1994). *The psychology of writing.* New York: Oxford University Press.

Kelley, C. M., & Jacoby, L. L. (2000). Recollection and familiarity: process-dissociation. In E. Tulving, F. Craik, & I. M. Fergus (Eds.). The Oxford handbook of memory (pp. 215–228). London: Oxford University Press.

Kelley, C. M., & Lindsey, D. S. (1996). Conscious and unconscious forms of memory. In E. L. Bjork & R. A. Bjork (Eds.), *Memory* (pp. 31–63). New York: Academic Press.

Kempe, V., Schaeffler, S., & Thoresen, J. C. (2010). Prosodic disambigua-tion in child-directed speech. *Journal of Memory and Language, 62,* 204–225.

Kensinger, E. A., & Corkin, S. (2003). Effect of negative emotional content on working memory and long-term memory. *Emotion, 3,* 378–93.

Keppel, G., & Underwood, B. J. (1962). Proactive inhibition in short-term retention of single items. *Journal of Verbal Learning and Verbal Behavior, 1,* 153–161.

Kershaw, T. C., & Ohlsson, S. (2004). Multiple causes of difficulty in insight: The case of the nine-dot problem. *Journal of Experimental Psychology: Learning, Memory, and Cognition, 30,* 3–13.

Key, A. P. F., Dove, G. O., & Maguire, M. J. (2005). Linking brainwaves to the brain: An ERP primer. *Developmental Neuropsychology, 27,* 183–215.

Key, B. W. (1973). *Subliminal seduction.* Englewood Cliffs, NJ: Prentice Hall.

Kihlstrom, J. F. (2004). An unbalanced balancing act: Blocked, recovered, and false memories in the laboratory and clinic. *Clinical Psychology: Science and Practice, 11,* 34–41.

Kihlstrom, J. K. (1998). Exhumed mem-ory. In S. J. Lynn & K. M. McConkey (Eds.), *Truth in memory* (pp. 3–31). New York: Guilford Press.

Kim, H., & Cabeza, R. (2007). Trusting our memories: Dissociating the neural correlates of confidence in veridical versus illusory memories. *Journal of Neuroscience, 27,* 12190–12197.

Kimball, D. R., & Holyoak, K. J. (2000). Transfer and expertise. In E. Tulving & F. I. M. Craik (Eds.), *The Oxford handbook of memory* (pp. 109–122). New York: Oxford University Press.

Kimble, G. A. (1985). *Psychology and learning.* Washington, DC: American Psychological Association.

Kimchi, R. (1992). Primacy of wholistic processing and global/local paradigm: A critical review. *Psychological Bulletin, 112,* 24–38.

Kintsch, W. (1974). The representation of meaning in memory. Hillsdale, NJ: Erlbaum.

Kintsch, W. (1988). The role of knowledge in discourse comprehension. A construction-integration model. *Psychological Review, 95,* 163–182.

Kintsch, W. (1998). *Comprehension: A paradigm for cognition.* Cambridge: Cambridge University Press.

Kintsch, W., Healy, A., Hegarty, M., Pennington, B., & Salthouse, T. (1999). Models of working memory: Eight questions and some general answers. In A. Miyake & P. Shah (Eds.), *Models of working memory.* London: Cambridge University Press.

Kintsch, W., & Keenan, J. (1973). Reading rate and retention as a function of the number of propositions in the base structure of sentences. *Cognitive Psychology, 5,* 257–274.

Kintsch, W., & van Dijk, T. A. (1978). Toward a model of text comprehension and production. *Psychological Review, 85,* 363–394.

Kirby, K. N. (1994). Probabilities and utilities of fictional outcomes in Wason's four-card selection task. *Cognition, 51,* 1–28.

Kirsner, K., Brown, H. L., Abrol, S., Chaddha, A., & Sharma, N.K. (1980). Bilingualism and lexical representation. *Quarterly Journal of Experimental Psychology, 32,* 565–574.

Kirsner, K., Milech, D., & Standen, P. (1983). Common and modality specific coding in the mental lexicon. *Memory & Cognition, 11,* 621–630.

Kirsner, K., Smith, M. C., Lockhart, R. S., King, M. L., & Jain, M. (1984). The bilingual lexicon: Language-specific units in an integrated. *Journal of Verbal Learning and verbal Behavior, 23,* 519–539.

Klatzky, R. L., & Lederman, S. J. (1995). Identifying objects from a haptic glance. *Perception & Psychophysics, 57,* 1111–1123.

Klatzky, R. L., & Lederman, S. J. (2008). Object recognition by touch. In J. Rieser, F. Ashmead, A. Ebner, & B. Corn, *Blindness and brain plasticity In navigation and object perception* (pp. 185–207). New York, NY: Erlbaum.

Klatzky, R. L., Lederman, S. J., & Metzger, V. A. (1985). Identifying objects by touch: An "expert system." *Perception & Psychophysics, 37,* 299–302.

Klatzky, R. L., Lederman, S. J., & Reed, C. (1987). There's more to touch than meets the eye: The salience of object attributes with and without vision. *Journal of Experimental Psychology: General, 116,* 356–369.

Klein, G. S. (1964). Semantic power measured through the interference of words with color-naming. *American Journal of Psychology, 77,* 576–588.

Kleunder, K. R., Diehl, R. L., & Killeen, P. R. (1987). Japanese quail can learn phonetic categories. *Science, 237,* 1195–1197.

Knoch, D., Gianotti, L. R., Mohr, C., & Brugger, P. (2005). Synesthesia: When colors count. *Cognitive Brain Research, 25,* 372–374.

Kohler, W. (1925). *The mentality of apes.* New York: Harcourt, Brace, and Jovanovich.

Kohnken, G., Milne, R., Memon, A., & Bull, R. (1999). The cognitive interview: A meta-analysis. *Psychology, Crime, and Law, 5,* 3–27.

Kolb, B., & Whishaw, I. Q. (1996). *Human neuropsychology.* New York: W. H. Freeman and Company.

Komatsu, L. K. (1992). Recent views of conceptual structure. *Psychological Bulletin, 112,* 500–526.

Koole, S. L., & DeHart, T. (2007). Self-affection without self-reflection: Origins, models, and consequences of implicit self-esteem. In C. Sedikides & S. Spencer (Eds.), *The self in social psychology* (pp. 36–86). New York: Psychology Press.

Koriat, A. (1991). How do we know what we know? Exploring a process model of feeling of knowing. Paper presented at the international conference on memory. Lancaster, England.

Koriat, A., & Lieblich, I. (1974). What does a person in a TOT state know that a person in a don't know state doesn't know? *Memory & Cognition, 2,* 647–655.

Kornell, N., & Bjork, R. A. (2008). Learning concepts and categories. *Psychological Science, 19,* 585–592.

Kounios, J., & Beeman, M. (2009). The aha! moment. *Current Directions in Psychological Science, 18,* 210–216.

Kounios, J., Fleck, J. I., Green, D. L., Payne, L., Stevenson, J. L., Bowden, E. M., & Jung-Beeman, M. (2008). The origins of insight in resting-state brain activity. *Neuropsychologia, 46,* 281–291.

Kounios, J., Frymiare, J. L., Bowden, E. M., Fleck, J. I., Subramaniam, K., Parrish, T. B. (2006). The prepared mind: Neural activity prior to problem presentation predicts subsequent solution by sudden insight. *Psychological Science, 17,* 882–890.

Kozar, B., Vaughn, R. E., Lord, R. H., & Whitfield, K. E. (1995). Basketball free-throw performance: Practice implications. *Journal of Sport Behavior, 18,* 123–129.

Kramer, A. F., & Larish, J. L. (1996). Aging and dual-task performance. In W. A. Rogers, A. D. Fisk, & N. Walker (Eds.), *Aging and skilled performance: Advances in theory and applications* (pp. 83–112). Hillsdale, NJ: Erlbaum.

Kramer, T. H., Buckhout, R., & Eugenio, P. (1989). Weapon focus, arousal, and eyewitness memory: Attention must be paid. *Applied Cognitive Psychology, 14,* 167–184.

Krueger, J. I., & Funder, D. C. (2004). Towards a balanced social psychology: Causes, consequences, and cures for the problem-seeking approach to social behavior and cognition. *Behavioral and Brain Sciences, 27,* 313–327.

Krueger, L. E. (1992). The word-superiority effect and phonological recoding. *Memory and Cognition, 20*, 685–694.

Kuhl, P. K., Andruski, J. E., Chistovich, I.A., Chistovich, L. A., Kozhevnikov, E. V. (1997). Cross-language analysis of phonetic units in language addressed to infants. *Science, 277*, 684–686.

Kuhl, P. K., Stevens, E., Hayashi, A., Deguchi, T., Kiritani, S., & Iverson, P. (2006). Infants show facilitation for native language phonetic perception between 6 and 12 months. *Developmental Science, 9*, 13–21.

Kuhl, P. K., Williams, K. A., Lacerda, F., Stevens, K. N., & Lindblom, B. (1992). Linguistic experience alters phonetic perception in infants by 6 months of age. *Science, 255*, 606–608.

Kuhn G., Amlani A. A., & Rensink R. A. (2008). Towards a science of magic. *Trends in Cognitive Sciences, 12*, 349–354

Kuhn, G., Tatler, B. W., Findlay, J. M., & Cole, G. G. (2008). Misdirection in magic: Implications for the relationship between eye gaze and attention. *Visual Cognition, 16*, 391–405.

Kutas, N., & Hillyard, S. A. (1970). Reading senseless sentences: Brain potentials reflect semantic incongruity. *Science, 207*, 203–205.

Kutas, N., & Hillyard, S. A. (1980). Reading between the lines: Event-related brain potentials during natural sentence processing. *Brain and Language, 11*, 354–373.

Kvavilashvili, L., Mirani, J., Schlagman, S., & Kornbrot, D. E. (2003). Comparing flashbulb memories of September 11 and the death of Princess Diana: Effect of time delays and nationality. *Applied Cognitive Psychology, 17*, 1017–1031.

Kvavilashvili, L., Mirani, J., Schlagman, S., Foley, K., & Kornbrot, D. E. (2009). Consistency of flashbulb memories of September 11 over long delays: Implications for consolidation and wrong time slice

hypotheses. *Journal of Memory and Language, 61*, 556–572.

Lachman, R., Lachman, J. R., & Butterfield, E. C. (1979). *Cognitive psychology and information processing: An introduction.* Hillsdale, NJ: Erlbaum.

Lachter, J., Forster, K. I., & Ruthruff, E. (2004). Forty-five years after Broadbent (1958): Still no identification without attention. *Psychological Review, 111*, 880–913.

LaBerge, D. (1983). Spatial extent of attention to letters and words. *Journal of Experimental Psychology. Human Perception and Performance, 9*, 371–9.

Lakoff, G. (1972). *Women, fire, and dangerous things.* Chicago: University of Chicago Press.

Lakoff, R. (1975). *Language and woman's place.* New York: Harper & Row.

Lam, K. C., & Buehler, R. (2009). Trips down memory lane: Recall direction affects the subjective distance of past events. *Personality and Social Psychology Bulletin, 35*, 230–42.

Lampinen, J. M., Meier, C. R., Arnal, J. D., & Leding, J. K. (2005). Compelling untruths: Content borrowing and vivid false memories. *Journal of Experimental Psychology: Learning, Memory, and Cognition, 31*, 954–963.

Lamy, D., & Tsal, Y. (2000). Object features, object locations, and object files: Which does selective attention activate and when? *Journal of Experimental Psychology: Human Perception and Performance, 26*, 1387–1400.

Lane, S. M., & Schooler, J. W. (2004). Skimming the surface: Verbal overshadowing of analogical retrieval. *Psychological Science, 15*, 715–719.

Laney, C., Morris, E. K., Bernstein, D. M., Wakefield, B. M., & Loftus, E. F. (2008). Asparagus, a love story: Healthier eating could be just a false memory away. *Experimental Psychology, 55*, 291–300.

Larsen, S. F. (1996). Memorable books: Recall of reading and its personal context. In R. J. Kreuz & M. S. MacNealy (Eds.), *Empirical*

approaches to literature and aesthetics (pp. 583–599). Norwood, NH: Ablex.

Lawless, H. T. (1997). Olfactory psychophysics. In G. K. Beauchamp & L. Bartoshuk (Eds.), *Tasting and smelling* (pp. 125–174). New York: Academic Press.

Lawless, H. T., & Engen, T. (1977). Associations to odors: Interference, mnemonics, and verbal labeling. *Journal of Experimental Psychology: Human Learning and Memory, 3*, 52–57.

Leach, J., & Griffith, R. (2008). Restrictions in working memory capacity during parachuting: A possible cause of 'no pull' vatalities. *Applied Cognitive Psychology, 22*, 147–157.

Leahey, T. H. (1992). *A history of psychology: Main currents in psychological thought* (3rd ed.). Englewood Cliffs, NJ: Prentice-Hall.

Lederman, S. J., & Klatzky, R. L. (1990). Haptic classification of common objects: Knowledge-driven exploration. *Cognitive Psychology, 22*, 421–459.

Ledoux, J. (2002). Synaptic self: How our brains become who we are. New York, NY: Viking Press.

Lee, J., Kwon, J. S., Shin, Y. W., Lee, K. J., & Park, S. (2007). Visual self-recognition in patients with schizophrenia. *Schizophrenia Research, 94*, 215–220.

Lee, Y., Lee, J. D., Boyle, L. N., & City, I. (2007). Visual attention in driving: The effects of cognitive load and visual disruption. *Human Factors, 49*, 721–733.

Lefly D. L, Pennington, B. F. (1991). Spelling errors and reading fluency in compensated adult dyslexics. *Annals of Dyslexia 41*, 143–162.

Lehrner, J. P. (1993). Gender differences in long-term odor recognition memory: Verbal versus sensory influences and the consistency of label use. *Chemical Senses, 18*, 17–26.

Lemaire, P., & Siegler, R. S. (1995). Four aspects of strategic change: Contributions to children's learning of multiplication. *Journal of Experimental Psychology: General, 124,* 83–97.

Lesch, M. F., & Hancock, P. A. (2004). Driving performance during concurrent cell-phone use: Are drivers aware of their performance decrements? *Accident Analysis and Prevention, 36,* 471–480.

Levav, J., & Argo, J. J. (2010). Physical contact and financial risk taking. *Psychological Science, 21,* 804–810.

Levelt, W. J. M. (1983). Monitoring and self-report in speech. *Cognition, 14,* 41–104.

Levelt, W. J. M. (1989). *Speaking: From intention to articulation.* Cambridge, MA: MIT Press.

Levelt, W. J. M., Roelefs, A., & Meyer, A. S. (1999). A theory of lexical access in speech production. *Behavioral and Brain Sciences, 22,* 1–75.

Levin, D. T., & Simons, D. J. (2000). Fragmentation and continuity in motion pictures and the real world. *Media Psychology, 2,* 357–380.

Levin, D. T., Simons, D. J., Angelone, B. L., & Chabris, C. F. (2002). Memory for centrally attended changing objects in an incidental real-world change detection paradigm. *British Journal of Psychology, 93,* 289–302.

Levine, L. J., & Edelstein, R. S. (2009). Emotion and memory narrowing: A review and goal-relevance approach. *Cognition, 23,* 833–875.

Lewald, J. (2002). Opposing effects of head position on sound localization in blind and sighted subjects. *European Journal of Neuroscience, 15,* 1219–1224.

Lewandowsky, S., Stritzke,W. G. K., Oberauer, K., & Morales, M. (2005). Memory for fact, fiction, and misinformation: The Iraq War 2003. *Psychological Science, 16,* 190–195.

Liberman, A. M., Cooper, F. S., Shankweiler, D. P., & Studdert-Kennedy, M. (1967). Perception of the speech code. *Psychological Review, 74,* 431–461.

Liberman, A. M., Harris, K. S., Hoffman, H. S., & Griffith, B. C. (1957). The discrimination of speech sounds within and across phoneme boundaries. *Journal of Experimental Psychology, 54,* 358–368.

Liberman, A. M., & Whalen, D. H. (2000). On the relation of speech to language. *Trends in Cognitive Sciences, 4,* 187–196.

Lichtenstein, S., P. Slovic, B. Fischhoff, M. Layman, and B. Combs. (1978). Judged frequency of lethal events. *Journal of Experimental psychology: Human Learning and Memory, 4,* 551–578.

Lichtenstein, S., & Slovic, P. (1971). Reversals of preference between bids and choices in gambling choices. *Journal of Experimental Psychology, 89,* 46–55.

Lichtenstein, S., & Slovic, P. (1973). Response-induced reversals of preference in gambling: An extended replication in Las Vegas. *Journal of Experimental Psychology, 101,* 16–20.

Lieberman, M. D. (2000). Intuition: A social cognitive neuroscience approach. *Psychological Bulletin, 126,* 109–137.

Lien, M., Ruthruff, E., & Johnston, J. C. (2006). Attentional limitations in doing two tasks at once: The search for exceptions. *Current Directions in Psychological Science, 15,* 89–93.

Lindsay, D. S. (1990). Misleading suggestions can impair witness' ability to remember event details. *Journal of Experimental Psychology: Learning, Memory, and Cognition, 16,* 1077–1083.

Lindsay, D. S. (1998). Depolarizing views on recovered memory experiences. In S. J. Lynn & K. M. McConkey (Eds.), *Truth in memory* (pp. 481–494). New York: Guilford Press.

Lindsay, D. S., Hagen, L., Read, J. D., Wade, K. A., & Garry, M. (2004). True photographs and false memories. *Psychological Science, 15,* 149–154.

Lindsay, D. S., Ross, D. F., Smith, S. M., & Flanagan, S. (1999). Does race influence measures of lineup fairness? *Applied Cognitive Psychology, 13,* S109–S119.

Lindsay, R. C., Mansour, J. K., Beaudry, J. L., Leach, A., & Bertrand, M. I. (2009). Sequential lineup presentation: Patterns and policy. *Legal and Criminological Psychology, 14,* 13–24.

Lindsay, R. C., & Wells, G. L. (1985). Improving eyewitness identifications from lineups: Simultaneous vs. sequential lineup presentation. *Journal of Applied Psychology, 70,* 556–564.

Linton, M. (1975). Transformations of memory in everyday life. In U. Neisser (Ed.), *Memory observed: Remembering in natural contexts* (pp. 77–92). San Francisco: Freeman.

Linton, M. (1986). Ways of searching and the contents of memory. In D. C. Rubin (Ed.). *Autobiographical memory* (pp. 50–66). Cambridge: Cambridge University Press.

Livesay, K., & Burgess, C. (1998). Mediated priming in high-dimensional semantic space: No effect of direct semantic relationships or co-occurrence. *Brain and Cognition, 37,* 102–105.

Llewellyn, T. (1962). Eye movements in speed reading. In *Speed reading: practices and procedures.* (pp. 104–114). University of Delaware Press.

Locke, E. A. (2009). It's time we brought introspection out of the closet. *Psychological Science, 4,* 24–25.

Loftus, E. F. (1975). Leading questions and the eyewitness report. *Cognitive Psychology, 7,* 560–572.

Loftus, E. F. (1976). Unconscious transference in eyewitness identification. *Law and Psychology Review, 2,* 93–98.

Loftus, E. F. (2005). A 30-year investigation of the malleability of memory. *Learning and Memory, 12,* 361–366.

Loftus, E. F., & Davis, D. (2006). Recovered memories. *Annual Review of Clinical Psychology, 2,* 469–498.

Loftus, E. F., Feldman, J., & Dashiell, R. (1995). The reality of illusory memories. In D. L. Schacter (Ed.), *Memory distortions: How minds, brains, and societies reconstruct the past* (pp. 47–68). Cambridge, MA: Harvard University Press.

Loftus, E. F., & Ketcham, K. (1991). *Witness for the defense: The accused, the eyewitness, and the expert who puts memory on trial.* New York: St. Martin's Press.

Loftus, E. F., Miller, D. G., & Burns, H. J. (1978). Semantic integration of verbal information into a visual memory. *Journal of Experimental Psychology: Human Learning and Memory, 4,* 19–31.

Loftus, E. F., & Pickrell, J. E. (1995). The formation of false memories. *Psychiatric Annals, 25,* 720–725.

Logan, G. D. & Cowan, W. B. (1984). On the ability to inhibit thought and action: A theory of an act of control. *Psychological Review, 91,* 295–327.

Logan, G. D. (1988). Toward an instance-based theory of automatization. *Psychological Review, 95,* 492–527.

Logan, G. D. (1997). The automaticity of academic life: Unconscious applications of an implicit theory. In R. S. Wyer (Ed.), *The automaticity of everyday life, advances in social cognition.* Vol. 10, (pp. 157–179). Mahweh, NJ: Erlbaum.

Logothetis, N. K., Pauls, J., & Poggio, T. (1995). Shape representation in the inferior temporal cortex of monkeys. *Current Biology, 7,* 645–651.

Lotto, A. J., Hickok, G. S., & Holt, L. L. (2008). Reflections on mirror neurons and speech perception. *Trends in Cognitive Sciences,* 1–5.

Lotto, A. J., & Sullivan, S. C. (2007). Speech as a sound source. In W. A. Yost, R. R. Fay, & A. N. Popper (Eds.), *Springer Handbook of Auditory Research: Auditory Perception of Sound Sources.* New York: Springer.

Lowery, B. S., & Eisenberger, N. I., Hardin, C. D., & Sinclair, S. (2007). Long-term Effects of Subliminal Priming on Academic Performance, *29*(2), 151–157.

Lu, L., & Gilmour, R. (2007). Developing a new measure of independent and interdependent views of the self. *Journal of Research in Personality, 41,* 249–257.

Lubart, T. I. (1994). Creativity. In R. J. Sternberg (Ed.), *Thinking and problem solving* (pp. 290–323). New York: Academic Press.

Luchins, A. M. (1942). Mechanization in problem solving—the effect of Einstellung. *Psychological Monographs, 54,* 95.

Lung, C., & Dominowski, R. L. (1985). Effects of strategy instructions and practice on nine-dot problem solving. *Journal of Experimental Psychology: Learning, Memory, and Cognition, 11,* 804–811.

Luo, C. R., Johnson, R. A., & Gallo, D. A. (1998). Automatic activation of phonological information in reading: Evidence from the semantic relatedness decision task. *Memory and Cognition, 26,* 833–843.

Lustig C., Matell M. S., Meck W. H. (2005). Not "just" a coincidence: frontal-striatal interactions in working memory and interval timing. *Memory, 13,* 441–448.

Lyon, G. R., Shaywitz, S. E. & Shaywitz, B. A. (2003). A definition of dyslexia. *Annals of Dyslexia, 53,* 1–14.

MacDonald, M. C., Perlmutter, N. J., & Seidenberg, M. S. (1994). The lexical nature of syntactic ambiguity resolution. *Psychological Review, 101,* 676–703.

MacDonald, S., Uesiliana, K., and Hayne, H. (2000). Cross-cultural and gender differences in childhood amnesia. *Memory, 8,* 365–376.

MacGregor, J. N., Ormerod, T. C., & Chronicle, E. P. (2001). Information processing and insight: A process model of performance on the nine-dot and related problems. *Journal of Experimental Psychology: Learning, Memory, and Cognition, 27,* 176–201.

Mack, A., & Rock, I. (1998). *Inattentional blindness.* Cambridge, MA: MIT Press.

MacKay, D. G. (1987). *The organization of perception and action: A theory for language and other cognitive skills.* New York: Springer-Verlag.

Macknik, S. L., King, M., Randi, J., Robbins, A., Thompson, J., Martinez-conde, S. (2008). Attention and awareness in stage magic: turning tricks into research. *Nature Reviews Neuroscience, 9,* 871–879.

Macpherson, R., & Stanovich, K. E. (2007). Cognitive ability, thinking dispositions, and instructional set as predictors of critical thinking. *Learning and Individual Differences, 17,* 115–127.

Maier, N. R., & Burke, R. J. (1967). Influence of timing of hints on their effectiveness in problem solving. *Psychological Reports, 20,* 3–8.

Maki, R. H. (1998). Predicting performance on text: Delayed vs. immediate predictors and tests. *Memory and Cognition, 26,* 959–964.

Malt, B. C. (1989). An on-line investigation of prototype and exemplar strategies in classification. *Journal of Experimental Psychology: Learning, Memory, and Cognition, 15,* 539–555.

Malt, B. C. (1995). Category coherence in cross-cultural perspective. *Cognitive Psychology, 29,* 85–148.

Malt, B. C., & Smith, E. E. (1984). Correlated properties in natural categories. *Journal of Verbal Learning and Verbal Behavior, 23,* 250–269.

Mandler, G., & Shebo, B. J. (1982). Subitizing: An analysis of its component processes. *Journal of Experimental Psychology: General, 111,* 1–22.

Mandler, G. (1980). Recognizing: the judgment of previous occurrence. Psychological Review, *87,* 252–271.

Mandler, J. A. (1987). On the psychological reality of story structure. *Discourse Processes, 10,* 1–29.

Maratos, F. A., Mogg, K., & Bradley, B. P. (2008). Identification of angry faces in the attentional blink. *Cognition & Emotion, 22*(7), 1340–1352.

Marcel, A. J. (1983). Conscious and unconscious perception: Experiments on visual masking and word recognition. *Cognitive Psychology, 15,* 197–237.

Margolis, H. (1987). *Patterns, thinking, and cognition.* Chicago: University of Chicago Press.

Markman, A. B., Taylor, E., & Gentner, D. (2007). Auditory presentation leads to better analogical retrieval than written presentation. *Psychonomic Bulletin & Review, 14,* 1101–1106.

Marian, V., & Neisser, U. (2000). Language-dependent recall of autobiographical memories. *Journal of Experimental Psychology: General, 129,* 361–368.

Markman, E. M., & Abelev, M. (2004). Word learning in dogs? *Trends in Cognitive Sciences, 8,* 479–481.

Marks, L. E. (1987). On cross-modal similarity: Auditory-visual interactions in speeded discrimination. *Journal of Experimental Psychology: Human Perception and Performance, 13,* 383–394.

Markus, H. R., & Kitayama, S. (1991). Culture and the self: Implication for cognition, emotion, and motivation. *Psychological Review, 98,* 224–253.

Marr, D., & Nishihara, H. K. (1982). Representation and recognition of the spatial organization of three-dimensional shapes. *Proceedings of the Royal Society of London, Series B: Biological Sciences* (pp. 269–294). Cambridge, MA: MIT Press.

Marsh, R. L., Landau, J. D., & Hicks, J. L. (1997). Contributions of inadequate source monitoring to unconscious plagiarism during idea generation. *Journal of Experimental Psychology: Learning, Memory, and Cognition, 23,* 886–897.

Marshall, P. J. (2009). Relating psychology and neuroscience. *Perspectives on Psychological Science, 4*(2), 113–125.

Marslen-Wilson, W. D., & Welsh, A. (1978). Processing interactions and lexical access during word recognition in continuous speech. *Cognitive Psychology, 10,* 29–63.

Martindale, C. (1991). *Cognitive psychology: A neural-network approach.* Pacific Grove, CA: Brooks/Cole.

Martindale, C., & Greenough, J. (1973). The differential effect of increased arousal on creative and intellectual performance. *Journal of Genetic Psychology, 123,* 329–335.

Martino, G., & Marks, L. E. (2001). Synaesthesia: Strong and weak. *Current Directions in Psychological Science, 10,* 61–65.

Massaro, D. W. (1972). Preperceptual images, processing time, and perceptual units in auditory perception. *Psychological Review, 79,* 124–145.

Massaro, D. W. (1975). *Experimental psychology and information processing.* Chicago: Rand-McNally.

Massaro, D. W. (1994). Psychological aspects of speech perception: Implications for research and theory. In M. A. Gernsbacher (Ed.), *Handbook of psycholinguistics* (pp. 219–263). New York: Academic Press.

Massaro, D. W., & Jesse, A. (2009). Read my lips: Speech distortions in musical lyrics can be overcome (slightly) by facial information. *Speech Communication, 51,* 604–621.

Massaro, D. W., & Loftus, G. R. (1996). Sensory and perceptual storage: Data and theory. In E. L. Bjork & R. A. Bjork (Eds.), *Memory* (pp. 67–99). New York: Academic Press.

Matan, A., & Carey, S. (2001). Developmental changes within the core of artifact concepts. *Cognition, 78,* 1–26.

Matin, E. (1974). Saccadic suppression: A review and an analysis. *Psychological Bulletin, 81,* 899–917.

Matsukura, M., & Vecera, S. P. (2006). The return of object-based attention: selection of multiple-region objects. *Perception & Psychophysics, 68*(7), 1163–1175.

Mattingly, I. G., & Liberman, A. M. (1987). Specialized perceiving systems for speech and other biologically significant sounds. In

G. M. Edelman, W. E. Gall, & W. M. Cowan (Eds.), *Auditory function: Neurological bases of hearing* (pp. 775–793). New York: Wiley.

Mattys, S. L., White, L., & Melhorn, J. F. (2005). Integration of multiple speech segmentation cues: A hierarchical framework. *Journal of Experimental Psychology: General, 134,* 477–500.

Maye, J., Weiss, D. J., and Aslin, R. N. (2008). Statistical phonetic learning in infants: Facilitation and feature generalization. *Developmental Science, 11,* 122–134.

Mayer, R. (1992). *Thinking, problem solving, cognition* (2nd ed.). New York: Freeman.

Mazzoni, G. A. L., Loftus, E. F., & Kirsch, I. (2001). Changing beliefs about implausible autobiographical events: A little plausibility goes a long way. *Journal of Experimental Psychology: Applied, 7,* 51–59.

McBain, R., Norton, D., & Chen, Y. (2009). Females excel at basic face perception. *Acta Psychologica, 130,* 168–173.

McBride-Chang, C., & Kail, R. V. (2002). Cross-cultural similarities in the predictors of reading acquisition. *Child Development, 73,* 1392–1407.

McClaughlin, G. H. (1969). Reading at "impossible" speeds. *Journal of Reading, 12,* 449–454.

McClelland, J. L., & Elman, J. L. (1986). The TRACE model of speech perception. *Cognitive Psychology, 18,* 1–86.

McClelland, J. L., & Rumelhart, D. (1981). An interactive activation model of context effects in letter perception, I: An account of basic findings. *Psychological Review, 88,* 375–407.

McClelland, J. L., & Rumelhart, D. E. (1985). Distributed memory and the representation of general and specific information. *Journal of Experimental Psychology, General, 114,* 159–188.

McClelland, J. L., Thomas, A. G., McCandliss, B. D., & Fiez, J. A.

(1999). Understanding failures of learning: Hebbian learning, competition for representational space, and some preliminary experimental data. In J. A. Reggia, E. Ruppin, & D. Glanzman (Eds.), *Progress in brain research* (Vol. 121). Amsterdam: Elsevier.

McCloskey, M., & Zaragoza, M. (1985). Misleading postevent information and memory for events: Arguments and evidence against memory impairment hypothesis. *Journal of Experimental Psychology: General, 114*, 1–16.

McCloskey, M., Wible, C. J., & Cohen, N. J. (1988). Is there a special flashbulb-memory mechanism? *Journal of Experimental Psychology: General, 117*, 171–181.

McClure, E. B. (2000). A meta-analytic review of sex differences in facial expression processing and their development in infants, children, and adolescents. *Psychological Bulletin, 126*, 424–453.

McConkie, G. W., & Rayner, K. (1976). What guides a reader's eye movements? *Vision Research, 16*, 829–837.

McDaniel, M. A., & Einstein, G. O. (2000). Strategic and automatic processes in prospective memory retrieval: A multiprocess framework. *Applied Cognitive Psychology, 14*, S127–S144.

McDaniel, M. A., & Einstein, G. O. (2005). Material-appropriate difficulty: A framework for determining when difficulty is desirable for improving learning In A. F. Healy (Ed.), *Experimental cognitive psychology and its applications. Decade of behavior* (pp. 73–85). Washington, DC: American Psychological Association.

McDaniel, M., Roediger, H. L., & McDermott, K. B. (2007). Generalizing test-enhanced learning from the laboratory to the classroom. *Psychonomic Bulletin & Review, 14*, 200–206.

McDowd, J. M., & Craik, F. I. (1988). Effects of aging and task difficulty on divided attention performance. *Journal of Experimental Psychology: Human Perception and Performance, 14*, 267–280.

McDonald, J. L., & MacWhinney, B. (1995). The time course of anaphor resolution: Effects of implicit verb causality and gender. *Journal of Memory and Language, 34*, 543–566.

McElree, B. (2001). Working memory and focal attention. *Journal of Experimental Psychology. Learning, Memory, and Cognition, 27*, 817–35.

McGeoch, J. A. (1932). Forgetting and the law of disuse. *Psychological Review, 39*, 352–370.

McGurk, J., & MacDonald, H. (1976). Visual influences on speech perception. *Perception & Psychophysics, 24*, 253–257.

McIntyre, S. E. (2008). Capturing attention to brake lamps. *Accident Analysis and Prevention, 40*, 691–696.

McKone, E., & Robbins, R. (2007). The evidence rejects the expertise hypothesis: reply to Gauthier & Bukach. *Cognition, 103*, 331–336.

McKoon, G. (1977). Organization of information in text memory. *Journal of Verbal Learning and Verbal Behavior, 16*, 247–260.

McKoon, G., & Ratcliff, R. (1992). Inferences during reading. *Psychological Review, 99*, 440–466.

McLaughlin, G. H. (1969). Reading at 'impossible' speeds. *Journal of Reading, 12*, 449.

McMackin, J., & Slovic, P. (2000). When does explicit justification impair decision making? *Applied Cognitive Psychology, 14*, 527–541.

McNally, R. J. (2003). Recovering memories of trauma: A view from the laboratory. *Current Directions in Psychological Science, 12*, 32–35.

McNally, R. J., & Geraerts, E. (2009). A new solution to the recovered memory debate. *Psychological Science, 4*, 126–134.

McNamara, H. J., Long, J. B., & Wike, E. L. (1956). Learning without response under two conditions of external cues. *Journal of Comparative and Physiological Psychology, 49*, 477–480.

McNamara, T. P. (1992). Theories of priming I: Associative distance and lag. *Journal of Experimental Psychology: Learning, Memory, and Cognition, 18*, 1173–1190.

McNamara, T. P. (1994). Knowledge representation. In R. L. Sternberg (Ed.), *Thinking and problem solving* (pp. 81–117). New York: Academic Press.

McNamara, T. P., & Altarriba, J. (1988). Depth of spreading activation revisited: Semantic mediated priming occurs in lexical decisions. *Journal of Memory and Language, 27*, 545–559.

McNealy, K. Mazziotta, J. C. Dapretto, M. Cracking the language code: Neural mechanisms underlying speech parsing. *Journal of Neuroscience, 26*, 7629–7639.

McNeil, B. J., Pauker, S. G., Sox, H. C., & Tversky, A. (1986). On the elicitation of preferences for alternative therapies. In K. R. Hammond & H. R. Arkes (Eds.), *Judgment and decision making*. New York: Cambridge University Press.

McQuiston-Surrett, D., Malpass, R. S., & Tredoux, C. G. (2006). Sequential vs. simultaneous lineups: A review of methods, data, and theory. *Psychology, Public Policy, and Law, 12*, 137–169.

McVay, J. C., & Kane, M. J. (2009). Conducting the train of thought: Working memory capacity, goal neglect, and mind wandering in an executive-control task. *Journal of Experimental Psychology: Learning, Memory, and Cognition, 35*, 196–204.

Medin, D. L., & Atran, S. (2004). The native mind: Biological categorization and reasoning in development and across cultures. *Psychological Review, 111*, 960–983.

Medin, D. L., & Coley, J. D. (1998). Concepts and categorization. In J. Hochberg (Ed.), *Perception and cognition at century's end* (pp. 403–439). San Diego, CA: Academic Press.

Medin, D. L., & Heit, E. (1999). Categorization. In D. Rumelhart & B. Martin (Eds.), *Handbook of cognition and perception* (pp. 99–143). New York: Academic Press.

Medin, D. L., Lynch, E. B., & Solomon K. O. (2000). Are there kinds of concepts? *Annual Review of Psychology, 52,* 121–147.

Medin, D. L., & Ortony, A. (1989). Psychological essentialism. In S. Vosniadou & A. Ortony (Eds.), *Similarity and analogical reasoning* (pp. 179–196). New York: Cambridge University Press.

Medin, D. L., & Rips, L. J. (2005). Concepts and categories: Memory, meaning, and metaphysics. In K. Holyoak & R. G. Morrison (Eds.), *The Cambridge handbook of thinking and reasoning* (pp. 37–72). New York: Cambridge University Press.

Megreya, A. M., & Burton, A. M. (2008). Matching Faces to Photographs: Poor Performance in Eyewitness Memory (Without the Memory). *Journal of Experimental Psychology: Applied, 14,* 364–372.

Mehl, M. R., Vazire, S., Ramírez-Esparza, N., Slatcher, R. B., & Pennebaker, J. W. (2007). Are women really more talkative than men? *Science, 317,* 82.

Meissner, C. A., & Brigham, J. C. (2001). Thirty years of investigating the own-race bias in memory for faces: A meta-analytic review. *Psychology, Public Policy, & Law, 7,* 3–35.

Melton, A. W. (1963). Implications of short-term memory for a general theory of memory. *Journal of Verbal Learning and Verbal Behavior, 2,* 1–21.

Melton, A. W. (1970). The situation with respect to the spacing of repetitions and memory. *Journal of Verbal Learning and Verbal Behavior, 9,* 596–606.

Menneer, T., Cave, K. R., & Donnelly, N. (2009). The cost of search for multiple targets: effects of practice and target similarity. *Journal of Experimental Psychology: Applied, 15*(2), 125–39.

Merckelbach, H., Smeets, T., Geraerts, E., Jelicic, M., Bouwen, A., & Smeets, E. (2006). I haven't thought about this for years! Dating recent recalls of vivid memories. *Applied Cognitive Psychology, 20,* 33–42.

Merikle, P. M. (1988). Subliminal auditory messages: An evaluation. *Psychology and Marketing, 5,* 355–372.

Mervis, C. B., & Rosch, E. (1981). Categorization of natural objects. *Annual Review of Psychology, 32,* 89–115.

Metcalfe, J. (1986a). Feeling of knowing in memory and problem solving. *Journal of Experimental Psychology: Learning, Memory, and Cognition, 12,* 288–294.

Metcalfe, J. (1986b). Premonitions of insight predict impending error. *Journal of Experimental Psychology: Learning, Memory, and Cognition, 12,* 623–634.

Metcalfe, J., & Greene, M. J. (2007). Metacognition of agency. *Journal of Experimental Psychology. General, 136,* 184–199.

Metcalfe, J., & Weibe, D. (1987). Intuition in insight and noninsight problem solving. *Memory and Cognition, 15,* 238–246.

Metzger, R. L., Boschee, P. F., Haugen, T., & Schnobrich, B. L. (1979). The classroom as learning context: Changing rooms affects performance. *Journal of Educational Psychology, 71,* 440–442.

Milkman, K. L., Chugh, D., & Bazerman, M. H. (2009). How can decision making be improved? *Perspectives on Psychological Science, 4,* 379–383.

Miller, G. A. (1956). The magical number seven, plus or minus two: Some limits on our capacity for processing information. *Psychological Review, 63,* 81–97.

Miller, G. A. (1990). The place of language in a scientific psychology. *Psychological Science, 1,* 7–14.

Mills, C. B., Boteler, E. H., & Oliver, G. K. (1999). Digit synesthesia: A case study using a Stroop-type test. *Cognitive Neuropsychology, 16,* 181–191.

Moè, A., & De Beni, R. (2005). Stressing the efficacy of the loci method: Oral presentation and the subject-generation of the loci pathway with expository passages. *Applied Cognitive Psychology, 19,* 95–106.

Monti, L. A., Gabrieli, J. D. E., Wilson, R. S., Beckett, L. A., Grinnell, E., Lange, K. L., & Reminger, S. L. (1997). Sources of priming in text rereading: Intact implicit memory for new associations in older adults and in patients with Alzheimer's disease. *Psychology and Aging, 12,* 536–547.

Moore, C. M., & Egeth, H. (1997). Perception without attention: Evidence of grouping under conditions of inattention. *Journal of Experimental Psychology: Human Perception and Performance, 23,* 339–352.

Moore, D. A., & Healy, P. J. (2008). The trouble with overconfidence. *Psychological Review, 115,* 502–517.

Moore, T. E. (1996). Scientific consensus and expert testimony: Lessons from the Judas Priest trial. *Skeptical Inquirer, 20.*

Moors, A., & De Houwer, J. (2006). Automaticity: A theoretical and conceptual analysis. *Psychological Bulletin, 132,* 297–326.

Moray, N. (1959). Attention in dichotic listening: Affective cues and the influence of instructions. *Quarterly Journal of Experimental Psychology, 11,* 56–60.

Morgan, C. A., Hazlett, G., Doran, A., Garrett, S., Hoyt, G., Thomas, P., Baranoski, M., & Southwick, S. M. (2004). Accuracy of eyewitness memory for persons encountered during exposure to highly intense stress. *International Journal of Law and Psychiatry, 27,* 265–79.

Morris, C. D., Bransford, J. D., & Franks, J. J. (1977). Levels of processing versus transfer-appropriate processing. *Journal of Verbal Learning and Verbal Behavior, 16,* 519–533.

Morrot, G., Brochet, F., & Dubourdieu, D. (2001). The color of odors. *Brain and Language, 79,* 309–320.

Morton, J. (1969). Interaction of information in word recognition. *Psychological Review, 76,* 165–178.

Most, S. B., Scholl, B. J., Clifford, E. R., & Simons, D. J. (2005). What you see is what you set: Sustained inattentional blindness and the capture of awareness. *Psychological Review, 112,* 217–242.

Motley, M. T. (1985). Slips of the tongue. *Scientific American, 253,* 116–127.

Motley, M. T., & Baars, B. J. (1979). Effects of cognitive set upon laboratory-induced verbal (Freudian) slips. *Journal of Speech and Hearing Research, 22,* 421–432.

Moulds, M. L., & Bryant, R. A. (2005). Traumatic memories in acute stress disorder: An analysis of narratives before and after treatment. *Clinical Psychologist, 9,* 10–14.

Mousty, P., & Bertelson, P. (1992). Finger movements in braille reading: The effect of local ambiguity. *Cognition, 43,* 67–84.

Mueller-Johnson, K., & Ceci, S. J. (2004). Memory and suggestibility in older adults: Live event participation and repeated interview. *Applied Cognitive Psychology, 18,* 1109–1127.

Multhaup, K., Johnson, M., & Tetirick, J. (2005). The wane of childhood amnesia for autobiographical and public event memories. *Memory, 13,* 161–173.

Murray, D. J. (1968). Articulation and acoustic confusability in short-term memory. *Journal of Experimental Psychology, 78,* 679–684.

Murray, J. E., Young, E., & Rhodes, G. (2000). Revisiting the perception of upside-down faces. *Psychological Science, 11,* 492–496.

Murray, W. S., & Kennedy, A. (1988). Spatial coding in the processing of anaphor by good and poor readers: Evidence from eye movement analyses. *Quarterly Journal of Experimental Psychology: Human Experimental Psychology, 40(4-A),* 693–718.

Myers, D. G. (2001, December). Do we fear the right things? *American Psychological Society Observer, 14,* 3.

Nadel, L., & Jacobs, W. J. (1998). Traumatic memory is special. *Current Directions in Psychological Science, 7,* 154–157.

Nadel, L., & Zola-Morgan, S. (1984). Infantile amnesia: A neurobiological perspective. In M. Moscovitch (Ed.), *Infant memory* (pp. 145–172). New York: Plenum Press.

Nairne, J. S. (1983). Associative processing during rote rehearsal. *Journal of Experimental Psychology: Learning, Memory, and Cognition, 9,* 3–20.

Nairne, J. S. (1990). Similarity and long-term memory for order. *Journal of Memory and Language, 29,* 733–746

Nairne, J. S. (1996). Short-term/working memory. In E. L. Bjork & R. A. Bjork (Eds.), *Memory: Handbook of perception and cognition.* New York: Academic Press.

Nairne, J. S. (2001). A functional analysis of primary memory. In H. L. Roediger, J. S. Nairne, I. Neath, & A. Surprenant (Eds.), *The nature of remembering: Essays in honor of Robert G. Crowder.* Washington, DC: APA.

Nairne, J. S. (2002a). The myth of the encoding-retrieval match. *Memory, 10,* 389–395.

Nairne, J. S. (2002b). Remembering over the short-term: The case against the standard model. *Annual Review of Psychology, 53,* 53–81.

Nairne, J. S., Pandeirada, J. N., Gregory, K. J., & Arsdall, J. E. (2009). Adaptive memory: Fitness relevance and the hunter-gatherer mind. *Psychological Science, 20,* 740–746.

Nairne, J. S., Pandeirada, J. N., & Thompson, S. R. (2008). Adaptive memory: The comparative value of survival processing. *Psychological Science, 19,* 176–180.

Nakayama, K., & Silverman, G. H. (1986). Serial and parallel processing of visual feature conjunctions. *Nature, 320,* 264265.

Nash, R. A., Wade, K. A., & Brewer, R. J. (2009). Why do doctored images distort memory? *Cognition and Consciousness, 18,* 773–780.

Nathan, D., & Snedeker, M. (1995). *Satan's silence: Ritual abuse and the making of a modern American witch hunt.* New York: Basic Books.

Navon, D. (1977). Forest before trees: The precedence of global features in visual perception. *Cognitive Psychology, 9,* 353–383.

Navon, D., & Gopher, D. (1979). On the economy of the human information processing system. *Psychological Review, 86,* 214–255.

Navon, D., & Miller, J. F. (2002). Queuing or sharing? A critical evaluation of the single-bottleneck notion. *Cognitive Psychology, 44,* 193–251.

Neath, I. (2000). Is "working memory" still a useful concept? *Contemporary Psychology, 45,* 410–412.

Neisser, U. (1967). *Cognitive psychology.* New York: Appleton-Century-Crofts.

Neisser, U. (1978). Memory: What are the important questions? In M. M. Gruneberg, P. E. Morris, & R. N. Sykes (Eds.), *Practical aspects of memory.* New York: Academic Press.

Neisser, U., & Harsch, N. (1992). Phantom flashbulbs: False recollections of hearing the news about Challenger. In E. Winograd & U. Neisser (Eds.), *Affect and accuracy in recall: Studies of "flashbulb" memories* (pp. 9–31). New York: Cambridge University Press.

Nelson, E. L., & Simpson, P. (1994). First glimpse: An initial investigation of subjects who have rejected their recovered visualizations as false memories. *Issues in Child Abuse Accusations, 6,* 123–133.

Nelson, K. (1993). The psychological and social origins of autobiographical memory. *Psychological Science, 4,* 7–14.

Nelson, K., & Fivush, R. (2004). The emergence of autobiographical memory: A social-cultural developmental theory. *Psychological Review, 111,* 486–511.

Newell, A., Shaw, J. C., & Simon, H. A. (1958). Elements of a theory of human problem solving. *Psychological Review, 65,* 151–166.

Newell, A., & Simon, H. (1972). *Human problem solving*. Englewood Cliffs, NJ: Prentice Hall.

Nicholas, J. S., Charles, J. M., Carpenter, L. A., King, L. B., Jenner, W., & Spratt, E. G. (2008). Prevalence and characteristics of children with autism-spectrum disorders. *Annals of Epidemiology, 18*, 130–136.

Nichols E. A., Kao Y., Verfaellie, M., Gabrieli J. D. E. (2006). Working memory and long-term memory for faces: Evidence from fMRI and global amnesia for involvement of the medial temporal lobes. *Hippocampus, 16*, 604–616.

Nickerson, R. S. (1998). Confirmation bias: A ubiquitous phenomenon in many guises. *Review of General Psychology, 2*, 175–220.

Nisbett, R. E., & Masuda, T. (2003). Culture and point of view. *Proceedings of the National Academy of Sciences, 100*, 11163–11170.

Nisbett, R. E., & Miyamoto, Y. (2005). The influence of culture: Holistic versus analytic perception. *Trends in Cognitive Sciences, 9*, 467–473.

Nisbett, R. E., Peng, K., Choi, I., & Norenzayan, A. (2001). Culture and systems of thought: Holistic vs. analytic cognition. *Psychological Review, 108*, 291–310.

Nisbett, R. E., & Wilson, T. D. (1977). Telling more than we can know: Verbal reports on mental processes. *Psychological Review, 84*, 231–259.

Noble K. G., McCandiliss B. D., Farah, M. J. (2007) Socio-economic gradients predict individual differences in neurocognitive abilities. *Developmental Science, 10*, 464–480.

Noice, H., & Noice, T. (2001). Learning dialogue with and without movement. *Memory and Cognition, 29*, 820–828.

Noice, H., & Noice, T. (2006). What studies of actors and acting can tell us about memory and cognitive functioning. *Psychological Science, 15*, 14–18.

Norenzayan, A., Choi, I., & Peng, K. (2007). Perception and cognition. In H. Kitayama & D. Cohen (Eds.), *Handbook of cultural psychology* (pp. 569–594). New York, NY: Guilford Publications.

Norman, D. A. (1981). Categorization of action slips. *Psychological Review, 88*, 1–15.

Norman, D. A. (1988). *The psychology of everyday things*. New York: Basic Books.

Norman, K. A., & Schacter, D. L. (1996). Implicit memory, explicit memory and false recollection. A cognitive neuroscience perspective. In L. M. Reder (Ed.), *Implicit memory and metacognition* (pp. 229–259). Hillsdale, NJ: Erlbaum.

Norris, D. (1994). Shortlist: A connectionist model of continuous speech recognition. *Cognition, 52*, 189–234.

Nosofsky, R. (1984). Choice, similarity, and the context theory of classification. *Journal of Experimental Psychology: Learning, Memory, and Cognition, 10*, 104–114.

Novick, L. R. (1988a). Analogical transfer, problem similarity, and expertise. *Journal of Experimental Psychology: Learning, Memory, and Cognition, 14*, 510–520.

Novick, L. R., & Holyoak, K. E. (1991). Mathematical problem solving by analogy. *Journal of Experimental Psychology: Learning, Memory, and Cognition, 17*, 398–415.

Nunes, A., & Kramer, A. F. (2009). Experience-based mitigation of age-related performance declines: Evidence from air-traffic control, *Journal of Experimental Psychology: Applied, 15*, 12–24.

Nygaard, L. C., & Queen, J. S. (2008). Communicating emotion: linking affective prosody and word meaning. *Journal of Experimental Psychology. Human Perception and Performance, 34*, 1017–1030.

Oberauer, K. (2002). Access to information in working memory: Exploring the focus of attention. *Journal of Experimental Psychology: Learning, Memory, and Cognition, 28*, 411–421.

Oberauer, K. (2006). Reasoning with conditionals: A test of formal models of four theories. *Cognitive Psychology, 53*, 238–283.

Ochsner, K. N. (2000). Are affective events richly recollected or simply familiar? The experience and process of recognizing feelings past. *Journal of Experimental Psychology: General, 129*, 242–261.

Okado, Y., & Stark, C. E. L. (2005). Neural activity during encoding predicts false memories created by misinformation. *Learning & Memory, 12*, 3–11.

Oliva, A., & Torralba, A. (2007). The role of context in object recognition. *Trends in Cognitive Sciences, 11*, 520–527.

Olive, T., & Kellogg, R. T. (2002). Concurrent activation of high- and low-level production processes in written composition. *Memory & Cognition, 30*, 594–600.

Olson I. R., Moore K. S., Stark M., Chatterjee, A. (2006) . Visual working memory is impaired when the medial temporal lobe is damaged. *Journal of Cognitive Neuroscience, 18*, 1087–1097.

Olson I. R., Page K., Moore K. S., Chatterjee, A., & Verfaellie M. (2006). Working memory for conjunctions relies on the medial temporal lobe. *Journal of Neuroscience, 26*, 4596–4601.

Olton, R. M. (1979). Experimental studies of incubation: Searching for the elusive. *Journal of Creative Behavior, 13*, 9–22.

Olton, R. M., & Johnson, D. M. (1976). Mechanisms of incubation in creative problem solving. *American Journal of Psychology, 89*, 617–630.

Ophir, E., Nass, C., & Wagner, A. D. (2009). Cognitive control in media multitaskers. *Proceedings of the National Academy of Sciences, 106*, 1–5.

O'Regan, J. K. (1980). The control of saccade size and fixation duration in reading: The limits of linguistic control. *Perception & Psychophysics, 28*, 112–117.

O'Regan, J. K., Rensink R. A., & Clark, J. J. (1999). Change blindness as a result of 'mudsplashes'. *Nature, 398*, 34.

Pagel, M. (2000) The history, rate and pattern of world linguistic evolution. In C. Knight, M. Studdert-Kennedy & J. Hurford (Eds.) The evolutionary emergence of language (pp. 391–416). Cambridge, UK: Cambridge University Press.

Palmer, S. E. (1975). The effects of contextual scenes on the identification of objects. *Memory and Cognition, 3,* 519–526.

Palmer, S. E. (2003). Visual perception of objects. In A. F. Healy & R. F. Proctor (Eds.), *Handbook of psychology: experimental psychology* (Vol. 4, 179–211). Hoboken, NJ: John Wiley & Sons, Inc.

Palmer, S. E., & Beck, D. M. (2007). The repetition discrimination task: an objective method for studying perceptual grouping. *Perception & Psychophysics, 69,* 68–78.

Palmer, S., Rosch, E., & Chase, P. (1981). Canonical perspective and the perception of objects. In J. Long & A. Baddeley (Eds.), *Attention & performance IX* (pp. 135–151) Hillsdale, NJ: Erlbaum.

Palmeri, T. J., & Tarr, M. J. (2008). Visual object perception and long-term memory. In S. Luck, (Ed.) *Visual memory* (pp. 163–207). New York, NY: Oxford University Press.

Parr, W. V. (2008). Application of cognitive psychology to advance understanding of wine expertise. In K. H. Kiefer (Ed.) *Applied psychology research trends.* (pp. 119–140). Hauppauge, NY, US: Nova Science Publishers.

Parr, W. V., White, K., & Heatherbell, D. A. (2004). The nose knows: influence of colour on perception of wine aroma. *Journal of Wine Research, 14,* 79–101.

Pashler, H. (1992). Attentional limitations in doing two tasks at the same time. *Current Directions in Psychological Science, 1,* 44–48.

Pashler, H. (1994). Dual-task interference in simple tasks: Data and theory. *Psychological Bulletin, 16,* 220–244.

Pashler, H. (1998). *The psychology of attention.* Cambridge, MA: MIT Press.

Pashler, H., & Carrier, M. (1996). Structures, processes, and the flow of information. In E. L. Bjork & R. A. Bjork (Eds.), *Handbook of perception and cognition: Memory* (pp. 3–29). New York: Academic Press.

Pavani, F., Spence, C., & Driver, J. (2000). Visual capture of touch: Out-of-body experiences with rubber gloves. *Psychological Science, 11,* 353–359.

Payne, J. D., Jackson, E. D., Ryan, L., Hoscheidt, S., Jacobs, W. J., & Nadel, L. (2006). The impact of stress on neutral and emotional aspects of episodic memory. *Memory, 14,* 1–16.

Payne, J. D., Nadel, L., Britton, W. B., & Jacobs, W. J. (2004). The biopsychology of trauma and memory. In D. Reisberg & P. Hertel (Eds.), *Memory and emotion. Series in affective science* (pp. 76–128). New York: Oxford University Press.

Paz-Alonso, P. M., Ghetti, S., Donohue, S. E., Goodman, G. S., & Bunge, S. A. (2008). Neurodevelopmental correlates of true and false recognition *Cerebral Cortex, 18,* 2208–2216.

Pelucchi, B., Hay, J. F. and Saffran, J. R. (2009), Statistical Learning in a Natural Language by 8-Month-Old Infants. *Child Development, 80,* 674–685.

Pennington, B. F., & Bishop, D. V. (2009). Relations among speech, language, and reading disorders. *Annual Review of Psychology, 60,* 283–306.

Pepperberg, I. M. (1999a). *The Alex studies: Cognitive and communicative abilities of grey parrots.* Cambridge, MA: Harvard University Press.

Pepperberg, I. M. (1999b). Cognitive and communicative abilities of grey parrots. *Current Directions in Psychological Science, 11,* 83–87.

Pepperberg, I. M. (2006). Cognitive and communicative abilities of grey parrots. *Applied Animal Behaviour Science, 100,* 77–86.

Perea, M., Acha, J., & Carreiras, M. (2009). Eye movements when reading text messaging (txt msgng). *The Quarterly Journal of Experimental Psychology, 62,* 1560–1567.

Perfect, T. J., & Harris, L. J. (2003). Adult age differences in unconscious transference: Source confusion or identity blending? *Memory & Cognition, 31(4),* 570–580.

Perlmutter, M. (1979). Age differences in the consistency of adults' associative responses. *Experimental Aging Research, 5,* 549–553.

Petersen, R. C. (1977). Retrieval failures in alcohol state-dependent learning. *Psychopharmacology, 55,* 141–146.

Peterson, L., & Peterson, M. J. (1959). Short-term retention of individual verbal items. *Journal of Experimental Psychology, 58,* 193–198.

Peterson, C., Wang, Q., & Hou, Y. (2009). "When I was little": Childhood recollections in Chinese and European grade-school children. *Child Development, 80,* 506–518.

Pezdek, K. (2003). Event memory and autobiographical memory for the events of September 11, 2001. *Applied Cognitive Psychology, 17,* 1033–1045.

Pezdek, K. (2007). It's just not good science. *Consciousness and Cognition, 16,* 29–30.

Pezdek, K., & Lam, S. (2007). What research paradigms have cognitive psychologists used to study "false memory," and what are the implications of these choices? *Consciousness and. Cognition, 16,* 2–17.

Pickering, M. J., & Ferreira, V. S. (2008). Structural priming: A critical review. *Psychological Bulletin, 134,* 427–459.

Pickering, M. J., & Traxler, M. J. (1998). Plausibility and recovery from garden paths: An eye-movement study. *Journal of Experimental Psychology: Learning, Memory, and Cognition, 24,* 940–961.

Pillemer, D. B. (1984). Flashbulb memories of the assassination attempt on President Reagan. *Cognition, 16,* 63–80.

Pillemer, D. B. (1992). Remembering personal circumstances: A functional analysis. In E. Winograd & U. Neisser (Eds.), *Affect and accuracy in recall: Studies of "flashbulb" memories.* New York: Cambridge University Press.

Pillemer, D. B. (1998). *Momentous events, vivid memories.* Cambridge, MA: Harvard University Press.

Pillemer, D. B. (2003). Directive functions of autobiographical memory: The guiding power of the specific episode. *Memory, 11,* 193–202.

Pillemer, D. B., Picariello, M. L., Law, A. B., & Reichman, J. S. (1996). Memories of college: The importance of specific educational episodes. In D. C. Rubin (Ed.), *Remembering our past: Studies in autobiographical memory* (pp. 318–337). New York: Cambridge University Press.

Pillemer, D. B., & White, S. H. (1989). Childhood events recalled by children and adults. In H. W. Reese (Ed.), *Advances in child development and behavior* (Vol. 21, pp. 297–340). San Diego, CA: Academic Press.

Pinker, S. (1991). Rules of language. *Science, 253,* 530–535.

Pinker, S. (1997). *How the mind works.* New York: Norton.

Pinker, S. (1999). *Words and rules.* New York: Basic Books.

Pinker, S. (2007) *The stuff of thought: Language as a window into human nature.* New York: Viking.

Pinker, S. & Jackendoff, R. (2005) The faculty of language: What's special about it? *Cognition, 95,* 201–236.

Pinker, S., & Jackendoff, R. (2009). The reality of a universal language faculty. *Behavioral and Brain Sciences, 32,* 465–466.

Pinker, S. & Ullman, M. (2002). The past and future of the past tense. *Trends in Cognitive Science, 6,* 456–463.

Platek, S. M., Wathne, K., Tierney, N. G., & Thomson, J. W. (2008). Neural correlates of self-face recognition: An effect-location meta-analysis. *Brain Research, 1232,* 173–184.

Plous, S. (1993). *The psychology of judgment and decision-making.* New York: McGraw-Hill.

Plucker, J. A., Beghetto, R. A., & Dow, G. T. (2004). Why isn't creativity more important to educational psychologists? Potential, pitfalls, and future directions in creativity research. *Educational Psychologist, 39,* 83–97.

Poldrack, R. A. (2006). Can cognitive processes be inferred from neuroimaging data? *Trends in Cognitive Sciences, 10,* 59–63.

Pollatsek, A., & Rayner, K. (1982). Eye movement control in reading: The role of word boundaries. *Journal of Experimental Psychology: Human Perception and Performance, 8,* 817–833.

Porcelli, A. J., & Delgado, M. R. (2009). Acute stress modulates risk taking in financial decision making. *Psychological Science, 20,* 278–283.

Posner, M. I. (1980). Orienting of attention. *Quarterly Journal of Experimental Psychology, 32,* 3–25.

Posner, M. I., Goldsmith, R., & Welton, K. E. (1967). Perceived distance and the classification of distorted patterns. *Journal of Experimental Psychology, 73,* 28–38.

Posner, M. I., & Keele, S. W. (1967). Decay of visual information from a single letter. *Science, 158,* 137–139.

Posner, M. I., & Snyder, C. R. R. (1975). Facilitation and inhibition in the processing of signals. In P. M. A. Rabbitt & S. Dornic (Eds.), *Attention and performance V* (pp. 669–682). New York: Academic Press.

Postle, B. R. (2006). Working memory as an emergent property of mind and brain. *NeuroImage, 30,* 950–962.

Postle, B. R., & Pasternak, T. (2009). Short-term and working memory. In L. R. Squire (Ed.), *Encyclopedia of Neuroscience, Vol. 8* (pp. 793–799). London: Elsevier.

Potter, M. C, So, K.-F., Von Eckardt, B., & Feldman, L. (1984). Lexical and conceptual representation in beginning and proficient bilinguals. *Journal of Verbal Learning and Verbal Behavior, 23,* 23–38.

Povinelli, D. J., Landry, A. M., Theall, L. A., Clark, B. R., & Castille, C. M. (1999). Development of young children's understanding that the recent past is causally bound to the present. *Developmental Psychology, 35,* 1426–1439.

Pratkanis, A. R., & Aronson, E. (2001). Age of propaganda: The everyday use and abuse of persuasion. New York: W. H. Freeman.

Premack, D. (1970). A functional analysis of language. *Journal of the Experimental Analysis of Behavior, 14,* 107–125.

Premack, D. (2007). Human and animal cognition: Continuity and discontinuity, *104,* 13861–13867.

Premack, D., & Premack, A. J. (1983). The mind of an ape. New York: Norton.

Prentice, D. A., & Miller, D. T. (2007). Psychological essentialism of human categories. *Psychological Science, 16,* 202–206.

Pretz, J. E. (2008). Intuition versus analysis: Strategy and experience in complex everyday problem solving. *Memory & Cognition, 36,* 554–566.

Principe, G. F., Kanaya, T., Ceci, S. J., & Singh, M. (2006). Believing is seeing: How rumors can engender false memories in preschoolers. *Psychological Science, 17,* 243–248.

Proctor, R. W., & Fangini, C. A. (1978). Effects of distractor-stimulus modality in the Brown-Peterson distractor task. *Journal of Experimental Psychology: Human Learning and Memory, 4,* 676–684.

Proffitt, D. R. (2006). Embodied perception and the economy of action. *Perspectives on Psychological Science, 1,* 110–122.

Proffitt, D. R., Bhalla, M., Gossweiler, R., & Midgett, J. (1995). Perceiving geographical slant. *Psychonomic Bulletin & Review, 2,* 409–428.

Proffitt, D. R., Stefanucci, J., Banton, T., & Epstein, W. (2003). The role of effort in perceiving distance. *Psychological Science, 14*, 106–112.

Proust, M. (1922/1960). Swann's way (part 1) (Trans. C.K. Scott Moncrieff). London: Chatto & Windus.

Quinn, D. M., & Spencer, S. J. (2001). The interference of stereotype threat with women's generation of mathematical problem-solving strategies. *Journal of Social Issues, 57*, 55–71.

Rabinowitz, M., & Hogan, T. M. (2008). Experience and problem representation in statistics. *American Journal of Psychology, 121*, 395–407.

Radford, B. (1999). The ten-percent myth. *Skeptical Inquirer, 23*.

Rajaram, S. (1993). Remembering and knowing: Two means of access to the personal past. *Memory and Cognition, 21*, 89–102.

Ramachandran, V. S., & Hubbard, E. M. (2001). Psychophysical investigations in to the neural basis of synaesthesia. *Proceedings of the Royal Society, 268*, 979–983.

Ranganath C., Cohen M. X., Dam C., D'Esposito, M. (2004) Inferior temporal, prefrontal, and hippocampal contributions to visual working memory maintenance and associative memory recall. *Journal of Neuroscience, 24*, 3917–3925.

Ranganath C., DeGutis J., D'Esposito, M. (2004) Category-specific modulation of inferior temporal activity during working memory encoding and maintenance. *Cognitive Brain Research, 20*, 37–45.

Rauschecker, J. P., & Tian, B. (2000). Mechanisms and streams for processing of "what" and "where" in auditory cortex. *Proceedings of the National Academy of Sciences, 97*, 11800–11806.

Rawson, K. A., Dunlosky, J., & Thiede, K. W. (2000). The re-reading effect: Metacomprehension accuracy improves across reading trials. *Memory and Cognition, 28*, 1004–1011.

Rawson, K. A. Touron, D. R. (2009). Age differences and similarities in the shift from computation to retrieval duringreading comprehension. *Psychology and Aging, 24*, 423–437.

Rawson, K. A., & Van Overschelde, J. P. (2008). How does knowledge promote memory? The distinctiveness theory of skilled memory? *Journal of Memory and Language, 58*, 646–668.

Rayner, K. (1998). Eye movements in reading and information processing: Twenty years of research. *Psychological Bulletin, 124*, 374–422.

Rayner, K., Binder, K. S., Ashby, J., & Pollatsek, A. (2001). Eye movement control in reading: Word predictability has little influence on initial landing positions in words. *Vision Research, 41*, 943–954.

Rayner, K., Foorman, B. R., Perfetti, C. A., Pesetsky, D., & Seidenberg, M. S. (2001). How psychological science informs the teaching of reading. *Psychological Science in the Public Interest, 2*, 31–74.

Rayner, K., Foorman, B. R., Perfetti, C. A., Pesetsky, D., & Seidenberg, M. S. (2002). How should reading be taught? *Scientific American, 287*, 85–91.

Rayner, K., & Morris, R. K. (1992). Eye movement control in reading: Evidence against semantic preprocessing. *Journal of Experimental Psychology: Human Perception and Performance, 18*, 164–172.

Rayner, K., & Pollatsek, A. (1989). *The psychology of reading*. Englewood Cliffs, NJ: Prentice Hall.

Rayner, K., & Well, A. D. (1996). Effects of contextual constraint on eye movements in reading: A further examination. *Psychological Bulletin and Review, 3*, 504–509.

Rayner, K., White, S. J., Johnson, R. L., & Liversedge, S. P. (2006). Raeding wrods with jubmled lettres: There is a cost. *Psychological Science, 17*, 192–193.

Reed, C. L., Klatzky, R. L., & Halgren, E. (2005). What vs. where in touch: An fMRI study. *NeuroImage, 25*, 718–726.

Reese, E., & Fivush, R. (1993). Parental styles of talking about the past. *Developmental Psychology, 29*, 506–516.

Reisberg, D. and Heuer, F. (2004). Remembering emotional events. In Reisberg, D.and Hertel, P. (Eds.), *Memory and emotion* (pp. 3–41). New York: Oxford University Press.

Rensink, R. A. (1997). How much of a scene is seen? The role of attention in scene perception. *Investigative Ophthalmology and Visual Science, 38*, S707.

Rensink, R. A. (2002). Change detection. *Annual Review of Psychology. 53*, 245–277.

Repp, B. H. (1984). Closure duration and release burst amplitude cues to stop consonant manner and place of articulation. *Language and Speech, 27*, 245–254.

Reyna, V. F., & Brainerd, C. J. (1995). Fuzzy-trace theory: An interim synthesis. *Learning and Individual Differences, 7*, 1–75.

Rhodes, M. (1961/1987). An analysis of creativity. In S. G. Isaksen (Ed.), *Frontiers of creativity research: Beyond the basics* (pp. 216–222). Buffalo, NY: Bearly.

Rikers, R. M., Schmidt, H. G., & Boshuizen, H. P. (2000). Knowledge encapsulation and the intermediate effect. *Contemporary Educational Psychology, 25*, 150–166.

Rips, L. J. (1974). Inductive judgments about natural categories. *Journal of Verbal Learning and Verbal Behavior, 14*, 665–681.

Rips, L. J. (1989). Similarity, typicality, and categorization. In S. Vosniadu & A. Ortony (Eds.), *Similarity and analogical reasoning* (pp. 21–59). Cambridge, UK: Cambridge University Press.

Rips, L. J. (1990). Reasoning. *Annual Review of Psychology, 41*, 321–353.

Rips, L. J. (1994). Deduction and its cognitive basis. In R. J. Sternberg (Ed.), *Thinking and problem solving* (pp. 149–178). New York: Academic Press.

Risko, E. F., Stolz, J. A., & Besner, D. (2005). Basic processes in reasoning: Is visual word recognition obligatory? *Psychonomic Bulletin and Review, 12,* 119–124.

Rivas, E. (2005). Recent use of signs by chimpanzees (Pan troglodytes) in interactions with humans. *Journal of Comparative Psychology, 119,* 404–417.

Robbins, R., & McKone, E. (2007) No face-like processing for objects-of-expertise in three behavioural tasks. *Cognition, 103,* 34–79.

Robinson, J. A. (1980). Affect and retrieval of personal memories. *Motivation & Emotion, 4,* 149–174.

Roediger, H. L. (1990). Implicit memory: Retention without remembering. *American Psychologist, 45,* 1043–1056.

Roediger, R. (2004, March). What happened to behaviorism? *American Psychological Society Observer, 17* (3).

Roediger, H. L., & Gallo, D. A. (2004). Associative memory illusions. In R. F. Pohl (Ed.), *Cognitive illusions: A handbook on fallacies and biases in thinking, judgment and memory.* New York: Oxford University Press.

Roediger, H. L., & Guynn, M. J. (1996). Retrieval processes. In E. L. Bjork & R. A. Bjork (Eds.), *Handbook of perception and cognition: Memory* (pp. 197–236). New York: Academic Press.

Roediger, H. L., & Karpicke, J. D. (2006). Test-enhanced learning: Taking memory tests improves long-term retention. *Psychological Science, 17,* 249–255.

Roediger, H. L., & McDermott, K. B. (1995). Creating false memories: Remembering words not presented in lists. *Journal of Experimental Psychology: Learning, Memory, and Cognition, 21,* 803–814.

Roediger, H. L., III, & McDermott, K. (1996). False perceptions of false memories. *Journal of Experimental Psychology: Learning, Memory and Cognition, 22,* 814–816.

Roediger, H. L., Meade, M. L., & Bergman, E. T. (2001). Social contagion of memory. *Psychonomic Bulletin and Review, 8,* 365–371.

Rogers, T. B., Kuiper, N. A., & Kirker, W. S. (1977). Self reference and the encoding of personal information. *Journal of Personality and Social Psychology, 35,* 677–688.

Rogoff, B., Paradise, R., Mejia Arauz, R., Correa-Chavez, M., & Angelillo, C. (2003). Firsthand learning through intent participation. *Annual Review of Psychology, 54,* 175–203.

Rosch, E. (1973). Natural categories. *Cognitive Psychology, 4,* 328–350.

Rosch, E. (1976). Basic objects in natural categories. *Cognitive Psychology, 8,* 382–439.

Rosch, E., & Mervis, C. B. (1975). Family resemblances: Studies in the internal structure of categories. *Cognitive Psychology, 7,* 573–605.

Rosenbaum, D. A. (2005). The Cinderella of psychology: The neglect of motor control in the science of mental life and behavior. *American Psychologist, 60,* 308–317.

Ross, B. H. (1987). This is like that: The use of earlier examples and the separation of similarity effects. *Journal of Experimental Psychology: Learning, Memory, and Cognition, 13,* 629–639.

Ross, B. H., & Spalding, T. L. (1994). Concepts and categories. In R. J. Sternberg (Ed.), *Handbook of perception and cognition,* Vol. 2: *Thinking and problem solving* (pp. 119–148). San Diego, CA: Academic Press.

Roth, E. M., & Shoben, E. J. (1983). The effect of context on the structure of categories. *Cognitive Psychology, 15,* 346–378.

Rothman, A. J., & Salovey, P. (1997). Shaping perceptions to motivate healthy behavior: The role of message framing. *Psychological Bulletin, 121,* 3–19.

Rubin, D. C. (1998). Beginnings of a theory of autobiographical remembering. In C. T. Thompson, D. J. Herrmann, D. Bruce, J. D. Read, D. G. Payne, & M. Toglia (Eds.), *Autobiographical memory: Theoretical and applied perspectives* (pp. 47–67). Mahwah, NJ: Erlbaum.

Rubin, D. C. (2005). A basic-systems approach to autobiographical memory. *Current Directions in Psychological Science, 14,* 79–83.

Rubin, D. C. (2006). The basic-systems model of episodic memory. *Psychological Science, 1,* 277–311.

Rubin, D. C., Rahhal, T. A., & Poon, L. W. (1998). Things learned in early adulthood are remembered best. *Memory and Cognition, 26,* 3–19.

Rubin, D. C., Wetzler, S. E., & Nebes, R. D. (1986). Autobiographical memory across the lifespan. In D. C. Rubin (Ed.), *Autobiographical memory* (pp. 202–221). Cambridge, UK: Cambridge University Press.

Rumelhart, D. E. (1975). Notes on a schema for stories. In D. G. Bobrow & A. M. Collins (Eds.), *Representation and understanding* (pp. 211–236). New York: Academic Press.

Rumelhart, D. E., & McClelland, J. L. (1986). *Parallel distributed processing: Explorations into the microstructure of cognition.* Cambridge, MA: MIT Press.

Runco, M. A. (2004). Creativity. *Annual Review of Psychology, 55,* 657–687.

Sachs, J. (1967). Recognition memory for syntactic and semantic aspects of connected discourse. *Perception and Psychophysics, 2,* 437–442.

Sacks, H., Schegloff, E. A., & Jefferson, G. (1974). A simplest systematics for the organization of turn-taking in conversation. *Language, 50,* 696–735.

Safer, M. A., Christianson, S.-Å., Autry, M. W., & Österlund, K. (1998). Tunnel memory for traumatic events. *Applied Cognitive Psychology, 12,* 99–117.

Saffran, J. R., Aslin, R. N., & Newport, E. C. (1996). Statistical learning in 8-month old infants. *Science, 274,* 1926–1928.

Salame, P., & Baddeley, A. D. (1982). Disruption of short-term memory by unattended speech: Implications for the structure of working memory. *Journal of Verbal Learning and Verbal Behavior, 21,* 150–164.

Saling, L. L. and Phillips, J. G. (2007) Automatic behaviour: Efficient, not mindless. Brain Research Bulletin, *73,* 1–20.

Sanfey, A. G., Loewenstein, G., McClure, S. M., & Cohen, J. D. (2006). Neuroeconomics: Cross-currents in research on decision-making. *Trends in Cognitive Sciences, 10,* 108–116.

Sapolsky, R. S. (2004). Why zebras don't get ulcers. New York, NY: Holt.

Sauerland, M., & Sporer, S. L. (2009). Fast and confident: Postdicting eyewitness identification accuracy in a field study, 15, 46–62.

Saufley, W. H., Otaka, S. R., & Bravaresco, J. L. (1986). Context effects: Classroom tests and context independence. *Memory and Cognition, 13,* 522–528.

Savage-Rumbaugh, E. S., & Brakke, K. E. (1996). Animal language: Methodological and interpretive issues. In M. Bekoff & D. Jamieson (Eds.), *Readings in animal cognition.* Cambridge, MA: MIT Press.

Savage-Rumbaugh, E. S., Rumbaugh, D. M., & Boysen, S. (1980). Do apes use language? *American Scientist, 68,* 49–61.

Schab, L. (1990). Odors and the remembrance of things past. *Journal of Experimental Psychology: Learning, Memory, and Cognition, 16,* 648–655.

Schacter, D. L. (1989). *Memory.* In M. I. Posner (Ed.), *Foundations of cognitive science.* Cambridge, MA: MIT Press.

Schacter, D. L. (1996). *Searching for memory: The brain, the mind, and the past.* New York: Basic Books.

Schacter, D. L. (2001). *The seven sins of memory: How the mind forgets and remembers.* New York: Houghton-Mifflin.

Schacter, D. L. and Addis, D. R. (2007). On the constructive episodic simulation of past and future events. *Behavioral and Brain Sciences, 30,* 299–351.

Schacter, D. L., & Moscovitch, M. (1984). Infants, amnesia, and dissociable memory systems. In M. Moscovitch (Ed.), *Infant memory* (pp. 173–216). New York: Plenum Press.

Schacter, D. L., Norman, K. A., & Koutsaal, W. (1997). The recovered memories debate: A cognitive neuroscience perspective. In M. A. Conway (Ed.), *Recovered memories and false memories* (pp. 63–99). Oxford: Oxford University Press.

Schacter, D. L., & Slotnick, S. D. (2004). The cognitive neuroscience of memory distortion. *Neuron, 44,* 149–160.

Schank, R. C., & Abelson, R. B. (1977). *Scripts, plans, goals, and understanding: An inquiry into human knowledge structures.* Hillsdale, NJ: Erlbaum.

Scherer, K. (1986). Vocal affect expression: A review and a model for future research. *Psychological Bulletin, 99,* 143–165.

Schlagman, S., & Kvavilashvili, L. (2008). Involuntary autobiographical memories in and outside the laboratory: How different are they from voluntary autobiographical memories? *Memory & Cognition, 36,* 920–932.

Schegloff, E. A. (1972). Sequencing in conversational openings. In J. J. Gumpetz & D. Hymes (Eds.), *Directions in sociolinguistic: The ethnography of communication* (pp. 346–380). New York: Holt, Rinehart, & Winston.

Scheck, B., Neufeld, P., and Dwyer, J. (2000). *Actual Innocence.* New York: Doubleday.

Schiano, D. J., & Watkins, M. J. (1981). Speech-like coding of pictures in short-term memory. *Memory and Cognition, 9,* 110–114.

Schilling, H. E. H., Rayner, K., & Chumbley, J. I. (1998). Comparing naming, lexical decision, and eye fixation times: Word frequency effects and individual differences. *Memory & Cognition, 26,* 1270–1281.

Schmader, T. (2010). Stereotype threat deconstructed. *Current Directions in Psychological Science, 19,* 14–18.

Schmader, T., & Johns, M. (2003). Converging evidence that stereotype threat reduces working memory capacity. *Journal of Personality and Social Psychology, 85,* 440–452.

Schmidt, H. P., & Boshuizen, H. G. (1993). On the origin of intermediate effects in clinical case recall. *Memory and Cognition, 21,* 338–351.

Schmidt, S. R. (2004). Autobiographical memories for the September 11th attacks: Reconstructive errors and emotional impairment of memory. *Memory & Cognition, 32,* 443–454.

Schneider, W., & Shiffrin, R. M. (1977). Controlled and automatic human information processing I: Detection, search, and attention. *Psychological Review, 84,* 1–66.

Schooler, J. W. (2001). Discovering memories of abuse in the light of meta-awareness. *Journal of Aggression, Maltreatment and Trauma, 4,* 105–136.

Schooler, J. W. (1994). Seeking the core: The issues and evidence surrounding recovered accounts of sexual trauma. *Consciousness and Cognition, 3,* 452–469.

Schooler, J. W., Bendiksen, M. A., & Ambadar, Z. (1997). Taking the middle line: Can we accommodate both fabricated and recovered memories of sexual abuse? In M. Conway (Ed.), *Recovered memories and false memories* (pp. 251–292). Oxford: Oxford University Press.

Schooler, J. W., & Eich, E. (2000). Memory for emotional events. In E. Tulving & F. I. M. Craik (Eds.), *The Oxford handbook of memory.* New York: Oxford University Press.

Schunn, C. D., McGregor, M. U., & Saner, L. D. (2005). Expertise in ill-defined problem-solving domains as effective strategy use. *Memory & Cognition, 33,* 1377–1387.

Schusterman, R. J., & Krieger, K. (1988). Artificial language comprehension and size transposition by a California sea lion (Zalophis Californianus).

Journal of Comparative Psychology, 100, 348–355.

Schutz, M. & Kubovy, M. (2009). Deconstructing a musical illusion. *Canadian Acoustics, 37*, 23–28

Schutz, M., & Lipscomb, S. (2007). Hearing gestures, Seeing music: Vision influences perceived tone duration. *Perception, 36*, 888–897.

Schütz-Bosbach, S., Tausche, P., & Weiss, C. (2009). Roughness perception during the rubber hand illusion. *Brain and Cognition, 70*, 136–144.

Schweickert, R., McDaniel, M. A., & Riegler, G. (1993). Effects of generation on immediate memory span and delayed unexpected free recall. *Quarterly Journal of Experimental Psychology: Human Experimental Psychology, 47*, 781–804.

Scoboria, A., Mazzoni, G., Kirsch, I., & Milling, L. S. (2002). Immediate and persisting effects of misleading questions and hypnosis on memory reports. *Journal of Experimental Psychology: Applied, 8*, 26–32.

Seabrook, R., Brown, G., & Solity, J. E. (2005). Distributed and massed practice: From laboratory to classroom. *Applied Cognitive Psychology, 19*, 107–122.

Sehulster, J. R. (1996). In my era: Evidence for the perception of a special period of the past. *Memory, 4*, 145–158.

Seidenberg, M. S., Petersen, A., MacDonald, M. C., & Plaut, D. C. (1996). Pseudohomophone effects and models of word recognition. *Journal of Experimental Psychology: Learning, Memory, and Cognition, 22*, 48–62.

Seidl, A. (2007). Infants' use and weighting of prosodic cues in clause segmentation. *Journal of Memory and Language, 57*, 24–48.

Seidenberg, M. S. (1997). Language acquisition and use: Learning and applying probabilistic constraints. *Science, 275*, 1599–1603.

Shallice, T., & Warrington, E. K. (1974). The dissociation between the short-term retention of meaningful sounds and verbal material. *Neuropsychologia, 12*, 553–555.

Shapiro, K. L., Arnell, K., & Raymond, J. E. (1997). The attentional blink. *Trends in Cognitive Sciences, 1*, 291–296.

Shapiro, P. N., & Penrod, S. (1986). Meta-analysis of facial identification studies. *Psychological Bulletin, 100*, 139–156.

Shapiro, S. L., Carlson, L., Astin J., Freedman, B. (2006). Mechanisms of mindfulness. *Journal of Clinical Psychology, 62*, 373–386.

Share, D. L. (2008). On the Anglo-centricities of current reading research and practice: The perils of overreliance on an "outlier" orthography. *Psychological Bulletin, 134*, 584–615.

Sharot, T., Delgado, M. R., Phelps, E. A. (2004). How emotion enhances the feeling of remembering. *Nature Neuroscience, 7*, 1376–1380.

Shaywitz, S. E., & Shaywitz, B. A. (2005). Dyslexia (Specific reading disability). *Biological Psychiatry, 57*, 1301–1309.

Shiffrin, R. M., & Nosofsky, R. M. (1994). Seven plus or minus two: A commentary on capacity limitations. *Psychological Review, 101*, 357–361.

Shih, M., Ambady, N., Richeson, J. A., Fujita, K., & Gray, H. M. (2002). Stereotype performance boosts: The impact of self-relevance and the manner of stereotype activation. *Journal of Personality and Social Psychology, 83*, 638–647.

Shih, M., Pittinsky, T. L., & Trahan, A. (2006). Domain-specific effects of stereotypes on performance. *Self and Identity, 5*, 1–14.

Shipherd, J. C., & Beck, J. G. (2005). The role of thought suppression in post-traumatic stress disorder. *Behavior Therapy, 36*, 277–287.

Shors, T. J. (2006). Stressful experience and learning across the lifespan. *Annual Review of Psychology, 57*, 55–85.

Siegler, R. S. (2000). Unconscious insights. *Current Directions in Psychological Science, 9*, 79–83.

Silverberg, S. & Samuel, A. G. (2004). The effect of age of second language acquisition on the representation and processing of second language words. *Journal of Memory and Language, 51*, 381–398.

Simons, D. J., & Chabris, C. F. (1999). Gorillas in our midst: Sustained inattentional blindness for dynamic events. *Perception, 28*, 1059–1074.

Simons, D. J., & Levin, D. T. (1997). Change blindness. *Trends in Cognitive Sciences, 1*, 261–267.

Simons, D. J., & Levin, D. T. (1998). Failure to detect changes to people during a real-world interaction. *Psychonomic Bulletin and Review, 5*, 644–649.

Simonton, D. K. (1994). *Greatness: Who makes history and why.* New York, NY: Guilford Press.

Simonton, D. K. (2000). Creativity: Cognitive, personal, social, and developmental aspects. *American Psychologist, 55*, 151–158.

Sims, V. K., & Mayer, R. E. (2002). Domain specificity of spatial expertise: The case of video game players. *Applied Cognitive Psychology, 16*, 97–115.

Singer, M. (1980). The role of case-filling inferences in the coherence of brief passages. *Discourse Processes, 3*, 185–201.

Singer, M. (1990). *Psychology of language.* Hillsdale, NJ: Erlbaum.

Singh, L., Morgan, J. L., & Best, C. (2002). Infants' listening preferences: Baby talk or happy talk? *Infancy, 3*, 365–394.

Sio, U. N., & Ormerod, T. C. (2009). Does incubation enhance problem solving? A meta-analytic review. *Psychological Bulletin, 135*, 94–120.

Slagter, H. A., Lutz, A., Greischar, L. L., Francis, A. D., Nieuwenhuis, S., Davis, J., & Davidson, R. J. (2007). Mental training affects distribution of limited brain resources. PLoS Biology, 5, e138.

Slevc, L. R., & Ferreira, V. S. (2006). Halting in single word production: A test of the perceptual loop theory of speech monitoring. *Journal of Memory and Language, 54,* 515–540.

Sloman, S. A. (1996). The empirical case for two systems of reasoning. *Psychological Bulletin, 119,* 3–22.

Slotnick, S. D., & Schacter, D. L. (2004). A sensory signature that distinguishes true from false memories. *Nature Neuroscience, 7,* 664–672.

Slovic, P. (1987). Perception of risk. *Science, 236,* 280–285.

Smallwood, J., & Schooler, J. W. (2006). The restless mind. *Psychological bulletin, 132,* 946–58.

Smári, J. (2001). Fifteen years of suppression of white bears and other thoughts: What are the lessons for obsessive-compulsive disorder research and treatment? *Scandinavian Journal of Behaviour Therapy, 30,* 147–160.

Smith, E. E., Langston, C., & Nisbett, R. E. (1992). The case for rules in reasoning. *Cognitive Science, 16,* 1–40.

Smith, M. A. (1983). Hypnotic memory enhancement: Does it work? *Psychological Bulletin, 94,* 387–407.

Smith, S. M. (1979). Remembering in and out of context. *Journal of Experimental Psychology: Human Learning and Memory, 5,* 460–471.

Smith, S. M. (1988). Environmental context-dependent memory. In G. M. Davies & D. M. Thomson (Eds.), *Memory in context: Context in memory.* New York: Wiley.

Smith, S. M. (1995). Getting into and out of mental ruts: A theory of fixation, incubation, and insight. In R. J. Sternberg & J. E. Davidson (Eds.), *The nature of insight.* Cambridge, MA: MIT Press.

Smith, S. M. (2003). The constraining effects of initial ideas. In P. B. Paulus & B. A. Nijstad (Eds.), *Group creativity: Innovation through collaboration* (pp. 15–31). New York: Oxford University Press.

Smith, S. M., & Blankenship, S. E. (1991). Incubation effects. *Bulletin of the Psychonomic Society, 27,* 311–314.

Smith, S. M., Ward, T. B., & Finke, R. A. (1994). *The creative cognition approach.* Cambridge, MA: MIT Press.

Snyder, M., & Swann, W. B. (1978). Hypothesis-testing in social interaction. *Journal of Personality and Social Psychology, 36,* 1202–1212.

Soderstrom, M., Blossom, M., Foygel, R, Morgan, J. L (2008). Acoustical cues and grammatical units in speech to two preverbal infants. *Journal of Child Language, 35,* 869–902.

Solomon, K. O., Medin, D. L., & Lynch, E. B. (1999). Concepts do more than categorize. *Trends in Cognitive Science, 3,* 99–105.

Sporer, S. L. (1994). Decision–times and eyewitness identification accuracy in simultaneous and sequential lineups. In D. F. Ross, J. D. Read, & M. P. Toglia (Eds.), *Adult eyewitness testimony: Current trends and developments* (pp. 300–327). New York: Cambridge University Press.

Sporer, S. L., Penrod, S. D., Read, J. D., & Cutler, B. L. (1995). Choosing, confidence, and accuracy: A meta–analysis of the confidence-accuracy relation in eyewitness identification studies. *Psychological Bulletin, 118,* 315–327.

Squire, L. A. (1987). *Memory and brain.* New York: Oxford University Press.

Squire, L. R. (1993). The organization of declarative and nondeclarative memory. In T. Ono (Ed.), *Brain mechanisms of perception and memory: From neurons to behavior.* New York: Oxford University Press.

Squire, L. R. (2004). Memory systems of the brain: A brief history and current perspective. *Neurobiology of Learning and Memory, 82,* 171–177.

Squire, L. A., & Zola-Morgan, S. (1988). Memory: Brain systems and behavior. *Trends in Neuroscience, 11,* 170–175.

Stanovich, K. E. (1999). *Who is rational? Studies of individual differences in reasoning.* Mahweh, NJ: Erlbaum.

Stanovich, K. E. (2004). Balance in psychological research: The dual process perspective. *Behavioral and Brain Sciences, 27,* 357–358

Stanovich, K. E., & West, R. F. (1997). Reasoning independently of prior belief and individual differences in actively open-minded thinking. *Journal of Educational Psychology, 89,* 342–357.

Stanovich, K. E., & West, R. F. (2000). Advancing the rationality debate. *Behavioral and Brain Sciences, 23,* 701–726.

Steblay, N., Dysart, J., Fulero, S., & Lindsay, R. C. L. (2001). Eyewitness accuracy rates in sequential and simultaneous lineup presentations: A meta-analytic comparison. *Law and Human Behavior, 25,* 459–473.

Sternberg, R. J. (2006). The nature of creativity. *Creativity Research Journal, 18,* 87–98.

Sternberg, R. J., & Ben-Zeev, T. (2001). *Complex cognition.* New York: Oxford University Press.

Sternberg, R. J., & Davidson, J. E. (1983). Insight in the gifted. *Educational Psychologist, 18,* 51–57.

Sternberg, R. J., Grigorenko, E. L., Singer, J. L. (Eds.), 2004. *Creativity: The Psychology of Creative Potential and Realization.* American Psychological Association, Washington.

Sternberg, R. J., & Lubart, T. I. (1996). Investing in creativity. *American Psychologist, 51,* 677–688.

Stevenson, R. J., Case, T. I., & Mahmut, M. (2007). Difficulty in evoking odor images: The role of odor naming. *Memory & Cognition, 35,* 578–89.

Stewart, N. (2009). The cost of anchoring on credit-card minimum repayments. *Psychological Science, 20,* 39–41.

Strayer, D. L., & Drews, F. A. (2006). Multitasking in the Automobile. In A. Kramer, D. Wiegmann & A. Kirlik (Eds.) *Applied attention: From theory to practice.* (pp. 121–133). New York, NY: Oxford University Press.

Strayer, D. L., & Drews, F. A. (2007). Cell-phone–induced driver distraction. *Psychological Science, 16,* 128–131.

Strayer, D. L., Drews, F. A., & Crouch, D. J. (2006). A comparison of the cell phone driver and the drunk driver. *Human Factors, 48,* 381–91.

Strayer, D. L., Drews, F. A., & Johnston, W. A. (2003). Cell phone-induced failures of visual attention during simulated driving. *Journal of Experimental Psychology: Applied, 9* (1), 23–32.

Strayer, D. L., & Johnston, W. A. (2001). Driven to distraction: Dual-task studies of simulated driving and conversing on a cellular telephone. *Psychological Science, 12,* 462–466.

Stroop, J. R. (1935). Studies of interference in serial verbal reactions. *Journal of Experimental Psychology, 35,* 643–662.

Subramaniam, K., Kounios, J., Parrish, T. B., & Jung-Beeman, M. (2009). A brain mechanism for facilitation of insight by positive affect. *Journal of Cognitive Neuroscience, 21,* 415–432.

Sulin, R. A., & Dooling, D. J. (1974). Intrusion of a thematic idea in retention of prose. *Journal of Experimental Psychology, 103,* 255–262.

Sutton, S., Tueting, P., Zubin, J., & John, E. R. (1967). Information delivery and the sensory evoked potential. *Science,* 155(3768), 1436–1439.

Symons, C. S., & Johnson, B. T. (1997). The self-reference in memory: A meta-analysis. *Psychological Bulletin, 121,* 371–394.

Talarico, J. M., & Rubin, D. C. (2003). Confidence, not consistency, characterizes flashbulb memories. *Psychological Science, 14,* 455–461.

Talarico, J. M. & Rubin, D. C. (2007) Flashbulb memories are special after all; In phenomenology, not accuracy. *Applied Cognitive Psychology, 21,* 557–578.

Tanaka, J. W. (2001a). The entry point of face recognition: Evidence for face expertise. *Journal of Experimental Psychology: General, 130,* 534–543.

Tanaka, J. W., & Farah, M. J. (1993). Parts and wholes in face recognition. *Quarterly Journal of Experimental Psychology, 46A,* 225–245.

Tang, Y., Ma, Y., Wang, J., Fan, Y., Feng, S., Lu, Q., et al. (2007). Short-term meditation training improves attention and self-regulation. *Proceedings of the National Academy of Sciences, 104,* 17152–17156.

Tang, Y., & Posner, M. I. (2009). Attention training and attention state training. *Trends in Cognitive Sciences, 13,* 222–227. Tannen, D. (2001). *You just don't understand: Women and men in conversation.* New York, NY: Harper.

Tarr, M. J. (2000). Visual pattern recognition. In A. Kazdin (Ed.), *Encyclopedia of psychology.* Washington, DC: American Psychological Association.

Tarr, M. J., & Bülthoff, H. H. (1995). Is human object recognition better described by geon-structural-descriptions or by multiple-views? *Journal of Experimental Psychology: Human Perception and Performance, 21,* 1494–1505.

Tarr, M. J., & Cheng, Y. D. (2003). Learning to see faces and objects. *Trends in Cognitive Science, 7,* 23–30.

Tarr, M. J., & Pinker, S. (1989). Mental rotation and orientation-dependence in shape recognition. *Cognitive Psychology, 21,* 233–282.

Telford, C. W. (1931). The refractory phase of voluntary and associative responses. *Journal of Experimental Psychology, 14,* 1–36.

Terrace, H. S., Petitto, L. A., Sanders, R. J., & Bever, T. G. (1979). Can an ape create a sentence? *Science, 206,* 891–902.

Thaler, R. H., & Sunstein, C. R. (2008). *Nudge.* New Haven, CT: Yale University Press.

Thiede, K. W., & Anderson, M. C. M. (2003). Summarizing can improve meta-comprehension accuracy. *Contemporary Educational Psychology, 28,* 129–160.

Thiede, K. W., Dunlosky, J., Griffin, T., & Wiley, J. (2005). Understanding the delayed-keyword effect on meta-comprehension accuracy. *Journal of Experimental Psychology: Learning, Memory, and Cognition, 31,* 1267–1280.

Thoma, V., Hummel, J. E., & Davidoff, J. (2004). Evidence for holistic representations of ignored images and analytic representations of attended images. *Journal of Experimental Psychology: Human Perception & Performance, 30,* 257–267.

Thomas, E. L. (1962). Eye movements in speed reading. In R. G. Stauffer (Ed.), *Speed reading: Practices and procedures* (Vol. 10). Newark: University of Delaware, Reading Study Center.

Thompson, P. (1980). Margaret Thatcher: A new illusion. *Perception, 9,* 483–484.

Thomson, D. M., & Tulving, E. (1970). Associative encoding and retrieval. *Journal of Experimental Psychology, 86,* 255–262.

Thomson, R., Murachver, T., & Green, J. (2001). Where is the gender in gendered language? *Psychological Science, 12,* 171–175.

Thorell, L. B., Linqvist, S., Nutley, B., S., B., G, Klingberg, T. (2009). Training and transfer effects of executive functions in preschool children. *Developmental Science, 12,* 106–113.

Thorndyke, P. W. (1977). Cognitive structures in comprehension and memory of narrative discourse. *Cognitive Psychology, 9,* 77–110.

Tinker, M. A. (1939). Illumination standards for effective and comfortable reading. *Journal of Consulting Psychology, 3,* 11–19.

Tinker, M. A. (1958). Recent studies of eye movements in reading. *Psychological Bulletin, 55,* 215–231.

Tolman, E. C. (1948). Cognitive maps in rats and men. *Psychological Review, 55,* 189–208.

Tolman, E. C., & Honzik, C. H. (1930). Introduction and removal of reward, and maze performance in rats. *University of California Publications in Psychology, 4,* 257–275.

Treffner, P. J., & Barrett, R. (2004). Hands-free mobile phone speech while driving degrades coordination and control. *Transportation Research Part F: Traffic Psychology and Behavior, 7,* 229–246.

Treisman, A. (1960). Contextual cues in selective listening. *Quarterly Journal of Experimental Psychology, 12,* 242–248.

Treisman, A., & Gelade, G. (1980). A feature-integration theory of attention. *Cognitive Psychology, 12,* 97–136.

Treisman, A., & Gormican, S. (1988). Feature analysis in early vision: Evidence from search asymmetries. *Psychological Review, 95,* 15–48.

Treisman, A., Sykes, M., and Gelade, G., 1977. Selective attention and stimulus integration. In S. Dornic (Ed.) Attention and Performance VI (pp. 333–361). Hillsdale, NJ: Erlbaum.

Treisman, A., & Souther, J. (1985). Search asymmetry: A diagnostic for preattentive processing of separable features. *Journal of Experimental Psychology: General, 114,* 285–310.

Trepel, C., Fox, C. R., & Poldrack, R. A. (2005). Prospect theory on the brain? Toward a cognitive neuroscience of decision under risk. *Cognitive Brain Research, 23,* 34–50.

Trick, L. M., & Pylyshyn, Z. W. (1994). What enumeration studies can show us about spatial attention: Evidence for limited capacity pre-attentive processing. *Journal of Experimental Psychology: Human Perception and Performance, 19,* 331–351.

Tronsky, L. N. (2005). Strategy use, the development of automaticity, and working memory involvement in complex multiplication. *Memory & Cognition, 33,* 927–940.

Trout, J. D. (2003). Biological specializations for speech: What can the animals tell us? *Current Directions in Psychological Science, 12,* 155–159.

Trueswell, J. C., and Tanenhaus, M. K. 1994. Toward a lexicalist framework for constraint-based syntactic ambiguity resolution. In C. Clifton, K. Rayner, and L. Frazier (Eds), *Perspectives on Sentence Processing.* Hillsdale, NJ: Erlbaum.

Tulving, E. (1962). Subjective organization in free recall of "unrelated" words. *Psychological Review, 69,* 344–354.

Tulving, E. (1972). Episodic and semantic memory. In E. Tulving & W. Donaldson (Eds.), *Organization of memory.* New York: Academic Press.

Tulving, E. (1983). *Elements of episodic memory.* New York: Oxford University Press.

Tulving, E. (1991). Memory research is not a zero-sum game. *American Psychologist, 46,* 41–42.

Tulving, E. (2002). Episodic memory: From mind to brain. *Annual Review of Psychology, 53,* 1–25.

Tulving, E., & Pearlstone, Z. (1966). Availability vs. accessibility of information in memory for words. *Journal of Verbal Learning and Verbal Behavior, 5,* 381–391.

Tulving, E., & Schacter, D. L. (1990). Priming and human memory systems. *Science, 247,* 301–306.

Tulving, E., & Thomson, D. M. (1973). Encoding specificity and retrieval processes in episodic memory. *Psychological Review, 80,* 359–380.

Tversky, B. (2006). Gestalts of thought. In L. Albertazzi (Editor), *Visual thought* (155–163). Amsterdam, The Netherlands: Benjamins.

Tversky, A., & Kahneman, D. (1971). Belief in the law of small numbers. *Psychological Bulletin, 76,* 105–110.

Tversky, A., & Kahneman, D. (1973). Availability: A heuristic for judging frequency and probability. *Cognitive Psychology, 5,* 207–232.

Tversky, A., & Kahneman, D. (1974). Judgment under uncertainty: Heuristics and biases. *Science, 185,* 1124–1131.

Tversky, A., & Kahneman, D. (1981). The framing of decisions and the psychology of choice. *Science, 211,* 453–458.

Tversky, A., & Kahneman, D. (1983). Extensional vs. intuitive reasoning. The conjunction fallacy in probability judgment. *Psychological Review, 90,* 293–315.

Ullman, M., Corkin, S., Coppola, M., Hickok, G., Growdon, J. H., Koroshetz, W. J., & Pinker, S. (1997). A neural dissociation within language: Evidence that the mental dictionary is part of declarative memory, and that grammatical rules are processed by the procedural system. *Journal of Cognitive Neuroscience, 9,* 266–276.

Ullman, S., Vidal-Naquet, M. , & Sali, E. (2002) Visual features of intermediate complexity and their use in classification. *Nature Neuroscience, 5,* 1–6.

Unsworth, N., & Engle, R. W. (2007). On the division of short-term and working memory: An examination of simple and complex span and their relation to higher order abilities. *Psychological Bulletin, 133,* 1038–1066.

Usall, J., Araya, S., Ochoa, S., Busquets, E., Gost, A., Márquez, M., et al. (2001). Gender differences in a sample of schizophrenic outpatients. *Comprehensive Psychiatry, 42,* 301–305.

Usher, J. A., & Neisser, U. (1993). Childhood amnesia and the beginnings of memory for four early life events. *Journal of Experimental Psychology: General, 122,* 155–165.

Uttal, W. R. (2003). *The new phrenology: The limits of localizing cognitive processes in the brain.* Cambridge, MA: MIT Press.

Van den Bussche, E., Van Den Noortgate, W., & Reynvoet, B. (2009). Mechanisms of masked priming: A meta-analysis. *Psychological Bulletin, 135,* 452–477.

Van Rullen, R., Carlson, T., & Cavanagh, P. (2007). The blinking spotlight of attention. *Proceedings of the National Academy of Sciences, 104,* 19204–19209.

van der Kolk, B. A., & van der Hart, O. (1991). The intrusive past: The flexibility of memory and the engraving of trauma. *American Imago, 48,* 425–54.

Van Der Linden, D., Keijsers, G., Eling, P., & Van Schaijk, R. (2005). Work stress and attentional difficulties: An initial study on burnout and cognitive failures. *Work & Stress, 19,* 23–36.

van Dijk, T. A., & Kintsch, W. (1983). *Strategies of discourse comprehension.* New York: Academic Press.

Van Orden, G. C. (1987). A ROWS is a ROSE: Spelling, sound, and reading. *Memory and Cognition, 15,* 181–198.

Van Orden, G. C., & Kloos, K. (2005). The question of phonology and reading. In M. Snowling & C. Hulme (Eds.), *The Science of Reading: A Handbook.* (pp. 61–78). Malden, MA: Blackwell.

Van Wert, M. J., Horowitz, T. S., & Wolfe, J. M. (2009). Even in correctable search, some types of rare targets are frequently missed. *Attention, Perception, & Psychophysics, 71*(3), 541–553.

Vecera, S. P., Vogel, E. K., & Woodman, G. F. (2002). Lower ground: A new cue for figure-ground assignment. *Journal of Experimental Psychology: General, 131,* 194–205.

Verhaeghen, P., & Basak, C. (2005). Aging and switching of the focus of attention in working memory: Results from a modified N-Back task. *Quarterly Journal of Experimental Psychology* (A), *58,* 134–154.

Vicente, K. J., & Wang, J. H. (1998). An ecological theory of expertise effects in memory recall. *Psychological Review, 105,* 33–57.

Vokey, J. R., & Read, J. D. (1988). Subliminal messages: Between the devil and the media. *American Psychologist, 39,* 1231–1239.

von Eckardt, B., & Potter, M. C. (1985). Clauses and the semantic representations of words. *Memory and Cognition, 13,* 371–376.

von Frisch, K. (1967). *The dance language and orientation of bees.* Cambridge, MA: Belknap Press.

von Restorff, H. (1933). Uber die Wirkung von Bereichsbildungen im Spurenfeld. *Psychologische Forschung, 18,* 299–342.

von Wright, J. M. (1972). On the problem of selection in iconic memory. *Scandinavian Journal of Psychology, 13,* 159–171.

Vroomen, J., van Zon, M., & de Gelder, B. (1996). Cues to speech segmentation. Evidence from juncture misperceptions and word spotting. *Memory and Cognition, 24,* 744–755.

Vul, E., & Pashler, H. (2007). Incubation benefits only after people have been misdirected. *Memory & Cognition, 35,* 701–10.

Wade, K. A., Sharman, S. J., Garry, M., Memon, A., Mazzoni, G., Merckelbach, H., et al. (2007). False claims about false memory research. *Consciousness and Cognition, 16,* 18–28.

Wagenaar, W. A. (1986). My memory: A study of autobiographical memory over six years. *Cognitive Psychology, 18,* 225–252.

Wagner, U., Gais, S., Haider, H., Verleger, R., & Born, J. (2004). Sleep inspires insight. *Nature, 427,* 352–355.

Wakefield, H., & Underwager, R. C. (1994). *Return of the furies: An investigation into recovered memory therapy.* Chicago: Open Court.

Walker and Yekovich (1987). Activation and use of script-based antecedents in anaphoric reference. *Journal of Memory and Language, 26,* 673–691.

Wallace, W. P. (1965). Review of the historical, empirical, and theoretical status of the von Restorff phenomenon. *Psychological Bulletin, 63,* 410–424.

Wallach, M. A. (1970). Creativity. In P. Mussen (Ed.), *Carmichael's handbook of child psychology* (pp. 1211–1272). New York: Wiley.

Wallas, G. (1926). *The art of thought.* London: J. Cape.

Wang, Q. (2006). Earliest recollections of self and others in European-American and Taiwanese young adults. *Psychological Science, 17,* 708–715.

Wang, Q. (2009). Are Asians forgetful? Perception, retention, and recall in episodic remembering. *Cognition, 111,* 123–31.

Wang, Q., & Ross, M. (2007). Culture and memory. In H. Kitayama & D. Cohen (Eds.), *Handbook of cultural psychology* (p. 645–667). New York, NY: Guilford Publications.

Warren, R. M. (1970). Perceptual restoration of missing speech sounds. *Science, 167,* 392–393.

Warren, R. M. Perceptual restoration of obliterated sounds. *Psychological Bulletin, 96,* 371–383.

Warren, P. & Marslen-Wilson, W. D. (1988) Cues to lexical choice: Discriminating place and voice, *Perception and Psychophysics, 43,* 21–30.

Warren, R. M., & Sherman, G. L. Phonemic restorations based on subsequent context. *Perception & Psychophysics, 16,* 150–156.

Warrington, E. K. and Shallice, T. (1972). Neuropsychological evidence of visual storage in short-term memory tasks. *Quarterly Journal od Experimental Psychology, 24,* 30–40.

Warrington, E. K., & Weiskrantz, L. (1970). Amnesic syndrome: Consolidation or retrieval? *Nature, 228,* 628–630.

Wason, P. C., & Johnson-Laird, P. N. (1970). A conflict between selection and evaluating information in an inferential task. *British Journal of Psychology, 68,* 325–335.

Waugh, N. C., & Norman, D. A. (1965). Primary memory. *Psychological Review, 72,* 89–104.

Weber, N., & Brewer, N. (2006). Positive versus negative face recognition decisions: Confidence, accuracy, and response latency. *Applied Cognitive Psychology, 20,* 17–31.

Weber, N., Brewer, N., Wells, G. L., Semmler, C., & Keast, A. (2004). Eyewitness identification accuracy and response latency: The unruly 10–12-second rule. *Journal of Experimental Psychology: Applied, 10,* 139–147.

Wegner, D. M. (1994). Ironic processes of mental control. *Psychological Review, 101,* 34–52.

Wegner, D. M. (2003). The mind's best trick: How we experience conscious will. *Trends in Cognitive Sciences, 7,* 65–69.

Wegner, D. M. (2004). Precis of The illusion of conscious will. *Behavioral and Brain Sciences, 27,* 649–692.

Wegner, D. M., Ansfield, M., & Pilloff, D. (1998). The putt and the pendulum: Ironic effects of the mental control of action. *Psychological Science, 9,* 196–199.

Wegner, D. M., & Sparrow, B. (2004). Authorship processing. In M. Gazzaniga (Ed.), *The cognitive neurosciences* (3rd ed., pp. 1201–1209). Cambridge, MA: MIT Press.

Wegner, D. M., Sparrow, B., & Winerman, L. (2004). Vicarious agency: Experiencing control over the movements of others. *Journal of Personality and Social Psychology, 86,* 838–848.

Weir, W. (1984, October 15). Another Look at Subliminal 'Facts'. Advertising Age, 55, p. 46.

Weisberg, R. W. (1992). Metacognition and insight during problem solving: Comment on Metcalfe. *Journal of Experimental Psychology: Learning, Memory, and Cognition, 18,* 426–431.

Weisberg, R. W. (1995). Prolegomena to theories of insight in problem solving. A taxonomy of problems. In R. J. Sternberg & J. E. Davidson (Eds.), *The nature of insight.* Cambridge, MA: MIT Press.

Weisberg, R. W., & Alba, J. W. (1981). An examination of the alleged role of "fixation" in the solution of several "insight" problems. *Journal of Experimental Psychology: General, 110,* 169–192.

Weiskrantz, L. (1986). *Blindsight: A case study and implications.* Oxford, UK: Oxford University Press.

Weiskrantz, L. (2009). Is blindsight just degraded normal vision? *Experimental Brain Research, 192,* 413–416.

Weldon, M. S. (2000). Remembering as a social process. In D. L. Medin (Ed.), *The psychology of learning and motivation* (Vol. 40, pp. 67–120). New York: Academic Press.

Wells, G. L. (1984). The psychology of lineup identifications. *Journal of Applied Social Psychology, 14,* 89–103.

Wells, G. L. (1993). What do we know about eyewitness identification? *American Psychologist, 48,* 553–571.

Wells, G. L., Cutler, B. L., & Hasel, L. E. (2009). The Duke-lacrosse rape investigation: How not to do eyewitness identification procedures. In M. L. Siegel (Ed.), *Race to injustice: Lessons learned from the Duke University lacrosse players' rape case.* Carolina Academic Press.

Wells, G. L., Ferguson, T. J., & Lindsay, R. C. L. (1981). The tractability of eyewitness confidence and its implications for triers of fact. *Journal of Applied Psychology, 66,* 688–696.

Wells, G. L., Leippe, M. R., & Ostrom, T. M. (1979). Guidelines for empirically assessing the fairness of a lineup. *Law and Human Behavior, 3,* 285–293.

Wells, G. L., & Luus, C. A. E. (1990). The diagnosticity of a lineup should not be confused with the diagnostic value of non-lineup evidence. *Journal of Applied Psychology, 75,* 511–516.

Wells, G. L., Malpass, R. S., Lindsay, R. C. L., Fisher, R. P., Turtle, J. W., & Fulero, S. M. (2000). From the lab to the police station: A successful application of eyewitness research. *American Psychologist, 55,* 581–598.

Wells, G. L., & Murray, D. M. (1984). Eyewitness confidence. In G. L. Wells & E. F. Loftus (Eds.), *Eyewitness testimony: Psychological perspectives.* New York: Cambridge University Press.

Wells, G. L., & Olson, E. (2003). Eyewitness testimony. *Annual Review of Psychology, 54,* 277–295.

Wells, G. L., Olson, E. A., Charman, S. D. (2002). The confidence of eyewitnesses in their identifications from lineups. *Current Directions in Psychological Science, 11,* 151–154.

Wells, G. L., Rydell, S. M., & Seelau, E. P. (1993). On the selection of distractors for eyewitness lineups. *Journal of Applied Psychology, 78,* 835–844.

Wenzlaff, R. M., & Luxton, D. D. (2003). The role of thought suppression in depressive rumination. *Cognitive Therapy and Research, 27,* 293–308.

Wenzlaff, R. M., & Wegner, D. M. (2003). Thought suppression. *Annual Review of Psychology, 51,* 59–91.

Wertheimer, M. (1938). Untersuchungen zur Lehre von der Gestalt, II [Investigations of the principles of gestalt II]. In W. D. Ellis (Ed.), *A source book of Gestalt psychology* (pp. 71–88). New York: Harcourt, Brace. (Reprinted from *Psychologische Forschung, 4,* 301–350, 1923)

Wetzler SE, Sweeney JA: Childhood amnesia: An empirical demonstration. In D.C. Rubin (Eds.), *Autobiographical memory.* Cambridge: Cambridge University Press, pp. 191–201.

White, S. J., Johnson, R. L., Liversedge, S. P., & Rayner, K. (2008). Eye movements when reading transposed text: The importance of word-beginning letters. *Perception, 34,* 1261–1276.

Wickens, C. D. (1984). Engineering psychology and human performance: Columbus, OH: Merrill.

Wickens, D. D., Dalezman, R. E., & Eggemeier, F. T. (1976). Multiple encoding of word attributes in memory. *Memory and Cognition, 4,* 307–310.

Wilke, A., & Barrett, C. (2009). The hot hand phenomenon as a cognitive adaptation to clumped resources. *Evolution and Human Behavior, 30,* 161–169.

Wilkins, M. C. (1928). The effect of changed material on ability to do formal syllogistic reasoning. *Archives of Psychology, 16* (102).

Williams, J. M. G., Barnhofer, T., Crane, C., Hermans, D., Raes, F., Watkins, E., et al. (2007). Autobiographical memory specificity and emotional disorder. *Psychological Bulletin, 133,* 122–148.

Williams, J. M. G., Ellis, N. C., Tyers, C., Healy, H., Rose, J., & MacLeod, C. (1996). The specificity of autobiographical memory and imageability about the future. *Memory and Cognition, 24,* 116–125.

Williams, J. M., & Scott, J. (1988). Autobiographical memory in depression. *Psychiatric Medicine, 18,* 689–695.

Williams, L. M. (1994). Recall of childhood trauma: A prospective study of women's memories of childhood abuse. *Journal of Consulting and Clinical Psychology, 62,* 1182–1186.

Wilson, M. (2002). Six views of embodied cognition. *Psychological Bulletin and Review, 9,* 625–636.

Wilson, M., & Emmorey, K. (2006). Comparing sign language and speech reveals a universal limit on short-term memory capacity. *Psychological Science, 17,* 682–683.

Wilson, M., & Emmorey, K. (1998). A "word-length effect" for sign-language: Further evidence for the role of language in structuring working memory. *Memory and Cognition, 26,* 584–590.

Wilson, M., & Emmorey, K. (1997). A visuospatial "phonological loop" in working memory: Evidence from American Sign Language. *Memory and Cognition, 25,* 313–320.

Wilson, M. P., & Garnsey, S. M. (2009). Making simple sentences hard: Verb bias effects in simple direct object sentences. *Journal of Memory and Language, 60,* 368–392.

Wimmers, P. F., Schmidt, H. G., Verkoeijen, P. P., & van de Wiel, M. W. (2005). Inducing expertise effects in clinical case recall. *Medical Education, 39,* 949–957.

Witt, J. K., Linkenauger, S. A., Bakdash, J. Z., Augustyn, J. S., Cook, A.,

Proffitt, D. R., (2009). The long road of pain: Chronic pain increases perceived distance. *Experimental Brain Research, 192,* 145–148.

Witt, J. K., Linkenauger, S. A., Bakdash, J. Z., & Proffitt, D. R. (2008). Putting to a bigger hole: Golf performance relates to perceived size. *Psychonomic Bulletin & Review, 15,* 581–585.

Witt, J. K., & Proffitt, D. R. (2005). See the ball, hit the ball: Apparent ball size is correlated with batting average. *Psychological Science, 16,* 937–938.

Wolfe, J. M. (1998). What can one million trials tell us about visual search? *Psychological Science, 9,* 33–39.

Wolfe, J. M. (2003). Moving towards solutions to some enduring controversies in visual search. *Trends in Cognitive Sciences, 7,* 70–76.

Wolfe, J. M., Cave, K. R., & Franzel, S. L. (1989). Guided search: An alternative to the feature integration model for visual search. *Journal of Experimental Psychology: Human Perception & Performance, 15,* 419–433.

Wolfe, J. M., & Horowitz, T. S. (2004). What attributes guide the deployment of visual attention and how do they do it? *Nature Reviews Neuroscience, 5,* 1–7.

Wolfe, J. M., Horowitz, T.S., Kenner, N. (2005). Rare items often missed in visual searches. *Nature, 435,* 439–440.

Wyer, T. K., & Srull, R. S. (1989). *Memory and cognition in its social context.* Hillsdale, NJ: Erlbaum.

Yang, C. D. (2004). Universal grammar, statistics or both? *Trends in Cognitive Sciences, 8,* 451–456.

Yan, G., Tian, H., Bai, X., & Rayner, K. (2006). The effect of word and

character frequency on the eye movements of Chinese readers. *British Journal of Psychology, 97,* 259–268.

Yantis, S. (1998). Objects, attention, and perceptual experience. In R. Wright (Ed.), *Visual Attention.* (pp. 187–214). New York: Oxford University Press.

Yin, R. K. (1969). Looking at upside-down faces. *Journal of Experimental Psychology, 81,* 141–145.

Young, A. W., Ellis, A. W., & Flude, B. M. (1988). Accessing stored information about people. *Psychological Research, 50,* 111–115.

Zacks, J. M, & Swallow, K. M. (2007). Event segmentation. Current Directions in Psychological Science, 16, 80–84.

Zattore, R. J., Evans, A. C., Meyer, E., & Gjedde, A. (1992). Lateralization of phonetic and pitch discrimination in speech processing. *Science, 256,* 846–849.

Zhang, Y., Yu, J., & Boland, J. E. (2010). Semantics does not need a processing license from syntax in reading Chinese. *Journal of Experimental Psychology. Learning, Memory, and Ccognition, 36,* 765–81.

Ziegler, J. C., and U. Goswami. 2005. Reading acquisition, developmental dyslexia, and skilled reading across languages: A psycholinguistic grain size theory. *Psychological Bulletin, 131,* 3–29.

Zimmerman, D. H., & West, C. (1975). Sex roles, interruptions, and silences in conversation. In B. Thorne & N. Henley (Eds.), *Language and sex: Differences and dominance* (pp. 105–129). Rowley, MA: Newbury House.

Photo Credits

Additional Text Credits

Name Index

Subject Index